The Conquest
of a
Continent

The
Conquest
of a
Continent

Siberia and the Russians

W. Bruce Lincoln

Random House New York

Library of Congress Cataloging-in-Publication Data
Lincoln, W. Bruce.
The conquest of a continent: Siberia and the Russians / by W. Bruce Lincoln.
p.   cm.
Includes bibliographical references and index.
ISBN 0-679-41214-X
1. Siberia (Russia)—History. I. Title.
DK761.L56   1993
957—dc20   93-22342

Manufactured in the United States of America
23456789
First Edition

To Mary, with love

Contents

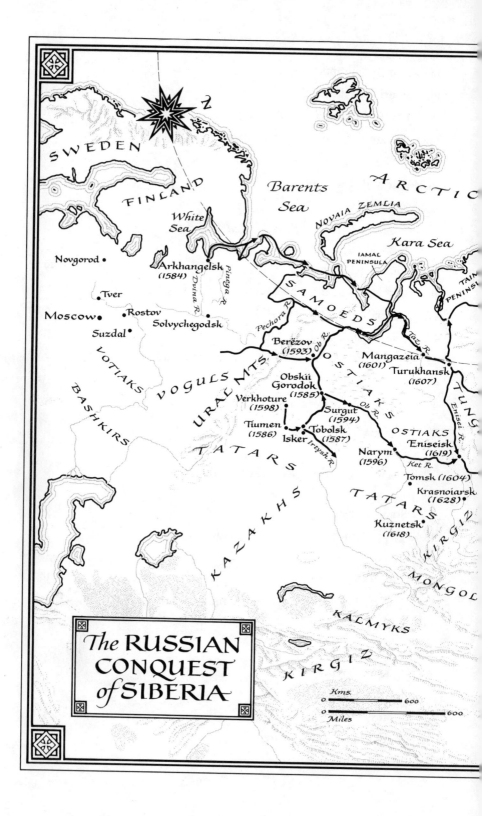

The RUSSIAN CONQUEST of SIBERIA

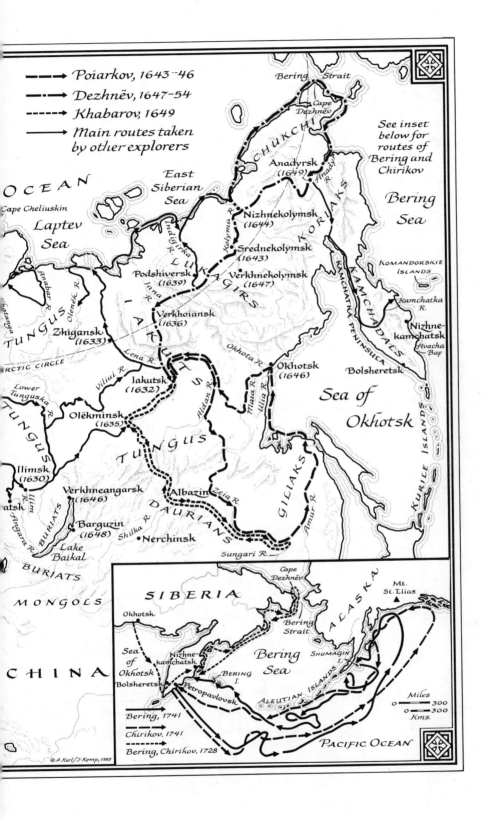

Bering Strait

Cape Dezhnëv

CHUKCHI

Anadyrsk (1649)

Anady R.

OCEAN

Cape Cheliuskin

Laptev Sea

East Siberian Sea

KORIAKS

Bering Sea

KOMANDORSKIE ISLANDS

Nizhnekolymsk (1644)

Srednekolymsk (1643)

Podshiversk (1639)

Verkhnekolymsk (1647)

Kamchatka R.

Nizhne-kamchatsk

Verkhoiansk (1636)

Zhigansk (1633)

Okhota R.

KAMCHADALS

KAMCHATKA PENINSULA

Avacha Bay

ARCTIC CIRCLE

Viliui R.

Iakutsk (1632)

Okhotsk (1646)

Bolsheretsk

Lower Tunguska R.

Olëkminsk (1635)

Maia R.

Ulia R.

Sea of Okhotsk

TUNGUS

TUNGUS

Ilimsk (1630)

Verkhneangarsk (1646)

Albazin

Zeia R.

DAURIANS

GILIAKS

Barguzin (1648)

Shilka R.

Nerchinsk

KURILE ISLANDS

BURIATS

Lake Baikal

Sungari R.

Amur R.

BURIATS

MONGOLS

SIBERIA

Cape Dezhnëv

ALASKA

Mt. St. Elias

CHINA

Okhotsk

Bering Strait

Sea of Okhotsk

Nizhne-kamchatsk

Bering Sea

SHUMAGIN I.

Bolsheretsk

BERING I.

Petropavlovsk

ALEUTIAN ISLANDS

Miles
0 — 300
0 — 300
Kms.

Bering, 1741

Chirikov, 1741

Bering, Chirikov, 1728

PACIFIC OCEAN

© A.Karl/J.Kemp, 1993

──▶ Poiarkov, 1643–46
─·─▶ Dezhnëv, 1647–54
----▶ Khabarov, 1649
───▶ Main routes taken by other explorers

See inset below for routes of Bering and Chirikov

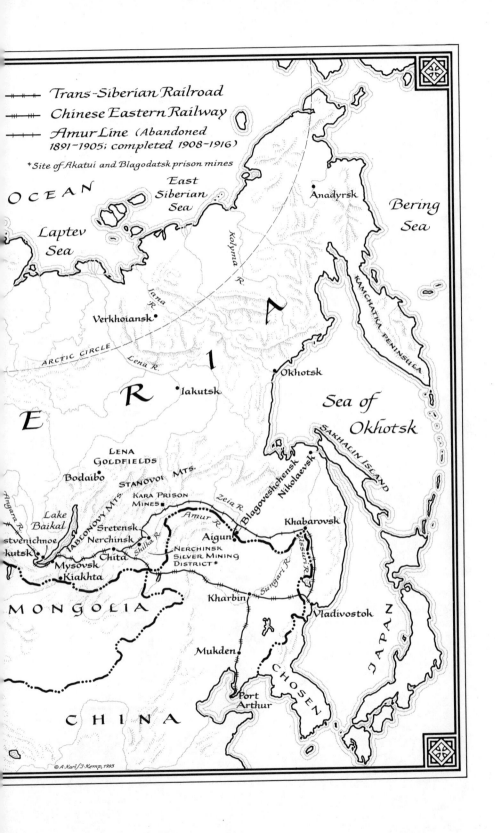

Trans-Siberian Railroad
Chinese Eastern Railway
Amur Line (Abandoned 1891–1905; completed 1908–1916)
*Site of Akatui and Blagodatsk prison mines

OCEAN

East
Siberian
Sea

Anadyrsk

Bering
Sea

Laptev
Sea

Kolyma R.

KAMCHATKA PENINSULA

Iana R.

Verkhoiansk

ARCTIC CIRCLE

Lena R.

Okhotsk

Iakutsk

Sea of
Okhotsk

SAKHALIN ISLAND

LENA
GOLDFIELDS

Bodaibo

STANOVOI MTS.

KARA PRISON
MINES

Blagoveshchensk

Nikolaevsk

Zeia R.

Amur R.

Khabarovsk

YABLONOVY MTS.

Lake
Baikal

Sretensk
Nerchinsk

Shilka R.

Aigun

stvenichnoe

NERCHINSK
SILVER MINING
DISTRICT *

Ussuri R.

kutsk

Chita

Mysovsk

Kiakhta

Sungari R.

Kharbin

Vladivostok

MONGOLIA

JAPAN

Mukden

CHOSEN

Port
Arthur

CHINA

Argara R.

© A. Karl/J. Kemp, 1993

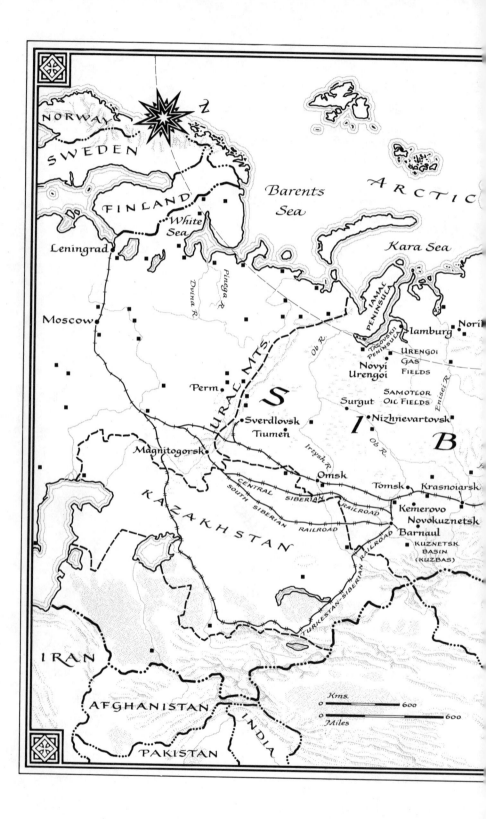

Trans-Siberian Railway System

• Forced Labor Camps
(One or more camps)
Information courtesy of the
National Geographic Society

OCEAN

Laptev
Sea

East
Siberian
Sea

ARCTIC CIRCLE

Anadyrsk

Bering
Sea

Kolyma R.

Iana R.

Lena R.

Viliui R.

Iakutsk

KAMCHATKA PENINSULA

Magadan

Okhotsk

Sea of
Okhotsk

SAKHALIN ISLAND

Ust-Ilimsk

BAIKAL-AMUR MAINLINE
RAILROAD (BAM)

Neriungri

Tynda

Komsomolsk

Zeia R.

Khabarovsk

Ust-
Kut

Lake
Baikal

Chita

Amur R.

Shilka R.

Ussuri R.

Irkutsk

atsk
ishet

garsk

MONGOLIA

Vladivostok

JAPAN

CHINA

SOVIET
SIBERIA

© A. Karl/J. Kemp, 1993

Prologue

Nations are born of battle, and conquest makes them great. Agincourt, Trafalgar, and El Alamein defined the greatness of England. France had some of her finest hours at Austerlitz and Jena, while modern Germany took shape against the background of her victories at Königgrätz, Sedan, and Tannenberg. The United States of America came into being at Concord and Yorktown, preserved her union at Gettysburg, and took the stage as a world power at Château-Thierry and the Battle of Midway. For Russia, the process of birth and conquest has taken longer, beginning with the triumph of Moscow's Prince Dmitrii Donskoi over the Mongols at Kulikovo Field in 1380. Since then, Russia has fought titanic battles against Europe—Poltava in 1709, Borodino in 1812, and Stalingrad in 1942—but the conquest that has defined her greatness has been in Asia. What has enabled Russia to rise among the great powers of the world and supplied her with the means to maintain that position once she achieved it has been her conquest of Siberia. Begun in 1582 with the victory of the cossack chieftain Ermak Timofeevich over the Sibir Tatars near present-day Tobolsk, Russia's Siberian conquest has extended across four hundred years, from the days of Ivan the Terrible until the end of the Brezhnev era.

The Russians took Siberia as part of a larger process of conquest and defeat that reached back more than three thousand years to the days when the political churnings of Inner Asia drove the Scythians westward along the great grass road that lay to Siberia's south. Some seven centuries before Christ, these nomads took the Western world by storm, marking the way for later waves of warriors to stake their claims to the steppe lands that divided Siberia from Central Asia. Some of the finest light cavalry the world has ever seen, these horsemen of the steppes presided over more than two thousand years of Asiatic triumphs against the armies of the West and the Near East. Never retreating and rarely tasting defeat, they shaped the history of the world's peoples from Cathay to Canterbury.

Moving slowly west around 700 B.C., the Scythians were the first to cross the steppes in search of grass for the horses and cattle on which they centered their daily lives. About four centuries later came the Sarmatians, advancing more swiftly and overwhelming their foes with their heavy cavalry, the likes of which the West had never seen. Cruel barbarians who consecrated their treaties with toasts of human blood drunk from a human skull, Attila's Huns followed the Sarmatians to build an empire that, by the fifth century A.D., reached into the plains of Hungary. Then, not long after the death of Charlemagne, the collapse of the Huns' empire opened the way for the Avars, the first of several new nomadic waves that struck against the edge of Europe before Christendom celebrated its first millennium. The Mongol armies of Batu Khan came last of all, more fearsome and brutal than any yet to reach Europe, but the last of the Asiatic invaders to ride out of the east.

On the eve of modern times, when the cutting edge of military technology—and, with it, the ability to claim Eurasia—shifted toward Europe, the pattern of Eastern triumphs and Western defeats began to change. Beginning in the 1580s, the Russians moved toward the east, taking a route that avoided the great centers of civilization that dotted the Eurasian steppe and shunning the massive battles with the armies of Central Asia that such a campaign in the steppe would have cost. Crossing Asia much farther to the north, the Russians worked their way along the great rivers and portages of Siberia so that the wild forests and tundras between the Urals and the Pacific became their prize, not the steppes and desert oases that the horsemen from Asia had conquered in years gone by. Bounded by the Ural Mountains on the west, the Arctic Ocean on the north, the lands of Kazakhstan, Central Asia, Mongolia, China, and Korea on the south, and the Bering Sea, the Sea of Okhotsk and the Sea of Japan on the east, Siberia increased the size of medieval Russia more than a hundredfold.

Once they entered Siberia, the Russians at first moved hesitantly into the valleys of the Irtysh and the Ob, the westernmost of the great

Siberian rivers that flowed from the highlands of Inner Asia to the seas that formed the Asiatic edge of the Arctic Ocean. Facing little opposition in lands whose average population was less than one person for every twenty-five square miles and finding the richest furs the West had ever seen, the Russians quickened their pace as the seventeenth century opened. Before 1620, they reached the valley of the Enisei, a thousand miles east of the Irtysh. Just a decade later, they crossed the Lena, a full twelve hundred miles beyond the Enisei and then, in 1639, reached the Pacific, more than three thousand miles east of their starting point. Nine years after that, they reached the Chukotka Peninsula, more than twelve hundred miles to the northeast and a scant hundred miles from Alaska's westernmost tip. At least in a formal territorial sense, with only a handful of cossacks and trappers marking their advance with a scattering of frontier forts and trading posts, Russia had conquered Siberia in sixty-six years.

Stretching for five thousand miles from the Urals to the edge of the Bering Sea and encompassing five and a third million square miles of territory, the Russians' Siberian conquest allowed them to build the modern world's largest land empire. On the eve of the First World War, the single Siberian province of Iakutsk was larger than all of India, and Eniseisk, Siberia's second largest province, encompassed more land than the combined territories of all the European combatants in the Great War except for Russia. Siberia was so large that almost two million square miles of space would be left over if the entire contiguous continental United States were placed into its center. Drawn to the scale used in Britain's famous Ordnance Survey maps, one nineteenth-century traveler explained to his readers, a map of Siberia would cover the entire tip of Manhattan from the Battery to Wall Street.[1] Western notions of time and space did not apply in this land where sunlight at midnight in one season became darkness at noon in the next. "When I thought I had covered at least half the ground between the Pacific Ocean and the Urals," one traveler from Vladivostok confessed, "I saw inscribed on the government notice-board at a post-station: 'To St. Petersburg, 5000 versts [3,300 miles].' "[2]

As rich in resources as it was large in size, Siberia brought the Russians a sixth of the world's gold and silver, a fifth of its platinum, and a third of its iron. A quarter of the world's timber grows within its boundaries, and its supplies of coal, oil, and natural gas are still difficult to estimate. Larger than Belgium and a mile deep, Lake Baikal, which stands midway between the Urals and the Pacific, holds a fifth of the earth's fresh water, and Siberia's navigable rivers are more than long enough to encircle the globe. Diverse and monotonous, sinister and romantic, rich and impoverished, Siberia to this day remains a virtual continent unto itself, in which nature and history have juxtaposed an endless array of contradictions and opposites.

The Russians' conquest did not immediately give them access to Siberia's vast resources. Its huge reserves of gold were not discovered until the nineteenth century, and its even larger stores of coal, oil, and natural gas did not become known until well into the twentieth. Historically, Siberia has been reluctant to yield her resources to her Russian conquerors, yet it has been those resources that have supported a large part of Russia's claim to greatness. In the new balance between East and West that has emerged during the past four hundred years, the possession of Siberia's vast natural wealth has thus become a vital element in determining the place that Russia occupies in world affairs.

To explore this vital process of conquest and integration is the purpose of the pages that follow. The story begins in the days before Russia became Russia, when Siberia was not yet called Siberia, and when the Mongol hordes stood at Europe's eastern gates in the last of the East's great victorious campaigns against the West. Mongols ruled in Peking, Samarkand, and the lands of the Near and Middle East. Their armies were about to turn the great medieval Ukrainian city of Kiev into a wasteland and ride over Roman Catholicism's eastern bastions at Krakow and Budapest. The West and Christendom stood at a crossroads. Faced with what seemed to be certain destruction at the hands of these "satellites of Antichrist,"[3] there appeared to be no escape from a course of events that men and women could explain only as the product of God's wrath. To the people of the West in the year 1238, it seemed that the cruel and dark forces of the pagan East stood poised to overwhelm them all.

PART ONE

The Beginnings

1

The Fury of God

Terrifying rumors began to spread across Europe soon after the New Year came in 1238. At first repeated only in dark whispers between people who dared not test their truth in the open, these formed an invisible undercurrent to which the lives of Europeans began to respond by spring. Recalling their sins, men and women who had forgotten their Christian duty turned their thoughts inward, wondering what atonement could shield them from "the rod of God's anger." "In consequence of heresy and many other sinful things arising among us Christians," a clerk in the archbishop of Bordeaux's chancery explained, "the Lord has ... become an angry devastator and most fearful avenger."[1] No one knew where or when God's rod might strike, and the busy trade that had once flourished all along the coasts of the North Sea and the Baltic dried up. "Owing to this," wrote Matthew of Paris, a monk at St. Alban's Abbey who spent his days recording the history of his times and knew well the importance of the fishing trade for England's people, "herrings in that year were considered of no value."[2]

The cause of these fears lay in the east, a source of danger for the people of Europe ever since the first steppe horsemen had ridden out of Asia nearly two thousand years before. Since their lands stood between the invaders and the West, the Saracens, against whom Rome's crusaders had fought in the Holy Land for more than two hundred years, felt the danger first. Seeking an alliance with their former enemies lest they

all perish separately, these "infidels" sent "a powerful and noble messenger" to the courts of France and England warning that "a monstrous and
inhuman race of men had burst forth from the northern mountains"
during the previous winter. After devastating a score of well-defended
towns and cities in the lands of Russia, the Saracens reported, these
fearsome horsemen had turned south and west. They were called "Tartars," Friar Matthew explained when he recorded the contents of the
Saracens' message. Always attacking in large numbers, he added, they
were "believed to have been sent as a plague on mankind."[3]

The Saracens' unexpected plea for common action challenged the
principles around which thirteenth-century Christians had shaped their
lives. Could sworn enemies who claimed divine sanction for their hatred
become allies? Should Christians take up arms alongside the Infidel?
Friar Matthew's bishop disdained their offer and advised his king against
it. "Let us leave these dogs to devour one another," he counseled after
the Saracen envoys had spoken. "When we proceed against the enemies
of Christ who remain, we will slay them and cleanse the face of the earth
so that all the world will be subject to the one Catholic church and there
will be one shepherd and one fold."[4]

After 1238, Friar Matthew's chronicle made no mention of the Tartars
until 1240, when he reported more atrocities in lands nearer to home. By
then, the Tartars had conquered all of Russia and their victims were
fleeing into Poland, Hungary, and Germany. All too ready to embroider
upon the horrors they had seen, some of these refugees were making
their way to the courts of Europe. Friar Matthew now wrote of warriors
"rather to be called monsters than men," for whom the exhilaration of
combat seemed as vital as food and drink. "They are short in stature and
thickset, compact in their bodies and of great strength," he explained.
"Invincible in battle, indefatigable in labor," he continued, "they have
no human laws." The Tartars showed no mercy. "Covering the face of
the earth like locusts," Matthew wrote of the invaders, "they rush forth
like demons loosed from Tartarus [that is, from Hell]."[5]

Sworn by England's King Henry III to record the truth,[6] Friar Matthew reported the march of the horsemen from Hell (*ad Tartaros* in the
Latin in which he wrote) with some restraint. There was fear in his
account, but there was caution too as he struggled to separate fiction
from fact and divide rumor from reality. Yet the caution that held him
in check did not constrain his contemporaries, especially those who did
not have the English Channel to protect them from the Tartars' advancing armies. Fear of these "satellites of Antichrist" overflowed into almost
every line that Europeans wrote about them. "They have hard and

robust breasts, lean and pale faces, stiff high shoulders, and short distorted noses," wrote one who claimed to be citing no less an authority
than an Englishman who had been forced to serve the Tartars. "Their
chins are sharp and prominent," his account continued, "the upper jaw
low and deep, the teeth long and few, their eyebrows stretch from the
hair to the nose, their eyes are black and restless, their countenances
long and grim, their extremities bony and nervous, their legs thick but
short below the knee." Here were true soldiers of Satan, "a fierce race
of inhuman beings," whose advance seemed certain to destroy the foundations of Christian civilization.[7]

After the Tartars routed the famed Livonian Knights at Liegnitz and
filled nine large sacks with right ears cut from the bodies of the slain,
Europeans' horror deepened.[8] On Palm Sunday 1241, one of the several
detachments into which the Tartars had divided their forces burned
southern Poland's lovely city of Krakow to the ground and moved into
the plain of Hungary, while another large army advanced through
Wallachia and Transylvania. Tales of their bestiality now ran rampant
in Europe. "The old and ugly women were given to their dog-headed
cannibals . . . to be their daily food, but those who were beautiful were
saved alive to be stifled and overwhelmed by the number of their
ravishers in spite of all their cries and lamentations," reported one
account of the Tartars' advance through Hungary toward the Adriatic.
"Virgins were deflowered," its author added, "until they died of exhaustion, when their breasts were cut off to be kept as dainties for their chiefs
and their bodies furnished a jovial banquet to the savages."[9] The writer
was certain that men such as these expected no quarter and gave none.
Whether the Tartars could be stopped no one knew, but the terrifying
tales of inhumanity that preceded their advance left many fearful that
nothing could stand in their path.

While their subjects lived in fear, the rulers of Europe spoke of unity
but drew apart. "This race of people is wild, outlawed, and ignorant of
the laws of humanity," the Holy Roman Emperor Frederick II wrote to
the king of England. Lest they all be destroyed, the kings and princes
of Europe must now "rise with alacrity and unanimously to oppose these
lately emerged savages."[10] But Europe was too divided for its princes to
unite. As the Middle Ages passed into history, a new world was taking
shape that was destined to be ruled less by the quest for salvation and
more by temporal concerns. As men and women turned their attention
from the hereafter to the here and now, warring princes and a warring
pope divided Europe into rival kingdoms that stood helpless before the
Tartar threat. "The notion that they will eradicate the name of Christian

shatters all our bones [and] dries up our marrow," Pope Gregory IX lamented. "We know not which way to turn."[11]

In such times, the pope himself was not above suspicion, and there were even those in later years who wondered if he had not plotted an alliance with the Tartars against his temporal enemies, none of whom was more thoroughly despised at the Papal Court than the recently excommunicated Holy Roman Emperor.[12] Could no one convince pope and emperor to set aside their differences and unite Europe against the Tartar threat? "I wonder that, when so terrible an extermination threatens all Christians, such stubbornness should have universally seized on kings and other potentates of the earth," one worried lord wrote to the archbishop of Bordeaux. Could not the archbishop, he asked, "move the hearts of the obstinate?" If not, ruin threatened every nation. "If all are united," the archbishop's correspondent concluded, the armies of Europe could "crush these monsters."[13] Singly, they would be destroyed one after the other, just as Russia, Poland, and Hungary already had fallen. The Tartars, who swept up people in their line of march and used them as shock troops to overwhelm the fortresses that barred their path, could now use Russians, Poles, and Hungarians to overwhelm Germans, Germans to defeat the French, and so on until all the kingdoms of Europe had been conquered. "They say," Friar Matthew wrote sadly, "that the Divine vengeance formerly purged the world by a deluge, and now it will be purified by a general depopulation and devastation."[14]

Yet Europe was to be spared. At the beginning of 1242, the Tartar commanders suddenly turned away from battlefields that stretched from China to Central Europe and rode straight for Karakorum, the capital that their great khan Chingis had built south of Siberia's Lake Baikal on the edge of Mongolia. There, more than seven thousand miles east of Friar Matthew's cell, these great captains of the world's largest empire gathered to elect a successor to the great khan Ugedei, the son of Chingis, who had died in December. Politics in a land that Europeans had never seen had taken precedence over Tartar conquest. Even though the cities and fields of Europe had lain open before them, the horsemen from the high plains of Asia had retreated as quickly as they had come.

The scourge from which Europe had been spared had had its beginnings more than half a century earlier in the rough highlands of Inner Asia, when Chingis Khan had welded the tribes of Mongolia and Siberia's Transbaikal lands into a nation. Nomads like the Scythians and Huns who had come before them, the Tartars, or Mongols as we shall call them in the following chapters, saw war as a way of life and were more brutal than any invader who had ridden out of the east in centuries past. Theirs was a discipline unsurpassed in any age, and their disdain for human life knew no bounds. The casualties they inflicted during the wars that built their empire numbered in the millions. "The score is staggering," one historian wrote of the Mongols when the carnage of the Second World War was still fresh in his readers' minds. "No other place and period have known such a concentration of wholesale killing."[15] Between their proclamation of Chingis Khan as the earthly representative of the great god Tengri in 1206 and their retreat from Europe, the Mongols became the masters of the largest contiguous land empire ever recorded in history.

2

"Great Khan of All the People Living in Felt Tents"

None of the men who drove the Lady Oelun-eke, her three sons and two stepsons into the Siberian wilderness in 1177 expected to see them again. Even for the most resourceful and strongest men, banishment into the brutal wilds of Siberia's Transbaikal lands usually meant death. For a Mongol noblewoman whose husband had just been poisoned by his enemies, the chances for survival seemed even more slim. Once well fed from Lord Esugai's numerous flocks and well tended by many slaves, Oelun-eke and her children now had only the small creatures of the forest, fish caught on hooks bent from needles, and the wild garlic, onions, and roots that grew beside the mountain streams to keep them alive. They were alone. "Apart from our own shadows," she told her children during those dark days, "we have no friends."[1]

Because the present seemed so fearsome and the future so very dark, Oelun-eke vowed that her sons must know the glorious saga of their past. Well practiced in the art of "citing ancient words" according to the Mongol chronicles,[2] she told them the story of their origins—of how a great "bluish wolf" had crossed over the waters of Siberia's Lake Baikal to mate with a "fallow doe" in the thick pine forests that clustered beneath the peak of Burkan-Kaldun. This was the home of Tengri, God of the Eternal Blue Sky and first among the ancient deities of the Mongols. And it was there, at the foot of Tengri's mountain, that the union of doe and wolf had given birth to the first of the line from which the children of Esugai and Oelun-eke had descended. As the generations passed, Tengri himself had blessed the descendants of this union when he had come to the beautiful Lady Alan after the death of her husband, entering her tent on the shafts of moonbeams and leaving on the rays of the sun after their sons had been conceived. From this union of god and woman had come Kabul Khan, whom the Chinese called King of the Mongols. His son had been Kutula, the Mongol Hercules, with hands like powerful bear claws and a voice that rolled and crashed through the mountain glens like thunder. Esugai had been Kutula's nephew. Oelun-eke's marriage to him had produced three sons. Temuchin, the eldest, had been born in 1167, the Year of the Pig.[3]

Amid the dark forests that spread out from the god Tengri's mountain toward the headwaters of eastern Siberia's Onon River, Temuchin grew tall and sturdy, with an iron constitution, a flint-hard will, and an amazing sixth sense that helped him to turn the weaknesses of others to his own advantage.[4] Often hungry and without shelter, he became inured to the discomforts of cold, heat, and rain as he struggled to survive in the wilderness. Outcast from the society of the steppe, he nonetheless observed its intricate social hierarchy of lords, knights, commoners, and slaves from afar and pondered how they could be made to serve his ends. With that knowledge, he would change the world. In less than twenty years after he reached manhood, Temuchin became Chingis Khan, the dreaded conqueror whose mighty legions raised his white standard with nine flames high above the ruins of Peking, Samarkand, and a score of great Eurasian cities.

Once he came of age, Temuchin reentered the arena of steppe politics that had claimed his father's life. Admired by those among whom he lived and fought, he had become the vassal of one of Mongolia's most powerful lords before he was twenty and built an army of supporters by offering unswerving protection to those who gave him their loyalty.[5] With them he triumphed in great battles and lived through narrow escapes. On one occasion he languished as a prisoner among his enemies for several weeks before he could break free; on another, only the devotion of a faithful comrade saved him from dying of a wound that had severed a vein in his neck. Always, Temuchin placed his faith in Jebe, Kubilai, Jelme, and Subudei, the four great generals who would fight with him throughout his life. Held in check by "chains of iron," these "four dogs" of Temuchin drew joy and sustenance only from the thrill of combat. On the day of battle, the chronicles said, "they eat the flesh of men." At such times, Temuchin soared above them "like a falcon which is become greedy for food."[6]

At the proper time, Temuchin wed the beautiful Lady Borte, daughter of an allied chieftain, only to have her abducted by men following the age-old Mongol tradition of seizing wives and concubines from the tents of their enemies. In a rage, Temuchin raised an army of forty thousand and pursued Borte's abductors into the thickly wooded lands of the Transbaikal. There, amidst the forests of pine overgrown with rhododendrons and orchids, near what is now Ulan-Ude in the Buriat lands of the present-day Russian Federation, Temuchin freed his wife. On the journey home, she gave birth to a son to whom she gave the name Juchi, uncertain whether his father was Temuchin or the enemy chieftain who had abducted her. One day, Juchi's son Batu would conquer Russia.[7]

After Borte's rescue, Temuchin proceeded to weld the warring Mongol tribes into a nation. In the spring of 1206, he summoned "all the people living in felt tents" to a solemn assembly, a Great Kuriltai, to decide their destiny. These were men and women born of want in the harsh circumstances of life in Inner Asia. Ignorant of writing, town life, and agriculture, they and their ancestors had tended their flocks, raided their neighbors, and worshiped the God of the Eternal Blue Sky Tengri for centuries on end. Nature, fate, and the predictions of shamans who consulted the gods in ways not understood by ordinary men and women shaped their lives. When their shamans proclaimed that Temuchin had won special favor in Tengri's eyes, the Kuriltai proclaimed him Chingis Khan.[8]

As "great khan of all the people living in felt tents," Chingis set out at the age of thirty-nine to build an empire that his sons would extend across three continents. A superbly disciplined, precisely organized cavalry force of more than a hundred thousand men supported by a corps of engineers that had mastered the best siege technologies known in East and West, his army was the most formidable fighting machine of its day. At times advancing in a "lake array" that spread their attack over a large area, at others marching in a "karaquana" formation, so named for the thorny karaquana bushes that grow in thick clumps on the Eurasian steppe, its men lived by the sword and thought only of the present.[9] "The greatest pleasure," Chingis Khan once said, "is to vanquish your enemies, chase them before you, rob them of their wealth, see those dear to them bathed in tears, ride their horses, [and] clasp to your bosom their wives and daughters."[10]

Able to travel long distances at great speed, the Mongol fighting men who shared this creed boasted astonishing powers of endurance. Their razor-sharp broad-headed arrows could inflict massive bleeding and almost instant death upon enemies at close range, while eagle-feathered shafts with lighter heads allowed them to kill at distances approaching four hundred yards. Every warrior carried a quiver of each type of arrow on his saddle and fired them from a large compound bow whose pull of at least 166 pounds far exceeded that of the famed English longbow. The high front and back of the Mongol cavalryman's heavy wooden saddle allowed him to sit firmly while shooting his arrows toward any point of the compass. In Mongol hands, such weapons had no equals. Not until the development of the breech-loading rifle in the 1860s did the world's fighting men again carry weapons that enabled them to surpass the accuracy and firepower of the thirteenth-century Mongols.

A cuirass of thick leather, sometimes reinforced by plates of copper or iron, a helmet of hide and iron that protected head, neck, and throat, a fur or sheepskin coat, a fur hat with ear flaps, felt socks, and heavy leather boots were the Mongol cavalryman's standard equipment for winter fighting. Dried meat, ten pounds of dried curds, a leather bottle filled with two liters of fermented mare's milk, at least two quivers, each with a side pocket to carry a file for sharpening arrowheads, an awl, and a needle and thread rounded out the supplies he carried unless he fought in the heavy cavalry, in which case he replaced his bow, arrows, and quivers with a saber, mace, and battle-ax, and a lance that had a cleverly designed hook at the base of its head for pulling enemies from the saddle. All Mongol horsemen led from one to four mounts that survived on whatever tufts of grass they could find along the way. In time of need, their riders could live on mouthfuls of blood sucked from their veins.[11]

Chingis Khan organized these horsemen, who could subsist on lice, the blood of their horses, and, in moments of real desperation, the flesh of their comrades, into tens, hundreds, thousands, and tens of thousands. Each unit shared a ruthless collective responsibility for the actions of its members. If a man fled in battle, the rest of his unit faced death for allowing him to do so, and Mongol commanders were expected to order the rest of a unit to be killed if they failed to rescue a comrade who had been taken prisoner. Such a force could be mobilized on short notice, moved toward an objective with great speed, and thrown into battle with devastating effect.[12]

Drawn south by the lure of booty and greater glory, Chingis Khan turned these fighting men toward the domains of the emperors of north China in 1211. Here was a land such as the Mongols had never seen, a land not wild like the steppe and forests whence they came but fully tamed, where fields of rice, maize, and millet had been cultivated for thousands of years by patient farmers skilled in drawing sustenance from the soil.

Yet access to this land did not come easily. Wild gorges, gloomy mountain passes, and the Gobi Desert guarded it from the north. Beyond them stood the Great Wall, the barrier that China's rulers had raised a thousand years before to protect their people from the ancestors of the Huns that Attila had led into Europe. Here was no steppe settlement of felt tents to be overridden by determined attackers, but a fortress formed by elements that man had tamed and turned to his advantage. To succeed here required more than raw courage; more, even, than the combined genius of the "four dogs" of Chingis Khan.

Not yet experienced in attacking heavily fortified positions, Chingis and his generals spent two years forcing a passage across China's Great Wall. Then they turned toward Peking, the capital of the King of Gold and one of the great metropolises of the world. Surrounded by a triple line of moats, its eighteen miles of stamped clay walls crowned by brick battlements along which twelve gates were interspersed with nine hundred towers, Peking was thought invincible. For two years the armies of Chingis stood before it, plotting its destruction and seeking to break through its defenses. With the help of captured Chinese engineers, they succeeded in May 1215, after which they carried away a vast hoard of gold, silver, precious stones, and rare silks.[13] Legend tells us that sixty thousand of Peking's women threw themselves from the city's walls rather than fall into the hands of the Mongol soldiers when the looting began. So many of its people were put to death that one eyewitness reported that "the bones of the slaughtered formed whole mountains, and the soil was greasy with human fat."[14] Then the Mongols razed Peking so completely that, when Chingis Khan's grandson Kublai decided to make his capital there a half century later, it had to be rebuilt from the ground up.

Although the Mongols continued to fight in China for another twenty years, Chingis Khan turned his main force westward soon after the fall of Peking. After overrunning the kingdom of the Kara-Kitans, which lay to the west of Lake Issyk-Kul, he led his armies into western Turkestan, where the Khorezm Empire stood as a flourishing island of civilization amid a sea of steppe lands and deserts. A powerful Muslim empire turned sour by palace intrigues and heavy taxation, Khorezm was ripe for attack.[15] Without popular support and with an army whose soldiers preferred to plunder than fight, Khorezm's sultan had to face the Mongols' cavalry army of nearly two hundred thousand men supported by the latest in Chinese siege technology. As the host of Chingis Khan entered the Khorezm lands, it brought with it hundreds of Chinese engines of war that could rain storms of stones and burning naphtha mixed with saltpeter upon a city's defenders from distances well beyond the range of their arrows and javelins.[16]

In the fall of 1219, Chingis Khan split his massive force into smaller units that ravaged the countryside and assembled hordes of captives to storm the walls of better defended cities. In February 1220, these forces reunited at Bukhara, the Central Asian center of learning and trade that produced the sumptuous silken carpets which still bear its name. Bukhara in those days was "the cupola of Islam," a city "embellished with the rarest of high attainments," in the words of the thirteenth-century Persian chronicler Ala-ad-Din Ata-Malik Juvaini.[17] Merchants thronged its bazaars and the Muslim faithful filled its mosques, but its defenses could not stand against Mongol attack. As they drove native captives against Bukhara's fiercely defended inner citadel, the surrounding moat filled with bodies and gave the Mongol shock troops easy access to the breaches that their siege engines had opened in its walls.[18] "It was a day of horror," an account of how the Mongols sent the survivors into exile concluded. "There was nothing to be heard but the sobbing of men, women, and children torn apart forever."[19]

Using captives from Bukhara to spearhead their advance, the Mongols advanced against Samarkand, a city of half a million people known for its graceful copper urns, fine cottons, silks, paper, and exquisite silver lamé fabrics. Its canals and fountains had made the desert bloom, and its melons, which were packed in leaden boxes filled with snow, were known and relished as far away as Baghdad.[20] "If it is said that a paradise is to be seen in this world, then the paradise of this world is Samarkand," one of Khorezm's poets had written. "A country whose stones are jewels, whose soil is musk and whose rain water is strong wine," another added,[21] Samarkand ranked among the greatest of Khorezm's treasures. Its defenses were thought to be the strongest in Central Asia, but that advantage was lost the moment the city's commander led its garrison into an ambush that claimed tens of thousands of its defenders. Attacking three days later to the traditional cacophony of drums, trumpets, and bellowing camels, the Mongols overwhelmed the last of Samarkand's defenders. After they sacked the city and leveled its ramparts, the Mongols herded the survivors together to be driven toward their next objective.[22]

Within a year, all of the major cities of the Khorezm lands had fallen to the terror of Chingis Khan. Chingis's youngest son butchered nearly three-quarters of a million innocents at Merv, according to Arab and Persian accounts. The same sources tell us that, after Nishapur was marked out for special vengeance because the great khan's son-in-law had been killed by an arrow shot from its walls, the Mongols held a blood carnival presided over by the dead prince's widow in which every captive was decapitated and their heads piled in pyramids. "Flies and wolves feasted on the breasts of religious dignitaries," the chronicler Juvaini wrote of the fearsome slaughter at Nishapur. "Eagles on mountain tops regaled themselves with the flesh of delicate women," he added, "and vultures banqueted on the throats of houris."[23] Because destruction had been the goal at Nishapur, the Mongols left a fortune in gold, silver, and precious stones among its rubble. In later years, it was said that thirty thousand dinars in treasure could be dug out of its ruins in a single day.[24]

In the weeks that followed, Bamiyan shared the fate of Merv. So did Gurganj, where the Mongols ended their victory celebration by destroying the main dam on the Amu-Daria and drowning the entire city. Herat was leveled to the ground after an orgy of killing that lasted a week. At Nisa, near present-day Ashkabad, the Mongols herded their victims into the fields, ordered them to tie each others' hands behind their backs, and then slaughtered them by firing arrows indiscriminately into their midst.[25] The stench of death lay heavily upon the fertile oases of Turkestan and eastern Persia. Such ruin would take a millennium to repair. "Even though there be generation and increase until the Resurrection," wrote Juvaini forty years later, "the population will not attain to a tenth part of what it was before."[26]

While Chingis watched the cities of Khorezm crumble, Jebe and Subudei, two of his "four dogs" of war, had ridden further west in search of Khorezm's sultan Mohammed, who had fled his kingdom during the summer of 1220. In hot pursuit, the two generals had chased their quarry into Khorezm's Persian provinces along the southern shores of the Caspian Sea. Darting back and forth like a trapped hare, the sultan had led them from Nishapur to Sebzevar, and from there to Ray, the greatest city of Persian Iraq. While the Mongols sacked Ray, Mohammed fled west, but Jebe and Subudei were at his heels again in an instant. Suddenly he turned to the southwest, perhaps intending to take refuge in Baghdad, and then, just as quickly, doubled back toward the Caspian. At one point, the Mongols' advance units came close enough to wound his horse with their arrows; on another, he escaped into the Caspian while a hail of Mongol arrows fell around his boat. Finally, at the very end of 1220 or the beginning of 1221, Sultan Mohammed died on the tiny Caspian island of Abeskun, leaving Jebe and Subudei free to pursue other ventures.

With twenty thousand horsemen at their command, the two Mongol generals looked for new kingdoms to conquer in the name of their master and the god Tengri. Galloping west across the high steppes that covered most of northwest Persia, they turned north into Azerbaijan, where they rested briefly in the Mugan steppes before they invaded Georgia. In late spring 1221, they swept back into Persia to fight a year-long campaign before they turned north again, forced their way through the Derbent Pass, and broke out onto the Black Sea steppes that make up the present-day Kuban. Now fully off their tethers, Jebe and Subudei entered the southern lands of Russia, where they smashed a small Russian army on the banks of the Kalka River in the southeastern Ukraine in June 1223. Then they crossed the Volga River near present-day Volgograd and rejoined Chingis's main army in Khorezm.[27] For the moment, what they had learned during their amazing foray into Russia had to be set aside while their chief planned a new war against China.

While the Mongols fought in China, the Russians resumed the dynastic feuds that had kept their land in turmoil for the better part of two hundred years. They made no attempt to forge new alliances for defense, nor did they reconnoiter the lands beyond the Volga to learn where the Mongols had gone. "We do not know where these evil Tartars came from," one chronicler of old Russia confessed. "Whither they went," he added, "only God knows."[28] For a decade and a half, the fearsome clouds of death that the horsemen of Jebe and Subudei had brought to the edge of the Russian land slipped back below the horizon. Then, in less time than it took for warriors born at the time of the Kalka battle to grow to manhood, the Mongols returned to find that the Russian land did not hold enough fighting men to stand against them.

The deaths of such great captains as Alexander the Great, Attila, and Charlemagne had destroyed their empires almost overnight, but the passing of Chingis Khan in August 1227 only spurred the Mongols to greater conquests. Chingis Khan bequeathed to each of his sons an *ulus*, that is, a number of tribes and the grazing lands needed to support their herds and flocks, but none of these bequests conferred the right to rule the Mongol Empire. The Grand Kuriltai bestowed that honor upon Ugedei, the third son, whom Chingis had chosen as his successor. While Ugedei reigned from the Mongol capital at Karakorum, his brothers and nephews spread their conquests deeper into China, Korea, western Persia, Russia, and Eastern Europe.[29] Later, each *ulus* became a powerful kingdom tied to Karakorum only by its loyalty to the great khan. The Persian khanate of the House of Hulegu, the khanate of Jagatai, which encompassed the old Khorezm Empire and the Kingdom of Kara-Kitai, the Mongol Empire of China under the House of Kublai Khan, and the

Golden Horde of Batu all grew out of the conquests that the sons and grandsons of Chingis Khan achieved before the middle of the thirteenth century.

Of these great inheritances, the *ulus* of Batu, second son of Chingis Khan's eldest son, Juchi, stretched westward from Siberia's borderlands and the steppes of Kazakhstan "as far as Mongol hooves have beaten the ground."[30] No one knew how far Mongol hooves actually had reached, nor did they know what lay beyond the lands they already had claimed. The expedition that Jebe and Subudei had led beyond the Caspian Sea during the Khorezm war therefore took on new importance in the mid-1230s, as Batu and his counselors looked west. Jebe, "the arrow" upon whom Chingis Khan had depended to lead lightning campaigns in years past, had joined his master in the world beyond the grave, but Subudei, although well beyond middle age, remained alive to tell the tale of the campaign on the Kalka fifteen years before. Batu therefore appointed Subudei, the last of the "four dogs" upon whom his grandfather had counted for the victories that had built his empire, to be his chief of staff for a campaign against the West. After crushing the Bulgars, whose kingdom centered around the modern-day city of Kazan and would become Ivan the Terrible's gateway to Siberia three hundred years later, Batu and Subudei were ready to attack Russia in the late fall of 1237.

3

Batu's Winter War

During the past thousand years, the Russians have fought four great winter wars. In 1708, one of the coldest winters on record destroyed the armies of Sweden's Charles XII as they wintered in Russia's southwest. A hundred and four years later, one of the nineteenth century's mildest winters transformed Napoleon's Grand Army into a starving, freezing rabble that left nineteen out of every twenty of its men behind in Russia. Then, in more recent times, the Wehrmacht of Nazi Germany suffered losses that rose into the millions as it froze in Russia's steppes. Only the horsemen of Batu Khan, who were bred to thrive in the rough storms that lashed the high Asian plains along Siberia's Mongolian frontier, have ever fought a successful winter war in Russia. Used to its rigors, they saw winter as a time of opportunity, when marshes turned solid underfoot and deep rivers became broad, smooth highways through the forest.

Preferring to fight in winter, Batu's host of 150,000 cavalry swept across the newly frozen Volga River into Russia's northeastern lands in November 1237 to attack Riazan, the first of several fortified towns that lay along their line of march. Because Riazan stood closest to the Bulgar lands that Batu's forces had ravaged earlier that year, its people had undoubtedly heard of the Mongols' atrocities, but they rejected the invader's traditional offer to spare them in return for a tenth of all they possessed.[1] From what the chronicles tell us, Riazan's prince believed that a stand had to be made lest the principalities of Russia's northeast fall to the Mongol armies one by one. He and his counselors therefore vowed to halt the Mongols' advance before it got fully under way, knowing full well that they had not the means to do so by themselves.

Like the Saracens (whose emissaries were on their way to the courts of France and England at that very moment to urge common action against the Mongol armies that Batu's uncles were leading into the Near East), the prince of Riazan called upon his neighbors for reinforcements. Yet Russia's princes paid no more heed to calls for unity than did the sovereigns of Western Europe. Civil wars had become yearly events in the Russian land, and the dominions of every prince were fair game for any other. Accustomed to internecine warfare and having no regrets about killing their countrymen, Russia's princes sent no reinforcements to help Riazan. As the Mongols closed their siege in December, the people of Riazan faced them alone.

The brutality with which Batu's generals developed their attack took the defenders of Riazan by surprise. Within five days Mongol sappers had ringed the town with breastworks and palisades to cut off every avenue of escape. Then, engineers who had practiced their art in sieges against the fortress cities of Central Asia attacked Riazan's walls with ballistae, catapults, and armored battering rams, weakening the defenses and preparing the way for an assault. When Mongol shock troops stormed the town's walls on the morning of December 21, fierce hand-to-hand fighting claimed lives by the hundreds on both sides. Men "fought with such intensity," one chronicle tells us, "that even the earth began to moan." Steel clashed against steel for hours until the Mongols overwhelmed Riazan's defenders.

In victory, the Mongols transformed one of northeast Russia's most picturesque towns into the first of the great hecatombs that would mark their campaign. "There was not even anyone to mourn the dead," the chronicle of Riazan's destruction concluded. "Neither father nor mother could mourn their dead children, nor the children their fathers or mothers. Nor could a brother mourn the death of his brother, nor relatives their relatives. All were dead."[2] Those whom Batu's archers shot for sport had to count themselves among the fortunate, for impaling, flaying, and crucifixion headed the list of torments that Riazan's survivors had to endure. Now the Russians knew what awaited those who refused to surrender to Batu's envoys. If they failed to triumph over their terrible foes, any who took up arms against the Mongols had to choose between dying with weapons in hand or being slaughtered without mercy.

After ravaging Riazan, the Mongols attacked Moscow, which, in those days, was one of Russia's smallest provincial towns. In political terms, this was hardly an objective worthy of the Mongols' effort because Moscow's ruler counted among the lowest ranking of the two dozen or more princes who ruled the Russian land. Yet Batu and Subudei did not decide to march more than a hundred miles to the west of their main objective at Vladimir merely to destroy a minor outpost. Endowed with the best reconnaissance of any army in the world, they knew that Moscow stood at the center of the upland in which the great rivers of European Russia had their beginnings and that it was a hub from which Russia's river highways zigged and zagged outward like the irregularly shaped spokes of a lopsided wheel. From Moscow, an army could move along Russia's frozen river highways in any direction or, if it was large enough, could advance in several directions at once.

From the Moscow hub, Batu and Subudei turned toward Vladimir, the largest city in Russia's northeast, the capital of its highest-ranking and most powerful prince and the headquarters of the one army that had to be destroyed before they dared to march farther west. Ruled at that time by Grand Prince Iurii II, Vladimir spread out for more than a mile along the Kliazma River. The onion domes of dozens of churches rose above its walls, and travelers from miles around used its brilliant white stone Cathedral of St. Dmitrii as a landmark. Although larger and better equipped than the force that had fought at Riazan, the army of Vladimir slowed Batu's advance for no more than a few days before the Mongols' siege engines breached the city walls and sappers once again built earthworks and palisades to close a siege around it. On Shrove Tuesday, the day when Russians traditionally feasted on thin pancakes in a final celebration before facing the denials of Lent, the Mongols burst into Vladimir and slaughtered the grand prince's mother, wife, and children, along with every other living soul they could find. The dawn of Ash Wednesday, February 9, 1238, found no one but Mongols alive in Vladimir.[3]

Hoping to raise a new army to fight in better circumstances, Prince Iurii had fled into the forest just before the Mongols had closed their ring around his capital. Spreading their forces to ravage the countryside as they had done in China and Khorezm, Batu and Subudei at first paid him no heed and spent the rest of the month destroying a dozen other Russian towns. Then, at the beginning of March, they overran Iurii's badly chosen new positions and slaughtered him and the rest of his men. Now free to turn toward Novgorod, the greatest commercial center in the Russian land and the eastern outpost of Northern Europe's powerful Hanseatic League, Batu and Subudei resumed their advance.[4]

As the Mongols approached Novgorod, fate and Nature turned against them. Perhaps grown too confident after their easy victories over a score of larger towns, Batu's force attacked the small outpost of Torzhok with every intention of taking no more than a day or two to clear one more minor obstacle from its path. But Torzhok held out for two full weeks, and, by the time its last defenders had fallen on March 23, the ice in the rivers and lakes of northwest Russia had begun to soften. With Nature threatening to turn their frozen river invasion routes into death traps that could swallow men and beasts in an instant, the Mongols halted just sixty miles short of Novgorod and turned toward Russia's southern steppe. There they rested for the next two years, replacing the men and mounts they had lost during their six months of furious winter fighting. Then, in the summer of 1240, Batu again divided his forces. Now joined by Mongka, a nephew who would become the next great khan, Batu and Subudei devastated the towns of southwestern Russia and then reassembled their armies near Kiev to strike a final blow against the Russians.[5]

A forest of gilded domes rising above white stone walls when seen from a distance, Kiev was one of the most beautiful cities in the lands of eastern Christendom, and one of the most important. St. Vladimir the Blessed, the prince who had brought Christianity to the Russian land in the tenth century, lay at rest in its great cathedral. So did his mother, the saintly Princess Olga, and the eleventh-century lawgiver, Iaroslav the Wise. During most of the Middle Ages, Kiev had been a center of art and learning, a steppe metropolis that had collected the rich influences of the Near and Middle East, integrated them with her Slavic past, and seasoned the resulting mixture with generous borrowings from the cultures of Central and Western Europe. Great brick palaces adorned its center, and libraries, hospitals, and schools enriched the lives of its people to an extent unknown in Paris or London at the time. The great epics of the medieval West mentioned Kiev and its people often, and its rulers were allied by ties of marriage to nearly every important royal family of Christian Europe. Aside from Constantinople, there was no greater prize between Baghdad and Vienna, and none more easily taken.

Standing at the crossroads where caravans carrying spices and silks from the Orient intersected with the traffic that moved along the "Great Amber Road" from the Baltic to Constantinople, Kiev was the "Mother of Russian Cities" and the bastion that had guarded the eastern frontier of Christian Europe against Eurasia's steppe nomads for more than two hundred years. Without Kiev, medieval Krakow, Budapest, and Vienna could not have flourished in the way that they had, for the fierce steppe horsemen who had been driven back from Kiev's walls so many times would have ridden farther west. But, as the thirteenth century approached its midpoint, Kiev had grown weak. Tarnished by the strife that continued to keep Russia's rival princes apart, its brilliance had begun to fade. No longer could Kiev's prince summon the armies of a dozen lesser rulers to his aid, nor had he the wealth to fight large wars as his ancestors had done. The ravages of politics had eroded the pillars that had elevated Kiev above ancient Russia's other cities, but it still remained a lavish final course for Batu's hordes, a worthy conclusion to the bloody banquet they had enjoyed since they had entered the Russian land three years before.

At Kiev, the Russians felt for the first time the full fury that the Mongols had unleashed against Peking and the cities of Khorezm. Prince Mongka, who would soon show that he had all the ruthlessness needed to rule an empire in which politics were becoming more divisive and the ruling class increasingly unstable, sent the usual envoys to offer subjugation, only to have the defenders of Kiev kill them to prevent the faction that favored peace at any price from negotiating.[6] Now there would be no mercy for man, woman, or beast if the Mongols breached Kiev's defenses. As at Riazan and Vladimir, the assault against Kiev would be a fight to the death, but its greater size and wealth meant that battle would be waged on a larger scale.

As the Mongols gathered before Kiev in "thick clouds," the ancient chronicles tell us, the clamor of creaking carts, bellowing camels and oxen, and neighing horses, all numbering in the tens of thousands, deadened reason and put men's minds on edge. Inside the city's walls, people had to shout to make themselves heard, and a sense of doom hung heavily upon them.[7] Once the Mongols had closed their ring, some of their siege engines began to batter Kiev's walls with boulders and rams, while others rained javelins and pots of liquid fire upon them. "Arrows darkened the daylight,"[8] and the howling of beasts and men filled the night to swell pangs of fear into waves of terror. Here was the onset of events so awful that none dared contemplate their outcome.

Attacks flowed one upon the other, their clamor never ceasing. After several days of desperate fighting (the chronicles disagree about whether the date was November 19 or December 6), the Mongols broke into the city, slaughtered all who remained, and ravaged the buildings and churches.[9] Frenzied horsemen scattered the relics of Russia's first saints to the four winds and destroyed the treasures of art and learning that had made Kiev famous. The evidence of their brutality would remain for years to come. "We came across countless skulls and bones of dead men lying about on the ground," the Franciscan friar Giovanni del Plano Carpini reported after his visit to Kiev six years later. "There are at the present time," he wrote, "scarcely two hundred houses there."[10] Friar Giovanni found cathedrals in ruins, destined to survive only as stones scattered through the foundations of churches to be built in centuries yet to come. More than two hundred years would pass before a new city would begin to rise from the rubble that the Mongols left behind when they moved westward into Poland and Hungary at the beginning of 1241. In the meantime, the people of the Russian land would be their vassals, destined to fight in Mongol armies as far west as Hungary and as far east as China.

At odds with their neighbors and divided among themselves, none of the princes and people whose lands Batu's armies had conquered between 1237 and 1240 had a sense of national destiny that could have united them against their enemies. Russia in those days was not yet Russia, and that made it a simple matter for Mongols guided by the imperial vision of Chingis Khan to hold them in servitude. Willing to pay tribute to their Mongol overlords just as weaker princes in the Russian land had paid tribute to their stronger cousins in the days before Batu's host had come, Russia's many princes continued their civil wars. Until they developed a sense of national identity that could unite them against a foreign enemy, neither the princes nor the people in the lands we now know as Russia could hope to free themselves from the yoke that the Mongols imposed.[11]

Insignificant at the time of Batu's winter war, the princes of Moscow eventually forged the Russians into a nation. Overcoming their rivals one by one, at times by diplomacy, at others by treachery, and resorting to arms only when every other course had failed, Moscow's princes slowly added Vladimir, Suzdal, Rostov, and a score of other principalities to their own, gaining new resources of men and treasure with every acquisition. This was the historic "gathering of the Russian lands" that Grand Prince Ivan I began in the 1320s. Six generations later, the gathering would be completed and Moscow's domains would have increased a full fortyfold. By that time, "Moscow" had become "Russia."

An obscure prince whose reign ended just a few years before the Black Death swept Europe, Ivan I was a schemer among schemers. Karl Marx once described him as a ruler who combined the "qualities of a Mongol hangman, a sycophant, and a slave-in-chief,"[12] but his people called him Ivan Kalita, that is, "Ivan the Moneybag," in recognition of his well-known reluctance to part with Moscow's treasure. Careful to curry favor with the Mongols, who by that time had taken the name of the Golden Horde and built a capital called Sarai in the vicinity of present-day Volgograd, Ivan Kalita became one of their chief tax collectors. A part of what he took in the name of the khan remained in Moscow, and he used that new treasure to gain the upper hand among his feuding rivals.

From the perspective of six hundred years' hindsight, the triumph of Ivan Kalita and his descendants seems all but inevitable, but, to the men and women who lived through it, the gathering of the Russian lands seemed to have been timidly undertaken and erratically completed. Others also knew how to turn Russia's political turmoil to their advantage, and the princes of Moscow were by no means the only ones to curry favor with Batu's successors at Sarai. What set Ivan and his successors apart from their rivals was their close alliance with the Russian Orthodox Church, the metropolitan of which became Moscow's chief ally. While their enemies fell by the wayside, the princes of Moscow used their unique combination of wealth, political power, and church support to become the Mongols' successors as the masters of the Russian land.[13]

The monkish chroniclers who recorded the gathering of the Russian lands called the rulers of Moscow the earthly agents of Christ, and pious churchmen proclaimed that any who followed them were doing God's work on earth. Moscow's rulers, so the church claimed, had a divine mission to unite the Russian land and destroy the Mongol yoke.[14] Combined with rivalries among the descendants of Batu Khan that produced muddled and erratic policies toward the Russians,[15] these urgings of the Church Fathers convinced the grand prince Dmitrii, Moscow's ruler between 1359 and 1389, to test the strength of his Mongol overlords at what history remembers as the battle of Kulikovo Field. Fought along the banks of the Don River on the Feast Day of the Nativity of the Virgin, September 8, 1380, this battle marked the first time in history that the Russians turned the tide of battle against the Mongo's.

4

On Kulikovo Field

Friday, September 8, 1380, dawned in dense fog on Kulikovo Field. Fog covered both banks of the Don River, and the Mongol soldiers of Khan Mamai, who were marching to punish Moscow's grand prince for attacking one of their raiding expeditions two years before, had gathered around large kettles of food to fill their stomachs after several days' forced march. This was the largest Mongol force to invade the Russian land since the days of Batu, and one that was expected to be even more effective than the army of steppe horsemen he had led. Elite infantry units from the Genoese settlements in the Crimea had been hired to anchor its center so that the Mongol cavalry would be free to fight on both flanks, and the armies of Grand Duke Jagiello of Lithuania, known to be one of the most formidable forces anywhere in Eastern Europe, were expected to join them in a few days' time. Together, Mongols and Genoese numbered about thirty thousand; Jagiello's force would increase their ranks by half that amount again.

In an age when an army of twenty-five thousand was thought to be very large, the union of two such forces promised to give Mamai overwhelming strength against the Russians. Certain of that and confident that the Russians were still far away, he had called in the shield of cavalry that usually served as the eyes and ears of advancing Mongol armies. Now he and his men were waiting at Kulikovo Field, the "field of snipes," until Lithuania's grand duke joined them. Once united, they planned to march together against Moscow.

While the Mongols had been advancing without the cavalry reconnaissance that had made them famous from China's Great Wall to the Mediterranean, an army of Russians was marching toward the Don. Like the Mongols, they numbered about thirty thousand, probably the largest force of Russians ever assembled against an enemy. From spies and informers they knew the Mongols' plans for a joint campaign with Jagiello's Lithuanians, and they knew that both forces thought they still were in Moscow. Hoping to take the Mongols by surprise and defeat them before the two armies joined, Moscow's prince Dmitrii advanced quickly, sending horsemen to reconnoiter the land far ahead of his main force. He had already chosen as his battlefield the same Kulikovo Field on which the Mongols were waiting for the Lithuanians.

A slightly rounded spit of grassland formed by the junction of the Don and Nepriadva rivers, Kulikovo seemed well suited to Prince Dmitrii's purpose. The deep streams and thickets that cut across it would prevent the Mongols from using their cavalry to sweep up his flanks once the battle had been joined, and the larger rivers on each side would prevent them from attacking his force from the rear. From Dmitrii's perspective, the only dangerous terrain lay on his right, where, if the Mongol cavalry won enough room to force his army against the steep banks of the Nepriadva, it would be hard pressed to escape. Otherwise, a shallow ford across the Don left the way open for retreat.

While the Mongols gathered around their kettles that morning, Prince Dmitrii moved his men into position under the cover of the heavy Don fog. Certain of salvation in the world beyond the grave if they shed their blood beneath their prince's black banner, the Russians looked for "a second baptism" in battle. "Let us place upon our heads the crown of victory!" Dmitrii told them as he set aside his richly ornamented weapons and donned the armor of an ordinary Russian warrior. "If I die, it will be among you," he told the men who would be fighting on his left and right. "If I survive, it will be while fighting among you also."[1] By then the fog had begun to lift, and the Mongols saw the men of Moscow advancing against them. As they seized their weapons, they did not see the reserves of cavalry that Dmitrii had placed in ambush in the large thicket that stood on the Russians' left.

The Battle of Kulikovo Field began at about eleven in the morning, when each side sent forth a champion to fight in single combat. The men, the chronicles tell us, struck each other with their lances simultaneously, and both died at the same instant. Then the Mongol and Russian armies fell upon each other, with Russian straight swords and Mongol scimitars slashing against each other all across the field. Neither side gave ground or gained it, and blood, the chronicle says, "flowed as in a cloudburst."[2] Some of Prince Dmitrii's men saw his horse fall beneath him right after midday. Others saw him remount, and still others remembered him fighting on foot after that, limping and wounded, but still in the battle when the balance began to tilt toward the Mongols in midafternoon. Then, just as the khan's armies seemed about to claim victory, the reserves that Dmitrii had hidden in ambush fell upon their rear and drove them from the field. Not until evening did the Russians find their prince, unconscious but still living, beneath a pile of corpses. Dmitrii had been spared, but twelve Russian princes, almost five hundred great lords, and nearly half of the army he had led to the Don had perished.

It took eight days for the Russians to bury their fallen comrades in a common grave before they left Kulikovo Field laden with trophies. Proclaimed "Donskoi" by his people in honor of his victory on the banks of the Don, Dmitrii had shaped a major watershed in Mongol-Russian relations, even though he would die before the age of forty from the internal injuries he had suffered during the battle.[3] Still another century would have to pass before the Russians' final liberation from the Mongol yoke. That would happen only when the princely conflicts that had darkened Russian political life since before the days of Batu Khan had been put to rest and the Russian lands gathered together under one sovereign.

Although a heroic moment in Russia's history, Dmitrii's victory at Kulikovo had done nothing to wipe away the political instability that had weakened the Russians for so long. Even though fear of Mamai's invasion had prompted some of the Russians to take up arms against him, others had sided with the Mongols all along. Four great princes, including the powerful rulers of Novgorod and Tver, had sent no troops to Dmitrii's army in 1380, and the victory over Mamai's host had divided even those who had. When the Mongols sent another expedition against Moscow two years later, no more than a handful of allies helped Dmitrii defend his capital. Half a century after Ivan Kalita had begun to gather the Russian lands, the Russians seemed more divided than ever.

At the same time, forces even more destructive than those working against Russia's unification were pulling the Mongols apart. Ever since Janibeg Khan had been murdered by his son in 1357, Mongols had been fighting Mongols throughout the lands of the Golden Horde, and

Mamai had been only one khan among several who had risen to rule parts of Batu's once indivisible realm during the 1360s and 1370s. From Central Asia to the Crimea, murderous men were vying for power, and they used assassination against their enemies as indiscriminately as modern-day politicians would use parliamentary debates. At one point, such murders claimed five khans in five years. As Mamai began his campaign against the Russians at Kulikovo, an explosively unstable situation continued to fester in his rear troops.[4] The forces that were pulling the Mongols apart in those days were thus even more destructive than those working against Russia's unification. Just as urgently as the Russians needed a strong man to unite them against the Mongols, the Mongols needed one to bind them together once again.

Just such a hero arose in Central Asia while Dmitrii was growing to manhood and fighting his first wars in Russia's northeast. Born in the city of Kesh in 1336, the Year of the Mouse, Timur the Lame (or Tammerlane, as he would be known in the West) was in every way the antithesis of the sign under which he had been born. A brilliant soldier, a patron of art, literature, and the law, and a prudent leader who viewed the world (in the words of a great historian of the steppe) from the perspective of "far-sighted Machiavellianism," Tammerlane became a practitioner of *realpolitik* in its most dynamic form and the builder of the last of the great Mongol empires in Eurasia.[5]

While Dmitrii fought against his rivals in northeast Russia, Tammerlane conquered much of the old Khorezm Empire and built a new capital at Samarkand. Reborn from the ruins left by Chingis Khan's hordes and adorned with a dazzling array of new buildings and monuments, this became the last of the great Mongol cities. Here Tammerlane built the Mosque of Bibi Khanum in honor of his favorite wife, its main portal flanked by minarets overlain with exquisite mosaic ornamentations and its courtyard dominated by a huge Koran desk formed from two colossal wedge-shaped stones. Farther on, Tammerlane's builders added a mausoleum for each of the khan's sisters, and on the other side of the citadel they placed his own tomb, the Gur Emir, whose massive sky blue dome still rises above his city.

In the late 1370s, Tammerlane struck an alliance with Prince Tokhtamysh, a disgruntled nephew of the khan of Kazakhstan and a brilliant general who needed only the smallest amount of encouragement to march against the fragmented lands of the Golden Horde. Quickly, Tokhtamysh conquered their eastern parts, and then, as Mamai marched against Dmitrii at Kulikovo, he advanced upon Mamai's rear, determined to pit Mongol against Mongol in a battle that would have been unthinkable in Chingis's time. Not far from the ancient field on which Jebe and Subudei had defeated the Russians in 1223, Tokhtamysh shattered Mamai's army in 1381. Then he, not the less able Mamai, took the field against the Russians.[6]

Supported by Dmitrii's Russian rivals, Tokhtamysh marched straight to Moscow and stormed its newly built bastions of stone and brick. After his armies had fought for three days and nights without success, Tokhtamysh used a flag of truce and a false promise of negotiations to induce Moscow's defenders to open its gates. Then his army fell upon the Muscovites, slaughtering them in the streets, in their homes, and in the great stone churches in which they sought refuge from the flames that consumed the city. "All at once her beauty perished and her glory disappeared," the chronicler of Voskresensk wrote of Moscow after the Mongols had finished their work. "Nothing could be seen," he added, "but smoking ruins and bare earth and heaps of corpses."[7] Having gone north to raise reinforcements before Tokhtamysh had begun his attack, Dmitrii returned with fewer troops than he needed to find more than twenty thousand corpses scattered in the ruins of his capital.[8] Already Russia's princes were hurrying to pay tribute to the Golden Horde's new ruler. Unable to unite his allies of the Kulikovo campaign behind him again, Dmitrii submitted as well.

When Dmitrii renewed his pledge to the Golden Horde at the end of 1382, it seemed that the gathering of Russia's lands had fallen upon very hard times.[9] Yet men like Tokhtamysh and Tammerlane could not remain allies for very long, and their rivalry soon rendered the Russians' situation less desperate. Throughout the 1380s and 1390s, the two Mongol princes fought each other in wars that raged across Dagestan, Transoxania, and Kazakhstan until Tokhtamysh was left with only a fragment of his once mighty host. Yet fate kept him and Tammerlane from that terrible, final clash in which the triumph of one would have meant the death of the other. Tammerlane died in February 1405 as he set out to conquer China, while Tokhtamysh, who had found refuge in the remote khanate of the Tatars in western Siberia, died at about the same time while trying to assemble one more army to hurl against his rival.[10] After that, the Mongols' power declined while that of the Russians, finally welded into a nation by Dmitrii's grandson Vasilii the Blind, grew too strong for the Mongols to oppose.[11]

The final confrontation between Mongols and Russians took place in October 1480, a century and a month after Mamai's defeat. Once again, the Mongol khan began his war by making an alliance with Lithuania, Russia's greatest enemy in Eastern Europe, only to have the Lithuanians fail him, just as they had failed Mamai. This time, there was no great pitched battle between Russian and Mongol as there had been at Kulikovo. After several months of facing each other from positions on opposite banks of the Ugra River, the Mongols retreated into the steppe, leaving the grand prince of Moscow to replace their khan as the supreme authority in the Russian land.[12]

At his death in 1505, Ivan the Great, the grand prince who had led the Russians against the Mongols in 1480, left only a few finishing touches to be added by his son to unite all of the lands of northern and eastern Russia firmly under Moscow's control. Moscow's grand princes were about to become tsars of all the Russias, the new overlords of the lands west of the Urals.[13] Yet if the grand prince of Moscow had become the greatest among the Russians, rulers more powerful than he stood to his north and west. To the north, Sweden barred Russia's way to the Baltic and Western Europe while Poland, now joined by ties of marriage to Lithuania, had become the most powerful state between Russia and the Holy Roman Empire.

With the road to further conquest closed in the west, the Russians turned east. Just as the Mongols once had reached from Inner Asia toward the rich grazing lands of the west, so in the second half of the sixteenth century the Russians began to reach east toward the treasure-filled fur lands of Siberia. Ivan the Great sent several punitive expeditions to punish the natives of Siberia's northwest corner during the last years of his reign, including one that captured some forty native villages and more than a thousand prisoners.[14] Yet to approach Siberia from that direction proved too arduous and difficult, even in the best of times. Some five hundred miles to the south lay an easier route, but in the days of Ivan the Great the Tatar khanate of Kazan barred the Russians' way. Before Moscow's rulers could think seriously about staking a permanent claim to Siberia, Kazan would have to be taken.

Ivan the Terrible, grandson of Ivan the Great and Russia's first true tsar, opened the way to Siberia through Kazan. By all contemporary accounts tall and strongly built, with small blue eyes that were piercing and quick, Ivan shaved his head and wore his beard thick and long in true Muscovite fashion. Daring, crafty, and cruel, he inspired fear in greater measure than had any of his predecessors. A recent examination of his skeleton by medical experts has shown that spinal disease crippled him during his later years, but we do not know how much it hindered his efforts to rule Russia. Nor do we know the extent to which the drugs and alcohol he consumed to deaden his pain affected his judgment. So murky are the sources about Ivan's reign that the very best modern scholars still cannot agree about whether he wrote some of the epistles that have been attributed to him. Some experts are not even sure if Ivan the Terrible knew how to read and write.[15]

When Ivan began to rule in his own right in 1547, the heritage of almost three hundred years of Mongol domination very naturally drew his attention to the east, where the grandsons of the men who had marched against his grandfather in 1480 ruled the broken fragments of the Golden Horde. Because the Tatars, a fringe element in the Golden Horde in Batu's time, had come decisively to the fore as the Mongol Empire fell apart, historians tell us that these warring factions should no longer be called Mongols, but Tatars. None of the small Tatar states scattered through western Siberia and Kazakhstan ever seriously challenged the tsars of Moscow as their forefathers had done, but each proved to be a nuisance, especially when they allied with the Ostiak and Vogul tribesmen who lived in Siberia's northwest. Young Ivan the Terrible made the stronghold of Kazan his first foreign venture because the Tatars of Kazan had become the most bothersome of all.[16]

While Russia's senior churchmen cheered his campaign as a crusade of the Cross against the Muslim Crescent, Ivan modernized his armies and reorganized his government to prepare for war. Using a newly formed corps of musketeers to supplement Moscow's traditional cavalry armies and supporting both with artillery, his generals took Kazan by storm at the beginning of October 1552, winning for Russia control of the river routes that flowed from the crest of the Ural Mountains to the Volga.[17] With the way to Siberia now open, daring entrepreneurs made ready to take advantage of the tsar's conquest. At their head stood Anika Stroganov, whose uncanny sense of timing and opportunity would make his family one of the richest in Russia. Using the Kazan gateway, he and his sons would build a private empire on the edge of Siberia that would elevate their heirs to the pinnacle of Russia's nobility.

The beginnings of the Russians' conquest of the continent that lay between the Urals and the Pacific exhibited none of the glory, pathos, or sheer terror that had marked the Mongols' march into Europe. The forces of Moscow and the Stroganovs advanced into Asia with no great host as Batu Khan had done, nor did mounds of dead mark their line of march. A flurry of skirmishes, a few small battles, and a handful of frontier forts and trading posts scattered along Siberia's westernmost rivers in the 1580s and 1590s marked the Russians' path. Until just a few years ago, historians were not even entirely certain of the year in which the events that began the "conquest" of Siberia took place.

PART TWO

The Russians Take Siberia

5

Anika and His Sons

Legend has it that the family of Anika Stroganov derived its name from the fate of Spiridon, an aristocratic Mongol ancestor who fled the khan's service to join the entourage of Dmitrii Donskoi. Spiridon had served the Russians for several years, converting to Christianity, marrying one of them, and earning a reputation as a faithful servant. The Mongols obviously saw him differently, and, during Tokhtamysh's war against Moscow, they arrested him as a traitor and executed him by peeling his flesh off in strips, layer by layer, until nothing but his bones remained. Spiridon's widow took refuge in the valley of the Dvina River in European Russia's northeastern corner, where hundreds of miles of virgin forest separated her and the son she had borne after her husband's death from the vengeful Mongols of Tokhtamysh. Commemorating her husband's martyrdom by taking the name of Stroganov (from the Russian verb *strogat*, meaning "to peel"), she founded the family who became the keepers of Siberia's western gateway and the Midases of early modern Russia.[1]

The early Stroganovs became traders in Solvychegodsk, a town that had sprung up along the shores of a recently discovered salt lake on the northeast Russian frontier. There, Spiridon's grandson Luka joined a number of enterprising Russians in dipping water out of the town's famed salt lake, boiling it in large rectangular iron pans, and collecting the fine residue that remained after the liquid had evaporated.[2] Russians in those days treasured salt nearly as much as they valued gold, because it was their only way of preserving food. Without native sources of salt before the discovery of the Solvychegodsk salt lake, the Russians had been obliged to depend for their supply upon North Europe's Hansa merchants and the Genoese traders who had colonized the Crimea. For centuries they had paid dearly for one of medieval life's greatest necessities. Now the Solvychegodsk enterprises, although worked on a scale too small to take the place of foreign salt in Luka's time, offered the Russians a chance to end the dependence that had tied them to foreign merchants. Eventually produced in quantities so huge that Russia became a salt-exporting country, salt was to become the cornerstone of the Stroganovs' fortune.

The records do not show how Luka rose above his fellow salt boilers, but he had become rich enough by the middle of the fifteenth century to pay part (some sources insist that he paid all) of the ransom demanded for Moscow's grand prince Vasilii the Blind by his Mongol captors.[3] In those days, Moscow's ruler had not yet gathered all the Russian lands, and Luka's loyalty stood to cost him dear if one of the grand prince's rivals won out in the struggle to rule Russia. Nonetheless, he took the risk, foreseeing the days when the grand prince of Moscow would become Tsar of All the Russias. Memories of those long-ago days would remain with Moscow's rulers for the next five hundred years while the Stroganovs served them as merchant adventurers, bankers, diplomats, courtiers, and patrons of the arts. Always loyal, always ready to take risks in their sovereigns' service, the Stroganov family stood as a pillar of the Russian throne until the Revolution of 1917. In return, Russia's tsars showered these loyal subjects with privileges and honors that raised Luka's descendants to the ranks of the richest and most famous men and women in Russia. Peter the Great would make the Stroganovs counts of the Russian Empire; in the nineteenth century, one of Luka's descendants would wed a daughter of the tsar.

By buying up the enterprises of his neighbors during the 1520s and 1530s, Luka's grandson Anika laid the foundations of the commercial empire that made the Stroganovs fabulously rich. Scorning the narrow vision of Russia's merchants and disdaining their interest in small profits, Anika stopped evaporating lake water as his father and grandfather had done and brought in experts from Europe who taught him how to pump water saturated with salt from underground springs that flowed through subterranean salt beds and evaporate it in heated sluices.[4] Quickly his vision paid handsome dividends. As Anika's enterprises gave the Russians their first native source of salt large enough to meet their needs, the Stroganovs made a fortune by having a monopoly on the sale of it.

The tsar knew Anika's worth and so did his counselors, but Anika was not content to live in the past or rest satisfied with the present. Thinking of the future and dreaming of empires, he traded his salt for furs, and as the pelts of sable and black Arctic fox flowed into his warehouses, he petitioned the tsar for permission to trade directly with the English merchants who had just found their way through the White Sea to the mouth of the Dvina River on Russia's northern coast. Anika offered furs to the English that were worth nearly their weight in gold in the markets of Europe and received in return Western luxuries that he traded to his countrymen for more furs.[5] Like all men of ambition and means, he knew where and how to bestow gifts; as the tsar's "humble slave," he sent the best of his furs to his royal master and his favorites so that when Russia's conquest of Kazan opened the way to the Siberian frontier, he and his sons stood at the head of the line of those seeking the chance to take great risks for greater profits in Russia's eastern borderlands.

By that time, Anika had built a massive wooden castle to serve as his headquarters at Solvychegodsk. Measuring more than two hundred feet across its front, its heavy wooden walls were punctuated by tiny windows that let in only a few shafts of light. Torches and oil lamps cast eerie shadows across its interior even at midday, as servants and accountants scurried to do their master's bidding. Gloomy and damp like the caverns that held the salt from which the wealth that built it had come, the Stroganov castle fell just short of being grotesque. Towers and turrets that vaguely reflected the style of Europe signaled Anika's effort to draw closer to the West despite a xenophobic Church and government that worked to preserve the old ways at the expense of progress.[6] At Moscow, tsar and patriarch insisted that travelers who came from the West be confined to a special section of the city and that Russians be taught to regard foreign ways and learning with deep suspicion. At Solvychegodsk, where Europeans came and went more frequently than in Moscow because of the Stroganov fur trade, Anika saw things differently.

Foreigners were one of the keys to the trade that built Anika's empire, and he therefore insisted that his sons learn the ways of the English, Dutch, and Germans with whom his agents exchanged furs, forest products, and grain. The West, he knew, had much to offer, especially the technology that allowed its explorers to sail the world's seas at a time when ignorance of the compass forced Russian sailors to remain within sight of land. Knowing that whoever in Russia possessed the West's science held the key to the future, Anika worked to bring the learning of the West to Solvychegodsk and to integrate it into the world around him. His experiment with architecture proved how awkward that undertaking could be, for the gap between the two cultures remained large and difficult to bridge. Nonetheless, the Stroganovs' castle held the largest private library anywhere in Russia, and it became a melting pot for the culture and politics of East and West. There, learning, wealth, security, and success blended together to form a firmly set anchor that guaranteed the family's fortune. For another century, Solvychegodsk— at odds with its surroundings and a monument to the tensions that East meeting West could produce—would remain the nerve center that animated the Stroganovs' empire, even after the focus of their vision had shifted from Europe to Siberia.

From the awkward keep that he had raised out of the north Russian forest, Anika presided over enterprises that reached from the White Sea coast to Moscow and beyond. As he passed fifty, there was much of the biblical patriarch about his way of doing business, and even more in his manner of ruling the lives of his three sons. Anika's eldest son, Grigorii, had inherited his love of learning, while Iakov was endowed with his practical interest in science. Semën, the youngest, had his father's thirst for beauty, traditionally focused, and expressed it by organizing the famous Stroganov school of icon painters in Russia's Siberian borderlands at the end of the sixteenth century.[7] In the mid-1550s, it became Semën's task to hold the Solvychegodsk bastion while his father and two elder brothers set out to conquer the Siberian frontier. Left behind, Semën became the patriarch of the Stroganovs' next generation before his time.[8]

The Russian conquest of Kazan had turned the attention of Anika and his sons to the lands that later would become the Russian province of Perm. Even while the Tatars still held Kazan, Stroganov agents had explored the territory beyond it and had found new salt springs at Solikamsk, where the land could be tilled more easily than in the far north.[9] In the Perm territory, from which river transport to Moscow was more direct, the Stroganovs could increase their salt production at lower cost, feed their workers more cheaply, and have easier access to Siberia's furs than at Solvychegodsk. A prize of great value to whoever could exploit it, the Perm lands were the reward the Stroganovs sought for their long years of giving gifts and loyal service to the tsar. They had but to ask, and Perm became theirs. Ready to reward their loyalty, Ivan the Terrible also intended to turn their genius for making fortunes in the wilderness to his treasury's advantage. Allowing the Stroganovs to develop European Russia's eastern frontier would be an investment in the future, even though its dividends would be some time in coming. Ivan understood that the taxes Anika's heirs would pay on their profits would add a fortune to the coffers of his successors in the years ahead. In the meantime, holding the eastern lands of the Perm territory gave the Stroganovs control of Russia's Siberian gateway, for the Kama and Chusovaia rivers that flowed through it connected the crest of the Ural Mountains directly to the Volga and the river route to Moscow.

In 1558, Ivan the Terrible leased nine and a quarter million acres of "empty lands, dense forests, wild streams and lakes, empty islands and pools" that lay "along both banks of the river Kama up to the river Chusovaia" to Anika's son Grigorii. Grigorii received full rights to develop the land as he saw fit so long as he reported any gold, silver, copper, or tin he found to the authorities in Moscow. Exempted from taxes on his new enterprises for twenty years, Grigorii received a royal dispensation to build forts along Russia's Siberian frontier and "to set up in it cannon and muskets, and station gunners, and musketeers and artillery men" to defend his saltworks and settlements against native attacks from the Siberian side of the Urals.[10] Here the Stroganovs reigned supreme, free even from the authority of the tsar's officials. "The tsar's officials cannot handle cases of the Stroganovs and their men," a supplementary charter stated in 1564, "unless the latter commit murder or are caught while plundering."[11] As the first line of defense on Russia's eastern frontier, Stroganov settlements and frontier blockhouses thus became the Russians' staging area for the conquest of Siberia.[12]

A decade after he had leased the lands along the Kama to Grigorii, Ivan the Terrible more than doubled the Stroganovs' holdings in Perm's Siberian borderlands by giving Iakov the same rights to the lands that lay along the Chusovaia River from its source in the Urals to the point where it emptied into the Kama.[13] From there, the Stroganovs could send their trappers, traders, and tribute collectors along the rivers of western Siberia to begin opening the empire that Anika had been dreaming of since his early days as a salt boiler in Solvychegodsk. Now the masters of a domain that was two thirds the size of sixteenth-century England, the Stroganovs had become the largest private landholders in Russia. Still loyal servants of a tyrannical tsar, they had risen in the space of two generations from humble salt boilers to Russia's richest entrepreneurs.

For Anika, the prize had come at least a decade too late. Over seventy when Grigorii received his first charter from the tsar, the old man had outlived two wives and was now ready to devote his last years to prayer and contemplation of the world to come. Leaving his sons and grandsons to carry on his work, the patriarch of the Stroganovs therefore took the name of Ioasaf, retired to a monastery, and lived out his final days as a monk while his sons took the first steps to shift the eastern edge of the empire he had built into Siberia itself. Nearly equal to their father in shrewdness, and with greater energy and more strength, Grigorii and Iakov Stroganov sent the first traders across the Urals to collect fur tribute from the natives and fill the Solvychegodsk warehouses with rare Siberian furs.[14]

While agents sent by Grigorii and Iakov moved the leading edge of the Stroganov empire into Siberia, their new settlements along the Kama River had to bear the brunt of the first Siberian counterattacks. Almost directly east of the point where the Chusovaia River had its beginnings near the Urals' crest, the khanate of Sibir, the sister state of the fallen Tatar khanate of Kazan, stood guard over Siberia's western fur lands.[15] As Stroganov expeditions moved eastward into the khan's lands, they confronted an enemy whose fighting strength no one in Russia knew and whose resources no one could accurately calculate. By itself, the army of the Sibir Tatars did not seem to be large, but neither was the force that the Stroganovs could send against it. The key question the Stroganovs faced in the 1570s was how many of the Siberian tribes who owed allegiance to the Sibir khan would honor their pledges. If other natives such as the Ostiaks and the Voguls added their fighting men to the khan's army, the Stroganovs might face a formidable enemy.

While the Tatars at Kazan had been fighting against the armies of Ivan the Terrible in the 1540s and 1550s, the Tatars of Sibir had faced other conflicts and different enemies. Rival clans had assassinated several of Sibir's khans during the half century before Kazan's fall, and the ensuing political turmoil had encouraged Ivan the Terrible to demand thirty thousand sable pelts from them as a yearly tribute. The Tatars sent seven hundred and, despite continued threats from the tsar's diplomats, never sent more than a thousand. Moscow, they now knew, had become too deeply embroiled in a war with Sweden and Poland to enforce its demands for tribute in the east so long as they sent a token payment.[16]

Even so, continuing feuds between its princes seemed certain to condemn Sibir to follow in Kazan's footsteps until Kuchum Khan, a descendant of the great Chingis, brought its rebel lords and feuding princes to heel in the 1560s. With the lands and lords of Sibir under control for the first time in half a century and with a large force of Crimean Tatars marching as allies of the Ottoman Empire against Russia from the south, Kuchum paid one last tribute of furs to the tsar in 1571 and prepared for war. Hoping to take advantage, as one report explained, of the natives' resentment at the way in which the Stroganovs' new settlers "seized the places where the natives hunted beavers and gathered honey and fished,"[17] Kuchum strengthened his alliances with his neighbors. Then, as the Crimean forces advanced against Moscow that summer, he thought his chance had come to reassert Sibir's independence and stop the Stroganovs' advance across the Urals.[18]

By the time of Kuchum's first campaign, the Stroganovs' frontier settlements held close to ten thousand freemen and another five thousand serfs. These men and women had built saltworks to boil the waters of Perm's salt springs and had carved farms out of the wilderness. As would be the case on the American frontier a hundred years later, they had built blockhouses and stockades to protect their homes and fields, and they were well prepared for any attack that might come against them from the east. At first, Kuchum sent his native allies to raid the Stroganov settlements along the Kama, where, in July 1572, they killed nearly a hundred Russians. An enraged Tsar Ivan responded by urging the Stroganovs to "live very much on your guard" but to assemble as many men as they could muster to defend their lands against the Tatars. For any natives willing to turn against the Tatars and join the Russians, he added, "We shall make all things easy for them."[19]

The next year, the Stroganovs faced a larger Tatar force under the command of Kuchum's nephew that massacred not only Russians but a number of the natives who had joined them. Fearful that larger, better-equipped expeditions might soon follow, the Stroganovs petitioned the tsar for permission to carry the fighting into the heart of Kuchum's kingdom rather than continue their defensive war, and their petition reached Moscow not long after Ivan learned that one of his own envoys had been killed by Kuchum's forces. In reply, he extended the Stroganovs' charters of authority into Siberia itself and gave them permission to build frontier forts on the edge of Kuchum's lands. As the tsar's agents, the Stroganovs now had permission to invade Asia.[20]

Measured by any standard, the Stroganovs' decision to fight Russia's first war in Siberia was a bold one. Once in Kuchum's lands, the Ural Mountains and several hundred miles of trackless wilderness would separate their forces from their bases of support in Perm and make it difficult to send reinforcements and new supplies. What made the situation all the more uncertain were the tsar's own second thoughts, for a quarter century of wars and half a lifetime of suffering from the pain of spinal disease had eroded the daring that had ruled Ivan the Terrible's decisions in earlier times. Remembering how stubbornly the Tatars had fought his armies at Kazan and in the Crimea and knowing how wars in the east had drained Russia's resources for almost half a century, the terrible tsar was by no means confident that the Stroganovs commanded the manpower and weapons needed to conquer Kuchum's kingdom. With Russian arms and diplomacy more deeply embroiled than ever against Sweden and Poland on the Baltic coast, where the war he had begun in the 1550s continued to grind on, Ivan in the late 1570s hesitated to risk opening a second war in the east. Knowing that his commanders would continue to call for more men and weapons for the Baltic war than he could supply, he ordered the Stroganovs to pull back from Siberia before they began to build the new bases beyond the Urals that he had urged them to begin a few years before.[21]

Yet it was in the character of the Stroganovs to take risks, and the grandsons were as amply endowed with that trait as their fathers and grandfathers had been. After Grigorii died in 1575 and Iakov in 1579, their sons Nikita and Maksim knew that they could not hold their settlers in the lands around Perm if the attacks from Siberia became stronger and more frequent.[22] Taking advantage of the great distances that separated Solvychegodsk and the Perm lands from Moscow, Nikita and Maksim Stroganov decided to ignore the tsar's orders and carry the war to Kuchum's capital. A victory in Siberia could win greater favor from a tsar who had grown weary of defeat elsewhere.[23]

This was perhaps the most daring decision that any of the Stroganovs ever made, for the tsar's rages were legendary and his readiness to ruin favorites who displeased him was well known. Committed to destroying Kuchum's army in Siberia's borderlands and knowing that the cost of defeat would reach far beyond the battlefield itself, at the end of the 1570s Anika's grandsons recruited several bands of cossacks to fight their war. Such adventurers had a long and inglorious history of banditry in the southern lands of Russia, but, as men who were equally at home on water or land, they had a well-deserved reputation for being some of Russia's most daring fighters. If the cossacks could work their way along the Kama and Chusovaia riverways and portage across the Urals crest, they could then sail their high-sided boats along the rivers that flowed into the heart of Kuchum's kingdom. Needing a leader whose daring matched the courage of these men, Nikita and Maksim chose a cossack chieftain known as Ermak Timofeevich. The most prominent among the brigands whom the Stroganovs took into their service, Ermak became the man who led the "conquest" of Siberia.

6

Ermak's "Conquest"

Folklore and legend fortified with a modest sprinkling of fact make up the image of Ermak Timofeevich that has come down to us. A product of the age of Ivan the Terrible, Queen Elizabeth of England, and Sir Francis Drake, he combined the brutality, cunning, and daring of all three as he opened the way to a new world that none of them had ever dreamed of. Until he entered the service of the Stroganovs in the spring of 1582, we know only that Ermak had once fought for the tsar against the armies of Poland and that, as a brigand of some renown, he had often plundered merchant ships upon which the tsar had bestowed his protection. Beyond that, not even one contemporary description of Ermak has survived, and, because the Church Fathers in those days condemned the painting of portraits from life, we can only guess at what he looked like. One Russian chronicle describes him as "flat-faced, black of beard with curly hair, of medium stature and thick-set and broad-shouldered,"[1] but that account was written more than a century after his death by a monk who had never seen him and did not even know the exact year in which Ermak's "conquest" had taken place.[2]

Measured against the great hosts that conquerors from the east had led against the West in earlier times, Ermak's "army" of 840 men was a tiny force, but it was remarkably similar in size to those European expeditions that had carried out the great colonial conquests of the New World earlier in the century. Only eighty-eight men had sailed with

Columbus to discover the New World, and Hernando Cortés had conquered Mexico's Aztec empire in 1519 with a force of 617.[3] Like the captains of Spain, Ermak would have the advantage of fighting with firearms against an enemy without them, and the Ural Mountains barrier would cut him off from his bases of supply nearly as completely as the Atlantic Ocean did the expeditions that conquered the New World.

Nikita and Maksim Stroganov spent twenty thousand rubles—a sum that not even the tsar could assemble at that moment—to equip and supply Ermak's "army" with the best weapons that could be found in Russia. Against the bows, arrows, and spears of Kuchum Khan's armies, Ermak's cossacks therefore carried matchlock muskets, sabers, pikes, and several small cannon when they set out on September 1, 1582, from one of the frontier forts the Stroganovs had built on the Chusovaia River. Divided into companies of fifty, each with a supply of rye flour, cracked buckwheat, salt, gunpowder, and lead, and with three priests and a runaway monk to give them spiritual comfort, Ermak's force set out in a flotilla of the high-sided boats that centuries spent on the rivers of southern Russia had taught their ancestors to build.[4]

At first, the cossacks pulled their boats up the Chusovaia toward the Urals' crest. Then, when the river narrowed and grew too shallow, they portaged across the mountains, until the land began to drop away toward the east allowing them to continue their journey on the widening, deepening rivers that flowed into Siberia's western borderlands. Within five weeks from the time they left the Stroganov fort on the Chusovaia, Ermak and his men were in Siberia, beginning the first leg of the five-thousand-mile journey that would carry the Russian flag to Bering Strait. Advancing as much as forty kilometers a day along the route that thousands of traders and trappers would follow in the years ahead, they passed small settlements from which Kuchum's native allies rained arrows upon them, but the high wooden sides of their boats served as shields and kept them safe.[5]

Less than two months after they left Perm, Ermak and his men reached the vicinity of Isker, Kuchum Khan's capital. Not far from the future site of Tobolsk, destined to become the leading Russian town in western Siberia until late in the nineteenth century, the cossacks fought the battle with the army of Kuchum Khan's nephew Mahmet-Kul on October 26, 1582, that was to change the course of Siberia's history. There, on the banks of the Irtysh, the westernmost of those great Siberian rivers that flow north from the mountains of Inner Asia to the Arctic Ocean, they met the Tatar charge with a volley of massed musket fire that wounded Mahmet-Kul and broke the spirit of his warriors before they could inflict a single casualty.[6] That evening Ermak and his men occupied Isker to celebrate what has traditionally been called the "conquest of Siberia"[7] and to divide in true cossack fashion the wealth of sable and black Arctic fox pelts that filled Kuchum's treasury.[8] Now burdened with their plunder and with the river highways along which they had come freezing in their rear, the Russians settled down to spend their first winter in Siberia.

Although Ermak fought in the pay of the Stroganovs, he claimed Siberia in the name of Russia and Ivan the Terrible, with whom he hoped to make amends for his earlier crimes as a river pirate. Early in the spring of 1583, he therefore dispatched a deputation led by his second in command to pay proper homage to Russia's fearsome tsar in Moscow at the same time as he sent word of his victory to his employers in Perm. To the tsar, Ermak sent a royal tribute such as few Russians would ever match. At a time when a prime sable pelt sold for ten times what a peasant family could earn in a year and a black fox fetched up to ten times the price of a sable, Ermak's cossacks carried the pelts of twenty-four hundred prime sable, eight hundred black fox, and two thousand beaver. Such a tribute was easily worth five times what the Stroganovs had paid to fit out Ermak's expedition, and it represented only the tiniest fraction of what the Russians would take from Siberia in the years ahead.[9]

From the point of view of winning the tsar's favor, Ermak's men reached Moscow at the best possible moment in the summer of 1583. The Russians finally had ended their war with the Poles and Swedes, and the tsar, now freed from the burden of his Baltic wars for the first time in a quarter of a century, was more than ready to support the Stroganovs in the east. As a mark of favor, Ivan the Terrible sent Ermak a long coat of fine chain mail, emblazoned with the gilded double-headed eagles that formed the crest of Moscow's rulers. He then added "Tsar of Siberia" to his many titles and ordered a force of three hundred musketeers under one of his leading commanders to march east to help the cossacks hold the prize they had won.[10]

In the meantime, Ermak fought against raiding parties that Kuchum continued to send out from a new base farther upriver. In February 1583, some of the cossacks captured Mahmet-Kul and sent him to Moscow, where the Tatar commander pledged his loyalty to the Russians at Ivan the Terrible's deathbed. But if Ermak won the larger battles against the remnants of Kuchum's armies, ambushes by the Tatars and their Ostiak allies continued to whittle away his tiny force. To live through a second winter in Siberia, he needed the supplies, gunpowder, and shot that the tsar had sent with his musketeers, but these failed to arrive before the snow fell, leaving Ermak with only a handful of the men who had crossed the mountains with him more than a year before. When the summer of 1584 still brought no supplies or reinforcements, the cossacks knew that their chances of surviving a third Siberian winter were very slim.[11]

Having used up or lost all the supplies they had brought with them, the tsar's musketeers finally reached Ermak's camp in November 1584, more than a year late. Kept busy fighting skirmishes with Kuchum's Tatars and expecting the reinforcements from Moscow to bring large quantities of supplies, the cossacks had stored up far fewer provisions than the amount needed to feed so many more mouths, and that made their situation truly desperate once the Siberian winter struck with full force. "Many people died," one of the chronicles reported. "Men were forced to eat the bodies of their companions who had died from hunger."[12]

As hunger and scurvy took their toll, more Tatar ambushes claimed a large share of the starving survivors. By summer, a new expedition from Moscow was searching for what remained of Ermak's force but had not yet found it when, on August 5, 1585, the Tatars ambushed the survivors during a night when Ermak and his exhausted men had fallen asleep without posting guards. Although the Tatars killed most of the cossacks in their first assault, Ermak broke free, raced to the river, and leapt from the high bank toward one of the boats that stood anchored near the shore. He misjudged the distance, missed his footing, and fell into deep water, where the weight of the coat of mail that his tsar had sent him in recognition of his "conquest" pulled him to the bottom. Without a leader, the remnants of Ermak's force began to withdraw toward the Urals lest they lose the booty they had won.[13]

As with so many popular heroes, Ermak's power over men grew with the passing of time. For the Russians, he became a folk hero, the conqueror not merely of a small Tatar kingdom but of all Siberia. Over the years, the historical folk songs from which the Russian masses drew comfort during times of oppression transformed this onetime river pirate into a gallant knight, a champion of the unfortunate, and a hero who knew no fear and suffered no reproach. Ermak became Russia's King Arthur embellished, depending upon the tastes of narrator and listeners, with touches of Roland, Siegfried, and Sir Galahad whenever lonely women and men on the run gathered around Siberian campfires.[14] Among the Tatars, Ermak in death became a brave spirit who could heal the sick and ensure victory to the downtrodden. Tatar legends told how his body had remained uncontaminated for many days after Kuchum's men had pulled it from the river and how, after they secretly buried their fallen foe on the riverbank, columns of fire visible only to Siberians marked his grave at night. Certain that it would make him invincible against his enemies, one Siberian ally of the Russians in later years even begged the tsar for Ermak's coat of mail.[15]

The gateway that Ermak's "conquest" had opened into Siberia never closed, although the Tatars reoccupied Isker briefly after the remnants of Ermak's last detachment retreated back into Russia. Even before news of Ermak's death reached Moscow, Boris Godunov, the regent for Ivan the Terrible's sickly and retarded son Tsar Fëdor, had sent another force to help stake out the Russians' claim by building small frontier forts along the river routes that Ermak had followed into Siberia. Almost every year after that, more expeditions added new sites to the list of the fortified places that were beginning to establish the Russians' claims to the vast new continent they had entered. Obskii Gorodok became the first such settlement in 1585, followed by Tiumen in 1586 and Tobolsk, not far from the site of Ermak's first battle with the Sibir Tatars, in 1587. The 1590s saw the Russians fortify a dozen more key points so as to tighten their grip on Siberia's western lands. By 1600, Moscow's musketeers and cossacks had claimed all of the territory between the Urals and the Ob River and were beginning to reach toward the Enisei, the next of Siberia's great river highways, which lay nearly a thousand miles farther east.

Ahead of the Russians stretched a vast domain, the breadth and limits of which no one knew or imagined. Fewer than two hundred thousand natives scattered in tiny settlements and nomadic stopping places across Siberia's five and a third million square miles were all that barred their advance, and only a handful of these offered more than sporadic resistance. Some were hunters and gatherers like many of the contemporary Indians in the central lands of the United States and Canada, while others lived as nomads, following their flocks and herds as the seasons dictated. Very few had yet learned to till the soil.

Siberians of the north had long since come to grips with the emptiness of the tundra that spread along Asia's entire Arctic coast, its barrenness being broken only by the dwarf bushes that marked the courses of the Ob, Enisei, and Lena rivers as they flowed northward toward the Arctic Ocean. South of the tundra in the taiga, a wild belt of unbroken forest that stretched from the Urals to the Pacific and covered lands several times larger than the nineteenth-century empires of the Hapsburgs and Hohenzollerns combined, the natives lived by hunting and fishing, while the Siberians of the south, whose domains touched the edge of the steppe, lived mainly as nomads, herding cattle and horses across Eurasia's million square miles of grasslands.

Without firearms and the accoutrements of seventeenth-century civilization, these Siberians could not stand against Russia's cossacks, who conquered lands many times the size of the Roman Empire to reach the shores of the Pacific in less than sixty years. As they moved ahead, fighting mainly against climate, terrain, and distance, these advance guards of Russia's new world order made the Siberians into payers of tribute, demanding from each a rich yearly ransom in furs and wreaking terrible vengeance upon any tribe or clan that refused. Siberians had faced such oppressions before, for some of northern Asia's most warlike tribes had imposed similar burdens upon their weaker neighbors in the years after the Mongols' decline. Yet, while their former oppressors had tempered their demands with the understanding that ruined people could not pay tribute, the Siberians' new Russian masters measured the value of their subjects' lives only in terms of the furs they could squeeze from them. As the Mongols had done to the Russians and to conquered peoples from China to Egypt, so the cossacks who served the Tsar of All the Russias now did to the Siberians. Any Siberian community that failed to pay its annual fur tribute faced cossack torches and sabers.

Before the Russians came, few of Siberia's hundred and forty-odd tribes and peoples had ever lived at peace for long, for the strong among them had always oppressed the weak. But they had lived in harmony with the world around them on the basis of time-tested principles that had preserved the wealth of their huge domain for thousands of years. Never exhausting the supply of wildlife upon which their survival depended and moving their flocks at proper intervals so as not to overgraze the steppe, these people had suffered natural disasters but never man-made ones. The coming of the Russians replaced that harmony with a system of exploitation based upon greed and arrogance. Draining one Siberian resource after another, the Russians over the next four hundred years would turn Siberia into one of history's greatest ecological catastrophes.

Arrogantly, and with all the self-righteous certainty of men and women who had proclaimed it their mission to bestow the blessings of their way of life upon the other peoples of the world, the Russians dated the beginnings of Siberia's history from October 26, 1582, the day of Ermak's "conquest." Yet Ermak had not entered a world without a past of its own. For the 175,000 men and women whom the forces of history had scattered across Siberia, "the beginnings" stretched back to a dimly remembered time when folk heroes had done great deeds and when great founders had brought new peoples into being. For most of Siberia's past, there is no written record. Only legends, folklore, and the remnants of people and places long since swallowed by time remain to tell the story of Siberia before the Russians.

7

The Siberians

No one knows why a few hardy men and women left the temperate lands of Eurasia's south and west to settle in its northern and central parts or why, after perhaps fifty thousand years of wandering, their descendants settled Siberia's first communities around 10,000 B.C. Organizing their lives around the mammoth, the great elephantine herbivore that served as their chief source of food, these prehistoric Siberians built their dwellings from huge mammoth femurs and set their floors several feet below ground for protection against the Arctic winds. They shaped flint in the same ways as did the cave dwellers of Paleolithic Europe, and, like the North American Eskimos and the ancient Finns, they called upon shamans to speak with long-departed ancestors and the spirits that ruled the sky and earth. In these ways, they came to grips with one of the earth's most brutal climates and lived at ease with the natural forces that ruled their daily lives.[1]

When the earth's climate warmed and the great Eurasian glaciers retreated, Siberia's mammoths died out and its people had to reshape their lives around herds of horses, cattle, and reindeer.[2] Gradually, the advent of agriculture and animal husbandry accelerated the pace of progress until, around 2500 B.C., the Afanasevo people of south-central Siberia's Altai highlands discovered how to produce bronze from the copper they extracted from the dull green rocks that Nature had scattered across the hills around them. During the next millennium, these

Afanasevo people evolved into the more sophisticated Andronovo societies that spread their culture across the Minusinsk and Altai highlands
from the edge of present-day Kazakhstan and the eastern Urals to the
lands west of Lake Baikal.[3]

Though far ahead of their neighbors in the taiga and the tundra
because of their ability to shape metal, the Andronovo people remained
well behind the civilizations that flourished at that time in both East and
West. These were the days when the Egyptians built the first pyramids
and when Babylonia's King Hammurabi wrote his famed code of laws.
The Third Dynasty of Ur had already passed into history by the time
the Andronovo people appeared on history's stage, and so had the
civilization of Crete.[4] The way of life portrayed in the *Iliad* and
the *Odyssey* ruled the West. In the East, the rich Bronze Age culture of
the Shang Dynasty flowered in China. Nothing comparable to these
civilizations had appeared in Siberia by 1000 B.C., but its southern parts
were being drawn into the more complex world of East and West
nonetheless.

Although life in the ancient world moved no faster than the pace of
its beasts of burden, trade was beginning to tie many of its outlying parts
together during the first millennium B.C. Sea-lanes connected the ports
of South China with India, Persia, and Egypt, and overland routes
through the Sinai and along the Euphrates River valley joined the trade
of Asia with that of Greece and Rome at the Mediterranean ports of
Alexandria and Antioch. Farther north, the great Silk Road stretched
across Eurasia like a slender thread from Luoyang in north China
through the oases of eastern Turkestan and the empire of the Parthians
to Baghdad and Antioch. In the slow-moving processions of packhorses
and two-humped camels that moved along its hard-packed lanes to
exchange sandalwood, aromatic resins, silks, and spices from the East for
the goods of Persia, Greece, and Rome, the Andronovo people played
a part. Sending their furs south to the bazaars of Central Asia, they
traded these for the treasures and luxuries that the richer civilizations
of East and West produced.[5] This trade provided the rich pelts that
lined the silken cloaks of Chinese mandarins and Roman aristocrats.
With their furs commanding a prince's ransom in the cities of China,
Bactria, Persia, and Rome, the people of Siberia's south-central highlands were more closely tied to the world's great centers in the days of
Alexander the Great and Julius Caesar than they would be at the time
of Columbus or the voyage of the *Mayflower*.[6]

Were it not for five burial mounds built by the Pazyryk people of the
Altai highlands around 600 B.C., it would not be possible to judge the

wealth that the trade from the Silk Road brought to Siberia's southern lands.[7] Discovered about a hundred miles north of the Mongolian frontier soon after the Bolshevik Revolution, these tombs held the bodies of Siberian grandees along with rare fabrics, furs, carpets, and a treasure trove of objects made from horn, bone, bronze, and clay. All perfectly preserved by two thousand years of permafrost, aromatic woods, spices, and all the luxuries of high civilization lay neatly arranged within these graves. So did red-brown steeds bred for elegance and speed, their bridles, saddles, shields, and ceremonial reindeer masks all intact, lying frozen in the chambers' anterooms. Golden jewelry and ornaments in the shape of stylized deer, tigers, horses, and mythical winged griffins showed that the art and culture of East and West had made a mark upon life in Siberia's south-central highlands in the centuries before Christ walked the earth.[8] Far-reaching and complex, this was a very different world from the isolated one the Russians would find two thousand years later.

Even as the Pazyryk valley descendants of the Andronovo people filled their chieftains' tombs with treasures from Rome, Persia, and the Orient, the Eurasian world that the ancient Silk Road had tied together was being pulled apart by a great stirring among the nomadic peoples who inhabited the steppes along Siberia's southern frontier. Around 700 B.C., the Scythians burst out of their homeland on the edge of present-day Mongolia and began the great westward campaign that would condemn Eurasia's great grass road to two thousand years of turmoil. One after another, the Sarmatians, the Huns, and the Mongols followed, each of their massive migrations helping to weaken the ties that had bound the Altai and Minusinsk lands with the East and West. On the verge of being drawn into the mainstream of world trade and civilization at the time of Christ, Siberia began to drift away, turned inward on itself, and fell rapidly behind. Siberia's fur trade began to shift to China and, once the Christian era was well under way, to Russia and the north of Europe.

Although much of Siberia's life and history remains obscure during these dark centuries when the nomads of Mongolia were fighting their way across Eurasia, the Kirghiz peoples formed one of its centers. Originally the masters of the lands between the upper reaches of the Enisei River and Lake Baikal, these fierce Turkic horsemen overthrew the Uigur Khanate in A.D. 840 and, for about three quarters of a century, ruled Mongolia in the Uigurs' stead. Driven back into their former lands around 920, some of the Kirghiz moved west to settle in the corner of the steppe that separates Central Asia's Tien Shan from the eastern shores of the Caspian Sea. Those who remained around the upper Enisei submitted voluntarily to Chingis Khan in 1207, barely a year after he had formed his confederation of "all the people living in felt tents."⁹

Aside from the Uigurs, the Kirghiz were the only Siberians who knew how to read and write. They tended not only flocks but fields, turned the ground with iron-tipped plows, and raised millet, barley, and wheat. Using slave labor, they built stone-paved roads and laid out extensive irrigation systems to bring semiarid lands into bloom. By the middle of the ninth century, they were trading furs to the Arabs for cloth, although they saved their finest pelts to send to the Chinese for luxury goods. Kirghiz smiths were famous for their artistry in casting gold and silver into ornaments and the skill with which they forged iron into fine weapons. These had a market in China too, especially at the Imperial Court, which valued Kirghiz blades above all others.

Because the Kirghiz had submitted voluntarily to the law of Chingis Khan, the Mongols allowed them to continue mining and working iron, sowing wheat, tending huge flocks, and—thanks to a large number of Chinese craftsmen who emigrated to their country—weaving brocade and crepe from silk. But as the Mongol empire began to break apart, so did the Kirghiz civilization it had allowed to flourish. Within the space of two hundred years, the Kirghiz people lost their written language, gave up their trades, and abandoned agriculture for their earlier no-madic way of life. By the seventeenth century, they had become so deeply embroiled in tribal and clan wars that some of them greeted the arrival of the Russians as a way of preventing political and economic chaos from overwhelming them. At that point, one master seemed better than several to the Kirghiz, and one tribute collector preferable to a dozen.¹⁰

Although Mongol domination weakened the Kirghiz, it left the war-like Buriats strong. In his early days, Chingis Khan had fought several campaigns against these distant relations who ruled the forests and upland pastures to the Mongols' north and shared a way of life very much akin to their own. The scattered sources tell us very little about these wars, except that the Mongols never conquered the Buriats but drove them farther north, where they continued to tend their herds and flocks in the rough lands of the Transbaikal. For many centuries, sha-mans ruled the Buriats' lives and required that a horse be sacrificed at each warrior's burial. But that, like many other aspects of Buriat life, eventually began to give way to influences from the south. By the time they clashed with the Russians in the 1640s, the Buriats were beginning to replace some of their tribal shamans with Lamaist priests and to trade

furs and leather to the Chinese. But shamanism remained strong, especially among those who lived farthest from Tibet, the source of the
Lamaism that the eastern Buriats had chosen to adopt.

While some of Siberia's natives offered little opposition to the Russians, the Buriats never missed an opportunity to strike against their new
enemies. Buriat uprisings flared up around Lake Baikal several times
during the seventeenth century, and Buriat arrows took the lives of
tsarist tribute collectors even in times of peace. Only in the middle of
the eighteenth century did the Buriats and Russians come to terms and
begin to intermingle, with Russian men marrying Buriat women but
rarely the reverse. In the nineteenth century, Siberia's Buriats formed
the backbone of the Transbaikal cossack regiments, intermarried frequently with the Russians, learned to farm, and became much more
Russified than such neighbors as the Tungus, an assortment of tribes
whose tents and far-flung stopping places dotted the eastern half of
Siberia from the point where the Taimyr peninsula jutted into the
Arctic Ocean to the shores of the Pacific Ocean.[11]

In ancient times, the Tungus people had lived in Manchuria and were
closely related to those Manchu lords who rose to rule China. But
political upheavals that spilled over into their homeland from north
China had uprooted the Tungus, and the warriors of Chingis Khan had
driven them far to the north. There in the taiga, a vast realm of towering
evergreens interspersed by clearings and open fields, most of the Tungus became hunters and reindeer herders. Moving with the seasons, they
used their reindeer for transportation and food, supplementing the meat
and milk they provided with the flesh of the animals they killed in the
forest. Like most Siberian natives, the Tungus relied upon shamans to
communicate with their gods and to guide their lives. They interred
their dead above ground by sewing them in reindeer skins and setting
the hide-wrapped corpses atop high posts because they dared not violate
the domain of the spirits that lurked beneath the forest floor.

Described by one nineteenth-century observer as "cheerful under the
most depressing circumstances, persevering, open-hearted, trustworthy,
modest yet self-reliant,"[12] the Tungus proved to be as easy for the
Russians to conquer as the Buriats had been difficult. The westernmost
Tungus paid their first fur tribute to the Russians in 1614, and within
forty years all of their eastern cousins were doing the same. Yet these
easily conquered wandering natives turned out to be more resistant to
modern ways than did those Siberians who opposed the Russians. Even
into the twentieth century, all but a handful of Tungus remained herders and hunters, resisting settlement, farming, and modernization and

living, as they had for centuries, from the bounty of the forest.[13] Only the massive resources that their new Soviet conquerors devoted to forced social engineering in the twentieth century would begin to bring the Tungus into the modern world. No longer allowed the choice of remaining apart, Tungus men began to mine coal and build railroads in the 1920s. Later they helped to raise the massive iron and steel mills at Komsomolsk.

Under pressure of the first Russian advance into Siberia's eastern lands in the 1620s and 1630s, some of the Tungus adopted the ways of the Iakuts, the Turkic-speaking Siberians whose settlements had long since established their claim to nearly all of the Lena River valley. Iron makers like the Buriats, the Iakuts built their lives around raising cattle and horses and supplemented the meat and milk their herds supplied with the game, fish, and roots that could be gathered from the taiga and the tundra. Iakuts made no cloth from animal hair or plant fibers, and they did not know how to spin like the Buriats and Kirghiz or make felt as the Mongols did. They cured hides and skins crudely, smearing them with oil and smoking them in earthen stoves since they did not know how to tan leather. Blacksmithing, in which they worked the ore they dug from river marshes, was their only trade, although they made some crude pottery, which they shaped without the aid of a wheel.

More numerous than the Tungus and more fecund, the Iakuts had once been more powerful than they were when the Russians found them. Tribal conflict and clan rivalries had made them easier to conquer, although the Russians had to put down four bloody Iakut rebellions in the 1630s before they had these proud people firmly under control. Then the Iakuts, who had been shamanists like their Tungus neighbors, became one of the few Siberian peoples to convert quickly to Christianity.[14] Ready to adopt many of the Russian ways, they continued to live in iurts made of hides or birch bark in the summer and of a mixture of bark, clay, and cattle dung in the winter. Directly connected to the sheds in which they protected their cattle from the Arctic winters, Iakut iurts became notorious for their stench and dirt. Exile to a Iakut settlement along the edge of the Arctic Circle was one of the punishments Russian revolutionaries of the nineteenth century feared most. "The excrement of the cattle and of the children, the inconceivable disorder and filth, the rotting straw and rags, and the impossibility of speaking a word of Russian," one such revolutionary confessed, "are positively enough to drive one insane."[15]

West of the Iakuts and Tungus, and therefore among the first Siberians to encounter the Russians, the Ostiaks herded reindeer, hunted, trapped, and fished along the Ob and Irtysh rivers. Related to the Finns and the Hungarians by language and to the neighboring Voguls in their way of life, the Ostiaks lived in large families but did not organize into tribes as did their eastern neighbors. While those among them who lived in the tundra followed their reindeer herds, most of the Ostiaks lived on the bounty of the forest, hunting moose, reindeer, bear, and fowl for food while they trapped sable, fox, squirrels, and rabbits for their pelts. Of the animals they killed, they ate the kidneys, liver, and marrow raw, drank the blood fresh, and dried or boiled the meat. In summer, they set aside hunting and trapping for fishing, using complicated traps to take large catches that they dried or ate uncooked. Until Soviet times, fish entrails soaked in oil continued to be one of the Ostiaks' great delicacies.

Trappers and traders from Novgorod began to trade iron tools and weapons to the Ostiaks for sable and Arctic fox pelts almost two hundred years before the Mongols came, and, when Moscow replaced Novgorod in Russia's far north, its agents kept the trade with the Ostiaks going. Ostiak furs found their way into the Stroganovs' warehouses almost a half century before Ermak's time, and, once Ermak's "conquest" allowed the tsar to claim Siberia, the Ostiaks were among the first from whom his cossacks claimed fur tribute. At first the Ostiaks paid. Then, when the tsar's officials demanded more furs as "gifts" in addition to the ten sable pelts for each man they required in tribute every year, the Ostiaks rose up in revolt. Just ten years after Ermak's victory, they besieged the Russians' newly built log fort at Berëzov. After being brutally suppressed but left free to plunder their Vogul neighbors, they attacked Berëzov again in 1607 and, the next year, tried to unite all the natives of Siberia's northwest against the Russians.[16] Less accustomed to paying tribute than those Siberians from whom the Mongols and Buriats had demanded payment in years past, the Ostiaks resisted Russian control for the better part of thirty years.

Not until they reached Siberia's northeastern corner almost fifty years and five thousand miles later did the Russians face similar efforts by Siberia's natives to unite against them. Beginning in 1640, the warlike Koriaks of Siberia's northeast allied with the neighboring Chukchi in the most successful attempt of any natives to oppose the Russians. For more than a hundred years, the Koriaks fought the Russians, refusing even to recognize Russian sovereignty until 1712 and then continuing to fight the tsar's tribute collectors for another half century after that. Even deeper in Siberia's northeast corner, on the Chukhotka peninsula, the Chukchi never did submit, even after the Russians built a strong frontier fort in the midst of their lands. At a cost of more than a million rubles, the

Russians held the Anadyr fort for more than fifty years and collected barely a fiftieth of that cost in furs. In 1764, they therefore decided to leave the Chukchi to themselves. A hundred and twenty-five years later, the Chukchi finally agreed to pay a token tribute of 247 rubles (about the amount of taxes that fifty serfs paid in European Russia) to the Russian government every year.[17]

Closely related by language and custom, Siberia's northeastern Chukchi and Koriaks built their lives around hunting and fighting, tales of which filled their legends from very early times. Theirs were among the roughest and coldest lands in Siberia, some of which became the scene of Stalin's Kolyma death camps in the 1930s. Based upon the reindeer, the whale, and the seal, the economy of the Chukchi and Koriaks combined elements of the lives of the reindeer herders farther west with those of the Eskimos on the other side of Bering Strait. In earlier times, kayaks made of seal and walrus skins seem to have carried early Siberians and native Americans back and forth across these narrow waters. Chukchi and Koriak tools, weapons, and ways of life bore striking similarities to those of the closely related Tlingit Indians in Alaska, as some of the survivors of Vitus Bering's famous expedition would point out in the eighteenth century. In both cultures, the skin of certain whales eaten raw with its layer of pink blubber still attached was thought to be a great delicacy.[18]

Whether dealing with Siberia's tundra reindeer herders, its southern steppe nomads, or its taiga hunters, the Russians thought only of furs as they crossed the five thousand miles that lay between the Urals and Bering Strait. The astronomical prices that Siberian furs fetched in the markets of Moscow made rich men out of some of the first Siberian explorers and left others even richer in tales to tell of the wealth to be found in the lands beyond the Urals. Working in groups as small as two or three or as large as sixty, these men—called *promyshlenniki* in Russian—plunged into the Eurasian wilderness for years at a time before they returned laden with what some were beginning to call "soft gold." Kept alive by a brand of raw courage that few humans possessed, the conquerors of Siberia sought the pelts of squirrels, foxes, ermines, martens, and, above all, the vulnerable sable.

Described by one expert as "an arboreal marten native to the taiga of Eurasia ... [with] fur ranging from gray to brown to black," the sable—in scientific language, the *Martes zibellina*—was about twenty inches long, lived alone, and fed on everything from squirrels and grouse to pine nuts, berries, and insects.[19] A dense, silky undercoat protected it against Siberia's ferocious winters, and that formed its chief attraction for the wealthy men and women from Europe to China who clamored for its fur. "A beast full marvelous and prolific," one seventeenth-century Russian diplomat wrote, the sable was "a beast . . . that the ancient Greeks and the Romans called the Golden Fleece."[20] In Siberia, this small animal that was scarcely larger than a house cat became the magnet that pulled the Russians across the entire Eurasian continent before 1650.

8

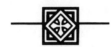

To the Great Ocean

The men who claimed Siberia for the tsar after Ermak's death were driven by a love of danger, a passion to explore the unknown, and raw, festering greed. "They behaved as if this land were in imminent danger of falling to an enemy forever, and thus they had to take out everything that the enemy might be able to use," Siberia's greatest living writer, Valentin Rasputin, once wrote. "They found," he added, "that vast Siberia, larger than any continent, became much less large and bottomless if they did nothing but scoop everything out."[1] Scoop everything out they did. Sables, martens, and foxes they took in the hundreds of thousands; squirrels they collected in the tens of millions. Almost every decade during the first half of the seventeenth century, the Russians' greed for furs pushed Siberia's fur frontier a thousand miles to the east. Before 1650, cossacks were trapping and collecting fur tribute along Siberia's Pacific coast.

Three large rivers flowing from south to north, their tributaries stretching east and west like the intersecting branches of three mammoth trees, divide Siberia into large segments that the Russians crossed in several large bounds, leaping from one river basin to the next. By 1600, they had taken the lands between the Urals and the Ob, the westernmost of these three great river trunklines. By 1620, they had moved on to the Enisei, and they reached the Lena before 1630. In 1639, fifty-seven years and three thousand miles after Ermak's victory at Isker, they reached the

Sea of Okhotsk, a part of the North Pacific. Twelve hundred miles and nine years later they were on the shores of Bering Strait, less than a hundred miles from Alaska's Cape Prince of Wales. Now at the easternmost tip of Eurasia, the Russians stood closer to the mainland of North America than had Columbus when his tiny flotilla first sighted land in the Caribbean.[2]

Cossacks, government officials, traders, and *promyshlenniki*—the Siberian counterparts of the famed *coureurs de bois* and Hudson's Bay Company men in North America—played prominent parts in the Russian conquest of Siberia, but historians continue to disagree about who played the leading role and when. In the 1920s, the dean of Soviet Siberian historians, Sergei Bakhrushin, argued that military commanders and government officials following a clear-cut program set down in Moscow had been the key factor in carrying Russia's flag to the Pacific. Thirty years later, Mikhail Belov, an expert who combined the study of geography and history, insisted that Bakhrushin's theory applied to the conquest only as far as the Enisei, and that *promyshlenniki* and cossacks acting on their own had taken the lead after that.[3] In fact, the conquest was more complex and its various elements more interdependent than either view indicates. At different times and under quickly changing circumstances, officials, cossacks, traders, and *promyshlenniki* all played important parts. On some occasions, they responded to the vision of the tsar's chief commanders and governors in Siberia. At other times, they followed orders sent from Moscow, and in some cases they searched for fame and fortune on their own.

Without significant logistical support from one of the tsar's military governors, trappers and traders found it next to impossible to amass the resources needed to explore Siberia's remote parts. Of necessity, traders, *promyshlenniki,* and government men therefore squabbled but worked together. At times, there was more conflict among various military governors, each of whom competed for recognition in Moscow, than there was between them and the leaders of privately planned expeditions. On other occasions, governors who saw every independent expedition as a challenge to their supreme authority worked against the men who struck out on their own. One thing always remained certain: Moscow's grip upon Siberia's conquerors weakened as the frontier moved farther east. It took the better part of a year for a messenger to travel from the tsar's palace in Moscow to the military governor of Iakutsk and even longer for one to reach Okhotsk.

However they viewed the balance of forces behind Siberia's conquest in its latter stages, experts agree that government leadership and soldiers sent from Moscow played the leading part before the Romanovs rose to power in 1613. Such consistent leadership from Moscow's Kremlin was all the more remarkable because it happened when national political life was falling apart during the Time of Troubles that engulfed Russia after Tsar Fëdor's death in 1598. Each claiming the throne as his own, several pretenders gathered armies along old Russia's frontiers, and, at one point, the army of Poland occupied Moscow for the better part of a year. Yet, however muddled the politics in Russia's European lands became, the conquest of Siberia continued. Tsars, magnates, and men who wished to make pretenders into sovereigns pursued contradictory goals, but they all sensed that Siberia's wealth in furs would help to shape whatever political world Russia found herself in once the turmoil of the Time of Troubles came to an end. Siberia's riches, which came to make up more than a tenth of the Royal Treasury's receipts during the seventeenth century, would help the Romanovs to rebuild Russia. To the present day, other forms of Siberia's natural wealth have helped to keep the Russians strong.

Built on the eastern side of the Urals on the road that connected the saltworks that Anika Stroganov's sons had founded at Solikamsk with the west Siberian forts of Tiumen and Tobolsk, Verkhoture became the Russians' gateway into Siberia until the first segments of the Great Post Road from Moscow to Irkutsk were opened in the 1760s. Founded in 1598, Verkhoture held the tsar's customs house, through which all goods and furs going across the Urals had to pass, for nothing would pass duty-free between Siberia and Russia before the 1770s. All winter long, trains of sledges worked their way across the Urals, bringing flour, gunpowder, lead, and salt from European Russia to be stockpiled at Verkhoture until the spring thaw opened Siberia's rivers. By the early 1600s, ninety river barges, each carrying up to thirty-six tons of supplies being sent on to Russian outposts on the lower reaches of the Ob and Enisei rivers, left Verkhoture every spring.[4]

While Verkhoture served as the gateway through which furs, supplies, and trading goods passed between Russia and Siberia, Tobolsk became the nerve center of the Russian conquest. After it became the headquarters of Siberia's first military governor in 1588 and the home of its first archbishop in 1621, power and wealth flowed to and from Tobolsk in all directions. By the 1650s, its merchants were selling over eighty thousand rubles' worth of goods a year and transshipping tens of thousands more.[5] No other town east of the Urals played so large a part in

Russian and Siberian affairs in the seventeenth century. One out of every four people who lived there worked in trade; one out of every two served in the army or the government.[6]

With Verkhoture as its gateway and Tobolsk as its nerve center, Russia's conquest of the lands between the Ob and Enisei rivers proceeded along two roughly parallel east-west courses that lay roughly five hundred miles apart. The northern route went through the tundra, marking its centers at Berëzov (on the Ob, founded in 1593), Mangazeia (founded above the Arctic Circle on the Taz River in 1601), and Turukhansk (founded in 1607 just below the Arctic Circle on the Enisei). Using these as their headquarters, Russian cossacks, working in squadrons of ten to thirty, ranged back and forth across the tundra, collecting fur tribute from the Ostiak hunters and Samoed reindeer herders. At the same time, traders and *promyshlenniki* brought foreign goods from warehouses that British and Dutch agents had built at the newly opened White Sea port of Arkhangelsk to trade with the natives for more furs. Yet the end purpose of their efforts was always gold. A nation without significant gold or silver mines, old Russia needed to exchange Siberia's "golden fleece" for the hard metal that all nations had to acquire to be strong.[7] Without Siberia's furs to convert into gold, Russia's poverty in the seventeenth-century international marketplace would have been astounding.

For something more than a decade beginning in the early 1600s, daring Russian seamen sailed through the Arctic seas from Arkhangelsk to Mangazeia, always hugging the coast, never letting land out of sight, but taking only a fifth as much time to make the voyage as was needed to travel overland and by river through Verkhoture, Tobolsk, and Berëzov. But, if Russians could sail from Arkhangelsk to Mangazeia without compasses in four or five weeks, foreign captains with modern instruments and better ships might do so even more easily. There are a number of documents that show that England's King James I was making plans to seize the tundra lands around Mangazeia just as the time of troubles came to an end in 1613. Fearful that foreign traders would use the Arkhangelsk-Mangazeia sea route to build their own direct links with the Siberian fur trade, the Romanovs closed it in 1619.[8] After that, the eclipse of the Russian tundra capital at Mangazeia became only a question of time, for the river and overland route to it was too long and dangerous to make it profitable.[9]

Cut off from the outside world for nearly six months out of every twelve, Siberia's Arctic frontier towns flourished during the first half of the seventeenth century and then began to wither as the Russians learned that the barren tundra, without wood for fuel or shelter, could not support their eastward march. By the 1720s, Berëzov had become so remote that the advisers of Emperor Peter II chose it as the place of exile for Field Marshal Prince Menshikov. Turukhansk fell into such disuse over the years that the Russian secret police condemned some of the most dangerous revolutionary leaders of the early twentieth century (including Stalin) to terms of exile there. The most important of all these tundra towns, Mangazeia, which once had held more than five hundred buildings and hosted a fair at which some two thousand people gathered each June to exchange furs, had all but disappeared by the end of the seventeenth century.[10] Except for a few charred log walls left over from a fire in the 1660s, all traces of it had vanished by the time the Imperial Russian Geographical Society began to publish the first comprehensive gazetteer of the Russian Empire in the 1860s.

While cossacks, *promyshlenniki,* and traders struggled to maintain Russia's tundra outposts during the first two decades of the seventeenth century, others advanced directly east from Tobolsk, working their way along the tributaries that flowed into the Ob. After reaching Surgut (on the southern edge of the lands that would become the huge Samotlor oil fields in the 1970s) in 1594 and Narym in 1598, cossacks and soldiers following this southern route founded Tomsk on the Tom in 1604 and Makovsk on the Ket in 1618. Sometimes, as at Tomsk, where they built a small fort to help a local Tatar prince defend his lands against his longtime Kirghiz enemies, the Russians took part in native wars. More often, they fought against Ostiak, Tungus, Tatar, and Kirghiz tribesmen, relying upon their muskets and small cannon to terrify their foes into submission. Native rebellions continued to plague the Russians, but, by the time they founded Eniseisk in 1619, they held nearly all the lands between the Urals and the Enisei. Eniseisk marked the point where the Russians' northern and southern routes of conquest intersected. Beyond it, they moved apart once again.

Founded more than a thousand miles east of Tobolsk, near the point where the Angara flows into the Enisei, Eniseisk became the staging area for the expeditions that would conquer Siberia's eastern lands.[11] To indicate how important he thought this new town would be, the tsar sent a military governor to rule Eniseisk just four years after the cossacks had raised the first logs of its palisades, and until the 1660s it stood as the main bastion of Russian authority east of Tobolsk. From Eniseisk, the Russians built new lines of frontier forts to the southeast, beginning in 1631 with Bratsk (destined to become the site of one of the Soviet Union's largest hydroelectric stations in the days of Khrushchev), followed by

Verkholensk in 1641, Verkhne-Angarsk in 1646, and Barguzin, the point
of departure for Russia's conquest of the Transbaikal, in 1648. By that
time, the cossack captain Kurbat Ivanov had led an expedition of seventy-five *promyshlenniki* to the shores of Lake Baikal to stake Russia's
claim to Eurasia's largest lake, which held a full fifth of the globe's
freshwater supply.[12]

Despite their successes in moving toward the southeast, the main
thrust of the Russians' march beyond Eniseisk lay directly east toward
the Lena, the third of Siberia's massive rivers. Leading a detachment of
ten cossacks, Vasilii Bugor reached the Lena in 1628 and became the first
Russian to collect fur tribute from the Iakuts living along it.[13] When
Bugor returned to Eniseisk without having built a base for further
exploration upon the Lena, the cossack lieutenant Pëtr Beketov set out
by a different route to set Russia's heel firmly upon the new lands Bugor
had discovered. Well known for his exploits in collecting fur tribute
from the Buriats and the Tungus, Beketov had every intention of repeat-
ing that success on the Lena. "I, your slave ... sailed down the great river
Lena and, having arrived at the Iakut lands, built a small fort, and made
all necessary defenses [for it]," he would report to Tsar Mikhail Fedorovich after his return to Eniseisk. "I shed my blood for you, Sire," Beketov
added, "and defiled my spirit and ate mare's meat and roots and fir bark
and all kinds of filth." Thus, in the flat, compacted official language of
the time, Beketov reported the founding of Iakutsk by his force of thirty
cossacks in 1632.[14]

Set on the right bank of the Lena River about halfway between its
source and its mouth, Iakutsk proved to be an incredibly rich source of
furs for the Russians. The natives in the huge territories around it placed
an even lower value upon sables than did those from whom the Russians
already were collecting fur tribute in the valleys of the Ob and Enisei,
and they willingly paid for each copper kettle that the Russians could
supply by filling it with sable pelts. Less than a decade after the first
cedar posts for the outer defenses of Iakutsk had been set into place, the
number of sable pelts passing through its customs house reached 150,000
a year. The pelts of Arctic foxes numbered in the thousands at the same
time and those of squirrels in the hundreds of thousands. For a time,
Iakutsk became the Tobolsk of the east, the home of more than three
thousand Russians by 1650 and the point of departure for tribute-gather-
ing expeditions that carried the tsar's standard to Siberia's remote northeast, into the Amur River valley and, most important, to the edge of the
Pacific.[15]

Just seven years after Beketov founded Iakutsk, the cossack captain

Ivan Moskvitin led twenty men up the Lena's eastern tributaries and portaged across the Dzhugdzhur Mountains to the headwaters of the Ulia River. After a five-day voyage down the Ulia, Moskvitin's tiny force reached the Sea of Okhotsk, where it built the wintering place that became the town of Okhotsk. Two years later, in 1641, Moskvitin and his men returned to Iakutsk carrying the pelts of 440 prime sable and 323 black foxes, a treasure well worth the hardships they had endured.[16] More than four thousand miles east of Moscow and just fifty-seven years after Ermak's victory, the Russians now had their foothold on the Pacific. But with every leap they had taken across Siberia's huge river basins, they had stretched further the lifeline that connected them to their bases of supply west of the Urals. By the time they reached Okhotsk, this slender thread had all but reached the breaking point.

Too far away from their European homeland to rely upon it to supply the shipments of food they needed, the Russians in eastern Siberia also could not feed themselves on what the land around them provided. There was no large beast that roamed in immense herds like the American bison, and nowhere were Siberia's lands blessed with a crop comparable to the Indian corn that sustained the trappers and settlers who crossed the North American continent. Not only did very few Siberian natives practice agriculture, but the Russians found that rye, wheat, and even barley often failed to ripen during the short, unpredictable summers in the lands east of the Enisei. Fruits and vegetables proved to be so difficult to grow in Siberia's eastern half that the Russians there suffered from scurvy until the end of the eighteenth century.[17]

With the Russians in Iakutsk and the lands beyond perpetually hungry, the question of food supplies concerned every military governor who served east of the Enisei during the seventeenth century. Because no crops grew in the forest and tundra lands that lay to the north and east, the tsar's governors looked south to the Siberian lands that still remained unexplored. What lay beyond the Stanovoi and Iablonovy mountains, the great natural barriers that divided eastern Siberia's wild taiga from the floodplains of the Amur River valley? Might not those lands hold the key to feeding the Russians? Hoping to answer these questions, upon which their survival seemed to depend, the vanguard of Russia's Siberian conquest turned south during the 1640s after half a century of moving east.

9

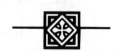

Searching for Grain

Very soon after they founded Iakutsk, the Russians began to hear of a great river valley, somewhere beyond the Stanovoi Mountains to the south, in which grain grew in abundance. Hoping that he might find more food for Siberia's hungry Russians, the military governor of Iakutsk sent 133 cossacks and *promyshlenniki* under the command of Vasilii Poiarkov to find the river, explore it, and learn if the natives who lived near it grew grain.[1] Only able to guess at the best route across the mountains, Poiarkov set out in June of 1643 and followed the Lena's Aldan River tributary southward toward its source only to discover that he had made the worst of all possible choices. No fewer than sixty-four rapids had to be portaged, and his men lost precious weeks as they shifted their supplies from boats to packs and back to boats again. The first snows came too early that year, and winter struck with full force before the cossacks even reached the mountains' crest. Nonetheless, Poiarkov decided to press ahead and risk spending the winter in whatever land lay beyond the mountains.

Anxious not to leave his line of communication unprotected over the winter, Poiarkov assigned forty-nine of his men to build a wintering place in the mountains with instructions to join him in the spring. Then he and the rest of his men crossed the Stanovoi passes in December and reached the Zeia River, one of the chief tributaries of the Amur, on which the Russians and the Chinese would start to build a massive hydroelectric dam in the early 1960s. Poiarkov's force now found itself in Dauria, a wild but fertile domain that stretched along the Zeia and Amur rivers for several hundred miles until it shaded into the lands of the Goldi and Giliak fishermen farther east. Here grain was the staff of life, as it was in the lands of Russia. For the first time since they had crossed the Urals, the Russians had found people who preferred farming to hunting.

From Poiarkov, the Daurians were about to learn—as Siberia's natives farther west already had—that no matter how much they gave or how readily they gave it, their Russian conquerors would demand more and devastate their villages if they failed to provide it. In this case, the Daurians offered fur tribute and food, including the oats and buckwheat that the Russians had hoped to find, but, when they insisted that they knew nothing about the silver, lead, and copper mines of which the Russians had also heard rumors, Poiarkov demanded hostages. Certain that the Daurians were concealing silver, even though (or perhaps because) they had offered up such generous supplies of food and furs so willingly, Poiarkov tortured the people who had fallen into his hands, thereby turning a land of willing tributaries into a nest of dangerous enemies. As the snow deepened and the small game disappeared, the Russians tried to take more food from the now hostile Daurians at gunpoint. When their victims fled and left them with no food at all, Poiarkov's men began to hunt the Daurians like wild game, shooting them and roasting their flesh over open fires.[2] These people remembered the cossacks' brutality for centuries to come. A full two hundred years later, the Russian explorer Aleksandr Middendorf would find that the wellsprings of Daurian hatred still ran very deep.[3]

A diet of pine bark, roots, pirated supplies, stray creatures of the forest, and the flesh of natives supplemented by that of comrades who died along the way left fewer than forty of Poiarkov's men alive by the time the remnants of the force he had left in the mountains joined him in the spring of 1644. As they worked their way down the Zeia to the Amur, the huge East Asian river that divides China and Siberia to this day, the Russians found that word of their deeds had gone before them. All along the river, the natives were on the defensive, forcing the unwanted explorers to fight their way through one ambush after another. For the first time, the raw brutality with which the Russians had pushed their advance across Siberia was turning against them.[4]

That fall, the Russians entered the land of the Giliaks, who lived near the Amur's mouth where the river broadens to a width of ten miles before flowing into the Sea of Okhotsk. Among the Giliaks there were no farmers, only hunters and fisherfolk who dressed in clothing made of fish skins warmed by robes of dog fur in the winter. To avoid a second hungry winter in the wilderness, Poiarkov and his men seized several Giliak chieftains and used them as hostages to guarantee regular deliveries of food. Again they abused their captives unnecessarily, making as many enemies among the Giliaks as they had among the people of Dauria the year before. With hatred rising in his wake and only a handful of his command still alive, Poiarkov dared not retrace his steps. He therefore continued to move ahead, destined to cover more than five thousand miles in a huge loop that circled the entire southeastern corner of Siberia before he returned to Iakutsk.

Kept strong by the Giliaks' reluctantly delivered provisions, Poiarkov's cossacks built boats in the spring of 1645 and made their way up the coast of the Sea of Okhotsk to the Ulia River, where they spent a third winter in the log shelters that Ivan Moskvitin had built six years earlier. The next spring, they followed Moskvitin's route back to Iakutsk, arriving just a few days after the third anniversary of their departure. Like so many of the men who helped to conquer Siberia, Poiarkov received no reward. His rough ways of command had turned some of his men against him, and their complaints convinced the military governor of Iakutsk to send him to Moscow for trial and an unknown fate.[5] At the same time, the governor reported enthusiastically that Poiarkov's campaign had brought the treasury five hundred prime sable pelts and confirmation that grain could be found in Dauria. Based upon the information Poiarkov had brought back, it seemed certain that the Daurian harvest could feed the hungry Russians east of Eniseisk and leave grain to spare. Russia, the authorities in Iakutsk insisted, must therefore conquer the lands beyond the mountains from Dauria to the Amur's mouth.[6]

To conquer Dauria and the rest of the Amur lands for Russia became the task of Erofei Khabarov, a man destined to be painted larger than life by history. Like many young men from European Russia, Khabarov had succumbed to Siberian fur fever in his late teens and had left the Stroganovs' salt town of Solvychegodsk in the mid-1630s to seek his fortune in the Mangazeia fur trade. There he ranged as far afield as the Taimyr peninsula, the northernmost lands of Eurasia, but he found only modest profit. The early 1640s therefore found Khabarov and his brother trapping sables and foxes in the valley of the Lena, their thirst for glory and wealth still unquenched.

For a while, Khabarov tried to follow the example of the Stroganovs by building a saltworks near Iakutsk. When the government took it away from him, he turned to farming, trying to use native workers and transported criminals from Russia to grow grain in the hostile Iakutsk climate. Among his newly plowed grainfields, he built a flour mill, but none of these enterprises satisfied the longings that had drawn him into Siberia's eastern depths. Knowing that fame and fortune awaited the man who conquered the grainfields of Dauria, Khabarov offered to explore them at his own expense. Not surprisingly, the military governor of Iakutsk gave him his blessing. Since the Russians now knew that the Olëkma River offered the best way into the mountains, Khabarov led a force of seventy volunteers along that route in the spring of 1649.[7]

Crossing the Iablonovy range rather than the Stanovoi peaks farther east, Khabarov entered Dauria at the beginning of 1650. He found the countryside deserted, its villages abandoned in haste, and the natives' stores of provisions hidden or burned. During a brief meeting with three Daurian princes, he learned through interpreters that their people had fled for fear that he would renew Poiarkov's reign of terror, and, instead of trying to win allies for Russia, he did little to ease their fears. Seeing only frightened natives in the lands around him, Khabarov anticipated an easy conquest.[8] The self-confidence that stemmed from having defeated Siberia's natives in almost every encounter since Ermak's battle in 1582 had made the Russians self-indulgent, too reckless, and too arrogant. A reign of terror still seemed the easiest way for Siberia's vastly outnumbered conquerors to keep its people firmly under control and, in Rasputin's wonderfully evocative phrase, "scoop everything out."[9]

Then Khabarov learned that a complex system of alliances tied the Daurians to Manchuria and thus to the new Manchu lords of China. Uneasy about risking a war with the Chinese, whose army was larger and had bases of supply much closer to hand, Khabarov hurried back across the mountains at the end of May 1650 to make a report and get new instructions from the military governor of Iakutsk. Emphasizing the contrast between the fertile fields of the Amur valley and the barrenness of eastern Siberia, Khabarov urged his superior to let him take the Amur for Russia. "This land of Dauria will be more profitable than the Lena," he promised, "and, in contrast to all of Siberia, will be a region beautiful and abundant." More than that, he went on, "in the great river Amur there are more fish than in the Volga [the largest of European Russia's rivers]."[10] There was enough grain in the Amur valley, Khabarov now insisted, to feed twenty thousand Russians every year, and it could be sent to Iakutsk in less than two months rather than the four years needed to ship flour from Verkhoture. But he also warned that China might be a formidable enemy if she chose to defend her vassals on the Amur.

Thirty men had been enough to take the Lena valley from the Iakuts, and twenty had claimed the lands of Siberia's Pacific coast. Against China, however, Khabarov estimated that Russia would need to send at least six thousand soldiers armed with muskets and cannon to hold Dauria and the Amur lands to its east. Since all the garrisons in Siberia put together numbered fewer than half that number, an army would have to be sent from Moscow so as to be ready if China intervened.[11]

For the first time, Khabarov and the military governor of Iakutsk faced the chronic problems of communication and transportation that would plague Russia's governors in eastern Siberia until the Trans-Siberian Railroad was built at the beginning of the twentieth century. It would take the better part of a year to get their message to Moscow, and, if the tsar supported their plan, it would take another two years for an army to reach Iakutsk. In the meantime, the shortage of grain continued, and there was no way of knowing whether the Chinese had already been stirred to action. While he waited for the tsar's reply, the military governor had to act on his own, knowing full well that he would have to bear the blame if his master chose a different course. Yet if he did nothing and the tsar supported the plan to take Dauria, he might be punished for not acting promptly. Given the choices, the tsar's chief official in Iakutsk gave Khabarov permission to assemble another force of volunteers, to which he contributed weapons and a unit of twenty-one men.[12]

With fresh horses, several small cannon, and nearly twice the men he had commanded the year before, Khabarov crossed the mountains again in the fall of 1650. This time, the Daurians refused to pay tribute and defended their land in several battles that pitted cossack muskets and sled-mounted cannon against native bows and arrows. After reinforcements had increased his force to over two hundred at the beginning of June 1651, Khabarov followed Poiarkov's route down the Amur valley, intending to establish a new line of frontier forts to cement the Russians' hold upon it, just as his predecessors had done in the basins of the Ob, Enisei, and Lena. Often, the natives fled. When they did not, the Russians battered down their defenses with cannon fire before butchering the men, raping the women, and driving off whatever livestock they found.[13] Decades of conquest still had not taught the Russians that devastated villages and burned fields produced ruined people, not reliable taxpayers. Over the next decade, they would ravage Dauria so thoroughly that its people could no longer produce the grain for which the Russians had come in the first place.[14]

By the middle of September, Khabarov's men had reached the mouth of the Sungari River, another of the Amur's tributaries. Two weeks later, they built a fort in the vicinity of present-day Komsomolsk-on-Amur and called it Achansk. Again the natives offered provisions and fur tribute and the Russians responded by demanding more and torturing hostages until the natives rose against them. Even though Khabarov's men killed nine hundred natives and suffered but one casualty in crushing the uprising that followed, the victory cost them dearly in other ways. Now convinced that they could not drive the Russians out of their lands, the peoples of the Amur valley turned to the Chinese. While the Russians wintered at Achansk, a well-armed Chinese army summoned by the natives was marching toward it.[15]

Not just the Russians' brutality but a complex series of events in Moscow, Peking, and Iakutsk broadened the conflict on the Amur during 1651 and 1652. Khabarov's first winter in Dauria had convinced him that Russia must colonize the Amur lands, not just conquer them, and he had urged that men and women condemned to Siberian exile be transported there to help the land yield the full measure of its fruits.[16] The military governor of Iakutsk had sent Khabarov's proposals on to Moscow, and the tsar had decided to send an army of three thousand men under Prince Lobanov-Rostovskii, one of his best commanders.[17] At the same time, with an absurd lack of understanding about Asian affairs, the governor had invited the Chinese emperor to become a Russian subject. Sensing that the Russians were serious about claiming the Amur and freed from the civil wars that had prevented them from acting earlier, the Chinese moved against them in 1652.[18]

On March 24, 1652, two thousand Chinese attacked Achansk and broke open its defenses with artillery. Here was an enemy against which the Russians were not prepared to fight, for even though most of the Chinese fought with bows and arrows, their cannon were superior and the few firearms they carried (called "rapid-firing" matchlocks in one report) surpassed the Russians' guns in firepower. Learning that the Chinese had orders to take them alive, Khabarov and his men managed to drive them off with moderate losses, but their victory only served to remind them that they faced dangers they still could not begin to measure. How many men could the Chinese put into the field, and how quickly? Had their main army attacked Achansk, or had the Russians faced only the vanguard of a larger force? If other armies were on the march, how large were they, and would they be even better equipped with firearms? The Russians had no way of answering any of these questions, yet they needed to know the answers to them all.[19]

With fear beginning to rule his calculations, Khabarov turned back up the Amur, plotting his line of march toward the Iablonovy Mountains to avoid the Chinese. At one point, a force of six thousand Chinese got ahead of him, but good fortune helped his men slip past the enemy under the cover of fog and darkness. Two hundred miles farther on, the Russians met 117 cossacks who had been sent out from Iakutsk to reinforce them more than a year before, but these turned out to be more anxious to plunder the natives than to fight the Chinese. When some of Khabarov's men joined the cossacks in a mutiny, he had to spend the rest of the summer chasing them down and trying to avoid the Chinese at the same time. Catching up with the mutineers in mid-October, Khabarov stormed their hastily built fortifications and flogged to death those who survived his attack. With the tensions of the mutiny still festering, the Russians faced a fourth winter in the Amur lands.[20]

While Khabarov had waited for new instructions, the authorities in Moscow had sent a detachment of 150 men under the nobleman Dmitrii Zinovev to reinforce his small force. When the two detachments finally met in the fall of 1653, Zinovev demanded full command, and, when Khabarov insisted upon seeing the orders that allowed him to claim that authority, Zinovev placed him under arrest and sent a formal complaint to Moscow. Khabarov's men protested. Unable to win their loyalty and not daring to remain in the Amur lands without it, Zinovev returned to Moscow and took Khabarov with him.

Once again, one of the tsar's explorers paid for his Siberian victories with disgrace. Deprived of his property and rank, Khabarov made the fifteen-month journey to Moscow and waited for the better part of a year before the tsar's Siberian Office acquitted him of Zinovev's charges and set him free. Eventually, he was given minor noble rank on the condition that he return to Siberia, but that proved a meager payment for the vast lands he had claimed in the tsar's name. "Because of my poverty," the man who had collected thousands of sable pelts for the Royal Treasury complained at one point, "I am perishing from hunger."[21] Then he fell from sight. The only other trace we find of Khabarov in the scattered records comes in 1658, when the Siberian Office issued orders that he be placed in irons if he refused to serve as a guide for an expedition that was on its way to the Amur. After that, the account breaks off. We do not know whether the expedition found Khabarov or if he went with it. We only know that he lived for at least ten more years. The fading historical record remains silent about where this poorly rewarded conqueror died or when.[22]

Khabarov's victories left a dangerous and uncertain legacy on the

Amur. Following in Poiarkov's footsteps, he had found the grain needed to feed the Russians in Siberia's eastern lands, but it would require centuries to undo the hatred that his brutality had stirred up among the natives. At the same time, the stories of wealth that his men had spread had infected the Russians in the Lena valley with what one historian has called an epidemic of "colonizing fever"[23] that drew them away from Iakutsk and into the Amur lands. By 1653, so many Russians had pulled up stakes and struck out across the mountains to plunder the lands of Dauria, according to a report that the military governor of Iakutsk sent to Moscow, that the valley of the Lena was becoming depopulated.[24] The damage they inflicted as they all tried to claim tribute from the Daurians wiped away the Russians' last chances for provisioning eastern Siberia from the nearby Amur valley grainfields.

When the outbreak of the First Northern War between Russia and Poland obliged the tsar to recall the regular forces he had sent to Siberia, only a small band of irregulars remained on the Amur to defend the flood of Russian immigrants against the Chinese. Strong enough to torment the Daurians, these men were no match for the Chinese, who killed or captured them all before the end of 1658. Then, having wiped out all the Russians on the Amur below Nerchinsk, the Chinese withdrew, leaving Dauria to become a haven for outlaws and renegade cossacks for the next fifteen years.[25] When the Russians returned to the Amur lands in 1672, they again treated its handful of Chinese and Manchurian hunters and traders with such brutality that China's rulers decided to go to war again in the 1680s.[26]

The Russo-Chinese conflict of the 1680s saw the Chinese take the frontier fort that the Russians had rebuilt at Albazin in 1685 and withdraw again, only to have the Russians return and rebuild more modern defenses a few months later. When the Chinese mounted a new siege in July 1686, Albazin had more than eight hundred defenders supplied with enough food and water to last for a year, a dozen cannon, and more than two tons of gunpowder. This time the Chinese were prepared to bring Albazin to its knees, and, after a four-month siege, the Russians asked for a truce. Even more than in the 1650s, the Russians had to negotiate from weakness, for the regency that ruled in Moscow at that moment was none too strong. Signed in September 1689, the Treaty of Nerchinsk forced the Russians to destroy Albazin and renounce all claims to the Amur lands.[27] For the time being, the Amur had been closed and the hope of using its grain to feed the Russians in Siberia's eastern lands brought to an end. With Siberia's southern boundaries fixed at the crest

of the Stanovoi and Iablonovy mountains until the middle of the nineteenth century, the Russians turned toward Siberia's northeast. Eventually, their quest for furs and food would carry them beyond Bering Strait
and the North Pacific to North America. In the process, they unwit-
tingly solved one of the greatest puzzles facing the geographers of the
seventeenth century.

10

Discovering a Passage Between Two Continents

Ever since the first caravans had made their way along the ancient Silk Road, the men and women of Europe had craved the luxuries of the Orient. Limited to the size of a camel's back, cargoes from the East in those days reached the West only in the smallest quantities and commanded the highest prices. Silk was worth nearly its weight in gold in ancient Rome, and spices cost only marginally less. After Rome fell and the Middle Ages came and went, the merchants of Europe continued to dream of bringing larger quantities of precious goods from the Orient more quickly and with greater safety. Visions of finding a sea route to Cathay seized their imaginations the moment that the discovery of the mariner's compass made it possible to sail beyond the sight of land. If trade could be shifted from the backs of camels into the hundreds-of-times-larger holds of ships, the prospects for profit seemed immense. Such visions drew the Portuguese around Africa's Cape of Good Hope and across the Indian Ocean, just as they guided Columbus on his voyage to the New World.

When Europe's navigators discovered that the continents of North and South America stood between them and the Orient, they began to search for a waterway that would carry them through. Ferdinand Magellan found such a passage eight thousand miles from Europe near South America's tip, but its waters were too treacherous for any but the most daring and skillful sea captains. The explorers of England and

Holland therefore turned to the north, hoping to find a less arduous passage that would be closer to their home ports. To England's Martin Frobisher, Henry Hudson, and William Baffin, a Northwest Passage through the lands of North America seemed the most likely way to reach the East. At the same time, Sir Hugh Willoughby, Richard Chancellor, and Holland's Willem Barents searched for a Northeast Passage that would carry them north of Eurasia to China.

On a voyage that became the high-water mark of the search for a Northeast Passage, Barents and his crew spent the winter of 1596–1597 on the ice-locked island of Novaia Zemlia, which separates the Barents and Kara seas almost directly north of the Urals' northern tip. Like his predecessors, Barents failed, but each failure enlarged navigators' knowledge of the world's geography and kept alive the hope that another path around the continents might yet be found. As the Europeans continued their search, the most vital of all questions remained unanswered: Were Asia and North America actually separate continents, or were they joined somewhere north of China? Even if the waters above North America or Eurasia could be navigated, would it be possible to sail south to China, or would land block the way?

Cut off from contact with the learned men of Europe during the Age of Discovery and therefore unaware of the questions that commanded their attention, the Russians explored Siberia alone and in their own way. It would seem that the Russians did not even become acquainted with the compass until the end of the seventeenth century and that, like travelers in days long since past, they took their bearings only from the sun and the stars.[1] With none of the accumulated learning of the West to guide them and in ships that could sail only before the wind, they had nonetheless worked their way along Eurasia's northern coast to establish direct connections between their settlements on the White Sea coast and those on the Ob and Enisei rivers. Sailing their small coastal vessels east from Arkhangelsk, Russian traders had reached the Ob Gulf, the Taz River, and Mangazeia not long after 1600. Just a few years later, they made their way to the mouth of the Enisei and sailed up it to Turukhansk.[2]

Using the Ob and Enisei river towns as their bases after Tsar Mikhail Fedorovich closed the sea route from Arkhangelsk to Mangazeia in 1619, other traders and explorers continued to work their way east along the Arctic coast until the Taimyr peninsula, the northernmost point of Eurasia, barred their way. Caches of coins and artifacts discovered in the 1940s clearly show that daring Russians made a number of attempts to sail from the Enisei to the Lena by way of the Kara and Laptev seas on the peninsula's western and eastern sides, but none of them succeeded.³ Filled with mountains of pack ice, that part of the Arctic remained impassable until the advent of steam-powered icebreakers in the 1870s.

Unable to round the Taimyr peninsula, the Russians moved on to the Lena River by a combination of river routes and portages and then resumed their sea voyages from its mouth. Faced by some of the continent's most hostile natives, sharp mountain crags, rivers whose tributaries no longer came close to connecting (as had those of the Ob, Enisei, and Lena), and four mountain ranges, all of which stood above the Arctic Circle, the Russians toyed for a time with the idea of conquering Siberia's northeastern lands from the sea rather than fighting their way overland. From one to twelve miles wide, the mighty Lena formed a majestic entrance to the new lands they hoped to explore. If the seas east of its mouth could be navigated, it would be relatively simple to ascend the rivers of Siberia's northeast and claim the lands around them. Some of the cossacks and *promyshlenniki* at Iakutsk were willing to try. Others preferred to face the howling storms that lashed the steep face of the Verkhoiansk Mountains and work their way into the northeast by land rather than venture into the ice-filled seas of the Arctic.⁴

In the late 1630s, those cossacks and *promyshlenniki* who thought Siberia's northeast could best be approached by sea set out to pit their flat-bottomed wooden boats—built without tar or nails and with rigging and cordage made of deerskin strips attached to stiff deerhide sails—against the perils of the Arctic. Able only to run before the wind, such craft bore no relation to the triple-masted vessels that seventeenth-century European explorers were sailing across the world's other oceans. Unsteady on even the tamest seas and with none of the nautical instruments that Europeans used to chart a course, the boats that Russia's cossack and *promyshlennik* Vikings sailed from cape to cape and bay to bay east of the Lena's ice-clogged delta seemed to be in every way unequal to the perils that lay ahead. Shifting masses of ice could crush whatever lay between them in an instant, and the jagged edges of pack ice could cut the twigs and thongs that held a boat's siding in place with predictable ease. Many of the men who entrusted their lives to these fragile vessels never returned, but a few became famous. Among them, Mikhail Stadukhin and Semën Dezhnëv, who explored both land and sea routes into Siberia's northeast in the 1640s, became noted explorers and bitter rivals.

Stadukhin and Dezhnëv had grown up on European Russia's White Sea coast, where the dangers of the northern seas had tested its men for centuries. In the 1630s, infected with the fur fever as Khabarov had been,

both men made their way to Iakutsk, where the more flamboyant Stadukhin became wealthy and won the friendship of the military governor.
By 1640, the first expeditions to explore the lands beyond Iakutsk had
discovered the Iana and Indigirka, the first rivers east of the Lena.
Returning with a wealth of prime sable pelts and stories of other, greater
rivers yet to be discovered, the men who had crossed the first barriers
to Siberia's northeast spoke particularly of the fabled "Pogycha" River,
along whose banks walrus ivory was said to be piled in heaps and coal
black sable ran in herds.[5] According to other reports, there was a lake
filled with pearls not far from the "Pogycha" and a mountain nearby
from which silver could be obtained by firing arrows into it and picking
up the fragments they knocked loose.[6] For men of a nation that would
continue to use sable pelts as auxiliary currency for another half century
because its European lands held virtually no silver or gold, the prospect
of silver mountains and black sable herds was irresistible. Having already been on earlier expeditions into the borderlands of the northeast,
Stadukhin and Dezhnëv threw themselves into the search for the "Pogycha."

Stadukhin's wealth and friendship with the military governor of Iakutsk won him command of an expedition sent out in the spring of 1642
on a forty-four-month overland journey to the Indigirka River valley.
After spending the winter in temperatures that fell to $-70°$ Centigrade
and losing nearly all their horses in a battle against the natives, Stadukhin and his men built boats on the Indigirka, sailed down it to what
they called the Freezing Sea, and made their way east for about three
hundred miles to the Kolyma River. There, at the end of the valley that
would become the site of some of Stalin's most notorious death camps
three centuries later, they laid the foundations of Nizhnekolymsk, the
frontier fort that would mark the eastern edge of Siberia's fur frontier
for the rest of the decade. In 1646, they returned to Iakutsk with a fortune
in sable pelts. Based on what he had heard from natives he had captured,
Stadukhin hastened to report to the military governor that the famed
"Pogycha" lay a scant three days' sail east of the Kolyma's mouth.[7]

Stadukhin's report unleashed a rush of trappers and traders into the
Kolyma basin. Believing that the "Pogycha" could be reached more
easily by sea, more than four hundred Russians applied to the authorities
in Iakutsk for permission "to sail down the Lena and to travel by sea to
the Indigirka and Kolyma rivers for trade and fur [tribute] collection."[8]
Those who were well connected with the governor and his circle now
looked to Stadukhin to lead the way to the "Pogycha," while some of
the newly arrived agents sent by some of Moscow's richest merchants

to search out new opportunities on the Siberian frontier turned to Dezhnëv, whose exploits in collecting fur tribute among the warlike Iugakirs had won him a reputation as a man who knew how to get things done. Although their best efforts had yet to locate any native who actually had seen the Pogycha's banks, they hoped that Dezhnëv's talent for turning adversity to advantage might yield rich returns.

With Dezhnëv setting out from Nizhnekolymsk on the Kolyma and Stadukhin sailing from a base on the Lena, the search for the "Pogycha" began in earnest during the summer of 1647. After unusually thick ice floes prevented either expedition from entering the Freezing Sea that summer, both spent the winter and spring making new preparations so as to be ready to try again in 1648. This time, Dezhnëv had better luck. Setting out with ninety men in seven boats, he was now destined to lead one of the scant handful of Russian sea voyages to make history. Although a storm wrecked two of their craft at the Kolyma's mouth, the rest of Dezhnëv's force entered the Freezing Sea without incident and began their voyage along the coast. Because the Kolyma was the easternmost Asian river to flow into the Arctic, they never found the "Pogycha" River. Instead, they reached the northeastern tip of Siberia at the beginning of September, rounded the Chukotka peninsula, and passed the East Cape (now called Cape Dezhnëv), thus proving that North America and Asia were separate continents.[9]

Ignorant of geography and unaware of the larger questions that commanded cartographers' attention in the West, Dezhnëv and his comrades had no sense of the importance of what they had done. In retrospect, their success in sailing their crude craft for more than a thousand miles through the East Siberian and Chukchi seas seems all but impossible, and as recently as two decades ago some experts still were challenging the claim that Dezhnëv's men had done so.[10] The distance was too great, they insisted, the men's experience too limited, and their knowledge of navigation nonexistent. Dezhnëv's boats were too fragile, and their motive power too weak. Yet Russian scholars have now proved beyond a doubt that the events that Dezhnëv recounted in a deposition taken down several years later actually happened, even though the rest of the world did not learn of them until a hundred years later.[11]

About the time that Dezhnëv passed the cape that now bears his name, the luck that had carried him around Asia's northeastern tip turned sour. A storm sank all but one of his boats, and only twenty-four of his men managed to reach the desolate southern coast of the Chukhotka peninsula. "All of us took to the hills," the almost certainly illiterate Dezhnëv explained in his deposition to the military governor of Irkutsk. "We were cold and hungry and without clothes and barefoot and I, poor Semeika and my comrades [it was important, in those days, to use the most self-denigrating terms in a report to such a high official], went to the Anadyr in just ten weeks, reaching the lower reaches of that Anadyr River near where it flows into the sea." Now, nearly six thousand miles east of Moscow, a full twelve hundred miles northeast of Iakutsk, and nearly half a world east of Greenwich, Dezhnëv and his men did not know where they were, nor how they could return. Their boats were gone. Marooned in the northeasternmost corner of Asia with only the sun and the stars to tell their location, they could only guess that Iakutsk lay far away to the southwest. Unable to find food or wood, Dezhnëv divided his men into two groups to search for a better wintering place. One group disappeared, but Dezhnëv and eleven companions survived to claim Siberia's northeasternmost corner for Russia.[12]

In his deposition, Dezhnëv added details which, had they become known to Europeans, would have shifted the focus of their explorations for a century to come. "Going by sea from the Kolyma River to the Anadyr River one comes to a cape that extends far out," he explained. From that point, he had sailed on to the mouth of the Anadyr River on the Bering Sea, thereby proving to the careful cartographers of Europe that Asia and North America were separate continents.[13] But, probably because the military governor of Iakutsk had favored Stadukhin as the man best able to enlist new tribute payers for the tsar, Dezhnëv's report never reached Moscow and remained buried in the Iakutsk archives for nearly a century. In the meantime, the eighteenth-century Russian sea captains Vitus Bering and Aleksei Chirikov, in addition to Captain Cook and a dozen other Europeans, continued to explore the waters of the North Pacific to prove that Asia and North America were separate. As happened so often in Russia, where, until the middle of the nineteenth century, every official document was classified as a state secret, the government's compulsion for secrecy meant that discoveries made in one century had to be repeated in the next.

Far away on the Anadyr River, Dezhnëv and his eleven companions tried to act as the tsar's proper agents. Like Poiarkov, Khabarov, and scores of other seventeenth-century Russians who found themselves in unknown Siberian lands, they collected fur tribute from the natives, trapped sable on their own, and collected walrus and mammoth ivory when they found it. In the summer of 1649, they worked their way some 350 miles west to the Anadyr's headwaters and built a new wintering place. Now in desolate lands where trapping was poor (the Anadyr region was one of the few places in Siberia too barren for fur-bearing animals to live in large numbers), they still did not know how to return to Iakutsk. For a while, Dezhnëv seems to have toyed with the idea of building new boats and trying to return the way he had come. But the currents of the Bering Sea flowed in the wrong direction. A clumsy cossack boat, tied together with thongs and willow twigs and powered by oars supplemented by a fixed deerskin sail, could never have taken the reverse course.

It is difficult to imagine how Dezhnëv and his men must have felt when a small detachment from Nizhnekolymsk suddenly appeared at their camp the next spring. A way home had been found at last, but in one of those supreme touches of irony that only fate can provide, their rescuer turned out to be Stadukhin, the archrival, who immediately insisted that his higher rank entitled him to full command of their combined force. After completing one of the most difficult voyages undertaken by any seventeenth-century explorer and spending almost two years in the wilderness, Dezhnëv now had to become the subordinate of the man whom he had just defeated in the race to claim Siberia's northeast.

But Stadukhin had not been alone in searching for a way across the mountains. For most of the way from Nizhnekolymsk, he had followed the trail of a smaller expedition led by Semën Motora, a cossack officer who had spent the previous two years searching for a passage to the coast, and he had overtaken Motora just days before his forces met Dezhnëv's. Thus it had been Motora who had done the work but Stadukhin who claimed the credit for finding a way across Siberia's last mountain barrier.[14] For the next eight months, these three proud, self-centered men feuded and fought. With Stadukhin refusing to relinquish command, several of his lieutenants defected to Motora and Dezhnëv, who eventually joined forces and left Stadukhin to search for richer sources of furs further south.

Now working together, Dezhnëv and Motora explored the lands along the Anadyr, finding a fortune in walrus ivory on the sandbar that filled the river's mouth at low tide. In a month, they dug up nearly three tons and then, with summer coming to an end, made their way back to their wintering place at Anadyrsk. The next spring, Motora was killed in a skirmish with the natives, but Dezhnëv continued to collect ivory in the barren lands that spread across Siberia's northeast for most of another decade. Yet he did not remain out of touch with the authorities in Iakutsk as he had in earlier times. Although no one repeated his voyage in the seventeenth century or, for that matter, the eighteenth, expeditions from Iakutsk traveled overland to Anadyrsk every year once

Motora and Stadukhin had found the way. It was a literate officer in one
of those expeditions who took down the deposition that contained the
details of Dezhnëv's historic voyage.[15]

If the broader significance of Dezhnëv's discovery remained unknown
for a century, his entry into the Chukhotka peninsula brought the
Russians into contact with natives more warlike and better able to resist
than any they had yet encountered. Unlike the weaker and smaller tribes
to their west, who had paid fur tribute to their stronger neighbors for
centuries, the proud Koriaks, whose settlements stretched south from
the Anadyr to the Kamchatka peninsula, were determined to resist its
degradation. When the Russians tried to weaken them by provoking
conflicts with their rivals, as they had done when they had pitted Ostiaks
against Samoeds, Tungus against Buriats, and Lukagirs against Chukchi,
the Koriaks quickly forged alliances with other tribes.[16] Determined to
defend their lands, the Koriaks used captured firearms along with the
most effective of their native weapons to keep the Russians north of
the Anadyr River until the very end of the century.[17] Only then would
the Russians manage to enter the Kamchatka peninsula, the last remaining reservoir of rare pelts in Eurasia.

11

Life on the Siberian Frontier

The cossacks, *promyshlenniki,* and frontier traders who formed the vanguard of Russia's advance across Siberia lived by their wits in groups of five to a hundred in frontier blockhouses and wintering places scattered across five million square miles of Siberian wilderness. Disaster threatened them at every moment, for a minor illness, a fractured limb, or even an unwary step could bring death in a land where distances greater than the length of the British Isles separated one tiny settlement from another.[1] Very few among these men had crossed the Urals to put down roots, and all dreamed of leaving the wilderness with a fortune in pelts and ivory. Furs they had come for, and furs they meant to have. Unrestrained by law and ruled by greed once they set foot in the wilderness, they abused Siberia's natives without mercy. All along the frontier, cossacks demanded tribute for the tsar and "gifts" for themselves. Robbery and extortion acquired nearly as many furs for *promyshlenniki* and traders as did trade. No matter how willingly offered, no amount of furs or food could satisfy Russia's Siberian frontiersmen for long. Always wanting more than their native victims could provide and brutal in the punishments they inflicted upon the people who could not meet their demands, the first Russians who came to Siberia raised around themselves a wall of native resentment that only hardened their lot.

Anyone with daring and enough cash to buy a few goods to exchange with the natives could enter the Siberian fur trade. Although such small

traders collected only what furs could be carried on one or two packhorses, they accounted for hundreds of thousands of sable, fox, and
marten pelts before the first flush of Siberia's fur rush subsided. Only
small fragments of data about the furs taken from Siberia have survived,
but from them we know, for example, that 436 traders and *promyshlenniki*
on their way back to Russia brought nearly 34,000 sable pelts through
Mangazeia during the summer of 1630 and that, in the summer of 1641,
they brought 75,000 sable pelts through the tsar's customs house in
Iakutsk. Some estimates have set the value of furs gathered annually by
private traders during the seventeenth century at something over a third
of a million rubles. At that time, a peasant family of four in Russia earned
less than a ruble a year from forty acres of good farmland.[2]

At the other end of the scale from the thousands of small traders and
promyshlenniki who braved the dangers of Siberia's taiga to collect a
comparative handful of pelts apiece stood the few men who never
crossed the Urals but sent agents and hired traders to work for them on
the fur frontier. Carrying trading goods by the boat- and cartload, such
traders stayed in Siberia from two to six years, depending on distance,
luck, and weather. It usually took a winter and two summers to make the
round trip between Russia and the towns and frontier forts of western
Siberia, and journeys from Tobolsk to Iakutsk and back could take up
to three times that long. A man could complete two such enterprises in
a decade, even fewer if he went into Siberia's northeast to spend a winter
or two working with local trappers. Because half a dozen journeys to
distant parts of the fur frontier would consume the best years of a
lifetime,[3] space and time held different meanings for any Russian who
ventured into Siberia. That one could move from the vigor of youth to
the brink of middle age in the course of two or three journeys from
Moscow to the Kolyma lands and back imparted an urgent "here and
now" quality to life that contrasted sharply with the huge amounts of
time that travel in Siberia consumed.

Under the best conditions, conquerors and traders had barely seven
months after the spring thaws before the Siberian winter drove them to
seek shelter in remote wintering places. Often no more than enlarged
peasant huts of roughly squared logs and windows made of mica or
translucent fish bladders, these became the centers of winter life on the
fur frontier. Mixed with the noxious fumes from a single earthen stove,
the stench of crowded bodies turned such shelters into monuments to
humans' ability to withstand suffocation as they ate, slept, and fornicated
in a single open room, fought against the boredom of the long Arctic
nights, dressed their raw furs, gambled for entertainment, and killed one

another for amusement. In the spring, such men set out again, moving into the hinterland with carts and packhorses or working their way up and down the network of tributaries that flowed into Siberia's great rivers, portaging across the land bridges that separated one river system from another, then taking to their boats once again.

It required ruthless governors to hold these frontiersmen and cossacks in check, and the men sent to govern and defend Siberia were no more upright than the rough-and-ready adventurers they came to rule. Although the laws of Muscovy banned the tsar's officials from pursuing Siberia's "golden fleece" for personal gain, most of them thought of very little else. Almost every man who wielded power in the tsar's name enriched himself by trading in furs or by stealing a portion of those that passed through his hands. Sanctified by centuries of tradition, bribery and theft had been commonplace among old Russia's officials since the days of the Mongols, but the raw avarice of the men who represented the tsar in Siberia rarely found parallels on the European side of the Urals. Murder, extortion, embezzlement, highway robbery, and selling women for furs and ivory all counted among their crimes. "They were without the fear of God and without feelings of shame," one commentator confessed. "Were it not for the fact that the evidence on this point is uncontradictory," he added solemnly, "one could hardly believe that these men were as low and as depraved as the contemporary literature paints them."[4]

The military governors whom the tsar placed in charge of the regions surrounding Tobolsk, Mangazeia, Eniseisk, Iakutsk, and a dozen other vaguely defined territories offended the laws of God and man more than anyone else. Given unlimited opportunities to enrich themselves at the expense of others, thanks to their monopoly on military power and civil authority in the vast lands over which they ruled, these men lived in opulence. One high official brought thirty-two household retainers, a personal priest, and supplies that included 2,500 gallons of wine and spirits to Mangazeia in 1635, and each new military governor who came to Tobolsk (the most prestigious appointment in seventeenth-century Siberia) typically brought with him at least twice that number of relatives and servants and double that quantity of supplies. By the end of the century, the baggage trains of Siberia's high officials had become so huge that they called to mind the progresses of kings and queens in medieval Europe. Since these men served so far away and ruled over such vast lands, the best that could be done in Moscow to control them was to restrict their terms of office to two years in the hope that a brief appointment would limit their opportunities to steal.[5]

Aside from furs, traffic in females was the most lucrative enterprise among Siberia's Russians. Because women rarely entered Siberia's lonely frontier world of their own accord, native women, deported women, women who had accompanied their husbands and been widowed, and any other women whom fate sent across the Urals all became prime objects for sale and trade. "They traded, gambled, mortgaged, and sold their wives and daughters as if they were chattel," one writer reported after examining the first official reports of such crimes.[6] Promising the women of their choice better food and housing, government officials and soldiers shared out among themselves females deported to Siberia for offenses ranging from adultery to murder. For women thrown into the raw life of the Siberian frontier, the difference between hunger and survival or between a life of deprivation and one of minimal comfort seemed very large indeed. With the "courtship" rituals of the 1940s and 1950s being remarkably similar to those used three hundred years before, women in Siberia would continue to face those choices into the second half of the twentieth century, when deportations to the frontier finally ended. Even the best born among Siberia's native women faced similar fates. One Russian official reportedly forced the wife of a Siberian prince into his harem. Different sources tell us that others followed his example.[7]

Circumstances drove the more common sisters of native princesses into the embraces of ruder conquerors. The Russians forced Siberia's natives to pay part of their annual tribute in women to be sold in garrisons and wintering places for two or three prime sable pelts apiece. Bought and sold in markets, won at card tables, or traded in barracks and resold after a winter's use without any loss of value, these women passed from hand to hand, season after season, never knowing what fate had in store for them from one year to the next.[8] From their passing unions with cossacks, trappers, and exiled criminals came children who combined the blood of their Iakut, Ostiak, Samoed, and Mongol mothers with that of the Russians who fathered them. These became the first element in a long and complex heritage that the Russians would bestow upon the Siberians over the next four centuries and that would end in the 1980s with massive environmental poisoning.

After furs and women, trade in illegal liquor held pride of place as the most lively enterprise on the Siberian frontier. Out-of-the-way stills and backyard breweries yielded immense profits from the rough-and-ready Russian woodsmen who were ready to drink as much of the moonshine that seared the throat and numbed the brain as Siberia's illegal distillers could produce. Quantity counted most, and alcoholic content mattered more than purity. Like their modern-day descendants, who have been known to produce moonshine from almost any organic material known to man, the Russians in seventeenth-century Siberia consumed any quantity of any spirit produced at any time from any substance. In vain the authorities condemned producers, sellers, and consumers of Siberian frontier spirits to public floggings, fines, and imprisonment. Nothing could stop the trade in bootleg spirits from following the Russians across the Urals, and nothing could eradicate it once it had taken root.

Even in a crime-ridden land, crime had a price, especially for those without influence or the means to buy it in high places. The tsar's officials sentenced those who could not protect themselves to flogging, mutilation, imprisonment, hanging, and an astounding variety of cruel tortures. In a petition to the Siberian Office, a group of insubordinate cossacks once complained that the military governor of Iakutsk "burned us over a fire, pulled our limbs out of joint, poured icy water over our heads, [and] pinched our navels and muscles with hot tongs." Others reported that the same high official fried men on large iron pans, drove needles under their finger- and toenails, and scattered burning coals onto their bare backs.[9] Criminals had noses, ears, and limbs cut off, tongues torn out, and cheeks, foreheads, and backs branded. Men sentenced to capital punishment actually fared better than many who were not, for the authorities usually allowed them to seek new sources of tribute for the tsar in the lands beyond the frontier instead of facing the executioner. At some point in their lives, several of Siberia's most famous seventeenth-century explorers—including, it seems, Khabarov—went in search of new tribute rather than face the tsar's hangman. For those guilty of lesser crimes, the old Russian proverb that "God is high above and the tsar far away" took on new meaning in a land where it took over two years for a petition for clemency to reach Moscow, be acted upon, and be sent back to Siberia.

Even more than the rough-and-ready frontiersmen whom the tsar's officials tried to intimidate by torture and punishment, Siberia's natives suffered at the Russians' hands. Although the Siberian Office in Moscow warned them not to "insult" them, Siberia's governors-general frequently took chiefs and tribal shamans hostage, kept them in irons, and fed them with the rotten meat kept for sled dogs in the winter. Reports from western Siberia complained that the tsar's officials tortured natives as a matter of course. The military governor of Iakutsk once hanged twenty-three chiefs (for which he received a reprimand), and an official in Okhotsk was reported to have abducted all the children from the local Tungus so that he could sell them back to their parents for a sable pelt apiece.[11]

Disputes about fur tribute usually lay behind these misdeeds. Although the Russians took part of the payment in native women, Siberians had to pay most of the tribute owed to their new masters in furs. Depending upon the time and place, each native male paid one to ten prime sable pelts each year, and extra furs were demanded as "gifts" for the officials who collected the tribute.[12] Siberians who lived within reach of a town or a frontier blockhouse, of which the Russians had built twenty-nine in western Siberia by 1640, took their tribute to the chief official in residence at the end of the trapping season, while special expeditions of cossacks and tribute collectors made the rounds of those who lived farther away. Then the Russians graded the furs, packing fox pelts in bundles of ten, sable in bundles of forty, and minks and squirrels in bundles of sixty or eighty before they shipped them to Moscow, where the Siberian Office calculated their value (noting the particular flaws and fine points of each), before storing them away or using them in trade.

Combined with the tax of one pelt out of every ten levied on private traders and *promyshlenniki*, the tsar's fur tribute amounted to over a hundred thousand pelts a year by the end of the seventeenth century. Furs paid the expenses of the tsar's court and the costs of his government and served as gifts to foreign sovereigns and their ambassadors. This was the "soft gold" that helped the Russians to recover from the time of troubles that had preceded the Romanovs' rise to power at the beginning of the seventeenth century and paid the cost of winning back the western lands that the Swedes and Poles had seized. Profits from the fur trade would also help to finance Peter the Great's massive campaign to modernize Russia at the beginning of the eighteenth century.[13] In later times, Siberian gold, silver, charcoal, and iron ore would help the Russian Empire to enter the Industrial Revolution. In the twentieth century, gold, diamonds, coal, oil, natural gas, and timber from Siberia would help to pay the costs of the massive experiment in social engineering that Stalin and his successors imposed upon the Soviet people.

Just as the men who vied for wealth in the great gold rushes of the New World took up other occupations when their gold fever abated, so the Russians in Siberia turned to other sources of livelihood as the fur frontier moved east. At the peak of the fur rush, cossacks, traders, and *promyshlenniki* had dominated the Siberian frontier, where they lived by violence and were ruled by it. But because the fur frontier advanced so rapidly, the men and women who settled in western Siberia in the 1640s and 1650s no longer had furs as their chief concerns, nor were they foremost in the minds of those who moved into the lands of the Enisei and the Lena in the 1670s and 1680s. As they put down roots, built homes and businesses, and set the stage for a new way of life, these first *sibiriaki*—Russians who had left their old lives on the European side of the Urals and began to think of themselves as Siberians—became the creators of a new Siberian culture. Eventually, some of them would become powerful voices for separating Siberia from the Russian Empire.

Among the men and women who came to build new lives, carpenters, blacksmiths, gunsmiths, boat builders, and scores of other artisans all found a large demand for their skills. Once the fur frontier had moved east, trade was no longer a matter of exchanging knives, kettles, beads, and trinkets for pelts, and by the 1650s Russian artisans in western Siberia were producing silver, leather, and iron goods to supply a growing demand. By the end of the century, commerce with the lands of Central Asia had added new dimensions to Siberia's economic life, and the growing market for Russian furs in China made the forces shaping Siberian trade even more complex. By the 1670s, furs from the frontier lands of North America were beginning to compete with Russian furs in Europe. With their monopoly of the European fur trade being challenged, the Russians saw the markets offered by China and the khanates of Central Asia as particularly attractive new prospects.[14] It was no accident that the tsar began to send diplomats to China during the second half of the seventeenth century nor that working out a trade treaty with the Chinese became an ongoing preoccupation for the Russians from the 1650s to the end of the 1720s.[15]

As the frontier forts of the fur rush days evolved into more settled towns and trading centers, Tobolsk emerged as the chief town of Siberia. The center of Russian government, religion, and commerce east of the Urals, Tobolsk boasted a monastery, a nunnery, and a seminary before the end of the seventeenth century. Bukharan merchants and Tatar traders brought goods from the East to its markets, while the prosperity of its own artisans added greater vibrance to its economic life.[16] Virtually all of Russia's Siberian trade passed through the hands of Tobolsk merchants in those days. By the end of the century, Tobolsk had the largest merchant arcade in Siberia and one of the most prosperous anywhere in Russia.[17]

Even without rivals, Tobolsk in 1650 was by no means a lonely island in the Siberian wilderness. By the second half of the seventeenth century, Tomsk had begun to play a similar role in south-central Siberia, while Eniseisk, the funnel for all trade passing to and from Iakutsk and Siberia's far east, did the same farther north.[18] East of Eniseisk, Iakutsk and Irkutsk had become the key towns, the first having been founded a full quarter century before the second but the latter eventually becoming more important. Furs, goods, and grain going to and from the lands that Dezhnëv and Stadukhin had opened in Siberia's northeast passed through Iakutsk, and for that reason it ruled all the lands beyond the Lena during the middle third of the seventeenth century. Then Irkutsk, an outpost founded at the intersection of the Angara and Irkut rivers in 1661, began to collect the tsar's fur tribute from the Buriat natives and take control of the Transbaikal lands. Within easy reach of the Chinese frontier, Irkutsk was well placed to become the important link that Moscow needed for developing trade with China, but it was also one of those rare regions in eastern Siberia that could grow its own grain. Unlike in Iakutsk and Eniseisk, hunger was rare in seventeenth-century Irkutsk. Its people never had to depend upon grain shipped across the Urals.[19]

In Siberia's western lands, dependence on grain from European Russia was also diminishing as the seventeenth century entered its second half. More Russians were turning from trapping to farming, and grants of livestock, seeds, tools, and cash subsidies from the Royal Treasury were drawing more peasants to Siberia from those parts of European Russia where the soil was poor and farming hard. In Siberia's new lands, a family could farm five acres of government land for themselves for each acre they tilled for the tsar and escape the poverty that had crushed them at home. Some of those who came to begin new lives on the land were government-sponsored settlers. Others were runaway serfs who knew that their former masters had little chance of finding them once they had crossed the Urals. In centuries to come, Siberia would become what one nineteenth-century Russian foreign minister called "a deep net"[20] into which all of Russia's riffraff and criminals could be dumped, but it was also a land of opportunity, where men and women oppressed by their masters or broken by misfortune could build new lives. Thus, long before the centennial of Ermak's victory, Russian soldiers, Russian craftsmen, Russian peasants, Russian churches, Russian government, and a Russian way of life were all taking their places in Siberia. By the end of the century, Siberia held more than ten thousand households of Russian peasants.[21]

The conquest that opened Siberia to these men and women also transformed the once obscure kingdom of Muscovy into the modern world's largest contiguous empire, about to claim a place among the great powers of Europe. Driven relentlessly into the modern era at the beginning of the eighteenth century by Peter the Great, a six-foot, eight-inch giant who was bursting with energy and scornful of tradition, Russia in less than a quarter century built the army and weapons industry she needed to challenge the West. This process, France's foreign minister wrote at the time, transformed backward Muscovy into an empire that was "formidable to its neighbors."[22] Europe now "feared the extreme power of the tsar," confessed the illustrious German philosopher Leibnitz (who had once predicted that the armies of Sweden would march across Russia to the frontiers of China). To the sovereigns and statesmen of Europe, Leibnitz said, Peter had become "the Turk of the North."[23]

The key to Russia's sudden appearance among the great powers of Europe lay in Siberia, where the government had been searching for other forms of natural wealth even at the peak of the fur rush. Just before the end of the seventeenth century, prospectors discovered rich supplies of iron ore in the Ural forests along Siberia's western edge. This was a far cry from the bog iron that Buriat and Iakut smiths had hammered out in olden times and a notable cut above the metal that Eniseisk blacksmiths had begun to forge in the 1640s and 1650s. Here was iron fit to make the massive quantities of cannon and muskets that would render Russia capable of waging modern war at the beginning of the 1700s. Sensing its possibilities, Peter the Great seized the opportunity to use Siberian frontier iron to raise Russia to a place among the great powers. Yet before he could challenge the nations of the West on their own ground, the iron of the Urals had to be smelted, forged, and tempered. To do that, he needed men who would dare to set aside what they had in Russia and take the risk of trying to make iron and steel on a massive scale in the Siberian wilderness. He found them in Nikita Demidov, a blacksmith and weapons maker from the central Russian town of Tula, and his eldest son, Akinfii, who was one of the rare Russians in those days to have studied science in the West.

PART THREE

The Russians Explore Their Conquest

12

The Demidovs, Frontier Iron, and Tsar Peter

At the end of the seventeenth century, the statesmen and sovereigns who ruled Europe believed that only those nations possessing unlimited access to natural resources and the technology to manufacture them could become rich and strong. This belief had led England, Holland, France, and Spain to build colonial empires, using their newfound abilities to project force across the seas to seize vast lands in the New World and the Far East. Always in search of new empires, the merchant adventurers of England and Holland viewed Russia in similar terms. A rude and barbarous kingdom to their way of thinking, Russia held a fortune in furs as well as the grain Europe needed to feed its growing cities. Russia also had hemp, tar, and timber in abundance, all of them vital for modern navies. For those reasons, Europeans had been reaching into Russia ever since the days of Ivan the Terrible. By the middle of the seventeenth century, the English had even built a ropewalk on North Russia's White Sea coast to manufacture cordage for their fleet.

The Russians therefore stood in danger of being exploited by nations with greater access to wealth and technology in much the same way as they were exploiting the Siberians. "When the natives sell their products in a raw state," one Russian statesman warned, "it is the inhabitants of other countries who work up the raw materials and receive the great return on their labors, while the former possessors receive only a meager sustenance."[1] Combined with his sixth sense that the merchants and kings of Europe would devour his nation if he did not make Russia their equal, such warnings made it clear to Peter the Great that he had little time to lose. Russia needed to build an army equal to any in the world. To do that, it could not continue to arm its soldiers with expensive weapons bought from the West with Siberian furs.

Prepared to lead by personal example as no other tsar had done, Peter took Russia's helm in 1689 with a clear sense of urgency and purpose. He understood that Russian armorers had to make Russia's weapons from Russian iron and steel if Russia hoped to stand among the nations of the West, yet Russia had no iron industry aside from a few small foundries and a handful of armories in Moscow and Tula. All of Peter's predecessors had ordered every military governor they sent across the Urals to look for iron ore in Siberia, and some had tried to enlarge Russia's iron industry by hiring foreign experts to work with imported iron. None of these efforts had succeeded. Small deposits of iron ore had been found near the Stroganovs' saltworks at Solvychegodsk and a few other places, but the vast reserves that later would make the Soviet Union the world's largest producer of iron and steel had yet to be discovered. At the end of the seventeenth century, most Russian iron still came from bogs, dug by peasants, heated in small smithy forges, and then hammered into small bars or strips. For higher-quality iron and steel, the Russians had to rely upon Sweden, the very nation she would have to fight to gain access to the Baltic.[2]

The discovery of high-quality iron ore at Neviansk near Siberia's western frontier transformed Russia's iron industry in scarcely more than a decade after Peter the Great came to the throne. Set in the midst of a large network of rivers and surrounded by forests that promised abundant supplies of fuel, this ore was pronounced by experts to be "better than that found in Sweden," which, at that time, produced the highest-quality iron and steel in Europe.[3] Now, foundries had to be built, a labor force assembled in the wilderness, and master workmen trained to work with iron on a scale never before attempted by the Russians. Peter had assigned that task to the military governor of Verkhoture, only to see him fail just as Russia went to war with Sweden. Tired of the "botched iron" and "wry-mouth cannon" that the new foundry at Neviansk sent his armies and arsenals, the tsar turned it over to Nikita Demidych Demidov, an ironmaster and weapons maker who had won his confidence.[4]

Demidov's powerful, sloping shoulders bespoke a life spent at the forge. Some accounts claim that he first won Peter's favor by making for one of his favorites a perfect copy of an intricately designed pistol that had come from the armory of one of Central Europe's most famous gunsmiths. Others insist that he rose above Tula's other armsmakers by producing modern flintlock muskets to Peter's specifications on very short notice, and still others maintain that tsar and gunsmith first met when Peter, always on the lookout for men of great size and strength, tried to enlist him in his elite regiment of Preobrazhenskii Guards.[5] All we know for certain is that the tsar stopped at Tula on one of several journeys he made between Moscow and the front during his first war with the Ottoman Empire and that sometime in late 1695 or early 1696 Demidov presented him with six firearms of his own design.[6] Impressed by Demidov's understanding of modern weapons technology and his ability to manage men, Peter made him a promise. "Strive to expand your factory," he told him then. "Strive to expand your factory, and I will not abandon you."[7]

For several more years Nikita Demidov worked at Tula. He became the first ironmaster there to use water power, and, after buying up several other small foundries, he began to produce flintlock muskets that met the government's specifications at a fraction of what it cost to import them from Europe. With the beginning of the Great Northern War between Russia and Sweden in 1700, government orders began to pour in, and in less than a year Demidov had contracts for twenty thousand flintlock muskets.[8] Peter, it seemed, had already kept his promise that he would "not abandon" him. Then his patronage took a different form. Anxious to turn the failed foundry at Neviansk over to private hands in return for pledges of cheap iron and well-made cannon, he offered it to the artful Nikita in 1702.

With more government orders than he could fill and the promise of a comfortable life in his native Tula, Nikita Demidov must have found Peter's offer to move to the Siberian frontier a mixed blessing. Nonetheless, he seized the chance, sensing the opportunity to build on a scale that he never could have achieved at Tula. At Neviansk and in the ten thousand square miles of land around it, Nikita and his son began to build an empire, the base of which lay along Siberia's western frontier, from which the Chusovaia River could carry bargeloads of iron and weapons into the heart of European Russia. The Chusovaia and (on the Urals' Siberian side) the Tagil and Neiva would eventually bind together a sprawling network of mines, timbering camps, forges, and foundries that would move men, metal, weapons, and supplies back and forth across the mountains.[9]

To make iron and guns for the tsar, the Demidovs needed not only ore that was plentiful but labor that was cheap. Nikita therefore took the unprecedented step of asking the tsar to let him buy serfs to work in his foundries, for the only sources of local labor around Neviansk were a handful of Russian peasants and a few scattered native settlements.[10] Only the tsar, the Royal Treasury, and the nobility had the right to own serfs in Russia, and Peter's readiness to grant that privilege to a commoner indicates how urgently he wanted an iron and weapons industry that did not depend upon metal or technicians from the West. With the tsar's support, Demidov became the first commoner to own serfs in modern Russia. By doing so, he made certain that some of Russia's best foundry masters, metalworkers, and gunsmiths in the eighteenth century would be serfs.

The move to Neviansk in 1702 cemented an alliance between the Demidovs and the Romanovs that would survive the comings and goings of six sovereigns over the next half century. Demidov iron became the first of Siberia's products to be exempted from the duties imposed upon goods crossing the Urals into Russia, and by 1720 the Demidov forges and foundries had become the exclusive suppliers of iron to the Russian navy. Obliged to organize large-scale logging operations to fuel their forges and foundries, the Demidovs began to cut timber for government shipyards. Reaping profits from Peter's war effort at every turn, they had grown rich enough by 1721 to bestow a gift of a hundred thousand rubles in gold upon their tsar and tsarina at the birth of a son they hoped would rule Russia one day.[11] Yet such gifts were not what bound the Demidovs to their sovereigns. The most successful frontier entrepreneurs in Russia since the Stroganovs, they gave Peter and his successors the iron industry Russia needed to win a place among the great powers of the West. By the time Russia became the world's leading producer of pig iron in the 1780s, two out of every five tons of it came from the foundries that Nikita and his descendants had built in Siberia.[12]

As tsar and blacksmith traded gifts and favors in the early 1720s, both were approaching the end of their reigns, for both would die in 1725. With weapons forged from Demidov iron, Peter's soldiers had won a foothold on the Baltic and carved a place for Russia among the great powers of Europe. Demidov iron had also anchored and braced Russia's ships and served a hundred other vital purposes in building Peter the Great's new empire. The same iron had also built a kingdom of forges and foundries, for Nikita added six more ironworks to the one at Neviansk before he died. Each of these increased his already unmatched ability to produce more of the metal that had made his fortune. In 1725, he therefore left behind the beginnings of an empire that his son would expand to dwarf his achievement. By that time, Demidov forges were producing more than ten thousand tons of iron a year, or more than half of all the iron produced in the Russian Empire.[13]

As with the second generation of so many of the dynasties that led Europe and America into the Industrial Revolution, Nikita Demidov's eldest son, Akinfii, built upon his father's achievement according to his genius and the laws of mathematical progression. Born in 1678, Akinfii learned to make iron and steel at Freiberg, one of the greatest centers of metallurgy in Europe, then returned to Russia to work with his father just before they took over the Neviansk foundry. For more than two decades, the two men labored to build their empire, yet they did so on the basis of Nikita's old-fashioned intuition and experience, not Akinfii's knowledge of modern science. Nikita remained a patriarch who ruled his enterprises and his son with equal sternness, and, although he had the good sense to allow him some latitude, much of what Akinfii had learned in Freiberg had to be set aside to do his father's bidding.

When Nikita's death freed his hands, Akinfii combined his technical training with the stubbornness, confidence, and entrepreneurial skill he had inherited from his father to expand the Demidov realm of forges and foundries in the Urals into a Siberian industrial empire. Even more than his father's, Akinfii's life revolved around the forging and casting of metal, and each of the enterprises he built in Siberia's western lands received devoted personal attention. Making metal was his passion, and no detail was too small or any problem too large to consider. "Just like small children," he once wrote, "factories incessantly demand careful supervision."[14] During the twenty-one years that separated his father's death from his own, Akinfii made certain that his enterprises were the best-watched industrial progeny in Russia.

Akinfii's genius for forging metal and managing metalworks allowed him to surpass all rivals in producing iron at lower cost and higher profit. Using only a fourth as much labor, his foundries yielded twice the output of their government-managed counterparts, and, by building better sluices and more efficient blast furnaces, he produced iron and sold it in Moscow and St. Petersburg at more than ten times the profit earned by foundries run by the government. At the same time, he towered over his handful of private competitors. No other Russian iron maker produced more than a sixth of what the Demidov foundries did during the first half of the eighteenth century, nor could any other iron forged in Russia match Demidov quality.[15] Russia could not even begin to consume the output of Akinfii's foundries. By the time he died in 1745, nearly seven out of every ten tons of metal that came from his ironworks were being sold abroad.[16] From a nation obliged to import iron at high cost from potential enemies in 1700, the Demidovs had transformed Russia into one of the world's largest iron exporters in less than fifty years, and the English, who in the days of Ivan the Terrible had tried to mine and smelt iron in Russia themselves,[17] had now become Russia's willing customers. "The iron is pure, even in width and girth, and of highest quality," one enthusiastic English buyer wrote in the 1730s.[18] Especially at the price at which the Demidovs sold it, it was well worth paying the cost to ship it to England.

Not satisfied to be Russia's largest producer of iron, Akinfii began to branch out into other areas. Like iron, copper had been in short supply throughout Russia's history, and every tsar since Ivan the Terrible had commissioned special prospectors and foreign experts to search for it in the far north and Siberia. In the sixteenth and seventeenth centuries, the handful of finds, whose meager yields of low-grade ore had played out quickly, underlined the importance of locating richer lodes.[19] Intrigued by tales of mines deep in Siberia that had been worked long before the Russians' coming and looking for new challenges to test his skill, Akinfii now set out to become Russia's largest smelter of copper. More expert in metallurgy than the men who had gone before him, he shifted the focus of Russia's search for copper away from the north to the Altai foothills near the frontier of Mongolia in Siberia's south. There, more than a thousand miles south and east of the Urals, he found the treasure in copper ore that prospectors had been seeking since the days of Ermak.

In 1724, after long months of searching, Akinfii's prospectors uncovered ancient forges in the valley of the Shulba River and then, on Christmas Day 1725, found the mines near the shores of Lake Kolyvan that once had supplied them. In the spring of 1726, Empress Catherine I granted him permission to mine copper in the Altai lands, and within a decade her successor, Empress Anna, forbade all others to mine or smelt that metal anywhere in the vast territories between the Urals and the Ob River.[20] Still, no matter how talented or powerful, no single man could exploit Siberia's mineral wealth to the fullest. Nor would the forces that shaped Russian politics permit so much power and wealth to be concentrated in the hands of one family. Others therefore had to be given a share of the opportunity, even though none could hope to rival the Demidovs until the heirs of Nikita and Akinfii shifted their interests from Siberia's metals to waiting upon Russia's sovereigns in St. Petersburg at the end of the century.[21]

Unlike their father and grandfather, who had served a tsar seeking to win for Russia a prominent place among the great powers of the modern world, the Demidovs who left iron making and copper smelting to become diplomats, statesmen, and aristocrats in St. Petersburg served empresses and emperors who ruled the world's largest contiguous empire. As one of Europe's great powers, this new empire formed an integral part of the alliance system that divided and united Europe at various times in the eighteenth century, and its armies fought in Europe's wars as well as its own. Cossack squadrons in the outskirts of Berlin at the end of the Seven Years' War in 1761 and the parade of Russian divisions down the Champs-Élysées in 1814 provided the most dramatic evidence of Peter's achievement in making Russia a European power, but other factors tied the empire he had created to Europe as well. Like the rest of Europe in the eighteenth century, the Russians devoted themselves to slavish imitations of the Versailles court, and the growing English market for Demidov iron became only one of many instances of Russia's growing involvement in the trade and commerce of Europe.

Trade and the quest for new technology had begun to draw Russia into the world of European learning even in Tsar Peter's time, and, as more Russians followed the path of Akinfii Demidov in studying in the West, Western science came to Russia along with European scientists. In search of new and fertile areas of scholarly inquiry and scientific exploration, these disciples of Western learning turned to Siberia. There, botanists, historians, geologists, and above all geographers found virgin scientific ground, all of it untouched by the hand of modern science and scholarship.

13

Bering's First Voyage

In his passion for Western science and technology, Peter the Great built an academy of sciences that became the outpost of the scientific revolution in Russia. All of its seventeen fellows named in 1725 had to be imported from Central Europe because no Russians at the time were sufficiently learned to hold an appointment, and it became their task to educate Russia's first scholars. While they taught the Russians, these Europeans studied the natural history and ethnography of the land to which they had come, but geography held their attention most of all. To them it seemed that the time had come to reopen the search for a Northeast Passage.[1]

For men anxious to know if Asia and North America were joined at the top of the globe, the mystery of northeastern Siberia's so-called "glacial cape" had to be solved. "A large strip of land extends far northward toward the so-called but as yet unknown glacial cape," the great German scholar Gottfried Leibnitz explained to one of Peter's advisers. "It is necessary to determine if this cape exists," he continued, "[and to learn] if this strip of land ends at the cape [or converges with America]."[2] Dezhnëv's long-ago voyage had answered Leibnitz's question, but not even Russia's powerful tsar knew about the long-forgotten account of his discovery, which had been gathering dust in the Iakutsk archives for the past seventy years. What guided Peter (but remained unknown to Leibnitz and most of his contemporaries) was a later account prepared by Vladimir Atlasov, the explorer who had led the Russians into the Kamchatka peninsula at the very end of the seventeenth century. "Between the Kolyma and Anadyr Rivers there is an impassable 'nose' or peninsula that extends into the sea," Atlasov had written in 1698. "Along the left side of this 'nose,' " he continued, "there is ice in the sea during summer; while in the winter this same sea is frozen over."[3] Ice, not an isthmus connecting Asia with North America, made the waters around Siberia's East Cape impassable, the natives had told Atlasov. While Leibnitz and his fellow scholars continued to ponder the land barriers that might stand in the way of a Northeast Passage through the Arctic, Peter the Great and his advisers contemplated how its waters might be charted and a pathway found through the ice.

Unlike the European scholars with their urgings for new explorations who continued to pour into St. Petersburg during the last decade of his reign, Peter had other concerns about the waters that stretched east from Siberia's East Cape. By the beginning of the eighteenth century, the Russians' rape of Siberia's fur lands had led to a sharp decline in the number of fur-bearing animals all across northern Asia, and, just as Peter's wars placed an immense new strain upon Russia's national treasury, the income from the Siberian fur trade began to decline. With no lands left to claim in Siberia and no new sources elsewhere that could compensate for the shortage of pelts that the Russians' greed had caused, Peter began to look beyond the sea to the fur lands of North America.[4] Farther south, the Spanish and British had already begun to reap rich fur harvests along the coasts of California and Canada, and there was every reason to expect that the unexplored North American lands that lay across the Pacific from Siberia's eastern coast could yield similar wealth. In the 1720s, these remained undiscovered, yet Peter and his advisers felt certain that North America's western lands must extend as far north as Europe and Asia. Fearful that Spain and Britain might well try to prevent Russia from staking a claim in the New World should they sense his intent to discover and explore lands their own ships had not yet reached, Peter therefore concealed his true purpose by explaining Russian explorations in that remote corner of the globe as part of a search for a Northeast Passage.[5]

After several failures to reach the lands he believed lay east of Siberia, Peter planned a more grandiose attempt, even as he felt the onset of what was to become his final illness. "I have been thinking over the matter . . . [of] finding a passage to China and India through the Arctic Sea," the tsar told the general admiral of his fleet just a few weeks before he died. "I have written out these instructions," he continued, "and, on account of my health, I entrust the execution of them, point by point, to you."[6] Signed on December 23, 1724, a little more than a month before his death, Peter's actual instructions turned out to have nothing to do with a Northeast Passage. Instead, they set in motion the expedition that the Danish sea captain Vitus Bering was to lead overland from St. Petersburg to Okhotsk. From there, Bering was to cross the Sea of Okhotsk to the Kamchatka peninsula and, after building a ship sturdy enough to navigate the waters of the North Pacific, sail north by northeast to the lands that we now know as Alaska, chart the coast, and collect information that could be used for further Russian enterprises that almost certainly involved colonizing the lands of North America's far northwest.[7]

Aged forty-four when he received Tsar Peter's orders, Vitus Bering was a Dane who had learned his trade on Dutch East India Company ships that had carried him from his native Baltic waters to the Indian Ocean and beyond. Like so many Europeans whom fame had passed by in the West, he had come to Russia to seek his fortune and had received command of his own ship just six years later, in 1710.[8] A brave captain whose modest talent for seamanship won him attention in the navy of a nation whose men preferred to fight on land, Bering seemed much better suited to play the role of explorer than he really was. Stubborn, rigid, and stern, he viewed the world through the prism of an incurious mind, and he had not the passion to explore the unknown that drives true explorers beyond old frontiers. Ready and willing to face adversity, Bering was not a man to shirk his duty—nor did he ever try to reach beyond it. That failing showed in his choice of Martin Spanberg to serve as his second in command. A Dane like Bering, Spanberg could be counted on to do his utmost to carry out difficult orders, but he had neither the vision nor the desire to do more than commanded.

Once described as "a competent officer notorious for his great boorishness and brutality toward subordinates,"[9] Spanberg understood Russian poorly, spoke it badly, and barely wrote it at all. A huge dog that he would turn loose upon anyone who made him angry (so rumor had it) went with him everywhere, and, like his commander, he interpreted orders in their narrowest sense. Spanberg's dull nature helped to blunt the buoyant daring of Bering's second lieutenant, Aleksei Chirikov, who, at twenty-one, was thought to be one of the most promising officers in the Russian navy.[10] He "had a pure heart," one of his superiors wrote, "and a great love of the sea."[11] But Chirikov had graduated from Russia's newly founded naval academy only four years before. He had an explorer's soul, but his inferior rank, limited experience, and tender years obliged him on this, his first voyage, to defer to his gloomy Danish superiors.

Except for their commander, Spanberg, and four others, all of whom caught up three weeks later, Bering's expedition of twenty-six men and twenty-five wagons set out from St. Petersburg on January 24, 1725. Carrying all the cordage and canvas needed to build a ship on the Pacific, they reached the governor's headquarters at Tobolsk in the middle of March and then, after the spring thaws, continued on by river barge to Eniseisk and Ilimsk, where they spent the winter. The next spring, they portaged across the land bridge that separated Ilimsk from the Lena, built new barges, and made their way to Iakutsk, some twelve hundred miles downriver. There, Bering collected the rest of the supplies and workmen he would need in Okhotsk to cut timber and build a ship. At the beginning of July 1726, he placed Spanberg in command of the thirteen rafts that were to carry the heaviest of their supplies over a network of rivers and portages to Okhotsk. Six weeks later, he set out himself, leaving Chirikov in Iakutsk over the winter with orders to bring the remaining men and supplies overland the next spring.[12]

When Bering reached Okhotsk at the end of October, he found not the seventy-five-year-old town he had been told to expect by his superiors but a squalid settlement of eleven crumbling huts. Without shelter for his men or horses, he set his advance party to work cutting what scant timber could be collected from a land that grew no full-sized trees. Certain that he could not find in the scrubby woods around Okhotsk the timber needed to build an oceangoing ship, Bering decided instead to put his men to work on building a small craft called a *shitik* (the name being derived from the Russian word that means "to sew") that was made by "sewing" planks to a rough-hewn keel with willow twigs and leather thongs. The *shitik* would carry the expedition and its supplies across the Sea of Okhotsk to a new base on the southern tip of the Kamchatka peninsula, where the large forests would yield the first-rate timber needed to build a more sturdy vessel that could stand against the storms and waves of the North Pacific.[13]

While Bering struggled to get his advance party settled in Okhotsk, Spanberg got caught in the mountains, his barges frozen in by an early winter storm. Storing the bulk of their supplies as best they could, Spanberg and his men continued overland, finding shelter at night in dens dug beneath the drifting snow. After losing nearly a dozen of his crew along the way, Spanberg reached Okhotsk at the beginning of January 1727 and spent the next three months sending parties back into the mountains to bring forward the supplies he had left behind. Until

Chirikov arrived from Okhotsk with fifty steers and forty more tons of provisions at the end of May 1727, the rest of the men worked at building shelters at Okhotsk and transporting by sled trees that could be cut into ship's timbers from the scrub forests that grew some twenty to thirty miles inland.

By the time Chirikov reached Okhotsk, Bering's shipbuilders had nearly finished the *shitik Fortuna*. After the ship carried its first consign-ment of shipbuilders and cargo to Kamchatka at the end of June, it returned to Okhotsk in August to take Bering and the rest of his men to Bolsheretsk, a tiny settlement near Kamchatka's southwestern tip that the Russians used as a base for collecting fur tribute. From there, Bering planned to move his entire force across the peninsula to the mouth of the Kamchatka River more than three hundred miles to the northeast, where, at the rude fort that the tsar's cossack tribute collectors had built at Nizhnekamchatsk, he planned to lay the keel of the ship that would carry them into the North Pacific the next summer.[14]

To travel from Bolsheretsk to Nizhnekamchatsk required a journey across two ranges of mountains even more dangerous than those that separated Iakutsk from Okhotsk. Several active volcanoes, the highest of which rose to nearly twelve thousand feet and spewed a column of smoke and ashes over a mile into the atmosphere above its summit, made up the easternmost range. The only passage between them was through the Kamchatka River valley, where the land turned swampy in summer and temperatures fell to $-50°$ Fahrenheit in the winter. Span-berg led about half of the expedition over that route late in the fall of 1727 so as to begin cutting ship's timber right after the beginning of the new year; the rest followed in two large groups in midwinter, fighting their way through violent Kamchatkan blizzards. "The wind began to blow with great violence, and, drifting the snow in quantities, thickened the atmosphere so that we could not see a yard before us," one traveler wrote of a similar storm a century later. "Clouds of sleet rolled like a dark smoke over the moor," he added, "and we were all so benumbed with cold that our teeth chattered in our heads."[15] After digging shelters beneath the snow to live through storms such as these, Bering and his men finally straggled into Nizhnekamchatsk in the spring. Now some fifteen hundred miles north of Japan and six thousand miles east of St. Petersburg, they had to build out of green timber a ship strong enough to sail through waters uncharted by anyone in Russia or the West.[16]

"We went to work on April 4, 1728," Bering reported, "and, with the help of God had . . . [our ship, the *St. Gabriel*] completed by July 10."[17] Although the ship's iron had been brought from Tobolsk and its cordage and canvas from St. Petersburg, tar had to be made on the spot. "Since we had not brought any with us and the natives had none on hand as they did not know how to make it, we manufactured [tar] out of a tree known there as *listvennik* [larch]," Bering later explained to Empress Anna. "For lack of anything better to take along on the sea voyage, we distilled liquor from grass by a process known in that country," he continued. "Salt we boiled out of sea water, butter we made from fish oil, and in place of meat we took salt fish. We had on board," he concluded, "enough provisions to last forty men [for] a year."[18]

On July 13, 1728, Bering, Spanberg, Chirikov, and a crew of forty-one set sail heading due north. A month later, they passed St. Lawrence Island, less than a hundred miles off Siberia's Cape Chukhotskii. Bering Strait lay dead ahead, and Alaska (although they did not know it) stood less than three days' voyage to the northeast. Then, as the *St. Gabriel* passed through Bering Strait, the land to the west began to slip away, convincing Bering that the sea passage between Siberia and North America had been completed. Fearful that he could not return to Nizhnekamchatsk before winter if he sailed much farther, Bering summoned his lieutenants to a meeting on August 13 to decide what course to set. Assuming that the *St. Gabriel* had just passed "the most easterly point" of the Asian mainland, Bering told them, they might now choose to continue on in search of new lands in which to spend the winter, or they could retrace their course to their home port. "Looking at it from the point of view of best serving our country," he asked, "where does it seem best to go for the winter in order to protect men and boat?"[19]

Spanberg suggested that the *St. Gabriel* continue north for three more days in the hope of discovering new lands and then, whether they sighted land or not, "turn about and betimes seek shelter and harbor on the Kamchatka River whence we came, in order to save men and boat." Apparently as yet unacquainted with the real purpose of the mission but well versed in European geographers' debate about the Northeast Passage, Chirikov urged that they sail west toward the Kolyma River and the settlements near its mouth so as to make certain that North America did not touch Siberia at some more westerly point.[20] Bering sided with Spanberg and held the *St. Gabriel* on her course to the northeast for another seventy-two hours. Then, when his crew could have sighted the still undiscovered shores of Alaska had a heavy fog not hidden them, he turned back. "I concluded that according to all indications the instruction of the emperor of glorious and immortal memory had been carried out," he wrote in his notes of the voyage. "I based my conclusion on the fact that there was no more land to the north. . . . To winter in these regions was out of the question," he added, "because there are no forests, and the people are not under Russian jurisdiction."[21]

After spending the winter in Nizhnekamchatsk, a wretched settlement of some forty shacks, a blockhouse, and a church, Bering sailed the *St. Gabriel* back to Okhotsk in June of 1729 and then set out to make his report to the Imperial Admiralty, which remained in St. Petersburg even though Russia's child emperor, Peter II, had moved the capital back to Moscow in 1728. Moving quickly west, he and his men reached St. Petersburg in March of 1730, only to be greeted by a reception that was scarcely one that men who had crossed Siberia, built two ships in the wilderness, and explored an unknown sea might have expected to receive. When Bering addressed Russia's senior officers and the Ruling Senate, one commentator wrote, "some clapped their hands while others shrugged their shoulders."[22] With Peter the Great dead and the secret vision of extending Russia's power to a third continent not yet known to them, the senators delayed voting Bering the thousand-ruble reward that noted explorers usually received. They let his salary go unpaid for another two years, and when he asked to be promoted to the rank of rear admiral in recognition of his service, the senators declined to act.[23] The slowness of Russia's new leaders to grasp the breadth of Peter's vision for a new empire beyond the seas would cost them dearly in the century ahead. "If [our] government . . . had consistently followed Peter the Great's prescient vision," one of the men who later helped to colonize Russian America wrote in 1806, "then it can be said with certainty that New California [that is, the lands around Fort Ross and Bodega Bay in northern California] would never have become the property of Spain."[24]

Bering had not the political savvy to restore himself to favor, but he had supporters, a few of whom held high posts in the government, who did. These men convinced him to propose an even more ambitious second expedition designed to appeal to the new empress Anna's pretensions for enlarging upon Peter the Great's dream of winning acclaim for Russia among the nations of Europe. This undertaking, which history would remember as the Great Northern Expedition, eventually became so complex that no one man could hope to keep its many strands from becoming tangled. What began as a new attempt by Bering to chart the far northwestern coast of North America soon expanded into what has been described as "one of the most elaborate, thorough, and expensive expeditions ever sent out by any government at any time."[25] As Imperial Russia's first effort to win acclaim among the geographers and scientists of the West, the Great Northern Expedition was to be as vast in scope as the lands it was sent to explore.

14

The Great Northern Expedition

To show the world what the newly Europeanized Russia of Peter the Great could accomplish, Empress Anna and her advisers used Bering's proposal as a starting point for conceiving the Great Northern Expedition in the grandest tradition of science. Its nautical program had three main divisions, each of which was a major undertaking in itself and which, when taken together, exceeded the scope of any enterprise yet planned by any European nation. Exploring the Kurile Islands on the way, Spanberg was to chart Siberia's eastern seas from Okhotsk to Japan and establish commercial relations with the island kingdom that Europeans had only just begun to enter. At the same time, Bering was to sail across the North Pacific from Kamchatka to find the northwestern coast of North America, chart it as far north as possible, and make contact with the natives with an eye to collecting fur tribute and finding new supplies of food for Siberia's far eastern lands. Then, while these enterprises were being launched from Siberia's Pacific coast, half a dozen other expeditions were to chart seven thousand miles of Siberia's shoreline, working their way east from Arkhangelsk on Russia's White Sea coast until they reached Bering Strait, where they were to turn south and follow the coast of the Chukhotka peninsula to Kamchatka.[1]

Blocked by massive ice fields for much of the year, most of the coastline to be charted by the Great Northern Expedition lay above the Arctic Circle. The men and ships of the Hudson's Bay Company would spend the better part of two centuries on a similar mission in North America, and they would not finish their work until 1847. But, with a degree of daring that can come only from being willing to sacrifice men's lives to win greater glory, the organizers of the Great Northern Expedition planned to finish all of their work in a single decade. Nor did they intend to stop at exploring Siberia's seas. As part of this immense undertaking, a contingent of learned men attached to the Great Northern Expedition from the Imperial Russian Academy of Sciences was to produce nothing less than a complete historical, physical, botanical, ethnographical, and linguistic description of Siberia.[2] For a time, some of the men in the Ruling Senate talked of having part of the expedition explore Central Asia, and the Admiralty even considered adding a voyage around the southern tip of Africa to the enterprises Bering was to command.[3]

As set down by the Ruling Senate, the Admiralty, and the Academy of Sciences, the tasks of the Great Northern Expedition were more visionary than precise, entirely without clear organizing principles or a workable structure of command, and so vast in scope that no single hand could control them all. Like a roomful of mad political alchemists, the expedition's planners mixed the principles of democracy and tyranny in the decision-making process of each enterprise, making the officers sent to chart Siberia's Arctic coasts directly responsible to the Admiralty for the success of the enterprises they commanded but allowing their crews to make vital decisions by majority vote. At the same time, the expedition's "learned guard," from whom the Ruling Senate instructed Bering to seek advice in all things, were to answer only to their colleagues in the Academy of Sciences.[4] Commanders of the expedition's separate enterprises might turn to Bering for more men, supplies, and equipment, but control of the funds that purchased them remained in the hands of the Ruling Senate in St. Petersburg. Only the rigid stance with which the Admiralty faced every obstacle kept the diverging strands of the Great Northern Expedition from coming apart. Sickness, accidents, faulty equipment, and unexpected tragedies all counted for nothing in the minds of the men who directed the Great Northern Expedition from the chanceries of faraway St. Petersburg. No matter what obstacles the explorers reported, the lords of the Admiralty always gave the same reply. Somehow, in some way, "the work must be done."[5]

Just as the Russians' cost of Siberia's conquest had been taken from Siberia itself, so the statesmen of St. Petersburg expected to pay the expense of Siberia's exploration from the same source. Originally estimated to require no more than twelve thousand rubles from the Imperial Treasury because most of the supplies were to come from government storehouses along its route, the Great Northern Expedition had cost the Russians more than three hundred thousand rubles before its work was halfway done. Then all the doubts that had plagued Russia's senior statesmen about their dour Danish admiral after his first expedition came surging back.[6] Could something not be done so that "the Treasury should not be emptied in vain?" the empress's cabinet asked at one point. Would it not be possible, they petitioned the Admiralty, "to look into the Kamchatka [that is, the Great Northern] Expedition and see if it can be brought to a head?"[7] Now embroiled in expensive wars with the Ottoman Empire and Poland, Russia's senior statesmen had lost some of their peacetime enthusiasm for science and exploration and worried instead that the Great Northern Expedition might strain the resources of the Imperial Treasury too far.

The costs of the Great Northern Expedition had soared because so many of its parts faced such huge difficulties in completing their assignments, especially in charting Siberia's Arctic coast. Unpredictable, treacherous, and controlled only by the whims of wind and temperature, the ice at those latitudes never disappeared, but only broke apart enough between the middle of June and the end of September for water to appear in the spaces that separated one iceberg from another. Russia's explorers had to work their fragile wooden ships through these perpetually shifting mountains of ice and, while doing so, take all the readings needed for charting the coast along which they sailed. At most, they had four months out of twelve in which to work—four months during which sunlight at midnight tempted them to go without sleep in order to extend the working time that the return of winter would cut short. Then the great frozen masses that had floated free for the summer became fields of solid ice that closed all navigation. Frozen fast in the ice, the small oar- and sail-driven ships of the Great Northern Expedition's explorers would then have to wait for the next summer to free them to continue their work.

On the advice of the Ruling Senate, the Admiralty, and the Academy of Sciences, the Great Northern Expedition's planners divided Siberia's Arctic coastline into four segments, starting at Arkhangelsk in the west and working east. The coast from Arkhangelsk to the mouth of the Ob comprised the first segment, from the Ob to the Enisei the second, from the Enisei to the Lena the third, and from the Lena to the mouth of the Kamchatka River on Siberia's Pacific coast the fourth. Each had its own special perils, almost none of which the Russians foresaw. Between Arkhangelsk and the Ob, the icebergs of the fog-filled Kara Sea created a gauntlet that even the most determined explorers found difficult to overcome. The same obstacles filled the passage from the Ob to the Enisei. East of the Enisei, the risk of being crushed by ice increased, for the explorers had to sail even farther north to round the Taimyr peninsula, the northernmost point of Eurasia. Then, from the Taimyr peninsula to the delta of the Lena River, the ice got worse, for the colder winters to the peninsula's east meant that the coastal waters of the Laptev Sea remained frozen well into July. From the Lena to Bering Strait, the desolation of Siberia's northeastern coast heightened the danger of the fog-blanketed seas filled with shifting mountains of ice. Although some of the first Russian *promyshlenniki* and traders had navigated these waters in their tiny flat-bottomed boats during the first half of the seventeenth century, they had left no charts.

The westernmost enterprise of the Great Northern Expedition was to chart the coast of northeastern Europe and western Siberia from the White Sea port of Arkhangelsk eastward to the Ob River town of Berëzov, once a center of the Arctic fur trade but now shrunk into obscurity.[8] This should have meant little more than following the route of the small coastal traders who had sailed without compasses, astrolabes, or sextants between Arkhangelsk and Mangazeia at the beginning of the seventeenth century, but the task proved more difficult than expected because the Kara Sea had greater quantities of ice in the days of Bering than when Mangazeia and Berëzov had flourished. When naval lieutenants Stepan Muravëv and Mikhail Pavlov set sail from Arkhangelsk in the summer of 1734 on a voyage that had taken from four to six weeks in the days of Siberia's first fur rush, they therefore got no farther east than the mouth of the Pechora River by fall. Less than halfway to their destination by the time the sea began to freeze, they spent the winter in Pustozersk, a lonely outpost to which a number of famous Russians had been condemned to exile in years gone by. The next summer, Muravëv and Pavlov sailed a short distance east, but masses of icebergs that lay shrouded behind the fogs of the Kara Sea forced them back to Pustozersk for another winter.

Like many men of equal rank, Muravëv and Pavlov were fierce rivals, and, by the time they returned to Pustozersk in the fall of 1735, their rivalry had turned to hatred. Charging each other with incompetence, corruption, and brutality, they flooded the Admiralty with complaints only to have their superiors reduce them both to the rank of common seaman "for numerous dishonorable, slothful, and stupid actions."[9] The work must be done and progress reported, the Admiralty insisted. There was no room in its plan for personal squabbles that slowed the pace of work that was to win acclaim for Russia in the West.

In the spring of 1736, the Admiralty sent Stepan Malygin to replace Muravëv and Pavlov. Before early frosts forced him into winter quarters in the middle of September, Malygin sailed his ships into the Kara Sea and reached the southwest coast of the Iamal peninsula, from which he continued on to Berëzov the next summer. Based on the detailed readings he had taken, Malygin could report that the southern tip of Novaia Zemlia, the landmass that rose from the sea north of the Urals, was neither a peninsula nor another continent but an island, and that the Iamal peninsula itself was not an isthmus leading to land farther north. Hundreds of newly discovered islands still had to be explored when Malygin made his report to the Admiralty, but the first segment of the Great Northern Expedition's work was done by the summer of 1737. If the ships and crews working on the remaining segments of Siberia's Arctic coast enjoyed similar success, the navigators and cartographers of the world would come to know its details long before they learned the particulars of the northern coast of North America.

Information was beginning to come in from segments of the expedition that were working farther east, but it would take more time to finish their work and evaluate its success. Sailing down the Ob River from Tobolsk with a crew of fifty-six in the summer of 1734, the young naval lieutenant Dmitrii Ovtsyn set out in the *Ob Postman,* an oddly named seventy-foot ship from the deck of which he hoped to chart the few hundred miles of Arctic coast between the Ob and the Enisei in a single summer.[10] Ice in the Kara Sea drove him back almost as soon as he left the Ob. After spending the winter in Obdorsk, a small settlement at the river's mouth, he tried again in the summer of 1735, but scurvy struck his crew with a vengeance and forced him to wait again. After doing no better in the summer of 1736, Ovtsyn finally reached the Enisei and sailed upriver to Turukhansk in 1737. Then, after taking his ship and crew on to Eniseisk the next spring, he hurried to St. Petersburg to make his report. The second segment of charting Siberia's Arctic coast was done, but very bad news awaited Ovtsyn in Russia's capital.

Between 1725 and 1741, St. Petersburg became a morass of political intrigue that brought seven sovereigns to the throne in sixteen years. Unaware of how the currents of Russian politics had shifted during his four-year absence, Ovtsyn became the victim of one of the many upheavals that caused this time in Russia's history to be known as the "Era of Palace Revolutions." Having been a friend of Prince Aleksei

Dolgorukov, who had fallen from favor during his absence, Ovtsyn was, like Muravëv and Pavlov, reduced to the rank of common seaman and sent to Okhotsk to join the expedition that Bering and Chirikov were preparing to lead to Alaska. There, he would become Bering's aide, a sailor whose experience in Arctic waters far exceeded that of his chief. When he returned, he would fall into obscurity.[11]

Although the work of the expeditions charting Siberia's coast from Arkhangelsk to the Enisei had been slowed by weather and misfortune, greater obstacles faced the men assigned to chart Siberia's Arctic coast east of the Enisei's mouth, where the Taimyr peninsula stretched far out into the icy waters of the Arctic to divide the Kara and Laptev seas. Almost perpetually icebound, this coast had to be charted if the Great Northern Expedition was to complete its work, but, as far as navigators knew at the time, no ship had ever rounded its northernmost cape from either east or west. Deciding to approach the peninsula from both directions at once, the Admiralty assigned Fëdor Minin to sail around it from the west at the same time as they ordered Vasilii Pronchishchev and his redoubtable wife, Mariia, the world's first female polar explorer, to sail toward it from the east.[12]

At the beginning of June 1738, Minin and a crew of fifty-seven boarded the *Ob Postman,* which Ovtsyn had just brought safely into Eniseisk. After following the Taimyr peninsula's coast to the northeast and passing its northernmost point, Minin's optimistic instructions from St. Petersburg read, he and his crew were to turn south and sail on to the mouth of the Khatanga River. If there were time, they should return to the Enisei by the same route. Otherwise, he and his men should winter on the Khatanga and return the following summer. For most of July, Minin's expedition fought ice in the long bay that separated the Enisei's mouth from the Kara Sea until heavy fog forced them to stop. By the time a south wind cleared the fog and allowed them to sail on, the water in the ship's casks was beginning to freeze and snow was starting to fall. When a boat sent ashore reported that the streams and small rivers had already frozen, Minin knew he would have to put his crew ashore to build winter quarters without ever having reached the Taimyr peninsula.

The next summer brought no more progress. After storms and ice drove his ship back into the mouth of the Enisei, Minin sent his second in command to chart the Taimyr coast by land, only to have him return empty-handed after the cold had frozen his instruments and the blazing light reflected from the Arctic snow had injured his eyes. In the summer of 1740, Minin and his crew fought their way through the icebergs to the mouth of the Piasina River, perhaps a hundred and fifty miles north of the winter quarters they had built two years before. By that time, his superiors had decided to replace him, despite the maps and charts he had been sending to St. Petersburg of the small segments of Siberia's coastline he had managed to explore. After the lords of the Admiralty relieved him in the fall of 1740, they debated his case for nearly a decade before they reduced him (like Ovtsyn, Muravëv, and Pavlov) to the rank of common seaman. Disgrace and punishment were becoming the regular rewards of even the most daring men who failed to conquer the ice and weather in Siberia's Arctic waters.

In the meantime, naval lieutenant Vasilii Pronchishchev, his wife, Mariia, and a crew of fifty-five were trying to round the Taimyr peninsula from the east in order to reach the ice-filled seas that had defied the best efforts of Minin's crew. Sailing in a near carbon copy of the *Ob Postman* called the *Iakutsk*, they had left Iakutsk at the end of June 1735, sailed down the Lena River to the sea, and begun to work their way west. Two months and a hundred miles later, they reached the mouth of the Olenëk River, where they built winter quarters and began to transfer the sightings and soundings they had taken during the summer onto detailed charts. The next summer, ice kept the *Iakutsk* bottled up in Olenëk harbor until the beginning of August, and, by the time the ship reached the Khatanga River some three hundred miles west, both of the Pronchishchevs were dying of scurvy. The expedition's remaining officers and crew then voted to retreat to the Olenëk for a second winter because "there were neither people nor any wood" to be found on the Khatanga.[13] By the time they reached winter quarters, both of the Pronchishchevs were dead. The next summer, their chief navigator Semën Cheliuskin took the remnants of the expedition back to Iakutsk. The Admiralty then transferred command of the *Iakutsk* to Khariton Laptev, an officer who had just been promoted to junior lieutenant.

We have no record of when or where Laptev was born or what sort of family he came from, but he was an immensely resourceful man who had been blessed with a deep understanding of what moves men in times of stress. Laptev knew that only proper rations, enough equipment, and a crew dedicated to their work could bring success in the Arctic, and he therefore asked the Admiralty to pay his men before they sailed and build storehouses for extra supplies along the course he expected to chart. The Admiralty agreed to all his requests, but no amount of material help could modify the terrible climate that Laptev and his men had to face. Only in July and August (according to twentieth-century calculations) were the average temperatures in the Taimyr peninsula's northern lands above freezing. For the rest of the year, they ranged from

$-21°$ to $-31°$ Centigrade (November through April) to a high of $-1.7°$ Centigrade in June.[14]

Like the Pronchishchevs, Laptev had to fight ice every foot of the way in the sea that now bears his name. Inching between the shifting floes and icebergs, the *Iakutsk* worked her way back to the Pronchishchevs' winter quarters on Khatanga Bay but then, after sailing north for just eight days, had to turn back. Finding neither food nor driftwood on shore, Laptev decided to winter back on the Khatanga, where men sent overland from Iakutsk had already built winter shelters and laid in supplies for his men. The next summer, while Minin was making his last effort to work his way up the Taimyr peninsula's western coast, Laptev tried again. This time icebergs crushed the *Iakutsk* and drove him and his crew back to their winter quarters at Khatanga Bay on foot.

With the *Iakutsk* gone and no means of replacing her, Laptev ordered Cheliuskin (the same pilot who had guided the Pronchishchevs) to take a small party across the peninsula on dogsleds and proceed north from the point of Minin's farthest advance. Five weeks later, at the end of April 1741, Laptev himself set out with a single soldier and a Iakut guide to meet Cheliuskin, and the two spent the summer charting the peninsula's western coast by land. After retreating nearly five hundred miles to the shelter of Turukhansk for the winter, Cheliuskin set out again and finally reached the northernmost tip of the Taimyr peninsula at the beginning of May 1742. After that, he rejoined Laptev and the two men returned to St. Petersburg to make their report to the Admiralty. Now that Eurasia's Arctic coast had been charted from Arkhangelsk to the mouth of the Lena River, both men agreed that even if there turned out to be no land barriers farther east, the hitherto impenetrable ice around the Taimyr peninsula made Siberia's Northeast Passage impassable.

While Laptev and Cheliuskin had been struggling to chart the coast of the Taimyr peninsula, another of the Great Northern Expedition's crews had been trying to make headway farther east. When the Pronchishchevs had sailed the *Iakutsk* north down the Lena to begin their explorations in June 1735, a slightly smaller sister ship, the *Irkutsk,* had followed in their wake under the command of naval lieutenant Pëtr Lasinius. Lasinius had then sailed the *Irkutsk* east to follow Dezhnëv's still unknown course to Bering Strait and the mouth of the Anadyr River, but he had none of Dezhnëv's good fortune.[15] Icebergs kept him bottled up in the Lena delta until the beginning of August and then stopped him just four days after he finally worked his way into the Laptev Sea. Scurvy killed Lasinius in December and left fewer than twenty of his crew alive by spring, when Dmitrii Laptev, a cousin of the young lieutenant who had taken the Pronchishchevs' place on the *Ia-kutsk,* arrived to take command.

Like Lasinius, Laptev made no headway at first. Convinced that the task was hopeless, he went back to St. Petersburg in the spring of 1737, where his superiors in the Admiralty told him that the work must still be done, if not in one year, then in two or three, and that, if the coast could not be charted by sea, then it must be done by land. Laptev returned to Siberia, took the *Irkutsk* to sea once again, and by the summer of 1739 had advanced somewhat more than four hundred miles to the mouth of the Indigirka River before the ice closed him in. The next year, Laptev fought his way through the ice to the Kolyma River and spent the winter building smaller boats that he hoped might be more maneuverable in the ice-filled seas farther east. When these managed to advance barely twenty-five miles in the summer of 1741, Laptev decided to go overland to Anadyrsk, the trading center that Dezhnëv had founded on the southern coast of the Chukhotskii peninsula after his shipwreck almost a century before. From Anadyrsk, Laptev tried again to approach Siberia's easternmost tip in 1742, but, although he and a number of others managed to reach it, its shores and waters could not be charted until 1823, when Lieutenant Ferdinand Vogel and a group of surveyors working from dogsleds finally mapped the last fragments of Siberia's northeastern coastline.

Except for the work done by Vrangel seventy years later, the contingents of the Great Northern Expedition that the Admiralty had assigned to chart Siberia's Arctic coast proved that the Northeast Passage, which men had dreamed about since the sixteenth century, did in fact lie along Siberia's northern coast. The obstacle to sailing that route was ice, not land, and, for the time being, that remained as formidable a barrier as any land could be. But the day would come at the end of the nineteenth century when Siberia's Northeast Passage would be opened to ships of the East and West. In 1875, for the first time, Sweden's Baron Nils Adolf Nordenskjöld sailed in the steam-powered *Vega* from Stockholm through Bering Strait, and by the early twentieth century timber from the Lena was being shipped regularly to mills in England by way of the Northeast Passage. In Soviet times, use of this route would become too common for comment. Perhaps most amazing of all, when Nordenskjöld took readings with his more precise modern instruments in 1875, the difference between them and those that Cheliuskin and Laptev had taken from their dogsleds proved to be less than three minutes.[16] In that sense, Russian science had accomplished more during the 1730s and 1740s than anyone had dared to hope. But the Great Northern Expedition's achievements did not end there. While men in fragile wooden ships had been fighting to make headway against the fog, ice, and cold of Siberia's northern coast, others had been at work in its interior in the largest scholarly venture to be undertaken by any group of scientists before the nineteenth century.

In 1733, the newly born Imperial Russian Academy of Sciences had contributed a detachment of scholars to the Great Northern Expedition and assigned them to produce a complete historical, physical, botanical, ethnographical, and linguistic description of Siberia. Four men, three of whom were not Russian, formed the core of this enterprise, and at their head stood Gerhardt-Friedrich Müller. An introspective Westphalian scholar who, although only twenty-eight, was known to suffer prolonged fits of morbid hypochondria, Müller went to Siberia to describe the customs and languages of all of the native tribes living between the Urals and Kamchatka and to search through whatever archives could be found to write the history of the Russian conquest. While he did so, Johann Georg Gmelin, a brilliant twenty-two-year-old Württemberg physician, professor of chemistry, and passionate student of natural history, assembled materials on Siberian flora and fauna. Less accomplished and somewhat older, their third companion was a mediocre French scientist by the name of Louis Delisle de la Croyère, who, despite a knowledge of astronomy that has been described as "very defective," had been assigned to determine the precise latitude and longitude of Siberia's main towns and landmarks. All three men looked down upon their Russian assistant, a young naturalist by the name of Stepan Petrovich Krasheninnikov. Two years younger than Gmelin and one of the first Russians to study at the Academy of Sciences in St. Petersburg, Krasheninnikov would return after eight years in the Siberian wilderness to become as renowned as any of the Europeans who had disdained him.[17]

Supported by an impressive host of artists, topographers, and scribes and traveling with a jumble of scientific paraphernalia including telescopes up to fifteen feet in length that de la Croyère insisted he could not work without, the academicians set out for Siberia in August 1733. It took them six months to reach Tobolsk and another six to get to Eniseisk. Now that the Russians had become firmly settled in Siberia, travel no longer had to be limited to the spring, summer, and fall, and the academicians therefore moved on from Eniseisk to reach Irkutsk at the beginning of March 1735. By then, Müller and Gmelin were squabbling with the local authorities about the quality of their accommodations and were finding east Siberian life distinctly less than pleasant. They spent most of the summer in Kiakhta, studying how this newly built gateway to China affected Russia's trade, and then returned to Irkutsk for the winter. Only in September 1736 did they finally reach Iakutsk, which was supposed to become the base from which they were to explore the peninsula of Kamchatka, the last part of Siberia to be occupied by the Russians.[18]

None too pleased with the primitive conditions under which they had been obliged to live and work in Irkutsk and Iakutsk, Gmelin and Müller (who carried bottles and casks of their favorite European wines with them wherever they went) decided to set aside the part of their assignment that required them to go on to Kamchatka, where Russia's grip was the weakest and the conditions the least comfortable, and concentrate their studies of history, ethnography, and botany farther west. Müller spent the next decade making forays to the archives of remote Siberian chancelleries and monasteries from headquarters in the more comfortable, congenial atmosphere of Eniseisk and Tobolsk, while Gmelin collected the specimens and made the observations needed to prepare the text of his massive four-volume *Flora Sibirica*, which is still remembered as a classic in the history of botany. When the two men returned to St. Petersburg toward midcentury, they had traveled some twenty-three thousand miles. Müller had copied thousands of rare documents that would make it possible for him to tell Siberia's story as part of the Russians' first effort to describe their national past.

Everywhere he traveled, Müller unearthed historical treasures that showed how the Russians had taken Siberia and at what cost. At Solvychegodsk, he found documents in the Stroganovs' private archives that told the details of Ermak's campaign, and among the long-forgotten documents in the government storerooms at Iakutsk, he unearthed Dezhnëv's amazing report describing how he and a handful of cossacks had done almost a century earlier what Lasinius and Laptev now had failed to accomplish. After verifying its age and authenticity, Müller immediately pronounced Dezhnëv's aging file to be genuine, but others, citing the difficulties that Lasinius and Laptev had just encountered, insisted that such a feat was impossible. Skepticism about the Dezhnëv file grew as the years passed, especially as explorers with larger ships, more training, and better equipment continued to fail in their efforts to round Siberia's East Cape. Not until well into this century, when the best Russian experts finally proved that Dezhnëv and his handful of cossacks had done precisely what they claimed to have done, could the debate be put to rest. In the meantime, Müller outlived seven Russian autocrats before he died at the age of seventy-eight in 1783. Using the notes and materials about the history, geography, languages, and ethnography of the lands and peoples east of the Urals that he and Gmelin had assembled, Müller, the German who spent nearly all of his adult life in Russia, became the father of Siberian history.[19]

While Müller and Gmelin studied the history of Siberia, the life and languages of its natives, and the flora and fauna between the Urals and Iakutsk, they had sent their assistant Krasheninnikov on to Kamchatka so as to avoid going there themselves.[20] Armed with detailed instructions about what he was to investigate and how, Krasheninnikov first traveled from Iakutsk to Okhotsk in nothing resembling the grand style of his superiors, fighting the terrain and climate as he went. Nearly a hundred years had passed since the first Russians had made their way across the mountains to found Okhotsk, but the passing of time had not made the journey appreciably more pleasant or less dangerous. As he and the handful of men who accompanied him clambered across boulder-filled streams and worked their way across bog-topped mountains, Krasheninnikov felt himself almost entirely at the mercy of the elements. "On the summits [of the mountains], there are terrible bogs and quagmires," he later wrote. "One is terrified," he added, "by the way the earth there quivers." Everywhere, the land seemed determined to stand against any man who tried to cross it. It would be very hard, Krasheninnikov remembered many years later, "to imagine a more difficult crossing."[21]

Things got no easier once Krasheninnikov reached Okhotsk, where the ancient *Fortuna* that Bering had built to ferry his first expedition to Kamchatka was still in service. Now much the worse for wear after a decade of carrying cargo between Okhotsk and Bolsheretsk, the *Fortuna* began to take on water soon after she left port with Krasheninnikov and his supplies and instruments aboard. Less than twelve hours after the ship had left Okhotsk, the men working the pumps in her hold were standing in water up to their knees, and all the crew were bailing with kettles and anything else they could find. Only by throwing the entire seven tons of cargo overboard could the crew lighten the *Fortuna* enough to get her to Bolsheretsk, where a storm stirred by an earthquake immediately drove her against the shore. "The next day, we found nothing but planks from the wreckage of our ship," Krasheninnikov reported. "Inside," he added, "they were all so black and rotten that one could break them by hand without difficulty."[22] Krasheninnikov now had no supplies, almost no instruments, and only his wits to support him, since Bering insisted that he had few supplies to spare.

Arriving at Bolsheretsk late in October 1737, Krasheninnikov worked on his own for much of the next four winters and three summers.

Wandering through the wilds of Kamchatka, he collected the specimens needed to piece together a full-scale portrait of the primeval land of earthquakes, volcanoes, geysers, quaking bogs, tidal waves, and avalanches into which his passion for science had brought him. He charted Kamchatka's rivers, mapped its trails and passes, crisscrossed its many mountains, discovered its hot springs, and struggled to understand the materials he had gathered and the things he had seen. "It has neither grain nor livestock and suffers frequent earthquakes, storms and floods," Krasheninnikov wrote of Kamchatka in the voluminous account he published some fifteen years later. "Almost the only diversion," he added, "is to look upon its towering mountains, whose peaks are continually covered with snow, or, if one lives along the sea, to listen to the crashing of the waves and observe the ways in which different species of sea animals live in hostility and friendship with each other."[23] This was hardly an enthusiastic portrait of the land in which Krasheninnikov spent more than three years, but, from the point of view of ethnography and natural history, Kamchatka was a veritable wonderland, and it was upon that that the young scientist concentrated.

What fascinated Krasheninnikov most about Kamchatka were the Kamchadals, who lived on the southern three quarters of the peninsula and who, during centuries of isolation, had managed to shape innocence and perversity into a way of life. "The natives of Kamchatka are as wild as the land itself," he wrote. "They are filthy and vile [and] ... they are so infested with lice ... that, using their fingers like a comb, they lift their braids, sweep the lice together into their fists and then gobble them up." As one of Russia's recently Europeanized elite and a man who enjoyed the good food, comfort, and leisure that life in the civilized world offered, Krasheninnikov found it hard to endure the society of the Kamchadals. He watched in disgust as they stuffed strips of seal blubber into the mouths of guests and insisted that they be swallowed whole, and he gagged upon delicacies made from fish that had been allowed to rot until the flesh had become gelatinous. "The stench" of such concoctions, he wrote, was sometimes "almost impossible to tolerate," yet he did so in order to better understand the people he studied and learn what impact their diet had upon the human organism.

Appalled by the Kamchadals' filth and unable to watch them prepare some of their meals "without feeling sick," Krasheninnikov still found virtue in their savage way of life. "They know nothing of wealth, honor, or glory," he reported, "[and] they do not suffer from greed, ambition, or pride. All of their desires," he continued, "are directed toward enjoying an abundance of whatever they want." The Kamchadals' measure of happiness therefore differed from that of civilized folk. "They think that it is better to die than not to be able to live in the manner they choose," he concluded. The Kamchadals used suicide, Krasheninnikov explained, as "a final means to achieve happiness."[24]

Krasheninnikov continued his lonely scientific vigil on Kamchatka until the fall of 1740, when Georg Wilhelm Steller, a physician trained at the University of Halle and a brilliant student of natural history, arrived from Central Europe. Steller had been a late addition to the contingent that the Academy of Sciences had contributed to the Great Northern Expedition, having reached St. Petersburg from Halle (with a number of less than respectable stops in between) only in 1735. Winning favor with some of the Academy's patrons almost immediately, Steller had set out for Siberia at the beginning of 1738. On the way to Okhotsk, he had met with Müller and Gmelin in Eniseisk and had been given their blessings for going on to Kamchatka and joining Bering. As part of the bargain, Steller had agreed to oversee Krasheninnikov's work. He had then proceeded slowly, collecting specimens and making meticulous notes, until he reached Iakutsk in the spring of 1740. Finding that town unpleasant and the authorities unhelpful, he was anxious to leave almost from the moment he arrived. "In wickedness, incredible deceit, perfidy and hypocrisy," he wrote of the people he met in Iakutsk, "they are as far removed from the other Siberian inhabitants and the native Russians as are the serpents from the doves."[25] Steller therefore hurried over the mountains and reached Okhotsk in the middle of August.[26]

There, he had his first meeting with Bering and impressed him immediately. Abrasive, dogmatic, usually without tact, and obsessed by his desire to explore the Alaskan coast, Steller could also be charming when the occasion demanded. He soon won Bering's confidence and made certain of a place on one of the ships he would sail to North America, but the problem of Krasheninnikov still remained. Steller had no intention of sharing his newly acquired place as Bering's chief naturalist, least of all with someone whose long study of Kamchatka and its natives might well have made him able to challenge the German's knowledge about the flora and fauna in that part of the world.

Steller therefore saddled Krasheninnikov with all sorts of burdensome tasks and on at least one occasion insisted that he set his work aside and travel half the length of Kamchatka just to translate into Russian a number of suggestions about governing Kamchatka and Christianizing its natives that he wanted to submit to the Ruling Senate. In this and other ways, Steller could make his Russian rival's life a torment, but what he could not do was order him back to the mainland. For that, he enlisted the aid of de la Croyère, the mediocre French astronomer and geographer who had parted company with Müller and Gmelin at Iakutsk in the fall of 1736 and had gone on to join Bering's expedition at Okhotsk. De la Croyère's high rank as a professor in the Academy of Sciences gave him the authority to dictate Krasheninnikov's fate, and he was more than ready to issue the order Steller wanted.

Evidently not relishing the prospect of working as Steller's humble assistant and, in any case, probably not reluctant to leave Siberia after eight lonely years, Krasheninnikov made no complaint.[27] His departure left Steller and de la Croyère alone to sail with Bering's expedition across the North Pacific in the summer of 1741. But there was still a final irony that would only become evident some years later. Although Steller would have the honor of being the first man of science to set foot on Alaskan soil, it would be Krasheninnikov who, when Steller died from acute alcoholism at the age of thirty-seven, fleshed out the gaps in his notes and published them as a part of his own huge study about Kamchatka. Krasheninnikov therefore had a key part to play in reporting some of the scientific findings of the enterprise that history remembers as Bering's second voyage, or the Russian "discovery" of America.[28]

15

The Russians "Discover" America

Ever since Ermak had crossed the Urals, the Russians had moved east, claiming new subjects for the tsar and scouring the Siberian countryside for furs. Then, as the tsar's cossacks worked their way into the Kamchatka peninsula and struggled to put down roots in the infertile soil around Okhotsk, only water stood on the horizon. What lay beyond Siberia? How far across the Pacific was it to North America from Kamchatka? What lay in between? Were there new lands from which fur tribute could be collected as the returns on the Siberian mainland continued their precipitous decline? The prospect of planting Russia's flag on a third continent was dazzling enough to induce Peter the Great, newly crowned head of the youngest of Europe's empires, to assign precious men and ships to exploring the North Pacific the moment that the pressures of the Great Northern War with Sweden eased. Two expeditions had preceded Bering's first voyage. Like his, neither had reached the New World.

Just three years after Bering had turned back from the voyage that had carried him through Bering Strait to within three days' sail of the Alaskan coast, the pilot Ivan Fëdorov and the surveyor Mikhail Gvozdev set sail in the *St. Gabriel* in search of a "big country" of great forests and high mountains that, Siberia's natives said, lay scarcely more than a day's voyage beyond the ocean.[1] Less than a month after they sailed from Kamchatka on July 23, the *St. Gabriel*'s crew reached the coast of the "big country" but could not land because of the head winds and shallow water. "We could see huts," Gvozdev remembered, "but in spite of our best efforts we did not come as close to them as we wished." Then, "because of the lateness of the season and the stormy weather,"[2] Fëdorov and Gvozdev sailed back to Kamchatka, still thinking that the "big country" was an island and not knowing that they had discovered America from the west.

A few months later, Fëdorov died. Soon after that, the ship's log disappeared, and the brief report that Gvozdev claimed to have sent to the authorities at Okhotsk seems never to have been forwarded to St. Petersburg. As the architects of the Great Northern Expedition made plans for Bering and Chirikov to search for North America once again, none of them knew that the "big country" and the northwestern corner of North America were one and the same, or that the *St. Gabriel* had reached it six years earlier. Still thinking that the "big country" was an island, the lords of Russia's Admiralty assigned Bering the task of sailing beyond it to North America.

Having decided to carry out their mission as soon as ships could be built at Okhotsk, Bering and Chirikov set out from St. Petersburg in the spring of 1733. Officially, in addition to the expedition he was to lead to the coast of North America, Bering also had responsibility for Spanberg's explorations of the Kuriles and the waters north of Japan, for every ship that sailed to chart Siberia's Arctic coast, for reforming the administration of Siberia, and for all of the work that the contingent sent by the Academy of Sciences was to accomplish. Only a man of stupendous energy, supremely Machiavellian outlook, and immense scientific genius could even have dreamed of controlling such an enterprise, and Bering was by no stretch of the imagination such a man. Nor would the plan according to which his superiors had organized all these undertakings have permitted him to exercise any real authority except over the voyage across the North Pacific that he himself was to command. But even though they limited Bering's control over the Great Northern Expedition, its planners made certain that he was well positioned to assume all of the blame for its failings. As the work slowed during the next half decade and the costs soared, the Ruling Senate hurried to accuse him of embezzlement, dealing in contraband liquor, and any number of other crimes, although not one of its charges ever proved to have any substance. In the meantime, the senators withheld Bering's pay for the better part of two years and continued to threaten him with court-martial.[3]

While he struggled to defend himself against these charges, Bering faced problems with the preparations for the expeditions that he, Chiri-kov, and Spanberg planned to lead into the Pacific. While he and Chirikov had been assembling a full complement of men and supplies in Iakutsk during the summer of 1735, Spanberg had gone ahead to Okhotsk only to find that the barracks promised for the expedition had not yet been started, that hardly any supplies had been laid in, and that the timber that was supposed to have been ready to build their ships had not even been cut.[4] Expecting that the ships that he, Bering, and Chiri-kov needed would be launched by 1736 or 1737 at the latest, Spanberg began to build barracks at Okhotsk instead.

In disgust, Bering hurried to join him. "We have sand and pebbles, no vegetation whatever, and no timber in the vicinity," he wrote after he had surveyed the situation. "Firewood must be obtained at a distance of four to five miles, drinking water one to two miles, while timber and joints for shipbuilding must be floated down the river twenty-five miles."[5] It was easy enough to fix the blame on officials whom the Admiralty had sent to prepare the way, and Bering certainly did his share of finger-pointing before his ships were ready to sail. But he was dealing with a navy that was less than half a century old and a country in which the tradition of corruption and shifting blame was as old as time itself. In the meantime, shipbuilders had to be put to work on cutting timber and building the barracks that should already have been finished. Only then could they move on to laying the keels for their ships.[6]

To make matters more difficult for the crews and officers who were to sail to North America, the first resources went to Spanberg's expedi-tion because it had been scheduled to sail before Bering.[7] With two new ships to sail along with the old *St. Gabriel,* Spanberg finally set out for the Kuriles in June 1738 and, the next year, sailed farther south to prove that the Kuriles formed a chain that stretched from Kamchatka to Japan. Yet Spanberg proved to be so careless in keeping his ships' logs that the lords of Russia's Admiralty had to order him to repeat his explorations be-cause they found it "quite impossible" to chart the course he had sailed from the readings he had taken.[8] Then, further misunderstandings with his superiors brought Spanberg to the brink of death three years later. Had the Danish government and several influential friends not in-terceded, he would have ended his career on the gallows.[9]

While Spanberg was exploring the Kuriles, help arrived for Bering in the form of two adjutants sent by the empress with full authority to impose his requests for men and supplies upon the uncooperative Sibe-rian officials who had been standing in his way.[10] By the end of June 1740, a pair of two-masted ships, each measuring eighty feet in length and carrying fourteen small cannon, had been launched at Okhotsk. That October, Bering and Chirikov sailed to Petropavlovsk, the harbor that was being built on eastern Kamchatka's Avacha Bay. Once the supplies that had been landed on the peninsula's more sheltered Okhotsk seacoast were carried across the mountains during the winter of 1740–1741, the second Bering expedition was ready to sail.[11]

When the *St. Peter* and *St. Paul* sailed out of Avacha Bay on June 4, 1741, each ship carried a crew of seventy-six, a hundred casks of water, about sixty-five tons of beef, pork, groats, flour, butter, and salt, and a list of signals to help each to keep in touch with the other. Chirikov commanded the *St. Paul,* to which de la Croyère had been assigned, while Steller, his arrogantly eccentric personality already having put him at loggerheads with most of the ship's officers, sailed with Bering aboard the *St. Peter.*[12] Bering and Chirikov had planned to keep their ships together so that each could help the other in the event of trouble, but a powerful storm set them on separate courses within a fortnight. Although the courses they sailed actually intersected no fewer than twenty-one times during the next four months, neither ship ever sighted the other again.[13]

After the storm, Bering searched for the *St. Paul* for several days and then set an easterly course that carried his ship into the Gulf of Alaska on July 16. Ahead stood Kayak Island, and behind it rose a soaring peak, the highest in North America, that the *St. Peter*'s crew named Mt. St. Elias in honor of the saint whose name day it was when they first sighted it. Here was the New World, the chance to extend Russia's power to a third continent and, perhaps, to end the food shortages that continued to plague Siberia's eastern lands. If food could be brought from the North American shores that stood only a few weeks' sail from Kamchatka, Okhotsk and Kamchatka would no longer have to depend upon the fragile lifeline of wagons and barges that still needed several years to carry grain from the Urals to the Pacific. A careful exploration of the new territories that spread out before Bering's ships could yield answers that might affect Russia's position in Siberia for decades to come, or so at least Steller thought. What was needed was time, manpower, and the will to explore.

Steller had the will, but neither the manpower nor the time. This was the land he had come halfway around the globe to see, yet Bering at first refused him permission even to go ashore when he sent a company of sailors to Kayak Island for fresh water. After a bitter argument, during which Steller threatened to report to the Admiralty what he called his captain's "intention to force me against my will to inexcusable neglect of my duty,"[14] Bering relented on condition that he return the moment that the crew had refilled the ship's casks. "I could not help saying that we had come only for the purpose of bringing American water to Asia," Steller wrote bitterly in his diary.[15] Now that land had been found, Bering thought only of returning to Kamchatka safely and with all speed. "Who knows but that trade winds may arise which may prevent us from returning?" he had said to Steller a day or two before the *St. Peter* reached the coast. "We do not know this country," he warned when Steller begged him to stay longer. "Nor are we provided with supplies for a wintering."[16] These were not the words of an explorer dedicated to discovery. Steller was talking to a man who, having fulfilled his duty in the most precise sense, longed to return home.

While Bering's crew filled water casks on Kayak Island, Steller worked frantically to gather samples of rock and vegetation. In just six hours, he collected 142 plant specimens, including not quite ripe salmonberries, a type of raspberry still unknown in Europe. Thanks to the marksmanship of his single cossack aide, Steller also brought back a western blue jay, "a single specimen of which I remember to have seen a likeness painted and described in the newest account of the birds and plants of the Carolinas," he later wrote. "This bird proved to me that we were really in America," Steller added. Nothing like it had ever been reported in Europe or Asia.[17]

In a deserted hut that gave every indication of having been inhabited until an hour or so before his arrival, Steller found utensils, a basket, weapons, and bits of food that he hastily scooped up, after leaving an iron kettle, tobacco, a Chinese pipe, and a piece of silk in exchange. Desperate for more time, he sent word to the *St. Peter* that he wanted to go inland, for he had seen smoke on another part of the island, which told him that people were very near. Already his bits of hastily assembled evidence had convinced Steller that the island's people were of the same origin as the Kamchadals of Kamchatka. But he thought that "in view of the great distance we have traveled ... it is not credible that the Kamchadals would have been able to get [here] in their miserable craft." The only explanation for their presence, he concluded, was that North America stood much nearer to Asia farther north of their landing place.[18] A few more hours of searching, Steller thought, would lead him to natives who could verify his conjectures.

Hours might as well have been centuries. When the crew still had twenty casks to fill, Bering suddenly ordered them to come aboard so that the ship could get under way and insisted that Steller return immediately or be left behind. In a rage, the German obeyed. What he said to Bering when he boarded the *St. Peter* we do not know, but he had plenty of vitriol left for the private journal to which he confided his innermost thoughts throughout the voyage. "The only reason why we did not attempt to land on the mainland is a sluggish obstinacy and a dull fear of being attacked by a handful of unarmed and still more timid savages," he wrote. "The time here spent in investigation bears an arithmetical ratio to the time used in fitting out," he added bitterly. "Ten years the preparations for this great undertaking lasted, and ten hours were devoted to the work itself."[19] Once again the broad interests of science had come into conflict with Bering's narrow sense of duty. The Dane's stubborn unconcern for the larger questions of science had cut short the process of discovery at its very threshold.

To be fair, Steller knew at that point that powerful forces were at work in Bering's mind, but for the time being he kept them in his heart and did not mention them in his journal. Struck by the first symptoms of scurvy soon after the voyage had begun, Bering had grown more gloomy and troubled as the days had passed. Deep within his inner being, in those dark corners of the soul that men try to wall off from contact with their consciousness, an icy voice was telling Bering that he had not long to live, even as the shores of North America rose before him. The detachment that separates a dying man from the living world had thus begun to isolate Bering from his officers and crew even before the *St. Peter* reached North America. Uninterested in all and everything around him, Bering seemed to be ruled only by the fear that death would overtake him before he returned to Kamchatka. With amazement, Steller noted in his journal that Bering had "even shrugged his shoulders while looking at the land" during their first hours in Alaskan coastal waters.[20] To a man such as he, who had left behind the comforts of his native Central Europe to explore new frontiers of science in an unknown world, Bering's detachment could not be explained. It was as if Columbus had lost interest in the New World the moment his lookout had sighted its shores.

As scurvy weakened Bering's limbs, he remained in his cabin and allowed the reins of command to slip into the unsteady hands of his lieutenants once he had ordered the *St. Peter's* course to be set for Kamchatka. Worried about the scurvy that was spreading among the crew and uncertain about precisely where Kamchatka lay, Bering's officers shifted their headings to produce a cat's cradle of backings and fillings that consumed forty precious days in sailing from Kayak Island to Alaska's westernmost tip. By the end of August, the *St. Peter* was struggling against contrary winds off the Shumagin Islands, which were normally less than a week's voyage from the point at which they first had sighted land on July 16.[21] By that time, most of the crew were so fiercely at odds with Steller that even when he urged them to search for a spring on one of the Shumagin Islands, they insisted instead upon filling the ship's casks at shoreside pools with water that inevitably turned brackish. When Steller spoke of collecting plants that could ease the ravages of scurvy, they rejected his advice. The lonely scientist now had to work with only the help of Friedrich Plenisner, an obscure German whom Bering had made his draftsman and who, in the course of the voyage, had become his friend.

Steller now had little to work with and less time in which to work. "Our medicine chest," he wrote in his journal, "was filled with enough plasters, ointments, oils, and other surgical remedies for four to five hundred men in case of a battle but had none whatever of the medicines most needed . . . against scurvy and asthma." Here Steller's knowledge of botany had put him well ahead of his time. Not until the 1750s would European mariners first discover that fruits and vegetables with a high content of vitamin C could ward off scurvy. But Steller already knew enough about the disease to think that infusions made from spoonwort could restore movement to its victims' limbs and that dock, one of the most common weeds of the field, could produce a tea that would fix their teeth firmly in their gums once again. He was amazed to find that both grew on the Shumagin Islands—yet the ship's officers, according to his angry journal account, would not assign men to help bring them aboard. Scorned and left to themselves, Steller and Plenisner had time on the Shumagins to gather only the small amount of herbs that would save their lives, prolong Bering's, and keep the crew alive for a few weeks longer. Many of the crew would perish in the days ahead for want of the medications Steller had begged them to collect during the last few hours they spent on land before winter.[22]

When the crew of the *St. Peter* set sail for Petropavlovsk from their sheltered anchorage in the Shumagins on September 6, 1741, they began a struggle against wind, waves, and scurvy that nearly took them over the brink of disaster. By the third week of October, the ship was wallowing in heavy seas because none of the sailors was strong enough to set the sails. "By now, so many of our people were ill that I had, so to speak, no one to steer the ship," Bering's second in command, Sven Waxell, later reported. "When it came to a man's turn at the helm," he went on, "he was dragged to it by two other of the invalids who were still able to walk a little, and set down at the wheel [where] . . . he had to sit and steer as well as he could [until] . . . he could sit no more." The weather grew steadily worse. "The winds were violent . . . to say nothing of the snow, hail and rain," Waxell remembered.[23] "There were . . . only three, one of them being the Captain Commander's man, [who] could come on deck," he added. "All others were sick unto death."[24] Too sick to take readings from the sun and stars for several weeks, the crew of the *St. Peter* had no idea of their location when October turned into November. "Our ship was like a piece of dead wood," Waxell wrote. "We had to drift hither and thither at the whim of the winds and waves."[25]

Then, two months after they had left the Shumagins, the *St. Peter's* crew caught sight of land. "It is impossible to describe how great and extraordinary was the joy of everybody at this sight," Steller wrote in his account of that day, November 5. "The half-dead crawled up to see it," he went on, "and all thanked God heartily."[26] The snow-covered mountains that loomed ahead seemed so like Kamchatka that the crew at first thought they had come directly to the entrance of Avacha Bay, the gateway to Petropavlovsk harbor. When a few hours' more sailing proved them wrong, the officers insisted that, even though the land ahead was not the Avacha headlands, they must be some part of the seven-hundred-mile-long Kamchatka peninsula nonetheless.[27] Once they were on land, Waxell explained, it would be only a matter of sending someone to Nizhnekamchatsk for horses to carry the sick. A council held in Bering's cabin voted to land, although Bering himself begged them to sail on to Avacha Bay. But Bering was too sick to rule his crew any longer. When one experienced seaman urged the men to follow Bering's advice, Steller reported, the others shouted him down with cries of *"Von!"* (get out!) *"Molchi!"* (shut up!).[28]

Led by Waxell and the first mate, the *St. Peter's* officers sent a boat ashore, and when they discovered that they were on an island, they decided to remain there for the winter nonetheless. Since the ground was by that time covered with snow and everyone was too weak to do any heavy work, the men scooped cavelike shelters out of the sand for winter quarters and then stretched scraps of canvas over them to ward off the snow, wind, and rain. These became the lazarets for the invalids who were brought ashore a week later. Some of the sickest men died the moment they were taken from the *St. Peter's* hold and the fresh air reached their lungs. Others reached the shore and lay in agony, slowly starving. "As their gums were swollen like a sponge, brown black, grown over the teeth and covering them," Steller noted in his journal account of their first days ashore, "they could not eat anything because of the great pain."[29]

His legs grotesquely swollen and already cold, Bering lingered at the edge of death for three long weeks. Then, on December 8, 1741, he passed into the next world, already half buried, Waxell remembered, because the sand from the sides of his dugout had kept trickling down upon his legs and lower body.[30] "He would undoubtedly have remained alive if he had reached Kamchatka and had only had the benefit of a warm room and fresh food," Steller concluded. "As it was," he added, "he perished . . . from hunger, thirst, cold, hardship, and grief."[31] Thirty others of the crew followed Bering in the next month, and it took several months more for the survivors to regain their strength. Only Steller and Plenisner remained unaffected by the ravages that scurvy visited upon the crew, most probably because of the herbs and plants they had gathered during the *St. Peter*'s brief stay on the Shumagins.[32]

Now condemned to spend the winter where driftwood was the only fuel and trying to hoard their small reserves of flour and groats in case they remained alive to sail away in the spring, the crew of the *St. Peter* had to live on what their island refuge provided. Stewed in oil rendered from the rank carcasses of two dead whales that washed up on shore, sea otters and fur seals, the flesh of the latter described by Waxell as "revolting, because it has a very strong and very unpleasant smell, more or less like that of an old goat," became their main food. Supplemented by potions that Steller prepared to help calm the ravages of scurvy from whatever roots and grasses could be found beneath the snow, this was all the crew had to eat until spring.[33] Some of them continued to linger at the brink of death, while others lived on the verge of madness. For the moment, there was no escape for anyone from the cold, the emptiness, and the blue foxes that had no fear of men.

"They attacked the weak and ill to such an extent that one could hardly hold them off," Steller wrote of the blue foxes that besieged their camp day and night. "One night when a sailor on his knees wanted to urinate out of the doorway," he went on, "a fox snapped at the exposed part and, in spite of his cries, did not soon want to let go." Angry and looking for diversion, the crew tortured the foxes in return. "Inasmuch as they left us no rest by day or night," Steller explained, "we indeed became so embittered against them that we killed young and old, did them all possible harm, and, whenever we could, tortured them most cruelly."[34] "Of some we gouged out the eyes," he explained in his description of the war that Bering's crew waged against the animals. "Others were strung up alive in pairs by their feet," he added, "so that they would bite each other to death."[35] Still, neither vigilance nor cruelty could drive the animals away. Instead, Waxell added, "they ate the hands and feet of the corpses before we had time to bury them."[36]

Chance had cast Bering's crew upon the island that now bears his name and that, ironically, stands less than three hundred miles from Avacha Bay. Yet that haven remained a world away for men whose ship had been damaged beyond repair by the winter storms. To build a new ship on an island without trees meant that every plank and spar of the old *St. Peter* had to be put to good use when the crew's forty-six survivors began to break her up under the command of Lieutenant Waxell in the spring. By midsummer, they had finished a vessel barely large enough to hold them all. "Exceedingly anxious for deliverance from this desert island," Steller wrote, they set sail on August 14, 1742.[37] Now the winds and the currents worked in their favor, and in less than three days they caught their first glimpse of Kamchatka. On August 27, 1742, they sailed into Avacha harbor and anchored at Petropavlovsk. It had taken fifteen months to complete a voyage that, under normal circumstances, should have taken less than three. "Surely," Steller concluded in one of his reports, "we could be all the more thankful not only for our rescue from the most imminent perils of the sea but also for our preservation."[38] Nonetheless, the scientist in Steller thought the sacrifice well worth the pain. "I would not," he wrote to a friend, "exchange the experience of nature that I acquired on this miserable voyage for a large [sum of] capital."[39]

Including the men who had sailed with Chirikov on the *St. Paul,* few others shared Steller's opinion. In keeping with the plan that he and Bering had agreed upon before they left Petropavlovsk, Chirikov had sailed east after their ships had become separated. A full thirty-five and a half hours before Bering sighted Mt. St. Elias, the *St. Paul* reached the North American coast, but farther to the south and east of Prince of Wales Island.[40] Yet Chirikov's crossing of the North Pacific proved to be only moderately less ill fated than Bering's, and misfortune actually struck the *St. Paul* sooner. When its crew lost both of the ship's boats trying to go ashore for fresh water just two days after they reached the New World, Chirikov's ship faced one of every seaman's worst nightmares.[41] "We had only 45 casks of water," Chirikov wrote in his report to the Admiralty, explaining why he and his officers had decided to return to Kamchatka before they had explored the North American lands that lay before them, "[and] we did not know whether they were full or [having leaked during the voyage] partly empty."[42]

With better navigation and more luck than the *St. Peter,* the *St. Paul* returned to Petropavlovsk ten weeks after it had sighted North America, but that was not soon enough to spare its crew, which had lived mainly on salt meat, from the ravages of scurvy. By mid-September, "some of the men were so feeble that they could not even come on deck," Chirikov reported. A fortnight later, he added, "all members of the crew were down with scurvy ... [and] I was so ill and so weak that I expected death at any moment."[43] When the *St. Paul* reached Petropavlovsk, Chirikov had to be carried ashore. De la Croyère, the astronomer and cartographer who had sailed with him that summer, died just before the *St. Paul* dropped its anchor.[44]

Although neither the *St. Peter* nor the *St. Paul* managed to explore the lands that would soon become known as Alaska, the expedition that Bering and Chirikov led into the North Pacific had unexpected and important consequences. Bering had set sail just more than a decade after the Kiakhta Treaty of 1727 had opened a larger market for Russian furs in China than ever before, and at precisely the time when the yields from Kamchatka, the last of the Siberian fur grounds to be invaded by Russian trappers and tribute collectors, had begun to wane. Where were the pelts for Russia's new China trade to come from? And how was the demand from Europe to be met? At this most critical of moments for the Russian fur trade, Bering's expedition found a source of new furs that shifted its center for a century to come.

The Russians had first found sea otters along the coast of Kamchatka at the beginning of the eighteenth century and had immediately dubbed them "Kamchatka beavers."[45] Larger than the best Arctic fox and more valuable than the blackest sable, the pelt of a sea otter might contain as much as twelve square feet of precious fur. Its gloss, Steller once explained, "surpasses the blackest velvet," and the silvery white hairs scattered here and there added highlights that no other fur could match.[46] Although sea otter pelts tended to stiffen in severe cold and were thus undesirable for coats or cloaks, the Chinese used them with particularly brilliant effect to trim garments made of other rich materials. At the time of the *St. Peter*'s voyage, a single prime sea otter pelt brought forty rubles in Irkutsk and as much as a hundred at Kiakhta. By the end of the century, when the Russians' greed and persistence in hunting sea otters had all but eliminated them from the waters around Kamchatka, the Komandorskie Islands, and the Aleutians, those prices rose by nearly ten times.[47]

Just at the time when the sea otters were beginning to disappear from the coast of Kamchatka, Bering's crew found them in abundance on Bering Island. No one had a moment's doubt that a new treasure had been found, and the men who remained alive when spring came in 1742 used every bit of their returning strength to hunt them down. The tiny ship they built from the wreckage of the *St. Peter* had barely enough room for men and food, yet somehow its crew stuffed in nine hundred precious sea otter pelts as well, knowing that they had found the new "golden fleece" to take the place of the declining numbers of sable, marten, and fox on the Siberian mainland. Within a year, the uninhabited islands of the North Pacific began to swarm with men in search of the sea otter. For another century, the Russians would follow this new source of wealth across the North Pacific and through the Aleutians to the lonely northwestern shores of North America.[48]

16

The "Russian Columbus"

Fur from the sea—a new golden fleece that had to be pursued through the icy waters of the North Pacific rather than in the remoteness of the Eurasian taiga—stirred a new frenzy in Siberia after the *St. Peter* returned. Once again, the prospect of new wealth drew men east, this time to the new frontier beyond Siberia's Pacific coast, where the emptiness of the ocean magnified tenfold the loneliness that men had felt in the tundra and taiga lands in years gone by. Much of the North Pacific remained uncharted, its islands still unexplored. Yet all that was needed to lure men into its unknown waters was the belief that sea otters in apparently untold numbers could be found there.

In contrast to the thousands of *promyshlenniki* and fur traders who had hunted the creatures of Siberia's taiga and tundra during the 1600s, only a handful of men could pursue the golden fleece of the North Pacific. To hunt sea otters required a ship and the promise of profits large enough to justify the danger to the men who sailed as her crew, for the risk to life and limb was very great. Bering had not dared to take his *shitik*, the *Fortuna*, into the ocean waters beyond the Sea of Okhotsk, but the men who hunted the sea otters of the North Pacific often sailed in similar craft because the iron needed for the spikes and braces of stronger ships could not be had on Siberia's Pacific coast. Their planks "sewn" to rough-hewn keels with willow branches and leather thongs, such ships could often not stand against the force of the winds and waves. During the second half of the eighteenth century, as many as two out of every five vessels that sailed into the North Pacific in search of furs were never heard from again.[1]

If the sea animals of the North Pacific were harder to reach than the forest creatures that had drawn the Russians into Siberia in the seventeenth century, they were easier to kill once they were found. "[A sea otter] prepares itself for death by turning on its side, drawing up its hind feet, and covering its eyes with its fore feet,"[2] Steller wrote in describing how his scurvy-weakened shipmates killed the defenseless animals on Bering Island with a single cudgel blow to the head. The first hunters to retrace the *St. Peter's* voyage found the sea otters such easy prey that they killed almost two hundred thousand of them during the half century after the *St. Peter's* return and hunted the larger and even more numerous fur seals in the hundreds of thousands. In one massive four-year hunt on the Pribylov Islands, the Russians butchered nearly a million fur seals and then, after realizing that their ships could not possibly hold that many pelts, left almost a third of them to rot on the beach.[3] Like the buffalo hunters of the American plains, Russian *promysh-lenniki* became caught up in an orgy of killing for its own sake. Also like the Americans, they moved on to new hunting grounds rather than limiting their kills so as to preserve the animals whose pelts provided their main source of livelihood. Because female sea otters had only one or two pups every other year, the onslaught of the Russians made their extinction all but certain.[4]

By 1750, expeditions sailing from Okhotsk and Petropavlovsk had wiped out the sea otters that once had flourished on the shores of Kamchatka and the nearby Komandorskie islands and had moved their hunting grounds into the Aleutians. Beginning with the westernmost island of Attu and working east to Unalaska and Unimak, they sailed farther and stayed out longer until only the largest and most elaborately organized expeditions could yield the profits their backers expected.[5] By 1780, the deadly combination of greater risks and shrinking catches had driven the ships of all but seven Russian merchant companies from the North Pacific. Sixteen years later, when Catherine the Great's son Paul replaced her as Russia's autocrat, the costs of outfitting ships and crews had reduced that number to three.[6]

The farther east they went, the more difficult it became for Siberia's *promyshlenniki* to hunt from ships that bobbed precariously at anchor nearly two thousand miles from their home ports. In waters where a lost longboat or anchor, a broken mast, or a hull shattered by an iceberg could mean disaster, expeditions needed permanent bases in which to find shelter and repairs, and that meant fighting the Tlingit Indians once the Russians reached the Alaskan mainland. Like the Koriaks who had barred the Russians' way into Kamchatka until the end of the seventeenth century, the Tlingits were a warlike people. "They are courageous by nature, and accustomed to enduring every deprivation and physical pain," one officer wrote three quarters of a century after the Russians had built their first settlement in Alaska. "If they were to unite under the leadership of a brave chief," he added, "they would easily conquer our settlements and kill all the Russians."[7] To carry the fur rush into the lands of the Tlingits therefore demanded courage and careful preparation, all the more so since the English seemed likely to challenge any Russian attempt to secure a foothold on the North American mainland. Unwilling to risk direct confrontation with British seapower, Russia's empress, Catherine the Great, dared not have the Imperial Navy carry her flag to Alaska as her predecessor had hoped Bering would do. That mission now would have to be accomplished by one of a handful of daring Siberian entrepreneurs who continued to send their ships into the North Pacific.

Perhaps the richest and most adventurous of those who hunted sea otters in the North Pacific, Grigorii Ivanovich Shelikhov took up the challenge and staked Russia's claim to Alaska. Celebrated as the "Russian Columbus" by the poet Derzhavin, Shelikhov came from the south-central Russian province of Kursk, which has been described as being "famous for its nightingales and race-horses"[8] but having nothing to do with the sea. Already middle-aged when he arrived in Siberia in the 1770s, he married a well-to-do young widow whom he took with him on his explorations and whose fortune he invested with such profit in the fur trade that he rose into the ranks of Siberia's richest merchants in less than a decade. Shelikhov ships, money, or goods played a part in two out of every five fur-hunting expeditions that sailed from Okhotsk and Petropavlovsk during the last quarter of the eighteenth century. To broaden his opportunities still further, Shelikhov joined forces with Ivan Golikov, a countryman from Kursk who shared his vision of raising an empire on a new continent. In just twelve years, the two men shipped almost ninety thousand pelts worth nearly a million and a half rubles from Siberia's Pacific ports to their headquarters in Irkutsk.[9]

In 1783, Shelikhov and Golikov formed a company "to sail to the land of Aliaska [Alaska], which is called America, to islands known and unknown, in order to trade in furs, make explorations, and arrange voluntary trade with the natives."[10] Intending to reach North America in time to build quarters before winter, Shelikhov and his wife, Natalia, set sail from Okhotsk late that summer in a new ship they had christened *Three Saints*. Foul weather forced them to spend the winter on Bering Island, and they did not reach Alaska's Kodiak Island until late the next summer. Just before the snows fell, they built the first huts and palisade defenses for Three Saints' Harbor and claimed Alaska for Russia.[11]

Working along with their crew, Shelikhov and his wife spent the next nine months collecting pelts, fortifying their settlement's defenses, and building a second outpost at Kenai Bay, now Cook Inlet. When they set sail on their return voyage with a cargo of precious furs in the late spring of 1786, they knew that settlements in Alaska would not be all they had hoped, but thought that the profits would be worth the cost nonetheless. How far their effort could go without direct support from St. Petersburg, they did not know. That would depend in part upon Empress Catherine the Great's estimate of the risks involved and the measure she took of her potential enemies in Europe.

Extending the Russians' empire to a third continent promised to create major new policy dilemmas for a nation whose rulers felt ill at ease with the sea. It also posed immense problems of supply and communication, for the imperial capital of St. Petersburg stood nearly half a world away from the tiny log blockhouse that Shelikhov had raised on the edge of Three Saints' Harbor. Between them stretched a fragile lifeline across six and a half thousand miles of Eurasia and two thousand more of the North Pacific. Nothing demonstrated more vividly how tenuous the connection between St. Petersburg and Russia's new eastern outpost could be than the Shelikhovs' own experiences in sailing to Alaska and back. Under good conditions, it took less than two months to travel from Irkutsk to Okhotsk and another three to sail to Alaska. Yet it had taken the Shelikhovs nearly a year to reach the North American continent and only a few weeks less to return to Irkutsk after fighting storms at sea and blizzards on land.[12]

Shelikhov returned to Irkutsk hoping (with his partner Golikov's help) to convince Siberia's governor-general, Ivan Iakobii, to put the case for his grand Alaskan venture before the empress, the Ruling Senate, and the Collegium of Commerce in St. Petersburg. A German nobleman who served Russia's sovereigns as his father had before him, Iakobii commanded the respect that Shelikhov and Golikov could not hope to win at a court whose empress had once spoken of Siberia's merchants as "irresponsible and malignant people,"[13] and they knew they could not succeed without his support. What the two men wanted, Iakobii later explained to the empress's advisers in phrases that fairly dripped with concern for the national interests of the Russian Empire, was soldiers to defend their company's holdings in Alaska, a subsidy from the Imperial Treasury to help finance future ventures, and a monopoly of the Alaskan fur trade.[14] In return, Shelikhov and Golikov would plant Russia's flag firmly on the North American continent.

Far too clever not to see what lay beyond all this, Catherine the Great listened to the case Iakobii presented, invited Shelikhov and Golikov to St. Petersburg, gave them honors that cost her nothing, and withheld the monopoly they sought. "To reward the zeal of the merchants Shelikhov and Golikov," she announced, "We bestow on each of them a sword and a gold medal to wear about the neck." A special citation from the Senate, she promised, would set forth "all their high-minded exploits and activities for the benefit of society," but, she added somewhat regretfully, "at present it will be impossible to provide their company with money or with a military detachment because of the need for troops in Siberia, where there are hardly enough for present demands."[15]

Privately, the empress remarked that the merchants' request for the Imperial Treasury to grant them an interest-free loan for two decades reminded her of a tale she once had heard about a man who promised to teach an elephant to talk in thirty years. Why would it take so much time to educate the elephant? someone asked. "Either the elephant or I will die," Catherine quoted the would-be educator as saying, "or else the man who gave me the money for the elephant's education will!"[16] She might also have added as reasons for treating the schemes of Shelikhov and Golikov with caution the facts that Spain's hurried movement of its garrisons into Upper California gave her little comfort and that she took no pleasure from the speed with which the British had begun to send their ships to trade for pelts on Vancouver Island and the coast farther north. Catherine knew that the confrontation that was brewing between Spain and Great Britain on the western coast of North America could expand to include Russia all too easily. Already at war with the Ottoman Empire and Sweden, she had no intention of burdening Russia with more enemies than she dared to fight at once.[17]

In the meantime, the Siberian magnate Pavel Lebedev-Lastochkin demanded a share of the North American fur trade and the handful of Russians in Alaska began to wage war against each other just when they needed to be united against the Tlingits, the British, and the Spanish. Soon after Shelikhov died in 1795, these conflicts spread to St. Petersburg. For the better part of a decade, Shelikhov and Golikov had been paying one of the empress's favorites handsomely to keep their competitors from making headway at court, but that line of defense collapsed when Catherine died in 1796 and her favorites fell out of favor. Without a defender at court, the future of the commercial empire the two partners had dreamed of building in North America seemed very dark.[18]

Amid a flood of lawsuits brought by her enemies after her husband's death, Natalia Shelikhova had to face the defection of Golikov, who joined the rival Irkutsk Company, headed by the powerful merchant Nikolai Mylnikov. Shelikhova held her own well enough for a time, but she could not fight enemies in Irkutsk, Alaska, and St. Petersburg all at once. She therefore gave greater authority to direct her company's Alaskan affairs to Aleksandr Baranov, the man her husband had chosen as his chief agent in North America. At the same time, she turned to her son-in-law, Privy Counselor Nikolai Petrovich Rezanov, to represent her in St. Petersburg.

Rezanov, whose patent of nobility dated back to the days of Ivan the Terrible, had become the commander of Catherine the Great's personal guards at the age of twenty-three and had managed to stay in the good graces of her son and heir at the same time. Rich, handsome, and powerful, his sad eyes and pouting lips making it appear that he had placed his heart ahead of his head, Rezanov had had his choice of any number of eligible young ladies whom hopeful parents pushed his way, but, perhaps sensing that any marriage in the capital would make new enemies as well as friends, he had looked to the provinces when he decided to take a wife. Charmed by the Shelikhovs' young and, according to some accounts, "extremely seductive" daughter Anna during a visit he made to Irkutsk on the empress's business in 1793, Rezanov married her before he returned to the capital that fall.[19]

The picture of aristocratic elegance, a close friend of the governor-general of St. Petersburg, and a favorite of the new emperor Paul, Rezanov had the influence at court to turn his mother-in-law's difficulties into astounding success. Combining his influence in St. Petersburg with Shelikhov ships and capital, Rezanov worked closely with her and Baranov to lay the groundwork for the enterprise that would give them control of the entire Alaskan fur trade. In 1797, he merged the Shelikhov American Company with Mylnikov's Irkutsk Company to form the United American Company and then transformed the United American Company into the famous Russian-American Company, which would dominate Russian ventures on the North American continent until it was liquidated in 1881.[20] With more power than old Shelikhov had ever dreamed of and with its foot firmly set in the New World, the Russian-American Company that Rezanov and Madame Shelikhova founded in 1799 became the main instrument for moving the Eurasian Russian Empire onto the continent of North America.

Aleksandr Baranov became the key to realizing Rezanov's grandiose vision in North America. In search of greater prospects and new worlds to conquer, Baranov at the age of thirty-three had left his wife and daughter in a town near Russia's Finnish border and had gone to Siberia in search of a chance to rise above the limited opportunities offered by life in European Russia. For a while, he had combined tax farming with distilling, glassmaking, and fur trading with some success, but his enterprises had eventually turned sour. On the brink of bankruptcy in the late 1780s, he had jumped at Shelikhov's offer to become his chief agent in North America. Like so many who crossed the North Pacific in those days, he had arrived at Three Saints' Harbor after a harrowing voyage.[21]

To the Shelikhov company outpost at Three Saints' Harbor, Baranov brought wisdom, energy, and daring. His wide-set eyes and balding head gave him more the look of a government official than a swaggering explorer, and he focused upon organizing the company's sparse human and material resources in ways that explorers rarely thought of. While Shelikhov had dreamed of founding a great metropolis on Yakutat Bay that, according to one of his last letters, would be distinguished by "great squares . . . on which, in time, obelisks would be raised 'in honor of Russian patriots,' "[22] Baranov concentrated more sensibly upon building the better-situated port of Novo-Arkhangelsk (present-day Sitka) on the island that today bears his name. There, where the sun shone less than a third of the year but the winters were so mild that raspberries sometimes bloomed in March and ripened in May, Baranov built the center from which the Russian-American Company would tighten its hold upon Alaska, reach out toward the lands of northern California, and, twenty-five years later, make a brief but spectacular lunge toward Hawaii.[23]

Tough, stubborn, and described by Washington Irving (in his memorable tales of *Astoria*) as "a rough, rugged, hard-drinking old Russian [who was] somewhat of a soldier, somewhat of a trader [and] above all, a boon companion of the old roistering school with a strong cross of the bear,"[24] Baranov labored to strengthen Russian authority on the North American mainland. The Russian-American Company was losing more than half of the ships it sent to Alaska in those days, and hostile Tlingit Indians, spurred on by rum and guns supplied by American and British traders who were trying to drive the Russians out of North America, burned several of the company's most prosperous settlements. Baranov lived on the brink of disaster for most of his twenty-nine years in North America. But his success in dealing with one seemingly impossible crisis after another helped the Russian-America Company to survive for another half century.[25]

Using Novo-Arkhangelsk as a base, Baranov extended the influence of the newly formed Russian-American Company southward at the beginning of the nineteenth century. When the expeditions he sent out in search of food and furs reported that the men of John Jacob Astor's American Fur Company already held the mouth of the Columbia River, he ordered them to continue on to the lands that the Russians called New Albion, where they built Fort Ross some twenty miles north of Bodega Bay on the coast of northern California. Yet the men sent to farm in northern California preferred to hunt sea otters, and the fertile lands around Fort Ross therefore never yielded enough grain (as Baranov and Rezanov had hoped) to feed the Russians in Alaska, let alone those in Kamchatka and along Siberia's Okhotsk coast. In desperation, Baranov expanded his vision of a Pacific empire to include the Hawaiian Islands, where tobacco, pork, beef, salt, vegetables, and tropical fruits promised rich profits to anyone able to carry them away. Yet Baranov's effort, which began with building a stone fort on the island of Kauai, turned sour very quickly. Less than two years of dealing with the Russians convinced Kauai's once friendly King Tomari (who had hoped that his new allies would help him against Hawaii's Kamehameha I) to expel them at the end of 1817 and end their dream of transforming the Hawaiian Islands into what the Russians' chief emissary once had called "a Russian West Indies and a second Gibraltar."[26]

Times were changing, even as Baranov tightened Russia's grip upon the lands around Fort Ross and reached toward Hawaii. In the less turbulent days that followed the liberation of Europe from Napoleon by the armies of Russia, Great Britain, and Prussia, men who were more concerned with national defense than about opening new frontiers came to power in Russia, and the less adventurous new directors of the Russian-American Company reflected that same outlook. In 1819, they replaced the roistering old bear who had served them so well for almost three decades with paler men who were less impulsive and more willing to observe the limits imposed upon them from St. Petersburg.[27]

By that time, the sea otters had been all but wiped out. For a time, the Russians hunted beaver as a replacement, but in the 1830s silk began to replace beaver in the manufacture of men's hats in the West, and political upheavals in China undermined the demand for furs there. By that time, China's growing weakness also made the Amur valley and the rich oases of Central Asia more accessible targets for Russian colonial ventures, for it had become clear even before the middle of the century that the Chinese could not defend their interests in the lands just beyond Siberia's southern frontier. With its interests turning in these new directions, the Russian government sold Alaska to the United States in 1867. As Kamchatka and the Pacific shores of Siberia became the easternmost boundaries of the Russian Empire, the tsars' dreams of ruling on three continents came to an end.

During the years when the Russians were pursuing their dreams of empire in North America, Siberia had changed from a land of scattered trading posts into a more closely held part of the Russian Empire. Towns and cities were beginning to flourish, trade was prospering, and colonists were beginning to put down deeper roots. Transportation was becoming more certain as roads took shape and distances shrank accordingly. By the end of the eighteenth century (according to a hopeful estimate produced by the Ruling Senate), a government courier could travel the sixty-five hundred miles from St. Petersburg to Okhotsk in less than eighteen weeks, and Nerchinsk could be reached in seventy-five days. A hundred days' journey separated Iakutsk from St. Petersburg, the same document reported, and the towns of western and central Siberia were much closer than that. The Ruling Senate claimed that Omsk, Tomsk, Tiumen, and even Eniseisk could all be reached from St. Petersburg in sixty days or less.[28] During the century since Peter the Great had mounted the throne, it had become possible for Russian sovereigns to make decisions and have their orders carried out—except in Alaska and California—within a matter of months.

Still, travel through the Siberian wilderness remained unpredictable and dangerous. Quagmires that offered neither shelter nor vegetation and ice fields created by permafrost continued to claim the lives of travelers and horses in the wild lands east of Irkutsk even into the nineteenth century. In 1822, it took Captain John Cochrane of England's Royal Navy a full seventy-five days to travel from the Kolyma valley to Okhotsk on a journey that he called one of the most trying of his life. "The difficulties I had to contend with," he wrote to Siberia's governor-general, Mikhail Speranskii, after he reached Okhotsk, "surpassed every thing of the kind I have seen before and required every exertion of mine to conquer."[29] Nonetheless, Siberia's shrinking distances were making the sum of its separate parts more measurable and accessible. No longer an exotic and isolated frontier land, Siberia now lay within easy reach of anyone who wanted to exploit it in the interest of the government that ruled it from St. Petersburg.[30]

17

At the Threshold of a New Era

Although the Great Northern Expedition had shown that eighteenth-century ships could not sail through Siberia's Northeast Passage, its explorations of the huge landmass that separated the Urals from the Pacific helped to open other trade routes between East and West. As East-West trade began to regain the importance it had held in Siberia's economic life during the long-ago days of the Silk Road, its center shifted farther south, away from the northern towns of Turukhansk, Eniseisk, and Iakutsk to the taiga trading centers of Tobolsk, Tomsk, and Irkutsk. This time not the ancient oases of Central Asia that had been the keys to international commerce in olden times but the newly built town of Kiakhta that stood on Siberia's Chinese frontier became the center through which much of this trade flowed. A barren spot of ground with neither trees nor shelter in the days of Peter the Great, Kiakhta became one of the greatest trading centers of the Russian Empire within a century.

A town built in the midst of nowhere, Kiakhta was the creation of a wily Herzegovinian nobleman by the name of Count Sava Lukich Vladislavich-Raguzhinskii. Before he appeared in Irkutsk in the spring of 1726 with an entourage of a hundred diplomats, officials, and trade experts escorted by fourteen hundred specially chosen Russian soldiers, Vladislavich had undertaken a number of delicate missions of state for Peter the Great, most of them under less than pleasant circumstances.

Now ambassador extraordinary and minister plenipotentiary in the service of Peter the Great's widow, Catherine I, he was to negotiate a treaty to guarantee the borders between China and Russia and open the Chinese frontier to Russian trade. Irkutsk, which Vladislavich reached after a five-month journey from St. Petersburg in the dead of winter, marked just the first stage of an odyssey that would take him across the empty Mongol steppes and the wastes of the Gobi Desert to Peking. There, China's emperor told him that his ambassadors would discuss trade between Russia and China in the Kiakhta valley, a bit more than four hundred miles from Vladislavich's starting point at Irkutsk.[1]

A heritage of cultural hostility and border conflict complicated the negotiations between Russia and China from the very first. So did the Russians' sour memories of the Treaty of Nerchinsk, for they had always felt that China's reluctantly yielded trade concessions had been poor payment for the Amur lands that they had been forced to give up in return. Depending upon their inclinations at the moment, China's Manchu rulers had been exasperatingly unpredictable about opening and closing the door to trade with Russia ever since the treaty had been signed. During one three-year period, Peter the Great had lost twenty thousand rubles in customs duties when China had closed her frontier to the Russians. Vladislavich's instructions therefore commanded him to negotiate regular access to China's markets for Russian merchants in order to ensure a predictable income for his mistress's cash-poor treasury from duties levied on goods leaving and entering her domains.[2] Given the Oriental mistrust of the West and Russian distrust of the East, that seemed a formidable assignment. Yet before the end of 1727, Vladislavich had opened the gateway to trade between China and Russia permanently. Its hinge, the Chinese insisted, must be set in the treeless Kiakhta valley, where they and Vladislavich had concluded the negotiations for the treaty that bore the valley's name.

The next fall, soldiers from Siberia's Tobolsk Regiment laid the foundations for the town of Kiakhta directly across the frontier from the Chinese border town of Mai-mai-cheng. Located 4,329 miles east of St. Petersburg and 1,021 miles north and slightly west of Peking, this was one of the most wretched sites for a town that could be imagined. The nearest source of drinking water stood a good half hour away, and firewood had to be carried for at least twenty miles on the backs of men or beasts. "The soil is so poor," England's Captain John Cochrane wrote when he visited the town ninety years after its founding "that even common vegetables are with difficulty raised."[3] A decade after Kiakhta's sesquicentennial had passed, the American journalist George Kennan still found it hard to think of Kiakhta as "the most important commercial point in Eastern Siberia."[4] Why, one Russian asked, "had two powers like Russia and China not treated themselves to something grander?"[5] The answer remained forever a mystery, perhaps known on the Russian side only to the sphinxlike Vladislavich. Outwardly, neither Kiakhta nor its Chinese counterpart of Mai-mai-cheng would ever reflect the wealth that flowed through them in the years to come.

China's Mai-mai-cheng was only slightly less primitive than the Russians' Kiakhta. Just a few hundred yards to the south, Mai-mai-cheng (meaning, literally, "buy-sell city" in Chinese) was more carefully laid out than its Russian counterpart, with larger houses, cleaner streets, and a better water supply, but remained a frontier outpost nonetheless. Here, in what one traveler called the "unguarded back door to China,"[6] there were no women, a fact that England's Captain Cochrane blamed upon its residents' preference for pederasty, "that dreadful degeneracy," he wrote, "which is said to pervade all ranks of society."[7] More probably, China's emperors banned women from Mai-mai-cheng to discourage merchants from settling permanently in a place where they ran a greater risk of becoming Westernized. For, if the Russians saw Mai-mai-cheng as an outpost of China on the Siberian frontier, the Chinese regarded it as the gateway through which Western culture could cross their northwest border.

In Kiakhta and Mai-mai-cheng, the Russians traded furs, skins, leather, ginseng, and coarse cloth for fine Chinese cottons, dried rhubarb root, silks, and tea for the next two hundred years. At the top of the list of goods coming through the Kiakhta gateway stood Chinese cottons, more than a million yards of which passed into Siberia every year during the eighteenth century.[8] Silk had its place too, for the foulards, brocades, gauzes, and crepes that made the journey through Kiakhta held honored places in the lives of eighteenth-century Russians and Europeans. Seamstresses and tailors from Moscow to London dressed their best customers in silken satins and velvets, but silk never challenged the position of cotton at the head of Kiakhta's list of Chinese imports. Tea, however, did.

Although often thought of (aside from vodka) as the Russian national beverage, tea did not become an important part of upper-class Russian life until the 1770s and 1780s. Before that, it was consumed more in Siberia than in Russia and was bought by the merchants of Kiakhta mainly in the form of hard-packed bricks, which the Siberians infused with mutton fat, salt, and rye meal. Durable, easily stored, and weighing about three pounds apiece, these bricks even served for a time as units of currency in specie-starved Kiakhta. Until the 1780s, the three hundred tons of brick tea that entered Siberia through Kiakhta each year far outweighed the more expensive, higher-quality loose leaf tea that Russian merchants and nobles were just learning to consume. Then, at the end of the century, the quantity of loose tea being shipped through Kiakhta soared to almost 700 tons a year and surpassed the 567 tons of brick tea that Siberians continued to purchase for their own use and for sale to the lower classes in Russia. By then, the value of Russia's yearly tea imports from China stood at nearly two million rubles.[9]

Dried Chinese rhubarb root, from which medicinal infusions could be brewed, was regarded as particularly important in the West and therefore became a prized commodity in the Kiakhta trade. Both a cathartic and an astringent, a twentieth-century pharmacopoeia tells us, rhubarb differed from other purgatives "in that it has a high tannic content thereby preventing free movement of the bowels after complete evacuation has been obtained."[10] Eighteenth-century European physicians also prescribed it as a cure for maladies ranging from liver disease to gonorrhea and intestinal worms, and thought that it grew best in the highlands of Tibet, Kansu, and Chinese Central Asia. Sought after to purge the heaving bowels of middle- and upper-class patients in every city west of Moscow, the supply of dried rhubarb coming across the Chinese frontier almost never satisfied the demand, even though a good twenty-five tons of high-quality dried roots passed through Kiakhta every year. There were times when rhubarb sold in St. Petersburg for fifteen times what it cost in Kiakhta, and merchants who bought it at those prices had little trouble selling it in Paris and London at a hefty profit.[11]

For much of the eighteenth century, the Russians used Siberia's furs to pay for the Chinese goods that passed through Kiakhta, where high-quality pelts brought up to ten times what they cost nearer to their source. Warm, durable, and inexpensive, Siberian squirrel headed the list of Chinese imports, with the merchants of Mai-mai-cheng buying more than seven million pelts a year from the Russians toward the end of the century. Ermine, muskrat, sable, fox, beaver, domestic cat, ferret, and rabbit accounted for over a million more pelts in some years. By the beginning of the nineteenth century, the Manchus' appetite for furs had outstripped even the combined resources of Siberia and the newly discovered Aleutian and Alaskan fur grounds, and the Russians began to import tens of thousands of beaver pelts from Canada and the American Northwest to sell in Mai-mai-cheng. Once the gateway at Kiakhta had been opened, the mandarins and merchants of China made Siberia's furs the Russians' true golden fleece, and nothing else the Russians sold abroad in the eighteenth century—not even the Demidovs' iron—equaled their value.[12]

The trade that flowed to and from Kiakhta during the eighteenth century helped the Siberian towns along its route to flourish too. Founded in 1661 as a base for collecting the tsar's fur tribute from the local Buriat natives, Irkutsk became the chief distribution point for all goods moving to and from Kiakhta and one of the most rapidly developing towns in Siberia as a result. Here in the Siberian wilderness, some 3,900 miles from St. Petersburg and farther east than Singapore, Russia's trade with China produced a prosperity that many urban centers farther west found hard to match. Profits from the Kiakhta trade built a stone cathedral, several wooden churches, half a dozen arcades for wholesale and retail trade, ten taverns, a brewery, and public baths, not to mention a host of government buildings and nearly a thousand privately owned shops and dwellings in Irkutsk before Catherine the Great mounted Russia's throne in 1762. During the next forty years, the economy of Irkutsk grew even stronger as more merchants and craftsmen settled there and accumulated greater wealth.

The Shelikhov-Golikov enterprises had their headquarters in Irkutsk, and so did the firms of Mylnikov and Lebedev-Lastochkin, their chief rivals in the Aleutian and North American fur grounds. The great Irkutsk commercial fair, at which the goods of East and West were traded between mid-November and the end of December and again from mid-March until the end of April, brought together merchandise from Europe, Russia, and China that grew more varied with each decade that passed. By the beginning of the 1780s, well over three hundred different kinds of Russian goods valued at more than two million rubles changed hands at the Irkutsk fair during the so-called "December market," and even more appeared in the spring. That was before the Shelikhov-Golikov and Lebedev-Lastochkin companies began to pour furs from the Aleutians and Alaska through the town's arcades toward the end of the 1780s. A decade after that, the value of Chinese and Russian goods moving back and forth through Irkutsk passed seven million rubles a year.[13]

Along with Tobolsk and Tomsk, two older towns that stood closer to European Russia, Irkutsk had become one of Siberia's leading urban centers long before its population passed the fifteen-thousand mark around the beginning of the nineteenth century. The first public library in Siberia opened in Irkutsk in 1782, thanks to a donation of more than thirteen hundred books from the Imperial Academy of Sciences. Before the end of the century Irkutsk had an amateur theater, a forty-piece orchestra (brought in by Governor-General Iakobii in the 1780s), and one of the first centers for smallpox vaccination anywhere in the world. On orders given by Catherine the Great, more than fifteen thousand people in and around Irkutsk, including many of Siberia's Buriat and Tungus natives, became some of the first in the world to be innoculated against smallpox.[14] Native Buriats, merchants from Moscow, St. Petersburg, Kazan, and a host of lesser Russian towns, Swedes, Germans, an occasional Englishman, an American or two, and traders from many other parts of the world all found places in Irkutsk in those days. One of the emperor's own counselors spoke of the "lively" society and "polished manners" he had found in Irkutsk around 1820, and England's Captain Cochrane, who passed through in the same year, thought that "its resources would be sufficient even for a capital of an independent kingdom."[15]

Although Eniseisk had once been more illustrious than Irkutsk, it had fallen far behind by the middle of the eighteenth century. Still, it remained the gateway to the Turukhansk region, the rich fur lands of the central Siberian north and the site (at the town of the same name) of the fair at which buyers and sellers of the best pelts of the Arctic gathered in June. In August, on the heels of the Turukhansk fair, came Eniseisk's own, where the natural products of Siberia competed with the work of skilled Eniseisk craftsmen for the attention of merchants from all over European Russia.[16] What was bought at the fairs of Turukhansk and Eniseisk was hauled in barges up the Angara to Irkutsk and sent overland to Kiakhta, or else shipped sixty miles overland to Makarskoi Fort, from which it traveled on barges down the Ob and then was hauled up the Irtysh to Tobolsk. Not until the 1760s, when Siberia's Governor-General Chicherin built a road across the Baraba Steppe, did Eniseisk begin to lose its importance as a key transit point between Irkutsk and Tobolsk. Then the line of Siberia's east-west trade moved south, following the completed sections of the Great Siberian *trakt* that connected Irkutsk with Tobolsk.[17]

Situated almost precisely at the halfway point between St. Petersburg and Irkutsk, Tobolsk stood in the midst of lands in which farming flourished. "It produces a great amount of grain and all the necessaries of life in great plenty," one visitor wrote at the beginning of the nineteenth century. "Vegetables of all kinds," he added, "grow here in a remarkably fine state, as well as pumpkins, melons, and cucumbers."[18] Tobolsk in those days had about the same population as Irkutsk, but it was thought to be more cosmopolitan, mainly because it stood so much closer to European Russia. One of the emperor's advisers thought that

Tobolsk around 1820 could "fairly stand a competition with that of some of the best provincial towns of Russia,"[19] although that may have been a backhanded compliment, in fact. Provincial towns in European Russia were almost universally considered by men and women from the capital to be backwaters in which pleasure could be found only in its grosser forms. Still, in comparison to other parts of Siberia, Tobolsk could lay a fair claim to enlightenment and culture. The fur trade provided a major source of wealth there, too, but Tobolsk in 1790 also boasted a dozen icon painters, a clockmaker, eighteen silversmiths, forty-five blacksmiths, thirty-five gunsmiths, and a host of tailors, dressmakers, bootmakers, and legions of other artisans.[20]

In 1775, Catherine the Great divided the "Tsardom of Siberia" into two parts and officially made Irkutsk the eastern counterpart of Tobolsk. Between the two "capitals" lay the great Baraba Steppe, the swamps and peat bogs of which formed a thousand-mile barrier of land so inhospitable that no one had yet settled within its boundaries. The Baraba Steppe had no villages, no land dry enough to grow grain, little firm ground, and almost no fresh water. Any goods or people being sent farther east had to be hauled in barges against the current along the route formed by the Ob and Angara rivers, even though the distance by water was more than twice as far as by land. To lay a road across the steppe, drain its swamps, and fill its bogs, the government used serf and convict labor upon whose lives it placed little value. "Exhaustion, brutal punishments, fever, typhus, scurvy, and the scourge of malignant anthrax took the lives of thousands," one writer wrote of these labor gangs. "Then new throngs fated for similar deaths took their place."[21]

Still far from being the sort of highway to which travelers had grown accustomed in the West, the Great Siberian *trakt* became Siberia's major east-west artery starting in the 1780s. Mud flowed axle deep in spring and fall, and clouds of dust choked every living thing that moved along it in summer, when many of the streams and ponds that supplied its water turned brackish and foul in the heat. With its closely spaced post stations, the Great Siberian *trakt* was most easily traveled in winter, when snow covered the dust and frost solidified the mud. Then goods began to move in quantities and at a speed not often seen in the West. In the 1790s, when Siberia had become a major link in the trade networks that spanned Eurasia, as many as ten thousand sledges gathered in Irkutsk to carry freight west from Kiakhta once the ground had frozen.[22]

Improvements in transportation narrowed the gap that had separated East and West since Ermak's "conquest." Certainly, Siberia's west continued to be better developed than its more distant eastern lands, but the space between the two was closing as the eighteenth century came to an end. Some commentators still complained of the "bourgeois aspirations of the merchant class, the despotic monopoly of the officials, [and] the dark ignorance and passive servility of the masses,"[23] but the fact remained that, because there was no titled aristocracy in Siberia, its merchants became the bearers of culture and civilization. Men and women like the Shelikhovs performed that mission more capably than Empress Catherine and her courtiers, who thought that enlightenment was destined to remain the exclusive domain of Russia's aristocrats, cared to admit. Even in the 1780s, Irkutsk had its small circle of literati, who discussed the works of Russia's leading writers.[24] Foreign tutors, the pride of affluent aristocratic households in Russia, appeared in Irkutsk and Tobolsk despite one governor's complaint that there was "almost no education [there] at all."[25] By the early nineteenth century, one visitor was amazed to see in Irkutsk "even the wines and other luxuries of Europe . . . sold at very moderate prices." "The traveler is truly surprised," he added, "not only to find a well-built populous town, but also a genteel pleasant society, and almost all the luxuries of life, in the very heart of Siberia."[26]

Greater opportunities and more abundant food supplies in all but Siberia's easternmost maritime lands began to bring more Russians into the lands beyond Tobolsk as the eighteenth century moved toward its end. In 1700, more than six out of every ten Russians living east of the Urals had settled in Siberia's western lands, but, a hundred years later, six out of every ten lived in its central and eastern parts. Between 1709 and 1797, the number of Russians in Siberia more than doubled, while the number of natives increased by scarcely two thirds.[27] More people, more trade, and more goods meant that Siberia needed better government. No longer could Siberia's Russians concentrate their energies upon exploiting native fur gatherers. Now they had to govern the vast colonial land that all of them recognized to be the largest part of the Russian Empire.

How could Siberia be held firmly within Russia's imperial framework? How could its resources be developed and utilized? How could its natives be transformed from exploited victims into useful citizens? And, most of all, how could the gross abuses of authority and the raw corruption that had been the chief characteristics of Siberia's governors for more than two hundred years be brought to an end? Siberia's seventeenth-century military governors had been crude and cruel men who had wielded raw power and abused it with impunity. Their eighteenth-century counterparts—the governors appointed by Peter the Great and the empresses Anna, Elizabeth, and Catherine the Great—had reflected the veneer of European civility with which the Russians had begun to overlay their Muscovite heritage, but they had been no less corrupt than their predecessors and no more willing to put the interests of the land and people they ruled ahead of their own. Prince Matvei Gagarin, a scion of one of Russia's most illustrious noble families, had been hanged for all he had stolen during his term as Siberia's governor-general in the days of Peter the Great.[28] Although few eighteenth-century Siberian governors combined that prince's greed and daring, they all claimed an illicit share of Siberia's wealth.

Such men fed upon the poor and weak as well as the strong and prosperous. Even after Governor-General Zholobov, one of Gagarin's successors, amassed a fortune in gold and precious furs, he continued to be petty enough to demand a piece of meat or a few eggs as a bribe from any victim who had nothing better to offer. A squadron of soldiers had to be sent from St. Petersburg to put Zholobov under arrest, yet his successors were only marginally better. The first inspector general sent to investigate some of the most blatant of Siberia's officials' crimes himself extorted 150,000 rubles from the citizens of Irkutsk during his visit, and one of the senators whom Alexander I assigned to wipe out corruption in Siberia proceeded to set himself up in Irkutsk as an Oriental potentate to whom, one chronicler wrote, everyone "bowed low and kept silent." After being raised to the rank of governor-general, this senator left his wife behind in Tobolsk and settled in Irkutsk with a French mistress.[29] Thievery, bribery, and graft flourished at every level of Siberia's government, and having unlimited power to get at Siberia's great natural wealth corrupted almost every official who wielded it.

As Siberia entered the nineteenth century, its governors seemed every bit as self-serving as had those who had wielded power in the days of Peter the Great, when the main difference between the tsar's officials (to quote one of them) was that some of them stole from the people they ruled "on a bigger scale and in a more conspicuous manner than others."[30] Even when some of these men began to think of governing Siberia more efficiently, they could not set corruption aside. Madame Treskin, the wife of the governor of Irkutsk during the second decade of the nineteenth century, was even reputed to have set up a special store to sell the bribes that petitioners showered upon her, while a much less exalted official who served her husband was found to have acquired furs and other goods worth more than a hundred thousand rubles by the time he was dismissed from office.[31]

Could such a government be transformed into one that put the interests of Siberia and its people ahead of its governors? That was the task Emperor Alexander I set for Privy Counselor Mikhail Mikhailovich Speranskii, his closest adviser on Russian domestic affairs in the years before Napoleon invaded Russia. Alexander named him Siberia's governor-general in 1819, and Speranskii, who had advised the emperor about domestic reforms at the beginning of his reign and later would become famous for codifying Russia's laws, found in Siberia his greatest challenge. There, in a world where everyone violated the law, he had to win respect for the law from governors and governed alike.

PART FOUR

The Largest Part of the Russian Empire

18

Governor-General Speranskii

Although he died a count of the Russian Empire, Mikhail Speranskii began life in very humble circumstances. Born on New Year's Day 1772, he grew up in a tiny Russian village, where he was known only as Mikhail, son of Mikhail the parish priest. In those days, last names were just beginning to be given to priests in Russia, and Mikhail did not receive his until he entered the theological seminary in Vladimir at the age of twelve intending to follow in the footsteps of his father, as custom dictated a priest's son ought to do.

The seminary usually condemned its students to wretched years of hunger and cold before sending them out to serve as clerics in some part of Russia, but Speranskii's brilliance won him the chance for further study at the new Theological Academy in St. Petersburg, where he soon earned a reputation for being the school's best student. He taught at the academy for several years after he finished his studies and then left to become private secretary to Prince Aleksei Kurakin, one of the most powerful magnates in the Russian Empire. At Kurakin's urging, he entered government service. By 1807, his genius for cutting to the heart of complex matters of state and writing clear reports about them won him a place as one of Emperor Alexander I's most trusted counselors. For the next several years, the priest's son Speranskii stood at the apex of Russia, close to the emperor and a part of the inner circle that discussed ways to modernize Russia's ineffective government. Yet he did not fit well into Russia's high society, and his methodical approach to life and government won him no friends at a court where influence could count for more than talent. The plans for reform that he prepared at the emperor's request challenged serfdom and undermined the sinecures of Russia's aristocrats, and his cold personality made him even more enemies than he might otherwise have had. Courtiers threatened by a commoner would want revenge, and they meant to have it at the first opportunity.

In peacetime, Alexander I preferred Speranskii's counsel to that of Russia's more self-interested aristocrats, but, when Napoleon invaded Russia in 1812, he had to send him away in disgrace in order to secure his nobles' support for the war he had to fight against the French. He did not dare to bring Speranskii back into government until 1817, when Napoleon had been beaten and Russia's lords were reveling in a renewed sense of self-esteem. Even then, the hatred for Speranskii among Russia's lords ran sufficiently deep for Alexander to keep his onetime confidant at a distance by naming him governor of Penza, an out-of-the-way province in central Russia. Speranskii hoped that success in Penza would restore his place at the emperor's side in St. Petersburg. Instead, two years of service in Penza won him an appointment to Siberia.[1]

Siberia needed an enlightened governor, and it needed reform. In the West, accountability and efficiency in the affairs of state had begun to produce the modern, effective governments that would guide Europe into the age of the Industrial Revolution, but the principles that reigned in the West had not yet found a place in Siberia's affairs, even though the Russian Empire had moved into the modern world in many other respects. Floggings, banishment to remote Arctic villages, and penal servitude in the mines and saltworks of the Transbaikal continued to be the chief instruments used by statesmen who spoke in the emperor's name but filled their pockets at his expense in the lands east of the Urals. The conditions under which their predecessors had been obliged to govern at the edge of Siberia's fast-moving frontier had helped to excuse such behavior in the days of the early Romanovs, but times were different now. More than a hundred years had passed since the days of Siberia's rapacious military governors, but the priorities of its high officials had remained the same.

True to this tradition, Governor-General Ivan Pestel and his close ally Nikolai Treskin, the civil governor of Irkutsk province, imposed a corrupt regime from one end of Siberia to the other between 1805 and 1819. By then, Siberia's merchants had stretched their trade networks from California and Canton to Cádiz and London, and they had become a part of the economic life of both East and West. Although they lived and traded in the modern world, the government that Pestel and Treskin imposed upon these traders dated from an era long since past, and the two inevitably came into conflict. Irate merchants sent a flood of petitions to the emperor complaining about his governors' high-handed attempts to curb their enterprises and the bribes they had to pay. As the bulwark of Russia's China trade and the emperor's main base of social and political support east of the Urals, Siberia's merchants had to be listened to, and their complaints about Treskin's and Pestel's tyranny eventually had to be taken into account.[2] This posed a fundamental question about Siberia's present condition. Could the beginnings of modern trade and the remnants of premodern government survive together?

After the fall of Napoleon, a strong feeling had begun to develop in St. Petersburg that the time had come to integrate Siberia more firmly into the structure of the Russian Empire, and some of the policies of Pestel and Treskin pointed in that new direction, despite the corruption with which they ruled. Convinced that only the government could lead Siberia's people to a better life, both men had granted subsidies to new settlers and pressed such natives as the Buriats to exchange their nomadic ways for more settled lives as farmers. Mainly by raising the amount of land under cultivation by nearly a half and by using treasury funds to buy grain at high prices for state-owned granaries, they had increased the size of the harvest in the grain-poor lands of eastern Siberia by fifty percent in just over a decade.[3] What needed to be done to make Siberia a full partner in the government of the Russian Empire was to continue these policies while doing away with the corruption and brutality that had made the regime of Pestel and Treskin so unpopular. Treskin and Pestel had to be replaced by a statesman who shared their interest in Siberia's development but had the integrity that the emperor could trust absolutely. When Speranskii's term as governor of Penza came to an end, Alexander turned to him to set things right in Siberia.[4]

To pacify Siberia's angry merchants, reform its government, and bring its settlers and natives into the mainstream of Russia's national life, Alexander gave Speranskii greater authority than any tsar had allowed a Siberian governor to wield before. "You are to correct everything that can be corrected," he wrote, "and you will put on trial whomever necessary."[5] Yet it was one thing to have the authority to "correct everything that can be corrected" and quite another to know how and against whom to proceed. As a rare statesman who knew the dangers of absolutism, Speranskii understood that the broad powers his emperor had bestowed upon him lay at the very root of the disease from which Siberia suffered. It was all too easy, Speranskii pointed out, for a benevolent governor to set the law aside while he tried to do good, but such intentions, no matter how noble they might be, threatened the only principles that could hold corruption in check. More than one well-intentioned Siberian governor had fallen into that trap. The law therefore had to stand above them all, and Speranskii wanted to institute a system of checks and balances that would prevent the highest officials from breaking the law, even for good reasons.[6]

More than most men who had lived all their lives in European Russia, Speranskii knew something about Siberia's history from reading the books Müller had published in the 1770s and from what other members of the Academy of Sciences had written after Müller's death. But he still knew almost nothing about Siberian life and the day-to-day problems a governor-general had to face. Speranskii therefore spent the better part of two years traveling through Siberia, observing, discussing, and, most of all, listening. Visiting the mines to which the government sent condemned prisoners at Nerchinsk, speculating about the (as yet undiscovered) mineral wealth of Iakutiia, and calculating ways to increase trade at Kiakhta and Okhotsk, he tried to see Siberia in broad perspective and up close at the same time. Reading at night, asking questions when the opportunity arose, and looking into complaints as he went along, he visited Tobolsk, Omsk, Tomsk, Eniseisk, and Krasnoiarsk in the summer of 1819. In the middle of August, he reached Irkutsk, Treskin's stronghold and, in the words of Speranskii's first biographer, Siberia's "true nest of corruption."[7]

In Irkutsk, Speranskii saw the consequences of the Treskin-Pestel regime and met Loskutov, one of the most feared district chiefs anywhere east of the Enisei. As district chief of Nizhneudinsk, Loskutov never entered a village without a detachment of cossacks and a cartload of rods to be used for punishing anyone who failed to pass his martinet-like inquiries into their daily lives. Everywhere he looked, Loskutov found fault: the state of a peasant's kitchen was as likely to bring punishment as the condition of her husband's fields, and there was no appeal from his sentence once imposed. Everyone feared this petty tyrant who ruled his district in the tradition of Siberia's earliest and cruelest military governors. Wherever Loskutov appeared, men and women bowed their heads and prayed that he would pass them by.

Just before Speranskii's arrival, Loskutov had confiscated all of the ink, pens, and paper in his district and stored them in government offices so that private citizens could not write any complaints, but Speranskii soon learned enough of the truth to arrest him in front of a crowd of his victims. "Can it be that you're saying this to Loskutov?" shouted one old man who could not imagine anyone daring to question the chief's authority. "Don't you know who Loskutov is?"[8] By that time, Speranskii knew all too well. Too cowed by their abusers to speak out in public, the people of Siberia's eastern lands had taken to stopping their governor-general's carriage in the midst of the forest and making their complaints in secret. Speranskii responded by removing men like Loskutov from office, but much more had to be done before Siberia could be governed on the same terms as European Russia.

There was a limit to how many corrupt officials could be dealt with summarily, for Siberia had far fewer officials than needed and not many candidates to take the place of the men Speranskii removed from office. In European Russia, the nobility formed a ready reserve of men to be recruited into government service when need be, but Siberia had never developed an aristocracy, nor, except for those working in the Demidov ironworks, did it have the serfs to serve them. As the Siberian social and economic pyramid had taken shape during two hundred years of Russian rule, the great merchants stood at its top, but the successors of Shelikhov and his Irkutsk rivals had no interest in serving the government and no training to do so. Speranskii therefore had to govern with the officials Siberia already had, and that meant trying to turn corrupt men into honest holders of the public trust rather than driving them away in disgrace. Deputy governors and even district chiefs like Loskutov might still be suspended. But smaller fry received a second chance for the asking.[9] Some repeated their crimes without hesitation, but Speranskii's conviction that a benevolent government could guide its people to greater prosperity began to draw Siberia's officials together to work toward more elevated public aims. From top to bottom, the atmosphere of Siberian government was changing under Speranskii's direction. Moderation and humanity were beginning to replace tyranny and brutality.

Determined to raise Siberia to the level of European Russia in all respects, Speranskii took its problems seriously and studied them carefully. Convinced that Siberia's real wealth had scarcely been touched, he urged its merchants to look beyond the profits from furs and the China trade and develop other resources. Siberia needed to manufacture goods on its own if it hoped to move beyond trading raw materials with the Chinese and the Europeans for finished goods, and Speranskii therefore wanted to see it develop modern industries and play a larger role in Europe's trade with the Orient.[10] Most of all, he understood that eastern

Siberia still had to find better sources of food. By the 1820s, agriculture had begun to flourish in Siberia's west and southwest, and the region around Irkutsk had long been able to supply its own provisions. In the rest of the lands east of the Enisei, such vitamin deficiency diseases as scurvy, beriberi, and pellagra still plagued Siberians in Speranskii's time. Not many years had passed since Captain Cook's second in command had reported that *all* of the residents of Petropavlovsk, the port on Kamchatka from which Bering had sailed, suffered from scurvy. As late as 1849, more than one sailor out of every five in the port of Okhotsk was sick and in the hospital, many from illnesses connected with malnutrition.[11]

Speranskii insisted that the solution to the food shortages in Siberia's eastern two thirds had to be found further east, not in the west. Trade with the Philippines and China might lessen Siberia's dependence on Russian grain supplies, especially if the Amur could be developed as an artery into the Siberian hinterland, and he also urged that the government consider provisioning Siberia's eastern seaboard by sending ships from Russia's Baltic ports rather than continuing to ship grain by overland convoy and river barges. But most of all, Speranskii thought that the solution to Siberia's food shortages would be found in North America. More than anyone since Shelikhov, he looked beyond the Pacific and saw North America's western coast as a part of Siberia's economic life. In his vision of Siberia's future, food from California could replace grain from European Russia.[12]

A man who believed in the civilizing power of Europeanized Russian culture, Speranskii saw Russification as the key to a better life for Siberia's natives. The march of civilization had driven such primitive peoples as the Ostiaks, Voguls, and Kamchadals toward the continent's outer fringes, where poverty, hunger, and disease had taken a heavy toll. Unable to set their lives as wanderers and hunters aside for the ways of civilization, these "stepchildren of the empire" seemed condemned to extinction,[13] but there were others—the Kirghiz, Buriats, Iakuts, and Tungus in particular—who seemed able to come to grips with the new world that was taking shape around them. To transform these onetime nomads and herders into settled farmers became one of Speranskii's chief aims. He therefore offered them greater access to education and economic opportunity, while leaving them as free as possible to lead their own lives for the first time since the Russians had crossed the Urals.[14]

During his three years as governor-general, Speranskii came to understand Siberia's great diversity and sense its vast opportunities in ways that the men who served in St. Petersburg did not. He was the first governor-general to require accurate reports about the people and lands Siberia's officials governed, the first to perceive the huge economic opportunities that lay beyond the fur trade, the first to propose doing away with tariffs on goods being imported from China for sale abroad, and the first to visit the mines of Nerchinsk. Yet Speranskii also understood how difficult it would be to remove the barriers that stood in the way of realizing any far-reaching program of reform. What Siberia needed, one resident of Irkutsk wrote with a touch of sarcasm at the time, was "to establish the rule of law, improve the judiciary, insure the safety of everyone, develop trade and agriculture [and], in a word, make Siberia completely happy."[15] A man whose personal fortunes had soared and plummeted, Speranskii knew how elusive happiness could be, but he also believed that progress and opportunity could raise the quality of life. To do so, he had to convince the emperor to transform his ideas, insights, and intuitions into laws.

Speranskii's greatest achievement as Siberia's governor-general came after he finished his term of office in 1822 and returned to St. Petersburg bearing the draft of a lengthy body of legislation that he convinced the emperor to approve. The product of his years of watching, listening, and governing in Siberia, these new laws divided the lands east of the Urals into more manageable units, established a hierarchical system of government, and limited the authority of governors and governors-general. Now Siberia was to be governed like the rest of the empire of which it was a part. Russia's imperial administration had its failings, to be sure, but it far surpassed the colonial regime that had ruled Siberia since the days of the first Romanovs.

Even more than making new laws for Siberia, Speranskii insisted that the law had to be obeyed. "I have discovered the true political problem of Siberia," he wrote after he realized the extent of its lawlessness. "Only Ermak," he added, "can compete with me in this respect."[16] Even if it was not realized easily or very often, the rule of law became the standard against which Siberia's government had to be measured once Speranskii had set his stamp upon it. For that reason, one of his admirers claimed a few years later, the history of Siberia was best divided into the period that came before him and the one that came after.[17]

With Speranskii's reforms, issued in 1822 as a body of eleven laws that took up more than two hundred pages in the thirty-eighth volume of *The Complete Collection of the Laws of the Russian Empire*, Siberia ceased to be a colony of Imperial Russia.[18] Like the lands west of the Allegheny Mountains, in which Americans at the same time were beginning to make new lives and seek greater fortunes, Siberia became Russia's land of opportunity, in which men and women could begin a new life while remaining full-fledged citizens of their country. Although the results of their efforts took shape slowly, builders, entrepreneurs, craftsmen, foreign traders, teachers, gold miners, and those peasants whom the government encouraged to settle in Siberia all began to make their way in the new world that Speranskii's laws helped to bring into being.

Yet for the million men, women, and children whom the government compelled to waste their lives in banishment and penal servitude between the time when the Russians first reached the Pacific and the Revolution of 1917, Siberia remained a land of tyranny and suffering. In another of Siberia's great contradictions, penal servitude and banishment were to be as much a part of its history in the nineteenth century as the laws and opportunities that Speranskii had created.

19

Katorga *and* Ssylka

When Russians talked of Siberia, they often said the words *katorga* and *ssylka* in the same breath. *Katorga*—forced labor or penal servitude—was by far the harsher punishment, for its conditions resembled the slave labor of the Soviet era, and a sentence of a decade or more often meant death. *Ssylka* involved several different types of banishment. In its most moderate form, it required the victim to live in one of Siberia's larger towns under the surveillance of the local police. Sterner types of *ssylka* transported prisoners to more remote Siberian villages, sometimes above the Arctic Circle and almost always cut off from all but the most infrequent contact with the outside world. In its severest form, *ssylka* condemned criminals to live among Siberia's natives and endure their primitive ways of life. Prisoners inevitably faced a term of *ssylka* after they had served their sentences of *katorga*, usually starting in a remote village and being allowed to move to larger towns as time passed. Somewhat in reverse, a term of *katorga* hung over the head of every man and woman serving a sentence of *ssylka*. Any violation of the terms of banishment, especially an attempt to escape, could condemn a prisoner to years of forced labor in Siberia's mines or convict prisons.

Starting with the First Northern War in the 1650s and continuing through the war in Vietnam, foreign prisoners joined the march of Russians being banished to Siberia. So did religious dissenters and statesmen, courtiers, generals, and princes who had fallen out of favor.

Because of the desperate shortage of educated people in Siberia, military governors and high officials sometimes appointed men sentenced to terms of *ssylka* to official posts in which they spoke in the name of the sovereign who had banished them. It became another of Siberia's many contradictions that men who had been judged too dangerous to live in European Russia were thought fit to serve the tsar in the remoteness of Asia. Even Mikhail Bakunin, the implacable nineteenth-century revolutionary enemy of tsarist Russia, once held an appointment as a minor government official in Siberia's remote eastern lands.

For three centuries, men and women condemned to *katorga* or *ssylka* spent their years of hard labor and banishment in Siberian outposts, where survival demanded their full attention and the outside world became a tenuously held memory. Peter the Great's onetime comrade in arms, Prince Aleksandr Menshikov, the young "Decembrist" officers who tried to overthrow their emperor in 1825, the great novelist Dostoevskii, the revolutionary populist Ekaterina Breshko-Breshkovskaia, and the Bolsheviks Lenin, Trotskii, and Stalin all endured terms of Siberian exile, as did at least a million other Russians before the Romanovs fell in 1917. Once the Bolsheviks seized power, the human tide flowing to Siberia rose to a flood that carried hundreds of thousands more across the Urals every year. These "enemies of the people" faced greater misery, were fed and sheltered more wretchedly, and were forced to live perpetually closer to death in Soviet slave labor camps than their tsarist forebears ever had because the system that sent them to Siberia was more capricious and cruel. The moral absolutism that encouraged Soviet camp commanders to let Gulag victims die by the tens of thousands was not part of Russia's penal system before the Great October Revolution of 1917.

Together, *katorga* and *ssylka* helped to provide the labor and settlers needed to incorporate Siberia into the Russian Empire. The Law Code of 1649 gave Russia's tsars the authority to condemn fugitive serfs, rebels, robbers, thieves, religious dissenters, counterfeiters, beggars, and "anyone who drove his horses into a pregnant woman and caused her to miscarry" to "eternal exile" in Siberia,[1] just as their fellow sovereigns in England and France sent criminals to settle their newly founded colonies in North America and the West Indies. Until the end of the seventeenth century, they sought mainly to remove men and women deemed to be unfit from their midst and populate distant lands over which they wanted to strengthen their control, not create a reserve of slave labor to do their bidding.

Starting in the early 1700s, when Peter the Great began to send criminals to the recently opened silver mines around Nerchinsk,[2] men and women sentenced to *katorga* began to supply the human power needed to work a network of mines that eventually stretched from Siberia's Altai foothills to the northeastern wastes of the Kolyma valley. Russians sentenced to *katorga* also helped to build the Great Siberian *trakt* and laid sections of the Trans-Siberian Railroad through the rough and remote lands east of Lake Baikal. During the Soviet era, they built factories, hydroelectric dams, and cities. Men and women whom fate sucked into Stalin's vast Gulag system cut timber and mined coal, iron ore, copper, and a dozen other nonferrous metals above the Arctic Circle to help take up the slack in economic development that plagued the capital-poor Soviet regime. Combined with *ssylka,* forced labor thus became a vital link in the historical chain that connected Siberia's past with its future.

Peter the Great's decision to use *katorga* in the mines of Nerchinsk did not mean that he had abandoned his predecessors' practice of banishing men and women to Siberia as well. Although his small inner circle remained immune from punishment, Peter deported to Siberia men who stole from his treasury just as quickly as he transported those who failed to pay his new taxes or produce the goods demanded by his quartermasters. At the same time, the many new opportunities for political action provided by Peter's modernization program increased the numbers of men and women sentenced to *ssylka* for reasons of state. During the Era of Palace Revolutions that followed Peter's death, the overthrow or death of a sovereign could change the personal fortunes of dozens of courtiers in an instant.[3]

Although particularly prominent, fallen statesmen and favorites made up only a handful of the men and women sentenced to Siberian banishment in those days. Beginning in the 1730s, the government sent to Siberia's eastern wilderness every year some two thousand runaway serfs, army deserters, and men and women guilty of crimes that ranged from begging to murder.[4] Then, when Empress Elizabeth decreed at the end of 1760 that Russia's nobles could deport troublesome serfs, credit them against the quotas of recruits they had to provide for the army, and receive direct payment for the women and children they sent with them, the numbers of Russians condemned to *ssylka* doubled. With thousands of officials and aristocrats having the power to banish men and women to Siberia, the chance for error now became as large as the number of people who had the authority to make it. By the time of Catherine the Great, chance and accident so ruled the lives of men and women condemned to *katorga* and *ssylka* that prisoners who had committed serious crimes often served light sentences, while those guilty of such misdemeanors as losing their identity papers or angering their masters sometimes ended up spending the rest of their lives at hard labor.[5]

How many convicts were condemned to *katorga* and how many to *ssylka* varied from one decade to the next. There are no accurate records for the early days, but during the 1830s and 1840s about one prisoner in seven, or more than twenty-three thousand of those who crossed the Urals, had received a sentence of *katorga*. Many of these served their time in government saltworks (the ubiquitous "salt mines" referred to by European writers of that era), one of which had been founded at the beginning of the 1640s by Khabarov. Others worked in state-owned distilleries, iron foundries, or the silver mines around Nerchinsk, which required more than three thousand men to work them at any given time.[6] For some, *katorga* became a sentence of death. Those who survived their terms of penal servitude usually continued to live in the same region to which they had been sent to do hard labor. Very few ever returned to European Russia. In 1840, the population of Irkutsk province included over sixteen thousand men and women who had served out their sentences, in addition to almost seven thousand more sick and decrepit exiles whom the government had released from *katorga* so it would not be responsible for feeding and sheltering them.[7]

At the very end of the eighteenth century, a new kind of exile— literate, well educated, and deeply concerned about Russia's future— began to appear among the men and women being sent to Siberia. Because the rights of man and social justice stood at the center of their dreams, a strong sense of moral and political commitment drove the most passionate among them to risk their wealth, health, and even their lives in an ongoing battle against Russia's establishment. Although these "politicals" eventually overwhelmed Romanov Russia in 1917, they numbered only in the tens during the years that separated the French Revolution from the end of Russia's Napoleonic wars. By the 1840s, their ranks had risen into the hundreds and, by the 1860s, into the thousands.

The first to seek the overthrow of Russia's autocracy was a group of aristocratic young army officers whom history remembers as the Decembrists. During the days when they had fought against Napoleon and shared the thrill of liberating Europe from his grip, these young men (like the European Romantics whose writings shaped their opinions) saw themselves as the noble opponents of an evil tyrant. They saw their victory in Europe bring constitutions to France and Poland, both of them at the urging of Russia's emperor. Then, thinking that their sovereign shared their hopes and dreams, they looked to him to grant similar rights to the Russians. When he disappointed them, they rose against his younger brother and successor, Nicholas I, on December 14, 1825, in what became known as the Decembrist Revolt. That day, several hundred young officers hoping to transform Russia into a constitutional monarchy or a republic led their men to St. Petersburg's Senate Square to challenge their emperor in a hopelessly unequal contest that ended in defeat, as such confrontations almost inevitably must. Five of these Decembrists were hanged and more than two hundred sent to serve as private soldiers in regiments stationed along the frontiers of the empire. Then the emperor condemned another ninety-six to long terms of *katorga* or *ssylka* in Siberia, from which only a handful ever returned to European Russia.

As they set out to serve their sentences in the lands east of Lake Baikal, few of the Decembrists realized what deep and bitter loneliness lay ahead. Nor did they know that two princesses and ten other brave women would join them to ease the pain and suffering that lay ahead. These women's sacrifices, one of their contemporaries remarked with admiration, were bound "to grant history a few beautiful lines,"[8] for they included all of the romantic idealism about which poetry is written and legends are made. "Models of self-denial and self-sacrifice, of love and extraordinary energy," one memoirist wrote of these twelve women, "they are examples the country can be rightly proud of and serve as ideal models for future generations."[9]

20

Two Princesses

Endowed with wealth, wisdom, and wit, Ekaterina Laval began her life at the apex of St. Petersburg's social pyramid.[1] Her mother's family was one of the richest in Russia, and the Kozitskii millions, of which her mother had received an ample share despite marrying against her parents' wishes, had built for the Lavals one of the most impressive palaces in the capital. The influence of the Kozitskiis had also assured that the émigré French captain whom their daughter had chosen to marry received the title of count from the emperor. Turn-of-the-century St. Petersburgers eagerly waited for invitations to the Laval palace on the Neva River's fashionable English Quay, where an evening rarely passed when some foreign ambassador or member of the imperial family did not join the guests. Only in the palace of the Iusupov princes on the nearby Moika embankment could one find a rival to the Lavals' grand ballroom with its stunning classical ceiling or their elegant dining room that one of the city's leading architects had decorated so elegantly in shades of gray, blue, and white. For the newly created Count Laval, all this was a far cry from his former life as Jean-Charles François de Laval de la Loubrérie, the second son of a small French winegrower.

Surrounded by a magnificent collection of art and thoroughly pampered by all of the comforts that her parents' wealth and popularity could bestow, Ekaterina Laval grew to womanhood during Russia's wars with Napoleon. Called Katasha by her friends, she was much like her mother: moody and at times touched by melancholia but genuinely kind, deeply pious, and able to face any crisis with the equanimity that only great faith can bestow. Beauty was never to be hers. "Bound eventually to assume the shape of a potato," one writer remarked,[2] her pug nose bore the scars of smallpox, and even the most elegant gowns could not conceal the robust solidity of her short figure. Common sense, concern for others, and loyalty to those upon whom she bestowed her friendship made Katasha Laval a commanding figure nonetheless. Few who crossed her path ever forgot her.

Like her mother, Katasha Laval married for love, but fate was kinder in the matter of her husband's origins than it had been when Aleksandra Kozitskaia had accepted the proposal of France's Captain Laval. Tall, handsome, curly-haired, and a promising diplomat in the emperor's service, Prince Sergei Trubetskoi traced his family roots back to the Gedemyn grand dukes of medieval Lithuania, and his name and wealth more than matched that of the woman he chose to marry. Katasha and her prince swore their marriage vows in the Russian Church of Paris in 1820, when she was twenty and he was thirty. At the end of Trubetskoi's tour of duty at Russia's embassy in Paris, the newlyweds returned to St. Petersburg, where they moved in an eternally charmed circle. There was no palace in Russia at which Sergei and Katasha Trubetskoi were not welcome. Health, wealth, and happiness all seemed to be theirs.

An equally charmed circle swirled around Mariia Raevskaia, the daughter of Russia's national hero General Nikolai Raevskii and great-granddaughter of Mikhail Lomonosov, eighteenth-century Russia's greatest scientist and one of the leading poets of its Elizabethan Age. While men and women who ruled the world of Russian politics gathered at the Laval palace, the salon of Raevskaia's parents attracted the leading lights of Russian art and literature. Vasilii Zhukovskii, one of the most celebrated poets of nineteenth-century Russia's second decade, shone among their guests. So did the greatest of all Russian Romantic poets, Aleksandr Pushkin, who, Zhukovskii once claimed, had been his pupil. Mariia Raevskaia's uncle, Vasilii Davydov, stood among the literary lions of St. Petersburg, and her brother-in-law, Mikhail Orlov, was one of the young generals who rode in the emperor's suite when the Russians occupied Paris in 1814.[3]

Carefree, charming, and utterly beautiful, Mariia Raevskaia grew up among heroes and poets. Masses of curls more shining than sunlight and darker than the night (in Pushkin's description) formed a lustrous frame around her heart-shaped face. With wide-set almond eyes, she was *"la fille du Ganges"* to the men who adored her, and none did so more attentively than Prince Sergei Volkonskii, who was as dashing as she was beautiful. A major general of the infantry and a hero of Russia's Napoleonic wars, Volkonskii wore the crosses of St. Vladimir, St. George, and St. Anne and carried a golden saber inscribed "For valor" from his emperor. After fighting Napoleon, Volkonskii had joined Russia's war against the natives of the Caucasus in a setting that only added to his romantic aura when he returned to St. Petersburg in 1824. When he was thirty-seven and she was not yet quite twenty, Prince Sergei won Mariia Raevskaia's hand.[4] As Princess Volkonskaia, Mariia Raevskaia looked forward to a life of happiness, fulfillment, and great comfort. In that, she and Princess Trubetskaia had very much in common. They also had in common a dark secret that neither of them knew, for there were things their husbands dared not tell them that would be the ruin of them all.

Ever since they had returned from fighting the armies of Napoleon, men such as Trubetskoi and Volkonskii had dreamed of making Russia more like the countries they had seen in the West.[5] Trubetskoi had become a leading figure among a group of conspirators in St. Petersburg, while Volkonskii, assigned to command divisions in Russia's south, had worked to strengthen revolutionary sentiment there even during the months when he was courting Mariia Raevskaia. During the fall of 1825, Volkonskii helped to work out a plot to assassinate the emperor when he came to south Russia to inspect the III Army Corps the following spring, and Trubetskoi committed himself to starting an uprising in St. Petersburg to support the southern rebels if they succeeded. At the same time, he and the leaders of St. Petersburg's secret Northern Society discussed how they might seize the reins of government before the would-be rebels began their revolt in the south.[6]

But events were to take a course that not even the wildest dreamers among the rebels could have anticipated. Without any warning, the childless Emperor Alexander I died in November 1825, just three weeks short of his forty-eighth birthday, and when his younger brother Nicholas ascended the throne, Trubetskoi and his fellow conspirators decided to act.[7] Hoping to convince the Imperial Guards to support them, the rebels of St. Petersburg chose Trubetskoi to become the "dictator" who would take up the reins of power in Russia and replace their nation's ancient autocracy with a constitutional monarchy on December 14, 1825, when all Russian statesmen, officials, and army units were to swear allegiance to their new emperor. They spoke of victory with the fatalism of defeat. "We shall die!" one of them exclaimed as they left their final meeting before the revolt. "But, oh, how glorious will be our death!"[8] How Trubetskoi would take charge of Russia remained unclear. Speaking only of victory or death, the rebels had no plan of action in the event that some of them should be captured.

According to Russian superstition, Mondays are unlucky days, and December 14, 1825—a Monday—dawned windy and wet, the temperature standing at eight degrees below freezing. At that time of year, daylight came late in the morning and the officers who planned to support Trubetskoi had begun to march their men toward St. Petersburg's Senate Square well before dawn. Although having learned of their plan only the night before, the new emperor, Nicholas, was ready, supported by the Preobrazhenskii Guards, selected from among the tallest and most handsome men in the empire, who had been the first to take his side. Then the Life Guard Grenadiers, followed by the Horse Guards, the Chevalier Guards, and the Guards Chasseurs joined the Preobrazhenskiis in surrounding the rebels on Senate Square. By late afternoon, the troops who had stood with their emperor had broken the revolt and scattered the conspirators. Well before midnight, they brought Prince Trubetskoi to Nicholas in chains after officers sent by Russia's Foreign Minister Nesselrode had found him hiding in the Austrian embassy, where his brother-in-law served as the Austrian ambassador.[9]

"What do you know about all this?" Nicholas asked Trubetskoi.

"I am innocent. I know nothing," the prince replied.

"You," Nicholas stated flatly, "are a criminal. And I—am your judge."[10]

With that, the emperor's younger brother remembered, Trubetskoi fell to his knees and begged for his life. "He fell at my feet," Nicholas wrote some years later. "He fell at my feet in the most shameful manner imaginable."[11]

The next day, an imperial messenger arrived at the Laval palace and placed a note in Princess Trubetskaia's hands. It read:

Do not be angry with me. I have ruined you and myself without evil intention. The Emperor requests me to tell you that I will be alive and am in good health.[12]

At that moment, Trubetskaia accepted her husband's rash act as a God-sent challenge to enrich their lives. "When the Lord sends us sufferings," she explained many years later, "He does that always for our own good, so that he brings us nearer to Him."[13] Immediately she wrote to the emperor, asking to see her husband. She was free to send whatever her husband needed, Nicholas replied, and she might write to him as long as the letters were left unsealed. But he continued to deny her request for a meeting for the better part of three months. When she finally visited Trubetskoi on Easter Monday, his princess vowed to follow him to whatever punishment he might be sentenced to.[14]

For Princess Volkonskaia, news of her husband's part in the revolt came more than a fortnight after Trubetskaia's world had crumbled, for Prince Volkonskii was arrested only after the men being interrogated in St. Petersburg implicated him. At first, the young princess seemed not to sense the seriousness of her husband's situation. Then, when she understood that neither rank nor wealth could spare him from a long term of *katorga*, she, like Trubetskaia, chose to go to Siberia with him. Told by the emperor that she could never return to European Russia if she followed her husband and that she would have to leave behind the son who had been born just a fortnight before the revolt, Princess Volkonskaia insisted that she had no other course. "My son," she wrote in explaining the agonizing choice she had to make, "is fortunate, my husband is unfortunate. Hence," she concluded, "my place is to be with my husband."[15] Her parents begged her not to go, and for more than a year General Raevskii remained adamant in condemning the "nasty man" his daughter had married.[16] Then he relented and gave her his blessing, complaining all the while of the pain it caused him to do so.

While the two princesses pleaded with the emperor to allow them to follow their husbands, the authorities decided to divide most of the ninety-six Decembrists who had been condemned to *Katorga* among the silver mines at Akatui, Blagodatsk, and Nerchinsk. At Akatui, prisoners lived in what a visitor described as an "inexpressibly dreary glen" in the damp bottomlands at the foot of mountains that closed around it from every side.[17] "The architect of Akatui prison," one of the Decembrists wrote some years later, "was without doubt the inheritor of Dante's imagination. My other prisons," he added, "were boudoirs by comparison."[18] Akatui, a Russian expert on prisons and forced labor concluded, was "gloomier than any place to be found anywhere in the Transbaikal."[19] The physical conditions at Blagodatsk and Nerchinsk were marginally better, but the jailers were more cruel. When he received orders to "take care of [his prisoners'] health," the commandant at Nerchinsk flew into a rage. "Without that 'catch' I would have them shot within two months," he fumed after the first Decembrists arrived, "but now, I ask you, how can I act with my hands tied in this fashion?"[20] For the moment, Volkonskii and Trubetskoi escaped the silver mines. Their first place of hard labor, which they reached at the end of 1826, was nearer to Irkutsk at the Nikolaevskii saltworks.

In late summer 1827, the emperor transferred most of the Decembrists
to Chita, a tiny settlement of fewer than fifty huts and outbuildings set
amid low hills at the confluence of the Chita and Ingoda rivers. Some
forty-five hundred miles east of St. Petersburg and endowed with all the
natural beauty that the Nerchinsk region so sorely lacked, Chita at first
seemed a more attractive prison. "The colors are bright and dazzling,"
one Decembrist wrote of the hills beyond Chita, and another spoke of
"views that might vie with the famed landscapes of Switzerland."[21]
Living conditions at Chita remained primitive, but Trubetskoi, Volkonskii, and their comrades found comfort in one another's company.
Obliged to build their own prison, the men lived in groups of twelve
packed "like sardines in a box" in each of Chita's one-room cabins.[22]
Between the spring thaw and the coming of frost, these onetime lords
repaired roads, reclaimed areas damaged by floods, and tended the
prison garden, while in winter they ground grain and did other work
within the prison compound.[23] They shared the learning that their
aristocratic educations had given them, and that, one of them confessed,
gave them "a political existence beyond political death."[24] One Decembrist lectured on higher mathematics, another on chemistry and physics,
and still others spoke about astronomy, history, and literature.[25] All of
them devoured whatever scraps of news about politics in Russia and the
West filtered through the curtain of surveillance that the emperor's
orders had drawn shut around them, and one mastered no fewer than
thirteen languages before he finished serving his sentence.[26]

While their men were moved from one place of hard labor to the next,
the princesses Trubetskaia and Volkonskaia, eight other wives, one
fiancée, and one sister were never far behind. Traveling by coach and
tarantass, the jolting, springless four-wheeled peasant cart that all Siberian travelers had to endure at one time or another, Trubetskaia had
been the first to reach Irkutsk in late September 1826. A few weeks later,
the authorities permitted her to travel into the wilderness for a brief
meeting with her husband. Then Volkonskaia arrived in January 1827,
and the two women began the friendship that endured for the rest of
their lives. They faced the stern officials who had been instructed to
discourage them at every step, and together they surrendered their
titles, ranks, and material wealth as the emperor insisted they must. "I
consider it my duty to repeat to you in written form," the governor of
Irkutsk told each of them, "that by following your husband and continuing your matrimonial relations with him, you [will] . . . lose your
former rank while your children born in Siberia will become state
peasants."[27] The women could carry no money or valuables beyond

Irkutsk, he warned, nor could they keep any of their serf servants.[28] As "wives of exiled hard labor convicts" according to the instructions issued by the authorities,[29] they shared a hut no better than those in which their families housed their serfs.

In Chita, Volkonskaia and Trubetskaia spent their days trying to find ways to survive on their meager government rations and waiting for those precious moments that came twice a week when they could visit their husbands for two hours.[30] Friends, companions, lovers, nurses, and special pleaders, they and the ten women who joined them during the summer and fall of 1827 became a bulwark for their husbands and their comrades. "It is hard to express what these women meant to us," one Decembrist wrote in later years. "One can never express in words the comfort they gave."[31] More than one poet eulogized their sacrifice. Many others cheered their bravery.

The jailers at Chita were more lenient than those in the silver mines, but they dared not be too generous. Kinder than most, the commandant at Chita prison was concerned that any leniency he showed his prisoners or their wives might reflect badly upon him in St. Petersburg, and he panicked when he heard that one of the Decembrists' wives had written to tell a friend in St. Petersburg that he was an honest man. "I am lost," he moaned as he held his head in his hands and paced up and down the room. "I am lost."[32] No act of kindness, Chita's commandant feared, would go unpunished, and regulations had to be interpreted in the strictest way, even against all common sense. "Allow me to say, mesdames, that you have no right to become pregnant," this officer stated flatly when he learned that several of the Decembrists' wives were anticipating motherhood. "When the babies are born," he added, as he fumbled to regain his composure after having been obliged to quote what he knew was an absurd regulation, "well, then it is a different matter."[33]

In August 1830, the governor-general of Siberia transferred the Decembrists to Petrovskii Zavod, some four hundred miles southwest of Chita. There each prisoner was to live alone in a tiny cell, the door of which opened onto a dark interior corridor of a prison the emperor himself had helped to design. Whether on purpose or through negligence, the cells had no windows, and it took nearly a year before the Decembrists' wives could persuade the emperor to allow small slits to be cut high in their outer walls.[34] Again they had to plead for permission to accompany their husbands, and again they traveled separately, jolting over the broken roads in peasant carts on a journey that took more than a month. "Here I am in the promised land at last," Mariia Volkonskaia wrote with sarcasm that was as obvious as it was bitter when she reached Petrovskii Zavod at the end of September.[35] Barren, and with only the most primitive housing, Petrovskii Zavod became home for Volkonskaia, Trubetskaia, and their comrades for the next decade. There they bore and raised the children that their marriages to state criminals produced. They buried husbands, children, and friends and waited for the years to pass until their husbands' sentences were commuted from *katorga* to *ssylka*. "What courage one needs to live in this country!" Mariia Volkonskaia wrote to her mother. "It is fortunate that we are forbidden to write to you frankly about it."[36]

His term of *katorga* finished, the first Decembrist left Petrovskii Zavod in 1833 to begin his life of perpetual Siberian banishment. A few more followed in 1834, and others left in the next few years after that. Prince Volkonskii finished his term of *katorga* in 1835, but Trubetskoi remained a prisoner until 1839. Scattered across wretched hamlets in Siberia's eastern lands, they and their friends sent petition after petition asking the emperor to allow them to move to larger towns and, if possible, to settle in Irkutsk itself. In 1854, soon after the Volkonskiis and the Trubetskois won permission to move to Irkutsk, the princess Trubetskaia died of cancer, leaving behind the husband whose health she had fretted over for so many years and a host of memories in the hearts of those whose lives she had touched. "The princess did not need funeral orations or public praise," wrote one of the Decembrists who attended her burial. "Her life spoke for itself."[37]

After an imperial amnesty allowed them to return to European Russia at the end of the Crimean War, the Volkonskiis settled in a small town in the Ukrainian province of Chernigov and lived for another decade. Princess Mariia died in August of 1865, and her prince died three months later in the midst of writing his memoirs. His last words, written on the lap desk that lay across his wheelchair, were: "The emperor said to me: 'I . . .' "[38] By that time, younger men and women had taken up the cause of Russia's "liberation."

Of course, most of the prisoners condemned to *katorga* and *ssylka* in the days of the Decembrists were common criminals, not "politicals." Before going to Siberia, they had lived in the raw Malthusian world in which survival of the fittest was the only law, and they brought that way of life with them to Siberia's prisons. History remembers little about this horde of exiles except for statistics that tell us that five times more men than women were among them. But faces do not emerge readily from this crowd of *neschastnye*—"unfortunates"—as the Russians called them, who found their destinies inextricably tied to that of Siberia.[39]

The next faces that come clearly into focus among the "unfortunates" appear at the end of the 1840s, when new tensions between tsar and people sent another contingent of "politicals" into hard labor and banishment. These men would not enjoy the special prisons that spared the Decembrists from the psychological terrors of serving sentences among hardened common criminals, for the men who ruled Siberia's prisons had learned more thoroughly how to inflict emotional pain. These new "politicals" therefore had to serve their sentences in some of Siberia's most fearsome convict prisons, among which history remembers Omsk prison as one of the most notorious. This was the "house of the dead" in which Russia's great nineteenth-century novelist Fëdor Dostoevskii endured the four long years of suffering that would influence his writing more profoundly than any other experience in his life.[40] Nor would any other book show more clearly than Dostoevskii's *Notes from a House of the Dead* what pain hard labor in a Siberian prison could inflict upon a man or woman who lived in the world of ideas and high-minded political beliefs.

21

Dostoevskii in the "House of the Dead"

During the late 1840s, a regime that the Russians would remember as the "Era of Censorship Terror" sent Fëdor Dostoevskii to Omsk prison. In those days, revolution was in the air all across Europe, and fear that winds blowing from the West would carry it to Russia hardened the resolve of the emperor and his counselors to fight against it. Anyone who dreamed of changing the course of Russian life faced grave danger if he shared his secret thoughts. Able to live only in the present, Russians dared not discuss their nation's future. "I absolutely *forbid* all articles, regardless of whether they are *for* or *against*," the emperor wrote of an essay that had defended his government's efforts to keep all but the upper classes out of Russia's universities.[1] An even more rigid prohibition forbade any discussion of revolution—even if only to describe what was happening in other countries. In Dostoevskii's case, it applied even to being within earshot when other men spoke about it.

The troubles that landed Dostoevskii in Omsk prison stemmed not from his own ideas but from those of a group of casual acquaintances whom he met through the offices of Mikhail Butashevich-Petrashevskii, a strangely complex young man who had managed to accomplish no more during the eight years after his graduation than to become a minor clerk in the Ministry of Foreign Affairs. The well-educated son of a well-known physician, Petrashevskii had invited Dostoevskii in the mid-1840s to join a number of lonely young men of wildly differing opinions who traded gossip in his St. Petersburg apartment. These petty clerks and sublieutenants drank too much, lamented their lowly positions too loudly, criticized their superiors too freely, and spoke of socialism as a way to avoid the economic traumas that were making Europe's cities into breeding grounds for revolution.[2] In the West, such talk was common; in Russia, where the authorities drew no line between thought and deed, such discussions were an act of rebellion.[3]

Attracted by the rising sound and fury of Petrashevskii's Friday evening gatherings, St. Petersburg's gendarmes arrested him, Dostoevskii, and a number of friends on April 23, 1849. Within a few days, more than seventy of the young men who had searched for comradeship and conversation at Petrashevskii's lodgings found themselves in the dungeons of the city's Peter and Paul Fortress, where they all faced charges of treason.[4] Eight months later, a company of guards marched Petrashevskii, Dostoevskii, and twenty of their comrades to St. Petersburg's Semenovskii Square, where three black execution stakes loomed above the snow. As a firing squad shivered in the predawn darkness, Dostoevskii heard his sentence read: "For taking part in criminal schemes, for circulating a private letter containing criticism directed against the Orthodox Church and the Emperor, and for attempting to circulate, by means of a private printing press, writings against the government, retired lieutenant of the engineers Fëdor Dostoevskii, aged twenty-seven, is sentenced to death by shooting."[5]

"We all were made to kiss the cross, a sword was broken over our heads, and we were told to don our white execution shirts," Dostoevskii wrote to his brother.[6] "My entire life," he added in a letter to a friend, "passed before me with lightning speed, its scenes shifting and blending into each other as in a kaleidoscope."[7] Just as the firing squad raised their muskets and took aim at the first three men who had been bound to the execution posts, an imperial aide-de-camp galloped onto the square to announce that the emperor had spared their lives. Dostoevskii, Petrashevskii, and seven others received sentences of *katorga*. The rest were banished to Siberia or assigned to frontline duty as privates with the Russian units that were fighting against the natives of the Caucasus.[8]

Spared from execution just three days before Christmas 1849, Dostoevskii had to leave behind everything he had known and treasured, including the literary acclaim that had greeted the appearance of his first published works. Too relieved at having been pulled back from the brink of death to think much beyond the present, he rejoiced. "Life is a gift," he wrote to his brother just before they took him from his cell on Christmas Eve and set him on the road to Siberia. "Each moment of life can be a century of happiness."[9] The psychological anguish of years to be spent in *katorga* still lay ahead. These would become a living death spent apart from everything that could give meaning to the life of an educated man or woman.

As the miles and days stretched out toward the east, Dostoevskii began to contemplate—as did the legions of "politicals" who would follow him in the half century to come—what a future lived without freedom and to no purpose beyond survival would be like. "All the past is behind me now," he wrote as he and his gendarme escort crossed the Urals. "Only Siberia and an unknown fate lie ahead."[10] On the sixteenth day, he reached Tobolsk, site of the transit prison at which the officials of the Imperial Bureau of Exile Administration decided whether a particular prisoner would serve his sentence of *katorga* in Siberia's mines, foundries, or labor battalions. Here at Tobolsk, one of the first Siberian exiles still remained as a monument to the raw tyranny of the system that now held Dostoevskii in its grip. This was the famed bell of Uglich, the ringing of which, in May 1591, had summoned its town's citizens to revolt. Tsar Boris Godunov had condemned the bell to lifelong banishment in Tobolsk, and thence it had been sent, where it rang to greet Dostoevskii's arrival almost two hundred and sixty years later.[11]

At Tobolsk transit prison, Dostoevskii descended into the netherworld of common criminals, where violence, brutality, and a singular unconcern for one's fellow beings created the very antithesis to the life of freedom that he had dreamed about during his student days. "Very heavy shackles and manacles," in the words of a physician who visited him, were riveted to Dostoevskii's wrists and ankles, and one side of his head was shaved to mark him as a convict.[12] While he waited at Tobolsk for the guard escort that would take him to begin his sentence of hard labor at Omsk maximum security prison, Dostoevskii began to sense how, as he later wrote, "the spiritual deprivations in prison are much harder [for an educated prisoner] to bear than the physical torment." Such a person, he explained, "is like a fish out of water—and his punishment turns out to be ten times more agonizing than it is for the common man."[13]

Fetters, chains, a deepening sense of fear, and a treasured copy of the Gospels were all that Dostoevskii carried when he left Tobolsk prison eleven days later. The Gospels' teachings combined with a belief that man was "hard to kill and by nature able to get used to anything"[14] would carry him through the difficult years he spent among men clad in rags, living on the precipice that divided human existence from lower forms of life.[15] In Omsk prison, crudely branded letters that marked

them as "exile convict prisoners" often scarred the inmates' cheeks and
foreheads, and the back of each one's clothing bore the large muddy
yellow diamond that marked all prisoners in the lands of Imperial
Russia.[16] Crowded into barracks, the floors of which were slippery with
human excrement, these men slept upon rough plank shelves impreg-
nated with infection that made disease their constant companion. Intestinal parasites and respiratory infections lowered their resistance.
Tuberculosis, typhus, dysentery, and a dozen other maladies claimed
their lives more quickly than any of the labors their jailers required them
to perform. "The worst feature of penal servitude in Siberia is not hard
labor in the mines," an American journalist concluded some years later,
"it is the condition of the prisons."[17]

At Omsk prison, men lived and worked and somehow survived
amid a din of clanging chains and manacles, hoarse curses, and stinking bodies, all of them condemned, as Dostoevskii explained, to "the
terrible and agonizing pain of never being alone for even a single
minute."[18] Murderers mixed with thieves, and noblemen lived with
peasants, for all distinctions of wealth and rank disappeared the moment a man or woman passed through the prison gates. In his *Notes
from a House of the Dead*, Dostoevskii recalled a nobleman who had
become a true "moral Quasimodo," a monument to "the lowest depths
to which a human being can sink" and a living example of "complete
moral degradation, absolute depravity, and insolent baseness."[19] There
were also in Dostoevskii's immediate circle a Jewish pawnbroker, a
highwayman who seemed able to bear any amount of flogging without
flinching, and scores of others who made up the convict society into
which he was thrown at Omsk.

Unlike the slave labor that would force men and women to cross the
divide that separated physical exhaustion from death under the Soviet
regime, *katorga* in the Omsk "house of the dead" inflicted its greatest
pain through the uselessness of the tasks it required of its victims. Men
and women sentenced to *katorga* had no choice about what they would
do or how they would do it, and they could derive no sense of accomplishment from anything they did. "To completely crush a man, to
destroy him utterly and subject him to a punishment so terrible that
even the worst murderer would draw back in fear," Dostoevskii later
explained, "one need only make him do work that is absolutely useless
and utterly absurd." The humiliation of doing such pointless labor
would break any man's spirit. "Compel [a convict] to pour water from
one tub to another and then back again, or make him grind sand or move
a pile of dirt back and forth," he concluded, "and he will hang himself

after a few days."[20] If Siberia's prison authorities had not understood that fundamental fact about human nature when they had allowed the Decembrists to live together at Chita and Petrovskii Zavod, they had learned to use it with a vengeance by the middle of the century.

The military despot who reigned as commandant of Omsk prison flogged prisoners without mercy and relied upon tyrannical underlings to make his whims the laws by which every prisoner lived.[21] As in the Russian army of that era, prison officials demanded instant obedience and tolerated no complaint, no matter what the provocation. On two occasions—once for complaining about a lump of feces found in the soup served to him and his comrades and once for saving a drowning prisoner after he had been ordered not to do so—Dostoevskii was flogged. The prisoners at Omsk had been so certain that he could not survive the second beating that they gave him the nickname *pokoinik* (the deceased) when he returned from the prison hospital some six weeks later.[22]

Four years in Omsk prison and five years of service as a private soldier in southwestern Siberia transformed Dostoevskii into a devout Christian committed to defending Russia's autocratic government. As he struggled to understand the true purpose of life, the pain of his experiences at Omsk prison helped to shape the vast and intricate tapestry of the human condition that he began to weave into his great novels. For some of his most alienated characters who failed to find their place in the everyday world of European Russia, Siberia offered the promise of redemption and a chance to build a new and better life. The complex blend of Mongol cruelty, Eurasian isolation, and European civilization that had shaped Siberia's history made that possible.

A living monument to the change that Siberian exile could work upon the minds of the tsar's enemies, Dostoevskii returned to St. Petersburg in 1859 to find Russia struggling to chart a course that would lead it into the modern world ruled by industry, technology, and an articulate citizenry that its European rivals had already entered. Russia needed to build railroads and factories, free its serfs, modernize its government, and instill in its people the sense of civic responsibility modern societies required. Men and women began to speak of *glasnost* as an antidote to the despotic power that had ruled their lives for centuries, and, just as their Soviet descendants did during the 1980s, they saw it as a key to progress and a freer life. "*Glasnost*," one Russian wrote then, "provides the oppressed with an opportunity to enjoy the protection of the law."[23] "We believe," a prominent radical added as the optimism sweeping Russia reached its peak, "that [the new emperor] Alexander II stands at the head of progress in Russia."[24] As part of this new movement for liberation and reform, Dostoevskii's "house of the dead" was demolished. By the time George Kennan visited the site of Omsk prison in the 1880s as a journalist for *Century Magazine,* all traces of it had vanished.

As others came to share Dostoevskii's belief that Siberia held the promise of redemption and a chance to build a new life, waves of settlers began to carve fields and farms out of virgin steppes and forests. But farms were not the only magnets that drew people from European Russia into Siberia in Dostoevskii's time. After centuries of forbidding anyone but government officials to search for gold in the Siberian wilderness, the Russian government reversed its policy in 1824 and announced, for the first time since Ermak's "conquest," that private citizens could dig for gold. By doing so, it opened the way for one of the greatest gold rushes in modern history.

22

The Search for Gold

For centuries, rare pelts had served the Russians as a substitute for gold. In part, this was because the demand for furs in Europe and Asia—like the demand for gold and silver everywhere—never declined, but it was also because Nature had bestowed very little gold and silver upon the lands of old Russia. With no mines that produced the metals that had been the soul of international trade since ancient times, the men who had ruled medieval Russia had been obliged to trade furs to the rulers of Saxony and Austria for the precious metals they needed to mint their coins. In the days of medieval Novgorod, furs had paid for the salt, fine cloth, and luxury goods that the Hansa merchants of northern Europe had brought to Russia.

Using furs as their "golden fleece," the Russians had taken Siberia and started to rule Eurasia without great reserves of precious metals, but this could continue only as long as their supply of rare pelts remained very large and the demand for them held firm. When the harvests of prime pelts began to diminish, the Russians needed gold and silver to replace them, and, because centuries of searching had uncovered very little treasure in Russia's European lands, her rulers again looked to the lands beyond the Urals. The men who had opened Siberia during the century after Ermak's "conquest" had been too busy plundering its furs to look for other treasure, to be sure, but, the tsars now asked, could gold not be found somewhere in its vast spaces? The discovery of carefully worked golden objects in the great Scythian burial mounds that dotted Siberia's southern steppe made it seem almost certain that the ancients had found gold there, and the writings in which Herodotus told of "huge quantities" of gold guarded by winged griffins in the northern—but imprecisely defined—lands of Eurasia added more substance to that belief. A score of legends told of ancient mines hidden deep in Siberia that rivaled those of Mexico and Peru, but gold continued to elude the Russians, no matter where they searched. The sources of the precious metal that the Scythians had shaped into fine jewelry and exquisite vessels before the time of Christ remained hidden by the shrouds wrapped around them by time.[1]

At the very end of the seventeenth century, foreign mining experts sent into Asia by Peter the Great discovered the first Siberian silver near the Chinese frontier at Nerchinsk.[2] For a moment, the silver seemed to be treasure enough, but the Russians soon found that every ton of smelted metal from these new mines would yield about a hundred ounces of gold as part of the refining process.[3] Silver from the Altai mines that Akinfii Demidov discovered and worked illegally around Lake Kolyvan and Zmeinogorsk during the 1730s showed similar traces of gold. Yet none of the explorers and cossacks whom Russia's sovereigns sent into Siberia's wilderness during the first half of the eighteenth century found the mother lode of gold ore that, they all believed, must lie somewhere between the Urals and the Pacific. Then, at midcentury, geologists sent out by the government discovered gold ore near Berëzov in Siberia's northwestern corner.[4] Once a place of exile for fallen royal favorites, Berëzov now became Siberia's first important gold mine and the only one up to that time that did not yield gold as a by-product of refining silver.

Berëzov's gold came from subterranean veins reached by large shafts dug by enserfed peasants and exiled criminals. Because the ore lay buried anywhere from a few feet to a hundred yards beneath the surface, miners had to work underground in water-filled shafts where the air contained barely enough oxygen to sustain a candle flame.[5] Cold, hunger, and disease took a heavy toll on the men who dug out the ore at Berëzov; yet, despite the great human cost, the return in treasure remained much less than the Russians needed. The mines at Berëzov produced only a bit more than four hundred ounces of gold a year, while those of the Altai yielded another sixteen hundred as a by-product of the silver smelting process. Even when another hundred or so ounces from the Nerchinsk mines were added in, the total scarcely reached a hundredth of the world's output. As the Russian Empire moved into the nineteenth century, it had no more than a fraction of the gold needed for a nation whose foreign policy required it to keep nearly a million men under arms.[6] Catherine the Great had issued paper money to make up the deficits in Russia's treasury, and her grandson Alexander I had printed a great deal more to pay the cost of Russia's wars against Napoleon. By the time of Alexander's death in 1825, these paper rubles had fallen to a fifth of their face value, and Russia had still not found a way to pay the costs of being one of the world's great powers.

For much of the eighteenth century, the quest for gold had posed questions that the Russians had found difficult to answer. In what sorts of terrain might gold be discovered? In what different forms did it exist in nature? Europeans had known some of the answers to these questions for centuries, but the first attempt to address them in the Russian language appeared only in 1763, when Mikhail Lomonosov, the first of eighteenth-century Russia's scientists to establish close ties with his counterparts in Europe, published a brief manual entitled *Fundamentals of Metallurgy*. In discussing how gold could be discovered, mined, and refined, Lomonosov explained that it could be found not only in veins, as at Berëzov, but in the sand and gravel that lined the beds of rivers and streams. This proved to be the first clue to unlocking the Siberian treasure house the Russians had been seeking.

A half century after Lomonosov published his book, a mining engineer by the name of Lëv Brusnitsyn discovered how to wash gold flakes from sand and gravel.[7] It then became possible for the Russians to think of extracting the gold that had remained hidden beneath Siberia's subsoil for so many centuries. Ignored until that time because of the difficulties in separating even the smallest amounts of gold from them, these vast alluvial deposits of auriferous sand now became the source of huge quantities of precious metal. Within thirty years, Siberia's yearly production of gold soared to nearly six hundred thousand ounces, and by 1845 Siberian miners brought in two fifths of all the gold being mined throughout the world. More than ten times the precious metal produced by Russia's European rivals and allies together came from Siberia in 1845—more, even, than the output of Europe, the rest of Asia, and all of Latin America combined.[8]

Because Brusnitsyn's technique of washing gold from sand made it possible for anyone who could turn a shovel and tilt a pan to prospect for gold, Russia's tsars either had to rescind their long-standing ban on private prospecting in Siberia or create an immense police force to guard the tens of thousands of miles of streams and rivers that flowed through it. Realizing that the second alternative was impossible, Emperor Alexander I opened Siberia's watercourses and valleys for exploration by prospectors in 1824. Soon men with picks, shovels, and pans began to work their way across the continent in search of the sands that could make them rich.[9] At first, they stayed mainly in the foothills of the Urals near Ekaterinburg, where Emperor Alexander I himself had once wielded a pick and shovel to emphasize the importance he attached to Russia's new search. When the Ekaterinburg lands yielded scarcely more gold than the mines of the Altai, prospectors working in groups of twenty or thirty began to move farther east, probing beneath Siberia's topsoil as they went.[10]

As their ancestors had done in the days of the great seventeenth-century fur rush, Siberia's nineteenth-century prospectors worked their way eastward to the Lena River and then struck out for Siberia's remote northeastern corner. They found gold near Tomsk in 1828 and along the southern tributaries of the Lena in 1829. They discovered auriferous sands near Krasnoiarsk and the ancient lands around Minusinsk in 1830 and at Achinsk and in the Transbaikal in 1832. The first golden sands were found in the tributaries of the Angara in 1836 and in the permafrost beyond Iakutsk in 1840. The harsher the climate, the richer the deposits seemed to be. Along with the northern parts of Iakutsk and Eniseisk provinces, the windswept lands of the Kara and Kolyma valleys proved to be the richest of all, even though they could not be fully mined until the days of Stalin's slave labor camps.[11]

In 1800, three thousand worn and beaten prisoners condemned to *katorga* had mined gold in Siberia. Almost entirely as a result of Brusnitsyn's discovery, the number of free gold miners stood at nearly sixty thousand half a century later.[12] Carting away as much as fifteen feet of topsoil before they could reach the gold-bearing sand beneath, these men moved some four million tons of dirt a year during the second quarter of the nineteenth century. Each spring found them in the gold-fields ready to begin work the moment the ground thawed, always trying to hurry the onset of the season by blasting away frozen topsoil or thawing it with huge bonfires. Working from sunrise to sunset with scarcely one day's rest out of thirty, they would fight the inevitable losing battle against the passage of time, knowing that the frosts must force them into winter quarters before the end of September. As they had in the spring, they again tried to stretch the mining season by building bonfires to keep the freezing soil soft enough to work, but they could squeeze out no more than two or three weeks of extra time at most.[13] Once the soil froze, the mining had to stop. Even in the days of Stalin, Siberia's golden sands could not be mined in the dead of winter.

The brutal Arctic climate was only one of many obstacles that miners faced on the world's wildest frontier. Not even the jungles of the tropics could breed rivals to the huge gray mosquitoes that rose from the meltwater swamps of Siberia's taiga and tundra every summer.[14] Yet the seas of icy muck in which miners had to stand knee deep when late and early snows combined with freezing rains every spring and fall were only marginally less unpleasant than the infamous "flying leeches" whose bites stampeded even the thick-skinned reindeer to seek the shelter of higher ground. Weekly pay in the goldfields was better than what could be earned in the mills of St. Petersburg and Moscow, but when calculated as a year's wage, less than five months' work in the goldfields seemed meager compensation at best, especially in the conditions under which the miners lived and worked.[15]

Rough huts, usually without floors, often lacking windows and chimneys and sometimes with nothing more than dirt walls topped with brush or canvas, sheltered from ten to forty men on the remote placers of Siberia. Although government inspectors often praised the cleanliness of such places in their reports, primitive stoves belched smoke and fumes directly into the quarters where the miners lived and slept. Latrines placed near streams infected miners with all the diseases associated with human waste, and the death rate in the camps was much higher than it ought to have been among men who, compared with their peasant relatives in European Russia, ate remarkably well. As they did among Russian peasants everywhere, sour rye bread and a watery cabbage soup known as *shchi* formed the basis of the gold miners' diet, and this was supplemented by a pound of meat a day, usually added in chunks to the *shchi* they ate at their evening meal. The danger of this diet was not hunger but disease, for there were never enough dried peas, sauerkraut, and salted cucumbers to offset the chronic lack of vitamin C–rich foods that made scurvy an ever-present danger.[16] Scurvy never left Siberia's mining camps. Neither did intestinal parasites and malignant fevers, all of which took a deadly toll.

When snow and ice ended the mining season for the year, lonesome miners set out for Siberia's towns to quench the thirst for cheap spirits that had been building all summer.[17] Often the wages of a Siberian summer's work disappeared in less than a fortnight, leaving the miner with a winter's worth of memories about days and nights spent in joyful communion with Bacchus while he looked forward to the pleasures that spending the next summer's wages in similar fashion would bring. This, not wealth, was a miner's reward for working in the goldfields. Those who invested in the thousand or so joint-stock mining companies that

had staked out claims all through Siberia by the middle of the nineteenth century were the ones who reaped huge profits, not the men who
dug the gold and fought cold and disease during the far northern
summer.[18]

The men who ran Siberia's mines shipped the gold their workers
collected to the government smelting works at Barnaul, where it was
cast into bars and forwarded to the treasury in St. Petersburg. At Barnaul, a town that had arisen not far from Akinfii Demidov's Altai mines,
private mine owners had to relinquish all control of their gold and rely
upon the tsar's officials to weigh and assay it accurately. Then the
treasury held privately mined gold for at least five months before making payment. This meant that the returns were slow in coming, but their
size made them worth the wait, for some of Siberia's joint-stock mining
enterprises yielded profits of more than eight hundred percent in a
single year. This made them particularly attractive to speculators looking for ways to invest the earnings they reaped from the trade that
continued to flow from Kiakhta into Irkutsk.[19]

More than ever, and on a scale never seen before, there were fortunes
to be made in Siberia as the nineteenth century passed its midpoint. As
the opportunities multiplied and the returns on investments became
more predictable, wealth no longer remained concentrated in the hands
of a few merchants as it had in the eighteenth century. Now those who
did not cross the Urals in chains found in Siberia a land of opportunity
and freedom the moment they entered it. A man and his family could
carve a farm out of the wilderness there, and they needed to recognize
no master but the tsar while they did so. Whole caravans, sometimes
with as many as a hundred families hoping to take advantage of the tax
exemptions and resettlement allowances the government offered, began
to make the journey in two-wheeled carts, their belongings piled high
and their livestock following behind. On the darker side, runaway serfs
crossed the Urals singly or in small groups to build "hidden" villages in
the Siberian wilderness. For decades, such folk lived, reproduced, and
died outside the law, their existence known to no one unless some
government official or stray traveler chanced to stumble upon their
community by accident.[20]

That entire communities of fugitives could settle beyond the Urals
without being detected showed that the Russians still had not managed
to tie Siberia as firmly to their empire as they wished. By transforming
Siberia from a colony into an integral part of the Russian Empire,
Speranskii had brought to it not only the empire's strengths but also its
failings, not the least of which was a tyranny of officials who placed their

devotion to the procedures of the bureaucracy in which they served ahead of their vow to do their soveriegn's will. Especially in the provinces, too many poorly educated officials who knew only how to move papers from one office to another thought neither of the importance of what they did nor of its meaning. Opposed to any kind of change for fear that new ways might prove to be too difficult to learn, the lower levels of Russia's bureaucracy had become a massive reservoir of passive resistance to progress. Rigid and unable to respond to the different needs of changing times, the bureaucracy that Speranskii had hoped would provide efficient government had, by Dostoevskii's time, become a barrier to modernization.

In European Russia, the emperor Nicholas I had tried to overcome the inertia of tradition-bound bureaucrats by assigning his most trusted adjutants to deal with Russia's thorniest problems. Throughout the 1830s and 1840s, specially chosen adjutants had worked to strengthen Russia's internal security, compile her laws, solve the problems of governing millions of state peasants, feed the starving masses during the famine of 1841–1842, and stem the ravages of cholera. Yet, as the 1840s passed their midpoint, the problem of Siberia—far-flung, ill attended, and undergoverned, its vastness magnifying all the problems that had been brought to it by bureaucratic government—still remained.

To confront the dilemmas created by Siberia's complexity and great distances required more than the emperor's trust; it demanded more, even, than an undisputed readiness to do his will. To speak for him in Siberia, the emperor needed an adjutant who combined absolute honesty and breadth of vision with an understanding of the ways in which the world around him was changing. For the better part of two decades, the emperor had searched in vain. Then, in 1847, he found his Siberian adjutant in the person of a thirty-eight-year-old general known for his bravery and his contempt for mediocrity. A poor aristocrat who fit awkwardly into the arrogantly predictable world of Russia's capital, Nikolai Nikolaevich Muravëv became his emperor's adjutant of adjutants, the governor-general whom Nicholas I sent to push Siberia into the modern age.

23

Muravëv Takes the Amur

Born in 1809 into a family whose men had served Russia in high office since the days of Dmitrii Donskoi, General of the Infantry Nikolai Muravëv was thirty-eight years old when the emperor Nicholas I passed over dozens of more senior officers to name him governor-general of eastern Siberia. Renowned as an officer who had fought with valor in Russia's campaigns against the Turks, the Poles, and the natives of the Caucasus, Muravëv disdained men of small talent and was known to be scrupulously honest. Yet he knew very little about Siberia or the nations he would have to face in that faraway part of the world where China's growing weakness was creating a vacuum that any one of Russia's several rivals in Europe might attempt to fill.[1] Anxious to play her stronger rivals against one another, China had begun to shift the world's Far Eastern trade away from Siberia's Kiakhta gateway toward Shanghai and Canton by ceding Hong Kong to the British and opening her southern ports to Western ships. To keep Russia firmly positioned in the Far East, Muravëv therefore needed to understand the complexities of dealing with the world's greatest maritime powers. At the same time, he would have to develop a sixth sense about the limits to which China might be pushed.

Not only the attention that the British and Americans were beginning to give to the Far East but a number of important discoveries of their own helped to turn the Russians' attention toward China as Muravëv prepared to take up his assignment in Irkutsk. After he had explored the Amur from its mouth to its source in 1843, Russia's Alexander von Middendorf had reported to his surprised superiors that the Chinese had never occupied the left bank that the Nerchinsk treaty had ceded to them. Seeing an opportunity for the Russians to seize one of Eurasia's greatest waterways, Middendorf had urged Russia to claim the Amur lands, but Foreign Minister Count Karl Nesselrode had spoken against doing so for fear of upsetting the diplomatic balance that his nation had established among the great powers of Europe.[2]

As part of the materials Muravёv read in St. Petersburg during the few weeks the emperor gave him to prepare for his assignment in Siberia, Middendorf's report convinced him that Siberia's true outlet to the sea was the Amur River—not the Ob, Enisei, and Lena, all of which emptied into the Arctic Ocean.[3] Convinced that Russia must take the Amur's left bank before some adventurous British or American ship captain found the river's outlet to the Pacific and staked a claim,[4] Muravёv thought Nesselrode too timid and Russia too cautious in pursuing her national interest in the Far East. "Whoever commands the mouth of the Amur will rule Siberia, at least as far as Lake Baikal," he wrote in one of the first reports he sent to St. Petersburg after he took up his new post. "We must," he concluded, "explain [to the Chinese] that the common interests of both governments demand that no one except Russia and China ought to have access to the Amur."[5] By way of explanation to the chief of Russia's Admiralty, he added that "a Russian force at the mouth of the Amur will serve to notify foreigners of our claim."[6]

Acting on Muravёv's orders, naval Captain-Lieutenant Gennadi Nevelskoi spent six weeks in the summer of 1849 charting the treacherous waters of the Amur delta before he found a channel that could carry ships from the Pacific through the sandbanks that separated the island of Sakhalin from the mainland and into the heart of Asia. There, more than a year before the statesmen of St. Petersburg decided to do so, Nevelskoi staked Russia's claim by building a small fort that he named Nikolaevsk. Hungry and outnumbered by the American and British ships that sailed that part of the Pacific, Nevelskoi and his small flotilla of lightly armed boats had to stand watch on the Amur for more than two years while Muravёv made the four-thousand-mile journey from Irkutsk to St. Petersburg to plead the case for the Amur's annexation with the emperor. Supported by the emperor's son, the grand duke Aleksandr (but still opposed by Russia's foreign minister), Muravёv eventually won cautious approval to move ahead in the Far East.

"Where once the Russian flag has been unfurled," the emperor now said of Nevelskoi's settlement, "it must never be lowered."[7] Half a century later, those words would be inscribed on a monument to Nevelskoi in Vladivostok, Siberia's far eastern port whose name meant "Mistress of the East."

Muravëv's dedication to claiming the Amur did not distract him from Siberia's domestic affairs or weaken his belief that good government held the key to its development. When he had faced eastern Siberia's assembled dignitaries on his first morning in Irkutsk, he had made clear his intention to remove the most corrupt of Siberia's high officials and break down Speranskii's rigid bureaucracy so that men of talent could rise quickly to the top. Silent and unsmiling, like a general officer inspecting new troops on the parade ground, Muravëv had passed from one man to the next that morning, stopping at each for only a moment before moving on. Not once had he offered his hand in greeting, nor had he even bowed. In the next room, he had accepted the traditional offering of bread and salt from the city's merchants, again without saying a word. In less than twenty minutes, he had turned on his heel and left. As he did so, his adjutant had stayed behind to announce that the governor-general required all senior officials to meet with him in his private office.[8]

"Where's Mangazeev?" Muravëv asked as he turned to face the assembled dignitaries. Thought to be one of eastern Siberia's most powerful men and one who, as head of the office that dealt with eastern Siberia's gold mines, had had the foresight to assure himself of support in St. Petersburg by transferring several goldfields worked by the treasury into the hands of a few well-connected aristocrats, Mangazeev stepped forward and bowed. "I hope," Muravëv stated flatly as he acknowledged his greeting, "that you will not continue to serve here."[9] Then, he relieved several other high-ranking influence peddlers, demanding that each resign that very day.[10] To replace them, he began to bring in well-educated young men from all over Russia to train the first corps of responsible government officials Siberia had ever seen, and he promised these new men greater opportunities than they could find in Russia's European provinces or even in the capital.[11] Although ability counted for much in Muravëv's eyes, he valued honesty even more. Guided by his integrity and his demand for efficient government, men of modern views and sound vision were beginning to move Siberia toward the modern age even before Nevelskoi staked out Russia's claim to the Amur.

In the meantime, Muravëv faced other problems, especially with the

English commercial agents who were trading in Siberia's eastern lands. "The activities of English [private citizens] in all corners of the globe," he wrote at one point, "are all directed toward realizing the interests of Great Britain,"[12] and the efforts of several Englishmen to explore the Amur lands made him more certain than ever that Russia must dare to seize them before it was too late. But Russia's statesmen were looking west, not east. At that moment, Austria and Prussia were struggling to unify Germany, France was being transformed into the Second Empire, and the tensions among Russia, France, and the Ottoman Empire were mounting in the Near East. As Russia went to war with the Ottoman Empire on October 4, 1853, the Far East was very far away. Then, when France and England joined the Ottoman Empire in the Crimean War against Russia six weeks later, Muravëv's warnings took on new and urgent meaning. Even Nesselrode had to admit that if the defenses of Okhotsk and Kamchatka should fail to stand against the frigates of the Royal Navy, Russia might have to face the British along the Amur's entire two-thousand-mile length.

Nesselrode's long-standing warnings about the dangers of angering England and France now seemed irrelevant, and St. Petersburg's policy makers began to shift their support to Muravëv. The time had come, the emperor now said, for the Russians "to set sail upon the Amur," although he asked "that there be no smell of gunpowder" accompanying their advance.[13] Confessing to his brother that "everything is turning out better than I had dared to hope,"[14] Muravëv began to build an armada of boats and barges in the winter and spring of 1854 along the banks of the Shilka, a tributary of the Amur that flowed through Russian territory. By early May, geographers, geologists, mining engineers, nearly a thousand soldiers, and a battery of artillery stood ready, together with all the horses, cattle, bread, and vodka rations needed for the long river voyage to the Amur's mouth.

On May 13, Muravëv and his men heard Mass before the icon of the Virgin of Albazin that had once occupied a place of honor in the fortress that the Russians had abandoned to the Chinese in 1689. Now vowing to return it to its proper place, Muravëv ordered his men to advance, leading the way in the sixty-horsepower *Argun*, the first steamer ever to sail the Amur. For the moment, he knew that his expedition was safe. The recently begun Tai Ping Rebellion had left the Chinese government with no troops to spare for reinforcing the small garrisons that guarded their northern frontiers, and the slowness of communications in the days before the telegraph and telephone meant that the British would not get word of their whereabouts before they reached the

Amur's mouth.[15] In the meantime, a two-thousand-mile voyage through some of eastern Siberia's most spectacular terrain lay ahead.

In less than a week, the Russians reached the ruins of Albazin. When the Chinese protested that they could not continue past the fortress of Aigun that lay farther down the Amur, Muravëv replied that he had orders to defend the river's mouth against the British and French, and they, knowing they could not bar his way, stood aside. As his flotilla neared the Amur's mouth, Muravëv learned that British and French frigates had been sighted not far away from several Russian warships that had gathered just to the south in De Castries Bay. Uncertain where his enemies might decide to attack, the governor-general loaded a third of his men onto the Russian warships and sent them to reinforce the small garrison at Petropavlovsk on the Kamchatka peninsula, and then ordered the rest to guard the outpost that Nevelskoi had built at Nikolaevsk. Now Russia had the foothold for which Muravëv had worked for nearly a decade. When his reinforcements drove off an Anglo-French naval attack against Petropavlovsk two weeks later, the world knew that Russia could defend her claim. After an Allied attack against Nikolaevsk failed in the summer of 1855, the great powers of the Western world knew that Russia was on the Amur to stay.[16]

In the meantime, Muravëv's vision had captured the imagination of an American who had formed a partnership as a gold-dust broker with the brother-in-law of Ulysses S. Grant almost half a world away in San Francisco.[17] "I had already fixed in my own mind upon the river Amoor as the destined channel by which American commercial enterprise was to penetrate the obscure depths of northern Asia and open a new world to trade and civilization," Perry McDonough Collins explained some years later as he recalled his state of mind in 1855. With the blessings of Russia's ambassador to Washington, D.C., and bearing his government's appointment as "Commercial Agent of the United States at the Amoor River," the energetic Collins had set off in search of profit and adventure the next spring.[18] After meeting with Muravëv at Central Europe's Marienbad spa, where the general was taking the waters for a stomach ailment, Collins traveled across the Russian Empire to Chita, by then a fledgling center of eastern Siberian trade, where he spent several weeks in the spring of 1857 waiting for the ice to break up so that he could take the soundings needed to learn whether the Amur's shallow waters could support steamboat traffic.

While he waited, Collins began to dream of connecting Chita by railroad to Irkutsk, so as to funnel the goods and raw materials of Siberia's hinterland to the Amur and the outside world.[19] Few had been so bold in their vision since the days of Peter the Great. And, like Tsar Peter, Collins had little sense of the obstacles that would stand in the way of anyone who embarked on such a venture. Still, his daring proposal to organize an "Amoor Railroad Company" that would bring twenty thousand men to Siberia to build a railroad showed that Muravëv had been well ahead of his time in understanding the importance of the Amur lands.[20] As an outlet to the Pacific, the Amur River could transform Siberia into a new El Dorado for traders from America and Europe.

Even though Americans like Collins regarded them as the Amur's new proprietors, the Russians still had to secure China's formal agreement to their claim. Certain that the Chinese had no means to resist, Muravëv went to Aigun to discuss the annexation in the spring of 1858 and insisted that Russia must have the entire left bank of the Amur, from the Argun River to its mouth. For the moment, he was willing to leave the right bank as far as the Ussuri River in Chinese hands. Beyond that, he agreed to consider the rest of the Amur's right bank common property until the two powers could agree upon a frontier. With two Russian gunboats sitting at anchor in the river just beyond Aigun's walls, the Chinese agreed to Muravëv's terms and signed the Treaty of Aigun on May 16, 1858. Muravëv then withdrew his men and gunboats a few miles upstream to the mouth of the Zeia River, where he held a Mass at the place where the city of Blagoveshchensk would rise in the years ahead. "We have not labored in vain, for the Amur now belongs to Russia!" his order of the day told his soldiers. "Russia gives you her gratitude," he added. "Long Live [the newly crowned] Emperor Alexander II and may these newly acquired lands flourish under his rule!"[21]

Time would fulfill that wish. In half a century, the spot upon which Muravëv's men celebrated Mass that day became a city of seventy thousand. Six hundred miles downstream, where the Ussuri flowed into the Amur and where China's claim to the river's right bank ended, the Russian settlement of Khabarovsk grew into another city of fifty thousand during the same period of time. Founded farther south just a few months before Muravëv ended his reign as eastern Siberia's governor-general in 1860, Vladivostok become the headquarters of Russia's Pacific Fleet and Siberia's largest city by 1900, even though it continued to have the unfinished quality that so commonly marks the urban centers of a frontier land in transition.

Muravëv had twenty more years to live when he left Siberia, but none left in which to serve Russia. Times were changing, and the dictatorial methods that had helped to take the Amur and bring eastern Siberia to heel did not fit well into the Russia of Alexander II, where modern methods of government were beginning to replace the caprice of absolute governors. Given the title of Count Amurskii by the emperor in honor of his achievements, Muravëv lived in retirement in Paris while others developed the lands he had opened along the Amur. Before he was laid to rest in Paris's Montmartre Cemetery in 1881, he had seen the focus of eastern Siberia's life and economy shift toward the new centers of Blagoveshchensk, Khabarovsk, and Vladivostok he had founded in its south and east. Ironically, the most dramatic epitaph to the new Siberia of Muravëv-Amurskii was penned not by one of his followers but by the anarchist Mikhail Bakunin, who had spent nearly four years as an exile in Siberia in the late 1850s. "Through the Amur [Siberia] was linked to the Pacific and is no longer a wilderness without an outlet," Bakunin wrote to his friend and fellow revolutionary Aleksandr Herzen. "Siberia was transplanted by Muravëv to another site," he added. "It is coming closer to America and Europe than to Russia, it is being ennobled and humanized. Siberia—a blessed country of the future, a land of renewal!"[22]

So far as his description went, Bakunin spoke the truth, but he ignored Siberia's darker side. By the middle of the 1870s, more than fifteen thousand men and women were being sent to serve sentences of *katorga* and *ssylka* there every year, with at least a third of that number being wives who followed condemned husbands, husbands who accompanied convicted wives, and children who went with their imprisoned parents.[23] As Siberia drew closer to the West, the fate of these "unfortunates" stirred the hearts of sympathetic men and women in other countries as never before. How terrible, they asked, was life in the mines or years lived in banishment? Some, like the Bible-thumping English clergyman Henry Lansdell, thought that prisoners lived better in Siberia than in England during the 1870s and insisted that their rations were more plentiful and the labor less hard.[24] But others judged the Siberian system to be so brutal as to be unworthy of any nation aspiring to membership in the world's community of great powers. None made that point with greater force than George Kennan, an American telegraphist and journalist whose journey through Siberia produced one of the most memorable accounts of Siberian prisoners and prisons ever written.

24

Kennan's Journey

On June 10, 1885, two police officers approached a pair of foreigners in the center of Perm, still Russia's European gateway to Siberia as it had been in the days of Ermak and the Stroganovs.

"Will you permit me to inquire who you are?" the younger of the two asked.

"Certainly," the visitors replied. "We are American travelers."

"Where are you going?"

"To Siberia," the Americans answered.

"Allow me to inquire what you are going to Siberia for?" the officer went on, his politeness not entirely masking his suspicion.

"We are going there to travel," was the noncommittal reply.

The conversation continued. Polite, inquisitive, and suspicious, the stern representatives of Imperial Russia's forces of order had no intention of allowing their unwanted guests to escape, especially since one carried an artist's sketch pad and both had been seen in the vicinity of the city prison earlier that day. The Americans, the senior officer stated in a manner that permitted no argument, must consider themselves under arrest while the police accompanied them to their hotel and examined their passports.

Thus it happened that George Kennan, whose integrity had won him an appointment as a special liaison between the White House and the rest of the world when President Garfield had been dying from an anarchist's bullet, fell into the hands of the tsarist police. "Our passports did not seem, for some reason, to be satisfactory," he later wrote, "but the production of the letter of recommendation [we had obtained] from the Russian Minister of Foreign Affairs," he added, "brought the comedy of errors to an abrupt termination." Then the Perm policemen began to speak of "an unfortunate misunderstanding" and regretted "the lamentable mistake" they had made. "This little adventure interested me as a practical illustration of Russian police methods," Kennan later wrote. But, he continued, "if we were arrested in this way ... for merely looking at the outside of a prison, what probably would happen to us when we should seriously begin our work of investigation?"[1]

Proposing to follow the routes taken by prisoners from European Russia to their destinations in Siberia, Kennan and the artist George Frost had come to Perm with the expectation of writing a defense of the tsarist government's prison policy and exile system. "I went to Russia to study the workings of its penal system, to make the acquaintance of exiles, outcasts, and criminals, and to ascertain how the Government treats its enemies in the prisons and mines of Eastern Siberia," Kennan explained. "I believed," he wrote of his opinions at the time, "that Siberia was not so terrible a country as Americans had always supposed it to be; and that the descriptions of Siberian mines and prisons in the just-published book of the Rev. Henry Lansdell were probably truthful and accurate. I also believed," he added, "that the nihilists, terrorists, and political malcontents generally, who had so long kept Russia in a state of alarm and apprehension, were unreasonable and wrong-headed fanatics."[2] In fact, the reality of Siberia's exile system would prove to be so different from what he had expected that Kennan's journey transformed him into one of the exile system's bitterest critics.

All of the condemned men and women whose paths Kennan followed across Siberia faced a hazardous, exhausting journey. Siberian exile began with an arrest for reasons that might not be known at the time and might never be revealed, for an anonymous denunciation was more than enough to land a man or woman in prison on suspicion of having committed a "political" crime. Once behind bars, such a prisoner might wait for more than a year for a trial, all the while being denied bail and not knowing for certain the crime with which he or she had been charged. The trial itself might well be little more than a formality, for men and women accused of political crimes almost never were tried by juries. In those days, an appearance before a tribunal, a judge, or some other high official was all that was needed to satisfy the requirements for a legal conviction. Then the prisoner would be sent to the city of Kazan, which by the 1880s had become the convicts' gateway to Siberia.[3] At Kazan, convicts boarded special trains and barges that carried them and any wives, husbands, or children traveling with them to Tiumen, a town of not quite twenty thousand that stood on the edge of Siberia, just beyond the Urals' eastern slopes.[4]

Designed to hold about eight hundred prisoners under uncomfortable conditions, Tiumen transit prison was bursting with 1,741 men and women when Kennan and Frost arrived in the summer of 1885.[5] "They all were dressed from head to foot in a costume of gray, consisting of a visorless Scotch cap, a shirt and trousers of coarse homespun linen, and a long gray overcoat with one or two diamond-shaped patches of black or yellow cloth sewn upon the back between the shoulders," Kennan wrote.[6] Kept separate from the men, the women at Tiumen prison dressed in similar fashion except that a shawl replaced the cap and a garment that one prisoner described as "a chemise of coarse cloth and a skirt reaching to the ankles" took the place of the men's shirts and trousers.[7] Like the men, they, too, had become victims of their jailers' tyranny and officials' whims by the time they reached Tiumen.

Inside Tiumen prison's main building, Kennan found 160 men crowded into a cell that measured thirty-five by twenty-five feet. "Down the center of the room, and occupying about half its width, ran a sleeping bench—a wooden platform 12 feet wide and 30 feet long, supported at a height of 2 feet from the floor by stout posts," he reported. "Each longitudinal half of this low platform," he went on, "sloped a little, roof-wise, from the center, so that when the prisoners slept upon it in two closely packed traverse rows, their heads in the middle were a few inches higher than their feet at the edges." Since these benches could not hold all the men crowded into the cell, the others slept on the rough floor, stifled by the foul air that marked all Siberian prisons. "Every cubic foot of it had apparently been respired over and over again until it did not contain an atom of oxygen," Kennan wrote of the air inside the prison's barracks. "It was laden with fever germs from the unventilated hospital wards, fetid odors from diseased human lungs and unclean human bodies, and the stench arising from unemptied excrement buckets."[8]

Although female convicts lived in less crowded, cleaner, and better-ventilated quarters at Tiumen, they could enjoy these very modest advantages only as long as they remained healthy, for men and women had to endure the same wretched conditions in the prison hospital. "Never before in my life had I seen faces so white, haggard, and ghastly as those that lay on the gray pillows in these cells," Kennan wrote of the hospital wards at Tiumen. "Both men and women," he added, "seemed to be not only desperately sick, but hopeless and heartbroken."⁹ At a time when fewer than one prisoner in twenty-five died in the prisons of France and Austria and one out of seventy in England, a third of the fifteen thousand or so prisoners who passed through Tiumen prison each year did not live to continue their journey. Tiumen's death rate in the 1870s and 1880s was twice that of London during the Great Plague of 1665 and higher, even, than the death rate of the bubonic plague that decimated a quarter of Europe in the fourteenth century.¹⁰

Some of the convicts sent on from Tiumen traveled no more than a few hundred miles to the north or south, but most were sent farther east to Tomsk on convict barges that privately owned passenger steamers towed along a U-shaped water route that followed the Tura, Tobol, Irtysh, and Ob rivers. A yellow-and-black floating prison, according to Kennan's description, each barge had a large cage of iron mesh for men and a smaller one for women and children on the main deck, with sleeping platforms set on the deck below.¹¹ Usually crowding six to eight hundred people onto each 250-foot barge for a journey that lasted about ten days, the authorities moved between eight and ten thousand prisoners from Tiumen to Tomsk in this way every year during the 1870s and 1880s.¹²

Impressed by the cleanliness of one of these barges when he saw the prisoners board it at Tiumen, Kennan thought that it "suggested a recently vacated wild-beast cage" by the time it reached Tomsk. "In the gray light of a cloudy day," he confessed, "its dark *kameras* [cells], with their small grated port-holes, muddy floors, and polluted ammoniacal atmosphere, chilled and depressed me."¹³ A young noblewoman being sent to Siberia for spreading socialist propaganda among the peasants complained of the coarseness, cruelty, and "disregard for the rights of body and soul" aboard such barges. Even the best quarters on the barge seemed to her "a horrid, foul hole,"¹⁴ and others of humbler origin and less refined tastes found them no better. At some points along their route, the convicts passed empty lands, where a dozen wooden huts became a town and aboriginal natives happily traded fish for bits of bread and shreds of cheap tobacco. "The deathly stillness, the absence of any sign of life at this awakening season of the year, [and] the piercing cold," a condemned revolutionary wrote after making the journey in June, "had an uncanny and depressing effect." A hundred years later, some of the most isolated of these lands would become the oil and natural gas fields of Samotlor and Urengoi. In Kennan's time, they seemed to be what one of Russia's first Marxist revolutionaries called the "waste places of the earth."[15]

At Tomsk, guards herded bargeloads of exiles into a transit prison that reminded Kennan of a settlement on the American frontier. Except for several sheds that had cotton sheeting for sides, Tomsk prison was built of logs, its low-lying barracks festering with "the same inconceivably foul air, the same sickening odors, and the same throngs of gray-coated convicts" that he had found at Tiumen.[16] The three hastily built large sheds that housed convict families were even worse. "The first to which we came was surrounded by a foul ditch half full of filth, into which water or urine was dripping here and there from the floor," Kennan reported. "The floor of unmatched boards had given way here and there, and the inmates had used the holes as places into which to throw refuse and pour slops and excrement."[17] From the end of May until winter closed down river travel at the end of October, Tomsk transit prison received nearly twice as many prisoners every week as the prisons farther east could accommodate.[18] To relieve the massive overcrowding that developed by the end of each summer, the authorities at Tomsk continued to send convicts overland to Irkutsk long after ice had shut down the river route from Tiumen.

Just over a thousand miles east of Tomsk stood Irkutsk, the point from which prisoners were dispersed to their places of banishment or hard labor in eastern Siberia. Almost all "unfortunates" in the days before the railroad had to make the journey from Tomsk to Irkutsk on foot, usually in groups of three or four hundred that covered about 330 miles every month. Depending upon the season, the infirm, sick, and "politicals" of noble rank rode in the rough two-wheeled carts that accompanied each convoy, while the rest of the prisoners stumbled along, their chains and fetters dragging them into the mud and snow or raising clouds of lung-clogging dust. Whoever fell sick or was hurt along the way had to wait until the convoy reached one of the prison lazarets that appeared every 75 to 150 miles along their route. Those whose illnesses or injuries could not wait for treatment cured themselves or died along the way.[19]

At intervals of twenty-five to forty miles, an *étape*, or guardhouse, punctuated the exiles' route, with a halfway shelter, or *poluétape*, set midway between the two. Like the cabins of the convict barges that plied the rivers between Tiumen and Tomsk, *étapes* were painted a dirty yellow, the color reserved for all things connected with prisons and exiles in Siberia. Built of logs and rough boards that had absorbed the filth and refuse of decades and with windows that had been nailed shut long before, these buildings by Kennan's time had become festering storehouses of disease. Every night, guards locked their prisoners into these crude shelters that had no toilets except for several large, uncovered wooden tubs. By morning, "the stench was truly unbearable," one convict later wrote. "In a word," he concluded, "this really was like Hell."[20]

Getting enough food on the journey from Tomsk to Irkutsk remained the main concern of Siberian convicts, for the Russian government never made effective arrangements for feeding its prisoner convoys. Prisoners generally had to buy their rations from peasant women who gathered at each day's stopping place to sell coarse rye bread, meat and fish pies, hard-boiled eggs, milk, and salted cucumbers, but these people had no way of knowing how many hungry men, women, and children would appear on any given day. Nor could the government estimate what the price of the food offered for sale would be at any particular time. Every second day, convoy commanders passed out twenty kopeks in copper coins to each lower-class convict and thirty to each aristocrat, but that sum sometimes could not buy even two loaves of black bread if crops had been bad or if food was in short supply for some other reason. At every town, village, or hamlet, the poorest prisoners begged for anything the villagers could spare them to eat. "They would station themselves before a hut and start a pitiful song," one eyewitness remembered. "Then the Siberian women would throw out pieces of bread to them."[21] At other times, convicts with extra money tried to bribe their guards to buy them food, tobacco, and vodka. "If one hand washes the other," an old peasant saying went, "then both will come out clean."[22]

Convicts' long-standing practice of organizing themselves into mutual aid societies called *artels* made it possible for them to negotiate with their guards to better their lot from time to time. Each artel, Kennan explained, "exercises all of its functions in secret and strives to attain its ends, first, by enforcing solidarity and joint action on the part of all its members and, secondly, by deceiving, outwitting, or bribing the officers and soldiers with whom it has to deal."[23] An artel could arrange for prisoners' fetters to be removed at night, for exhausted convicts to ride, for floggers to wield their whips lightly, and for extra rations of food, tobacco, and vodka. In return for such favors, an artel could guarantee that no one would try to escape along specified segments of the route. Disobedience to an artel's decisions meant death to any offender, no matter where he might take refuge or how far he might flee. Whoever betrayed this body politic of the convict world asked to be placed in solitary confinement rather than live among his fellow prisoners because he knew that at some moment another convict would leap upon him to carry out an artel's sentence of death.

With chains jangling, feet shuffling, and bodies aching, convicts eventually reached the transit prison at Irkutsk from which they were sent to their final destinations. Irkutsk transit prison was less crowded than those at Tiumen and Tomsk, and was better lighted and not so foul, but it was in poor condition nonetheless. "It seemed to me an extremely dreary, gloomy, and neglected place," Kennan wrote of his first visit there. "Although I held my breath almost to the point of suffocation rather than take such terribly polluted air into my lungs," he added after a visit to its hospital wards, "I came out feeling faint, sick, and giddy."[24]

Compared to those who had been sentenced to *ssylka*, the lives of men and women condemned to *katorga* followed a very different course when they left Irkutsk transit prison. Some six hundred miles to the southeast lay the Nerchinsk Silver-Mining District, spread over several thousand square miles of rough terrain, and about three hundred miles farther north of its center at Nerchinskii Zavod lay another chain of mines and prisons for convicts who worked gold placers along the Kara River. The first and worst of the Kara valley's prisons was a scattered collection of buildings set in marshy ground at Ust-Kara near the junction of the Kara and Shilka rivers. "We ascended two or three steps encrusted with an indescribable coating of filth and ice an inch and a half thick, and entered through a heavy plank door, a long, low, and very dark corridor, whose broken and decaying floor felt wet and slippery to the feet, and whose atmosphere, although warm, was very damp and saturated with the strong peculiar odor that is characteristic of Siberian prisons," Kennan wrote after his visit there during the fall of 1885.[25] "It is so unlike any other bad smell in the world that I hardly know with what to compare it," he confessed as he searched his memory for words to transfer the reality of the prison's stench to paper. "To unaccustomed senses," he concluded, "it seems so saturated with foulness and disease as to be almost insupportable."[26]

There was worse to come when Kennan visited Ust-Kara's cells. "We stepped across the threshold into a room about 24 feet long, 22 feet wide, and 8 feet high, which contained 29 convicts," he began in an account that noted that "the walls were blotched in hundreds of places with dull red blood-stains where the convicts had crushed bedbugs." Except for the ubiquitous sleeping platforms, the room had no furniture, and the brick oven could be used only for heat and not for cooking. "When the door was locked for the night each one of these 29 prisoners would have, for 8 or 10 hours' consumption, about as much air as would be contained in a packing-box 5 feet square and 5 feet high," Kennan explained. "If there was any way in which a single cubic foot of fresh air could get into that cell after the doors had been closed for the night," he concluded, "I failed to discover it."[27]

Three pounds of black bread, a handful of barley, a small quantity of cheap tea, and about four ounces of meat that, when cut into dice-sized pieces, reminded Kennan of "small refuse scraps intended for use as soap-grease" made up the daily rations at Kara prison.[28] A few years before Kennan's journey, the Reverend Lansdell had pointed out that such rations were better than those given to prisoners in England,[29] but the men and women who worked the Kara mines also faced heavier labor than did the inmates of British prisons. Ten to twenty feet of clay and stones had to be dug away to reach the region's gold-bearing sand, which then had to be shoveled into large iron hoppers, mixed with water, and run through a series of shallow inclined sluices to trap the particles of gold. Although even the hardiest workers left the goldfields in privately owned mines before the end of September, Kennan found Kara's convicts still struggling against the ice and snow at the beginning of November 1885, their leg irons and chains still in place, while their cossack guards huddled around a small fire over which they tried to boil water for tea.

Struggling to keep their bearings as they went, Kennan and Frost began their journey from the prisons of the Kara valley to the Nerchinsk Silver-Mining District just as the first snows began to fall. "There was hardly a sign of life or vegetation except in the shallow haystack-dotted valleys," Kennan remembered. As the two Americans passed Aleksandrovskii Zavod, the countryside "looked like a boundless ocean suddenly frozen solid in the midst of a tremendous Cape Horn gale," and, as the mines at Algachi came into view, they reminded Kennan of "a little collection of floating driftwood, caught in the trough of the sea at the moment when the tremendous billows were suddenly turned to snow and ice."[30] The prison mine at Algachi was the one Kennan had chosen to measure against the ones he had just left at Kara.

Kennan's first impressions of Algachi prison gave him little ground for optimism, and his descent into the mines only deepened his disquiet. Surrounded by perpetual permafrost, Algachi's convicts worked in air that retained barely enough oxygen to sustain a candle flame and seemed never to rise above freezing. From these frost-filled subterranean chambers, no man took more than ten pounds of ore in a day, and many did not work at all because the shafts were too small to accommodate them all. "Probably not more than one-third of these men, and certainly not more than half of them, were actually engaged in hard labor," Kennan reported. "The rest lived, month after month, in enforced idleness" in what he lamented as a terrible waste of manpower and human spirit.[31]

Together with the nearby Pokrovskii mine, Algachi yielded about four hundred tons of ore in a year, of which one pound in five was lead and less than one out of every five hundred was silver. A believer in the power of American ingenuity to solve problems on the spot with the materials at hand, Kennan was appalled.

"Why don't you provide yourself with suitable iron machinery, furnish your laborers with improved modern tools, set up steam-pumping, hoisting, and ventilating apparatus, and work your mines as they ought to be worked?" he asked the engineer who escorted him.

"Do you realize what iron costs here?" the engineer replied. "We can't afford to put in iron machinery."

"But," Kennan said, "isn't there iron ore in this vicinity?"

"Yes," the engineer replied, "but it has never been gotten out."

"Why don't you get it out, set up smelting furnaces, and make your iron here on the ground where you needed it?" Kennan persisted. "More than half of your convicts lie constantly idle in their cells—why don't you utilize their labor?"

"We can't open an iron mine without a permit from St. Petersburg," the engineer explained, apparently amazed that anyone could not comprehend the magnitude of the problem.

"Then why don't the proper authorities give you a permit?" Kennan replied. "I don't see how the present state of affairs can be profitable to anybody."[32]

In the passive resistance to decision making that perpetually paralyzed the Russian bureaucracy, American practicality—the awesome force that had opened the North American continent, laid the largest railroad system in the world, bridged the world's oceans with telegraph cables, and invented thousands of the instruments that shaped the modern world—had met its match half a world away from the blast furnaces of Pittsburgh and the oil fields of Oklahoma. "His only reply," Kennan later wrote of the official with whom he had spoken, "was a shrug of the shoulders which I interpreted to mean either that he did not know or that it was not his business."[33]

Even though they offended his sense of efficiency—a word that does not exist in Russian even to this day—Kennan concluded that "as places of punishment the Nerchinsk mines did not seem to me so terrible as they are often represented to be," and he pronounced them "less prejudicial to health than unbroken confinement in a dirty, overcrowded, and foul-smelling convict prison."[34] Some convicts disputed that assessment. Even after he had spent more than a year in dungeons, prisons, and *étapes* farther west, Lev Deich, a Marxist revolutionary whose path nearly crossed Kennan's in the fall of 1885, found the prison at Nerchinsk a truly awful place. "I shall never in my life forget the picture that prison presented," Deich wrote in his memoirs. "A circle of the Dantean Inferno was the only possible comparison."[35]

Kennan left Siberia in March 1886, convinced that the exile system he had expected to justify was the most repressive in the Western world. All of its victims, and especially revolutionaries like Deich, won Kennan's sympathy. "I have not a word to say in defense of their crimes," he wrote, "but I can fully understand, nevertheless, how an essentially good and noble-natured man may become a terrorist when, as in Russia, he is subjected to absolutely intolerable outrages and indignities and has no peaceful or legal means of redress."[36] What had stirred these revolutionaries to action, Kennan insisted, was a government that had "first set the example of lawlessness in Russia . . . treating as a criminal every citizen who dared to ask why or wherefore."[37] For such "politicals," Siberia held its own special terrors. The Decembrists and Dostoevskii had already discovered some of these, but many of the men and women who followed them to Siberia during the half century before the Russian Revolution found that even more painful sufferings awaited them.

25

The "Politicals"

Combined with Kennan's observations, the memoirs of the men and women who survived terms of penal servitude tell us that "politicals" sentenced to Siberian *katorga* faced particularly painful and hopeless lives. Forced to toil among hardened felons who despised them for not having a true criminal past, young men and women who had lived in the world of ideas in the comfort of Russia's largest cities entered a world more violent and unpredictable than any they had ever imagined. In an ironic parallel with those Dostoevskian characters who had thought themselves able to live outside the law, revolutionaries condemned to live among thieves and murderers now had to learn to survive without the law's protection.

While "politicals" condemned to *katorga* struggled to find places of safety in the violent world around them, those sentenced to *ssylka* fought against Siberia's isolation. Not until their numbers had grown large enough for them to form their own groups within Siberia's exile communities at the very end of the nineteenth century did these "politicals" begin to find relief from the intellectual loneliness that had tormented earlier revolutionary exiles. Yet the company of other revolutionaries created new problems in Siberia's communities of exiles as the twentieth century opened. Disputes about the theory and practice of the revolution that none of them had ever seen often drove former comrades apart and deepened their isolation. Iulii Martov, at one time a comrade of

Lenin and a man of real brilliance when it came to revolutionary theory, lived a life of torment in Turukhansk partly because he could tolerate departures from revolutionary "truth" no more easily than he could forgive political betrayal.[1] "The saddest thing is how, under the conditions of exile and prison, a man reveals himself in all his petty characteristics," the Bolshevik Iakov Sverdlov once told his wife. "The comrade with whom I stayed turned out to be impossible in personal relations," he wrote of the man who would later be known as Stalin. "We had to stop seeing and speaking to each other."[2] There seemed no end to the divisions that could arise over questions of revolutionary tactics with which no one had had any practical experience. "May God save us," exclaimed Vladimir Ulianov, who later ruled the Soviet Union under the name of Lenin, "from 'exile colonies' and exile 'dramas'!"[3]

More than two out of every five of those banished to Siberia for revolutionary activities during the last quarter of the nineteenth century were students, and a growing number were women, the most dangerous of whom were sent to the terrible mine-prison at Ust-Kara that Kennan had thought so appalling.[4] There, beginning in 1880, the daughters of generals and great lords lived with children of peasants and village priests, all of them united by their common dedication to revolution and their belief that assassination could become a prime instrument of political action. One of the women at Ust-Kara had tried to kill the governor of the Transbaikal. In an armed robbery that had turned sour only at the very last moment, another had nearly succeeded in stealing a million rubles from a branch office of the Imperial Treasury, and still another had helped to assassinate the emperor Alexander II in March 1881.

Perhaps best known among the women of Ust-Kara was Mariia Kovalevskaia, the daughter of a prominent nobleman and sister of a famous political economist, who had devoted more than a decade of her life to serving the lower classes before she had been sentenced to thirteen years of penal servitude at the age of thirty. The authorities had separated Kovalevskaia from her daughter when they sent her to the Kara mines, and they had exiled her husband to the western Siberian town of Minusinsk, even though he had taken no part in her revolutionary activities. "In any other country she would have played a distinguished part," one of Kovalevskaia's comrades later wrote.[5] In Russia, the authorities were determined to keep her in prison.

Kovalevskaia arrived at Kara ready to fight against the system that had sent her there. Complaints poured from her pen, and, while she awaited the official action that never came, she broke windows and smashed furniture in anger. "Whether the matter were really serious or a comparative trifle, whether the offense was committed by a functionary of high position or by the meanest underling," one of her revolutionary comrades explained, "her determination knew no compromise."[6] Whenever she found occasion to protest, wherever she discovered room for action, Kovalevskaia confronted the men who represented the system she despised. She therefore became one of the first to join the hunger strike that history would record as the "Kara tragedy" after it caused the deaths of three women and two men in November 1889.

In her determination to protest, Kovalevskaia found a close ally in Nadezhda Sigida, a woman several years younger who had grown up in the southern port city of Taganrog. A dedicated teenage revolutionary, Sigida had been arrested at the age of twenty-one for running a clandestine printing press and had been condemned to eight years in Kara's mines. There she joined Kovalevskaia and several other women in a hunger strike to protest the authorities' mistreatment of one of their comrades. When their strike had no effect, Sigida insulted (or struck, according to some accounts) Kara's commandant, who sentenced her to a hundred lashes despite the prison doctor's warning that her hunger strike had left her too weak to survive.

Of all the punishments they faced in Siberia, Russia's revolutionaries feared flogging the most, not only because of its pain but also because, at some point before the whip ceased to fall, the victim almost invariably lost all self-control and begged for mercy. Anton Chekhov, Russia's master teller of short stories, who once witnessed a flogging on Siberia's prison island of Sakhalin, never forgot the scene. "His teeth were chattering, his face yellow and damp, and his eyes were wandering," he wrote of a man who had just received nearly a hundred strokes with the fearsome three-pronged *plet* that had cut away his flesh at every stroke. "When they gave him the medicinal drops in a glass of water," he added, "he convulsively bit the glass."[7]

Rather than face the lash at Kara, Sigida took poison. Then Kovalevskaia and two other women protested her death by killing themselves in the same way, after which twenty male "politicals" tried to follow their example, even though only two actually managed to take enough morphine to end their lives.[8] In the end, their protest went without notice. "Everything remained as of old," a prisoner who had not shared their attempt at self-destruction wrote some years later. "Only we ourselves were as though transformed by the tragic events that had taken place. A heavy weight seemed to oppress us," he added. "Most of us still suffered acutely from shaken nerves."[9]

At least in a symbolic sense, that weight was about to be lifted when the death of the stern Emperor Alexander III and the accession of his weak-willed son Nicholas II in 1894 gave Russia's radicals their first real chance for revolutionary action in a decade. Freed at last from the heavy-handed repression of a regime that had confined them to the realm of small deeds and timid hopes for the better part of fifteen years, these young men and women began to move among their country's newly born industrial proletariat to build the movement that would eventually overthrow the Romanovs' autocracy. Hesitantly at first and then more resolutely as the century reached its end, the young men and women who had dedicated their lives to the revolutionary cause began to shape the working folk of Russia's cities into the standard-bearers of class struggle. Beginning in the Lithuanian city of Vilno, then in Odessa, Kiev, Moscow, and finally St. Petersburg, factory workers laid down their tools and took to the streets to demand shorter hours and better wages. For the first time in history, Russian politics had entered the arena of mass action.

As the dozens of revolutionaries of the 1880s grew into the hundreds of the 1890s, the emperor's ministers, governors, chiefs of police, and hundreds of minor officials began to wield an old weapon with new sophistication and greater energy as they sent into exile men and women whose continued presence might be "prejudicial to public order" or "incompatible with public tranquillity." This practice of exile "by administrative process" remained one of Romanov Russia's last and most vicious instruments of tyranny, for it destroyed the lives of people who were innocent of any wrongdoing as well as those whose quest for social justice had led them to take up political views of which their government did not approve. Some of their stories were among the saddest of any in the history of Siberia's exile system.

26

"By Administrative Process"

Pure chance and pure meanness ruined the lives of many innocent men and women during the half century before the Revolution of 1917. Almost everyone in Russia knew of someone victimized "by administrative process," although few spoke about it too loudly because doing so could cause the teller to be sent into exile too. According to some of Kennan's investigations, one man was banished "by administrative process" to a remote northern village in Iakutsk province because the police accused him of keeping a "dangerous" and "pernicious" manuscript in his lodgings. A few months later, one of Russia's most widely circulated magazines published the manuscript with the censors' full approval, but the man remained in exile nonetheless. The authorities exiled the well-known novelist Vladimir Korolenko to Siberia "by administrative process" because of a mistake so obvious that the government later had to order his liberation. And still another "unfortunate" found himself in Siberia because a local police official worried (as it was later reported) that he might be guilty of having at one time had "an intention to put himself into an illegal situation."[1]

Mistakes were as numerous as the men who possessed the power to make them, and their errors were compounded because the accused had no defense or right of appeal. An Imperial High Commission that reviewed hundreds of cases of men and women exiled "by administrative process" found in 1880 that at least half of them were so obviously innocent that they should be released at once, and, when the men, women, and children who followed condemned spouses and parents are taken into account, it seems that as many as two out of every three Russians who crossed the Urals into Siberian exile during the last years of the nineteenth century may have been guilty of no wrongdoing at all![2]

All this reminded Kennan of the *Gulistan,* in which the twelfth-century Persian poet Saadi wrote of a fox who, when asked why he was fleeing in terror, replied that he had heard that the authorities had decided to conscript a camel. When assured that he looked nothing like a camel, Saadi's fox insisted that, in a world where all officials were tyrants, it made no difference. If someone should point to him and say: "that is a camel," he explained to his questioner, his fate would be sealed. "Who," the panic-stricken fox asked, "would be so solicitous for my relief as to order an inquiry? . . . Before the antidote can be brought from Iraq," he added sagely, "he who has been bitten by the serpent may be dead."[3]

If exile "by administrative process" poisoned the lives of innocent Russians by sending them to Siberia, it also imposed upon Siberia's communities large numbers of undeniably guilty thieves, drunkards, embezzlers, and other people whose character had been judged by the authorities to be flawed in some way. Transported criminals in Turinsk made up a third of the population, while in Ialutorovsk, according to complaints filed by its burghers, exiles outnumbered the town's residents by at least two to one.[4] In eastern Siberia, the townsfolk were fewer and the proportion of forced colonists even larger.[5] Without training, education, or friends, such exiles found it hard to make new lives and often returned to their former criminal trades to keep body and soul together.[6]

Although obviously better off than *katorga* convicts, men and women sent into exile "by administrative process" usually faced spiritually deadening lives of great poverty. Even though a hundred pounds of flour, ten pounds of meat, a dozen eggs, a half pound of sugar, half a "brick" of the cheapest tea, a quart of kerosene, a pound of the poorest tobacco, and the rent for a cheap room cost more than these exiles' monthly government allowance of twenty kopeks a day, the authorities forbade them to use any of their professional skills to help make ends meet.[7] Men and women banished to Siberia could not practice medicine, pharmacology, or law. Nor could they teach, work as photographers, lithographers, librarians, editors, printers, reporters, actors, or booksellers. They could not work for the government (as some exiles had done in earlier times), nor could they build new lives around business or "public activity." When some of the exiles in Akmolinsk complained to the governor-general of western Siberia that they could not feed themselves under such conditions, he suggested only that they try working as hired hands for the local Kirghiz tribesmen. "This," Kennan remarked, "was almost as cruel and insulting as it would be to tell postgraduate students of the John Hopkins University, who had been banished without trial to the mountains of the Sierra Nevada, that if they needed employment they might catch grasshoppers for the Digger Indians."[8]

At every turn, bureaucrats' tunnel vision tormented men and women who had been banished to Siberia. At one point, the frantic mayor of a small county seat in the province of Tobolsk begged a surgeon who had been sent to his town "by administrative process" to operate on his wife, who had suffered an accidental gunshot wound that the local doctor lacked the skill to treat. The exiled physician reminded the mayor that government regulations forbade him to practice medicine under pain of imprisonment, but he eventually succumbed to the man's pleadings and saved his wife's life. The next day, the local police chief threw the surgeon into prison for violating the terms of his banishment and began the convoluted legal proceedings that were officially designated as "The Affair of the Unauthorized Extraction of a Bullet, By the Administrative Exile Nifont Dolgopolov, from the Leg of Madame Balakhina, Wife of the Mayor of Tiukalinsk." When the people of Tiukalinsk protested against Dolgopolov's imprisonment, the police ordered him to be moved to another prison, even though he was by that time suffering from prison typhus. Racked by fever, the poor doctor had to travel more than a hundred miles under military escort in the dead of winter. Only the provincial governor's intervention at the last possible moment spared Dr. Dolgopolov from being transferred to Surgut, a small outpost on the Ob River just south of the Arctic Circle.[9]

Left to the mercy of local Siberian police officers whose integrity remained so open to question that Kennan once wrote, "I should hesitate to meet [some of them] anywhere at night unless I had a revolver,"[10] the victims of exile "by administrative process" lived without the law's protection even though no judge or jury had ever taken their civil rights away. Yet there was another form of exile in Siberia that surpassed even the worst indignities that such "felons in police uniform" could inflict.[11] Again by "administrative process," those upon whom the authorities wanted to inflict a particularly painful form of exile could be sent to live in the remote Iakut settlements that lay along the Arctic Circle. "The Iakuts live in winter [about eight months of every year in that part of the world] in the same buildings with their cattle," a man who had been condemned to such punishment later wrote as he described the filth and stench that permeated every native dwelling.[12] "The food of the Iakuts can hardly be eaten," another exile added. "It is carelessly prepared, without salt, often of tainted materials, and the unaccustomed stomach rejects it with nausea."[13] To become sufficiently "Iakutified" to adapt to the physical demands of such a life demanded great fortitude and greater patience.[14] "Man essentially is very adaptable," a "political" sent to live among the natives in Siberia's northeastern Kolyma lands wrote once he had overcome his initial disgust at their way of life. "At the front, in the trenches, and even in certain hard labor prisons," he continued grimly, "life is incomparably more terrible than in a Iakut cowshed."[15]

Even if men and women condemned to such banishment could grow accustomed to the filth of the Iakuts' hovels, they could never overcome the loneliness of life among them. "In this entire territory that is larger than France there were at that time only about 6,500 inhabitants [of which fewer than a thousand were Russians]," one exile wrote of the days he spent living on the Kolyma frontier. "Cut off from the entire world by some thirteen hundred miles of marshy, mountainous wilderness," he added, "we had been sent to a living death." The winter nights, "the nightmarishly long, long nights," seemed endless. "For a month and a half," he remembered, "you would go to sleep in the dark and get up in the dark," while the cold silence of temperatures that stood at fifty degrees below zero froze all thought of life. "Each night is a year, and a year is an eternity," this man lamented. "Even the memory of the time you spent in prison," he concluded, "seems like a sweet dream."[16]

Cut off from the world they had known, the young men and women who endured this most severe form of exile "by administrative process" became disoriented and despondent. "I have nothing to read—neither books nor newspapers—and I know nothing of what is going on in the world," one of them wrote. "Beyond this," he concluded morosely, "there remains nothing to do but to tie a man to the tail of a wild horse and drive him into the steppe, or chain him to a corpse and leave him to his fate."[17] When mail reached these settlements three or four times a year, it brought what one exile called an "electric shock" that stirred a brief moment of "mad ecstasy." Then, he explained, "the ecstasy would fade and you would fall again into hopeless melancholia."[18] Feeling desperately alone and utterly abandoned, such people frequently killed themselves. When allowed to resume life among Siberia's Russians, many "politicals" returned in broken health.

Yet, in a government in which so many were corrupt servants of the system they served and even the lowliest official could tyrannize others, there were a few cases in which exile proved to be moderately pleasant. Of no one was that more true than of Vladimir Ulianov, whom history remembers as Lenin. Like virtually every important revolutionary who lived between the assassination of Alexander II in 1881 and the Revolution of 1917, Lenin had to endure a term of Siberian banishment, but, unlike so many of his comrades, he spent his days east of the Urals in relative comfort. Lenin's days of exile under the tsars show that every system has its exceptions and that tyranny arbitrarily applied may, on occasion, be humanized in an equally arbitrary manner.

27

Lenin in Exile

The great strikes that helped to bring the Russian revolutionary movement back to life in the mid-1890s sent a new wave of "politicals" to Siberia.[1] For many of these revolutionary young men and women, Siberian exile remained a time of physical suffering and mental anguish that condemned them to watching history advance while they remained behind. Yet conditions in Siberia were changing in ways that, for some at least, could make the loneliness of *ssylka* not as desperate as it once had been. For one thing, a few of the colonies of exiled "politicals" had grown large enough by the end of the century so that the men and women sentenced to banishment sometimes found themselves in villages where at least a few others shared their views, and it was sometimes even possible for such people to rent rooms in the same house. Beyond that, the telegraph and railroad had crossed the Urals by then, allowing people to move between Europe and Asia in large numbers. Some of the new wave of "politicals" therefore found Siberia less unpleasant than their predecessors had. One such "fortunate" among the "unfortunates" was Vladimir Ulianov, better known by his revolutionary name of Lenin.

A short, balding young man who was soon to become the founder of the Bolsheviks, Lenin was one of the most dangerous revolutionaries to fall into the hands of the tsarist police at any time before the Revolution of 1917, yet exile in Siberia was far less difficult for him than it might have been. Being a hereditary nobleman and the son of a government official whose rank equaled that of a major general had advantages, even for a sworn enemy of the tsar, and Lenin therefore spent three years in Siberia under conditions very different from those endured by his less fortunate comrades.

Not yet twenty-six at the time of his arrest in December 1895, Lenin traveled to Siberia in his own way and at his own expense. He left St. Petersburg's Preliminary Detention Prison on February 14, 1897, spent three days gathering what he needed for his journey, and stopped at Moscow to bid farewell to his family and friends. His was not to be the agonizing journey by slow stages that had moved men and women condemned to Siberian exile from one *étape* to another along the Great Siberian *trakt* in earlier days. After the Petersburg prison cell in which he had just spent more than a year, the open sky and space of western Siberia gave Lenin a sense of liberation. "Snow and sky—that's all I've seen for the last three days," he wrote to his mother after he had crossed the Ob. "The steppe air is fine indeed," he added. "It's easy to breathe."[2]

Less than two weeks after he left Moscow, Lenin reached Krasnoiarsk, where the railroad ended and where he was to wait for the authorities to decide where he would be sent to serve his sentence. While they discussed his case, he rented a comfortable room in the home of a woman known to be sympathetic to "politicals" and spent the next two months working in the magnificent private library of the noted Siberian merchant and bibliophile Gennadii Iudin to assemble the materials that would help him to write his famous *Development of Capitalism in Russia*.[3] (A decade later, Iudin would sell his rare collection of books about Siberia to the Library of Congress for a fraction of its value in the hope that his gesture of goodwill would help to bind Siberia and the United States together more closely.)

While Lenin worked in Iudin's library, the wheels of Siberia's bureaucratic prison administration began the slow movements that would determine where he would spend his three-year term of banishment. In the same way as any other part of the Russian government, the exile system could be manipulated, and long experience with Russia's official world had taught Lenin's mother the ways of the system that had executed her eldest son in 1887 and was now sending her next one into exile. "My own poor health would make it very difficult for me to travel very far beyond the railroad," she wrote to the governor-general of Irkutsk. If her son could serve out his term in Krasnoiarsk or at least in the southern part of Eniseisk province, where the climate was more moderate and the railroad within easy reach, she explained, it might be possible for her to visit him once the doctors thought her strong enough to make the journey.[4]

In response to Madame Ulianova's petitions, the authorities decided to send Lenin to Shushenskoe, a village of some fifteen hundred dwellers on the upper Enisei in the foothills of the Saian Mountains that divided southern Siberia from Mongolia. There, in what Lenin later called "the Siberian Italy,"[5] he hunted in nearby woods that swarmed with game. From time to time, he went in search of bear, deer, and wild goats in the deeper forests that were only a bit farther away, and he soon acquired a mongrel pup that he hoped to train into a "hunting dog" because, as he wrote to his mother, "it would cost a mint to send one from Russia."[6]

From the moment he reached Siberia until the day he left, Lenin bombarded family and friends back in European Russia with requests that showed he was living at a level far above that of most Siberian exiles:

"I am sorry I did not bring an oilcloth cape," he wrote. "It's really necessary. Could you send one?"

"Have you subscribed to a paper for me?"

"Send me all sorts of catalogues, especially catalogues of secondhand and foreign books."

"I should very much like to have the classics of political economy and philosophy in the original."

"I still have no newspapers. . . . Send me your newspapers after you have read them."

"An alarm clock would be very useful."

"I need some paper, *ruled in squares,*" and so on.[7]

Lenin could not be where he wanted to be—at the center of the revolutionary struggle—nor did he have the newspapers and books of the Western world at his fingertips as when he had lived in European Russia. But he was far from isolated, and he was in constant contact with what was going on in the world he had left behind. Close to a dozen of his Marxist comrades from St. Petersburg had been exiled to villages within a fifty-mile radius of Shushenskoe, and the men sometimes visited each other for as long as a week. They celebrated Christmas and Easter together with dinners and long arguments about how to organize the working men and women of the empire, and during 1897 and 1898 wives, mothers, and fiancées joined them.

In the course of Lenin's thirty-three months in Siberia, he and his revolutionary friends celebrated three weddings. Certainly this was not the life that banished populists and terrorists had endured a generation before. Neither was it the one that terrorists and socialist revolutionaries

THE SIBERIANS

Born in the forests of Siberia's Transbaikal in 1167, Chingis Khan conquered a realm that stretched from China to the steppes of Russia. Three centuries later, the fall of his Mongol empire opened the way for the Russians to begin the conquest of Siberia. (Sovfoto/Eastfoto)

Shamans such as this one from the Altai region helped to link primitive men and women, who worshiped the spirits that ruled the sky and earth, with the world beyond the grave.

At one time masters of the lands that lay between the Enisei River and Lake Baikal, the ancestors of these Kirghiz nomads submitted to the armies of Chingis Khan to escape the devastation that the Mongols inflicted upon any who opposed them.

As the Mongols spread their empire across Eurasia, the ancestors of these Tungus hunters and reindeer herders retreated northward into the Siberian forest.

Turkic-speaking Siberians whose ancestors ruled nearly all of the Lena River valley, the shamanist Iakuts became some of the first Siberians to convert to Christianity.

The Goldi fisherfolk, who dressed in clothing made from fish skins and dog fur, lived along the lower reaches of the Amur River. (World Transportation Commission Collection, The Library of Congress, Washington, D.C.)

CONQUERORS AND SETTLERS

From their "castle" in the northeastern corner of European Russia, the Stroganov merchants launched Russia's conquest of Siberia.

Three years after the cossack chieftain Ermak Timofeevich led the Stroganovs' first campaign into Siberia, the Siberian Tatars killed him and all his men in an ambush.

Crude ships with deerskin sails and rawhide rigging carried Russia's explorers eastward along tributaries that flowed into the Ob, Enisei, and Lena rivers.

Vitus Bering led the Russians from Siberia's Pacific coast to the Aleutian Islands and Alaska. (Historical Pictures/Stock Montage)

Applauded by his countrymen as the "Russian Columbus," Grigorii Ivanovich Shelikhov founded Russia's first permanent settlement in the New World.

As new wealth from the Alaskan fur trade made Siberia's officials more corrupt, the emperor appointed Mikhail Mikhailovich Speranskii to reform its government.

General Nikolai Muravëv opened a waterway to the Pacific for Siberia's traders by seizing the Amur River valley from the Chinese.

Hundreds of small traders bought and sold their wares at the Irkutsk bazaar on market day during the early years of the twentieth century.

Villages scattered through the lands around Irkutsk remained very much a part of Siberian frontier life on the eve of World War I.

Even after the coming of the Trans-Siberian Railroad, Siberians continued to rely upon horse-drawn sledges for transportation during the winter.

Transported in boxcars that bore the inscription "To carry twelve horses or forty-three people," millions of Russian peasant settlers went to Siberia at the beginning of the twentieth century.

Shelters fashioned out of logs, animal skins, and canvas provided housing for Siberia's new settlers.

Determination and a sense of adventure helped to sustain Siberia's new settlers while they struggled to tame the wilderness.

A few modern entrepreneurs had begun to wash gold from Siberia's ore-bearing sands with machinery by the end of the nineteenth century.

PRISONERS AND EXILES

The Russians used Siberia the way the English used Australia, as a place of exile. Before the days of the Trans-Siberian Railroad, convicts had to make the journey to Siberia on foot.

In some of Siberia's worst prisons, convicts were given no more than two square yards of sleeping space on wooden benches. (World Transportation Commission Collection, The Library of Congress, Washington, D.C.)

Floggers such as this one punished the inmates of Siberia's prisons with a *plet*, an eight-pound whip whose three lead-weighted lashes could cause permanent injury or death.

Before they began their Siberian journey, male prisoners had their heads shaved on one side.

Until the 1840s, Siberian convicts were branded on their cheeks and foreheads.

Among the most famous of Siberia's women prisoners in the 1880s, Mariia Kovalevskaia was sentenced to thirteen years of penal servitude for plotting to kill one of Russia's high officials.

Shortages of able-bodied workers obliged the builders of the Trans-Siberian Railroad to assign more than ten thousand convicts such as these to lay track through Siberia's eastern lands.

All male convicts wore a long gray overcoat, a shirt and trousers of coarse home-spun linen, and a gray wool visorless Scotch cap. Women received a gray wool skirt instead of trousers.

Set at the foot of mountains that closed around it from every side, the site of Akatui prison was described by one Russian penal expert as being "gloomier than any place to be found anywhere in the Transbaikal."

As more roads and railroads made escape easier, Siberia's new Soviet masters built electrified barbed-wire barriers to contain their prisoners. (Sovfoto/Eastfoto)

THE TRANS-SIBERIAN RAILROAD

As one of the last great statesmen of Imperial Russia, Sergei Iulevich Witte urged his government to build the Trans-Siberian Railroad.

To enter Siberia, the builders of the Trans-Siberian Railroad cut a passageway through the Ural Mountains, which divide Europe from Asia.

The Trans-Siberian's builders had to cross four rivers that were larger than the Mississippi. This bridge across the Ob River stretches for almost half a mile.

To move trains across Lake Baikal while construction crews built a spur around its southern tip, the Trans-Siberian's operators used a steam-powered ferry that could carry an entire train on its lower deck.

Peasant immigrants rode in boxcars, but the handful of travelers who could afford berths on the opulent Trans-Siberian Express enjoyed the comfort of leather chairs and a library that included books in several languages.

Built during the 1930s, Magnitogorsk was the world's largest iron and steel plant. (Sovfoto / Eastfoto)

SOVIET SIBERIA

Some twelve hundred miles east of Magnitogorsk, the huge metallurgical plant at Kuznetsk (now Novokuznetsk) served as a key anchor of the Siberian industrial bastion that supplied the Red Army during World War II. (Sovfoto / Eastfoto)

Siberia's Bratsk Dam still stands as one of the greatest construction projects of the Khrushchev era. (Sovfoto/Eastfoto)

Today, these ruins of a Gulag camp in Siberia's remote Chita region stand as a lonely reminder of the power that the Bolsheviks once wielded so brutally in Siberia. (Sovfoto/Eastfoto)

would suffer in the years ahead. Partly the product of circumstances, partly the consequence of the government's momentary uncertainty about its course, and partly the result of influence brought to bear by Lenin's mother, this was a brief halcyon interlude to be savored by only a handful of revolutionaries. Soon the government would return to its view that Siberian banishment should be used to punish any who disagreed with it, not merely to isolate them from the masses they hoped to convert.

Of course, the daunting Siberian winter had to be faced, even in southern Shushenskoe. Longer and colder than any in central Russia, it began in late September and lasted into May, when the ubiquitous Siberian mosquitoes appeared in such hordes that Lenin considered wearing kid gloves to protect his hands.[8] Nor was the daily company in Shushenskoe the brightest or the best. Apart from the peasants, who came to Lenin's lodgings on Sundays seeking advice about settling their disputes, only a drunken, card-playing schoolmaster, a Polish hatmaker, and a rebellious Finnish factory worker from St. Petersburg broke the loneliness of everyday village life. Still, there was plenty to eat, plenty to read, plenty of work to be done, and plenty of time in which to do it. The authorities allowed Lenin to receive a steady stream of books and journals from Moscow and abroad, and they seem not even to have objected to the prodigious amounts of mail that came his way.[9] All in all, Lenin decided, Shushenskoe was "not a bad village" in which to live out a term of banishment.[10] "Shu-shu-shu," he once called it. "Shu-shu-shu, the place in which I eventually will find peace."[11]

One of the three weddings celebrated by the revolutionaries of Shushenskoe region during the late 1890s was Lenin's own. In the spring of 1894, when St. Petersburg's Marxists had met to discuss the problems of revolutionary tactics under the cover of a Shrove Tuesday supper, Lenin had met Nadezhda Krupskaia, a typical turn-of-the-century radical woman with short-cropped hair, an upturned nose, and eyes that were just beginning to protrude as a result of the goiter that would plague her for the rest of her life. Two years older than Lenin, Krupskaia had devoted herself to serving Russia's masses since the age of fourteen, and she had committed herself to Marxism at about the same time as he had in 1891. The clarity of Lenin's thought and writing had captured Krupskaia's loyalty even before they had met, and that attraction quickly turned to adulation. A Marxist courtship soon cemented their shared Marxist dedication to revolution. After Lenin's imprisonment, Krupskaia continued to organize the workers of St. Petersburg until she was arrested and sentenced to a three-year term of exile in Ufa, on the

European side of the Urals. Rather than go to Ufa, Krupskaia had asked to join her "fiancé" at Shushenskoe. In typically unpredictable fashion, the tsarist authorities agreed.

Traveling with her mother and at her own expense, Krupskaia set out for Siberia to join Lenin in the spring of 1898. For weeks before, her intended had flooded his family and friends with lists of things for her to bring: gloves, the straw hat he had bought in Paris, moleskin trousers, a new suit, pen wipers, sealing wax and seals, scissors, and a special kind of pencil that he particularly liked all had to be packed. Before she left St. Petersburg, Krupskaia also had to arrange for subscriptions, the publication of a volume of Lenin's essays, and more translation work and reviews (two enterprises that Lenin used to supplement his meager exile's stipend), as well as do a score of other errands. And, Lenin insisted in a letter to his mother, she "must be loaded down with as many books as possible."[12] Not for the last time, Lenin's adoring disciple became a willing packhorse.

Krupskaia arrived in Shushenskoe at the beginning of May, bearing Lenin's baggage and a unique injunction that could only have been conceived by one of the thousands of petty officials who issued internal passports in Imperial Russia. "They have placed upon Nadezhda Konstantinovna the tragi-comic condition that, if she does not marry *immediately* she must go back to Ufa," Lenin wrote to his mother. "We hope," he added, "to be married before the Feast of St. Peter. Can we allow ourselves," he asked rhetorically, "to hope that the strict authorities will think this a sufficiently 'immediate' marriage?!"[13]

The red tape was cut in time for Lenin to wed Krupskaia in July. "In the mornings, Vladimir Ilych [Lenin] and I set to work and translated the Webbs' [*History of Trade Unionism*]," Krupskaia wrote of their first months together. "After dinner we spent an hour or two jointly rewriting *The Development of Capitalism in Russia*."[14] Theirs was a relaxed, easy life, with Krupskaia tending the household during the hours when they were not working and Lenin giving himself over to hunting. "Vladimir Ilych was an ardent huntsman, but too apt to become heated over it," Krupskaia wrote of those days when the chase had become Lenin's passion and chess his obsession. "At one time he was so taken up by chess," Krupskaia added, "that he even cried out in his sleep: 'If he puts his knight here, I'll stick my rook there!' "[15] Eventually Lenin gave up the game entirely. "Chess," he stated sternly some years later, "gets hold of you too much and hinders work."[16]

Easy though life was after Krupskaia's arrival, Lenin was beginning to chafe at the restraints of banishment. He resented the distance that separated him from the revolutionary circles of European Russia, yet, in comparison to that of so many of those who had been sent to Siberia before and after, his exile was a truly amazing interlude. With Krupskaia's help, he completed *The Development of Capitalism in Russia*, one of his greatest books. He also translated several important works by European socialists and laid plans for strengthening the Russian Marxist movement in the years ahead. Was this still the banishment to miasmal lands from which exiles in earlier times had sought escape in suicide or madness? "These were liberal times in the Minusinsk region," Krupskaia later explained. There was, she wrote, "practically no surveillance at all."[17]

That was not true of the lands of the far north or those to the east of the Lena and Lake Baikal. There exiles still had terrible tales to tell of trying and painful conditions. Just two years after Lenin completed his exile, young Lev Bronstein, later to become known to the world as Trotskii, was sent to the godforsaken village of Ust-Kut on the upper reaches of the Lena River, where, while "brushing the cockroaches off the pages," he studied Marx's *Das Kapital* in temperatures so cold that, when he and his wife were transferred to Verkholensk, they had to keep checking to make certain that the infant daughter they had wrapped in heavy furs had not suffocated along the way.[18]

Others suffered fully as much. In the tiny settlement of Kureisk, two thousand miles farther west and fifty miles north of the Arctic Circle, other revolutionaries found banishment every bit as miserable as did the Trotskii family. "There is absolutely no kerosene [and] we use candles," the Bolsheviks' future general secretary, Iakov Sverdlov, wrote a few years later. "Since that provides too little light for my eyes, I do all my studying in the daytime now. As a matter of fact," he added, "I don't study much. We have virtually no books." Even the cold, unyielding Stalin, with whom Sverdlov shared a room for a time, felt the desolation of this empty land, where the frozen soil produced no food and winter lasted for eight months out of every twelve. "Nature is bare to the point of ugliness," Stalin wrote. "In summer, a river, in winter, snow. That's all nature offers here." When Sverdlov was sent elsewhere, Stalin remained behind to live among the native Ostiaks. Alone with his dreams and visions of a violent revolutionary future, Stalin spent most of his years in Kureisk in almost complete isolation.[19]

Still, even the lives of exiles in Siberia's remotest corners were changing somewhat. While the exile route that Kennan had followed in the 1880s had taken months to travel, Stalin and Trotskii could return to Russia's centers of power in a matter of weeks a quarter of a century later, for the vast dimensions of Siberia's time and space were shrinking as it entered the twentieth century. As on the world's other virgin lands, steam power and the railroad came to Siberia at the end of the nineteenth century, and with them came all of the problems and progress they had brought to human civilization elsewhere. Now the technology that had brought San Francisco within a week's journey of Chicago and New York brought Irkutsk to within a fortnight of Moscow and put Vladivostok less than a month's distance from St. Petersburg. The Trans-Siberian Railroad that tied these ends of the Russian Empire together became one of the most ambitious undertakings of the world's industrial age and an engineering feat that stood on a par with cutting a path through the isthmus of Panama to join the Atlantic and the Pacific.

28

An Iron Road Across Asia

Railroads projected the power of the world's industrialized nations more forcefully than any other invention of the nineteenth century. Natural barriers and great distances all shrank before the march of this amazing instrument of progress as it opened new markets, settled remote lands, and extended the reach of nations far beyond the limits that time and space had imposed in earlier days. Once the railroad had tamed the wild western lands of the North American continent, men began to speak of linking Cairo to Cape Town and Buenos Aires to Valparaíso. Yet, as the century neared its end, the greatest of all challenges remained unmet, for the railroad had still not conquered Eurasia. A railroad from Moscow to the Pacific would rival in magnitude the paths cut between the seas at Suez and Panama. It would, the Russian statesman Sergei Witte announced, "occupy one of the first places in the ranks of the largest and most important undertakings of the nineteenth century."[1]

A trans-Siberian railroad would be one of the most difficult in the world to build, not only because it would be the longest but because construction crews would have to work thousands of miles away from their bases of supply. Rails and bridge iron would have to be brought to Siberia from foundries as far away as St. Petersburg and Warsaw, ties would have to be cut in European Russia and shipped across the Urals because almost no hardwoods grew in the steppe or the taiga, and stone for bridge piers and abutments would have to be transported from quarries on the western frontier of Mongolia.² Then, as the tracklayers moved deeper into Siberia, terrain and climate would magnify the obstacles. The endless forests, the gorges cut from solid rock, the mountains of the Transbaikal, the treacherous permafrost, the short winter days, and the deep, deep Siberian cold all presented obstacles on a scale that the world's builders had yet to face.

Midpoint in the railroad's path stood Lake Baikal, larger than Belgium and rimmed by cliffs and gorges that would require more than a hundred miles of roadbed to be cut from solid rock as the tracklayers worked their way around its southern tip. Beyond Baikal, mountains and vast wastes had to be crossed before the land started to slope toward Siberia's Pacific lowlands. Many asked if the hoped-for benefits could be worth the cost and if Russia, the poorest of the world's industrialized nations, could afford to build such a railroad. Champions of the idea insisted that the prestige alone would be worth the price. The "numerous benefits" of such an undertaking, one of them wrote, "were not subject to direct arithmetical calculation."³

Debates about cost, routes, and design postponed the beginnings of a trans-Siberian railroad for several decades. By the middle of the 1880s, Russia's state debt was approaching six and a half billion rubles, and a full quarter of the national budget—more than the costs of the army and navy combined—had to be spent to pay the interest.⁴ Conservative fiscal experts worried that the loans needed to pay for laying five thousand miles of track across Siberia would undermine Russia's credit in the money markets of Europe, and none feared that more than Finance Minister Ivan Vyshnegradskii. Thought by some to be "[more like] a cashier than a minister,"⁵ Vyshnegradskii saw in the proposals for a trans-Siberian railroad an immense Pandora's box filled with inflated expenditures and lined with such immense costs that he wanted Russia to have no part of it. Himself a kopek pincher of legendary prowess, Russia's Emperor Alexander III shared Vyshnegradskii's reluctance to spend money, but he wanted the railroad for reasons of national security, international prestige, and hoped-for economic advantages nonetheless. Alexander thought that it would be enough to say, as he wrote in the margin of a report at the end of 1886, that it was "high time" to build the railroad⁶ and insist that it must be done "quickly and cheaply."⁷ Once he had opened the way for the railroad, he left it to others to find the means with which to build it. The emperor had set the course; others would have to plot its precise headings.

The wave of strident nationalism that had surged up after revolutionary terrorists had assassinated his father had shaped Alexander III's vision of Russia's course in the 1880s. A chauvinist pure and simple, he was powerfully drawn to a railroad that could make Siberia more "Russian" and strengthen the political forces that he and his advisers thought would serve Russia best. "The entire future of Siberia lies in its close unity with the rest of Russia," one supporter of that point of view wrote. "Siberia is not a colony of Russia," he added, "but Russia itself."[8] Others disagreed and insisted that Siberia must follow a more independent course because its interests no longer coincided with those of the empire that ruled it. A railroad built to move Russian armies more quickly into the Far East, these men warned, would make it more difficult for Siberia to choose an independent path and would bind it more closely to an empire of which it ought not to be a part. In 1882, such "regionalists" seized upon the tercentenary of Ermak's "conquest" to emphasize their views. Among them, Nikolai Iadrintsev, a distinguished scholar whose massive corpus of work in archaeology, ethnography, history, geography, and journalism could have provided enough in the way of accomplishment to satisfy half a dozen lesser men, pleaded Siberia's case against the railroad with the greatest eloquence.[9]

Iadrintsev insisted that the men and women he called "Siberians" were a "unique ethnic type" produced by the union of Russian trappers, soldiers, and colonists with Siberian natives. These new "Siberians," he argued, were more practical than their forebears, more self-reliant, and more capable of shaping their destiny. Such men and women had lived a different history than the Russians had. Because there had been no serfdom in Siberia, the political, economic, and social tensions that stemmed from the centuries-long oppression of serfs by masters in European Russia had not touched their lives. Such "Siberians," Iadrintsev wrote, thought of modern-day Russians as exploiters. Bent upon abusing the people and resources of less developed lands for the gain of the Russian "metropolis" (to use the colonialist language current all across Europe and the United States at the time) they hoped to find better ways to strip Siberia of its treasures. Talk among such "foreigners" about building a trans-Siberian railroad made Iadrintsev's "Siberians" very wary indeed.[10]

Led by Iadrintsev, Siberia's regionalists feared that a transcontinental railroad would make Siberia's people the subjects of Russian masters. "The invasion of a railroad civilization, grasping and greedy," one of them wrote, would give the Russians an even stronger grip on Siberian affairs and pull Siberia away from the course that promised to bring it closer to China, Japan, and the United States of America. "With the construction of the railroad," one regionalist newspaper warned, "the old familiar Siberia will disappear forever." In the orgy of speculation that inevitably would follow, "people of easy money, shady characters, [and] swindlers" would destroy "the healthy traits of Siberian life."[11] Siberia and the "Siberians" would become the prey of absentee landlords, absentee mine owners, and absentee industrialists. In a massive repetition of the British and Belgian experience in Africa, the "Siberians" would become victims of Russia's imperialists.

But Iadrintsev and the regionalists were neither so backward nor so blind that they failed to see the advantages that railroads could bring to the society they served. A trans-Siberian railroad could place Siberia at the crossroads between the Orient and the West and enable it to play a key part in "the unification of the worlds of Europe and Asia."[12] Especially if a branch of the railroad were built to Peking, they pointed out, Siberia might become "heir to the prosperity of Venice and the Cape of Good Hope," both of which had "served as way stations between Europe and Asia" in earlier times.[13] The danger therefore lay not in the railroad, but in the Russians' intention to use it to strengthen their authority in the Far East and tighten their grip on Siberia's people and resources. Before the railroad came to Siberia, Iadrintsev and his followers wanted to build defenses against the Russians.

The regionalists insisted that Siberians needed to be educated and modernized before they could reap the railroad's advantages and that Siberia needed more people, more factories, and more regional trade before it needed a transcontinental railroad.[14] "Why is it that people who want to do good for Siberia and . . . speak so heatedly of billions for a railroad do not apply themselves to . . . maybe more significant tools of civilization [such as people's schools and technical institutions]?" the regionalists asked.[15] "Building a railway into Siberia," one of Iadrintsev's friends wrote, "means beginning the matter from the tail end first."[16] Self-government, such limited civil rights as the great reforms of the 1860s had bestowed upon the men and women of European Russia, modern law and law courts, and widespread education all needed to come first. Otherwise, everything that made Siberia and the "Siberians" unique would be lost.

Finance Minister Vyshnegradskii agreed with part of that view but defined the objective of cautious spending differently. A priest's son who had become a professor of mechanical engineering at St. Petersburg's Technological Institute before he entered government service, Vyshnegradskii wanted Russia to build no more railroads anywhere until "salutary thrift in government expenditures" could be achieved.[17] Even though prices on the world grain market were plummeting, he tried to increase his country's grain shipments to Western Europe during the late 1880s and, in the process, created one of the worst famines of the nineteenth century. Vyshnegradskii's failed plan added the burden of massive famine relief to the obligations of the Imperial Treasury at just the moment when the advocates of the Trans-Siberian Railroad seemed to have victory within their grasp.

In February 1891, just a few months before the famine struck, Alexander III and the Imperial Committee of Ministers had agreed that "*a continuous line* from the Urals to the Pacific Ocean"[18] (and not a fragmented series of west-east rail portages to connect Siberia's river transport routes as Vyshnegradskii had proposed) must be begun "very soon."[19] Part of the reason for their decision lay not in the politics of the Imperial Court but in the reaction of Russia's archconservatives to the pressures that Iadrintsev and his allies had been exerting upon the government for the better part of a decade. Fearful that a railway into Siberia would open the floodgates of colonization and deprive landlords in European Russia of the migrant workers who tilled their fields for very low wages, several reactionary Moscow newspaper editors, including some of the emperor's most trusted supporters, had begun to urge Russia to defend herself against the forces of political change that modern technology was beginning to unleash. Chauvinism, they believed, was Russia's best weapon against the forces of constitutionalism and reform that reigned in the West. Foreigners, they said—and Jews most of all—were carrying these evil forces into the Russian Empire. "Permit the construction of the Siberian Railroad today," the tsar's friends warned, and "tomorrow Siberia will be given up forever to the Jews of the whole world."[20]

If Russia's archconservatives harbored an "apocalyptic fear" of what damage the Jews might inflict upon Siberia,[21] they also worried that Iadrintsev and his regionalist comrades might bring to Russia the liberalism that reigned in the West. Could the Russians, they asked, claim that they had brought Siberia fully under their control in the three hundred years since Ermak? Some insisted that they could not and that the railroad was the best instrument for tightening their grip upon lands and natural wealth that might otherwise slip away. This set the stage for the unlikely alliance between archconservatives and progressive imperialists that overwhelmed Vyshnegradskii's attempts to put off beginning the Trans-Siberian Railroad.

Work on the railroad began in 1891, the year of the great famine. Symbolic of the unstable forces that made its beginning possible, the first shovelful of earth on the Trans-Siberian Railroad was turned at its easternmost terminus of Vladivostok, while the real work of building it began more than four thousand miles farther west in the foothills of the Ural Mountains. Would the railroad become, as one source later claimed, "such a mighty influence on the growth of economic life in Siberia that its commercial success ... [would exceed] the most extravagant expectations"?[22] Or would it, as others remarked with unconcealed disdain, simply become thousands of miles of "rusty streaks of iron through the vastness of nothing to the extremities of nowhere"?[23]

The ceremonies at Vladivostok that marked the Trans-Siberian's beginning were presided over not by the emperor who had ordered it to be built nor even by the ministers who had supported him in doing so. On Sunday, May 19, 1891, Grand Duke Nicholas Aleksandrovich, soon to ascend the throne as Emperor Nicholas II, stood before a crowd of dignitaries, set his spade firmly into the soil of Imperial Russia's "Mistress of the East," turned its contents into a small wheelbarrow, and then held a ceremonial breakfast to celebrate the event. The railroad's purpose, he announced as he read the decree that his father had written for the assembled guests, was "to connect the natural abundance of the Siberian lands with [Russia's] network of rail communications." St. Petersburg's imperialists had triumphed over Iadrintsev and Siberia's regionalists.

To reach Vladivostok for the ceremonies that began work on the railroad, the future Nicholas II had traveled by sea on a grand tour that had carried him from St. Petersburg to the pyramids of Egypt, the jungles of India and Ceylon, and the recently medieval (but now rapidly modernizing) islands of Japan. To symbolize Russia's claim to Siberia, the tsarevich then returned to St. Petersburg by land, visiting cities in which none of his dynasty had ever set foot. During the summer of 1891, Nicholas visited Lake Baikal and from there moved quickly west along the great Siberian *trakt* that many nineteenth-century travelers had cursed as the worst road in the world. In the course of his three-month journey Nicholas saw no ruts, no vermin-infested public rooms, and no fly-speckled menus that advertised such delicacies as *rostbif* and *bifshteks* but offered only stale bread and salted fish. The road had been smoothed, the crumbling bridges repaired, and the post stations cleaned, painted, and freshly supplied. Russia's tsarevich saw Siberia at its very best, as only the heir of an absolute sovereign could hope to see it.[24]

No other Romanov had ever been seen in most of the parts of Siberia that Nicholas visited, and the Siberians' enthusiasm for their emperor-to-be seemed to speak against the regionalists' passionately stated distrust of their Russian masters. Buriats, Tungus, and Kirghizes cheered the tsarevich in Irkutsk and Krasnoiarsk. At Tomsk, he visited Siberia's first university, opened just three years before as a concession to those regionalists for whom Iadrintsev continued to speak so eloquently.[25] Then, toward the end of his journey, Nicholas reached Tobolsk, now more than three centuries old, to which fate had bound him most closely of all. From the province of which Tobolsk was the capital would come Grigorii, "a man of God" as Nicholas later wrote, who would be known to the world as Rasputin.[26] In Tobolsk, as prisoners of the Bolsheviks, Nicholas, Aleksandra, and their children would spend the last winter of their lives in 1917–1918.

Not only would Siberia retain a special significance for Russia's last emperor, it also initiated him into the complexities of statecraft when his father named him to preside over the special committee formed on December 10, 1892, to oversee the railroad's construction. At first, Nicholas moved timidly, unsure of his own ground, aware of his father's lack of confidence, and dependent upon Russia's new minister of finance, Sergei Witte. One of the last great statesmen of Imperial Russia and the Trans-Siberian's guiding genius, Witte used his influence over Russia's inexperienced tsarevich to push ahead with the Trans-Siberian Railroad at full speed. Soon convinced that the railroad would help the Russians to pursue their mission to "civilize" the Asians with greater success, Nicholas began to speak of exporting autocratic and Orthodox Christian principles to the East. He began to think that Siberia must become Russia's first line of defense against the "yellow peril" that he and his countrymen feared was about to arise in Asia.[27]

Born into a family of Baltic Germans who were allied by marriage to some of Russia's most illustrious aristocrats, Sergei Iulevich Witte at the age of forty-two combined a Spanish conquistador's thirst for adventure with a politician's love of behind-the-scenes intrigue. No less than Cecil Rhodes or Lord Curzon, he thought that colonization could bind the underdeveloped lands of the world more closely to the "metropolis" of Europe, and he saw Siberia's natural resources and industrial potential as one of the guarantees of Russia's greatness in the century that lay ahead. Unlike so many of his Russian contemporaries, who looked to Europe and thought of their homeland as part of the West, Witte believed that the Eurasian empire he served was fated to play a pivotal role in shaping the destinies of both continents. Russia, he insisted, must look west and east, and in the near term, he thought, the east would be more important.[28]

With most of her coastline icebound for much of the year, Russia had never been able to challenge her Western rivals in international trade, but Witte looked forward to a day when the world's east-west commerce could be shifted from the high seas to the Trans-Siberian Railroad. He therefore wanted to build the railroad quickly, but, because the great famine of 1891 had shattered the fragile foundations upon which Vyshnegradskii had erected his façade of prosperity, he had to restore Russia's economic stability at the same time. With his grandiose belief that "a minister cannot practice economy in the administration of a state"[29] standing in stark contrast to Vyshnegradskii's rigid fiscal conservatism, Witte insisted that it was "better [for a government] to lose money than prestige."[30] Only deficit financing could accomplish both tasks at once. "Money," Witte once explained, "can only be found by spending it lavishly."[31]

Yet Witte drew his sense of mission from more than abstract political principles. No matter how a transcontinental railroad might improve Russia's standing among the great colonial powers of Europe, the real force that drove him to build the Trans-Siberian was the will of his emperor. "The Emperor Alexander III told me of his desire, of his dream, that a railroad be built from European Russia to Vladivostok," he later wrote. "He asked for my word that I would complete this task," he added, "[and] I tried to do so as quickly as possible."[32] Witte's efforts to accomplish that feat from the security of St. Petersburg's chanceries revealed the breadth of Siberia's potential and the limits of the Russian bureaucracy's ability to shape the economic and political development of the empire it labored to govern. Using his influence over Russia's tsarevich to push ahead too quickly, Witte make the world's longest railroad a flawed gem at best.

29

Building the World's Longest Railroad

Built by workers and engineers who struggled to lay track across the largest landmass on the globe, the Trans-Siberian Railroad was planned by bureaucrats in the chanceries of St. Petersburg. Even though Witte's Committee on the Siberian Railroad was supposed to stand apart from the rivalries of chancery politics, interagency squabbles and bureaucratic mind-sets reduced many of the broader debates about how the railroad should be built to questions of personal preference and political necessity. Despite Witte's grand words about deficit financing, budgetary constraints forced curves to be cut more sharply than sensible engineers thought safe and grades to be inclined more steeply. Building the railroad cheaply and quickly remained the bureaucrats' first concern; safety and efficiency therefore had to count for less than in the West, where American and European entrepreneurs built railroads to move goods and people at speeds that would reap greater profits. There seemed to be something in the Russian psyche that could overlook the failings that this process produced, even though many of the trains averaged barely thirteen miles an hour once the Trans-Siberian was finished.[1] "Why go so fast?" one Russian asked when he heard that European trains traveled at up to four times greater speed. "If a man is in such a hurry to get somewhere, can he not take an earlier train?"[2]

At first, Russia's massive national debt made it difficult to see where the funds for building the Trans-Siberian would come from. Proclaiming that "whatever the government's needs may be, they must be satisfied,"[3] Witte insisted that the railroad could be financed by "surpluses" in Russia's budget, and he then tried to create those surpluses by floating new foreign loans and reporting them as "income."[4] In part, Russia's improved relations with France helped to bring in the funds Witte needed. So did the political stability that Alexander III had imposed upon Russia and the Imperial Treasury's scrupulous attention to paying the interest on its foreign debt on time and in gold. In the end, money for the Trans-Siberian therefore proved to be less difficult to come by than Vyshnegradskii had feared, but Witte's policy of spending now and paying later had to have its day of reckoning. Inevitably, Russia's workers and peasants would have to shoulder the cost by paying higher taxes.[5]

If new borrowing threatened deeper poverty for the masses, there was a promise of prosperity, too, for Witte insisted that the Trans-Siberian should be built with materials and equipment manufactured in Russia. Never had the nation's industries been called upon to produce so much so quickly, and rarely had its resources been so strained. Rails, spikes, and bridge iron for the railroad promised to consume at least a third of Russia's entire yearly output of pig iron, and the need for coal, iron, and steel spurred new searches for mineral wealth all across the empire. Between 1894 and 1896, fifty-eight geological expeditions explored western Siberia and the Altai Mountains and forty-four more looked for minerals in the lands farther east. Almost overnight Siberia became, as one writer remarked, "a fashionable place for all types of research"[6] as geologists and mineralogists combed its lands for the resources that would feed its industries in the century ahead.

As prospectors discovered new deposits of coal, iron, copper, graphite, lead, granite, silver, and gold, Siberia began to open up, even before the railroad was finished. Foundries, brick kilns, sawmills, and cement factories all had to be built, and each required massive loans from the government. Witte's freely given subsidies made it possible for men to make fortunes as contractors by collecting advances from the government but never supplying the goods and services they had agreed to provide. Others claimed to have gone bankrupt and pocketed the funds they had been given in trust without delivering the materials they had been paid to produce. Contractors often lowered the technical specifications set for gradings and curves to increase their profits. Then, when their crews fell behind schedule, the same men demanded bonuses to complete the work, sometimes at a higher price.[7]

Almost from the beginning, the surveys used by the railroad's builders proved to be dangerously flawed, and there was a strong suspicion among some experts that up to half of the route had not been surveyed at all before the tracklayers began their work.[8] The railroad's builders were amazed to learn that they would have to dig wells on the Baraba Steppe, whose many lakes, they learned too late, held water that was unfit to drink and too laden with caustic minerals even to be used in locomotive boilers. Nor did anyone guess that in the Transbaikal lands, more than two hundred miles of track would have to be relaid at higher elevations because the surveyors had chosen a route that was submerged by floodwaters nearly every spring and summer. The same problem occurred along the Ussuri River in Siberia's far east, where floods undercut hillsides and turned them into landslides that buried the track beneath hundreds of tons of rock and mud.[9]

Even where the surveys had been done properly, no one knew for certain how to take into account the problems of Siberia's climate and topography. In the eight hundred miles that separated the Urals from the Ob River, the railroad's gradient rose less than five hundred feet, but there was virtually no wood within easy reach. The next twelve hundred miles of dense taiga forest between the Ob and Irkutsk provided huge amounts of wood for fuel and temporary bridges, but none that was hard enough for ties. Then, to lay track between Irkutsk and Lake Baikal, the railroad builders had to blast a roadbed out of the Angara River's sheer rock banks and wedge bridges into deep crevasses that its tributaries had cut thousands of years before. Working in such terrain, it took the better part of four years to cover the forty miles that separated Irkutsk from the lake's western shore.

Intersected by the rugged, heavily forested Iablonovy Mountains and cut by the deep gorges of the Ingoda and Shilka rivers, the lands beyond Lake Baikal spread across an area larger than France and Imperial Germany combined. Here in the Transbaikal the permafrost provided a treacherous foundation, solid one day but apt to become a morass of quaking mud the next. Farther east, almost fourteen hundred miles of riverways separated the eastern end of the main railroad at the town of Sretensk from the Ussuri Railroad, which ran south near Siberia's Pacific coast from Khabarovsk to Vladivostok. The tsarevich Nicholas had turned the first shovelful of earth for the Ussuri Railroad in 1891, but, because the government's surveyors had decided (before they surveyed the route) that the tracks should follow the Ussuri River, scores of bridges had to be built across its many tributaries.[10]

When the railroad's builders set to work, Siberia's entire population totaled scarcely more than five million, some two thirds of whom lived in a narrow belt that extended fifty miles to the north and south of the railroad's planned route. But nomads and herders who asked more readily about the health of a man's herds and flocks than about his family could not make the transition to the modern world of steam engines, steel track, and dynamite quickly enough to become part of modern-day construction gangs, and Siberia's Russian settlers therefore had to provide the bulk of the labor.[11] As the track moved east, away from the western lands in which most of the Russians had settled, Witte's Committee on the Siberian Railroad had to fill in the thinning ranks of the tracklaying crews with more than fourteen thousand convict laborers and supplement them with army labor battalions and thousands of migrant workers from Japan, China, and Korea.[12] One out of every four of the stonemasons who built bridge abutments and piers for the Trans-Siberian had to be hired from as far away as Italy, for all of European Russia could not begin to supply enough men with the needed skills.[13] Italians, not Russians, thus built many of the massive stone structures that support the Trans-Siberian's bridges and have stood against the force of the huge ice floes that have risen as high as thirty feet every spring for the past hundred years.

As they mounted their huge iron-and-steel structures atop the stonemasons' piers, the bridge builders proved to be the most vulnerable of all the Trans-Siberian's workers, for hypothermia took a high toll among men who had to work unshielded from the wind in subzero temperatures. "They allow their body temperature to run down more than they are aware, with the result that some of them make a slip or find that they cannot get their numbed fingers to grasp a support in time," one contractor explained. Without safety devices to break their fall, frost-numbed riveters and bolters lost their grip and fell to the rock-hard ice below.[14] "This ain't railroad building," some of the workmen were heard to mutter at one point. "It's a battle, a war to the death."[15]

Russians and Europeans who worked on the Trans-Siberian received forty-five rubles a month, or about $23 at the rate of exchange that prevailed at the end of the nineteenth century, considerably more than most factory and farm workers received. Asians earned a little more than half that sum, and convict workers were paid less.[16] These men all ate the roughest food and lived in conditions that grew worse with every mile they moved toward the Pacific, for the Committee on the Siberian Railroad did not arrange for the first dugout shelters to be built until the tracklaying crews had been on the job for the better part of a year. Without sanitation facilities, worried public health officials reported, these workers' camps suffered so much sickness that it was "impossible [for men] to live under such conditions and retain any shred of human dignity."[17] There was very little difference, in fact, between the barracks along the Trans-Siberian and the housing in Siberia's *katorga* prisons.[18]

During Siberia's long summer workdays, men whose backs took the place of the machines that railroad builders used in the West needed at least four thousand calories, but local supply systems could not provide provisions on such a grand scale. Bread, vegetables, and other staples almost always turned out to be the poorest that money could buy, and contractors sometimes delivered beef cattle to the workers' railside camps that were too sick even to stand. One newspaper reported that some crews received rations of meat and bread "that were so bad that even the local pigs refused to eat them." Other exposés told about rotten food crawling with maggots and tainted with all sorts of filth not fit for human consumption. "The food's so bad around here that it makes you want to puke," an old-timer was heard to tell a detachment of new recruits. "While half of our guys are eating," he went on, "the rest are around the corner puking all over the place."[19]

Even though such working conditions turned the thoughts of do-gooding journalists and later-day Soviet historians to the Hebrews' days of bondage in ancient Egypt, most contemporaries were not overly concerned. Large-scale construction projects at the end of the nineteenth century inevitably produced hazardous working conditions and a great deal of sickness that cost large numbers of lives.[20] While malaria and yellow fever scourged thousands of workers digging the Panama Canal, the men who built the Trans-Siberian faced cholera, typhus, dysentery, scurvy, and the raging carbuncles of anthrax. Bubonic plague struck some of the crews working in Siberia's eastern lands during the summer of 1899 and returned again in 1900.[21] Europeans had not seen some of these diseases since the Middle Ages, but they were common in Asia.

The chronic shortage of medical facilities all along the Trans-Siberian's route raised the toll of lives these diseases claimed.[22] With combined territories of more than nine hundred thousand square miles, the provinces of Tobolsk and Tomsk in those days had only 187 doctors and about five hundred orderlies, midwives, and nurses. Farther east, the province of Eniseisk had sixty-five doctors and no more than three hundred clinic beds for an area larger than all of the United States east of the Mississippi, while the province of Iakutsk, which was larger than all of India, had five doctors assisted by a dozen orderlies and midwives.[23] Workers who got sick from spoiled rations, contracted diseases that had become rare in more advanced countries, or got hurt in any one of a hundred different ways usually had to cure themselves or not be cured at all.

By the fall of 1900, the Trans-Siberian's builders had laid just over two thousand miles of track to connect Cheliabinsk in the eastern foothills of the Urals with the tiny harbor of Listvenichnoe on Lake Baikal's western shore and had continued another seven hundred miles beyond the lake's eastern bank to Sretensk in the Transbaikal. Fourteen hundred miles farther east, the Ussuri Railroad connected Khabarovsk with Vladivostok, but this still left two great gaps to keep Witte's dream of rails stretching from Moscow to Vladivostok from taking shape. The only link between Sretensk and the beginning of the Ussuri Railroad at Khabarovsk continued to be the Shilka and Amur rivers, and the Transport Ministry's initial surveys showed that more than a hundred bridges and several times that many embankments and cuttings would have to be built before a railroad could connect the two towns. Farther west, the great chasm created by Lake Baikal still remained. Before the 162 miles of track around its southern tip could be laid, two hundred gorges would have to be bridged, thirty-three tunnels cut through rock, and dozens of miles of roadbed hewn from the cliffs that rose sharply from the lake's fog-draped shores.[24] Committed to opening the railroad before the end of 1900 and knowing that it would take a good half decade more to complete these last two segments, Witte's Committee on the Siberian Railroad decided to use riverboats and sledges to link Sretensk and Khabarovsk and steam ferries to bridge the Baikal gap.

The *Baikal*, a huge icebreaking steam ferry that measured nearly three hundred feet in length and displaced over four thousand tons, became the centerpiece of the Russians' plan for connecting Lake Baikal's eastern and western shores. Designed and built during the first half of 1896 by the British firm of Armstrong, Mitchell, and Company, Ltd., the *Baikal* was powered by three 1,250-horsepower engines and able to force its way through thirty-eight inches of ice while carrying twenty-eight loaded freight cars. Because it took two and a half years for all of its components to reach its home port at Listvenichnoe from England, the *Baikal* did not begin service until the spring of 1900. Once afloat, it was a marvel to behold, the first such monument to Western technology ever to reach Siberia's interior. Britain's John Fraser thought the *Baikal* "by no means pretty and rather like a barn that had slipped afloat" when he first saw it, but he hastened to add (for reasons of national pride and respect for the work it had to accomplish) that the ship was "one of the most wonderful vessels in the world."[25]

Laden with locomotives, passenger cars, freight, and up to eight hundred passengers for each crossing, the *Baikal* struggled against ice, fog, and violent summer storms, but with less success than the railroad's planners had hoped. Goods piled up on both sides of the lake and then began to back up all along the line. At one point, seven thousand freight cars were backlogged, leaving tens of thousands of tons of food products to rot on sidings. Then, when Russia's War Ministry sent a hundred and twenty thousand troops to the Far East during the Boxer Rebellion, the congestion at the Lake Baikal gap created chaos all along the railroad.[26] Reluctantly, Witte and his Committee on the Siberian Railroad concluded that the *Baikal* would have to be replaced by a circum-Baikal link that would be laid around the southern tip of the lake.

The bottleneck created by the *Baikal* experiment was only one instance of problems that could have been avoided had the Trans-Siberian's planners paid less attention to short-term savings and concentrated upon building their railroad according to proper specifications. To lay track more quickly and at lower cost, the railroad's builders chose rails that were half the weight of those normally used in the West and proceeded to set them on ties that were more widely spaced. They built the railroad's embankments narrower and lower than their counterparts in the West, left the curves sharper, and graded the inclines more steeply so as to lessen the amount of dirt that had to be moved by men whose main tools were wooden shovels and wheelless barrows. The lightweight rails buckled, and ties set in undrained roadbeds rotted to make the entire railroad unsafe from the moment it opened. Forced to maneuver around hairpin curves and ride on loose rails, the wheels of the Trans-Siberian locomotives wore out sooner than anyone expected, leading an exasperated engineer to remark that "after a spring rain, the trains run off the tracks like squirrels."[27] During the Trans-Siberian's first year in operation, wrecks occurred at the rate of nearly three a day and took the lives of ninety-three crewmen and passengers.[28]

To lessen the chance of accidents, engineers drove their trains at a crawl. Between Krasnoiarsk and Irkutsk in central Siberia, they ran without timetables, usually taking more than four days to complete the 670-mile journey, and they moved even more slowly once they got farther east. "I know of only one slower railway in the world," one traveler wrote in frustration. "[On the line] from Jaffa to Jerusalem," he added, "I have seen the driver alight, without actually stopping his engine, to gather wild flowers!"[29] Even after the circum-Baikal link was finished and the Lake Baikal gap closed in 1905, one railroad expert calculated, the old Nikolaevskaia Railroad that had been built to connect Moscow and St. Petersburg in the 1840s could still handle thirty times more traffic than the Trans-Siberian.[30]

In terms of resources, labor, lives, and treasure, the cost of the Trans-Siberian Railroad proved to be immense. To build it in a decade, more than seventy thousand men had moved seventy-seven million cubic feet of earth for gradings and had felled over a hundred thousand acres of forest. Even before the extension across Manchuria and the link around Lake Baikal had been built, more than twice the planners' original estimates had been spent, making the Trans-Siberian, as one expert estimated, "the most expensive peaceful undertaking in modern history up to that time."[31] Yet these huge expenditures had not produced the railroad Witte had envisioned. When Russia proudly announced the Trans-Siberian's opening in 1900, riverboats of the grandly named Amur Steam Navigation Company still formed a vital link in its operation. Until Russia completed the Trans-Siberian's Manchurian connection in 1903, steamboats remained as much a part of any journey across Siberia as locomotives and parlor cars.

30

Amur River Boats and Russia's Manchurian Connection

When Alexander III and his Council of Ministers had decided that the Trans-Siberian must be built as *"a continuous line* from the Urals to the Pacific Ocean,"[1] they had rejected the plans of Witte's predecessor, Vyshnegradskii, for building east-west rail portages to link Siberia's river transport routes. Yet Witte and his Committee on the Siberian Railroad had to reconsider that decision once they learned how difficult it would be to lay track through the rough lands along the Amur River to connect Sretensk with Khabarovsk.[2] The easiest and most obvious solution to these huge construction problems lay in rerouting the Trans-Siberian across territory held by the Chinese in Manchuria, but delicate diplomatic negotiations had to be undertaken before that could be done, and Witte knew that these could not be accomplished in time for the work to be finished in a decade. Until the negotiations for building a Manchurian connection could be concluded, he and his allies in Imperial Russia's Transport Ministry decided to use steamboats to carry passengers and freight along the fourteen-hundred-mile course of the Shilka and Amur rivers, which separated Sretensk from Khabarovsk.

Using rivers as highways had been common in northern Eurasia since prehistoric times. If placed end to end, Siberia's navigable rivers were long enough to encircle the globe with mileage to spare, and these, in olden days, had formed the pathways that had enabled men to move through the trackless taiga. Even after the great Siberian *trakt* was built in the 1770s, river barges continued to carry much of Siberia's freight and passengers in the summer. Immigrants, prisoners, and that crowd of simple folk in high leather boots, greasy sheepskins, calico print dresses, and faded black trousers whose itchy feet kept them forever on the move had all made their way along Siberia's rivers in the days before the railroad.

Once the three thousand miles of track had been laid from Siberia's western frontier at Cheliabinsk to the eastern edge of the Transbaikal at Sretensk, these travelers shifted from the lower decks of riverboats to the crude boxcars of the Trans-Siberian, upon which the words "to carry twelve horses or forty-three people" had been stenciled. "If there were fifth-class cars, there were plenty of sixth- and seventh-class people— some in rags, and many in tags, but few in velvet gowns," the New England cleric Francis Clark wrote of the travelers he had seen when he had crossed Siberia in the summer of 1900. Clark was amazed at the dirtiness of his fellow passengers, especially the "half-naked children, filthy with grime that had accumulated since their birth, and alive with unmentionable parasites."[3] Siberia's migrant masses, he learned during the four days before he could escape from the fourth-class car in which he had been obliged to travel by an accident, lived at a level of existence far below any New England preacher's line of vision.

Seven hundred miles east of Lake Baikal, travelers en route to Vladivostok exchanged their train accommodations for riverboats at Sretensk, "the most lively center of the Transbaikal," according to the official *Guide to the Great Siberian Railway* that the Imperial Russian Transport Ministry published in 1900. A century of progress since its founding as a convict prison at the end of the eighteenth century had brought Sretensk two churches, two schools, a flour mill, a tannery, a factory that produced ninety tons of soap, and commerce to the value of nearly seven million rubles ($3,500,000) each year.[4] Yet wealth had not changed the town's appearance, and in 1900 it retained all the primitiveness of an overextended eastern Siberian village. "A few old barns stuck anyhow on a humpy wilderness of dust," the English journalist John Fraser wrote disdainfully in his description of what he had seen when he had approached Sretensk from the west. On closer acquaintance, Fraser dismissed it as a town of "squalid raggedness."[5] To others, Sretensk seemed a "melancholy-stricken hole" whose "wretched inns" offered nothing to induce travelers to break their journeys any longer than necessary.[6]

At Sretensk, passengers traveling east boarded the creaking vessels and flat-bottomed rafts of the Amur Steam Navigation Company, which offered cabins to its first- and second-class passengers and posted notices that "third class [passengers] are placed on the decks of steamers and barges under awnings."[7] This "tatterdemalion throng [of third-class passengers] . . . carrying bedding, bundles of clothing, chunks of bread, a jangling kettle, and often a big flapping-tailed dried fish which would slap the face of the next person," Fraser wrote, fought their way onto the steamers' lower decks after the first- and second-class passengers had been boarded and the cargo stowed below.[8] That same year, "uncounted tow-headed babies tucked into every nook and cranny" on the crowded deck caught the eye of the Reverend Clark. "Every available foot of deck room," he reported in amazement, "had its two human feet to occupy it."[9]

Once under way, steamboat passengers traveling between Sretensk and Khabarovsk found themselves in unusual and unforeseen company, no matter what class of ticket they held. "I've an idea some fastidious Britishers would think this rather disgusting," Fraser remarked about the snorting and slurping of the passengers with whom he dined in the first-class saloon. "The most distinguished man at table," he explained, "was the colonel of a Tartar regiment . . . [who] ate with his fingers and salivated after the manner of a Mexican cow-puncher." To add insult to injury, the cabin that Fraser shared with a Siberian school inspector proved to be even worse than the ship's dining room. "I've known cleaner stables than our cabin," he complained. "[At] night I felt things dropping on my neck and crawling on my cheek, and making excursions along my arm."[10] Obliged to make the Amur journey at a time when a drought had left the river too shallow for steamboats, another traveler found himself in a flat-bottomed barge towed by a small tug that drew no more than a couple of feet of water. "The first class accommodation consisted of a stuffy cabin in which I could barely stand upright," he reported. "The food," he added in disgust, "was beyond anything I have ever experienced or even pictured."[11]

To add to everyone's discomfort, Amur steamboats often ran aground on the sandbars that filled the river's shallow channels. A few hours of pulling and prodding with poles and levers usually managed to heave the vessel clear, sometimes only to have it get stuck again just a few miles farther on. Mississippi River captains, those champion tellers of the tall tales that Mark Twain recorded with such relish, had been known to claim that they could cross a sandbar so long as "the sweat of an ice-pitcher" remained between the keel and the river's bottom.[12] Judging by the frequency with which they ran their boats aground, the captains of the Amur Steam Navigation Company tried to outdo their Mississippi counterparts at every bend. "Going down the Amur when the water is low," one traveler concluded wryly after he had made the journey in a small private steamer, "is as exciting as skating over thin ice."[13]

Those who did not travel during the scant 140 days when the Shilka and Amur rivers were open for navigation had to follow the river's frozen surface on sledges. Stopping only at post stations to change horses that had been driven across the snow and ice at breakneck speed, travelers needed at least twenty days to cover the distance between the two railheads. "The rule of the Russian road," the adventurous American engineer Lindon Bates explained, "[is that] one always starts at top speed, however bad the way ... [and] finishes at a gallop, however jaded the horses." Bates warned that such travel was not for the faint of heart. "Clothes and the nervous system," he wrote, "are at a discount in Siberian sledging." Day and night the weather maintained an unrelenting assault upon the human organism. "The cold is intense," Bates remembered. "Eyeglasses are unwearable, for the rising vapor from one's breath is caught and frozen on them in an opaque film. Fingers exposed but a moment become numb and useless, and uncovering the hand is an agony."[14]

Few travelers had Bates's fortitude or shared the enthusiasm of Lionel Gowing, the doughty Englishman from Hampstead who once insisted that "sledging in the moonlight nights had a charm which the brightest starlight could never give." Jolting against the chunks of frozen soup, meat, and milk that filled his sleigh, Gowing claimed to have found the forty-degree-below-zero temperatures in which he had crossed Siberia at the end of the 1880s invigorating. The "stern grandeur of the wintry landscape" and "the beautiful scenery [and] the clear bright weather" had enthralled Gowing but charmed very few others.[15] Most Trans-Siberian Railroad passengers therefore made the journey when the river between Sretensk and Khabarovsk was open for navigation.

Of the forty-two villages and hamlets that had arisen between Sretensk and Khabarovsk during the nineteenth century, the only one of any consequence was Blagoveshchensk, whose most striking landmark was a gigantic triumphal wooden arch built to commemorate the tsarevich Nicholas's visit in 1891. Founded in 1856, Blagoveshchensk was a Siberian boomtown whose population had grown from three thousand in 1880 to more than thirty thousand by 1900, mainly as a result of the discovery of gold in the nearby Zeia River. Blagoveshchensk had a gold town's economy of high prices and conspicuous waste that juxtaposed the elegant upon the tawdry. All across the town, impressive public buildings built of brick rose above one-story log cabins, yet Blagoveshchensk lacked the pulsating vibrance of its North American counter-parts. "It is a huge, straggling, prosperous village," the Reverend Clark wrote. "Of all the inland towns of Russia in Asia," he added, "this is the one which has had the greatest opportunities."[16] In 1900, no one knew for certain how these opportunities would be used or what direction the development of Blagoveshchensk would take.

A town whose name in Russian means "the Annunciation" or, more freely translated, "glad tidings," Blagoveshchensk soon became known to Europeans for the "black crime" that occurred after some sporadic rebel rifle fire from the Chinese side of the river during the Boxer Rebellion of 1900 drove a nervous cossack garrison to murder all of its Chinese workers. Fearful that another massacre such as was rumored to have taken place at Peking was about to begin, the cossacks herded several thousand Chinese into the river at lance point and drowned them all. Western observers were appalled at the Russian government's reluctance to punish the killers. "The drowning of these poor defense-less Chinamen," Fraser wrote with the self-righteous moral outrage that European travelers found so easy to muster in foreign lands, "has fixed a brand on Blagoveshchensk never to be forgotten."[17]

From Blagoveshchensk, steamboats from Sretensk had to continue east for another six hundred miles before they reached Khabarovsk, where about a quarter of the inhabitants were Koreans and Chinese and men outnumbered women by more than three to one. The town's first bank had only opened in 1899, and the local wine, made by an enterpris-ing Russian merchant by the name of Khlebnikov, was generally conceded to be very bad and equally expensive. "By reason of its uninhabited valleys, very wide, unpaved, unmade streets, and extensive barracks and government buildings," one traveler wrote as he passed through Khabarovsk, "the town seems desolate and stagnant."[18] Khaba-rovsk attracted comment from few other visitors, most of whom concen-trated upon putting it behind them as quickly as possible. "The conditions of life in Khabarovsk," the official *Guide to the Great Siberian Railway* stated blandly, "are not attractive on account of the absence of comfortable dwellings and the expensiveness of the most necessary articles."[19]

So long as Amur River steamboats continued to move passengers between Sretensk and Khabarovsk, the Trans-Siberian's schedule con-tinued to be little more than a fondly expressed hope. "It is impossible to calculate exactly, or even within a fortnight, the time that may be taken [for the journey]," the Reverend Francis Clark wrote after spend-ing thirty-eight days en route by train and riverboat from Vladivostok to Moscow. "I can well imagine," he concluded after a thirty-six-hour delay caused when a locomotive's fireman dumped coals onto a wooden bridge and set it afire, "that the trip might take three or four months instead of as many weeks."[20]

If the Trans-Siberian were to tie East and West together, the uncertainties of which Clark had complained had to be removed. Witte had therefore opened negotiations with the Chinese for the rights to build a thousand-mile railroad across Manchuria that would cut almost 350 miles off the Amur River route and pass through considerably less rugged terrain. His success in clearing the way for the Trans-Siberian's Manchurian connection offered the Russians a chance to dominate Manchuria, gain a foothold in Korea, establish an ice-free far eastern port on the Yellow Sea, and replace the Amur River steamboat route with a railroad.

Witte chose the coronation of Nicholas II and Empress Aleksandra in the spring of 1896, when some of the world's most prominent statesmen and the grandest of Russia's courtiers had gathered in Moscow, to plead Russia's case with Li Hung Chang, first chancellor of the Chinese Empire and representative of China's empress dowager at the Court of Imperial Russia.[21] Before the end of May, Li had agreed to Witte's demands in return for a Russian treaty of alliance against Japan, and the railroad's justification thus became the need to move Russian troops quickly to the far east if the Japanese should attack China. To conceal Russian ownership of the railway, Li insisted that the eighty-year concession China would grant to the land on which the railroad would be built must be given to the Russo-Chinese Bank, which was controlled by the Imperial Russian Ministry of Finance but had a Chinese diplomat as its chairman.[22] In return, Witte paid Li a bribe of three million rubles in gold through the Russo-Chinese Bank and wrote it off as part of the railroad's construction costs.[23]

Once Li's agreement had been converted into diplomatic documents, the Russians set to work on the Chinese Eastern Railway only to confront a host of unexpected problems. Bubonic plague swept Manchuria in the summer of 1899, and scientists, physicians, and public health experts had to be brought in to prevent the epidemic from raging out of control. No sooner had the plague been dealt with than the Boxer Rebellion broke out in China in the spring of 1900, and the Russians' hired coolies joined the rebels in ravaging more than five hundred miles of newly laid track. Another epidemic of bubonic plague struck during the summer of 1901, followed by Asiatic cholera, which broke out in 1902 as the Russians struggled to cut a two-mile tunnel through the Greater

Khingan Mountains, the last natural obstacle between Manchuria and the Russian frontier.[24] By the time the Russians opened the Chinese Eastern Railway to regular traffic in February 1903, it had cost them eleven million rubles more than they had spent to build all the rest of the railroad put together.[25] Yet Nicholas II and the Russian statesmen who hoped to win control of Manchuria thought the money well spent. A direct rail line now ran from Moscow to the western bank of Lake Baikal and from Lake Baikal's eastern shore to Vladivostok and Port Arthur, the newly acquired Russian naval base on the Yellow Sea. Only the link around the great lake's southern tip remained unfinished. Once that was done, Witte's vision of a railroad from the Baltic to the Pacific would be fulfilled.

31

Lake Baikal

Almost twenty-five million years before the first humans walked the earth, a series of seismic events created Lake Baikal in the middle of Siberia. Its name, in the language of the ancient Kurykans who lived there in the sixth century, means "much water," and those who have taken their place have called it, similarly, "natural sea" (*baigal-dalai* to the Buriats) and "rich lake" (*bai kel* in the language of the Iakuts).[1] Regarded by all who have lived around it as a "holy sea," the islands of which have long been venerated as places of worship, Lake Baikal fills an abyss as long as England, fifty miles wide, and more than a mile deep. The deepest body of fresh water anywhere on earth, Baikal's surface area of 12,162 square miles is larger than Belgium, and its 5,513 cubic miles of water comprise a fifth of the earth's freshwater supply. Something over three hundred rivers and mountain streams pour into it from the surrounding mountains, but only one—the mighty Angara River, which is more than a third of a mile wide where it joins the lake—exits from it. Although more than three and a half million cubic feet of water pour from Lake Baikal into the Angara each minute, Russian scientists estimate that it would take more than five hundred years to drain the lake if all of the water flowing into it could be shut off. According to another estimate, it would take most of the annual flow from all the world's major rivers to refill Lake Baikal, if that could be accomplished.[2]

The Russians managed to cross Siberia during the first third of the seventeenth century without seeing Lake Baikal or even guessing its existence. Their route carried them farther north, closer to the line that divides the taiga from the tundra, and it was only after they had reached the Pacific and begun to explore the southern parts of the lands they had discovered that they reached this "holy sea" of the Buriats and Iakuts. The first Russian to drink Baikal's waters was Kurbat Ivanov, a cossack captain who led seventy-five men to it in 1643 to collect fur tribute from the Buriats.[3] Soon after that, explorations beyond Lake Baikal uncovered irrigated valleys that once had been sown in grain. This discovery had been one factor in making Poiarkov and Khabarov so confident of finding cereals in the Daurian lands beyond the Amur River.[4]

A tangle of historical and geological contradictions, Lake Baikal continues to defy the best efforts of scientists and engineers to unravel its deeper mysteries. How did the types of flora one would expect to find in the high Swiss Alps come into being a mere fifteen hundred feet above sea level in the center of Asia? And how could such a lake, so fresh, cold, and stormy, nurture emerald green, chlorophyll-laden tropical sponges less than seven hundred miles below the Arctic Circle? Other lakes have rarely lasted longer than a million years before filling with sediment, but Baikal is more than twenty-five times that old. Although the layer of sediment on its bottom is nearly five miles thick (deep enough to bury Mount Everest with room to spare), the lake seems to be growing wider but not shallower.[5] As the world's oldest lake, Baikal continues to display aquatic plants and animals that have evolved over the past twenty-five million years of the earth's history. At every level, it is a zoological and botanical wonderland that continues to confound and fascinate scientists all across the world.

Lake Baikal contains two and a half thousand species of animals and plants, more than half of which cannot be found anywhere else on earth. Among them is the *golomianka*, or oil fish, so named because half of its body weight is oil. Iridescent, semitransparent, and prized by Baikal's natives for its medicinal qualities, the *golomianka* lives singly, not in schools, and is one of the few fish that gives birth to live offspring. Like fifteen hundred of Baikal's other creatures, it is unique to the lake's waters. So is the *epischura*, a tiny, whiskered crustacean no more than a sixteenth of an inch long. As many as three million of these tiny scavengers have been counted on a single square yard of Baikal's surface, and it is to their voracious appetite for algae and bacteria that the lake owes its extraordinary clarity. Scientists say that most of Baikal's water is so pure, in fact, that water collected in a laboratory beaker from its center becomes contaminated by the glass. Thanks to the *epischura*'s ability to remove its impurities, Lake Baikal is populated all the way to the bottom, unlike, for example, Africa's huge Lake Tanganyika, which sustains life for only the first five or six hundred feet below its surface.[6]

Lake Baikal's brilliant blue waters can turn violent in an instant, with waves rising to heights of six or seven feet.[7] "It is only on Baikal in the autumn that a man learns to pray from his heart," John Fraser wrote after living through one of its frequent storms. His crossing had begun "like a holiday cruise" on "a delicious afternoon" in September, only to turn sour when "billows of clouds tumbling from the [surrounding] mountains . . . filled the rigging of the ship with Valkyrie cries."[8] For several hours, the winds tore at the *Baikal* as it struggled to ferry Fraser and his fellow passengers across the lake. Then the storm, another of those natural phenomena that make Lake Baikal so complex, subsided as quickly as it had begun.

In 1901, the task of building a railroad around the southern tip of this treacherous and restless lake fell to Aleksandr Pertsov, once described as "a dynamic architect and civil engineer who preferred hard jobs to easy ones."[9] It may have been an exaggeration to claim, as one high official did in those days, that the circum-Baikal line "surpassed in difficulty and amount of work all those [railroads] constructed in the Russian Empire up to the present,"[10] but the undertaking certainly tested Pertsov's abilities as a railroad builder to the utmost. Embankments requiring an average of a hundred thousand cubic yards of stone and dirt per mile, a roadway that had to be blasted out of precipitous cliffs, thirty-three tunnels totaling more than five miles in length, and more than two hundred bridges and trestles all had to be built within the space of 162 miles before the link around Lake Baikal's southern tip could be finished.[11]

After three years of work, Pertsov opened this final segment of the Trans-Siberian Railroad to traffic in the fall of 1904, just in time to transport the huge quantities of men and supplies that the Russians needed to mount their campaign against the Japanese in Manchuria in February 1905. Then, for the first time in history, it became possible to travel by train from the Baltic to the Pacific. Able to move men and goods from European Russia to the Far East in less than three weeks, the Trans-Siberian Railroad had become, in the words of a British commentator, "a political weapon, the force and significance of which still are difficult to determine." Now the Russians had the means to build an empire that promised to be sufficient unto itself. "It makes Russia a totally self-contained state, no longer dependent upon the Dardanelles or the Straits [for shipping goods, armaments, men, and supplies from one end of the empire to the other]," the same writer explained. "It will give her an economic independence with which she can attain a degree of power such as no state has yet dreamed of."[12]

"After the discovery of America and the construction of the Suez Canal," one of France's future foreign ministers stated with admiration, "history has never recorded an undertaking with greater significance, or one with such profound direct and indirect consequences, than the construction of the Trans-Siberian Railway."[13] Like the United States of America on the North American continent, Russia now strived to fulfill what she regarded as her manifest destiny to rule Eurasia from the Baltic to the Pacific. "Siberia is for Russia," one Russian journalist explained. "Siberia is . . . Russia herself."[14] It seemed that a new era was about to begin and that the vision expressed more than fifteen years earlier by the editor of the Transport Ministry's official journal was about to be realized. "The ancient routes of the Huns and Mongols to Europe will open themselves anew," he had written then of the plans for a Trans-Siberian Railroad. "Along these paths," he went on, "steam engines will whistle and dart, bringing life and culture to the land of bears, sable, and gold!"[15] But war, it turned out, was destined to come before either culture or business. Even as the circum-Baikal link was being finished, Russia's armies were being tested against those of Japan in the Far East. To the amazement of those who had feared that the Trans-Siberian would make the forces of Russia dominant in Asia, the armies of the tsar were found wanting.

32

"A Small
Victorious War"

Before the days of the Trans-Siberian Railroad, Russia's tsars had defended Siberia's far eastern lands with a few scattered garrisons and cossack regiments. For much of the eighteenth and nineteenth centuries, China's attention had been elsewhere, and Japan, destined to become the major force in Asia in the twentieth century, had remained turned inward upon herself until the 1860s. The only threat to Russia's interests in Asia had seemed to be the British, who from their firmly held positions in India were reaching toward Afghanistan and aspiring to play an important part in the affairs of China. Yet, even from these new footholds, the British were in no position to threaten Siberia directly. Against natives untrained in modern warfare and too few in number to mount any large-scale campaign against them, the Russians continued to feel confident that their hold on Siberia remained secure.

Limited defenses in the Far East served the tsars of Russia well enough until Chinese settlers began to pour into northern Manchuria in the 1880s.[1] Then, they began to worry about how outnumbered their frontier outposts would be if the Chinese spread across the shallow Amur into Siberia. "In Manchuria there are more than ten million [Chinese] while there are fewer than a hundred thousand [Russians] in all the Siberian coastal lands," a colonel from the General Staff reported to a meeting of the Imperial Russian Geographical Society in 1891.[2] Although exaggerated to command his listeners' attention, the colonel's speech stirred age-old fears that the Asian menace, which once had brought the hordes of Batu Khan to the Russians' lands, was about to rise again. Then, as the armies of China and Japan began to modernize, many in Russia began to fear that a new Mongol horde might be forming in the east to destroy the civilization of the West.[3] Russia's poets began to speak of hearing the "iron tread" of new Hun armies echoing in the east. Their advance, the Symbolist Valerii Briusov warned, would drive "thinkers and poets, keepers of mysteries and the faith" into hiding "in catacombs, in deserts, and in caves." Everything else might "perish without a trace."[4]

Worries about holding back the "yellow tide" of Asia had played a part in the decision to build the Trans-Siberian Railroad, although Alexander III's caution and Witte's warnings about the dangers of imperialist ventures had kept the most ardent of Russia's expansionists from reaching beyond Siberia's frontiers. "Russia's mission in the East must be protective and educational," Witte had warned when more reckless men urged the tsar to seize lands coveted by the Japanese in Korea and Manchuria. "It is Russia's natural task," he explained, "to guard her neighboring eastern lands which lie in her sphere of influence against the excessive political and colonial claims of other powers."[5] Witte might protest Britain's incursions into China and worry about Japan's growing foothold on the Asian mainland, but he was not prepared to support diplomatic pressures with military force. First, Russia's economy had to be put into order, its budget balanced, and its grip upon Siberia made more firm. In the early 1890s, Witte was not prepared to risk his efforts to achieve those vital goals by launching his nation upon ill-advised undertakings in Siberia's southern borderlands.

When he ascended Russia's throne at the end of 1894, Nicholas II shared neither his father's caution about Asia nor Witte's good sense about avoiding foreign entanglements that might further tax the empire's already strained budget. Although Witte had in earlier times helped to shape Nicholas's views about the Far East, his timid student had grown too quickly into an incautious emperor who supported a more aggressive policy there than either his father or his mentor thought wise. Being thus set at odds with his emperor forced Witte to fight for his political survival in a government in which, as he once wrote, "intrigue plays an unseemly role."[6] At the same time, the emperor's lack of caution undermined Witte's efforts to restrain those reckless courtiers who hoped to reap large profits from the lands beyond Siberia's frontiers.

Yet Witte's commitment to building the Trans-Siberian Railroad eventually drew him deeply into the politics of the Far East nonetheless.

In negotiating the concessions that made it possible for Russia to build the Chinese Eastern Railway across Manchuria, Witte at one stroke weakened China, strengthened Russia's position, and threatened the designs that the Japanese had on Korea and parts of Manchuria. By moving into Manchuria, Russia embarked upon a collision course with Japan that made war between them all but inevitable unless one or the other retreated from Siberia's far east.

Unlike the tradition-bound mandarins and corrupt warlords who served themselves first and China last, the rulers and statesmen of Japan had built a modern army and an industrial base to support it during the last third of the nineteenth century. By 1900, they could mobilize over a million men, and they showed no hesitation about using force to defend their newly announced claims on the Asian mainland.[7] Japan had already gone to war with China over these interests in 1894, when it had advanced into Korea and the Liaotung peninsula.[8] When Nicholas II allowed speculators at his court to extend Russian influence into the Korean territories that the Japanese had just claimed, the tension between the two nations mounted.[9] "He is in an excited state," Witte wrote of his emperor then. "Ideas of some kind or another are seething inside him."[10] Anxious to make common cause with a circle of adventurers who urged him to view Russia's destiny in the Far East in bolder terms, Nicholas removed Witte from office in 1903.[11]

Sensing that Russia had crossed a Rubicon in embarking upon this new course, Witte left the tsar's government, warning as he did so that "an armed clash with Japan would be a great disaster,"[12] because the "elements, the distances, the oceans and the seas all were against Russia."[13] The Far East was too far away and Russia's ability to supply a modern army there still too limited to be worth the risk. "I do not desire war between Russia and Japan," Nicholas replied, "and I shall not permit it."[14] Japan, he insisted, must cede her sphere of influence in northern Korea to Russia, and he continued to speak of Russia's generous forbearance toward the people whom he habitually described as "little short-tailed monkeys."[15] Russia's emperor thus persisted in believing that the course of Far Eastern affairs could be controlled from St. Petersburg and that war would come only if—and when—the Russians desired it.

Despite the warnings of Witte and Minister of War General Aleksei Kuropatkin, Nicholas II and his advisers never seemed to take seriously the possibility that the Japanese might attack Russia or that a war against Japan might pose a serious test of their empire's strength. "The tsar remained supremely confident," Witte later wrote, that the Japanese "would be smashed to smithereens" in any war between the two nations.[16] In fact, now that the Trans-Siberian Railroad had been completed except for the circum-Baikal link, some of Nicholas's advisers were beginning to think that a war in Asia could help to calm Russia's domestic turmoil. "In order to hold back the tide of revolution," one high official wrote, "we need a small, victorious war."[17] "War is war, and peace is peace," Nicholas told the uneasy Kuropatkin soon afterward. "But this business of not knowing either way is agonizing."[18]

Confident that Russia's might far outweighed Japan's, Nicholas and his advisers showed no particular concern when the Japanese ambassador left St. Petersburg with his entire staff near the end of January 1904. The Russians had not yet planned how to finance a war in the Far East, nor had they begun to move the men and matériel that such a war would require into position. Nicholas seems simply to have assumed that the Japanese would wait for Russia to take the initiative in resolving the issues that divided them. Now ready to combine their samurai tradition with modern weapons to meet any challenge in the Far East, the Japanese had no intention of doing so.

When Nicholas and the empress Aleksandra attended a performance of the Imperial Opera on St. Petersburg's Mariinskaia Square on the evening of January 26, they did not know that Japan's fleet had steamed into Russia's newly built naval bastion at Port Arthur and attacked the battleships of the Far Eastern Fleet under the cover of darkness just eight hours before. Because Russia's Far Eastern High Command failed even to send proper word of the attack to the capital, the first news of it reached St. Petersburg from a commercial agent in the Far East, whose telegram his counterpart in Russia's capital took to the now retired Witte, who relayed it to Russia's incredulous war minister.[19] For the first time in modern history, Russians and Asians armed with modern weapons faced each other to test the myth of white supremacy. With its links across Manchuria to Vladivostok and Port Arthur now complete, the Trans-Siberian Railroad had made that confrontation possible for the Russians and unavoidable for the Japanese.

The Japanese attack against carelessly defended battleships and unprepared land fortifications marked the beginning of an eleven-month debacle at Port Arthur that ended on December 20, 1904, when, after reporting that he could hold the fortress for "only a few days more,"[20] the Russian commander surrendered more than thirteen thousand able-bodied men, hundreds of tons of supplies, over six hundred field guns, 200,000 artillery shells, and 2.5 million rounds of machine-gun and rifle ammunition to the dumbfounded Japanese.[21] Not only had the Russians lost a major fortress to a foe they had disdained as inferior but they had done it in full view of a world that had become linked by transoceanic telegraph, faster ships, and railroads as never before. For the first time, New York, London, Paris, and Berlin knew what had happened in the Far East only yesterday. And, as the world became smaller, the Russians' ignominious defeat at Port Arthur loomed larger in newspaper headlines. For the first time in modern history, Asians had defeated Europeans. No longer small and far from victorious, the Russo-Japanese War was beginning to spawn revolutionary discontent among the workers of St. Petersburg and Moscow at the same time that a shortage of overcoats and winter boots (sent from European Russia in the fall of 1904 but destined not to arrive in the Far East before the war ended almost a year later) undermined the morale of the troops at the front.

After the fall of Port Arthur, the Russians centered their hopes upon the large army that General Kuropatkin had withdrawn to Manchuria's capital of Mukden after an indecisive battle at Liaoyang in August and September. Now both sides needed a victory, the Russians to avenge their defeats at Port Arthur and in Korea, the Japanese to finish a war that was beginning to strain their reserves of men, money, and matériel to the breaking point.[22] "It is essential," Japan's commander told his generals at the beginning of February 1905, "that the enemy be dealt a heavy blow."[23] That was to be tried later that month at Mukden, where more than half a million men fought along a hundred-mile front for twenty days in what became history's first modern battle.

At Mukden, commanders had to rely for the first time upon telephone and telegraph to shape their vision of a battlefield that stretched far beyond the horizon, and victory became more than ever the achievement of corps and division commanders who had the foresight to turn unexpected shifts in the tide of battle to their advantage. In a battle in which reconnaissance and mobility became the key to victory, Kuropatkin moved his forces ponderously, predictably, and with appalling lack of imagination. Although he had the resources to develop reconnaissance far superior to that of the Japanese, the Russian commander had no idea what forces faced him or how they were positioned, and he made assumptions about his enemy's strategy that even the scant available evidence did not support. Japan's energetic generals therefore drove the Russians back at every point, although both sides were bled white in the process. By the time Japan's Marshal Iwao Oyama entered Mukden on February 25, more than 160,000 men had been killed, wounded, or listed as missing in action.[24]

Oyama had not the resources to press the fighting, but the war could not end at Mukden, for the Russians still had one more card to play. In October 1904, the Russian Admiralty had ordered the Baltic Fleet to the Far East, and at the moment of Kuropatkin's defeat, it was steaming around the tip of Africa to attack the Japanese in their home waters. The emperor, Witte remembered, expected that this badly trained force "would reverse the entire course of the war,"[25] a view in which he was encouraged by several soothsayers who had predicted in the fall of 1904 that peace would be concluded in Tokyo and had insisted that "only kikes and intellectuals could think otherwise."[26] With ships manned by inexperienced crews and defended by untrained gunners, this desperate venture came to a catastrophic end in the Strait of Tsushima in the middle of May 1905. In this first of the twentieth century's great naval battles, it cost the Japanese three torpedo boats and 116 men to send twenty of Russia's warships and five thousand of their crew members to the bottom of the sea in a single day.[27]

For the better part of eighteen months, the Japanese had defeated the best forces the Russians had in the Far East, but they had done so at a cost that threatened to turn the war against them if the fighting continued. "We now must be prudent," Japan's Field Marshal Marquis Yamagata Aritomo insisted. "The enemy still has powerful forces in its home country, but we have already exhausted ours."[28] The Japanese therefore accepted President Theodore Roosevelt's offer to mediate the conflict, although Nicholas delayed doing so in the hope that time and the weight of the new divisions that could be sent by way of the now completed circum-Baikal link might turn the war in Russia's favor. If Russia's armies could maintain their will to fight, and if Russia's factories could provide them with the weapons they needed, defeat might yet be averted.

Russia's tsar had neither the public support nor the domestic peace needed to follow such a course. With discontent among the workers in their largest cities about to explode into revolution, Russia's statesmen urged their emperor to end the war rather than risk new battles at home and in the Far East at the same time. Yet two more months had to pass before the Russians and Japanese had their first meeting at Portsmouth, New Hampshire. "Did you ever know anything more pitiable than the condition of Russian despotism?" President Roosevelt asked his ailing secretary of state at one point. "The Tsar is a preposterous little creature," he concluded. "He has been unable to make war, and he now is unable to make peace!"[29]

Thanks in large measure to Witte, who, although opposed to the war from the beginning, now negotiated a better peace than his emperor had any reason to expect, the Russo-Japanese War ended twenty days after the Russians and Japanese arrived at Portsmouth. Although Russia retained all of Siberia and lost only the Liaotung peninsula, the South Manchurian Railway, and the southern half of Sakhalin Island,[30] these losses were enough to convince her statesmen that the time had come to turn inward to develop Siberia rather than reach beyond its frontiers for new lands. Russia had too many problems at home. Her peasants were too poor, the yields of their fields too low, their villages too crowded, their taxes too high. A way had to be found to give more Russians better opportunities to rise out of the poverty that had ruled their villages for so long, and Siberia again seemed to offer the answer. With hundreds of thousands of peasants in European Russia suffering from land hunger, the tsar's government began to encourage massive migrations to the rich farmlands of Siberia's southwest. As had already happened in North America, South Africa, and Australia, Siberia became a land of promise for millions of immigrants in search of new and better lives.

33

The Immigrants

Fifty years after Ermak's "conquest," nine out of every ten of the 196,000 souls living in Siberia were natives whose ancestors had roamed the lands east of the Urals for millennia. By the time Russia and Japan made peace in 1905, Siberia's population had grown to 9.4 million, nine out of ten of whom were Russians. In the course of a little more than three centuries, the Russians' numbers had multiplied by a factor of 365, while those of the native Siberians had increased by less than six. Immigration, which became especially massive in the 1890s, accounted for this overwhelming increase in Siberia's Russians. Just between 1897 and 1911, three and a half million men, women, and children moved to Siberia from European Russia.[1]

As one high official wrote, the Russian colonization of Siberia had been "the free migration of unfree peasants" until after the Emancipation Acts of 1861 had taken effect in European Russia.[2] Once across the Urals, enterprising peasants in olden times had been able to live free of the many disabilities they had suffered in their former homes, where masters and government officials claimed the fruits of their labors and village communes reduced them all to the lowest common denominator. Siberia had been the place in which a peasant could leave behind the bonds of serfdom and begin life anew in a land that was as fresh as the immigrant's life itself. "Nowhere in the United States," England's John Fraser wrote as he compared Siberia's southwest with the Great Plains of North America, "have I seen such an expanse of magnificent agricultural land waiting for man and his plough."[3] "Oh, for a hundred families of my own North-country yeomen to settle here," he exclaimed further on. "In half a generation [they would] go home with fortunes made."[4]

Although Fraser attributed to Siberia's immigrants all of the laziness for which Europeans usually criticized Russia's peasants, the men and women who crossed the Urals were in fact a different breed compared to the countrymen they had left behind in European Russia. As an Englishman who traveled from Peking to St. Petersburg by way of Kiakhta in 1861 explained, beginning a new life in Siberia was not for the timid or unadventurous. "They have something of independence in their bearing," he wrote as he compared the lives of Siberia's peasants to the "poverty, negligence, and misery" of those he had met in European Russia. "The condition of their families," he concluded, "evinces a certain amount of self respect." There was a sense of "rude comfort" to be found in Siberian villages,[5] as well as signs of individual initiative such as were rarely seen in the peasant communities of Russia's European lands. "The great and varied wealth of the country has developed in the Siberian a passion for gain," one expert wrote at the beginning of this century.[6] Unlike their brethren who had remained behind, the Russians in Siberia were ready to take risks in the hope of greater profit.

Because they had run away from estates to which they had been bound as serfs, many of the peasants who fled to Siberia before 1861 crossed the Urals individually or in small groups. There were fewer than six hundred thousand Russians in all of Siberia in 1800, and twice as many exiles and prisoners entered Siberia from Russia between 1800 and 1850 than did peasants and runaway serfs. Only in the 1880s did the number of peasants hoping to begin new lives in Siberia began to climb into the tens of thousands. In 1889 alone, more than forty thousand crossed the Urals, and in 1891 that number more than doubled. Drawn by the prospect of opportunities that life had denied them at home, this flood of immigrants began to change Siberia.

Traveling in barges towed by steamboats or in carts drawn by horses or oxen, Siberia's new settlers moved mainly toward the Altai lands that made up the southern parts of the provinces of Tomsk and Tobolsk. Poor before they set out, they were even poorer now, for they had taken promissory notes from equally indigent friends and neighbors as payment for the crumbling cottages, barns, and livestock they had left behind. Without cash to meet the emergencies that inevitably occurred, one in ten would die before they reached their new homes; children would perish at three times the rate of adults.[7]

The tide of immigrants entering Siberia in the 1880s and 1890s became a flood once trains began to run on the western sections of the Trans-Siberian Railroad. Beginning every May, when the government reduced the fare for a family of four to less than a month's wages in a Petersburg or Moscow factory, special trains moved Russia's masses eastward by the tens of thousands. "They were horribly dirty," John Fraser wrote of the immigrants that filled the train he took to Siberia in 1901. "They carried all their worldly possessions with them" and lived on wet black bread, tea, and the watermelons that were sold at the train stations. The women, with the "patience of cows on their plain faces," Fraser noted, seemed to be happy. So did the men and especially the children.[8] "There is nothing to be seen like it at present in any other part of the world," one of Fraser's contemporaries wrote of the immigrants he saw when he crossed Siberia from east to west in 1898. "Every day one passes long trains laden with them."[9] Those who traveled by cart and wagon spent most of their nights under the stars in much the same way as the wagon trains that had crossed the American prairie half a century earlier. "The scene is very picturesque," a French journalist added, "the men unsaddling the horses, the women going to the well for water, and the children playing about, while some old man, seated on the wayside, reads the Bible out aloud to a group of eager listeners."[10] Except when Russia was fighting her war with Japan, the number of new settlers coming to Siberia never fell below a hundred thousand a year after 1895. Soon it rose above half a million.

Suffering was as much a part of the journey as adventure, although this hard and brutal side of Siberian migration had no place in the idealized accounts of travelers. Nor was it featured in the optimistic reports of officials whose superiors were beginning to see Siberian migration as a solution to the problems of overpopulation and land hunger that peasants suffered in the more crowded lands of European Russia. "The transfer of workers and capital from . . . a country where they have little into a country where they have a greater productivity," John Stuart Mill had once written, "increases the sum of riches in the old as well as in the new country."[11] No one quoted that remark with more enthusiasm than Pëtr Stolypin, Russia's first prime minister and an ardent advocate of free Siberian immigration.

The great migration that followed the Trans-Siberian Railroad continued to accelerate after the Russo-Japanese War, as peasants rushed to take advantage of the free land that the government continued to offer. In 1907, more than half a million Russians crossed the Urals, and a year later the number rose to three-quarters of a million, or more than the entire Russian population of Siberia a hundred years earlier.[12] Nearly three quarters of these immigrants continued to settle in Siberia's west and southwest, at roughly the same latitude as southern England, but one out of every five now went on to the lands beyond Lake Baikal. "Siberia is growing fabulously," Prime Minister Stolypin wrote to his emperor in 1910. "The mixed current of rich and poor, strong and weak, registered and irregular migrants bursting through from Russia into Siberia is in general a wonderful and powerful colonizational element."[13] Stolypin thought that the rugged individualism that the migration seemed to foster would strengthen Russia against the rising tide of revolution, but he saw dangers in Siberia too. An *"enormous, rudely democratic country, which soon will throttle European Russia,"* Stolypin warned, could be the result of the new spirit of independence that was growing among Siberia's immigrants.[14]

Such independence made Siberia's peasants more responsible citizens than their countrymen in European Russia. Whether they found land to till in already established communities or claimed holdings on newly opened government lands, Siberia's immigrants lived in villages rather than on isolated homesteads as their North American counterparts had done. Always the shape of the village was the same, with peasant cottages lining a single main street, the length of which was determined by the number of households along it. This was the way that peasants lived in European Russia, too, but in Siberia there were obvious differences. "The cottages of the peasants in the southern districts of Tobolsk province startled me by their spaciousness in comparison with the cramped, chimneyless huts of the peasants of Great Russia's Black Soil provinces," the famous Russian geographer Pëtr Semënov wrote when he first visited Siberia. "Usually they had six windows facing the street, and sometimes as many as twelve. Their roofs were built of planks," he added, "and sometimes these buildings had a second story."[15] By comparison, the peasant huts in Great Russia were almost always in bad repair. "Almost all cottages have thatched roofs which often leak, and in the winter the walls are generally covered with dung to keep the place warm," a government report on peasant life in Great Russia stated in 1902. "In brief," it concluded, "the poverty of the peasant establishment [in European Russia] is astounding."[16]

Siberia's new wealth in grain, meat, and timber led farsighted men to revive the dreams of a Northeast Passage that had tantalized their ancestors since the days of Ivan the Terrible and Queen Elizabeth. In 1876, Aleksandr Sibiriakov, whose huge silver-smelting works at Nerchinsk had made his family the richest in Siberia, had helped to finance voyages that brought the English merchant captain Joseph Wiggins and the Swedish explorer A. E. Nordenskjöld from the waters of northern Europe into the mouth of the Enisei River, and before another decade had passed, Nordenskjöld had sailed from Sweden to Cape Dezhnëv and through Bering Strait to the Pacific.[17] For a time, the triumphs of Wiggins and Nordenskjöld had remained little more than scientific curiosities, but as the harvests that millions of immigrants reaped from eighty million acres of virgin farmland transformed Siberia into a land of food exporters for the first time in its history, they took on new significance.[18] By 1910, Siberian farms boasted a yearly surplus of over a million tons of wheat, and their annual production of butter had risen to 63,000 tons in 1907 from just over 7,000 in 1894. Once men had proved that cargo-laden steam-powered ships could cross the icebound seas that had halted sailing vessels in earlier times, fortunes awaited those who could ship Siberia's surplus to Europe.

If immigrants so transformed Siberia's agriculture as to make the Northeast Passage profitable at the beginning of the twentieth century, they also built Siberia's cities. While only Tomsk and Irkutsk had populations of over fifty thousand in 1897, they—in addition to Vladivostok and Omsk—had over a hundred thousand by 1911. Eleven other Siberian cities had grown to fifty thousand by that time, and their rapid growth had created a boomtown atmosphere that was every bit as rough and raw as that seen in the American West. Still, the first years of the twentieth century also brought education and the finer amenities of life, especially to the cities west of the Enisei. Omsk, Semipalatinsk, Krasnoiarsk, and Tobolsk each boasted more than a dozen secondary and technical schools before the first decade of the twentieth century had closed, while Tomsk had more than thirty in addition to Siberia's first university.[19] Drawn together within Siberia's vastness by its opportunities, immigrants from European Russia soon began to think of themselves as "Siberians" rather than as people from Moscow, Kiev, Tambov, or some other province. This new sense of regional identity gave birth to the rude peasant democracy that Stolypin both admired and feared.[20]

Turn-of-the-century observers found it hard to resist drawing parallels between this new Siberia and the American West. East of the Enisei, there was that same roughness, that same devil-may-care world of fast money and fast women that had been so much a part of the American West at roughly the same point in its history. With the same poorly fitted cultural and economic overlays, there were the same amazing contrasts, too. The public-minded citizens of Irkutsk contributed nearly two hundred thousand rubles to build a theater but left its streets unpaved and sewage flowing in open ditches. "It is very gay—very, very gay," the American engineer Lindon Bates wrote at that time of an evening spent in the dining room of the city's Metropol Hotel, in which moss had been stuffed into the crevices of the log walls to keep out the cold. "Corks popped, and sweet champagne flowed," he remembered, and the bottles had come "thick and fast" all night long.[21] Army officers, tea merchants, gold miners, trappers, and anyone else with money to spend all gathered to share the "thriving, jostling, gay" life of this city that reminded one visitor of "a restless, bustling Western American town near the region of gold diggings."[22] This was Russia's Wild East, and it was every bit as wild as the West of the United States to which travelers so often compared it.

34

Siberia's Wild East

Irkutsk was the center of Siberia's Wild East, just as San Francisco and Denver were centers of America's Wild West. Gambling in Irkutsk was a passion, and conspicuous consumption of luxuries that travelers never expected to find so far from Europe was a matter of local pride. Fine port, French champagne, and a score of other signs of life at the top in the capitals of Europe and America could all be made to appear in an instant if the buyer could pay the price in faraway Irkutsk. "If, of the towns I know, I sought one that Irkutsk is really suggestive of, I would select San Francisco," John Fraser wrote after he had crossed Siberia in 1901. "The social atmosphere is the same," he explained, "and there is the same free-and-easy, happy-go-lucky, easy-come, easy-go, devil-may-care style of living."[1] Irkutsk had its demimonde and its high society, both set apart and intertwined in ways that can happen only in a city in a state of ceaseless flux.

With a population of 51,434 in 1897, Irkutsk had begun its history as a lonely frontier outpost just thirty-two years after the *Mayflower* had sailed into Plymouth harbor, but its development had progressed much more slowly than the region around the Pilgrims' landing place. Irkutsk had celebrated its sesquicentennial before its population reached ten thousand, and, despite its importance in the East-West trade that flowed from Kiakhta in the eighteenth and nineteenth centuries, there was little to remind visitors of those trading centers of Europe and America that dealt in similar volumes of goods. By the end of the nineteenth century, Irkutsk had become the second largest city in Siberia with more than twelve thousand buildings, but its way of life still remained wilder and closer to the frontier than its size led visitors to expect.[2] Set in the midst of the Siberian taiga a thousand miles from anywhere, Irkutsk remained a city of contradictions in which the unexpected became a part of everyday life.

Like all Siberian towns, Irkutsk came alive in winter, when its un- paved streets disappeared beneath a veneer of hard-packed snow and the lumpy muck and mud of progress turned solid, white, and smooth. "We found ourselves in the midst of a scene of civilization such as we had not witnessed since setting foot on Russian soil," a London doctor who arrived in midwinter from Siberia's far east wrote. "Sledges with beautiful well-groomed horses and glittering harness were galloping along the road, and ladies paced the sidewalks dressed in furs of designs which showed that Parisian fashions are not neglected by the mantle- makers of Irkutsk."[3] In winter, visitors to Irkutsk were fascinated by the way in which its merchants offered their wares for sale in frozen form: fowl piled like bricks and sturgeon stiff as boards and sometimes stacked in threes, tail down, nose pointing skyward, like the rifles of an en- camped infantry battalion. Milk and soup came in bricks or cakes into which lengths of twine had been implanted so that buyers could carry them away conveniently.[4] It was, in short, a world in which the ravages of winter were used to make life more convenient than it had been before the frosts set in.

In Irkutsk, men and women discovered what they had come to find. The founder of the Young People's Society of Christian Endeavor, Reverend Francis Clark, saw it in 1900 as a "small city dominated by a score of great churches."[5] Others found it more bawdy than pious, with citizens more dedicated to living in the here and now than to contem- plating life in the hereafter. Bootleggers, tea merchants, smugglers, thieves, traders, trappers, gold miners, soldiers, frontier whores, and ex-convicts all thronged to whatever places served food and liquor, and the city's best hotel in 1900 was still a rambling log structure in which travelers slept on straw mattresses in rooms hung with velvet curtains.[6] With *cafés chantants* that, in the words of one visitor, featured "maidens in a minimum of skirt and a maximum of smile,"[7] many of the city's amusements were, as another traveler remarked, "of the grosser order, unredeemed by wit."[8]

In Irkutsk, eating and gambling were pastimes but drinking was a way of life. "He who does not drain his glass is slighting the lady of the house" was a motto that often hung over the table of hors d'oeuvres, or *zakuski*, with which Russians habitually began an evening of gambling and dining. Siberians amused themselves at such gatherings with cards and dice until about midnight, when hosts invited their guests to share dinners that often included suckling pig, veal, game, sturgeon, and other kinds of fish, all washed down with immense quantities of alcohol. "I must have drunk at least three bottles of port that night, to say nothing of vodka," a fellow of Britain's Royal Geographical Society wrote of a similar dinner given by a merchant in Kiakhta. "We then adjourned to the drawing room," he continued, "where all sang and shouted at the top of their voices, regardless of time or tune, till past 4 A.M." Until sunrise, the outside world was forgotten. Then, the traveler concluded, "[you] bundle down the steps into the yard, where dogs snarl around your legs, open the big gate, and emerge into the street."[9]

In 1879, a fire burned four thousand of Irkutsk's buildings, destroyed goods valued at more than thirty million rubles, left some twenty thousand people homeless, and consumed so much of the city's grain reserves that the mayor ordered local distillers to cut their production of vodka in half for the next two years.[10] The fire, which began not long before noon on a Sunday, ravaged the dwellings of rich and poor alike and left the Reverend Henry Lansdell (who had come to Irkutsk to open a branch of the Bible Society) looking on in amazement while "no one took charge" and the city burned. "A river was flowing on either side of the city," Lansdell remembered, "but the firemen had no means of conducting the water by hose, and carried it in large barrels on wheels." As he and his companion crossed the Angara River to escape the burning city, men with "blanched faces and fear-stricken countenances," women screaming in fright, and children bawling in panic crossed their path. Terror built upon terror, making it seem that everything was lost and nothing could be saved. When they returned the next day, the Englishmen found the residents of burned-out Irkutsk already making light of their losses. "The people's demeanor was in strange contrast with their pitiable condition," Lansdell wrote. "Many having saved their samovars were drinking afternoon tea and on all sides were joking and laughing at their comical situation."[11]

The fire of 1879 helped to move Irkutsk decisively toward the modern age. The city rebuilt itself quickly, and new stone and brick buildings gave it a more elegant, stable appearance. The modern luxuries of electric lighting and telephone service came to Irkutsk very soon after the railroad, and contributions from wealthy citizens supported two companies of actors in an impressive theater. Although the streets remained unpaved and "all the sanitary arrangements" (in Fraser's words) "were unsanitary," the city was beginning to put on airs and think of itself as "the Paris of Siberia." "Even a grimy millionaire in red shirt and dirty top-boots will not be tolerated in the fashionable restaurants," Fraser explained. Nonetheless, one of the city's finest dining establishments, in which the cuisine was Parisian and the decor reasonably elegant, still featured a huge hurdy-gurdy organ for its patrons' entertainment. "Fancy 'A Bicycle Made for Two' being played in Eastern Siberia!" Fraser wrote in amazement. "It is just like a mushroom city in Western America."[12]

Even though the population of Irkutsk would "mushroom" by two and a half times between 1900 and the First World War, there were other cities in Siberia's east to which Fraser's description applied as well or better. Krasnoiarsk, where waiters in the railroad station restaurant served dinner in full evening dress around 1900, nearly tripled in size between 1897 and 1911. So did Vladivostok, Russia's rapidly growing "Mistress of the East," in which the grime and slime of too-rapid progress made a memorable impact upon travelers at the beginning of the new century. "The phenomenal filth of the place beggared description," a traveler wrote of one of Vladivostok's best hotels in the mid-1890s.[13] Although a more charitable commentator a few years later spoke of the city's "remarkably cosmopolitan" character, he nonetheless described it as being at a "raw, half-baked stage of its existence."[14] Even at its worst, this far eastern bastion of Russian power radiated energy and vibrance. "No man can not be amazed by what Russia has done in a generation," Fraser wrote after he had seen Vladivostok. "Russia has laid hold on the East."[15]

If the growth of Vladivostok was impressive after the opening of the Trans-Siberian Railroad, that of Chita was even more amazing. Originally the lonely outpost to which the Decembrists had been exiled in 1827, by George Kennan's time Chita had become a straggling trading town of four thousand.[16] Like the capital of the Transbaikal, it had remained a backwater until the railroad made its people conscious of fashion and anxious to ape the styles of manners and dress that they imagined applied in more civilized parts of the world. By the early 1900s, the population of Chita had passed eleven thousand. Scarcely more than a decade later, it had grown sevenfold.[17]

Perhaps most amazing among Siberia's "mushroom cities" was Kharbin—the "Aladdin City," as some called it—that had sprung up next to the Chinese Eastern Railroad about two thirds of the way between Chita and Vladivostok. The home of a few Chinese merchants and traders in

1900, Kharbin became in less than a decade a frantic, throbbing city of eighty thousand, with railway shops, army barracks, mills, stockyards, and a distillery that produced three million gallons of vodka a year. On the eve of World War I, two American travelers spoke of the "profusion of color" to be seen when East and West intermingled on a Saturday night on Kharbin's Kitaiskaia, the central thoroughfare whose name translates as "Chinese Street." "Soldier, sailor, tinker, tailor of half the races of the Occident and the Orient pass to and fro with gay laughter and chatter," these visitors wrote. Here in the middle of northern Manchuria Russian soldiers "with bayoneted rifles slung across their backs and big wooden revolver holsters at the hip" tried to keep order among a throng that had dedicated itself to achieving exactly the opposite.[18] Kharbin had a wildness that made Irkutsk seem tame by comparison. "What sort of revolver are you carrying?" was a standard question among casual acquaintances. Weapons made by Colt (which had supplied side arms to the Russian army during the Crimean War) and Smith & Wesson (maker of the standard side arm of the Russian army in the 1880s) were the ones most preferred.[19]

Everywhere, signs of conspicuous wealth began to punctuate the poverty that had dominated Siberia's Wild East in earlier times, just as the Diamond Jim Bradys and Bet-a-Million Gateses left their mark on turn-of-the-century America. In the mid-1880s, Kennan found one such magnate by the name of Butin in Nerchinsk, which was then a lonesome town of four thousand near the Manchurian frontier. "As I entered the splendid ballroom and caught the full-length reflection of my figure in the largest mirror in the world, I felt like rubbing my eyes to make sure that I was awake," Kennan wrote of his visit to Butin's mansion. "Marquetry floors, silken curtains, hangings of delicate tapestry, stained-glass windows, splendid chandeliers, soft Oriental rugs, white-and-gold furniture upholstered with satin, old Flemish paintings, and marble statues" all seemed amazingly out of place more than three thousand miles east of the Urals. So did the mansion's "extensive conservatory filled with palms, lemon-trees, and rare orchids" in a land in which winter temperatures fell to − 50° Centigrade. Compared with the town's only hotel, Kennan concluded, going to Butin's "was like going into Aladdin's palace from an East Siberian *étape.*"[20]

But if Butin was an early Siberian Croesus, there were any number of others to be found by the beginning of the twentieth century. One Englishman met a merchant in Irkutsk who used a large gold nugget as an ashtray and boasted of the three thousand rubles in yearly interest he lost by doing so. Another slept beneath a rare antique ebony bed draped with a seventeenth-century Gobelin tapestry because it was "too good to use." A gold-mine owner gave half a million rubles to rebuild the Cathedral of the Nativity in Krasnoiarsk, and Kiakhta's tea merchants contributed a sum half again that large to build a cathedral of their own. Thanks to men of similar means, among them the same Aleksandr Sibiriakov who had financed Wiggins and Nordenskjöld in their explorations of Siberia's Northeast Passage, the University of Tomsk had more than four million rubles donated as an endowment for scholarships. But the most notable patron of learning in turn-of-the-century Siberia was Gennadii Iudin, the Krasnoiarsk distiller who had made millions in the liquor trade and built Siberia's greatest private library. When Iudin presented his library to the Library of Congress in 1907, it required five hundred large packing cases to move it to Washington, D.C.[21]

Such wealth produced the beginnings of Siberia's own high society, in which women doused in French perfume wore clothes imported from Paris and men swilled vintage port and French champagne. Yet, whether in Irkutsk, Tomsk, Krasnoiarsk, or Omsk, Siberian society inevitably retained a provincial quality, with similar entertainments and the same people in attendance: the governor, the mayor, senior army officers, high officials, wealthy merchants and industrialists, and a sprinkling of well-born exiles, all with wives, marriageable daughters, and, if possible, eligible sons. In that sense, it remained a world similar to that which the great Russian writer Nikolai Gogol had captured in his tales of the 1830s, but with the technology of the modern age laid upon it.

If there were beginnings of social stratification in Siberia's Wild East at the beginning of the twentieth century, there was rough democracy, too. Rich merchants had no hesitation about rubbing elbows with poor tradesmen, and, as one might expect in a land to which more than a million men and women had been sent under sentences of banishment or penal servitude, a criminal past was no impediment to social success. The Butin brothers, whose mansion Kennan had so admired, had once had all their property taken into receivership, and some of the lions and grandes dames of society in Irkutsk had served time in prison for crimes that ranged from murder and robbery to violating the rules of censorship. Siberia's risks and opportunities were great levelers. Men and women who could flourish in this world of daring and danger had little concern about the kinds of lives their neighbors might have led in years gone by.

Gold, furs, iron, coal, liquor, and a score of other enterprises lay at the base of the fortunes that supported such men and women. But, if they were "democratic" in their willingness to consort with lesser folk, they were ruthless in exploiting the workers whose labor made their fortunes. By 1908, Siberia's enterprises were producing more than three percent (in terms of value) of the Russian Empire's industrial products with only one percent of its labor force.[22] Led by the railroad workers of the Krasnoiarsk repair shops and the ironworkers of the Ural and Altai lands, Siberia's first strikes broke out in the late 1890s and became more frequent as the twentieth century opened. Accompanied by choruses of *La Marseillaise,* shouts of "Down with autocracy!" were heard for the first time in Siberia in 1903. Organizations of Bolshevik workers took shape in Krasnoiarsk, Tomsk, Chita, and Irkutsk soon after that, and, before the end of 1905, soviets of soldiers' deputies had been formed in Vladivostok and Krasnoiarsk.[23]

Beginning in 1906, such labor protest fell upon hard times as the tsar's policemen began to choke out strikes all across the empire. Six thousand Russians had been sentenced to *katorga* in 1903, but that number rose to thirty-two thousand by 1910. Almost two million men and women, or about one out of every seventy-five who lived within the Russian Empire, were processed through its jails and prisons in 1912, and although most of them continued to be common criminals who were set free in a matter of hours or days, there were more "politicals" among them than ever.[24] "There is no place to put all those who have been seized," Lenin wrote, "[and] no way to send all those condemned to banishment to Siberia by the usual means of transport."[25]

All of the abuses that workers had suffered at the hands of foremen and factory owners in days gone by now returned with a vengeance, and even as late as 1910 men and women could be found living in shelters hollowed out of Siberia's hillsides. Nowhere were conditions worse than in the Lena goldfields, situated about midway between Irkutsk and Iakutsk, where nearly thirteen thousand men and women labored under conditions so dangerous that seven hundred out of every thousand among them suffered injuries in the course of any given year. When these workers went on strike and the government responded by killing and wounding more than five hundred of them in the spring of 1912, the workers of the Russian Empire came storming back into the arena of labor protest in greater numbers than ever before.[26] The infamous Lena Goldfields Massacre was the most brutal suppression of labor protest at any time in Imperial Russia's history. As Lenin once wrote, it was to be the "pivotal event in transforming the masses' revolutionary mood into a [new] revolutionary upsurge."[27]

35

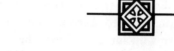

The Lena Goldfields Massacre

As immigrants and investment capital followed it across Asia, the railroad gave a tremendous boost to Siberia's economic development. In 1894, there had been only five banks in all of Siberia. Fifteen years later, Vladivostok alone had twice that number, and nearly seventy banks were doing business in other Siberian towns and cities.[1] With the United States taking the lead in developing trade and mining in Siberia's northeast, England, France, Germany, and half a dozen other countries worked to develop railroads, mines, and factories in other parts of the lands between the Urals and the Pacific.[2] More than a dozen nations had opened consulates and foreign trade offices in Vladivostok before the Russo-Japanese War broke out, and Irkutsk, Omsk, and Tomsk had all become centers of industry, foreign trade, and investment by that time.

Industries that processed food products and those that extracted or refined metals were the magnets that drew investment into turn-of-the-century Siberia. Flour mills to grind the wheat grown by Siberia's new immigrant farmers sprang up in Omsk, Semipalatinsk, Barnaul, Novonikolaevsk, and Blagoveshchensk, and a broadly based feeling of prosperity began to take hold.[3] After a group of Danes introduced dairy farming in the grasslands around Tiumen and Omsk, such an intense "butter fever" swept western Siberia that by 1910 the Siberians were exporting seventy tons of butter to the West every year.[4] Using the railroad to Arkhangelsk and the newly opened sea-lanes of the Arctic to export sawn timbers, the British started to develop Siberia's lumbering industry, while the Dutch, French, and Latin Americans from a number of countries shipped timber from the Transbaikal by way of the Amur to the Pacific.[5] At the same time, men with connections at court began to develop the Kuznets Basin near Siberia's southwestern Altai region. Owned by the imperial family before the Revolution of 1917, this became the famed Kuzbass of the Soviet era, with an estimated 450 billion tons of coal in mines that eventually extended over ten thousand square miles. On the eve of the First World War, Siberia's mines were producing almost two million tons of coal a year, mainly for the railroad, and the productivity of its coal miners was higher than anywhere else in the Russian Empire.[6]

Still, the opening of Siberia to investors and foreign trade in the early twentieth century did not bring growth everywhere. Even though its output of coal continued to rise, Siberia's production of iron and steel declined during the first decade of the new century as the railroad brought in cheaper metal from the Urals and the Ukraine and forced the more backward foundries and forges around Irkutsk and in the Transbaikal to shut down. By 1908, Siberia's output of iron had fallen to scarcely a quarter of what it had been a decade earlier, and yearly imports of iron and steel from European Russia had risen to more than a quarter of a million tons.[7]

Although butter, wheat, timber, and coal all showed Siberia's growing prosperity, gold still attracted investors most of all. By 1910, Siberia was mining forty tons of gold a year, the bulk of it in the Lena goldfields, which covered sixty thousand square miles of rough terrain in the depths of the taiga some twelve hundred miles northeast of Irkutsk. Bounded by the Lena River on the west and its tributary, the Vitim, on the south, this wilderness had seen only Tungus reindeer herders and Iakut hunters until the middle of the nineteenth century, when an Irkutsk merchant visiting one of the small fairs that the Russians organized during the summer months to trade grain and trinkets to the natives for furs had noticed a gold nugget being worn as an ornament by a Tungus trapper. Once the Russians learned that the native had found his nugget in the Lena-Vitim triangle, gold fever swept Siberia's eastern lands. As in other parts of Siberia, some of the ore lay in veins that could be mined, but most of it was in gold-bearing sands covered by hundreds of tons of topsoil that had to be moved before the sands could be washed to rinse out the gold.[8]

By the early 1870s, the Lena miners were washing more than a third of a million tons of sand a year to produce just over a ton of gold, and a number of small enterprises were at work finding more. Among them was the Lena Gold Mining Joint Stock Company, which its owners reorganized in 1896 into the Lena Gold Mining Company with a capital of nearly seven million rubles. Known by its Russian acronym, Lenzoto, and with influential backers in St. Petersburg, the company became the most powerful enterprise in eastern Siberia and took control of most of the Lena goldfields in scarcely more than a decade. Soon after a group of British investors bought a controlling interest in Lenzoto and reorganized it into a joint-stock company called Lena Goldfields Ltd. in 1908, it was working more than four hundred placers. The dowager empress Mariia Fëdorovna was one of its stockholders. So were Witte, Vyshnegradskii, the St. Petersburg magnate Aleksei Putilov, and several other influential statesmen, all of whom received dividends that, in 1911, amounted to 252 rubles on each 500-ruble share of stock.[9]

As their predecessors in Lenzoto had done, the managers of Lena Goldfields Ltd. purchased their immense profits at a high price in human misery. "Work in the pits and shafts of Lenzoto went on without interruption, day and night, winter and summer," one worker wrote.[10] Wages in some cases were higher than in Russia's European factories, but fines lowered them substantially while food and supplies from company stores in Siberia's goldfields cost from two to four times as much as in European Russia.[11] Nor were these the miners' only miseries. The most fortunate had barracks with dirt floors and rotting log walls, while the rest lived in dugouts built of sandbags over which canvas and empty sacks were stretched to form a roof. To keep out the cold, miners spread wet snow—"freezing plaster" some called it—on their shelters' outside walls, but wet boots still froze to the floor before morning. The stench of unwashed flesh, dirty clothes, and food cooked on kerosene heaters choked anyone who entered such a place, and one group of government inspectors found barracks in which the sleeping space had been reduced to a single square meter per person.[12] For these and other reasons too numerous to list, government investigations in 1911 pronounced nine out of every ten workers' "barracks" maintained by Lena Goldfields Ltd. unfit for winter use.[13]

Obliged to add the burdens of cooking, washing, and child care to their daily labors, the Lena women lived even more wretchedly than did their husbands, brothers, and sons. Raped and tormented by foremen and managers if they accepted work as servants and assigned to physical labor that was beyond their strength if they did not, they endured lives akin to slavery from which liberation seemed impossible. A Russian senator who visited the goldfields in 1911 received no fewer than fifty petitions from women and girls about the abuses they had suffered. The same statesman described the lives of their children, of which there were more than two thousand, as "absolutely horrible."[14]

Such conditions stirred anger among the immigrant workers from European Russia more quickly than among those who had spent their working lives in Siberia, and these became the most volatile group of miners in the goldfields. Labor protest was not new to men from Russia's west, and some of the miners driven to Siberia by the depressions that European Russia suffered periodically had even helped to lead strikes in the oil fields of Baku, the coal mines of the Donbass, and the textile mills of Moscow in earlier times. The Mensheviks and Bolsheviks among these workers quickly joined ranks with men and women who had been banished for their part in the revolutionary events of 1905, and they began to talk about how to transform the miners' sporadic grumbling into open protests. Their efforts proceeded slowly because the police and government officials gave their full support to the mine owners, and it took a full half decade for the seeds that revolutionary workers from European Russia sowed in the Lena goldfields to bear fruit.[15]

On February 29, 1912, the workers at the Andreevskii mine of Lena Goldfields Ltd. went on strike. The next day and the day after, three thousand miners at ten other mines laid down their tools and joined them in calling for an eight-hour day, better food and medical care, improved housing, and higher wages to be paid regularly in cash, not company scrip. When the mine managers refused these demands, the miners organized a strike committee that spread their protest all across the goldfields by the middle of March.[16] Violence was in the wind, and the governor of Irkutsk province feared that the oft-quoted axiom "where there is gold there is bloodshed" was about to be proved once again.[17] With only 215 soldiers garrisoned in the entire Lena goldfields region, and the nearest reinforcements twelve hundred miles away in Irkutsk, the provincial governor telegraphed for instructions to the minister of internal affairs in St. Petersburg. He was told that Captain Treshchenkov, a brutal officer of the imperial gendarmes, was being sent to keep order at the mines and that the government was prepared to see blood shed if the strike continued.[18] "The experienced hand of the gendarmes," one striker wrote, "would not hesitate to make an example of the Lena miners so as to intimidate anyone else who dared to rise against the existing order."[19]

With none of their demands met, the workers' representatives assembled on Easter Sunday, March 25, and voted to stay on strike.[20] Treshchenkov immediately telegraphed to his superiors that "the miners absolutely refuse to return to work until their demands are met" and received a coded order to "liquidate the strike committee without delay."[21] On the night of April 2, the gendarme captain started to round up the strike leaders. That same night, the miners began to organize a mass protest to demand that the authorities release their comrades.[22]

On the morning of April 4, Mikhail Ivanovich Lebedev, a Bolshevik sailor who had been sentenced to *katorga*, took his place near the head of a column of men and women marching toward the Lena Goldfields' Nadezhdinskii mines. Keeping the river on their right and a narrow-gauge railroad on their left, he and his comrades advanced along the lower road from the district capital of Bodaibo until they came within range of Treshchenkov's men, their vicious quadrangular bayonets fixed as Russian soldiers always did in the field. "No, brothers," the marchers assured each other, "they won't shoot at us if we just march past, not toward, them."[23] Then, as the miners started forward again, Treshchenkov ordered his soldiers to fire. His military training taking command of his reflexes, Lebedev fell to the ground. "I scarcely had time to take a breath before another volley rang out," he remembered, "and then it was quiet."[24] Lebedev saw one worker stand up, holding his wounded right arm with his left, and walk slowly toward the soldiers. "What sort of animals are you?" he heard him shout. "Why are you shooting at us?"[25] The wounded miner stood for only a moment. Then a soldier cut him down with one well-placed bullet.

"People lay scattered all along the roadway like rocks," Lebedev later wrote. "You couldn't tell who was dead and who was alive." He made his way to a comrade who lay nearby to find "blood spurting from his arm like a fountain." With the help of another miner, Lebedev had just enough time to drag his wounded friend behind a pile of logs before the shooting started again. "I looked over and saw a man fall just five paces away from me," Lebedev remembered. "He got back up onto his knees and then fell over." When the shooting stopped again, Lebedev ran to drag the wounded man behind his shelter. At that moment, the soldiers opened fire again and Lebedev felt a bullet tear into the flesh above his elbow. Then another bullet cut a furrow across his forehead and his right eye began to fill up with blood. "They kept firing for a long time," Lebedev wrote. "Then the shooting died away and people began to move about." Some ran away. As others hurried to help the wounded, Treshchenkov's voice rang out. "Get away from them," he shouted, "or we'll start shooting again!"[26] For the next two hours, Treshchenkov's soldiers rifled through the pockets of the dead and wounded, taking any money or valuables they found. Then they left the miners to gather up their comrades. By the next morning, 250 bodies lay outside the infirmary morgue piled like cordwood and another 270 wounded were being treated wherever they could find shelter. It was well below zero, but some of the wounded still lay in the snow waiting for help.[27] One widow asked for a photograph to be taken of her husband's body so that she could give it to her five-year-old child later. "They said," she remembered, "that such a thing was forbidden."[28]

The massacre in the Lena Goldfields brought grief to its victims but gave new life to labor protest all across Russia and Siberia. Gold miners in Eniseisk and Tomsk provinces went on strike that summer, and so did the copper miners in Akmolinsk. All along the railroads, workers put down their tools. In the Ukrainian cities of Kharkov, Kiev, and Ekaterinoslav, in the Latvian capital of Riga, and in the imperial capital of St. Petersburg, new strikes broke the calm that had settled upon the empire's factories. In 1910, the empire of Nicholas II had counted only two hundred strikes, but the number increased to two thousand in 1912 as three-quarters of a million workers joined the strikers' ranks.[29] More than ever before, Russia's workers were on the move. No longer was it a struggle of revolutionaries and workers against the men who owned Russia's mines and mills. Now the men and women who went on strike focused their hatred against the emperor Nicholas II himself, and, as they did so, the number of men and women sent to Siberia by the government soared.

36

"I Hate the Autocracy
So Much"

As the Russian government had gained new confidence after crushing the Revolution of 1905, it had broadened its net of police surveillance, hired hundreds of new spies to infiltrate the workers' ranks, and sent anyone suspected of sympathizing with the workers' cause to Siberia. By the end of 1906, one out of every forty adult Russian men was in jail for one reason or another, and the authorities were spending almost thirty million rubles a year (about $15,000,000) to keep them there. Taking its much larger population into account, Russia was spending more than twice as much on prisons as did England or Austria. Siberia's forced labor prisons filled to overflowing. Just between 1905 and 1912, thirty thousand Russians died in prison or in penal settlements.[1]

As the avenging furies who wore the tsar's uniform condemned five thousand men and women to be shot or hanged during the half decade after 1905, extremism spawned extremism and terrorism begat terror. In 1906, revolutionary terrorists claimed nearly 1,600 victims, ranging from village policemen to a minister of internal affairs and the emperor's uncle. The next year, they killed another 2,500 before the government's antiterrorist campaign began to take effect.[2] Among those who had waged war against Russia's old regime after the Revolution of 1905, women hated the autocracy with even greater passion than did the men alongside whom they fought. Women became some of the most effective killers the forces of order in Russia had ever had to face.

Once described as looking "for all the world like Olga, the schoolmis-
tress in Chekhov's *Three Sisters*,"³ Mariia Spiridonova stood prominently
among the women terrorists who fought against the tsar after the Revolution of 1905. Raised in a small country town, she felt more akin to
Russia's peasants than to its proletariat and derived no comfort from the
rigid economic laws that shaped Marxist dogma. Finding the "soulless
chessboard" upon which the Bolsheviks sought to play out history's
forces too impersonal and cruel, she turned to Russia's Socialist Revolutionaries, who fought hand to hand with the authorities and took moral
responsibility for the terrorist acts they committed. In her late teens,
Spiridonova therefore became a terrorist. Before her twenty-first birthday, she shot a general who had been unusually brutal in suppressing
peasant uprisings in central Russia and was sentenced to be hanged.
When told that the emperor had commuted her sentence to lifelong
katorga, she was angry. "I hate the autocracy so much," she explained to
a friend, "that I do not want to receive any favor from it."⁴

Spiridonova became an icon of terrorism whose life stood as a bench-
mark against which Russia's revolutionaries measured one another's
dedication. In the summer of 1906, the authorities moved her from
Moscow's infamous Butyrka jail to Maltsev, the hard-labor prison in
Siberia's Nerchinsk Mining District in which female terrorists were
confined after the authorities had closed Kara prison in 1890. Among the
other terrorists who joined Spiridonova during her four years at Maltsev, Aleksandra Izmailovich, a general's daughter who had tried to kill
the governor of the west Russian city of Minsk, became her closest
companion. There was also Fania Kaplan, the anarchist terrorist who
later shot Lenin in 1918, and Anastasiia Bitsenko, a taciturn peasant who
had killed a tsarist general and later became a member of the delegation
that Trotskii led to make peace with the Germans at Brest-Litovsk. In
later years, Bitsenko reminded one observer of "a beast of prey seeing
its victim at hand and preparing to fall upon it and rend it."⁵ These
women all hated Russia's tsar and any who spoke in his name. None of
them feared death. Indeed, they found a certain exaltation in facing it.
"Between the act [of assassination] and the scaffold there lies a whole
eternity," one terrorist wrote. "It is perhaps the supreme happiness of
man."⁶

Once described as "a white square patch in a depression amid the hills
with a few gray wooden buildings huddled beyond it," Maltsev was a
desolate outpost near Siberia's Chinese frontier.⁷ Its main building
stretched out long and gray "like a desolate, abandoned barracks" that
reminded Irina Kakhovskaia, a lifelong terrorist who arrived there two

years after Spiridonova, of a lizard. For the Maltsev women, there was
no forced labor, only enforced isolation from the outside world in which
each day was like the next and the one that had gone before. In one
corner, one of them spent her days dissecting pigeons, desperately
trying to believe that she was continuing the scientific work her imprisonment had interrupted. On another side of the prisoners' common
room, a student of Assyrian languages compared ancient texts, while
others worked on translations or mathematical exercises. "In these moments of dead silence," Kakhovskaia wrote of the long winter nights
when ice formed on Maltsev's inner walls and spilled water froze solid
on its floors, "your excited thoughts absorbed your entire being and,
when you came to yourself again, it was already four o'clock in the
morning. Then," she explained, "when you awoke the next day, your
first hazy memory would be that something beautiful had happened the
day before."[8]

Such introspection was part of a search for inner peace among women
who called themselves the "Thirty-three Monsters." "In some way, we
had to compensate ourselves for being deprived of nature, civic activity,
and political struggle," Kakhovskaia once wrote. "Otherwise, life and
activity would retrogress ... [and], when the day came for us to be freed,
we should have become spiritual cripples." To guard against the psychological erosion that prison life could bring, the Maltsev women set
one of their cells aside for discussions that helped them to share the
burdens of prison life and draw strength from one another. "This was the
center of our civic life," Kakhovskaia remembered. "Here we argued,
quarreled, and made up." Some of the women at Maltsev tried to
develop revolutionary theories that could support their terroristic faith.
"We had to rethink all of the intellectual baggage we had brought with
us," Kakhovskaia confessed in her brief memoirs. "We had to think
everything through again from the very beginning. Seriously and con-
scientiously, stone by stone, we had to build a foundation for our
philosophy of life."[9] In their moments of silence, Maltsev's women
ruminated about the writings of Nietzsche, Dostoevskii, Tolstoi, the
Bible, and a host of other books that the prison authorities allowed to
come their way. Because they were dedicated to Russia's peasants, only
a handful studied the writings of Karl Marx.[10]

In Maltsev's communal cell, the better-educated women taught their
less fortunate sisters. Kakhovskaia taught French while Izmailovich
concentrated on Russian literature and others shared their knowledge of
medicine, mathematics, science, and philosophy in much the same way

as the Decembrists had done at Chita almost a hundred years before. "We had only two sources of consolation," Kakhovskaia wrote in her recollections of those times, "our own community of comrades and the world of books. For many years these remained an inexhaustible source of life, interest, and happiness."[11] In that way, the loss of freedom produced a life of moral superiority among them. "It was thanks to *katorga* alone," Kakhovskaia explained, "that many of us managed to learn how much one human being can give to another."[12]

Such a life was less brutal than the terrible conditions of *katorga* that George Kennan had chronicled twenty years earlier, and the fact that Spiridonova and her comrades had had their death sentences commuted showed a humanitarian dimension to the tsar's government that few of its enemies cared to recognize. Yet the quality of life in Siberia's forced-labor prisons on the eve of the First World War depended upon how individual commandants chose to enforce the regulations, and Maltsev was a rare exception to the regimes of punishment and mistreatment that "politicals" endured elsewhere. Beatings, floggings, and isolation in dark, freezing cells all continued to be common coin. "Each prison had a governor who tortured the prisoners in his charge in his own way," one inmate explained. "Some of them were motivated by devotion to duty and obsequiousness to the higher authorities. . . . Others were motivated by hatred and fear, others again were motivated by pure sadism."[13]

Of all the torments they faced, "politicals" feared floggings the most, for no matter how strong-willed or proud, men and women lost control of their reflexes and begged for mercy if the whip was allowed to do its work long enough. Especially the three-thonged *plet*, which tore away the flesh at every stroke, destroyed prisoners' mastery of their emotions, and reduced them to shattered masses in human form, and revolutionaries who took pride in spitting in the face of authority could not bear such humiliation. Such beatings became more widespread in Siberia's prisons when a new governor general took command of the Transbaikal lands after the assassination of Russia's Prime Minister Pëtr Stolypin led the authorities to declare a new war on terrorism in 1911. "I am not the kind of general who gets hanged," this officer announced as he took office. "I'm the kind that hangs others."[14] Under this new regime, "politicals" lost their books, writing materials, soap, tobacco, and right to receive letters from family and friends. Any who declared hunger strikes in protest were allowed to starve, just as those who took poison were left to die even when they could have been saved. "Your business is to die, ours is to bury you," one prison commandant told his prisoners when they protested against these new restrictions with a hunger strike. "Pigs," his superior added as he ordered all "politicals" to be chained, fettered, and locked in their cells, "must be treated like pigs."[15]

Although Siberia's jailers spoke harsh words, their ability to live by them was weakening, for public opinion was beginning to change the way in which the tsar's officials ruled. As the political culture of the West came to Russia during the two decades before revolution would sweep the Romanovs from their throne, it began to moderate the tyranny that reigned in Siberia's prisons, forced-labor mines, and government distilleries and saltworks. Once the Revolution of 1905 had eliminated censorship, word of the authorities' misdeeds began to reach the outside world from such formerly remote places as Verkhoiansk, Olëkminsk, and Srednekolymsk, and reports about prison hunger strikes and protest suicides began to appear in Russia's newspapers. On occasion, even Russia's newly formed National Assembly, the Duma, debated prisoners' mistreatment, and such European notables as Sir Arthur Conan Doyle, Anatole France, and Claude Debussy responded by pleading for the Russian government to moderate its exile system.[16] Siberia had become too much a part of the outside world for the Russian government to hide the brutality of its penal system from public scrutiny. Closer to the modern world than ever before, Siberia still had a long way to go before public opinion would begin to shape national policy as it did in Europe and the United States, but it was well positioned on its edge and moving forward more rapidly with every year that passed. As in Australia a few decades earlier, it seemed at the beginning of 1914 that Siberia's penal colonies were about to become a thing of the past.

37

Before the Storm

In 1911, Siberians bought twenty million rubles' ($10,000,000) worth of farm machines and tools. Not only did they own nearly thirty-seven thousand mowing machines and thirty-nine thousand horse-drawn rakes, but they relied heavily upon horse- or steam-powered threshers while the peasants of European Russia still threshed their grain by hand. Siberian farmers at the beginning of 1914 had more than three times as many horses, twice as many oxen, nearly five times as many sheep, and nineteen times as many goats as did their countrymen west of the Urals, and they produced larger surpluses of grain. After setting aside a bit more than seven hundred pounds of grain to feed each man, woman, and child among them, and not counting the huge quantities of grain they used to feed the five and three-quarters of a million cattle in their meat and dairy industries, Siberia's peasants had a million and a half tons left over for export every year.[1]

With much of its eighty thousand tons of butter being sent to Europe by means of the best refrigerated cars the technology of the age could manufacture, Siberia's newly founded dairy industry was producing more butter by 1914 than Holland or Australia and only slightly less than Denmark. Twice a day, seven days a week, trains pulling as many as twenty-five such cars at a time made their way to Russia's ports to transfer the products of Siberia's creameries to the refrigerated ships that would carry them to London, Hull, and a score of other cities in the

West. In scarcely more than a decade, butter had become one of Siberia's most important cash "crops." By 1914, its returns were exceeded
only by gold, wheat, and furs.[2]

The twentieth century brought new life to Siberia's old enterprises,
too. Fishing and hunting had supported Siberia's natives in the centuries
before the Russians came, and they flourished anew at the beginning of
the modern age. Two hundred thousand tons of salmon and close to
three-quarters of a million tons of herring formed the backbone of the
catches the Siberians took from the sea, but the Ob, Enisei, Lena, and
Amur all yielded tens of thousands more tons of sturgeon, sterlet, pike,
roach, and carp. In some places, fish still packed Siberia's rivers so tightly
when they swam upstream to spawn that the pressure of their movement
forced thousands onto land. Near the village of Kuninskaia, on the part
of the lower Ob River that the Soviets would later turn into a pumping
ground for oil and natural gas, fishermen once took seventeen thousand
tons of fish from a single deep hole.[3] Especially in the Amur River, the
quantities of red caviar collected as a by-product of salmon fishing
soared, and although their ancestors had taken the best in ages past,
Siberians continued to trap fur-bearing animals in large numbers. The
sea otters of the eighteenth century were gone, but the pelts of seventy
thousand sables, ten times that many ermines, five million rabbits, and
fifteen million squirrels still accounted for almost half of the world's furs
in 1910. All across Siberia, men hunted for meat and killed animals for
sport. Fowl of all sorts, deer, bear, wild sheep, and wolves all added up
to a yearly kill that accounted for more than two thousand tons of game
that Siberians sold in European Russia and Europe.[4]

The consequences of this new prosperity for the natives whose ancestors had ruled Siberia in ages past are less clear than those for the
transplanted Russians themselves. Perhaps the people affected most
painfully by the pressures of the new century were the Tungus, whose
settlements had once spread across eastern Siberia from the Enisei to the
Pacific and from the Arctic Ocean to the Chinese frontier. Described by
some as the "filthiest of any Siberian tribe" and by others as "a fearless
race of hunters born amidst the gloom of their dense pine forests," the
Tungus found it all but impossible to come to grips with the modern
world the Russians had thrust upon them.[5] By the beginning of the
twentieth century, epidemics and famines had reduced the numbers of
these onetime hunters and reindeer herders to fewer than sixty-five
thousand. "Of all the Ural-Altaic peoples," a commentator wrote in 1914,
"the Tungus are losing their identity the most rapidly."[6] Some of them
eventually became Russified and took up farming. Others tried to take

on the ways of life of their Buriat and Iakut neighbors, and those who remained in the tundra continued to herd reindeer. By 1927, Soviet census takers found that their numbers had fallen to less than two thirds of what they had been just thirty years before.[7]

Numbering more than a third of a million, the Buriats fared better, in part because they entered the twentieth century in larger numbers than the Tungus but also because they adapted more quickly to the new world that was taking shape around them. More warlike than the Tungus, the Buriats had resisted the Russian advance in the best tradition of their Mongol forebears until conquest had finally reduced them to loyal allies in the eighteenth century. Then they formed the backbone of the cossack regiments in the Transbaikal and often intermarried with their Russian conquerors. As the Buriats began to farm instead of raising cattle in the nineteenth century, they also began to exchange their felt iurts for Russian-style wooden houses, especially in the lands of Irkutsk province to the west of Lake Baikal. By the beginning of the twentieth century, these western Buriats were beginning to buy modern farm implements and machines from European Russia, although they kept to their traditional ways longer in the Transbaikal lands farther east. There they continued to raise and herd cattle, but, as Siberia's modern age began, even these Buriats drew closer to the Russians, whose veterinarians made it possible for their herds to survive the epidemics that had decimated them in centuries past.[8]

Although they lived in Siberia's largest province of Iakutiia, the Iakuts were less numerous than the Buriats, numbering slightly fewer than a quarter of a million at the beginning of the twentieth century. In close contact with the Russians since the 1630s, the Iakuts had turned to agriculture more slowly than the Buriats, and they continued to lead their herds and flocks to and from summer pastures in May and October as their ancestors had done. Unlike the more modernized Buriats, the Iakuts continued to supplement their food supplies by hunting, fishing, and gathering even as the twentieth century opened. Lily roots, wild onions, horseradishes, sorrel, and the inner layer of pine and larch bark gathered when the sap was rising in the spring all remained part of the Iakut diet, even as the Russians brought electricity and the first modern conveniences into their land. Despite their homeland's vast reserves of coal, iron, diamonds, gold, silver, platinum, salt, and semiprecious stones, the Iakuts remained poor. Although most of their clans were breaking up under the impact of contact with the modern world, they maintained slavery into the twentieth century.[9]

The Russians exerted a growing influence upon the Iakuts, the Buriats, the Tungus, and dozens of less numerous Siberian native tribes as the twentieth century opened. This was mainly because the Russians outnumbered their native neighbors by an overwhelming ratio, and because Siberia's natives needed their knowledge of science to cure disease in man and beast. Nor could the natives avoid the Russians' technology, which had made Siberia's great distances more manageable. As the twentieth century opened, these influences combined to draw peoples who had lived for millennia outside the mainstream of progress into the modern world. Railroads, river steamboats, better roads, the telegraph, and, as the twentieth century entered its second decade, electricity and telephones all were beginning to transform Siberia, although the full impact of these innovations would not be felt until the 1930s.

Electricity especially changed Siberian life as the twentieth century began. The first industrial hydroelectric station anywhere in the Russian Empire was built at the emperor's Zirianovsk silver mines in the Altai highlands in 1892, and the six hydroelectric stations that the owners of the Lena Goldfields built on the Bodaibo River between 1900 and 1914 accounted for a sixth of tsarist Russia's entire output of electricity on the eve of the First World War. As the second decade of the new century opened, the use of electricity spread to Siberia's coal mines, especially the Cheremkhovo pits near Irkutsk. Krasnoiarsk received its first facilities for domestic electric lighting in the 1880s, not long after London, Paris, and St. Petersburg, and Irkutsk had electric street lighting by 1896, even before its main streets had been paved. Tomsk, Chita, and half a dozen other cities had municipal electric stations in operation before the First World War. In faraway Iakutsk, a hydroelectric station freed people from the perpetual kerosene shortage that the difficulties of shipping fuel oil into Siberia's far north had inflicted upon them for a century.[10] Yet Siberia's greatest power resource of all—the immense potential of its huge rivers to produce electricity—continued to go unused. The massive hydroelectric dams of Siberia's modern age would come only in the time of Stalin and Khrushchev.

Although the technology and know-how of the Russians changed the lives of indigenous Siberians, the ways of life of Siberia's tribesmen made little imprint upon the immigrants who streamed across the Urals in the nineteenth and twentieth centuries. In olden times, Russian trappers and traders had used the Siberians' ways to survive in a wilderness that threatened to consume them all, but the settlers who came to build new lives in Siberia after that clung tenaciously to their Russian customs and ways of life. Dedicated to making their communities in Siberia a reflection of those they had left behind in European Russia, these men and women designed and decorated their homes in the old way and planned their villages and towns in similar fashion. As in European Russia, the dwellings in Siberian villages lay along a single main street, with barns and gardens in the rear, and it was rare to find farms scattered across an entire township, as in the North American Midwest. As they had in their homeland, Russians preferred to live cheek by jowl rather than be isolated on a farm that stood a mile or more from any neighbor.

Larger towns and cities such as Omsk, Tomsk, Tobolsk, and Irkutsk all bore a strong resemblance to the towns of European Russia, with churches and cathedrals designed in similar fashion and with public buildings that could just as easily have been found in Moscow, St. Petersburg, or a score of lesser cities. Always the Russians built their government offices, barracks, city halls, and jails in Siberia in the grand imperial style. The buildings that lined Liubinskii Prospekt in Omsk bore a striking resemblance to those along parts of St. Petersburg's Nevskii Prospekt, and it was only in the towns and cities east of Lake Baikal that Oriental styles continued to survive. This would be even more true in Soviet times, with the badly proportioned, lumpy buildings favored by Stalin being scattered from the Urals and the Arctic to the edges of Bering Strait and the Gobi Desert. Later would come the sterile styles in which the Soviets built in the 1970s and 1980s, as Red Siberia became even more Russian in appearance than its pre-Soviet predecessor.

Opening Siberia to the modern world meant giving foreigners access to Siberian markets. Siberians produced less than one twenty-fifth of tsarist Russia's exports in 1910 but purchased over a seventh of its imports.[11] Danish cement, British mining machinery and consumer goods, agricultural implements from the United States, and high-voltage electrical equipment from Germany all played a visible part in Siberians' daily lives as they entered the second decade of the twentieth century, and this demand drew crowds of foreign businessmen to Siberia's main cities.[12] Siberia was easier for foreigners to visit between 1900 and 1914 than it would be at any other time before the Gorbachev era, and it attracted not only businessmen but journalists and ordinary travelers too. "Off to Siberia! There is something uncanny about the phrase," the British journalist John Fraser confessed as he began his journey in a second-class car on one of the Trans-Siberian's ordinary trains in 1901. "The very word Siberia is one to make the blood run chill," he added. "It smells of fetters in the snow."[13]

Fraser saw Siberia's potential as well as its problems. With "millions of miles of corn-growing land, minerals waiting to be won, and great tracks of country to be populated," this, he thought, could become "the Canada of the eastern world." Everywhere there was promise. "Nowhere [else]," he concluded, "have I seen such an expanse of magnificent agricultural land waiting for man and his plough."[14] Other foreigners who visited Siberia just before World War I shared those opinions. Whether it was the adventurous fellow of the Royal Geographical Society Harry de Windt, the tough young American engineer Lindon Bates, or George Frederick Wright, the "Instructor in Quaternary Geology and Professor of the Harmony of Science and Revelation" at Oberlin College who predicted that Siberia's population would increase tenfold in the coming century,[15] all saw the land's promise and praised its potential. But perhaps only the young Englishman Phillips Price fully sensed the Russians' ability to exploit Siberia and the Asians. "Because in character and habits he is so Asiatic himself," Price concluded, "the Eastern Slav is born to conquer and assimilate the Asiatic races."[16]

38

War and Revolution

A third of a world and ten time zones to the east, midmorning in Vladivostok was still evening of the previous day in St. Petersburg. The sun was therefore up and the day well begun when the brief message sent from St. Petersburg's Central Telegraph Office on the evening of July 18, 1914, reached Siberia's far east. Signed by the tsar and counter-signed by his ministers of war, the Admiralty, and internal affairs, the tape carried the following words:

HIS IMPERIAL MAJESTY ORDERS: THE ARMY AND NAVY TO BE PLACED ON WAR FOOTING. TO THIS END, RESERVISTS AND HORSES TO BE CALLED UP ACCORDING TO THE MOBILIZATION PLAN OF THE YEAR 1910.[1]

Russia was mobilizing all along its western front in response to the fighting that had broken out between Austria and Serbia six days before. Because its generals had never drafted the plan for partial mobilization that could have made it possible to march against only Austria, Russia's armies were massing from the Baltic seacoast to Bessarabia. For the next four days, messages flashed back and forth along the telegraph wires of Europe. Then, when the final deadline of the German ultimatum to Russia passed on midnight, July 19 (August 1, according to the Western calendar), the telegraph keys fell silent. "The lamps are going out all over Europe," England's foreign secretary told a friend. "We shall not see them lit again in our lifetime."[2] In the lands of the Russian Empire, the last moments of peace that people would know for 2,383 days slipped away. Then Russia and the rest of the world went to war almost without trying. "The die is cast!" France's ambassador to Russia wrote with an awed sense of amazement in his diary that night. "The part played by reason in the government of peoples is so small that it has taken merely a week to let loose universal madness!"[3]

War came to Siberia, too, as bright red cards appeared on signposts, in the windows of government buildings, and in post and telegraph offices to summon men who could not read to their mobilization points. Broad-shouldered, phlegmatic Buriats with square faces, high cheekbones, and jet-black hair; fierce Kirgiz tribesmen from the wild lands of the upper Ob and Irtysh valleys; sheepskin-hatted, saber-wielding cossacks; a scattering of Siberian Tatars; and hordes of blond, blue-eyed, strong-backed, stolid-faced young Russians all went to war. Some of them had met the Germans and Austrians against whom they now were going to fight among the flood of foreigners who had come to do business in Siberia. In a similar manner others had encountered the Englishmen and Frenchmen who were about to become their comrades in arms.

Even those Siberians who had come to know Europeans at first hand knew little or nothing about the world from which they came. If foreign lands and politics had no place in the narrowly defined and uncomplex world of European Russia's peasants, they held even less interest for the majority of Siberians. How the average Siberian called to the colors would fight—or if he and his comrades would fight at all—remained the great unknown for the leaders of the Russian Empire at the beginning of the First World War. In those days, a politician remembered, "eternal silence reigned in the depths of rural Russia."[4] Could Russia's—and Siberia's— masses be convinced to make the cause for which their tsar had gone to war their own? That was the riddle that tormented Nicholas II and his advisers from the Great War's beginning to its end, for the peasants, as one revolutionary remarked, had always been "the sphinx" in Russia's political history.[5] "A Tambov peasant is willing to defend the province of Tambov," Russia's first wartime Chief of Staff once explained, "but a war for Poland [where much of the fighting took place in 1914 and 1915], in his opinion, is foreign and useless."[6]

To the people of faraway Siberia, that statement applied most of all. If Russians whose villages stood a few hundred miles away from the battles of 1914 and 1915 could dismiss the war as irrelevant unless the fighting reached their doorstep, how much less relevant it seemed to the men and women who lived beyond of the Urals. Nonetheless, Siberians fought in the very first battles of the Great War. The Fifth Siberian Corps fought with distinction on the Galician front in the fall of 1914, and the Sixth was all but wiped out in the battle for Łódź in December. Siberians fought at the Masurian Lakes, at Tannenberg, and in a score of lesser battles before 1914 ended, and they fought throughout Russia's great retreat, which began the next spring and lasted through the summer.[7]

Although hundreds of thousands of its men were called to the colors, Siberia's greatest contribution to Russia's war effort was as a supplier of raw materials and as an entry through which its allies could ship weapons and munitions. After the Central Powers closed the Dardanelles and the Baltic to Allied shipping at the beginning of the war, German submarines played havoc with shipments of war matériel bound for Russia's White Sea ports of Murmansk and Arkhangelsk, and the Trans-Siberian Railroad became the faltering empire's lifeline to the outside world. Throughout 1915 and 1916, the Allies poured cannon, rifles, shells, and bullets into Vladivostok, from which they were shipped along the Trans-Siberian to Moscow to keep Russia's western front from collapsing under the weight of the forces that the Austrians and the Germans threw against it.

Russia's soldiers therefore fought the First World War with Japanese Arisakas, American Winchesters and Krag-Jorgensens, British Lee-Enfields, and outdated French Gras-Kropatcheks in addition to the Mosin-Nagant rifles produced by their nation's own armories. America's Westinghouse Appliance Company produced several hundred thousand Mosin-Nagants for the Russians in 1916, as did the Remington Arms Company in upstate New York. Field guns came from France, England, the United States, Japan, and Canada along with more than thirty-seven million (about two out of every three) of the artillery shells that Russia's armies fired by the end of 1916. Before the February Revolution drove Nicholas II from the throne in 1917, Russia's allies had sent more than three-quarters of a billion rifle and machine-gun cartridges through Siberia to the western front and the storage depots of central Russia, as well as tens of thousands of tons of other vital war supplies.[8]

The Russians were never able to move weapons and supplies along the Trans-Siberian as rapidly as their allies poured them into Vladivostok. As the war dragged on, the backlog of matériel to be moved across Siberia grew so large that British officers in Vladivostok complained that tons of precious nitrates were being left in uncovered muddy storage areas near the docks.[9] More than fifty thousand tons of supplies had backed up at Vladivostok by the beginning of 1916, and the backlog had risen to nearly 400,000 tons a year later, even though the opening of the great Khabarovsk bridge and the Amur River railroad line offered an alternative route to relieve the congestion between Vladivostok and Sretensk. So many supplies and weapons had been shipped by the Allies to Vladivostok by the beginning of 1917 that their combined weight caused some of them to sink into the ground when the spring thaw began.[10] Many of these never reached their destinations before Russia withdrew from the war and were used during the Civil War of 1918–1921 instead.

In the spring of 1917, the U.S. government sent a Railway Advisory Commission to Vladivostok to get Siberia's railroads moving. Headed by the former chief engineer of the Panama Canal, John Frank Stevens, and supported by the Railway Service Corps, which the United States sent under the command of the Great Northern Railway's general manager, George Emerson, American advisers eventually took over the management of Siberia's railways. Not concerns for Russia's welfare, but a modern-day version of the vision that Perry McDonough Collins had conceived in the 1850s, lay behind their effort. Collins had envisioned linking America and Russia by means of a railroad from Siberia's hinterland to the Amur and the Pacific. Stevens and Emerson were part of a group of American financiers who dreamed of linking the Great Northern Railway in the United States with the Trans-Siberian by means of shipping lanes that stretched from Seattle to Vladivostok.[11]

That Russia depended upon the weapons and munitions that its allies had shipped through Siberia did not mean that it failed to increase its own industrial capability during the First World War. At the beginning of 1916, the Russian Empire had 1,797,000 men and women working on defense contracts in 3,846 factories, and a year later the number of plants and mills producing war goods had risen to 5,200. The number of Siberian industries involved in the war effort had more than tripled to nearly a thousand by then. Some of the iron-and-steel works that had been unable to compete in peacetime reopened, and the coalfields of the Kuzbass and Cheremkhovo found their product in greater demand than ever. At the same time, Western investments poured into Siberia's capital-starved far east in a flood. After investing just more than a million dollars in Siberia's eastern lands during the first half of 1914, American financiers and industrialists increased their investment by 118 times to more than $124,000,000 by the middle of 1916.[12]

The growth of Siberia's already booming agriculture was as impressive as the expansion of its wartime industry, in large measure because the military authorities sent more than a million captured Austrians,

Germans, Hungarians, and Turks to work in its mines and fields.[13] Like other Europeans during the Great War, the Russians saw such prisoners as part of the war's spoils and assigned them to work in regions that were far from the front, where virtually all of them received no pay and lived in camps that were ridden with disease. In Siberia, prisoners who had enjoyed higher standards of living in their homelands lived in the most primitive sorts of shelters and ate food their countrymen would have considered unfit for humans. Some camps held as many as thirty-five thousand men, often in dugout shelters, with minimal sanitation facilities and virtually no medical services. Typhus killed more than half of the prisoners at Krasnoiarsk and Novonikolaevsk, where Red Cross observers saw thirst-crazed victims of the disease greedily drinking water that they described as "flowing yellow with human excrement from the latrines."[14] At Omsk, sixteen thousand prisoners died in less than ten months from similar causes, and tens of thousands more died in other camps.[15]

Prisoners seized any opportunity that would take them beyond the prison walls, where the chances of escape were better even if the work was harder. Prisoners sent to build railroads or work in Siberia's mines and factories all complained of ill treatment, but there was humor as well as pathos in the lives of those who tilled Siberia's fields. Elsa Brändström, who, as the daughter of Sweden's ambassador to St. Petersburg, spent the war years championing the cause of prisoners of war in Russia, tells of an Austrian prisoner who had managed a Siberian peasant woman's farm for several years. During the course of his stay, the woman had borne him a son, and then, when it came time for her husband to return from the war, the authorities had assigned the prisoner elsewhere. According to Brändström's account, the authorities soon had a visit from the returned peasant, who demanded to see the man who had been managing his farm and, quite obviously from the age of the son, sleeping with his wife. Expecting the worst, they brought the prisoner forward, only to see the peasant embrace him in gratitude. "How can I thank you for what you have done for my farm!" he exclaimed. "The pigs are fat, the cows are healthy, there are four calves and, I say, the boy is just splendid!"[16] Such exceptions were rare. By 1917, riots against the terrible conditions under which they had to live and work had become common among Siberia's prisoners of war, and they would be an important factor in the revolutionary chaos that swept the land during the next several years.[17]

The hordes of prisoners, the breakdown of the railroads' track and rolling stock, and the shortage of farm equipment and consumer goods that induced Siberian peasants to hoard grain rather than sell it at low fixed prices all added to the crisis that led the Russian Empire down the road to revolution. During January 1917, strikes by more than a quarter of a million workers cost the war effort nearly three-quarters of a million lost working days.[18] The price of bread was rising at the rate of two percent a week in Petrograd, potatoes and cabbage were rising at three percent, and meat at seven. Firewood became so expensive that common city folk had to choose whether to be warm and live on the verge of starvation or buy food at the cost of doing without heat.[19] As life started to slip out of focus, fatalism turned to cynicism and cynicism to dull, deadening indifference. People no longer asked if there would be a revolution but only when it would break out. "The revolution was ready," one conservative remembered, but "the revolutionaries were not yet prepared for action."[20] One of Russia's leading liberal orators spoke more bluntly. "The revolutionary path is inevitable," he concluded. "The only question is when to start the fight."[21]

The tensions that had heated discontent to the ignition point in Petrograd had been building in Siberia, too. Siberia's peasants continued to store their grain rather than sell it at the government's fixed prices, and that drove the prices of rye up by two thirds, wheat by a half, and potatoes by nearly ninety percent before the end of 1915. The next year, the prices of flour and butter doubled and tripled, while real wages plunged to a quarter of what they had been before the war. People's feelings about the war changed from cynicism to bitterness. As people grumbled about the government "taking more men for the army although victory never comes," gendarme officers all across Siberia began to send in reports about war weariness.[22] Everywhere, men and women who had used Siberia's opportunities to escape poverty began to lose the ground they had gained. Soaring prices and falling real wages were driving them back toward the lives of destitution they had suffered in European Russia.[23]

Once the workers of Petrograd set into motion the events that were to be remembered as the February Revolution of 1917, the revolutionary labor organizers in Siberia's cities and the tens of thousands of men and women who had been sent into exile after the Revolution of 1905 stepped forward to help overthrow the autocracy. In the railroad centers of Omsk, Krasnoiarsk, Irkutsk, Chita, and Khabarovsk; in the mining towns of Barnaul and Ekaterinburg; in the "Aladdin city" of Kharbin; and in Vladivostok, Siberia's "Mistress of the East," the Romanovs and their government found few defenders. Bitter, angry, and sullen, Siberians shed no tears of grief when Nicholas II abdicated in March 1917.[24]

When the Romanovs fell, Siberia's factory owners, merchants, well-to-do farmers, army officers, and clergy formed committees of public safety in each provincial capital, industrial center, and county seat to press for caution, moderation, and gradual change instead of the massive social and economic upheaval that Russia's revolutionaries demanded. Yet, as 1917 moved ahead, the course of events began to turn against these defenders of order as a host of new forces that the Romanovs' overthrow had unleashed vied for places in the new world that was taking shape around them. Everyone spoke about what needed to be done, but no one dared to govern. Revolutionaries, the masses, and the defenders of order all struggled to get their bearings, and the authority of workers, soldiers, industrialists, merchants, and army officers ebbed and flowed from one month to the next.

Tension mounted as workers' factory committees demanded higher wages and an eight-hour day while Siberia's committees of public safety worked to continue Russia's war effort. In such out-of-the-way places as Turinsk, Nizhneudinsk, Achinsk, Kansk, and Minusinsk, crowds spoke out in support of demands that their comrades in such better-known cities as Omsk, Tomsk, Krasnoiarsk, Irkutsk, Chita, and Vladivostok had already set down, and strikes increased. Workers put down their tools, trains stopped running, and a host of newspapers whose editorial policies ranged from extreme right to far left kept Siberia's cities in turmoil. Even before the Bolsheviks seized power in Petrograd in October 1917, radical workers had begun to organize Red Guards for "self-defense" all across Siberia.[25]

Historically, Russians had gravitated to their frontiers to escape the conflicts that tore life apart in the Moscow heartland during times of turmoil, and the year after the Bolsheviks seized power proved to be no exception. Socialist Revolutionaries, Mensheviks, Constitutional Democrats, followers of the Constituent Assembly, anarchists, and a growing number of monarchists all attempted to establish regimes to rival the new masters of Petrograd and Moscow. Prisoners of war added to the heavy cloud of dissent that hung over the land, and so did Asians, who dreamed of breaking away from their long-hated Russian masters. Combined with armies of bandits, these dissident forces transformed Siberia into a cauldron of violence. None of them agreed with any other, but some were willing to strike temporary alliances to fight against their common Bolshevik enemies. Most prominent and best known in the West, the Czech and Slovak prisoners of war formed themselves into the famed Czech Legion, which fought the Reds all along the Trans-Siberian Railroad, hoping to win the freedom that would allow them to leave Siberia and fight the Germans on the fields of France.

PART FIVE

Red Siberia

39

The Czech Legion

Although the Czech Legion played a key part in the Civil War east of the Urals, its beginnings had nothing to do with Siberia. Organized during the first days of World War I as an oversized company of Russian-born Czechs and Slovaks, its purpose was to spread propaganda among the many Czechs and Slovaks who had been drafted into the Austrian army and to carry out reconnaissance behind enemy lines. Yet, if this small Czech and Slovak force served Russia well, it also represented those nationalist forces that would threaten the stability of Eurasia in the century ahead. Ukrainians, Georgians, Armenians, Lithuanians, Latvians, Estonians, Finns, and a dozen more peoples from Central Asia and Siberia had all begun to think of breaking free from the Russian Empire in the days before the Great War began, just as the Czechs and Slovaks hoped one day to claim a homeland from the Austrians. Fearing that any organized dissident nationality group might draw others to it, tsarist statesmen therefore insisted that the "Czech Legion" must remain small enough not to be noticed by any who might want to do Russia harm at home.

The Provisional Government that took up the reins of power in Russia after the February Revolution of 1917 remained as wary of the Czech Legion as its predecessor had been. Then, in recognition of the part that its soldiers played in the offensive of July 1917, Prime Minister Aleksandr Kerenskii gave the legion permission to open its ranks to any

Czech or Slovak prisoner of war who wished to volunteer. Before the
end of 1917, the legion had swelled into a corps of sixty thousand men,
and, as Russia's defenses collapsed along Europe's eastern front, it became the best-organized and most formidable fighting force to be found
anywhere on unoccupied Russian soil. What role it would play in the
chaos that reigned in the lands of the fallen Russian Empire was anyone's guess, and how it could be used to support the cause of the Allies
became a matter of heated debate from Tokyo to Paris and London.[1]

As Russia's armed forces broke apart after the Bolsheviks seized
power in October 1917, a handful of Czech exiles who dreamed of
building an independent Czecho-Slovak nation from the debris of the
crumbling Austrian Empire worked from London to keep the Czech
Legion from being engulfed by the turmoil that boiled beyond Europe's
eastern front. At the end of March 1918, these exiles won the Bolsheviks'
permission to move the entire legion across Siberia to Vladivostok, from
which Allied ships were to carry it across the Pacific, through the
Panama Canal, and across the Atlantic to France, where it would take
the field against the Germans. Then, if the Central Powers could be
defeated, the Czech leaders reasoned, the forces of the Czech Legion,
not the armies of France, England, or the United States, could claim the
honor of liberating the Czecho-Slovak homeland. Yet the Treaty of
Brest-Litovsk, which the representatives of Lenin's revolutionary Russia
had signed with the Central Powers to end the fighting on Europe's
eastern front almost a month before the Bolsheviks made their agreement with the Czechs, stood firmly in the way. Why the Bolsheviks did
not turn the Czech Legion over to the Austrians for punishment as the
treaty required remains uncertain to this day. Most probably, they saw
it as a potential ally against the disorganized White armies that were
beginning to form along their frontiers.

During April and May 1918, shortages of fuel and provisions transformed the well-organized Czech Legion into a sporadic procession of
seventy trainloads of men and equipment scattered across Eurasia from
the eastern borderlands of European Russia to Vladivostok on the
Pacific. Not long afterward, the Bolsheviks' commissar of war forbade
the legion to move any farther without surrendering its weapons and
threatened to divert those units that had not yet crossed into Siberia to
the ports of north Russia while allowing the rest to continue on to
Vladivostok. Fearful that Lenin's government had at last decided to turn
them over to the Germans and Austrians, the legionnaires grew restless
about the uneasy peace that had kept them from coming to blows with
the Russians.[2] Then, when Trotskii announced at the end of May that

"every Czech who is found carrying a weapon anywhere along the route of the railway [is] to be shot on the spot," the Czech Legion went to war.[3] Determined to get to Vladivostok at any price, the legionnaires reclaimed the weapons they had surrendered and began to fight their way east across the Urals and Siberia. At Novonikolaevsk, a key point on the Trans-Siberian line that has since been renamed Novosibirsk, an eyewitness reported that their battle with the Red Guards "was over in forty minutes."[4]

Forty-eight hours after they had overwhelmed the Red Guards at Novonikolaevsk and the nearby stations of Marianovsk and Mariinsk, Czech Legion units seized the important railroad center of Cheliabinsk. Before the middle of June, they added Tomsk, Semipalatinsk, Biisk, and Krasnoiarsk to their list of conquests and went on to take Omsk and its armory.[5] For the moment, they had no plan beyond joining those fifteen thousand or so of their comrades who had reached Vladivostok before the fighting had broken out, but the sudden appearance of an effective armed force in Siberia that might overthrow the Bolsheviks and reopen a second front against the Austro-German armies proved to be too tempting an opportunity for the Allies to let slip away.

Even before the Czechs and Red Guards had come to blows, Britain and Japan had committed themselves to limited intervention on the side of the Bolsheviks' White enemies. Now, as the legion's successes convinced the remaining allies to follow the British and Japanese, France's Premier Clemenceau set aside his demand that "all detachments of the Czech Corps be transported by the swiftest means to the western front" and urged that "all efforts now must be directed toward diverting the action of the Czechs to the complete occupation of the Siberian Railway."[6] Although President Wilson continued to resist intervention for a while longer, a number of U.S. diplomats supported the Czechs even more energetically than the British or French did. "It would be a serious mistake to remove the Czecho-Slovak troops from Siberia," the chief American attaché in Peking wrote. "If they were not in Siberia already," he added, "it would be worthwhile to bring them there."[7]

June 1918 therefore saw the Czech Legion change its objective from trying to join its countrymen in the trenches of France to remaining in Siberia to hold the Trans-Siberian Railroad and establish a beachhead for Allied intervention. As its units moved triumphantly back and forth along the railroad that summer, Bolshevik-held towns and industrial centers fell like ninepins and civil war began to flow back and forth across Eurasia. This was to become history's first railroad war, in which the fighting moved quickly along key rail lines and bypassed those regions into which the railroad did not reach. With no easily definable fronts and without territory being held decisively by either side, the Russian Civil War scarcely touched some of Siberia's remotest parts. As it had throughout its history, Siberia continued to move at a different pace and according to another sense of time. After the war's official end in 1921, fighting continued to sputter in out-of-the-way Siberian corners for the better part of a decade.

During the summer of 1918, no fewer than nineteen anti-Bolshevik governments took shape in Siberia, several of which were the creation of corrupt and self-serving men whom history would remember more readily as bandits than as politicians or statesmen.[8] Such men understood that anyone who commanded an armored train and a few hundred troops had the strength of an army in Siberia's far-flung spaces, and they used their armored trains much as naval commanders used battleships to bombard enemy ports. The *Orlik*—the famed "Eaglet"—that fought as part of the Czech Legion had cannon mounted in an armored turret similar to those on heavy battleships and protected its machine gunners with half-inch armored plate backed by eighteen inches of reinforced concrete. Carrying their own fuel, weapons, fighting men, and food, these track-bound dreadnoughts became fighting machines unto themselves, attacking key towns and supply centers and then steaming away if resistance became too fierce.[9]

Few understood the tactics of Siberian railroad warfare better than Grigorii Mikhailovich Semënov, the most tenacious and perhaps the most vicious of the self-serving captains churned up by the fighting east of the Urals. The son of a cossack father and a Buriat mother, Semënov at the age of twenty-seven looked every inch the bandit he was. "The whole pose of the man," the commander of England's forces in Siberia wrote of Semënov a few years later, "is at first suspicious, alert, determined, like a tiger ready to spring, to rend, and to tear."[10] Semënov had grown up in Siberia's Transbaikal, and like those of so many able men of obscure origin, his fortunes had soared after the February Revolution. The fall of 1917 had found him trying to recruit a Mongolian division to fight on Russia's western front. Then, when the Bolsheviks seized power, he used his soldiers as an independent army to turn the Transbaikal into a private fiefdom upon which he unleashed a reign of terror from his capital at Chita.

Fighting with gold, weapons, and munitions supplied by the Japanese, who preferred not to see a stable government in Siberia, Semënov gave no quarter, and his slightest whim sent men and women to their deaths. Between 1918 and 1920, he and his lieutenants stole anything that passed along the Trans-Siberian Railroad between Sretensk and the eastern shore of Lake Baikal, at one point demanding a ransom of fifteen thousand rifles as a fee for allowing another thirty-five thousand to pass on to White forces who were fighting against the Reds farther west. Innocent victims who had stirred Semënov's anger dangled from telegraph poles in the vicinity of Chita, and his men machine-gunned freight cars full of victims at execution fields along the railway.[11]

Semënov owed some of his success to Baron Roman Ungern-Sternberg, his cruelest lieutenant and one of the most bizarre men to cross the pages of Siberia's history. Once described as "the type that is invaluable in wartime and impossible in times of peace," Ungern-Sternberg was a tangle of contradictions in every physical, mental, and moral sense. "War was his natural element," one of his superiors wrote. "He was not an officer, but a hero out of one of Mayne Reid's novels."[12] Ungern-Sternberg's staff physician described one of his written orders as "the product of the diseased brain of a pervert and a megalomaniac affected with a thirst for human blood."[13] Grown too used to killing and perhaps unhinged by having held for too long the power of life and death over others, Ungern-Sternberg killed his victims by beating, hanging, beheading, disemboweling, and an array of even more bizarre tortures. Although one observer described him as having "the shyness of a savage," most recognized him as a pathological killer who found in Siberia's turmoil of 1918 and 1919 the perfect opportunity to give free rein to a bloodlust that appalled everyone who crossed his path.[14]

Farther to the east, Semënov and Ungern-Sternberg were supported by their onetime comrade Ivan Kalmykov. All three had fought in the ranks of the Nerchinsk cossacks during the First World War before returning to their native Siberia in search of wealth and power once the Civil War began. More than Semënov and fully as much as Ungern-Sternberg, Kalmykov was a sadist who tortured for pleasure and killed men and women for sport. With snakelike eyes that darted from one victim to another and jet-black curls that spilled over his forehead from beneath his tight-fitting cossack fur hat, Kalmykov held men's attention precisely because he seemed more reptilian than human. Not yet thirty when the Civil War began, he owed his position as ataman of the Ussuri cossacks entirely to having murdered his predecessor. Kalmykov established his headquarters at Khabarovsk, whose chilly, dreary atmosphere matched the dark thoughts and cold blood that distinguished him from ordinary men. Complicity in every sort of murder, rape, and robbery bound his men to him as they, like those who followed Semënov, Ungern-Sternberg, and half a dozen others, violated the laws of nature, man, and God in Siberia's far east during the dark and bloody days of 1918 and 1919.[15]

Men such as these imposed what the Russians called the *atamansh-china*—the reign of terror by cossack atamans and robber chiefs—that held the eastern third of Siberia in its grip as long as Japanese weapons and gold kept them in the field. Perhaps more than any other force, *atamanshchina* drove the common men and women of Siberia into the arms of the Bolsheviks, whose tyranny was less capricious and more predictable. "*Atamanshchina* is helping Bolshevism more than all the preachings and propaganda of Lenin and Trotskii put together," one observer wrote from Irkutsk in the spring of 1919. The product of such tyranny was becoming all too clear, and the people who hoped to free Siberia from the Bolsheviks knew it. *"Finis Rossiae!"* one diarist exclaimed. The loss of Siberia to the Bolsheviks would mean the end of Russia as its people had known it for more than two hundred years.[16]

If the architects of the *atamanshchina* concentrated on personal enrichment, there were others whose vision of Siberia's welfare was broader and more generous but no less contentious. Within a week of the Czech Legion's first victories, a group of intellectuals and politicians who had made their way to Tomsk formed the Provisional Government of Autonomous Siberia and raised a green-and-white flag as a symbol of the forests and snows of the land they hoped to rule. A month later, they moved their government to Omsk, annulled all the laws issued by the Bolsheviks, and restored to their former owners all the lands the Reds had confiscated. Their vision of Siberia's future remained clouded by a lack of any clear purpose around which Siberians could unite. Like so many of the White forces that took shape in the borderlands of the fallen Russian Empire that year, the Provisional Government of Autonomous Siberia fought with its potential allies almost as readily as it did against the Bolsheviks.[17]

Most of all, the enemies of the Provisional Government of Autonomous Siberia included the Committee of Members of the Constituent Assembly, whose leaders proclaimed their support for a "United Independent Free Russia" from the Volga River city of Samara as soon as the westernmost units of the Czech Legion drove the Bolsheviks from it. Known by the Russian acronym Komuch, this government looked west, not east, and vowed to reopen a front against the Austrians and Germans in return for Allied aid. Yet Komuch wanted Siberia too, and its efforts to take hold of Siberia's western lands brought it directly into conflict with the forces of the Provisional Government of Autonomous Siberia farther east.[18] Disputes about precedence divided the two governments more than debates over principle, and the pettiness of their squabbling damaged both irreparably in the end.

The intervention of the Allies, each with a different purpose and none with the interests of Siberia foremost in mind, magnified the tension between the Provisional Government of Autonomous Siberia and Komuch during the summer and fall of 1918. In response to a small incident in which a Russian crowd killed three of their citizens, the Japanese sent five hundred marines ashore at Vladivostok on April 5, and the commander of Britain's HMS *Suffolk*, unwilling to allow the Japanese to gain an undisputed foothold on the Asian mainland, sent fifty British soldiers ashore to "support" them.[19] "It is . . . almost inevitable that the Japanese will advance," Lenin warned when he received news of the landing. "Undoubtedly," he added, "the Allies will help them."[20] As was often the case, Lenin's foresight proved all too accurate. Within six months, the handful of forces that the admirals of Britain and Japan had landed had swelled into invading armies. By the fall of 1918, 73,000 Japanese, 2,500 British, 1,000 French, and 1,500 Italians had entered Siberia.[21]

The Americans came last. Reluctant to intervene in the internal affairs of the fallen Russian Empire yet unwilling to allow Japan to gain undisputed access to Siberia's mineral wealth, President Wilson changed course abruptly in the summer of 1918. Insisting all the while that America had no intention of interfering "in the internal affairs of Russia" and promising to "guarantee" that its troops would "not impair the political or territorial sovereignty of Russia," Wilson announced at a special meeting of his closest advisers on July 6, 1918, that the United States was sending arms, ammunition, supplies, and men to Vladivostok in support of the Czech Legion.[22] "Military action," the American president explained in a famous *aide-mémoire* that went out over the signature of his secretary of state eleven days later, would be "admissible in Russia . . . only to help the Czecho-Slovaks consolidate their forces, get into successful cooperation with their Slavic kinsmen, and to steady any efforts at self-government or self-defense in which the Russians themselves may be willing to accept assistance."[23] That assistance, it turned out, included an armed force of more than eight thousand well-armed, well-trained men.

40

"Pitch-forked into the Melee"

On the afternoon of August 2, 1918, Major General William S. Graves, newly promoted and recently appointed commander of the U.S. Army's 8th Division, received a coded telegram at his headquarters at Camp Fremont in California. "You will not," it began, "tell any member of your staff or anybody else of the contents of this message." The telegram then instructed Graves "to take the first and fastest train out of San Francisco and proceed to Kansas City, go to the Baltimore Hotel, and ask for the Secretary of War." There was no hint about the purpose of the meeting, nor did the message explain when he might expect to return to his command. It was, Graves later confessed, "one of the most remarkable communications I ever saw come out of the War Department."[1]

Graves packed his traveling bag and caught the train to Kansas City just two hours later. At Kansas City, the general found Secretary of War Newton Baker waiting with orders for him to lead an (as yet unannounced) American expeditionary force to Siberia. "You will be walking on eggs loaded with dynamite," Baker warned as he hurried to catch the train that would take him back to Washington. "Watch your step. God bless you and goodbye."[2] To use his own picturesque description, Graves had just been "pitch-forked into the melee at Vladivostok."[3] He had hoped to lead the 8th Division into battle somewhere in France.

Now he was to command it, along with the 27th and 31st Infantry Regiments from the Philippines, on exactly the opposite side of the world.

At age fifty-three, General Graves knew nothing about Russia, even less about Siberia, and had no instructions other than his government's ambiguously worded *aide-mémoire* of July 17. "I have often thought it was unfortunate that I did not know more of the conditions in Siberia than I did," Graves once wrote with his usual candor. "At other times," he added, "I have thought that ignorance was not only bliss in such a situation, but was advisable."[4] Certainly, ignorance about the Russians did not pose the greatest danger to Graves's success in Siberia. That came from the armed forces of Imperial Japan, which outnumbered the Americans in Siberia by a margin of nine to one.[5]

America and Japan both wanted access to Siberia's natural resources, but each set out to gain a foothold on the Asian mainland in different ways. After making its first major foray onto the continent in the Sino-Japanese War of 1894–1895, Japan had used the turmoil of the First World War, when the attention of the Western world's great powers had been focused on the battlefields of Europe, to seize German territories in the Far East. Then the turmoil of Russia's revolutions in 1917 and the onset of civil war in Siberia had turned the attention of Japan's warlords and diplomats to Siberia's far eastern railways, which promised access to some of Eurasia's richest natural resources. There the Japanese had come into conflict with a group of American politicians and financiers, who dreamed of using the shipping lanes that stretched from Seattle to Vladivostok to link their nation's Great Northern Railway with the Trans-Siberian. Fearful that the Japanese would cut off their access to key markets and resources in Asia, these men had pressed the United States to strengthen its commercial interests in Siberia.[6] Partly for that reason, the U.S. government had sent the Railway Advisory Commission to Vladivostok in the spring of 1917.

Headed by John Frank Stevens, former chief engineer of the Panama Canal, and Colonel George Emerson, general manager of the Great Northern Railroad, the Railway Advisory Commission and the Railway Service Corps that followed it to Siberia later in 1917 shifted from advising the Russian government about its railways to managing them after the Bolsheviks seized power.[7] Both hoped to rebuild a strong Russia—"one mighty, aspiring democracy," in the words of an American diplomat—that would block Japanese expansion in the Far East while granting the Americans the trade concessions they wanted.[8] Japan, on the other hand, preferred to strengthen its foothold on the Asian mainland by direct military intervention.[9] Graves therefore faced large Japanese forces in Siberia.

With the sympathies of their supporters ranging from socialist to monarchist, Siberia's anti-Bolshevik forces were nearing the point of spontaneous combustion when Graves reached Vladivostok in September 1918. Throughout the summer and fall, the Western Allies had struggled to bring Siberia's contentious Whites together, with the French and Czechs organizing two conferences at Cheliabinsk at which they had urged a single course of action upon them all. Such efforts achieved nothing beyond emphasizing the conflicts that divided them. "There are rumors about revolutions in the purely Mexican style," one Russian officer wrote at the time,[10] and a Siberian politician concluded that "a *struggle for power* between [the Komuch government in] Samara and [the Provisional Government of Autonomous Siberia in] Omsk has become inevitable."[11] Any effort to create a unified front against the Bolsheviks, one participant added, was "an absolute farce."[12] Anti-Bolshevism no longer seemed enough. "Evidently it never occurred to them," a White general later wrote, "that this would make it possible for the Reds to destroy their enemies one by one."[13]

Supported by France, England, and the United States, all of which wanted to replace Siberia's shifting political centers with a stable White government, a number of senior White army officers urged the politicians to cut short their "senseless chatter" and concentrate on fighting the Reds.[14] At the beginning of September, soldiers and politicians therefore assembled once again, this time at Ufa, the capital of Bashkiria and the last city on the railroad from Moscow before it crossed the Urals and linked up with the Trans-Siberian. Founded during the reign of Ivan the Terrible as an outpost from which Moscow's tsar could impose tribute upon the warlike Bashkirs, Ufa in 1918 remained scarred by the boredom of life in Russia's provinces. Despite its population of slightly more than a hundred thousand, the arrival of more than a hundred and fifty delegates representing nine political parties and fourteen different Siberian "governments" to attend the grandly named Ufa State Conference therefore created a stir. Large crowds carrying placards and chanting political slogans were not usually a part of Ufa's daily scene.[15]

When the Ufa State Conference opened on the evening of September 8, 1918, its organizers insisted that Siberia and Russia could no longer afford the luxury of fragmented political allegiances, for the Reds were on the move and anxious to regain the territories they had lost that summer. Just two days after the conference opened, the Reds' first major victory at Kazan, Russia's gateway to Siberia since the days of Ivan the Terrible, hammered that point home and put Siberia's Whites on notice that the time left for settling differences had grown very short. As they debated what form a unified Siberian-Russian state should take, one Siberian government after another relinquished its claims against the others so that the delegates could announce on September 23 that "Supreme Authority throughout the entire Russian state [including Siberia] has been entrusted to a Provisional All-Russian Government" that was to be composed of an elected five-member Directorate.[16] This had been agreed upon, one observer explained, "in the name of saving our homeland from final ruin" and at the "unanimous request of representatives of all classes and sections of the population."[17] Yet the truth was that no such request had ever been made. The unity proclaimed at Ufa was so hollow that two of the first five men named to the Directorate refused to serve.[18] On the right, conservatives continued to insist that only a dictatorship could unify Siberia's diverse political forces. On the left, Siberian Socialist Revolutionaries repudiated the Ufa Conference as a "Walpurgis Night"—a night of witches and sorcerers.[19]

Such was the murky political world in which General Graves and his advisers had to find their bearings. While the members of the Directorate retired from Ufa to Omsk and tried to form a government, clouds of intrigue even thicker than those that had hung over Ufa in September settled upon them. "There's murder in the streets," one general wrote as knives, pistols, garrotes, and all the other weapons of back-alley assassination began to claim victims.[20] "We live, as it were, on a volcano, which is ready to erupt at any moment," two members of the Directorate warned in a joint letter. "Every morning," they added plaintively, "we sit and expect that they will come to arrest us."[21] Disgusted at the Directorate's vacillation, even the Czechoslovak legionnaires abandoned the struggle, seeing no reason to continue what seemed to be a hopeless fight in the east while Czechoslovak independence was being proclaimed in Prague. "They had fought enough for Russia," one observer explained. "Now it was time to go home to a free Czechoslovakia."[22]

As October 1918 turned into November, plots and counterplots festered in back rooms, army headquarters, and a host of out-of-the-way corners all across Siberia. "The conditions were such that you could not render any assistance to any Russian, without throwing overboard the policy of non-intervention in their internal affairs," General Graves later wrote. "Before I could take any steps . . . some decision had to be made as to what faction constituted the Russians referred to in the policy [set down in the *aide-mémoire* of July 17]." "That decision," he added, "could only be made in Washington." In the meantime, Graves saw his mission as being "to guard military stores, which may subsequently be needed by Russian forces" and to confine his units to the passive role that he believed his instructions required.[23] For the time being, his singular, uncomplicated view of the limits that the American Constitution placed upon his freedom to make policy on the spot kept peace among the Allies. "It was equally unconstitutional to use American troops in hostile action in Siberia against any faction of Russia [without a declaration of war by Congress]," he explained, "as it would have been to send them to Russia with a view to using them in hostile action against the Russians."[24]

Convinced that he could not order his men to fight for or against any group or government until he received specific instructions from his president, Graves took no sides in the jockeying for position that was about to bring the Omsk Directorate to an end. While he stood aside, insisting that "there were basic differences in our policies which could never be reconciled as long as my instructions remained,"[25] the French and British continued to pit various factions among Siberia's Whites against one another, and the Japanese continued to hold the key points that they had occupied along Siberia's railroads just before Graves had arrived. Then, in a single day, a new government emerged in Omsk. Led by Admiral Aleksandr Kolchak, the man who was destined to be remembered as Siberia's supreme ruler, this was to be the dictatorship that everyone had feared (or hoped) would impose common purpose upon the Siberians.

41

Siberia's Supreme Ruler

While the statesmen of Komuch and the Provisional Government of Autonomous Siberia squabbled over preference and precedence, others considered the question of Siberia's destiny. Among the men and women who had assembled to fight the Reds, every shade of political opinion had its advocates, each as uncompromising as the Bolsheviks themselves. On the left, anarchists vied with Socialist Revolutionaries while regionalists struggled against republicans and democrats in the center. Farther to the right stood the monarchists. Beyond them, Russia's nascent fascist movement shaped its own vision of the world to come. Should Siberia be a commonwealth? A federation? A republic? A dictatorship? Or, some asked, should the monarchy be restored?

During the summer of 1918, those who favored monarchy turned their thoughts toward the western Siberian mining center of Ekaterinburg, where the fallen emperor Nicholas II, the former empress Aleksandra, and their five children languished as prisoners of the Bolsheviks in the large stone-and-stucco building that had once been the home of a prosperous merchant family by the name of Ipatiev. Now known simply as "the House of Special Designation," the Romanovs' jail was surrounded by sentry posts, machine-gun emplacements, and a high fence of rough-sawn boards that allowed no one but its guards to have access to its interior. There were, of course, the inevitable rumors of plans for escapes and daring rescues, none of which materialized. Then, when units of the Czech Legion advanced against the city at the beginning of July, it seemed that the Romanovs' liberation might be possible after all. A secret message intercepted by the jailers at the House of Special Designation proclaimed that "the long awaited hour is at hand." Another added that "the days of the usurpers are numbered."[1]

Fearful that the Czechs and their allies might liberate their prisoners, the Regional Soviet of the Urals replaced the untrained Red Guard jailers at the House of Special Designation with elite Cheka guards from whom the Romanovs could expect no mercy. Headed by Iakov Iurovskii, a Jew who had converted to Lutheranism and whose family remembered him as an "oppressor" and a "despot," these guards had dedicated their lives to the Bolshevik cause. To kill a Romanov had long been Iurovskii's hope; the prospect of killing Russia's former emperor and heir at one stroke exceeded his wildest dreams. Iurovskii and his men were thus ready to execute the Romanovs at a moment's notice. All they required was the command to do so.

While he awaited further instructions about his prisoners, Iurovskii installed iron grates over the windows in the House of Special Designation and ordered that the glass be painted over so that no one could see out or in. "We like this type less and less," Nicholas wrote in his diary after Iurovskii had put his new security measures into effect. "We have no news whatever from the outside."[2] What the fallen tsar did not know was that soldiers of the Czech Legion were just a few days away from breaking into Ekaterinburg. By that time, a high-ranking Bolshevik reportedly explained some days later, Lenin had concluded "that we shouldn't leave the Whites a live banner to rally around."[3] That meant that the Romanovs could not leave Siberia alive.

On July 16, 1918, Nicholas, Aleksandra, and their children ate a meager supper and spent the evening chatting and reading before they went to bed around midnight. Two hours later, Iurovskii awakened them with word that they were about to be moved to a new prison. Hurriedly Nicholas and his son, Aleksei, donned army tunics and forage caps, while Aleksandra and her daughters put on ordinary dresses. Then Nicholas, carrying his son, who was still recovering from a massive hemophiliac hemorrhage, led his family down the stairs to the ground floor, where Iurovskii motioned them to wait in a nearby room until the cars that had been ordered for them arrived. All the while, the rumble of the Czech Legion's artillery could be heard in the distance as it bombarded the Bolshevik positions that guarded the approaches to Ekaterinburg.

At 2:45 A.M., Iurovskii led a detachment of ten Cheka guards into the room in which the Romanovs were waiting. "Nicholas Aleksandrovich," he announced simply, "You and your family are to be shot by order of the Regional Soviet of the Urals." Nicholas barely had time to gasp "*Chto?*"—"What?"—and leap to his feet before Iurovskii shot him in the head. Then, in the moments that followed, Iurovskii and his men methodically killed the rest of their prisoners. "Their blood flowed in streams," one of the Chekists testified later. It lay in puddles on the floor, "thick, like livers." Fifteen minutes later, the major line of the Romanov dynasty was no more. Then Iurovskii and his men hurried to do away with the bodies and erase the signs of their deed before the Whites arrived.[4]

When the Czechs and their White allies stormed into Ekaterinburg eight days later, a detachment of monarchist officers raced to the House of Special Designation to liberate their emperor, only to find the building deserted. A quick examination of the floor and walls of the room in which the Romanovs had spent their last moments produced twenty-two bullets but no clues about the victims' whereabouts. Only when the Whites captured one of the Cheka guards six months later did the world begin to learn the details of the Romanovs' brutal execution. "The execution of the Tsar's family was needed not only to frighten, horrify, and dishearten the enemy, but to shake up our own ranks and show them that there was no turning back," Trotskii later wrote.[5] As killers of their country's fallen sovereigns, the Bolsheviks now had to triumph or face the fate of regicides. All across the lands that once had been the Russian Empire, terror became one of the main weapons in their struggle for victory. Nowhere was that more the case than in Siberia.

Once the execution of Nicholas, Aleksandra, and their children had eliminated the figureheads around whom they might have rallied most easily, Russians and Siberians began to look for a "dictator" into whose hands Siberia's fate could be placed. Liberals and conservatives now agreed about the need for a strong government. "In a country . . . where the passions of civil war are raging," one liberal spokesman concluded, "there must inevitably be established a firm one-man authority capable of saving the state."[6] As winter returned in full force to Siberia in 1918, the cossacks and tsarist army officers who thronged the cafés and assembly halls of Omsk began to speak of overthrowing the crumbling Directorate. The tens of thousands of conservative Siberian peasants who feared that the turmoil of civil war would wipe out the prosperity that had made their lives comfortable in comparison with those of their countrymen in European Russia heartily seconded their opinion. "In political and military circles, the preference for a dictatorship grows stronger and stronger," the commander in chief of the Directorate's armed forces confided to his diary at the end of October. "Most likely," he added, "this idea will in some way be tied to [Admiral] Kolchak."[7]

A friend of Britain's Admiral Jellicoe and a famed explorer of the Arctic whom the head of Britain's military mission to Siberia praised as "the best Russian for our purpose in the Far East,"[8] Rear Admiral Aleksandr Vasilevich Kolchak turned forty-four on the day when the floundering politicians of the Directorate chose him to be their minister of war and navy. Tall and dark with a well-shaped aristocratic nose, an elegantly cleft chin, and piercing black eyes, he looked every inch the savior Siberians hoped he would become. In contrast to the politicians and intellectuals who had struggled to govern Siberia in the turbulent days of 1917 and 1918, Kolchak insisted that anyone who wanted to defend Siberia against the Bolsheviks "must lean on armed force." Any government that did not, he had already told England's military attaché, would "be a fiction."[9]

In a lightning coup that began in Omsk just after midnight on the morning of November 18, 1918, and was over before daylight lightened the leaden winter sky, Kolchak took power from the hands of the crumbling Directorate to become the "supreme ruler" and "dictator" of Siberia. "They call me a dictator," he told the assembled editors of Siberia's newspapers at a special meeting ten days later. "Well, let it be so." The Roman Senate had appointed dictators to guide the republic in times of crisis, he reminded his listeners, and he viewed his task in similar terms. The Siberians must dedicate everything to a "merciless, implacable struggle against the Bolsheviks." In return, Kolchak promised that he would make Siberia the key to the "resurrection of Russia."

Although ready to concede that "a government can function and develop in our times only on the basis of firm democratic principles," Kolchak insisted that Siberia's army must come first.[10] Siberia must be reunited and the petty fiefdoms of the cossack atamans Semënov and Kalmykov broken up. That went against Japan's policy of keeping Siberia weak, but it brought Kolchak the firm support of Great Britain, whose statesmen wanted someone to head Siberia's government who would crush dissent and do their bidding. Convinced that Siberia had at last found a champion who was "honest, patriotic, and capable"[11] and delighted with Kolchak's promise to "undertake to pay in full . . . all legitimate financial obligations of the [tsarist] government," England became his armorer, financier, and chief supporter.[12] Somewhat half-heartedly and with only a handful of forces in Siberia in any case, the French joined the British. Alone among the Allied representatives,

America's General Graves continued to stand aside. Skeptical yet hopeful, he still insisted that his troops must take no side until they received direct orders from Washington.[13]

Convinced that Kolchak's government represented the best hope for regaining what the revolutions of 1917 had taken from them, men of high birth and low principle descended upon Omsk with their wives, mistresses, children, and retainers. Once the masters of great mansions in the country and luxurious apartments in Moscow and St. Petersburg, these fallen courtiers, bankers, and high officials of Imperial Russia now lived in single rooms in a city whose population had grown nearly sixfold during the month after Kolchak rose to power. Speculation ran rampant in Omsk, and, as the prices of meat and bread doubled, Siberia's economy began to come apart.[14]

The men and women who flocked to Omsk in search of favors during 1919 brought with them the worst excesses of tsarism and none of its virtues. Senior staff officers sold the contents of whole supply trains on the black market while their men, clad in rags and bark shoes, fought and died in snowdrifts.[15] At the same time, Kolchak's pleas that "officers and soldiers exclude all political discussion and party conflicts from their midst" fell on uncaring ears.[16] "There's too much intrigue, too many power struggles, too much personal ambition and greed," one of the few honest statesmen in his government wrote in his diary.[17] By the summer of 1919, Siberia's supply networks had become so corrupt that desperate commanders at the front had begun to take supplies from one another at gunpoint.[18]

Such desperation stood at the opposite pole from what the military situation had seemed when Kolchak had come to power. Then, victory had appeared to be almost within the grasp of Siberia's armies, and the poorly armed, badly supplied Bolsheviks were retreating all along the front. On the day before Christmas 1918, Siberia's fighting men drove the exhausted Reds from Perm, a key mining center that held one of Imperial Russia's largest arsenals. There Kolchak's forces seized nearly fifty thousand tons of coal, almost a million and a quarter tons of iron ore, and close to 350,000 tons of smelted metals. About three hundred locomotives, ten times that many freight cars, enough machine guns and rifles to equip several divisions, and ten million rifle cartridges fell into the hands of Siberia's fighting forces on that day, making Perm the largest White victory up to that point.[19]

During the spring of 1919, Kolchak's armies continued to advance. By the middle of April, they had conquered nearly two hundred thousand square miles along the eastern frontier of European Russia, and their forward units stood within sixty miles of the Volga River. Then the corruption of Kolchak's self-serving subordinates started to take its toll. In Siberia's cities, proletarians who feared a regime that bore too many similarities to the tsarist government they had so recently overthrown grew restless. In response, Kolchak's lieutenants unleashed a reign of terror against innocent and guilty alike. "All over Siberia . . . there is an orgy of arrest without charges, of execution without even the pretense of trial, and confiscation without color of authority," America's Ambassador Roland Morris reported from Tokyo that summer.[20] "We are returning to the prehistoric period of human history," one of Siberia's leading newspapers warned as the repressions continued. "We are verging on the death of human civilization and its culture."[21]

Such senseless acts of violence eventually begat violence on an even greater scale. "The sweetness of living beyond the law has penetrated too deeply everywhere," one of the scant handful of Kolchak's advisers who cared about right and wrong wrote in his diary. "The acrid, heavily charged atmosphere of political struggle, of party and personal interests, of greed [and] speculation by politicians, merchants, and contractors," he added elsewhere, "has enshrouded us in a stinking fog."[22] Even those who had seen in Kolchak's Siberia a last hope for avoiding the terror of Bolshevism began to think that there was not much difference between the two. "This is not the avant-garde of a renovated system of government," one of them concluded. "This is the rear guard of a past that is slipping into eternity."[23]

As greed, corruption, and mindless cruelty poisoned life in the lands east of the Urals, Kolchak's armies started to collapse along Siberia's western front. On June 8, Red armies led by Mikhail Frunze, a thirty-three-year-old mill worker who was winning a place in the annals of the Civil War as one of the Bolsheviks' most brilliant commanders, took Ufa, where Kolchak's commanders had launched their first offensive six months before. By the end of the month, the Reds had crossed the Urals to begin reclaiming the plains of western Siberia.

As Frunze's forces advanced, partisans who saw little difference between the terror of Bolshevism and the tyranny of Kolchak rose all across the three thousand miles that separated Cheliabinsk from Vladivostok. Seeing no vision of a better future in Kolchak's privilege-ridden Siberia, these men and women attacked supply trains and harassed detachments of White regulars from the shelter of Siberia's taiga. In the wilderness of the Transbaikal, they called themselves the Forest Commune. Farther west, the men and women who gave themselves the title of the Peasant Red Army of Western Siberia claimed to have as many as fifteen thousand in their ranks.[24] Deadly certain in their hatred of the Kolchak regime, they fought to smash a yoke that seemed even more repressive than in tsarist times. "Their hatred is terrible to behold," one White officer reported. "Even women and twelve-year-old children are fighting against us."[25]

At first, the Whites had stood firm against partisans and Red armies alike, giving ground slowly and winning the grudging respect of their enemies for the valor with which they defended their positions. At Ufa, shock battalions in which every man had won the Cross of St. George for valor during the First World War had marched against Frunze's machine guns "with fixed bayonets, silent, holding their fire" until three thousand of Russia's bravest and best soldiers lay dead before the Reds' positions. "With the skull and crossbones insignia mounted on their caps, sleeves, and epaulets," Frunze's adjutant reported, "they made a terrifying impression."[26] But the soldiers who had placed duty and honor above survival were gone by summer's end, and the raw conscripts who had taken their places were surrendering by the thousands. Uralsk, Ekaterinburg, and Cheliabinsk were all in Red hands before fall. By late October, the Reds stood within striking distance of Kolchak's capital at Omsk.

As Frunze's armies advanced during the summer of 1919, Kolchak began to turn against those who spoke the truth too openly. With all the frustration of a man unable to bear the burdens that fate had placed upon him, he raged against the advisers he could not trust and the corruption he could not control. "He pounded the table with his fist, flung everything onto the floor, seized a penknife, and angrily slashed the arm of his chair," the executive secretary of the government remembered about a meeting between the Supreme Ruler and his ministers.[27] Another complained of Kolchak's "childish temper and conceit" and spoke of the "kaleidoscopic changes in his moods and decisions."[28] "People are packing suitcases, and the 'poor' openly rejoice and wait for the Bolsheviks to arrive," a sober statesman who had come from Moscow to serve in Kolchak's government wrote that summer.[29]

Everything was falling apart. "Can one really call this a government?" one of the few businesslike men who still served Kolchak asked himself in mid-July. "Can one really call this clique of second-rate citizens who have fastened themselves onto Omsk a government?" What had been the last great hope of liberals and conservatives alike, the same statesman wrote eight weeks later, had become such "a ghostly mirage"[30] by the time the Reds occupied Kolchak's capital on November 14 that they met no resistance. The government and armed forces of Siberia's once proud leader had left behind three armored trains, two hundred locomotives, three thousand freight cars, and half a million artillery shells. As the Reds entered Kolchak's abandoned capital, more than forty thousand soldiers, including a thousand White officers, raised their hands in surrender.[31] By that time, the hangers-on of Omsk were struggling to regroup in Irkutsk, to which they had been fleeing throughout October.

Deserted by his personal guards and traveling in a single second-class Pullman car that flew not the flag of Siberia but the standards of England, the United States, Japan, France, and Czechoslovakia, Kolchak struggled in vain to rejoin the shards of his government that had reached Irkutsk some weeks earlier.[32] On Christmas Eve 1919, a revolt led by a coalition of Mensheviks and Socialist Revolutionaries calling itself the Political Center broke out in Irkutsk, and on January 5 its leaders announced an end to the war against the Reds. After the Political Center abdicated in favor of the Bolsheviks and surrendered Kolchak into the hands of his bitterest enemies, the Irkutsk Cheka shot him on the morning of February 7, 1920, and cast his body into a hole cut in the ice of the Angara River.[33]

Kolchak's execution did not end Siberia's turmoil. While the Bolsheviks struggled to reestablish dependable transportation along the western half of the Trans-Siberian Railroad during the winter of 1919–1920, the men responsible for the *atamanshchina* in the lands east of Lake Baikal slipped completely out of control. Semënov continued to wage his campaign of terror and destruction until October 1920, when the pro-Bolshevik forces of the short-lived Far Eastern Republic seized his headquarters at Chita. Semënov's chief lieutenant, Baron Ungern-Sternberg, went on fighting from a base in Outer Mongolia until the summer of 1921, and the Japanese did not send their last shipment of arms—twelve thousand rifles, fifty machine guns, and well over a quarter-million cartridges—to the Bolsheviks' enemies until the end of 1921. Being reluctant to surrender their dreams of empire in Siberia's easternmost lands, the Japanese kept their occupation forces in place for more than two years after General Graves had withdrawn the last of his Americans in the spring of 1920.[34]

Remnants of the *atamanshchina* prevented the Bolsheviks from reclaiming Khabarovsk until mid-February 1922 and did not allow them to capture Vladivostok until the following October. A few weeks later, they absorbed the Far Eastern Republic into the Russian Soviet Federated Socialist Republic, around which the Union of Soviet Socialist Republics would be shaped that December. By then, the men and women who had dared to take the first steps along the uncharted road to communism had taken a firmer hold upon the lands farther west, hoping to use Siberia's vast resources to build socialism all across the territories of the Union of Soviet Socialist Republics. For the next few years, Siberians would enjoy a brief era of hope during which men and women ready to sacrifice their lives for a greater cause set out to build a society dedicated to economic opportunity and social justice.

42

The Bolsheviks Take Siberia

A grim prospect greeted the leaders of the newly formed Union of Soviet Socialist Republics when they surveyed their domain at the end of 1922. In human terms, the cost of the Revolution and Civil War that had ravaged the territories of the fallen Russian Empire may have run as high as thirteen or fourteen million, only a seventh of whom had died as the result of military action. Almost two million men, women, and children had fallen victim to typhus and typhoid in 1919 and 1920 alone, and more than twice that number had starved during the famine of 1921–1922. Millions more had died from the Spanish influenza pandemic of 1918–1919 and other diseases, while more than a half million had been executed, died in prison, or perished in the terrible death camps that the Cheka had opened in the far north. By the time the fighting ended, the Bolsheviks had seven million homeless children on their hands, and soaring child mortality may have accounted for as many as three million additional deaths between 1918 and 1921.[1] Never had the modern world witnessed a national catastrophe of such horrifying dimensions.

Combined with the devastation that the First World War had inflicted upon Imperial Russia's western provinces, the economic destruction of the Civil War had been nearly as ruinous as its human cost. In 1921, the Bolsheviks' domains produced fewer than a quarter of a million tons of steel, or less than a twentieth part of what Imperial Russia's mills had manufactured at the beginning of the First World War. Workers in the lands that became the Soviet Union produced less than a third of the coal, about the same percentage of the oil, and a mere one twenty-fifth of the cotton cloth that the people of tsarist Russia had enjoyed eight years earlier. Altogether, the value of the commodities mined, pumped, or manufactured in the lands of the former Russian Empire amounted to a scant seventh of what it had been before the fighting had begun. In this domain, which covered a sixth of the earth's surface, the quantity of foodstuffs harvested in 1921 and 1922 fluctuated between a fifth and a sixth of what it had been just a decade before, and the national income was only two-fifths as much. Combined with the massive breakdown of rolling stock all across Eurasia, the wartime destruction of railroad track and bridges had reduced the movement of freight by almost three quarters since the last days of peace. "Such a collapse," a Soviet expert wrote in 1924, "is unparalleled in human history."[2]

In Siberia, distance, industrial backwardness, and a shortage of railroads magnified the impact of these losses. Although it boasted more than a quarter of the world's timber supply, Siberia in those days had only a handful of sawmills, two match factories, two veneer works, and just one paper mill. Its population of about thirteen million consumed less than a third of a cord (forty cubic feet) of wood per person, and, despite their wealth of iron ore and coal, Siberians imported many more manufactured products from European Russia and abroad than they produced. Foodstuffs and precious metals had accounted for nearly nine tenths of the value of Siberian production at the outbreak of the First World War, a key sign of an underdeveloped national economy.[3]

Moving raw materials to factories and shipping manufactured goods to markets in Asia and Europe posed some of the greatest challenges the Bolsheviks faced in developing Siberia. With the exception of the Amur in the far east, all of Siberia's great rivers flowed north into the Arctic Ocean, and that, combined with the short navigation season, meant that railroads would have to play the major role in bringing the entire region into the modern world. Yet, in 1922, most of Siberia's raw materials lay beyond the reach of the railroad, for the Trans-Siberian Railroad, like the Great Siberian *trakt* before it, ran much nearer to Siberia's southern frontier than to its center. The goldfields of Bodaibo and Olëkminsk lay nearly 1,200 miles north of the railroad; the immense mineral resources of Iakutsk were eight hundred miles beyond that.

To restore the shattered industrial base they had inherited, the Bolsheviks set out to build factories closer to Siberia's sources of raw materials. There must be "a rationalization of our industry . . . by a significant transfer of industry to the East," the Soviet Union's founders insisted.[4] This made good sense in terms of moving industrial centers away from regions that were the most vulnerable to invasion, and it also fitted in with the Bolsheviks' massive propaganda effort to distance themselves from the oft-denounced "imperialist" policies of their tsarist predecessors. But the lakes of oil that flowed beneath the roadless Arctic tundra and the waterless deserts of Central Asia and the gold, copper, nickel, tin, and coal that nature had buried in the permafrost of Siberia's northeast could be reached only by building railroads, roads, hydroelectric stations, processing plants, and metallurgical combines on a scale never seen in human history. In other countries and under normal conditions, such gigantic undertakings would have required massive preparation. Nothing was normal about the situation the Bolsheviks faced in 1922.

Starting in March 1921, the ruin left by the Civil War and the economic disasters created by their first mad dash to build a classless society forced Lenin and the Bolsheviks to retreat into the "prudent pragmatism" of the New Economic Policy. This meant changing the economy of the Soviet Union not "by one stroke of the revolutionary sword" as a high-ranking Bolshevik once said, but by more gradual means.[5] By allowing Soviet peasants to sell most of their crops on the open market, permitting the thousands of tiny artels that had dotted the countryside in tsarist times to come to life once again, and insisting that even heavy industries—the "commanding heights" in Bolshevik parlance—must pay their way and show a profit, Lenin and his comrades set out to renew their nation's economy by using those very forms of private enterprise they had once condemned.[6] After five years of the New Economic Policy, Siberia's fields yielded more grain than they had during the bumper crop of 1913, and its herds had increased at a similar rate. By 1926, its agriculture was well on the road to recovery.[7]

The requirements of Bolshevik theory and the need to parcel out scarce resources and machinery meant that much of Siberia's mining and heavy industry had to be centralized rather than allowed to respond to the market forces that had spurred the recovery of its agriculture. During the year after the Civil War, the Bolsheviks therefore combined nearly two hundred of Siberia's largest prewar enterprises into thirty-eight "trusts" that employed more than three quarters of the miners and mill hands working east of the Urals. By the end of 1922, this new centralization had raised Siberia's gold production by six hundred percent, so that it stood at a fifth of what it had been in 1913. Yet even this slow pace of recovery was far from even. Although Siberia's mines responded to the Bolsheviks' policies, the output of its factories continued to decline. By the end of 1923, Siberia's industrial output still amounted to a little more than a sixth of what it had been at the beginning of the First World War.[8]

Even though its workers were mining more coal and exporting fifteen times more logs and sawn timber than they had before the Great War, all of Siberia in 1925 still had only 4,342 telephones, 269 automobiles and trucks, and 19 radio stations, and most of its 125,000 industrial workers still had jobs in reborn small workshops, not heavy industry.[9] When Stalin rose to power during the late 1920s, the transformation that would make Siberia into the industrial colossus the Bolsheviks envisioned lay in the future. Siberia's backwardness still had to be overcome, but time was short and growing shorter. "We are fifty or a hundred years behind the advanced countries," Stalin concluded. "We must make good this distance in ten years," he warned, "or we shall go under." Insisting that the world's first socialist state would soon have to face even more powerful attacks from the capitalist nations that surrounded it than those the Allies had launched to crush the Bolshevik Revolution, Stalin called for speed—what he called "a genuine Bolshevik tempo"—to modernize the Soviet Union in record time.[10]

The keys to Siberia's industrial transformation, or—to use the Soviet term—"socialist reconstruction," were to be speed and size. Colossal enterprises had to be built to match its huge natural wealth and tremendous distances, and Soviet planners began to think in ever enlarging proportions as Stalin took the reins of government more firmly into his hands. If the Soviet Union were to survive, Stalin said, Siberia's resources must be used for the purposes of producing "on a mass scale all modern means of defense and of equipping its army with them in the event of an attack from abroad."[11] Behind the Urals, where the vast distances and harsh climate could serve as two lines of natural defense, he and his advisers now planned to build an industrial complex that would lie beyond the reach of any foreign attack.

Spreading over thirty thousand square miles of rough territory along the headwaters of the Tom River in the southeastern part of western Siberia, the Kuzbass was to form the eastern anchor of this new Siberian industrial fortress. Destined to become the greatest of Soviet coalfields, with reserves estimated at more than nine hundred billion metric tons, its key centers were the hamlet of Shcheglovo, which was combined with the equally obscure village of Kemerovo to become Shcheglovsk in 1918 (only to regain the name of Kemerovo in 1932); Kolchulgino, founded in 1864 and renamed Leninsk-Kuznetskii in 1925; Prokopevsk, not to be found on any tsarist maps because it was not settled until 1918;

and Stalinsk (called Kuznets in tsarist times and, after 1960, Novokuznetsk), which, although founded in 1617, had remained of little consequence until a massive iron-and-steel plant took shape there in 1929.[12] By 1928, there would be two and a half times as many miners working in the Kuzbass as there had been at the end of the Civil War, and the output of coal would have nearly tripled. Eight years later, the Kuzbass mines were producing nearly two and a quarter million tons of coal, almost twice as much as they had at the beginning of the First World War.[13]

According to the grand Soviet plan, high-grade coking coal was to be transported from the mines of the Kuzbass to Magnitogorsk, an industrial city that was to be built at the base of western Siberia's Magnetic Mountain, some twelve hundred miles west of the Kuzbass. Estimated to hold at least half a billion metric tons of some of the highest-grade iron ore in the world, this Magnetic Mountain, according to an estimate made in the 1960s, could provide enough steel to build the skeletal structures of 7,938 Empire State Buildings or 3,969,140 diesel locomotives.[14] Using local ore in combination with Kuzbass coking coal, Magnitogorsk was to become the largest steel mill in Eurasia and the western anchor of Stalin's huge Urals-Kuznets Combine.

When the Great Depression seemed to challenge the most fundamental accomplishments of capitalism in the West, the Urals-Kuznets Combine became a monument to the daring of the Soviet vision. While the unemployed workers of the West faced a future that seemed to be moved by unseen and unforseeable forces, the men and women of the Soviet Union were laboring to build a world that, they promised, would enlist all the wonders of science and technology in the service of humanity. Nothing seemed impossible to men and women who saw blast furnaces rising from empty steppes while endless trains of hopper cars carried coal and iron ore back and forth across the wastes of southern Siberia.

To those looking at its rise from abroad, the Urals-Kuznets Combine seemed to prove that men and women might indeed reach their greatest potential and enjoy the best standard of living while working for the common good rather than for personal gain. Many of the participants in the Soviet experiment shared that view. Built in part by huge armies of forced laborers, the mines and metalworks of the Ural-Kuznets Combine were the product of work carried out by tens of thousands of free Soviet citizens as well as hundreds of foreign Communists who dedicated themselves to building the brave new world the Bolsheviks had envisioned.

Even before the Great Depression tightened its grip on the United States, the legendary "Big Bill" Haywood and the Dutch-born "Wobbly" John Rutgers urged America's workers to enlist in what would become known as the Autonomous Industrial Colony of the Kuzbass. Here, they announced from their headquarters at 110 West Fortieth Street in New York City, was the chance for "full chested men, open air men, men who can do things while they get their dinner from the river and snap it up on the wing" to build a new world. The Kuzbass colony needed up to six thousand such heroes who could "stand lonely nights on the edge of the earth and do it willingly because of the big thing that stands as a beacon before them."[15] Each would have to pay his own travel expenses and put up two hundred American dollars in cash before he left the United States to cover the cost of his food and tools. But the rewards could be beyond all imagining. Here, Haywood told a friend, was the chance they had been waiting for to begin building a new world in which working men and women would "not feed a parasitic society" but have the full product of their labor returned to them.[16]

Although Haywood's campaign failed to attract even a tenth of the workers needed for the Kuzbass colony during the 1920s, many of the men and women of the American and European Left believed with all their hearts that the Bolsheviks had found the key to a better future. Among those who were fired by the Soviet dream as the Great Depression settled upon the Western world was Jack Scott, a young student at the University of Wisconsin. Enthralled by the vision of a society so different from Depression America, Scott set out, as Haywood had urged, to volunteer his body and skills for the Soviet experiment. In 1932, this American student radical became a Soviet welder, working to raise the gigantic blast furnaces of Magnitogorsk from the emptiness of the southwestern Siberian steppes.

43

Jack Scott and Siberia's Magnetic Mountain

In 1931, a Great Depression paralyzed the West. Half a world away from Siberia, legions of men and women faced a future without hope, their dreams darkened by the prospect of living without work or pay. Bread-lines formed grim monuments to the apparent failure of the dream that had established the United States as the Promised Land for the world's poor and dispossessed. Now the lengthening specter of unemployment challenged the belief that hard work, thrift, and a readiness to seize the brass ring of fortune could assure men and women of better lives than their parents'. Many thought that capitalism had come to its final crisis. Was it possible, they asked, to shape a world without unemployment, hunger, or poverty? Was there a realm somewhere beyond capitalism in which there could be prosperity and social justice for all?

At that very moment, Stalin's massive experiment with building so-cialism in one country moved toward its crescendo. The Soviet Union could find a place for every pair of working hands, and there were to be no hunger, poverty, or want in its future, where opportunity and pros-perity would lie within the reach of every citizen. To those witnessing the tragedy of America and Europe, the Soviet Union became the "Country with a Plan," the nation that had conquered capitalism's curse of unemployment. One American magazine editor called the Soviet experiment "the most important human step since the birth of Chris-tianity." The Soviet system, its future enemy Arthur Koestler wrote in those days, was "the future," while the Western world had become "the past." That the vast social-scientific laboratory formed by the land of the Soviets stood open to one and all impressed such people deeply. "I have seen the future," one of them exclaimed. "And it works!"[1]

Jack Scott, son of well-educated American Communist parents and a second-year student at the University of Wisconsin's new Experimental College, thought that America offered painfully "few opportunities for young energy and enthusiasm" while the Soviet experiment promised vast new fields to plow. "The place where there is work to be done now is among the workers themselves," Scott wrote as he surveyed Depression America in one of his student essays. Convinced that his place was "with the workers helping to set up a new world,"[2] he vowed to "lend a hand," as he later wrote, "in the construction of a society which seemed to be at least one step ahead" of the United States.[3] Scott therefore set out for Moscow in the spring of 1932, the hordes of able-bodied men without work in every American and European city through which he passed confirming the rightness of his belief that the future lay elsewhere.[4]

August 1932 found Jack Scott—by then the proud possessor of a welder's certificate earned by working as an apprentice at General Electric's plant in Schenectady, New York—applying for a visa at the Soviet embassy in Berlin. A month later, he reached Moscow, visa and portable typewriter in hand, and got his first glimpse of Soviet life. To his chagrin, its separate parts seemed too often to work against the whole. Officials at Moscow's welders' union explained that they could not sign him up for work until the visa department gave him permission to stay in the Soviet Union; the visa department insisted that it could grant such permission to foreigners only after they had found jobs. After ten days of running from office to office in a city in which he knew not one word of the language, Scott finally got a resident alien's permit and an assignment as a welder in Magnitogorsk—the city of the Magnetic Mountain—in Siberia's bleak southwestern borderlands.

At the southern end of the Urals, some seventy miles east of the line that divides Europe from Asia, Siberia's Magnetic Mountain rises eight hundred feet above the wooded steppe. For centuries, the native Bash-kirs had tended their flocks in the sparse fields around it, knowing nothing of the high-grade iron ore that lay beneath their feet. Thus it had been left for the Russians to discover the mountain's treasure when they arrived at the beginning of the eighteenth century and noticed how its pull drew the needles of their compasses away from the magnetic pole. After giving the name "Magnitnaia"—"the Lodestone"—to the tiny Bashkir village that stood nearby, they began to mine the iron ore that had caused their compasses to fail. By 1913, the Magnetic Mountain and the blast furnaces that fed upon it were producing about fifty thousand tons of iron and steel a year. Considering that the mountain's ore contained up to sixty percent iron and ranked among the richest in the world, that output represented only the tiniest fraction of what the region had the potential to produce.[5]

In the late 1920s, the Magnetic Mountain came to the attention of Siberia's new Bolshevik rulers. Two thousand miles east of the Soviet Union's western frontier and protected on all sides by the vastness of Eurasia's space, the Magnetic Mountain seemed the perfect place to build the western bastion of Stalin's new industrial fortress. Here, within a realm of five hundred square miles that stood as far east of Moscow as Moscow was from Berlin, gold, platinum, silver, copper, nickel, lead, iron, and aluminum all lay in abundant supply. Once connected to the rich coal deposits of the Kuzbass, the Magnetic Mountain's iron ore could be transformed into the steel that would build the industrial colossus Stalin envisioned.

Siberia's Magnetic Mountain thus held the raw material from which to shape the ultimate socialist dream: a planned factory and a planned city to house its labor force. Magnitogorsk was to be a monument to the superiority of socialism, the largest iron-and-steel plant anywhere in the world, surrounded by a model workers' city in which everything done by the people with resources owned by the people would be done for the people. At Magnitogorsk, the grinding, dirty labor of steel making was to be consigned to the dustbin of history like all the other remnants of the capitalist world that Siberia's new rulers so disdained. "Built on the basis of the most up-to-date technique," a propaganda booklet published in 1932 explained, "the Magnitogorsk plant will ring the death knell of many hard and exhausting trades in the metal industry. . . . The unskilled worker will be a rare figure," it continued. "The whole of the production process from beginning to end will be permeated by electrical power."[6] Soviet propagandists promised that Magnitogorsk was to "be clothed in virtue." In the midst of the arid steppe, it would become "a garden city" where cesspools, mud, and slum housing all would be eradicated from workers' experience. "Every spare piece of ground," the purveyors of the Magnitogorsk vision wrote, "will be used for planting flowers, shrubs and trees."[7]

Nothing was to be wasted in this garden city, in which electricity and technology were to lift the burden of heavy labor from Siberia's masses. There would be no problems with sewage- and waterborne diseases, and all of the noxious gases released by the coking and smelting processes would be put to good use. "Special machinery will draw off the gases from the ovens" and convert them into a host of useful chemical products, the propagandists of Magnitogorsk promised. Ammonium sulfate for fertilizing the lands that would grow the city's food, tar for paving its roads, saltpeter to make the cotton fields of Uzbekistan more fertile, and even fuel for the open-hearth furnaces themselves—all would come from the by-products of Magnitogorsk, which, in earlier times and in different places, had poisoned the lungs of the men and women who had made steel. Now the workers were to be celebrated as the most precious resource of all, and every person at Magnitogorsk was to be educated to the highest level.[8] "The heights of metallurgical technique," Soviet propagandists insisted, "will be attainable for all workers at the Magnitogorsk plant."[9] Nothing would be overlooked. "The rotten inheritance of capitalism does not hinder anybody here," the men who wrote of Magnitogorsk in its early years insisted.[10] Freed from that burden, socialism would "cover in ten years the path that capitalism had taken over a century to travel."[11]

Modeled on the ultramodern plant the United States Steel Corporation had built twenty years before at Gary, Indiana, Magnitogorsk was thus to become the world's greatest maker of steel.[12] In the early 1930s, tens of thousands of Soviet citizens were working to raise this vast steeltown from the barren lands around the Magnetic Mountain, and Jack Scott was delighted to join them. "I was going to be one of many who cared not to own a second pair of shoes, but who built blast furnaces which were their own," he wrote later. "It was September, 1932, and I was twenty years old."[13] Four days later, Scott reached his destination. Now deployed on "the iron and steel front," he would become a part of the Soviet Union's struggle to overcome centuries of Siberia's technological backwardness in a single decade.[14]

In the fall of 1932, Magnitogorsk seemed more like a battlefield than the shining socialist city of steel and concrete promised in Soviet propaganda pamphlets. A tangle of steel girders, gigantic pipes, rough planks, and half-used brick, the "city" in which Jack Scott joined the furious "battle of ferrous metallurgy"[15] was a jumble of hastily built huts and shabby barracks without paved streets, running water, sewers, or any sort of safety equipment. Food was scarce, heat even more so, and diseases that stemmed from filth and malnutrition were rampant. The propagandists of Magnitogorsk might well disdain the "rotten heritage of capitalism," but the living and working conditions that Russia's workers found there at the beginning of the 1930s were worse than any in the

West. The difference, Soviet apologists insisted, was that filth and poverty had been a way of life under capitalism; under socialism, they were to be part of a passing (and very brief) moment.

Scott found his new home in Barracks No. 17, by far the best in Magnitogorsk but still without toilets or running water and dependent upon jerry-rigged sheet-steel stoves for heat.[16] Half a world away from the cozy college room with maid service that he had left behind at the Experimental College in Madison, Magnitogorsk was for Jack Scott a vast leap backward into an era in which men and women, whose lives were thought to be more expendable than the materials they used, did the work of machines. Yet if he had never seen such bleakness, Scott had also never witnessed such dedication. "Tens of thousands of people were enduring the most intense hardships," he wrote. "Many of them did it willingly, with boundless enthusiasm."[17] Everywhere there was a sense that the impossible was about to be accomplished.

Scott sensed Siberia's promise at the same time as he shared its problems. Among the quarter of a million men and women who had poured into Magnitogorsk since 1930, there were many who had never seen an electric light, a machine, or even a staircase, and these had to come to grips with the marvels of electricity, steam power, and all the paraphernalia of modern technology in an instant. Native Siberians saw their lives change more in one year than those of their ancestors had since the days of Tammerlane. Hunters, fishermen, trappers, and herders, they now had to become electricians, welders, and steel cutters, working with machines whose existence their parents had never even imagined.

Aside from hordes of human backs and hands, everything needed to build the great blast furnaces and hearths was in short supply. Foremen waged a constant battle for the rivets, welding rods, insulators, and wire their men needed for each day's work. There were not enough planks for scaffolding, and, when a power surge destroyed much of the construction site's lighting, there were not even any spare bulbs to replace the ones that had been damaged. The most elementary safeguards against accident had to be done without, and everything had to be patched, eked out, and reused while the Soviet Union's inexperienced planners struggled to bring the necessary raw materials, equipment, and workers together in the same place at the proper time.

At Magnitogorsk, work on the great ovens, blast furnaces, and rolling mills that would make Soviet steel took precedence over everything else. Workers lived on leftovers and the scant supplies that Soviet planners managed to send, but the equipment they installed was some of the best the world produced. Electrical equipment from General Electric, rolling mill parts from the German firm of Demag, and the best technical know-how gold could buy anywhere in the West all came together in Magnitogorsk to proclaim that, whatever the obstacles, the mills would be built and steel would be made.[18] Necessity, not idealism, shaped the daily lives of workers who froze inside the pipes they welded, fell from tottering chimneys and towers, and lived at the edge of survival in the belief that the day would soon come when life would be better. A brisk commerce in extra ration cards flourished at Magnitogorsk, where men and women ate more even if they did not eat well and warmed themselves with precious stolen planks set alight in stoves that would have stayed cold without them. "It did not take me long to realize," Scott later confessed, "that they ate black bread principally because there was no other to be had and wore rags because they could not be replaced."[19]

All told, Jack Scott spent five years in Magnitogorsk, working as a welder alongside men who, like himself, had never seen a welding torch until the dream of building socialism had entered their lives. Now, as the tangle of girders, pipes, cables, and iron rails took the shape of buildings, pipelines, and railroads, they saw the great chimneys of the blast furnaces, the blooming mills, and the coke and chemical plants rising against the Siberian skyline. Progress was being made, but the men and women who were making it knew all too well its cost. "They froze, hungered, and suffered," Scott remembered when he looked back on his days at Magnitogorsk, "but the construction work went on with a disregard for individuals and a mass heroism seldom paralleled in history."[20]

Even as its mills and apartments took shape, very little in Magnitogorsk resembled the garden city of steel about which its planners had dreamed. This was an enterprise built from compromises made with natural conditions and human failings that technology and science could never overcome. Yet the dedication of its builders and their willingness to learn while they worked were not to be denied. Thousands spent long evenings every week in hastily organized technical schools that transformed skilled workers into engineers, chemists, and economists and their once unskilled successors into welders, machine operators, and draftsmen. Almost overnight, peasants, nomads, and thousands of men and women whose only trade had been living by their wits were being made into telegraph operators, truck drivers, office workers, writers, and teachers to bring Siberia more quickly into the modern world.

The new world of socialism demanded that its citizens be shaped into whatever Siberia needed most. While attending the fledgling city's Communist University, Jack Scott met Masha Dikareva, the daughter of a poor peasant, who had become a teacher and a dedicated believer in the new world that seemed to be taking shape around her. A few months later, she and Jack were married and dedicated their lives to working together for the dream in which they both believed. Then, in 1935, the main energies of the men and women at Magnitogorsk shifted from building to producing the goods for which the vast new plants and industries had been built.[21] Along with his comrades, Jack Scott laid his welding torch aside and became a producer, working in the benzol department of Magnitogorsk's vast coking plant, where he helped to produce benzol and naphthalene from the gas given off by the coking process.

As Jack and Masha became parents, it seemed that life was becoming "better and more joyful," as Stalin himself promised, and as production at Magnitogorsk rose by astounding multiples, it seemed that perhaps they and their comrades were going to succeed in cramming a hundred years of Western experience into ten. Although it had been a wasteland when the first ground was broken in June 1929, Magnitogorsk was producing two million tons of iron ore, eight hundred thousand tons of coking coal, somewhat more than a half million tons of pig iron, and nearly a hundred thousand tons of steel just four years later. By 1937, the quantities of coking coal had doubled, iron ore and pig iron production had tripled, and the output of steel had risen by sixteen times to nearly a million and a half tons. The Scotts could count fifty schools, three colleges, eight theaters, seventeen libraries, twenty-two clubs, and eighteen clinics where there had been an empty steppe nine years earlier. Magnitogorsk still seemed "in a primitive state," to be sure, but its sod huts were beginning to give way to concrete apartment buildings, a city park had been built, streetcar lines had been laid, and paved, well-lit streets were replacing the mud ruts of earlier times.[22]

Yet ominous clouds were gathering even as a better life for the workers of Magnitogorsk was taking shape. With the obvious accomplishments at Magnitogorsk came the equally evident problems caused by a work force that had not yet become educated enough to run the complex machinery that modern-day steel making required. Jack Scott saw a worker ruin nearly a million gold rubles' worth of imported firebrick in a single moment of carelessness, while another accidentally set off an explosion that cost a million and a half rubles to repair. Scarcely a month went by without some sort of accident, wreck, or costly mistake. Foremen struggling to increase production abused ma-

chines in ways that cost more to repair than the added output could ever
be worth, yet no one dared, as Stalinism tightened its grip upon Siberia,
to place the blame for these costly accidents squarely upon the system
itself.

All across the Soviet Union the search began for "wreckers" and
"traitors" who could be blamed for accidents caused by carelessness,
fear, ignorance, and stupidity. From the very beginning, the work force
at Magnitogorsk had included men and women thought to be in need
of political reeducation by reason of their family backgrounds, and these
became the first to be swept up in the purges that struck the Soviet
Union in the mid-1930s. But these were by no means the only victims.
Foremen whose crews did not fulfill quotas, shop stewards who had been
on duty when an accident occurred, even department directors and
plant managers all came to know the terror of a knock in the dead of
night, an arrest without charges, and the agony of forced confessions.
Guilt by association, by implication, even by definition (in the cases of
men and women unfortunate enough to have been reared in families
now condemned as "enemies of the people") brought ruin to people who
had given the best of their energies and talents to the cause of socialism.

Jack Scott barely escaped. After visiting the United States in 1937, he
returned to Magnitogorsk to find that he was under suspicion simply for
being a foreigner. No longer allowed to work in the mills, he decided to
leave, but it took more than three years before the authorities granted
permission for Masha and their children to go with him. The Scotts left
behind a country torn by fear and suspicion even as it stood at the brink of
a new war. Disillusioned by the purges that took the lives of so many of
the men and women with whom he had worked to build Magnitogorsk,
Scott repudiated his Communist faith and became a dedicated anti-
Communist during the years after the Second World War. Before he died
in 1976, he helped to found Radio Liberty and served as an editor at Time
Inc. for the better part of three decades, all the while warning of the
dangers that the Soviet Union posed to the United States and Europe.[23]

In the meantime, millions of Soviet citizens fell victim to the system
that Scott had helped to create. But there was more than simple madness
or unreasoned fear to be blamed for the process that brought so many
of Scott's friends to ruin. Further to the east and north, the Soviet Union
stood in desperate need of working hands to mine gold, cut timber, and
build the foundations for scores of new cities and mills. Swept into labor
camps for reasons they did not understand, some of the most dedicated
builders of Siberia's new order in the 1920s and early 1930s now joined
the slave-labor armies needed to transform their visions into reality.

44

Edible Fossils

Toward the end of the 1950s, a brief scientific note describing how "frozen specimens of prehistoric fauna tens of thousands of years old" had been discovered near the Kolyma River reminded Aleksandr Solzhenitsyn and a few of his friends of days that had darkened their lives forever. Although the account supplied few details other than to report that the ancient creatures had been so well preserved by the permafrost that "those present broke open the ice . . . and ate them on the spot WITH RELISH," Solzhenitsyn and his comrades found it all too easy to picture how the discoverers of these edible fossils had thawed the flesh that had been frozen in the days of Siberia's first cave dwellers over a bonfire and, without even waiting for it to cook, had bolted it down. "We understood," Solzhenitsyn explained, "because we were the same kind of people." Like millions of other Soviet citizens, they too had known the torment of living without hope and working to the point of exhaustion for a tiny piece of meat or an extra quarter pound of bread in Siberia's slave-labor camps.[1]

By a strange evolutionary process that most early Bolsheviks had not foreseen, the Soviet slave-labor system had grown out of one of the most generous theories about crime and punishment yet to emerge from the crucible of human experience. Embracing Lenin's view that "crime is a form of social excess,"[2] the first Soviet jurists had proclaimed that correction and reeducation must be their task. Erasing such words as "guilt," "prison," and "punishment" from the criminal code in the belief that they smacked too much of vengeance, such men had insisted that society alone must bear the guilt for the crimes of its members. Whoever broke the law must therefore be regarded as a person who had gone astray and not be subjected to the abuse that capitalist prisons heaped upon their victims. "The system of squeezing golden sweat" from prisoners by sentencing them to terms of hard labor, Lenin's chief of "corrective institutions" wrote in the 1920s, was "entirely inadmissible in Soviet places of confinement."[3] Such was the theory of prison reform that was to have removed from Soviet Siberia all of the places of hard labor in which men and women had endured long years of suffering under the tsars.[4] It was precisely this humanitarian fairness combined with a strong sense of social justice that appealed to so many in the West during the terrible days of the Great Depression.

Like so much else that underlay the Soviet system in its early days, the theory about why crime occurred and how offenders could be rehabilitated had little basis in fact. Crime soared so dramatically that the number of prisoners in Soviet jails more than doubled between 1922 and 1927. "Places of detention" became so crowded that scarcely an eighth of the four hundred thousand men and women sentenced to prison terms could actually serve them. "If we were to carry out all the sentences imposed by the courts," a highly respected member of the Soviet Supreme Tribunal told the assembled Fifteenth Party Congress in December 1927, "we would have to spend millions [more] for prisons."[5] The time had come for idealistic principles and theories to give way to what Soviet leaders were beginning to call a "new realism." If crime could not be wiped out and rehabilitation not achieved, then punishment and forced labor must take the place of correction and reeducation. "We must overcome sugary liberalism," a leading Soviet legal journal warned its readers. "A prison is a prison," it concluded, "and punishment is punishment."[6] The Siberian vastness that had once been known as the "tsar's cow pasture" was about to be transformed into what Solzhenitsyn would call "that amazing country of Gulag, which, although broken up into an archipelago [of slave-labor camps] geographically was, in the psychological sense, forged into a continent."[7]

Toward the end of the 1920s, the immense cost of building the Soviet Union's industrial base without Western investment capital added an economic incentive to the moral and political justifications that jurists were beginning to develop to justify forced labor.[8] To purchase from the West the advanced machinery and know-how needed for Stalin's drive for industrialization meant that greater quantities of gold would have to be wrested from their natural havens in Siberia's remotest lands. Forced labor could send workers into lands to which free men and women would not willingly go, require them to work under conditions that free labor would not tolerate, and help to offset the shortage of machines on such newborn industrial sites as the Urals-Kuznets Combine. Therefore, the Cheka—renamed the OGPU in the 1920s and the NKVD in the 1930s—stepped up its efforts to uncover "enemies of the people," whose crimes, by definition, demanded punishment, not rehabilitation. Given its many failings, the Soviet system itself produced the new enemies the OGPU required.

Even before Stalin rose to power, the Soviet founders' belief that virtually every worker could be educated to perform any task had elevated legions of incompetents to positions of authority. To make matters worse, Soviet planners in 1928 set inflated goals for the First Five-Year Plan that no amount of effort by even the most dedicated workers could achieve. Because actual production could never reach the plan's inflated goals, the men who served Stalin had to face the hard fact that repeated failures, expensive accidents, and widespread corruption would all have to be explained to a leader who had been led to expect a great deal more than Soviet workers could ever hope to produce.

Charges of subversion, "wrecking," and outright treason eliminated any need to question the precepts upon which Stalin's crash industrialization program rested and guaranteed the livelihood of the tens of thousands of agents employed by the OGPU, whose survival depended upon the continued threat of subversion. "Enemies of the people" were everywhere, the OGPU insisted, and Stalin's lieutenants hurried to agree rather than admit their mistakes or accept the blame for costly failures. Every factory, construction site, mine, and government office, the OGPU now warned, had its "wreckers" and "shirkers" who worked to prevent the success of socialism. In the countryside, hundreds of thousands of peasants who resisted surrendering their small farms and livestock to newly formed collectives had to be considered part of the same group. By the middle of 1930, the population of the OGPU labor camps had risen to more than 600,000, nearly all of whom had been classified as "enemies of the people."⁹

Once the OGPU and its allies had decided that forced labor was a fitting punishment for this growing army of "wreckers," "shirkers," and "subversives," it followed that their labor in prison should be used to help build socialism in the Soviet Union. By 1929, forced labor was beginning to figure as a commodity in Soviet economic planning. "Places of confinement, having at their disposal excess labor in great quantities," a conference of high prison officials declared that fall, "can come to the assistance of those economic enterprises which experience an [unskilled] labor shortage." A few months later, the central planning agencies of the Soviet Union received orders to "incorporate the work performed by those deprived of liberty into the planned economy of the country and into the Five-Year Plan," and an infamous new department of the OGPU called the Central Administration of Labor Camps—the *Glavnoe Upravlenie Ispravitel'no-trudovykh Lagerei,* from which the acronym Gulag was derived—came into being.[10] In 1930, the value of such labor equaled two thirds of the output of the entire Soviet motor vehicle industry. A year later, the value of Soviet motor vehicle production had doubled, but that of slave labor had nearly tripled, even though the great purges that would send a tidal wave of Soviet citizens into the camps of the Gulag Archipelago were still several years away.[11]

Like a cancer of the most deadly sort, the network of Gulag forced-labor camps metastasized across the Soviet Union. In European Russia, it stretched from the western lands near Minsk and Kiev to the White Sea islands of the far north and the shores of the Black and Caspian seas in the south. In Siberia, Gulag camps first took shape along the Urals, reaching from the Arctic coast to Magnitogorsk. Then they spread east through the lands bordering on Central Asia to the Amur and the Siberian far east. Sakhalin, the prison island that Chekhov had described with such horror in the days of the tsars, held a large camp. So did Kamchatka, the great peninsula that had been among the Russians' last discoveries in Siberia's eastern lands. In northeastern Siberia, Gulag camps clustered along the Kolyma River, where huge goldfields had just been found in some of the most inhospitable climate and terrain on the face of the earth. From the Kolyma, they spread along the Arctic Circle to the tip of the Chukhotka peninsula in the east and back to the Lena River delta in the west.

Although manufacturing, canning, farming, mining, heavy construction, and a score of other Soviet enterprises eventually made use of Gulag labor, logging was the first task at which prisoners were put to work as the Soviet Union tried to sell enough timber abroad to pay for the hard currency that had been lost when Stalin's collectivization program cut into grain exports. In the dense taiga of Siberia and the forests of northern Russia, prisoners worked in snow up to their chests, trampling down small islands in which to swing their axes and work their saws. They called three weeks of this sort of work a "chilly execution,"[12] but hundreds of thousands (on some occasions well over a million) of men and women labored in the forests for months at a time nonetheless. Usually they worked in pairs, cutting trees, trimming boughs, and sawing trunks into proper lengths. Because woodcutting burned more energy than the prisoners' meager rations supplied, they collapsed from exhaustion, fell sick, starved, and died.

After a few weeks of malnutrition in the Gulag camps, many prisoners began to notice that blood appeared on their bread when they bit into it. That was the first sign of scurvy. "From then on, your teeth begin to fall out, your gums rot, and great sores appear on your legs," Solzhenitsyn explained. "Your flesh begins to fall away in chunks," he added, "and you begin to stink like a corpse." Other prisoners noticed their faces beginning to darken and their skin starting to peel. After that came diarrhea, violent and never ending, to mark the onset of pellagra. Sometimes starvation left a man's or woman's body "covered with blue-black pea-sized boils," which, when they came to a head, Solzhenitsyn wrote, burst, "forcing a thick, wormlike stream of pus out of them."[13] All three maladies brought death, and many of the prisoners agreed that the quicker it came, the better. "How simply a human being dies," Solzhenitsyn mused after watching his fellow prisoners cross the boundary between life and death. "He was talking—and he fell silent; he was walking along the road—and he fell; a shudder—and that's it."[14] So it would be for millions of the Soviet men and women who gave their lives in the fearsome realm of Siberia's Gulag Archipelago in the name of building socialism.

As the 1930s moved ahead, Siberia's taiga lumber camps lost their pride of place as the worst assignments in the Gulag to the newly discovered mines in the northeastern Kolyma lands, an area that endures the coldest temperatures in the northern hemisphere and holds a thousand kings' ransoms in lead, tin, silver, tungsten, uranium, and gold. Prisoners condemned to work in the wastes of the Kolyma usually made the journey from Moscow to Vladivostok in stinking freight cars with no ventilation or sanitary facilities, almost no light, little food, and only the most meager rations of water. "Water was a precious luxury," one woman remembered. "Sometimes," she added, "we were so thirsty we tried licking the round iron plates set in the wall [of the freight car], which were encrusted with hoarfrost because of the cold."[15] "We received coal or coal dust at most once every three days," this same woman went on. "We eagerly filled the stove with our bare hands . . . [but] the fire lasted only an hour. Then we crawled silently back on our planks, each one of us alone, a helpless, abandoned creature with too few blankets, too few clothes, and too thin blood to combat the icy

Siberian winter that whistled through many cracks in the frame of the car."[16]

Sometime between the twenty-eighth and forty-second day of the journey, the great iron doors of the freight cars slid open and the prisoners from Moscow found themselves in Vladivostok, where they spent anywhere from a few days to several months in unheated, unlighted barracks waiting for one of the several tramp steamers that ran between Vladivostok and Nagaevo, the grim prison port that served as the Kolyma's gateway. Running only with signal lights at night, their hatches covered by tarpaulins, these steamers were the slave ships of the twentieth century, the ghostly successors to those sailing vessels that had once carried cargoes of captive Africans from the Gulf of Guinea coast to the auction blocks of the New World.

Aboard these twentieth-century reincarnations of the ghost ships of olden times (ironically, their smokestacks were painted with bands of bright blue—the color of hope and, incidentally, of the insignia worn by the OGPU, NKVD, and the tsarist Okhrana before them), the "enemies of the people" entered a realm of terror ruled by common criminals. "Within five minutes we had a thorough introduction to the law of the jungle," wrote Evgeniia Ginzburg, a Jewish woman writer who made the voyage in 1939 among a horde of "counterrevolutionaries" and a handful of women convicted of murder, robbery, and prostitution. "Some of us wept," she remembered, "some panicked, some tried to reason with the whores, some spoke very politely to them hoping to restore their self-respect."[17] All was to no avail. "The retching, the wild cries, the dancing and stamping of feet, the brawling, fornicating, and wild-cat fighting went on day and night," another woman added. "I said to one woman: 'You are so young, you are even beautiful, and yet you are as evil as the fiend himself. Why?' She looked at me with an expression of which I can give no idea," she concluded, "[and said] 'Why should I be otherwise?'"[18]

On the ships that made the Vladivostok-Nagaevo run, the brutality of the women's hold appalled anyone not accustomed to living among thieves. "My eyes beheld a scene which neither Goya nor Gustave Doré could ever have imagined," an "enemy of the people" assigned to serve as a doctor on one voyage wrote. "In that immense, cavernous, murky hold were crammed more than 2,000 women. From the floor to the ceiling, as in a gigantic poultry farm, they were cooped up in open cages, five of them in each nine-foot-square space. . . . [There was] a giant cask," he continued, "on the edges of which, in full view of the soldiers standing on guard above, women were perched like birds, and in the most incredible positions. There was no shame, no prudery, as they crouched there to urinate or empty their bowels. One had the impression," he concluded, "that they were some half-human, half-bird creatures which belonged to a different world and a different age."[19]

Between eight and fourteen days after they left Vladivostok, the prison ships docked at Nagaevo. Here, the "enemies of the people" would be told the law of the wastelands into which they were being sent:

- "Never expect to eat soup and bread together."
- "What's gone from your hands is lost forever."
- "You must repay with sweat and tears the crimes perpetrated against the Soviet State and the Soviet People."
- "Those who do not fulfill The Plan are saboteurs and traitors."[20]

The first to learn these rules had been the prisoners who built Nagaevo harbor and the grim town of Magadan, which lay just beyond the swamp to its north. Put ashore on the desolate coast of the Sea of Okhotsk in the summer of 1932, these men had cut roads through the stone cliffs that protected Nagaevo from the tides and set pilings into the sea at their edge. A sawmill, a brickyard, a plant for salting fish, repair yards for the ships, a power station, buildings for government offices, and housing for officials all had taken shape while the prisoners continued to live in tents and larch-limb huts. Compelled to work as long as they could stand, the builders of Nagaevo-Magadan had died in the thousands, while the grimy steamers from Vladivostok had brought in thousands more to take their places.

Once the labor needs of Nagaevo-Magadan had been met, the prisoners began to lay out the rough roads that would carry their successors into the Kolyma lands, where winter temperatures dropped to $-70°$ Centigrade and the topsoil was frozen for all but a hundred days of the year.[21] In the winter, workers starved and froze. In the summer, they starved and fought the swarms of insects that rose from the meltwater swamps that formed atop the region's permafrost. Now, after the revolution to liberate the peoples of the Russian Empire from the tsar's tyranny, there were hundreds of times more prisoners in Siberia than during the worst days of *katorga*. The Kolyma valley and the lands that stretched from Bering Strait to the Lena River had become a new realm, the tsardom of Dalstroi (the Russian acronym for the Far Northern Construction Trust) that the OGPU had organized in 1931 to rule Siberia's northeast.

The first head of Dalstroi was Edvard Berzin, a Latvian Communist who had begun life as a herdsman. After the Bolshevik Revolution, he had worked in the Cheka and then the OGPU, where he had won a reputation for being a ruthless taskmaster who could be counted upon to carry out every assignment. Yet, despite Berzin's cruelty, the Kolyma slaves would remember his regime as the best days of Dalstroi, for, unlike his successors, he regarded slave labor as an important resource, not as an easily expendable commodity. Berzin therefore saw to it that prisoners working in the Kolyma mines had enough food to keep them healthy and (according to at least one account) "were given fur coats, fur caps, and warm felt boots" during the winter.[22] That way, the labor of every man and woman could be used to yield the largest possible return in gold and other minerals. Unlike those who followed him as head of Dalstroi, Berzin saw forced labor as a way of producing wealth for the state, not as a means of doing away with "enemies of the people."

In 1937, the OGPU's successor, the NKVD, began to criticize Berzin for treating prisoners too kindly and his superiors hatched an elaborate plot to get rid of this man who wielded more power in Siberia's northeast than any tsar ever had. First, a special wire arrived from Moscow to announce that as a reward for the great quantities of gold taken from Kolyma during the five years since the first Dalstroi slave workers had landed at Nagaevo, Berzin was to receive the coveted Order of Lenin, the highest honor the Soviet Union could bestow. In due course, a plane carrying a copy of the issue of *Izvestiia* that had published the decree announcing his achievement arrived to fly the Dalstroi commandant to Moscow, where, it was said, Stalin himself intended to award the medal. But the issue of *Izvestiia* proved to be a hoax, and the NKVD agents who had flown from Moscow to serve as an escort soon announced that they had orders to arrest Berzin for "coddling" prisoners (Stalin's phrase), surrounding himself with "Trotskyites," and plotting to hand the Dalstroi lands over to Japan or the United States.[23]

From the time the NKVD shot Berzin and his chief lieutenants, the killing of prisoners by beatings, shootings, disease, and starvation became almost as important in the Kolyma mines as getting the gold out of the ground. "A batch of convicts would arrive somewhere in the snow-covered taiga, be given shovels, axes, and iron bars, and told to start felling trees and building their own barracks," one convict wrote in describing how a new mine was opened. "Those who died were replaced by others," he went on. "Those who did not meet the norm were shot, but the work went relentlessly on."[24]

According to the best estimates, sixty-six mines requiring nearly half a million slave workers in any given year were operating in the Kolyma lands before the end of the 1930s.[25] At some of these mines, thousands of "enemies of the people" worked deposits of gold-bearing sand that lay near the surface, while others dug gold from veins buried deep within the rock. For those assigned to the surface mines, preparations for the hundred or so summer days when the rivers and upper crust of the permafrost would be unfrozen began in the dead of winter, when prison brigades blasted away the topsoil that covered the gold-bearing sands so as to be ready to wash the gold from them the moment the thaw began. "In some places, the deposits were incredibly rich," one prisoner reported, "and there were days when each of the five pieces of panning apparatus took off as much as 40 to 50 pounds of gold at each shift." Nuggets of three to four ounces were not at all rare, and there were cases of nuggets being found that weighed as much as four pounds.[26] Yet, even during Berzin's comparatively benevolent regime, this work had claimed huge numbers of lives. "Frequently this happened all of a sudden, sometimes even while the man was at work," a former Leningrad student wrote of his days in the Tumanny goldfields. "A man would be loading a barrow, prodded by the shouts of a foreman or a guard, then unexpectedly he would sink to the ground, blood would gush from his mouth—and everything was over."[27]

Men who worked underground lived in a different world from those who panned for gold. "Work in the mine held one vast advantage—it was relatively warm," the same prisoner wrote. But there also were disadvantages. "The felt boots that we were given," he explained, "were always wet, never quite drying out [and] rheumatism was guaranteed."[28] Miners also had to face the poisonous fumes released by the ammonal used to blast away the rock, for there were no ventilating fans of any sort below the surface. "Mines were 120–150 feet deep," one imprisoned leader of the Polish Socialist Party later explained. "Accidents below the surface were frequent, as many as five or six a day [for] the underground corridors were narrow and the ceilings not propped." "The unfortunate victims of accidents," he remembered, "were hauled to the surface, their hands cut off in proof of death (to be shown to the authorities) and the bodies then thrust below the brushwood."[29] Always, the appallingly high work quotas tormented every prisoner who remained alive. A hundred years before, the tsar's jailers had required each Decembrist to mine 108 pounds of ore a day, but the NKVD chiefs of Dalstroi set their prisoners' daily norms at 267 times that amount.[30] For fully a quarter of the men and women sent to the Kolyma in any given year, such work quotas became a sentence of death.

Whether they worked above or below ground, the days of the Kolyma prisoners centered around food and work, each being dependent upon the other. Those who could produce the full work quota received somewhere between twenty-eight and thirty-five ounces of rough rye bread a day, supplemented, in the best of times, by a bit more than two ounces of barley, millet, or oats, a fifth of an ounce of meal or starch, half an ounce of vegetable oil, three and a half ounces of salted fish, ten ounces of coarse salted cabbage, a third of an ounce of sugar, and a tenth of an ounce of herb tea. By comparison, the Japanese POW camps on the River Kwai, notorious throughout the West for their horrors during World War II, provided daily rations that included just under twenty-five ounces of rice, twenty-one ounces of vegetables, three and a half ounces of meat, almost three-quarters of an ounce each of sugar and salt, and a fifth of an ounce of oil. At that time, the accepted international standard for a man required to work "very actively" for eight hours was 3,100 to 3,900 calories, and the Japanese rations yielded 3,400. Kolyma rations—on those infrequent occasions when they were delivered in full—produced somewhere between 2,100 and 2,600 calories for men who had to work thirteen to sixteen hours a day in the coldest temperatures known in the Northern Hemisphere.[31]

That their diet produced at least 2,500 fewer calories than the minimum that a prisoner working a double shift needed to survive was only one of the difficulties that men and women suffered in the Kolyma mines. Kolyma rations provided almost no fats or vitamins and were consistently of the poorest quality. What vegetables, fats, and animal proteins there were usually took the form of rotten cabbage and the worst parts of (often spoiled) fish, but even so there were distinctions to be made. Would the half a herring a worker sometimes received at breakfast be a head or a tail, for example? "The tail end of a herring is almost all edible, except for a tiny portion," one prisoner explained, "while the head amounts to the same in weight, even though little of it can be eaten."[32]

Then there was the matter of the bread ration, the staff of life for every man and woman in the Kolyma lands. Would the chunk of bread placed into a prisoner's hands at mealtime be a middle section or an end? Was there a difference? "The end is crisper," a longtime woman prisoner explained. "It looks more attractive and seems to be heavier, but more than that, an end mysteriously fills you up more than the middle section of the bread although it too weighs only seven ounces. A middle section," she added, "is a stab wound to the heart. It is a confirmation from Providence that you are abandoned for good and all. It is the beginning of a day on which everything will surely go wrong. And you almost always get a middle section." For every seventy bread rations distributed, the men who ran Dalstroi allotted an extra one to make up for what would be lost in crumbs and evaporated moisture. Because the prisoners who handed out bread held those extra rations back for themselves, that assignment became one of the most sought-after in every camp.[33]

The terrible rations in the Kolyma camps made prisoners suspicious of anything that deviated from the norm. After five days of being cut off from the outside world by a blizzard, the starving workers at one mine were treated to large plates of soup with meat. "Large chunks of meat floated in it . . . but I was seized by a sudden suspicion," a prisoner remembered. "I called the cook, whom I knew, to ask what kind of meat it was. The cook laughed, immediately guessing my thought. His fat face shone. 'So, you are afraid it is human meat? No, not yet. Calm down and eat it. Today they slaughtered three horses at the stable. They say that one died himself, but what's the difference?' "[34]

Prisoners lived for food, thought mainly of food, and dreamed of food. Some even combined their dreams of food with fantasies about sex. "My own dreams assumed a cannibalistic, erotic form," a Polish officer captured by the Russians in 1940 confessed in the memoirs he published eleven years later. "Love and hunger returned to their common biological root," he continued, "releasing from the depths of my subconscious images of women made of fresh dough whom I would bite in fantastic orgies till they streamed with blood and milk, twining their arms which smelt like fresh loaves round my burning head."[35] Hunger drove others to the brink of madness. "One often saw prisoners in camp who stood on all fours, growling and rooting about in the filthy garbage near the tents and, especially near the kitchen, looking for anything even remotely edible and devouring it on the spot," a victim remembered. Such people, he concluded, "had become semi-idiots, whom no amount of beating could drive from the refuse heaps."[36]

In the Kolyma slave-labor camps, men generally outnumbered women by a ratio of about twenty to one. Because women were usually spared from working in the goldfields, female "enemies of the people" did the farming and fish processing that fed prisoners all across the Dalstroi lands and also moved earth, cut wood, worked in construction, and supplied menial labor for government officials and free workers in the town of Magadan itself. Women seemed to have an inner resilience that men lacked, and this helped them to adapt to lives of slave labor more readily, even though, as Solzhenitsyn wrote, "everything was harder for women in the camps than for us men."[37] "Women are far more enduring than men," wrote Elinor Lipper, a European Communist who spent eleven years in Soviet camps after the NKVD arrested her at an international congress that met in Moscow in 1937. Although convinced that "the transition from working as a stenographer, housewife, or teacher to wood chopping is no easier than the transformation of a [male] intellectual into a gold miner," Lipper thought that women were more successful in making the change. In the Kolyma camps, men killed themselves at a considerably higher rate than women.[38]

Every woman swallowed into the Gulag knew the horrors of rape. In the prisons where they were interrogated, on the trains and ships that carried them a third of a way around the world, and at the camps in which they served their sentences, women were at the mercy of prison officials, guards, and anyone else who had the strength to force his will upon them. In some cases, the prelude to these assaults took on aspects of courting in the outside world, with men offering to provide the essentials of food, clothing, and comfort that women who refused their advances would be denied. Women who had once dreamed of hearing the phrase "I love you" now found the words "butter, sugar, and white bread" a proper substitute in the Kolyma wilderness.[39] Life there could have no deeper meaning.

For many women, sexual favors provided the key to survival; for others, they offered a chance to recapture, if only for a few fleeting moments, a sense of physical and emotional closeness to another human being. "I knew and he knew that we would never meet again, but we played lovers and tried to make the best of it," one woman said of her seduction by the ship's captain on the voyage between Vladivostok and Magadan. "I drank to his health and he to mine, and we did so till dawn. Then I had to make my way back to the squalor of the hold. The dream was over."[40]

Sooner rather than later, women who resisted such advances faced the inevitability of rape. "There was even a common expression for it: 'she fell under the trolley,'" Elinor Lipper explained after describing a rape in which some twenty men attacked a young Polish elementary school teacher.[41] "A trolley for gang rape," was the way Solzhenitsyn remembered the expression. "Manifest old age and extreme ugliness were the only defenses for a woman," he added. "Attractiveness was a curse."[42] For the Polish schoolteacher, as for so many others who suffered the ravages of forced sex, venereal disease—in her case both syphilis and gonorrhea—added to their misery.

The architects of the Gulag system designed rituals that destroyed any vestiges of femininity that survived the indignities of repeated rape. "Hundreds of naked women in Indian file, heads bowed, silent, had to submit to the indignity of having their hairy parts shaven by a man," a Romanian intellectual imprisoned by the Russians after the Second World War wrote of a time when he had witnessed the monthly inspection of female prisoners at Magadan. Once in a while, a new woman would resist violently. "I was so shocked about it at first that I refused," one woman confessed. "Two soldiers kept my hands behind my back, while another two forced my legs apart. The razor cut into my flesh and they had to give it up for the moment, but later they forced me again." The outcome was inevitable. Eventually, this woman said, "I resigned myself to be handled by one man instead of five."[43]

Before many months passed, the burdens of hard labor and ill treatment consigned everything connected to a woman's femininity to her past. "Everything that is feminine in a woman, whether it be constant or monthly, ceases to be," Solzhenitsyn explained at one point. "She becomes ageless, her shoulders stick out at sharp angles, her breasts hang down like dried-out little sacks ... [and] there is so little flesh above her knees that a gap has opened that is big enough for a sheep's head or even a soccer ball to go through."[44] No one who entered the lands of Kolyma remained unchanged for very long. There the terms male and female reverted to a more rudimentary meaning from which the trappings of thousands of years of civilization and culture had been stripped away.

"A Soviet camp is an incubator for the vilest human instincts," Elinor Lipper wrote. "The thief steals, the speculator speculates, and the prostitute sells herself," she went on. "The normal person is perverted, the honest man becomes a hypocrite, the brave man a coward, and all have their spirits and bodies broken."[45] Of none did these comments ring more true than the corrupt rulers of the Dalstroi tsardom, who held the power of life and death over millions of their fellow beings. Here was the "new class" at its worst, reveling in the fruits produced by the suffering and dying of others.

At the very top of Dalstroi's ruling hierarchy stood its chief, larger than life and dedicated to making a mark that others would envy. Directly under him stood eight others who were distinguished from all the rest in that vast domain by their access to the special store at Magadan—the "Deviatka," or, in English, the "Store for the Nine"—that supplied them with every conceivable luxury (in Soviet terms) from American cigarettes, French cognac, and fine shoes and clothing to the sorts of fresh fruits and vegetables to be seen nowhere else in the entire Soviet far east.[46] All of these men held high positions in the Communist party, and they reveled in the material comforts enjoyed by high party members all across the territory of the Soviet Union. They controlled the camps, all of the regular army troops, and all of the NKVD forces in Dalstroi as well as every aspect of the region's economic life. As the experience of Berzin had shown in 1937, the footing on the peak of the Dalstroi pyramid could be very slippery, but, as long as a man could keep his hold, it was a life of luxury, surpassing even the comforts enjoyed by the Siberian potentates of old.

High among these new Soviet lords, Lieutenant General Ivan Fedorovich Nikishov stood proud and tall. Chief of Dalstroi throughout the Second World War, Nikishov at the age of fifty had divorced his first wife, shipped her back to Vladivostok, and married a fanatical twenty-nine-year-old Young Communist by the name of Gridassova with whom he shared a palatial country house surrounded by a private hunting preserve. Elinor Lipper described Gridassova as a "primitive, crude, avaricious creature" whose greed was exceeded only by her callous unconcern for the misery she inflicted upon the tens of thousands of men and women who came under her control after Nikishov named her commander of Maglag, the prison camp district of Magadan.[47] After he had met them in mid-1944, America's vice president, Henry Wallace, described this pair as a charming couple dedicated to building a brave new world in Siberia's northeast with the labor of men and women whom he once called the "pioneers of the machine age, the builders of cities."[48] Like Lipper, those who felt the perpetual lash of the Nikishovs' cruelty did not share Wallace's idealized impressions.

The successors of Nikishov and Gridassova, General Panteleimon Panteleimonovich Derevenko and his wife, Galina, lived even better after the war. "I often had the opportunity to see and hear how absolute the power of an individual may be in a Communist country," the Romanian intellectual Michael Solomon wrote of his years in Siberia's labor camps, "but never was I to see anything which surpassed in ruthlessness and grandeur of the romantic figure of Derevenko."[49] Solomon described Derevenko as "a refined Oriental satrap . . . [who], like Louis XIV, had organized his own theater, had his own court, artists, wrestlers, and clowns." Derevenko's wife was every bit as imperious as her husband. "She was a huge woman weighing over 250 pounds," Solomon remembered, who "kept the camp seamstresses and dressmakers working day and night" to keep her dressed in the latest Paris fashions. Galina Derevenko once ordered one of Solomon's imprisoned countrymen to make her a pair of white brocade shoes that stretched the shoemaker's abilities to the utmost. "She gave me strict orders that no shoe must weigh more than 150 grams [five and a quarter ounces]," this man explained as he described the difficult task the tsarina of Dalstroi had set for him. "How," he asked Solomon, "does one make a dainty shoe for an elephant?"[50]

Unlike Nikishov, who became a candidate member of the Central Committee of the Communist party and a colleague of Kosygin and Brezhnev,[51] the Derevenkos eventually fell on hard times. Fated to rule Dalstroi when its boundaries had been stretched as far west as the Enisei River, Derevenko had to deal with a massive rebellion at Norilsk, the northernmost city in the Soviet Union, which had been built entirely by forced labor near the base of the once impenetrable Taimyr peninsula. In May 1953, the prisoners of Norilsk went on strike and held out against the authorities for almost two months, despite Derevenko's efforts to force them back to work. Eventually, elite NKVD troops attacked with fixed bayonets and killed over a thousand with cold steel, but it took fifty-five days before they could claim victory. Afterward, Derevenko's superiors in Moscow charged him with incompetence and put him on trial. Like the potentates of old, the fallen master of Dalstroi took his own life rather than face execution.[52]

Although the Dalstroi lands produced huge quantities of gold, silver, platinum, uranium, copper, nickel, lead, and coal during the reigns of Nikishov and Derevenko, they also killed the prisoners who mined them at an appalling rate. In any given year between 1937 and 1953, the Kolyma camps held between two hundred thousand and half a million slave laborers, about four fifths of whom mined gold. Although we have only limited clues about how high the death rate in the gold camps really was, we know that their Soviet masters killed Siberian forced laborers at a rate not seen since the days of the Mongol hordes. One account reports that only five hundred out of the three thousand men sent to the Maksim Gorkii gold mine in 1944 remained alive to be transferred to another mine a year later.[53] "[Work] brigades that began the gold-mining season designated by the names of their brigadiers," another prisoner reported, "at the end of the season did not have a single man left of those who had started except the brigadier himself, his orderly, and some of his personal friends. The rest of the brigade had been replaced several times during the summer."[54] Some of the best estimates we have calculate that every two pounds of gold that came from Kolyma between 1931 and 1956 cost one life, and there was a time in the 1940s when the yearly output exceeded three hundred tons.[55] On top of that, virtually all the prisoners in the lead mines on the Chukhotka peninsula died because they worked without any safety devices, while those who cut logs, mined coal, and built roads through the Arctic wilderness died in the tens of thousands from exposure, hunger, and overwork.

Including those not directly involved in the actual work of mining, the annual death rates for the Kolyma camps probably averaged about one out of every four. For the decades between 1933 and 1953, that means that *at least* three million men and women (on the average, 150,000 every year) died at slave labor. If one uses what are admittedly exaggerated Soviet sources to calculate the total number of revolutionary men and women killed by the tsarist authorities between 1850 and 1900, the total comes to ninety-four, or fewer than two a year, all of whom were guilty of armed rebellion or killing government officials (six had murdered Emperor Alexander II), the only crimes that carried the death penalty during the last century of tsarist Russia's history. By contrast, as someone who has studied this question in some detail once pointed out, virtually all of the victims sent to Kolyma's slave-labor camps "were entirely innocent even from the Soviet point of view."[56] According to memoirs written by men and women who lived through the Stalin era, even a hint of guilt meant execution. Sentences of ten, fifteen, or even twenty years in labor camps were handed out only to those "enemies of the people" who were innocent of any actual "counterrevolutionary" activity. "Prove first that you are 100 percent crystal pure and you'll get ten years," one survivor remembered an interrogator telling him. "Otherwise, [you'll get] a lump of lead."[57]

Unwilling to believe that anything so appalling as the enslavement of millions of innocent men and women really could be happening, Europeans and Americans greeted the first accounts of Soviet slave labor with disbelief. To encourage their skepticism, Stalin's faithful lieutenant Viacheslav Molotov worked to discount such claims from the moment he became premier of the Soviet Union in 1930 by insisting that labor camps were nothing more than settlements that had been established to help those who had transgressed against Soviet law become "useful members of society." Promising that "many an unemployed worker of the capitalist countries will envy the living and working conditions of the prisoners in our northern regions,"[58] Molotov announced that foreign correspondents and delegations of foreign workers were welcome to visit the Soviet Union and see the truth for themselves.[59]

If some of the survivors are to be believed, when Westerners took Molotov at his word, the OGPU performed the remarkable feat of obliterating slave-labor camps from the areas their visitors asked to inspect. "In preparation for this visit [of an American commission], all lumber camps were liquidated in a few days," a prisoner who spent several years in the far north wrote. "Everything that could be burned was set on fire [and] a special agent of the OGPU made a tour of inspection to ascertain that no sign was left which might indicate that prisoners and not free lumbermen had been at work there. Then, whether day or night, prisoners were driven out of the woods to the railroad," he continued. "If a train appeared in the distance while the large crowds of prisoners were being driven along the railroad tracks, they were made to lie down in the swamp, in the snow, and remain hidden until the train had passed. . . . The OGPU," he concluded, "was afraid that somebody might see them from the car windows."[60] Another prisoner described how he and his comrades, "while waiting for the trains [to carry them to more remote camps], spent several nights in the forest, hungry and freezing. Prisoners suffering from fever, scurvy, or tuberculosis," he added, "formed no exception and endured the same privations."[61]

The Western world dared not—or at least wished not to—believe in the vastness and brutality of the Soviet slave-labor system as the 1930s moved toward their end. Every account published by a survivor was greeted in the Western press by a flood of denials from high-placed Soviet officials, and these continued throughout the Second World War and beyond. At times, these denials were supported by Westerners who ought to have known better, but few accounts were so amazingly—and purposefully—off the mark as that which Owen Lattimore published about his visit to the Kolyma camps in *National Geographic* magazine at the end of 1944.

At various times a professor at Johns Hopkins University, high-ranking official in the Office of War Information, head of the Institute on Pacific Relations, and editor of *Pacific Affairs* journal, Lattimore had accompanied Vice President Henry Wallace on a visit to the Soviet Union earlier that year and produced a glowing appraisal of life in the Kolyma lands. To this day, his account remains startlingly at odds with everything that was known about Soviet slave labor at the time and is comprehensible only if one remembers its author's long history as an apologist for some of Stalin's worst excesses. In 1938, Lattimore had described the now infamous Moscow purge trials as evidence that democracy was working well in the Soviet Union. He had spoken in support of Stalin's regime again and again, and his Institute on Pacific Relations had advocated a pro-Stalinist line so consistently that, by the early 1950s, even *The New Republic* had to conclude that it had given up "its objective research function" in order to speak for the policies of Stalin and Mao in China.[62]

Dalstroi, Lattimore told readers of *National Geographic,* was "a remarkable concern ... which can be roughly compared to a combination of the Hudson's Bay Company and TVA." Nikishov and his wife, Gridassova, whose reign of terror had by that time claimed hundreds of thousands of lives, seemed to him to be people blessed with "a trained and sensitive interest in art and music and also a deep sense of civic responsibility." Lattimore thought it worth noting that "instead of the sin, gin, and brawling of an old-time gold rush, extensive greenhouses growing tomatoes, cucumbers, and even melons, to make sure that the hardy miners got enough vitamins" could be found in the Kolyma lands.[63] It was all pure nonsense, the product of the wishful dreams of a noted scholar who desperately wanted to believe that Stalin had blazed a pathway into a future that glowed with social justice and equal opportunity for all. To the Kolyma slave miners—who starved for want of bread and gruel, dressed in rags, wore shoes soled with worn-out automobile tires, and were not allowed even to pick wild berries when they ripened in the forest—fruits and vegetables in any form other than salted or pickled cabbage had become an almost forgotten dream by the time of Lattimore's visit.

Starting in 1931, the suffering of slave laborers produced huge quantities of gold and the beginnings of an industrial base upon which Siberia's economy could develop. Magnitogorsk was a part of that base. So were Magadan, the factories and processing plants of Norilsk, the mines of the Kuzbass, and a score of new cities that arose across Siberia between 1931 and 1964. Unlike the lands of the Kolyma valley, where nearly all of the labor was provided by men and women sentenced to forced labor, some of these other centers had a larger component of free citizens. Nonetheless, forced labor remained a constant and vital part of Siberian economic life until the end of the Khrushchev era.

45

Socialist Reconstruction

During the winter of 1932–1933, railroad engineer Vladimir Tregubov received orders from the Kremlin to build a train for the leaders of the Soviet Union. This was to outshine the most comfortable trains of Europe and America, be so well insulated that not a sound from the outside could be heard, and run so smoothly along the tracks that a glass filled to the brim would not spill a drop as it moved toward its destination. Tregubov chose ten of the best cars he could find and proceeded to rebuild them. First he had his workmen pour a thick coating of lead over the floor of each car. Then he had them cover the lead with felt, on top of which they laid a layer of cork and another layer of felt. Tregubov's men installed in each car a wooden floor, over which they placed a third layer of felt that they covered with an exquisite carpet that cost, according to the best estimates at the time, the better part of fourteen years' pay for an average Soviet worker.

With some variations on their interior layouts, Tregubov built each of the ten cars for his train in the same way. The car designed for Stalin had an office, a sitting room, two bedrooms, an office for his secretary, a bathroom, a kitchen, and a separate compartment for anyone who might be traveling with him. The walls were paneled in fine mahogany, and the furniture was made especially to match the panels. For Lazar Kaganovich, the tanner and shoemaker whom Stalin had placed in charge of collectivizing agriculture and the purge of 1933–1934 before naming him people's commissar for transport, a similarly designed car was paneled and furnished in Karelian birch. Prime Minister Molotov's car was made to be a carbon copy of Stalin's own. Combined with the best that Siberian gold could buy abroad, each car offered the greatest comfort and luxury that Soviet ingenuity could produce.

Aside from these ten, Tregubov built several more cars that had eight compartments in each for regional party secretaries and high-ranking military officers. In these, every two compartments shared a toilet, and at the far end of the car was a large bathroom. Tregubov had each car painted deep azure, with a roof of sky blue. After carefully rubbing each coat of paint, his workmen polished and lacquered the final coat. Then they built a dining car that was to be kept filled with exquisite delicacies, choice wines, fresh fruits and flowers, and anything else the most discriminating traveler might wish to have. The final product of Tregubov's effort was named the Lux Blue Express. NKVD guards patrolled every station through which it passed, and special agents guarded every tunnel and bridge along the way.[1] Once put into service, the Lux Blue Express became a monument to what Stalin's system could achieve and an admission that it could achieve it for only the tiniest handful of the people in the Soviet Union.

Lesser party officials, military personnel, and ordinary Siberian citizens lived and traveled in an entirely different world. "Half an hour before the train arrives," a *Chicago Daily News* correspondent wrote in describing a journey he took on the Siberian Express in 1926, "the ticket office opens, usually a round hole in the wall no larger than a saucer." Hundreds of people, many of whom had waited in the station for days, fought for the handful of places available. Then the cashier slammed the ticket window shut "as coldly as a pay-car passes a wayside tramp."[2] What became of the hundreds of travelers who remained without tickets was of no concern to him. That was becoming the way of the new Soviet system too. All the evidence of slovenly maintenance—torn carpets, broken windows, cracked wheels—welcomed the handful who succeeded in boarding this Soviet version of the old tsarist Great Siberian Express. The dining car, the Chicago correspondent wrote, was unrelievedly grim, serving fish soup that turned out to be "greasy hot water poured over cold pieces of fish which had been cooked earlier in bulk" and, for a main course, roast veal that had been "cooked weeks earlier and was now dry and hard." When one of the diners managed to order "a beautiful confection of tomatoes and lettuce," it turned out to have a thick slice of laundry soap in the middle.[3]

An immense gulf separated this—the very best available to the masses—from the opulence of the Lux Blue Express. For the mass of Siberians who lived far below the lofty elevations at which the Lux Blue Express operated in the 1930s, a long process of "socialist reconstruction" lay ahead. Progress toward the better life promised by the makers of the Bolshevik Revolution continued to be slow. Life remained hard for average Soviet citizens, but the hope that it would get better still encouraged them to make new sacrifices in the name of greater achievements. Whether in mining gold, iron, or coal, making steel, building canals, collectivizing agriculture, exterminating "enemies of the people," or carrying out countless other tasks, the process of "socialist reconstruction" was changing the lives of Siberians in the 1930s in ways no one had imagined a generation before.

Most obvious of all, Siberia was beginning to fill up. In 1914, its population had been estimated at about 2.4 per square mile, but, because a good three quarters of its lands were considered unsuitable for settlement, virtually all of Siberia's population of 12,800,000 in those days was concentrated in the area of just over a million and a quarter square miles that lay along the Urals and to the north and south of the railroad. That meant that Siberia's inhabited lands at the beginning of the First World War were in fact more densely populated than the states of North and South Dakota, Montana, Idaho, Utah, Oregon, and Colorado and that its agricultural lands had about the same population per square mile as Kansas, California, and Maine.[4] Starting in the late 1920s, Siberia's population soared as people flooded into its cities and newly built industrial centers. From a population of less than four thousand in 1926, Stalinsk grew to nearly 170,000 by 1939. The population of Novosibirsk increased by six times to over 400,000 during the same time, and that of Sverdlovsk (tsarist Ekaterinburg) grew by the same multiple to 423,000. Cheliabinsk quadrupled in size. Irkutsk grew from 90,000 in 1917 to a quarter of a million twenty years later. Chita rose from 44,000 to 121,000 during those years, and Khabarovsk and Ulan-Ude (tsarist Verkhneudinsk) grew from 34,000 and 29,000 in 1923 to 207,000 and 126,000 in 1939.[5]

Everywhere, massive construction and industrialization spurred Siberia's growth. During the First Five-Year Plan, which stretched from 1928 to 1932, the Soviet government allocated nearly a billion rubles for the development of industry in Siberia and earmarked three quarters of it for new construction. All through the Kuzbass, where a chemical plant arose at Kemerovo in addition to its coal mines and where steel mills were beginning to appear at Stalinsk, men and women organized themselves into brigades of "shock workers" and made up for the lack of proper tools and machines with longer hours and harder work.[6] Waged in the name of the welfare of the community as a whole, "socialist competition" raised outputs among workers who, until a year or so before, had tended flocks or trapped for furs.

But the process of "socialist reconstruction" was by no means limited to the Siberian industrial fortress that was rising from its anchors in the Kuzbass and at Magnitogorsk. Once a railroad line had been built to connect Magnitogorsk with the Trans-Siberian at Cheliabinsk some 260 miles to its north, new plants arose there to transform the products from the furnaces and mills of "Steeltown USSR" into tractors and agricultural machinery. Moving a hundred miles or so north of Cheliabinsk to Sverdlovsk, the railroad brought Magnitogorsk-made steel to other new factories that produced heavy industrial equipment. Not far away, the Soviet Union's largest railway-car factory took shape at Nizhnii Tagil, at what had once been a hub of the Demidovs' iron-making empire. By the end of the First Five-Year Plan in 1932, these new enterprises had increased Siberia's output of metalworking machines and heavy equipment by sixteen times.[7]

Between 1933 and 1937, the Second Five-Year Plan continued the pace of Siberia's industrial development in the region anchored by the Ural-Kuznets Combine—that is, the Kuzbass, Magnitogorsk, and their subsidiaries—at high speed. At the same time, Siberian industry moved east, crossing the Enisei River and bringing plants to build heavy equipment and agricultural machinery to the lands around Irkutsk and the once desolate emptiness of the Transbaikal. New sawmills tripled Siberia's output of sawn lumber, and railroads began to reach beyond the Trans-Siberian and its handful of connecting lines. In 1937, Siberia's Soviet builders opened the first Arctic railroad anywhere in the world—a short line from Dudinka which provided Norilsk, the new center of coal, nickel, copper, platinum, and uranium mining, built above the Arctic Circle in 1935, with an outlet to the sea.[8]

Slave laborers built most of Siberia's new railroads and made up the human swarms that completed its other massive construction projects during the first two Five-Year Plans. Although not built within the boundaries of Siberia, the first great Soviet construction project to use forced labor was "The Belomor Canal Named After Stalin"—a massive waterway that connected the White Sea with the Baltic. The grotesquely distorted official account produced by Maksim Gorkii and a score of leading Soviet writers (some of whom later fell afoul of the system themselves) claimed that the numbers were far smaller, but the best estimates are that as many as three hundred thousand prisoners worked on the canal between late November 1931 and its opening in August 1933. Winter and summer they dug and hauled earth with the crudest shovels, picks, and wheelbarrows to raise a monument to social- ist reconstruction in Russia's far north. This, their masters claimed, demonstrated how socially useful labor could "reforge" men and women who had gone astray.[9]

After amnestying about a quarter of the prisoners who survived the Belomor Canal project, the Soviet authorities moved the rest to Siberia, where they built the Turkestan-Siberian Railroad, started the Baikal- Amur line, opened the Karaganda coal mines, and worked on a score of other large industrial projects. Especially in the early stages, which required large numbers of unskilled workers, Magnitogorsk consumed several tens of thousands of forced laborers, and the same was true of Stalinsk and the other mills of the Kuzbass. Slave labor built Norilsk above the Arctic Circle, helped to double-track the seventeen hundred miles of railroad that separated Ulan-Ude from Khabarovsk, and laid the track for a railroad between Khabarovsk and the new industrial and shipbuilding center of Komsomolsk-on-the-Amur, which grew from 160 inhabitants in 1932 to 71,000 in 1939.[10]

The Third Five-Year Plan, which began in 1938, called for building at least seven thousand miles of new roads, more than six times that mileage of railroads, and the extension of the Soviet Union's internal waterways by another eighty thousand miles. That most of these tasks were assigned to the NKVD meant that forced labor, the ranks of which had now grown to nearly seven million, or about one out of every thirteen people living in the Soviet Union, was expected to do the work. The NKVD therefore assigned about three and a half million of its penal army to construction work as the Third Five-Year Plan began. Beyond that, it sent something over a million more forced laborers to Siberia to mine gold, platinum, copper, nickel, silver, zinc, tin, lead, and other nonferrous metals, as well as iron and coal. Another four hundred thousand "enemies of the people" worked in lumber camps scattered through the taiga of Siberia and Russia's far north, and about half that number worked in farm labor gangs. The NKVD hired out still another million to other government enterprises, and the remainder of the Soviet forced-labor armies worked in NKVD factories, which, according to the Third Five-Year Plan, were expected to produce four and three- quarters million pairs of boots (probably for the Red Army), more than eleven million pieces of underwear, a million pieces of outer clothing, and slightly more than two and a quarter million pairs of hosiery.[11]

The nucleus around which the Soviet leaders shaped this huge penal labor force was the "kulaks," the so-called "rich" peasants. These were among the first "enemies of the people," often being distinguished from their neighbors by the fact that they owned an extra horse or cow or employed a hired man to help out during planting and the harvest. Proclaiming that "we have passed on from a policy of *limiting* the exploitative tendencies of the kulaks to a policy of *liquidating* the kulaks as a class,"[12] Stalin had declared war against these people as part of his program to force Soviet peasants into collective farms, which, the theorists of Marxism-Leninism promised, would be more efficient and productive.[13] "Everyone is against us who has outlived the epoch allotted to him by history," the writer Maksim Gorkii told the readers of *Pravda* when he defended collectivization in November 1930. "The logical consequence of this," he concluded, "is that, if the enemy does not surrender, he is to be exterminated."[14]

Experts disagree about the number of kulaks at the beginning of the First Five-Year Plan and still debate how many actually became victims of Stalin's effort to remove them from the countryside. The best estimates now stand at about ten million,[15] a minority of whom were killed outright with the rest being sent to Siberia and Central Asia to become the first wave of Gulag inmates. As these peasants killed their farm animals rather than surrender them to collective farms, the number of horses in the Soviet Union fell by a half (a loss of almost seventeen and a half million head) between 1928 and 1932. The number of cattle lost for the same reason amounted to more than thirty-two million, while the number of sheep and goats fell by almost two thirds, or about ninety-seven million.[16]

Collectivization proceeded more slowly in Siberia than in the European lands of the Soviet Union, in part because more Siberian peasants fell into the kulak category and also because Siberians tended to be more independent-minded. By October 1929, when the First Five-Year Plan had been in effect for a year, only about one Siberian homestead in twelve had been brought into a collective farm despite the efforts of the local police, OGPU, and Red Army Units.[17] When Stalin published his famous "Dizzy with Success" article in *Pravda* the next spring claiming that eighty percent of the Soviet Union's peasants had been brought into collectives, about one Siberian peasant homestead in five had been forced to join, but the resistance of those who remained had stiffened. In vain *Pravda* published letters from peasants who applauded collectivization, including one account that boldly announced that "the collective farm has freed us from poverty and bondage to the kulaks."[18] But even though the number of Siberian farms that hired workers for more than fifty days out of the year had fallen by two thirds, fully as many peasant farms as had joined collectives continued to use hired labor.[19] Soviet planners claimed that collective farming would produce more food; the harvest at the end of the First Five-Year Plan yielded a fourth less than it had five years earlier.[20]

Despite the fact that virtually all of the peasants in the European parts of the Soviet Union had been forced into collective farms, two out of every five of Siberia's stubborn peasants continued to resist as the Second Five-Year Plan got under way. In Siberia, it would take five years more to finish the collectivization process, and the suffering it inflicted proved to be so immense that it drove peasants to take up arms against the Bolsheviks.[21] This was not the class struggle of which the Bolsheviks had spoken so often. Peasants who watched the output of their lands fall off and the size of their earnings decline rose against the Bolsheviks from anger born of pure desperation.

If collectivization came slowly—and at great cost—to the peasants of Siberia, it brought even greater trouble to those natives who continued to live as nomads. Herders who roamed across the vast steppes of Kazakhstan, Central Asia, and southern Siberia fitted poorly into the rigid frameworks cast by Communist ideology. As a decidedly lower form on the Marxist evolutionary socioeconomic scale, nomads stirred the Bolsheviks' hatred in the same way that the principles of Marxism-Leninism brought disdain from men and women whose ancestors had followed their flocks for centuries. Nomads resisted collectivization even more fiercely than did Siberia's kulaks, but the result was no less inevitable. Soon Bolshevik commissars supported by the Red Army and the secret police destroyed the way of life upon which entire peoples had depended for centuries.

The ideological rigidity of the Bolshevik determination to collectivize Siberia's nomads and farmers was all the more astounding in view of the food shortages that plagued most of the Soviet Union's European lands. As one of the few foreigners to witness the brutality and senseless waste of the Bolsheviks' effort, an American mining engineer lamented the loss of "animals which might easily supply enough meat, dairy products, and wool for the whole of Russia. . . . My sympathies went out to those nomads who had forcibly resisted their conversion into 'proletarians,'" he added in describing a drive he had taken across the steppe in the summer of 1934. "There was pasturage here for millions of milk-mares and camels and sheep, and it was now going to waste," he concluded. "The herds had disappeared, and the nomads with them."[22]

Descendants of those fierce nomads who had once ruled Kazakhstan and parts of southern Siberia, the Kazakhs slaughtered their herds or fled to China rather than set aside their nomadic ways. Victims of Bolshevik impatience, which had decreed that nomadic life must be destroyed even before alternatives to it had been created, these men and women saw their ranks decrease by a fifth between 1926 and 1939, while their herds of sheep and goats declined by more than four fifths. Even after the Stalin era had passed into history, the economy of Soviet Kazakhstan still had not regained the ground it had lost during the first two Five-Year Plans. It did not begin to do so until the 1960s.[23]

Despite the waste and the tens of millions of lives lost or ruined, Siberia was becoming industrialized by the time war broke out along the Soviet Union's western frontier on June 22, 1941. Far from the lands in which the armies of the tsar had fought against Western invaders in centuries past, Red Siberia's great distances were now expected to render its vast new industrial fortress safe from foreign attack as the world stood on the brink of the greatest, most devastating war mankind had ever fought. Now Siberia was to be called upon to play to the fullest the new role that Stalin had envisioned for it. Only if it succeeded could the Soviet Union survive.

46

The Great Relocation

On June 22, 1941, 175 divisions of the Third Reich's Wehrmacht crashed across the Soviet Union's western frontier. For the first few weeks, Hitler's armies measured their progress in hundreds of kilometers, as their armor, artillery, and air forces smashed the poorly armed, badly supplied Russians. At Bialystok, Minsk, and Kiev, Soviet armies surrendered. By late fall, Germans ruled the great breadlands of the Ukraine and were pressing on toward the oil fields of the Caucasus. Hoping to close their ring around Moscow before the end of the year, Hitler's generals took up positions on three sides of the Soviet capital, and at Leningrad they had already begun the siege that would be remembered as the city's heroic "Nine Hundred Days." Then the Russian resistance stiffened and transformed the *Blitzkrieg* into a grinding fall and winter war for which the Germans were not prepared. Moscow would not fall, nor would Leningrad, nor Stalingrad on the Volga.

Set beyond the range of Germany's best bombers and surrounded by thousands of miles of unconquered Soviet territory, the factories of the Urals and west Siberian lands began to turn out the tanks, planes, and heavy guns needed to shatter the undefeated Wehrmacht even as the Red armies retreated before it. Yet the mines and metalworking plants of the Kuzbass, even when combined with the great mills that Jack Scott had helped to build at Magnitogorsk, did not have the capacity to replace all the weapons the Soviet forces lost in 1941. Nor could they alone produce the added weight of armaments needed to launch the huge offensives that could recapture the conquered lands. Soviet planners knew that more machines, more foundries, and more machine tools than could ever be found behind the Urals would be required before the tide of war could be turned.

To accomplish that feat, Stalin and his advisers replaced their Third Five-Year Plan with a War Economic Plan that shifted the Soviet economy onto a war footing and began to move its key factories to the east.[1] This "great relocation of the productive powers of the USSR to the east" (in the words of Chief of the Soviet State Planning Commission Nikolai Voznesenskii)[2] helped to make up for the Soviet losses in the west and change the direction of the war. Between June and December 1941, Soviet workers removed the machinery from hundreds of the mills and factories that lay in the Germans' path and sent them to reinforce the industries of the Urals and western Siberia. "Millions of people, hundreds of mills and factories, tens of thousands of machine tools, rolling mills, presses, turbines, and motors were all on the move," Voznesenskii wrote of those days, when nearly a million and a half freight cars crossed the Urals. In Siberia, this was setting the stage for a battle of war production that would pit the mills and mines of Magnitogorsk, the Kuzbass, and the Urals against the might of the Nazi Ruhr.[3]

The industrial fortress anchored by the Kuzbass and Magnitogorsk, the Urals metalworking plants and foundries farther north, and the heavy industrial facilities of Kazakhstan to the south now became magnets for the turbines, machine tools, rolling mills, and skilled workers who had made steel, weapons, and machines in European Russia during the days before the war. The Kuzbass attracted a host of electromechanical plants from the Ukraine and the lands of south Russia, while Omsk and Tiumen drew in many more. By early 1942, the great tractor plant from Kharkov in the Ukraine had been reborn to produce heavy weapons in the Altai town of Rubtsovsk, while the Rostov agricultural machine plant reappeared in Uzbekistan's capital of Tashkent to start making textile machines and metal-cutting lathes. The great Ivanovo nonferrous metal plant, the products of which were vital to modern weapons making, reappeared on the shores of Lake Balkhash in Kazakhstan, while plants that had been evacuated from Moscow and Leningrad sprang up all across Central Asia.[4]

Construction materials had to be brought in, housing built for machines and workers, and new networks created for supplying raw materials. Machines from soap factories in Moscow and Kharkov were incorporated into a soap factory in the Tadzhik city of Stalinabad (known today as Dushanbe), while the looms from Moscow's silk-weaving mills helped the Leninabad (Khudzhand) silk combine produce the materials needed to make parachutes for the Red Army's divisions of airborne infantry. Whether new plants and mills had to be started from scratch or incorporated into those already at work, the speed with which workers got their factories back into operation amazed even the most sour skeptics. Sometimes in as little as two months, workers in relocated factories began shipping armaments and war supplies again.[5]

Despite the Soviet Union's amazing success in rescuing workers and machines from the German advance in 1941, they alone could not provide the industrial capacity needed to support the war effort. While evacuated and reinforced factories beyond the Urals' crest stormed ahead to produce new armaments for the tattered divisions on the Soviet Union's western front, a host of new plants took shape. A new metallurgical plant and thermoelectric station at Cheliabinsk added to Siberia's ability to produce for the war effort, and so did the two huge new blast furnaces that came on line at Magnitogorsk. A whole series of new hydroelectric power stations produced additional electricity for Kazakhstan and Uzbekistan, where the output of electric power had fallen short of industrial needs in the years before the war, and, by the end of 1942, the Urals region's output of electric power had risen to four times what it had been in 1940.[6] Cost was no object. "Such a gigantic relocation of our nation's productive forces under such difficult wartime conditions," one Soviet commentator concluded proudly, "could only have been accomplished under the socialist economic system."[7]

Once the plants and power stations had been built, raw materials and workers became the keys to the Soviet war effort in Siberia. Proclaiming that "the destruction of Fascism is the most noble and greatest task that has ever confronted science," and that "all the knowledge, the strength, and the very lives of Soviet scholars must be dedicated to this task,"[8] the president of the Soviet Academy of Sciences, Vladimir Komarov, took command of a special commission for mobilizing the resources of the Urals, western Siberia, and Kazakhstan. A botanist who had dedicated his life to the study of the flora of Manchuria and Siberia's eastern lands, Komarov dedicated the full force of the Soviet scientific establishment—of all those "who toiled in science," in the language of the times—to discovering and producing raw materials from new sources.[9] Under Komarov's direction, Soviet scientists perfected new techniques for producing copper, lead, and nickel while an army of geologists searched for new iron deposits in the Urals and uncovered precious new reserves of manganese in Kazakhstan and western Siberia.[10]

If the distances that protected the lands beyond the Urals against German attack helped the Soviet Union to strengthen its Siberian arsenal, they also made it more difficult to move raw materials, ship finished products, and recruit more workers. Those evacuated to the Omsk and Novosibirsk regions from the war zone fell more than a quarter million short of the number needed, and it became necessary to use teenagers and women to make up the difference. By the end of 1943, more than half of the workers in the factories of Omsk, Novosibirsk, Tomsk, and Irkutsk were teenagers, who went to school by day and worked at night. Half again as many women worked in the metalworking and machine tool plants of the Kuzbass at the end of 1942 as had been there a year earlier, and they accounted for a full third of the workers in Siberia's coal mines.[11] By the middle of 1942, more women than men worked in the mines of the Transbaikal lands. That was also true in the Buriat and Iakut "autonomous republics," where tradition had kept women out of mines and heavy industries before the war.[12] To be a woman in the Soviet Union had always meant shouldering a larger portion of the national workload than in the West, but during the war years in Siberia, the weight of physical labor upon women became heavier than at any time since the Soviet Union had come into being.[13]

Feeding the hundreds of thousands of evacuees and new workers pouring into the towns and cities of Siberia's rising industrial fortress proved to be as difficult as finding workers and raw materials. Because the Wehrmacht held the lands that had produced almost two fifths of the Soviet Union's grain, two fifths of its cattle, and almost two thirds of its hogs during the year before the war,[14] Voznesenskii's and Komarov's planners had to look to southwestern Siberia for new food supplies just as the call-up of millions of able-bodied men into the armed forces halved the ranks of Siberia's collective farm workers. This meant that the burden upon the Siberian peasants who stayed behind was heavier than anywhere else in the Soviet Union. With fewer draft animals and machines and with more work being done by women and children, it took up to three times as long to sow, tend, and harvest an acre of grain in 1942 as it had in 1940.

While their women and children worked at home, the men of Siberia took up arms against the Germans. Siberians helped to turn the tide at Moscow at the end of 1941, when General Georgii Zhukov threw the fresh Siberian divisions that Stalin had withdrawn from the Far East into the Red Army's first counteroffensive. Five of the twenty-eight men who won Hero of the Soviet Union medals in the defense of Moscow came from Siberia, and General Konstantin Rokossovskii spoke proudly of the "steel grip" of Siberia's 78th Rifle Division, which fought as part of his Sixteenth Army that winter.[15] "The Siberian . . . is tougher and stronger and possesses considerably more capacity to resist than his European countrymen," the Chief of Staff of Germany's Fourth Army reported ruefully as his men retreated from Moscow. "Our men panicked," another general confessed. "This panic," he added in retrospect, "was a serious warning."[16]

Throughout 1942, the Japanese continued to ignore German pleas (including German-drafted operational plans) to open a second front against the Soviet Union. Combined with the information provided by Richard Sorge,[17] the grandson of Karl Marx's personal secretary, who until his arrest in late 1941 had used his position as Berlin's chief correspondent in Tokyo to organize a spy network for the Russians, this allowed Stalin and his commanders to shift four hundred thousand men, five thousand guns, more than three thousand tanks—a total of three field armies, thirty-nine divisions, and another three dozen support groups—from the Transbaikal and Siberia's far east to the Soviet Union's western front. Iakutsk and Krasnoiarsk became the receiving points for U.S. Lend-Lease aircraft, which American pilots flew from Alaska at the rate of ten a day. From there, Russian pilots took the planes west to fly them against the Germans.[18]

Siberian frontiersmen fought hand to hand against the Germans at Stalingrad and gave no quarter. Trained as children to hunt and shoot, Siberian snipers killed Germans in Stalingrad's streets, and men who had fought as Red partisans against the White armies of Kolchak in their youth returned in middle age to train and lead partisan units in German-occupied Belorussia and the Ukraine. As 1943 shaded into 1944, Siberians who had grown up on the banks of the faraway Amur and Ussuri rivers helped to drive the Wehrmacht from the shores of south Russia's quiet Don. Men from the Lena and the Enisei fought on the Vistula in Poland, on the Danube in Hungary, and, finally, on the Oder in Germany. Buriats, Iakuts, and men from a dozen other tribes of native Siberians all joined with their former conquerors against the forces of Nazi Germany in a war that the people of the former Soviet Union still remember as the most tragic and heroic days of their history.[19] Together, they marched a quarter of the way around the world from their native villages to Berlin. "We Siberians are in Berlin," some of the Omsk

Guards wrote on the wall of the conquered Reichstag. "We have come to Berlin so that it can be free."[20]

On May 9, 1945, cheering throngs of Soviet citizens in tens of thousands of towns and cities whose names were unknown to Westerners celebrated a victory over Nazi Germany that had cost their country more than any other combatant nation. Large parts of the Soviet Union's greatest cities had been reduced to rubble, and nearly five million peasant cottages and urban apartments had been destroyed. According to the best estimates, the material losses of the war on Soviet territory amounted to 357 billion U.S. dollars, and all that was destroyed had to be rebuilt or replaced.[21]

The Soviet government hoped that the product of its gigantic capital investments in Siberia during the war years could help to produce the machines and materials needed for that task. The gigantic mills of the Kuzbass and Magnitogorsk had the capacity to shape the mountains of structural steel that would be needed for rebuilding shattered cities, and Siberia's forests held the hundreds of millions of board feet of lumber that could resurrect new collective farms from the charred remnants that the retreating Nazi forces had left in their wake. Siberian coal, iron, oil, and natural gas would eventually produce more wealth than the goldfields along the Lena and the Kolyma, but it would require time, money, and vast amounts of human labor to develop them.

Siberia thus held a key to rebuilding the war-torn European lands of the Soviet Union, but the age-old problems still remained. Climate, distance, and the need to move armaments from factories to the front as quickly as possible had concentrated the resettlement and industry of the great relocation in Siberia's western lands, while its remaining two thirds had remained much as it had in earlier times. Because the war had drawn men and women away from the land, Siberia now produced less food than before, and the lands beyond the Enisei River continued to suffer from too few railroads, too few settlers, and mines and plants that remained too reliant upon the forced labor of the Gulag system. Siberia needed settlement, not resettlement, as did the ruined European lands of the Soviet Union, and it required construction, not reconstruction. Yet Stalin's last years saw Siberia facing the same problems in the same way it had in earlier times. New waves of prisoners began to flow into the Gulag. As the men in Moscow, themselves the product of thinking from times long past, continued to propose age-old solutions to age-old problems, the people of Siberia's eastern lands continued to endure the problems of backwardness and underdevelopment.

PART SIX

Siberia's Modern Age

47

Stalin's Last Years

During the summer of 1945, Siberians from Cheliabinsk to Vladivostok greeted trainloads of returning soldiers. In city squares named after Lenin and Stalin and in town parks named after their followers, bands played, workers cheered, and dedicated Communists vowed once again to build a better future. Idealism replaced the heroism of the war years and diluted the cynicism of the purge era. There was work to be done, and Soviet planners expected that the hundreds of thousands of demobilized men clad in the brown-green drab of the Red Army would be ready to take the jobs that every part of Siberia had for the taking. "Of course, during the first years after the war it was not possible to create good living conditions for every demobilized veteran," one commentator wrote. "But the most important thing of all—the opportunity for peaceful labor—was given to every one."[1] Peaceful labor, Soviet men and women thought, could overcome the shortages of housing and material goods and the massive destruction the war had left in its wake.

Now that the war was won, Siberians were promised more consumer goods, more food, and more medicines. There was to be new housing and better communications, and the fruits of twentieth-century technology were to play a greater role in their daily lives.[2] More railroads and roads were to be built, the Fourth Five-Year Plan of 1946 stated. More telegraph and telephone lines were to be strung, and more hydroelectric power generated to bring Siberia's remote regions into the mainstream of modern life. What had been begun in the 1930s was to be built upon, and the progress of the wartime years carried further. Especially in Siberia's eastern two thirds, where the wartime need for armaments had not touched local life as dramatically as it had farther west, Soviet planners hoped to weld people and land together so that both could play their intended parts in the Soviet future.

If the first three Five-Year Plans and the slave labor of the Gulag had been a part of what Soviet writers have called the "third discovery" of Siberia (the second having begun in the middle of the nineteenth century),[3] the great relocation of the Second World War had moved its western lands decisively to the brink of the modern age by transforming the Urals into the most powerful industrial region of the Soviet Union. The Soviet government had poured the equivalent of more than three and a quarter billion U.S. dollars into the economy of these lands every year during the war and had increased their industrial output by more than four times before the fighting ended. Aside from the Kuzbass, the Urals region (including, of course, Magnitogorsk) produced most of the Soviet Union's high-quality steel in 1945, and its plants turned out more nonferrous metals than the entire USSR had yielded in 1940.[4] Here, at the dividing line between Europe and Asia, the standard of daily life came closest to approximating that of the Soviet Union's more developed European lands. Towns and cities clustered more closely together than in any other part of Siberia, and the network of railroads was more dense. The populations of Sverdlovsk and Cheliabinsk had both passed four hundred thousand by 1945, and Magnitogorsk was not far behind. All across the lands in which the Stroganovs had built their Siberian gateway during the days of Ivan the Terrible, life had become decidedly more urban than rural.

Just a few hundred miles to the east, western Siberia was developing in a similar fashion but on a smaller scale. Novosibirsk and Omsk each had nearly half a million residents, and Tomsk had almost two hundred thousand. With industrial production at more than three times its prewar level and with the output of its tool-and-die industries nearly a dozen times greater in 1943 than in 1941, western Siberia had the capacity to produce the machine tools, tractors, ball bearings, and electrical equipment needed to help restore the Soviet Union's collective farms and rebuild the shattered factories that the retreating Germans had left behind. Farther to the south, nearly a million workers had settled in the industrial and mining towns of the Kuzbass, which formed a third Siberian industrial center. Although technically not part of Siberia in the strict geographical sense, the lands of northern Kazakhstan and parts of

Central Asia (where chemicals, metallurgy, and a host of light industries were beginning to dominate an economy that had once been ruled by nomadic herders and small oasis farmers) were nevertheless becoming a fourth industrial center in the lands east of the Urals.[5]

Comparatively little of this wartime development had reached the Gulag lands beyond the Enisei, where the eastern two thirds of Siberia continued to be undeveloped and undersettled.[6] Before they could prosper, these lands needed not more armies of the slaves that Stalin had used to mine gold and coal but a mass migration of men and women who would build new lives in the towns, cities, and collective farms of Siberia's east. "Until [free] labor is attracted [to the lands east of the Enisei]," the Siberian Department of the Soviet Academy of Sciences warned flatly, "the huge resources of the East will not be properly developed."[7] Realizing that starving prisoners could not become the attentive, efficient workers that eastern Siberia required to move into the modern world, some of the men who stood high in the party's inner circles had begun to wonder if forced labor had not outlived its usefulness even as Stalin sent a new wave of victims into the Gulag. Then the death of Stalin and the execution of Lavrentii Beria, his chief henchman in charge of the secret police, helped to bring that view into the open.

After the losses their country had suffered during the war, some of Stalin's heirs had to ask each other if the Soviet Union wanted to continue having more than a tenth of its adult male population incarcerated in labor camps, especially under conditions that promised to kill them long before their time. Their orders to increase rations, issue better clothing, and provide medical care for Gulag prisoners pulled tens of thousands of men and women back from the brink of death. At the same time, the experienced Red Army officers and partisans with whom Stalin had replaced the frail intellectuals and untrained peasant convicts of the 1930s provided leaders for any among them who dared to rise against the NKVD. After one more wave of vicious suppressions, this combination of factors brought the worst abuses of the Gulag Archipelago to an end.[8]

In 1953 and 1954, major uprisings in several Gulag camps forced the authorities to call in tanks, airborne infantry, and dive-bombers to support faltering NKVD detachments that had been used to crushing such resistance in a matter of hours. This time, the Gulag rebels held out for weeks, often finding unexpected allies among the peasants and women who had been sent there before them. When tanks broke into one slave-labor compound, dozens of women linked arms to block their path. "We all thought the tanks would halt before the serried ranks of these defenseless women," one horrified eyewitness remembered, "but they only accelerated [and] . . . drove straight over the live bodies. There were no cries," he added. "All we heard was a horrible sound of bodies being crushed and cracking bones."[9] Such brutality seemed to weaken the will of the Gulag authorities to use force again.

As the massive flood of prisoners began to dry up, eastern Siberia had to face the full burden of its chronic underpopulation.[10] As late as 1959, fewer than three people per square mile lived between the Enisei and the Pacific.[11] Nearly a million peasants from that region had left the land during the Second World War, and that exodus continued into the 1950s as the lives of country folk continued to be harder than those of anyone else. Consumer goods remained scarce, housing crude and cramped, and the conditions of work harsh enough to offset any incentives that the government's miserly resettlement bonuses might offer. As the twentieth century entered its second half, the people of Siberia's east had to get along with fewer than half the number of retail shops that their country-men who lived farther west enjoyed. A similar ratio applied to the numbers of doctors, medical technicians, hospitals, teachers, and schools in their communities.[12] Workers therefore left Siberia's east and north whenever they could. Not counting the men and women who still remained in the Gulag, six out of every ten workers in the timber industry had been on the job for less than three years when Stalin died. Then, when the government repealed the laws that forbade the "unau-thorized termination of employment," even the workers in western Siberia began to leave their jobs in search of better lives in European Russia. By the early 1960s, Siberia's labor force was shrinking at the rate of nearly a hundred thousand workers a year.[13] To reverse that statistic required more productive farms, better irrigation facilities, new hydro-electric stations, and many, many more miles of railroads. Only these could attract the massive human and scientific resources needed to exploit Siberia's natural wealth and bring its people firmly into the modern world.

48

Virgin Lands

Just when more food was needed to feed the millions of men and women whom Stalin's industrialization drive had taken off the land, his decision to send the Soviet Union's most productive and prosperous peasants to forced labor in Siberia had undermined his nation's agriculture. This condemned the nation that had financed its first industrial revolution in tsarist times by exporting surplus grain to massive food shortages throughout the 1930s and 1940s.[1] Even by the mid-1950s, average yields had still not regained the levels that tsarist Russia had enjoyed on the eve of World War I. Collective farms were still not working, but ideological constraints forbade Stalin's successors from abandoning them.

As long as there was not enough grain for bread, feeding livestock and poultry remained a luxury that government planners could ill afford, and Soviet citizens therefore continued to consume too little meat, eggs, and milk in the years after World War II. As growing more grain became a pressing concern, Nikita Khrushchev urged that collective farms be combined into gigantic "rural cities" or "agrotowns" in the hope that even more massive agricultural units would make farming more productive. Khrushchev's plan proved to be a fiasco, but that passing failure did not prevent him from becoming first secretary of the party's Central Committee in 1953 and prime minister within four years of Stalin's death.

Of all the solutions to the agricultural problems facing Siberia and the Soviet Union that were being considered in the mid-1950s, Khrushchev, the miner-turned-metalworker-turned-politician, chose the one that offered the quickest returns but carried the greatest risk of failure. According to the plans for which he began to campaign in the fall of 1953, the "virgin lands" of the semiarid steppes of southern Siberia and northern Kazakhstan (a vast region just beyond Siberia's southern boundary), which were similar to the southern prairies of Canada's Saskatchewan province, would be made to bloom, bringing tens of millions of acres of wild grasslands under cultivation.[2] Foreign experts warned that large amounts of these fragile lands had to be left fallow each year to prevent erosion of the light topsoil and cited the unfortunate experiences of farmers in the western Great Plains of Canada and the United States during the 1930s to prove their point. Utterly ignorant of soil and water conditions in southern Siberia and the much larger areas of northern Kazakhstan, Khrushchev scoffed at their warnings. With no conception of how devastating wind erosion could be or how easily the natural forces that held it in check could be destroyed, he placed his faith (as Soviet leaders so often did) in limited numbers of machines supplemented by massive amounts of human labor. "Merciless plowing,"[3] Khrushchev insisted, would enable the workers and peasants of the Soviet Union to "conquer" the virgin lands.[4]

Between 1954 and 1961, more than half a million "young patriots"[5] answered their party's summons to turn nearly 115 million acres of virgin lands—an area nearly three and a half times the size of England and equal to the sown area of England, France, West Germany, Sweden, Norway, Denmark, and Belgium combined—into huge state farms that were expected to show how productive socialist agriculture at its best could be. Because drought almost never occurred in the European and Asiatic Russian steppes at the same time, Khrushchev's planners believed that poor harvests in the breadlands of the Ukraine could now be offset by bumper crops from these new farms, thereby freeing the Soviet Union from its perennial food shortages.

In 1956 and 1958, unusually good weather and better-than-average rainfall produced harvests that made it seem that Khrushchev had discovered the panacea for which Soviet leaders had searched since the Bolshevik Revolution. But these proved to be such rare exceptions that, aside from one good harvest in 1964, the virgin lands during the rest of the Khrushchev era yielded barely half of what they had in the beginning.[6] In working with soil and climate that required careful attention to the details of fragile climatic and ecological conditions, Khrushchev and his planners had abandoned any thought of long-term planning to concentrate upon filling each year's quota. As with so much else of the

Soviet experience in Siberia, concern for the here and now had obscured every attempt to see what lay ahead.

No matter how certain the Bolshevik belief that bigness and efficiency went hand in hand, the two had proved incompatible from the moment the virgin lands program had shifted into high gear in 1954. On state farms whose average size approached 250 square miles (the size of about seven nineteenth-century townships in the American Midwest), workers had had to spend part of the summers in tents in the midst of the newly plowed steppes in order to be within a day's journey of their fields. Far from their families and homes, they had led spartan, lonely lives in which cold food had been the rule, and the smallest amenities had become nearly as difficult to acquire as they had been in the forced-labor camps of Stalin's time.

While these pioneers lived from hand to mouth in the open spaces of Eurasia, their families suffered from want at home, for Moscow's planners had relegated housing for the hundreds of thousands of "virgin landers" to a very distant second place in order to concentrate upon grain production. The new state farms provided workers with barely half as much living space as elsewhere, and even fewer schools, hospitals, and other public services. Because the population of these once sparsely settled districts had grown by ten and fifteen times in just a few years, consumer goods remained scarce.[7] Conditioned by forty years of Soviet experience to expect that better times did not in fact lie ahead, the virgin lands settlers began to plot their escape even before the failure of their crops showed that the experiment had fallen upon hard times.

If Moscow's officials provided too little in the way of housing, public services, and consumer goods in the virgin lands, they did no better with farm machines. Although Khrushchev's planners earmarked nearly half of the tractors and combines coming off Soviet production lines for the virgin lands, the pioneers of northern Kazakhstan and southern Siberia had only one tractor for every 538 acres of grainfields in the late 1950s, while American farmers had one for every 86. Even these few never worked at full capacity because only one farm in four had a repair shop and those never had enough spare parts. Shortages of windshield wipers idled trucks in the rain, and an unexplained lack of headlight bulbs kept desperately needed tractors from working after dark. On one occasion, Khrushchev himself complained that expensive combines often wore out in less than a year because of poor maintenance and abuse.[8] "The agricultural machine building industry," a high official admitted in 1959, "is not capable, under any conditions, of delivering within the next two or three years the quantity of machines [needed in the virgin lands]."[9]

Farm managers found it difficult to keep even machines in good repair working in the fields because operators remained in such short supply. It had been one thing to convince Young Communists graduating from high school to take jobs in the steppes of Asia, but it was much more difficult to entice experienced truck and tractor drivers to the frontiers of Siberia and Kazakhstan when their services were in great demand in more developed parts of the Soviet Union. Even though the government sent tractor drivers and combine operators from the Ukraine to help with the harvest in the virgin lands after they had finished their work at home, there were never enough to bring in all the grain before the snow fell. In 1959, four million acres had to be left standing for want of drivers and combines.[10]

Under the best of circumstances, only part of what virgin lands farmers harvested ever reached Soviet consumers. While the Soviet Union developed the technology to explore outer space and build long-range delivery systems for its nuclear weapons, farmers in the virgin lands had to store part of their harvests in the same crudely dug storage trenches that their ancestors had used hundreds of years before. Even in the 1960s, as much as a tenth of every year's crop in the virgin lands rotted for want of modern grain elevators.[11] Tens of thousands of additional tons had already been spilled from leaking and warped truck beds as the harvest was driven along the backcountry dirt roads of southern Siberia and northern Kazakhstan to storage facilities that were too small to hold it.

More money and better planning might one day have overcome such difficulties, had it not been for the terrible "black storms" of northern Kazakhstan that lay beyond the control of party and people alike. Villages struck by such storms had to be dug out by bulldozers, while the dunes of topsoil that the winds left behind buried newly sprouted crops in minutes and filled riverbeds in the space of a few hours. Here was the chief danger of the annual deep autumn plowing that Khrushchev had demanded when he had dismissed as nonsense the warnings of agronomists who had foreseen the erosion problems that lay ahead. By the early 1960s, even *Pravda* had to admit that "incorrect tillage practices" had eroded the better part of fifteen million acres.[12] "If we do not cease mercilessly plowing up all virgin lands fields, there will be no escape from erosion," one agronomist stated flatly in 1962. "We must," he warned, "stop it immediately."[13]

Instead, Khrushchev drove such critics from their posts, and when the "black storms" continued, he went on to blame the farmers themselves, firing as many as seven out of every ten state farm directors in some of the virgin lands districts.[14] By then, crops were failing on a huge scale and the space-age pioneers of Eurasia had begun to desert their lands in droves.[15] They had, *Pravda* explained, become "unwilling to remain on scorched fields."[16] By 1964, the virgin lands disaster, which was being discussed more and more frequently in the Soviet press, had grown visible enough to drive Khrushchev from power and force his successors to look seriously for solutions to the crippling problems of wind erosion and hopelessly botched planning. "Erosion," one expert wrote in retrospect, "is relatively easy to prevent, difficult to contain, and still more difficult to eliminate."[17] Perhaps even more difficult to eliminate were the foibles of centralized planning and the Soviet system's endless capacity for self-delusion. As in Stalin's time, agricultural development in the virgin lands continued to be ruled by ideologically driven directives framed by urban bureaucrats who knew nothing about farming and disdained the farmers' personal experience.[18]

High-ranking officials now admitted that there "had been some blunders in solving a number of organizational-economic and agro-technical questions," and, as Leonid Brezhnev and Aleksei Kosygin took power in the mid-1960s, one of their first tasks had to be the restoration of the virgin lands. "Through the efforts of scientists and production workers," one official explained in *Pravda*, the failings of Khrushchev's time were being overcome and "a new system of agriculture corresponding to local conditions . . . [was] being enforced."[19] This meant leaving the eroded lands fallow, abandoning the deep plowing that had exposed great quantities of semiarid topsoil to the wind, and bringing large amounts of potent fertilizers and herbicides into use whenever the chronic shipping problems connected with their distribution could be overcome. For a time these efforts improved the virgin lands' performance and even allowed Moscow's planners to begin concentrating the production of wheat in Kazakhstan and start planting such badly needed fodder crops as corn and sugar beets in the Ukraine. Two decades later, however, these new efforts helped to produce a new crisis of massive environmental poisoning in Kazakhstan and Siberia that proved to be even more irreparable than the erosion and failed crops of earlier times.

Because of monumental mistakes such as the virgins lands fiasco, the output of Soviet agriculture in general—and Siberia's farms in particular—had risen only sporadically during the quarter century after Stalin's death. Despite Soviet planners' oft-spoken vows to do better, the numbers of livestock in Kazakhstan were not yet double what they had been when Stalin had launched his collectivization drive thirty-five years earlier, and the situation was very much the same farther north in

Siberia proper, where it took nearly half a century after the beginning of collectivization before the numbers of sheep, cattle, and goats began to rise.[20] For a time, Brezhnev's highly touted agricultural reforms increased the number of beef cattle in Siberia by about a fifth, but the quantity of grain delivered by its farmers was actually lower in 1969 (by a third) and 1970 (by two percent) than it had been in 1960, when Siberia had produced more than a sixth of the Soviet Union's grain and about a tenth of its milk and meat, even though it had contained only a fifteenth of its farmers.[21]

The problems that had plagued Siberia's farms immediately after the Second World War continued throughout the 1960s and 1970s. Even in western Siberia, where distances were shorter and communications better, seed grain arrived late all through the 1970s, and the quantities of mineral fertilizers that crossed the Urals continued to be too small even after the Soviet Union had become the world's second largest producer.[22] Machinery continued to arrive without key parts, new tractors purchased to work in cold weather reached Siberia without enclosed cabs, and volunteer workers sent by various Young Communist organizations to help in the fields too often had no experience in the work for which they had been recruited.[23] Most of all, the Soviet effort to develop Siberia suffered from a chronic shortage of settlers.

Between 1945 and 1959, the population east of the Urals increased by less than a quarter million a year, despite government resettlement bonuses that amounted to an entire year's pay. During the 1960's, Siberia's population rose more rapidly, but in the 1970s, its rate of growth fell back to that of the 1950s, except in such new cities as Bratsk, where the population grew a hundredfold between 1956 and 1984.[24] During the Khrushchev era, about eighty thousand men and women left Siberia every year, most of them from its agricultural regions. Then, when discoveries of oil and natural gas drew new waves of men and women into Siberia's northwest, they refused to stay for want of decent housing and public services. "More often than not," Brezhnev told the party's Twenty-sixth Congress not long before he died, "a person leaves Siberia not because the climate is not suitable or the pay is small, but because it is harder to get housing and put a child in kindergarten."[25] On Siberia's collective and state farms, from which three-quarters of a million skilled farmhands left during the first half of the 1960s, the problems were even worse than in the cities.[26]

Lenin had seen hydroelectric power as a key to the development that would stem the persistent flight of Siberia's workers, but the production of hydroelectricity languished in Siberia's western lands until the Second World War.[27] Farther east, its development had to wait until the 1950s, when Khrushchev turned his attention in that direction after his imagination had been fired by visions of the part that Siberia's "enormous resources" could play in developing new energy sources. At the apex of Khrushchev's vision stood the unbuilt Bratsk Power Station, which, as he told the assembled delegates at the Twentieth Party Congress, would produce as much electricity in a year as the two most powerful stations in the European part of the Soviet Union. The Bratsk Power Station—immense, expensive, and built in the midst of a wilderness in which a demand for electric energy had not even begun to develop—was to become the industrial counterpart to Khrushchev's grandiose plans for the virgin lands.

49

Bratsk Power Station

Over the centuries, Siberia's Russian masters had calculated its wealth according to its furs, gold, timber, iron, and coal, but they did not begin to fully reckon its wealth in terms of hydroelectric power until Lenin began to speak about "electrifying Russia."[1] Then rural electrification became a means of communicating with citizens who remained illiterate, as well as a symbol of the progress that communism hoped to achieve. No other ruler sensed more quickly or clearly than Lenin how readily radio and motion pictures could tie people to their government or how they could be used to build public support for national policy. Well before the Russian Civil War ended in 1921, the men and women of Russia and Siberia therefore had a better idea of what Lenin looked like and what he hoped to accomplish than they had ever had about the fallen tsar Nicholas II.[2] Proclaiming that "communism means Soviet power plus the electrification of the entire country," Lenin's followers worked to bring the twentieth century's newest source of power to each peasant cottage, every Iakut hut, and every cabin in the wilderness. In the days before the world learned to build nuclear plants on a large scale, electricity generated by brown coal, natural gas, and, most of all, water held the key to transforming Soviet life.

For men looking to increase the Soviet Union's output of cheap energy, the huge rivers of northern Asia, each of which drained more than a million square miles of land, offered the prospect of producing hundreds of millions of kilowatt-hours of electric power. Closest to the Urals, the Ob flowed for 2,300 miles from the Altai Mountains to the Kara Sea. To the east, the Enisei flowed 2,100 miles to the same sea from the Saian Mountains, carrying well over half a trillion cubic yards of water to the Arctic in a single year.[3] These rivers could produce electric power for the mills of the Urals and western Siberia, including the massive industrial complexes that were being built at Magnitogorsk and in the Kuzbass. Krasnoiarsk, Novosibirsk, Omsk, Cheliabinsk, Tomsk, and Eniseisk could all draw upon any hydroelectric stations built along the upper half of the Ob and Enisei, and any excess power could be sent across the Urals to European Russia, where, during the first decades of Soviet history, the demand for energy continually outstripped the supply.

East of the Enisei, the Lena rose in the mountains near Lake Baikal and flowed to the Arctic's Laptev Sea. Nearly 2,700 miles in length, it cut through the Central Siberian Plateau before it reached the Central Iakut Lowlands on the edge of the Arctic and spread into a riverbed that stretched nearly twelve miles from bank to bank. Some four hundred miles to the southeast of the Lena's headwaters, the Argun River flowed north from Inner Mongolia to the Shilka. From that point it became the Amur, flowing on to the Tatar Strait some 1,700 miles to the east. The Ob, Enisei, Lena, and Amur totaled nearly nine thousand miles in length and drained lands a third larger than the contiguous United States. Soviet experts calculated in the 1950s that these four "rivers of electricity" and their chief tributaries could produce nearly a trillion kilowatt-hours of electric energy every year, or about half the world's entire supply.[4] But to dam and harness these rivers, the Soviets had to start virtually from scratch. At the end of the Civil War, Siberia's sixty-eight tiny power stations generated less than a single thirty-three millionth of the electricity that men spoke of producing when work began on the Bratsk Power Station in 1954.[5]

Although the first two Five-Year Plans increased the Soviet Union's electrical output dramatically, the network of high-voltage interlocking grids that would span Siberia in the 1970s did not begin to develop until the great plants of Magnitogorsk and the Kuzbass took shape. During the 1930s, the capacity of Siberia's power stations grew by more than fifteen times, and their output increased by twice that amount. As always, most of the development took place in Siberia's western third, leaving the energy of some of Siberia's most powerful rivers still to be harnessed. Eventually, the Lena, Vilui, Iana, Kolyma, and Amur rivers were to become the sites of the gigantic Siberian power stations that tantalized

Khrushchev with visions of unlimited energy produced at a fraction of what it cost in the West.[6]

On the eve of the Second World War, Stalin urged the Eighteenth Party Congress to set aside the wasteful "gigantomania" that had built the huge industrial complexes at Magnitogorsk and in the Kuzbass in favor of smaller, more manageable enterprises. But less than two decades later, his heirs shifted course again. Convinced that he could succeed where Stalin had failed, Khrushchev began to dream of harnessing the force of Siberia's giant rivers to send endless supplies of electric current across Eurasia, just as he had hoped to end his nation's food shortages by bringing huge modern agro-towns to the virgin lands. Fired by visions of Nature being harnessed in the service of communism, Khrushchev vowed to make Bratsk, a tiny town northwest of Lake Baikal, about halfway between Irkutsk and Eniseisk, the center of his effort to master the "enormous resources of the eastern regions."[7] Bratsk was to become the most powerful hydroelectric station in the world, a lasting monument to what communism could achieve.

Founded by a detachment of cossacks as a frontier outpost in 1631, Bratsk had celebrated its two-hundredth anniversary as a village of fewer than sixty buildings and a population of slightly more than six hundred people.[8] By 1956, when Khrushchev spoke to the Twentieth Party Congress about the crimes of Stalin and the wonders of electric power, Bratsk had grown to 2,500.[9] A year later, as the first contingents of the men and women sent to build its four-hundred-foot-high dam poured in, the village boomed into a town of twenty thousand. Fifteen thousand more came the following year and another fifteen thousand the next, all working to raise a dam that would bury 232 towns and villages beneath its waters to form a four-thousand-square-mile lake. Seventy thousand people would have to be resettled before the dam would begin to stem the 200 billion cubic yards of water that would generate more than twenty-two billion kilowatt-hours of electricity every year.[10]

At Bratsk, the dam builders faced scorching heat and Siberia's inevitable hordes of mosquitoes and gnats in summer only to have the mercury fall to forty degrees below zero four months later. Although the surface of the fast-moving Angara never froze, huge beds of sludge ice formed at its bottom that sometimes raised the river's waters as much as twenty feet in a single night to create floods in the midst of blizzards. While they struggled against heat, cold, storms, and floods, the Bratsk builders had to string high-voltage lines across four hundred miles of wild taiga to the power station at Irkutsk in order to have light and heat.[11] Only then could the real work on the great dam begin.

The Bratsk Dam fired the imagination of everyone, from Khrushchev to the "conquerors of the Angara,"[12] who shoveled away nearly ten million cubic feet of dirt and poured concrete in its place. Here was the dam of dams, the beginnings of a hydroelectric station that, Soviet propagandists hurried to point out, could produce more energy in a single day than could be generated by the muscle power of the entire population of the United States.[13] At the peak of his fame as the Soviet Union's (officially tolerated) dissident poet, Evgenii Evtushenko wrote a 170-page poem, *The Bratsk Power Station*, to call down the blessings of history upon its builders and dedicate their labors to a future "in which communism will be built among us not according to self-interest but in keeping with Lenin's teachings." Looking into the future, Evtushenko promised that the Bratsk Power Station was being built "so that women won't bear orphans, so there will be bread enough for everyone, so that innocent people won't be locked up in jail, so that no one will ever shoot himself again."[14] The Bratsk Dam, its builders believed, would transform Soviet life and change the course of history.

Enthusiasm for the task at hand and a belief in a better world to come could not overcome the shortages of food, shelter, building materials, and machines needed to do the work that willing men and women alone could not accomplish. Poor planning and the Soviet leaders' endless capacity for self-delusion stretched the work at Bratsk beyond its expected time of completion by a full seven years, and, even when it was finished, delays in building the great Bratsk aluminum plant condemned the power station to work at less than half its capacity for half a decade more. Yet by 1971 the Bratsk Power Station was in full swing, supplying not only the aluminum plant but a host of new timber-processing, paper, and cellulose mills that were to spring up within its reach.[15] For a while, it seemed that power from Bratsk might indeed transform Siberia, especially if more dams like it could be built.

The completion of the Bratsk Power Station in 1967 thus marked the beginning of a network of hydroelectric facilities that would form a roughly shaped oval along Siberia's Mongolian frontier, the circumference of which cut through Irkutsk, Bratsk, Ust-Ilimsk, and Krasnoiarsk. Even before the Bratsk Dam had been finished, builders were already working to build a slightly smaller version at Ust-Ilimsk, 175 miles downstream. Like Bratsk, whose completion had brought an array of new industries to Siberia's eastern lands, the Ust-Ilimsk Power Station was planned to support three new iron mines that were to become the center of an entirely new industrial area.[16] Farther west, a full three years before the Ust-Ilimsk Power Station was finished in 1974, an even larger one at Krasnoiarsk forced its counterpart at Bratsk to yield pride of place as the Soviet Union's largest.

Supported by smaller hydroelectric facilities scattered among them, the power stations at Bratsk, Ust-Ilimsk, and Krasnoiarsk could provide the eastern lands of central Siberia with more than fifteen million kilo-watt-hours of electricity every day, and there were plans to build more than a dozen additional stations to form a network of eight interlocking circles stretching from the Irtysh River to Lake Baikal and from Bratsk in the northeast to the Altai highlands in the southwest. By the late 1970s, the station at Krasnoiarsk had already been obliged to surrender its claim as the Soviet Union's largest to the Saiano-Shushenskoe Power Station, built in the vicinity of Lenin's place of exile, which soared to nearly twice the height of the giant concrete wall at Bratsk.[17]

As in all the gargantuan construction projects that had dominated Siberian life since the 1920s, people took a distant second place to steel, concrete, and machines at Bratsk and the power stations that followed it. "The failure to provide living accommodation, children's institutions, shops, and schools for a number of new enterprises," Leonid Brezhnev reported of the industrial complex that had been planned around the great Saiano-Shushenskoe Power Station, "has retarded the completion of production units and caused a great flight of labor."[18] What workers' housing was built continued to follow the predictably ugly pattern that had scarred the Soviet urban landscape since the days of Stalin. "It is a beautiful country," one commentator wrote of the Saiano-Shushenskoe lands that Lenin had once called the "Siberian Italy." "It is to be hoped that its natural beauty will not be destroyed by the tasteless industrial-ization characteristic of Soviet development."[19]

While workers were struggling to find minimal comforts in the huge industrial complexes at Bratsk, Ust-Ilimsk, Krasnoiarsk, and Saiano-Shushenskoe, other Soviet builders were working in the far eastern lands beyond Lake Baikal to harness the energy of the Lena, Vilui, Iana, Kolyma, and Amur rivers. Because winter temperatures fell to $-70°$ Centigrade, the Vilui Power Station had to be built underground, and the problems with its construction became so complex that it took nine years longer than expected to finish it. In the meantime, newly opened diamond mines in the vicinity languished for want of heat and power, just as the gold mines in Siberia's far northeast suffered in similar ways because of delays in building hydroelectric stations on the Kolyma River, where dam builders struggled against permafrost, winter storms, and unpredictable summer floods. Roads, bridges, barracks, and cook houses all had to be built from scratch, and specially designed equipment had to be sent over almost 2,500 miles of rough roads from the Vilui Power Station. Then, before the massive amounts of building materials needed for the Kolyma dams could be brought in, the port of Nagaevo, once the gateway for hundreds of thousands of prisoners the NKVD had poured into the Kolyma death camps, had to be rebuilt. Everywhere, workers fought against the climate, the isolation, and the botched schedules of bureaucratic planners who had no sense of the terrible conditions under which they had to work.[20]

By the end of the 1970s, such efforts had increased Siberia's ability to produce electricity by more than five times, but only at the cost of immense human suffering.[21] As the vast lakes formed by Siberia's huge dams spread across thousands of square miles, tens of thousands of people had been resettled in areas in which no housing, food supplies, or jobs had yet been created. Yet Soviet leaders' visions of huge accomplishments that could show communism's power to dominate even the forces of Nature did not end at Bratsk or on the fragile virgin lands, for Khrushchev's successors proved to be every bit as ready to undertake such ventures as he had been. Leonid Brezhnev, the man who ousted Khrushchev in the fall of 1964, worked on a similar scale in the far north, where he presided over the construction of mile-deep mines to tap the nickel and platinum reserves at Norilsk at the same time as he built immense petrochemical complexes at Tomsk and Tobolsk to make use of the newly discovered oil and natural gas reserves of the Siberian northwest. Beyond that, Brezhnev set out to build the Baikal-Amur Main Line across more than two thousand miles of territory in which some form of seismic activity occurred on the average of four times a day all year long, and avalanches, meltwater bogs, permafrost, floods, encephalitis, anthrax, toxoplasmosis, and a score of other diseases and natural dangers threatened its builders at every step.[22] Known to all who planned and worked on it by the acronym BAM, this railroad was expected to open a brilliant new chapter in the development of Siberia's Transbaikal lands while it lifted some of the burden of freight traffic from the Trans-Siberian.

Planned by the Tsarist Railroad Ministry on the eve of World War I and then abandoned as a project that could not be built because of the roughness of the lands through which it had to pass, the BAM had fascinated the Bolsheviks from the moment they had taken power. For the better part of a quarter century, Lenin and his heirs had grappled with its difficulties until war and circumstances had forced them to set it aside. Then, after three thousand designers and surveyors had revised and updated the work their predecessors had accomplished since tsarist times, Brezhnev and his advisers decided to build the railroad in 1971. Probably no one will ever be able to calculate how much they spent during the next twenty years, but estimates of the sums lavished on the BAM have run as high as eighteen billion U.S. dollars, an immense sum for a country in which the entire gross national product has been estimated at only thirty-six times that amount.[23] So complicated, wasteful, and ill coordinated was the project that it took until 1984 to lay the track and another half decade before full-scale train service could begin. Of all the massive construction projects conceived by Siberia's Soviet rulers, the BAM was easily the most grandiose, took the longest to complete, required the largest labor force, and was by far the most expensive.

50

The BAM

No matter how resolute the pioneers who settled its frontier or how grandiose the illusions (and self-delusions) of the men who ruled it from Moscow, Siberia continued to struggle against its vastness as the Brezhnev era began. As they had in olden times, its tens of thousands of miles of navigable rivers continued to freeze solid in the winter, and "roadlessness" continued to slow the movement of people, raw materials, and goods. Unlike in the United States and Western Europe, where the bulk of commercial traffic moved along well-paved highways, railroads remained Siberia's most reliable form of transportation in the 1970s. Yet as the decade opened, huge sections of its eastern lands—including some of its richest reserves of timber and strategic minerals—still lay hundreds of miles beyond the railroad's reach. Mines could not be developed, new stands of timber could not be cut, and oil and natural gas reserves could not be tapped without first building railroads through some of the roughest terrain on the face of the globe.

As the most heavily used transportation system in a country that boasted the most heavily traveled railway network in the world, Siberia's railroads had become overloaded almost to the breaking point by 1970. Soviet railroads generally carried three times as much freight as their American counterparts, and the Trans-Siberian hauled nearly twice that much to make it the busiest of all Soviet railroads. In the 1930s, men and women condemned to forced labor had given the Trans-

Siberian a second track, and during the 1950s they had electrified it from Moscow to the edge of the Transbaikal lands. Aside from those changes, the Trans-Siberian at the beginning of the 1970s was scarcely different from what it had been sixty years before. Still the main stimulus to Siberian economic development, it remained the only means of intercity travel for hundreds of thousands of Siberians. Oil going east and west, coal moving west from the Kuzbass, timber being shipped west from the lands around Lake Baikal, and foodstuffs traveling to the lands east of the Enisei, where, in the scant one percent of the land that was considered arable, local farmers produced no more than two fifths of what the region's settlers required—all flowed along the Trans-Siberian.[1]

If the Trans-Siberian served as the main artery for the lands east of the Urals, it was also their spine, the central cord through which flowed the impulses that directed Siberia's movements. But there its parallel with vertebrate anatomy ended, for the Trans-Siberian spine had few ribs, each poorly formed and all set very far apart. Faced by the problems of terrain, climate, and the huge construction costs that such obstacles imposed, Siberia's Soviet masters had struggled to supplement the Trans-Siberian with new railroads ever since the First Five-Year Plan began in 1928. At first, they had done so only in the spasmodic fashion typical of early Soviet planning, using prisoners and army units to lay the Turkestan-Siberian Railroad from Barnaul through Semipalatinsk, the onetime garrison town on the upper reaches of the Irtysh River to which Dostoevskii had been exiled after his release from Omsk prison. Then they had continued the track through the semiarid steppes of Siberia's southwest to Lugovoi, halfway between Kazakhstan's capital of Alma-Ata and the Uzbek capital at Tashkent. When completed in 1931, this "Turksib" Railroad made it possible to bring west Siberian grain to the cotton growers of Central Asia, so as to free their irrigated grainlands for growing more cotton and making possible one of those exchanges of resources with which Soviet planners dreamed of making Siberia self-sufficient.[2]

During Stalin's last days, the architects of the Fourth Five-Year Plan had assigned armies of forced laborers to build the South Siberian Railway to link the massive industrial complex of Novokuznetsk (called Stalinsk in the days of Stalin) with the equally large iron-and-steel plant at Magnitogorsk. By the mid-1950s, the South Siberian was moving coal, iron ore, pig iron, and steel east and west. Then, as the first harvests from Khrushchev's virgin lands project came in, the South Siberian hauled grain west, except for that grown along the new lands' eastern flank, which was sent to grain-hungry workers beyond the Enisei in the east.

In anticipation of still richer harvests from the virgin lands, Soviet builders began to lay track for the Central Siberian Railroad just a year after the South Siberian went into operation. Originally planned to link the industrial complex at Cheliabinsk with that at Barnaul, the Central Siberian had a spur that could divert shipments of coal from the Kuzbass southward to Magnitogorsk and ease the pressure on the Trans-Siberian and South Siberian during peak periods.

Once the Central Siberian was finished in 1980, these three railroads, linked by a handful of north-south feeder lines, tied much of the western third of Siberia together, especially after the Tiumen-Surgut-Urengoi line connected the huge, newly opened Samotlor oil fields near Surgut and the massive natural gas reserves discovered near Urengoi with the refineries of Tiumen.[3] With its areas for producing food, oil, gas, coal, iron, steel, and machinery well connected by the early 1980s, western Siberia was beginning to function as the modern, integrated economic unit that Soviet planners had envisioned since the 1930s, although the heavy traffic on even its new railroads still slowed the movement of goods and raw materials. Farther east Siberia's economic life continued to falter despite the many new discoveries of valuable minerals that Soviet scientists reported. For all practical purposes, the Trans-Siberian, which ran perilously close to Siberia's southern frontier, still remained the only major means of transportation between the Enisei and the Pacific, just as it had been at the time of the First World War.

Beyond the Enisei, about four hundred miles of track connected the Trans-Siberian terminus of Taishet (the northernmost point before the railroad turned south toward Irkutsk) with the city of Ust-Kut on the Lena. Then, much farther east, a spur of about half that length connected the Pacific ports of Vanino and Sovetskaia Gavan to Komsomolsk, the "City of Youth" that had taken its name from the Young Communist League members who had built it in the 1930s. Nearly 2,100 miles of wild taiga and swamplands separated Ust-Kut from Komsomolsk. Hundreds of miles north of the Trans-Siberian, these lands held some of Siberia's richest mineral deposits, but the outside world had no way to reach them.

"Virtually the whole of Mendeleev's table of elements," one distinguished Soviet academician told an *Izvestiia* reporter in 1984, was represented in these wild lands.[4] Around Udokan, Nature had concentrated an estimated 1.2 billion tons of high-grade copper ore—the largest deposit anywhere in the Soviet Union—into an area fourteen miles square. Farther north, along the Vilui River in southern Iakutiia, huge reserves of oil and natural gas, the latter estimated at more than thirty trillion (perhaps as many as 460 trillion) cubic feet, added to this storehouse of wealth, while the coalfields centered around Neriungri, a few hundred miles farther to the north and east, held some forty billion tons of coal. Just north of Neriungri, the Aldan mines opened the way to twenty billion tons of high-grade iron ore. Two hundred miles had separated the coal of the Donbass from the iron ore of Krivoi Rog when the entrepreneurs of Imperial Russia had developed that industrial complex at the end of the nineteenth century, and more than twelve hundred miles lay between Magnitogorsk and the Kuzbass. Yet the coking coal of Neriungri and the iron ore of the Aldan lands stood only sixty miles apart. If a railroad could connect them, Soviet planners could bring another huge iron-and-steel complex into being. The still rich Lena goldfields around Bodaibo stood not far away. So did hoards of vital lesser-known ores. Tin, molybdenum, mica, zinc, nickel, bauxite, a fortune in diamonds, and a hundred million acres of mature forests headed a long and luxurious list of the treasures to be found in these wild lands.[5]

After debating for the better part of three-quarters of a century whether a railroad could be built through the mineral-rich lands of the Transbaikal, Siberia's Soviet masters began in 1971 to build the Baikal-Amur Main Line to connect Ust-Kut to Komsomolsk. Including the segments already in service at each end, the BAM would be about half the length of the Trans-Siberian and would bisect nearly 2,700 miles of the world's roughest lands. A territory somewhat more than three times the size of France, the BAM zone held less than a fiftieth part of the Soviet Union's population. Aside from the vegetation that filled its bogs in summer and the wild forests of stone pine, spruce, fir, and larch that spread around them, very little grew on its poor soils. Seven out of every eight potatoes, five out of every six eggs, and fifteen out of every sixteen quarts of milk had to be shipped from other parts of the Soviet Union. So did virtually all the flour. Because of the short growing season in the BAM territory, grain could grow in only a few isolated valleys.[6]

To cross these wild lands, the BAM builders had to cut through seven major mountain ranges, build nearly four thousand bridges and culverts (nearly a hundred and fifty of which were more than three hundred feet long), bore fifteen miles of tunnels, construct seventy million square feet of shops and housing, and move about a billion cubic feet of earth in a climate cold enough to shatter steel in winter and wet enough to rot everything in summer. Near Lake Baikal, the northern tip of which the BAM would skirt, repeated earthquakes had raised cliffs almost fifty feet high and opened cracks sixty feet wide. Just in the western half of the BAM route alone, these earthquakes triggered an average of 350 avalanches and landslides a year. East of the earthquake and avalanche zone, permafrost that reached as deep as a thousand feet created ground ice up to fifteen feet thick in winter; in summer, the frozen subsoil's inability to absorb thawing ice and snow created bogs that bred hordes of mosquitoes and gnats.[7]

In contrast to the builders of the Trans-Siberian, who had worked with raw manpower, hand tools, and a minimum of primitive machinery at the end of the nineteenth century, the BAM workers drove dump trucks from West Germany, cranes and bulldozers from Japan, and the never absent Caterpillar bulldozers from the United States, supplemented by even larger quantities of equipment supplied by the factories of the Soviet Union. At a minimum, 1,200 excavators, more than 700 bulldozers and graders, 800 cranes, and nearly 7,500 eight-ton trucks worked on the BAM project, not to mention huge switching locomotives and more than 1,500 railroad dumper cars. In ways that the builders of the old Trans-Siberian had never dreamed of, the BAM engineers moved frozen dirt, laid track, and poured ballast. Into the mid-1980s, they and their machines spread four hundred thousand tons of ballast a year to set ties firmly into the BAM's roadbed. Added to that each year, the BAM builders shaped eleven million cubic feet of crushed rock, forty thousand tons of lime, and eighty million bricks into embankments, bridge abutments, and tunnel facings.[8]

Aside from the quarter million or so people living in its three major centers, a mere four thousand people lived along the BAM route when the tracklayers set to work in 1971. In desperate need of more workers, Brezhnev made the BAM the centerpoint of his speech to the Young Communist League Congress in 1974, calling upon its members to set their personal lives aside and volunteer for the great work ahead. Amazingly, and for the last time, thousands of young men and women heeded his appeal, many of them leaving directly for the BAM region when the congress ended in Kazakhstan's capital of Alma-Ata. By mid-1975, the BAM work force had risen to thirty thousand workers, of whom four out of every five had at least high school educations and were under the age of thirty. To keep them from abandoning eastern Siberia, as so many workers had abandoned the oil and gas fields farther west, Brezhnev offered these men and women two and a half times the average Soviet salary if they would stay on the job for at least three years. At the same time, the Soviet media showered the BAM's "heroic workers" with praise and attention, focusing upon the greatness of their accomplishment and romanticizing the difficulties they were struggling to overcome.[9]

Combined with the idealism that had drawn them to the Transbaikal, public attention and generous financial incentives kept more than four out of every five BAM builders on the job for the first year, but as Soviet-made machinery continued to break down and even the most basic necessities continued to be scarce, the young men and women who had postponed their careers to fulfill their duties as Young Communists soon began to have second thoughts. Even in Tynda, the town that had been designated as the capital of the BAM zone, shoes, coats, and hats could not be purchased, and, much as at Magnitogorsk in the days of Jack Scott, scarcely a third of the customers could be seated at the town's cafeterias. Like the hired navvies and criminals condemned to hard labor who had built the Trans-Siberian, the cream of Soviet youth lived in "tent cities" and dugouts while planners delayed building proper housing in order to deliver rails, ballast, and crossties.

As at Magnitogorsk in the early 1930s, there were no sewers, no plumbing, and shortages of water at Tynda in the mid-1970s. In another town, according to a well-known *Pravda* correspondent, the railroad's planners "forgot" to include a railroad station, and at Niia, a town built by BAM's Georgian workers, the same correspondent thought it worth noting that food shops and a cinema had actually been built. Elsewhere, the authorities at one point built barracks for bachelors only to find that most of the people arriving to work on the railroad were married couples. And so the ubiquitous litany of mismanagement, misappropriation of funds, and mistakes so familiar in the daily life of every Soviet citizen came to dominate what Brezhnev had designated as communism's major construction project of the 1970s. By the time of Brezhnev's death in the fall of 1982, the BAM remained unfinished.[10]

According to the Eleventh Five-Year Plan, which the party adopted in 1980, all of the BAM track was to be in place by 1985, with the railroad being opened to full-scale operations before 1990. In the spirit of "friendly socialist competition," Young Communist League construction gangs working eastward from Taishet and Ust-Kut announced that they would finish their section by the sixty-sixth anniversary of the Young Communist League's founding on October 29, 1984. In reply, the officers in charge of the army work crews that were laying track west from Komsomolsk vowed that they would complete their work in time to celebrate the thirty-ninth anniversary of the Soviet Union's victory over Germany on May 9. Both began to "storm," to use the Soviet term, meaning that everyone worked harder and put in longer shifts so that, by the end of 1983, only 300 of the original 2,100 miles of track remained to be completed. At that point, shortages of crossties slowed the track-layers' progress, and it required a series of heavy-handed appeals to the factories that produced them to finish the railroad.[11] This time, all of the construction gangs working on the BAM met their goals, and the railroad was officially opened in April 1985 by the "first through journey" of the "Science Express," a special trainload of scientists sent to study what still needed to be finished.[12]

Sufficiently completed to make propaganda claims, however, did not mean completed in fact. Too often, the "Science Express" traveled on hastily laid service tracks that bypassed unfinished tunnels, all of which still had immense construction problems to overcome. To make matters worse, the shortcuts taken by the "storming" work crews of the early 1980s came back to haunt their successors during the second half of the decade, as track beds sank into thawing permafrost, rails buckled, and carelessly cut tunnel walls began to break apart. And the Moscow planners, who in Brezhnev's time had showered praise and attention upon the BAM builders, lost interest once the track had been "officially" completed. "Today," a noted correspondent for *Pravda* confessed in August 1985, "there is coldness to their concerns and needs, where yesterday they received congratulations."[13] Even in Neriungri, the huge coal town that had grown from a few hundred to more than 120,000 in fifteen years and had enjoyed the benefits of some three billion dollars that the Japanese had invested in return for promises of five million tons of coking coal every year, workers still lived without running water in shacks built from packing crates.[14]

The BAM was exceptional only in terms of the attention the Soviet press lavished upon its workers during the Brezhnev era. What the Young Communist League workers suffered in building the BAM, others endured in even larger measure in the oil and gas fields of Siberia's west. Beginning a decade earlier than the builders of the BAM, the men and women who had gone to open the Urengoi gas fields on the edge of the Arctic Circle, and to tap the huge reserves of oil that flowed beneath the dead lake of Samotlor a few hundred miles to the south, faced similar privations caused by the same callous unconcern on the part of the men who sent them there. As with so much else in Siberia, immense natural wealth was again collected by men and women who lived in the worst conditions imaginable, not because they had no money but because housing, clothing, food, and life's simpler pleasures simply could not be had at any price. Virtually everywhere in the half-million square miles of land that held the treasures of Samotlor and Urengoi, massive riches and mass poverty stood juxtaposed. As always, when it came to fulfilling the production quotas of the Five-Year Plans in these new lands, Soviet planners put the needs of Siberia's people in a very distant second place.

51

The Riches of Samotlor and Urengoi

Ever since the fur trade moved beyond the Enisei in the middle of the seventeenth century, the Russians had avoided the marshy wilderness that lay along the lower reaches of the Ob River. As they followed their reindeer in search of the lichens that fed them, handfuls of native Ostiaks and Voguls (known in Soviet times as Khanty and Mansi) had continued to scatter their settlements of deerskin tents across these lands, but even they had found better grazing lands farther to the south and east. At best, the Ob River served as a highway to Siberia's more distant, desirable parts. Russian explorers and trappers had made their first expeditions to the fur-rich lands of Mangazeia in the early 1600s by way of the Ob River, and others had followed them along its tributaries to build the outpost of Turukhansk on the Enisei River not long after that.

Once flourishing centers of trade set at the edge of the Arctic tundra, Mangazeia and Turukhansk slipped into obscurity when the fur trade moved on. The eighteenth and nineteenth centuries saw traffic across Siberia shift farther south as Russians moved up the Ob to the Narym and crossed overland to Eniseisk or followed the Ob still farther upstream to Tomsk before crossing the shorter land bridge to Krasnoiarsk. By the time Catherine the Great's governors built the Great Siberian Post Road in the 1760s and 1770s, Mangazeia had disappeared. Shrunk to a tiny hamlet, Turukhansk survived at the beginning of the twentieth century only as a remote place of exile.

So this out-of-the-way part of Siberia remained until the late 1950s, when a group of Soviet geologists uncovered traces of the oil and natural-gas reservoirs that eventually came to be recognized as some of the world's richest. These first small discoveries gave no hint of the vastness of the source whence they flowed, and they therefore failed to appeal to Khrushchev's passion for huge projects that might serve as monuments to Soviet achievement. Already convinced that opening the virgin lands and building the Bratsk Power Station offered the best possibilities for transforming Siberian life, Khrushchev had little interest in men who wanted to probe remote forests and barren tundras for oil and gas deposits, which, his advisers warned him, would almost certainly turn out to be too small to justify the cost of development. Gosplan—the huge, unwieldy, poorly coordinated central state economic planning agency whose inept efforts had crippled the Soviet economy for decades—had no intention of wasting resources on further explorations by men who had become known in influential Moscow circles as the "Siberian fanatics."[1] During the late 1950s and early 1960s, the men who believed that an ocean of oil flowed beneath the Ob marshlands could not even get supplies through official channels to equip their expeditions.

Even if oil could be found, the bureaucrats cloistered in the sprawling Gosplan offices looking out on Moscow's Marx Prospekt had no interest in grappling with the problems connected with drilling through thousands of feet of permafrost in a land where winter temperatures fell to nearly −60° Centigrade. Beginning a few hundred miles south of the Arctic Circle and reaching well above it to the Iamal peninsula, which jutted into the Kara Sea, these barren lands were lonely, empty, and cold. A traveler—or even a small group of travelers—could cross them with difficulty, but the many rivers and marshes made it next to impossible to build roads and railroads. Whoever drilled for oil and gas there would have to ship in all of the necessary heavy equipment between the time the ice thawed in May and the freeze in September or do without it until the next year. In a nation whose planners had gained worldwide renown for their inability to meet schedules and anticipate needs, such problems could cripple the best of efforts.

But the "Siberian fanatics" insisted that the treasures hidden beneath the wilderness of the middle and lower Ob valley could transform Soviet life in ways that behemoth dams and drought-ridden fields could not. Led by Aleksandr Trofimuk, a stubborn and resourceful scientist from the Academy of Sciences, they continued to press for the wherewithal to probe the remote corners of Siberia's northwestern wilderness. No iron or coal had ever been found there, and only scattered handfuls of gold. Was it possible that these lands, thought worthless for so long, could hold huge stores of the liquid black gold that had become the lifeblood of modern industrial societies?

After a few grudgingly permitted expeditions during the last years of the Khrushchev era, explorations during the mid-1960s uncovered oil and natural-gas fields the likes of which not even the most daring scientists had imagined. When geologists discovered the huge Samotlor reserves north of Surgut and Nizhnevartovsk in 1968, they estimated them to hold up to two billion tons of proved and probable reserves of crude oil, only to learn a few years later that they held twice that amount. At about the same time, others had hoped that the lands north of the Arctic Circle around Urengoi might hold up to six trillion cubic meters of high-quality natural gas. Ten trillion cubic meters turned out to be a more accurate figure.

No sooner had the discovery of natural gas been reported at Urengoi than other reports from lands even farther north in the Taz and Iamal peninsulas marked the location of huge gas wells that held trillions of cubic meters more. Because Soviet oil and natural-gas statistics have been published only sporadically since 1938, there is still no way of knowing how much these wells actually hold, but the gas field at Urengoi is certainly the largest in the world, and the oil fields of Samotlor are nearly in the same category. Just as the reserves of the Soviet Union's oldest wells in Azerbaijan and the middle Volga valley were beginning to shrink, the persistent "Siberian fanatics" had uncovered new reserves far richer than the ones that were being consumed.[2]

Difficult as it had been, discovering some of the world's richest deposits of oil and natural gas proved to be much easier than extracting, processing, and shipping them to potential users. In 1970, the Tiumen Region was producing twenty-eight million tons of oil, roughly four fifths of Siberia's entire output. Fifteen years later, the same region was producing eleven twelfths of Siberia's oil, but instead of the twenty-eight million tons of 1970, the output of 1984 had risen to thirteen times that amount. To draw that much raw crude oil from beneath the permafrost, tens of millions of meters of exploratory holes had been drilled and thousands of wells brought into service. In the Urengoi fields farther north, natural gas had to be released from reservoirs as deep as two and a half miles, again through permafrost and in winter temperatures that were among Siberia's lowest. How was the permafrost to be kept from melting and shifting beneath the weight of oil rigs? How could gas and oil be kept at the proper temperatures for processing and shipping? Drilling wells into such terrain required new technology that involved, first of all, building huge artificial islands of sand dredged from the bottoms of lakes and rivers to shield the tundra beneath. Only then could the heavy rigs be put into place and the drilling begun.[3]

Drilling and pumping under such conditions were a nightmare made worse by bureaucrats who shipped drilling equipment designed for the deserts of Central Asia to the far north. But fully as complex as the drilling were the tasks of laying pipelines and building railroads to move the gas and oil to refineries and processing plants. The first pipeline in the Ob River lands was built to give the relatively small Shaim oil field access to the Trans-Siberian Railroad by connecting it with Tiumen. After that, a series of pipelines began to link the larger fields at Samotlor with refineries at Omsk, Angarsk, Tomsk, Tobolsk, and European Russia. By 1984, no less than 365 million tons of crude oil were flowing from the huge oil fields at Samotlor and slightly smaller ones at Noiabrsk, Kholmogorsk, Mamontovo, and Krasnoleninsk. By that time, Soviet planners were expecting to add another eighty or ninety million tons to their output before 1990.[4]

An even larger and more extensive network of pipelines had to be built to send natural gas from Urengoi, Iamburg, and the Iamal peninsula to southern Siberia and European Russia. Here the Russians built fewer pipelines and treatment plants than needed, although the massive increase in natural-gas production would have made it difficult to keep pace in any case. In 1984, the gas fields of the Tiumen Region, which had been producing fewer than 10 billion cubic meters of natural gas just fifteen years earlier, increased their output to 326 billion cubic meters. Within a decade, Soviet planners spoke of raising the output at Iamburg, the gas center on the Taz peninsula that had been opened only in 1983, so that it would produce more than half that amount.[5]

More and more, the production of natural gas and oil from the Tiumen Region was being geared to bring in desperately needed hard currency for the Soviet Union with little thought given to the ecological dangers that massively increased output might produce. Especially in the Iamal peninsula, that New York State–sized thumb of tundra sticking out into the Kara Sea, Soviet experts were warning, as one commentator remarked, that "intensive development may cause this peninsula to melt away." The tundra ecology was so fragile that the whole peninsula was "almost like an iceberg with a green skin stretched over it."[6] What impact the breakup of the Soviet Union now will have upon that process remains anyone's guess. Unlike such stern predecessors as Stalin, Khrushchev, and Brezhnev, the leaders of present-day Russia now face vehement opposition from those environmentalists whose protests Soviet authorities ignored for so long, but how they will respond is far from certain. Those who would protect the tundra by drilling more slowly for gas and oil face an inglorious history of environmental unconcern in high places. Combined with an urgent need for foreign technology to develop the fields more safely and a desperate desire not to disrupt one of Russia's major sources of hard currency, these forces may well overwhelm those who see Siberia's tundra as a priceless natural treasure.

Certainly, the discoveries at Samotlor and Urengoi have already begun to transform lands that were once remote and inaccessible. Tiumen, the famed "Gateway to Siberia" until it was bypassed by the Trans-Siberian Railroad in the 1890s, has now become the entry to the oil and gas fields that lie to its north. Long since dwarfed by Sverdlovsk, Cheliabinsk, and Omsk, Tiumen's population tripled during the quarter century after 1960, as it became a hub that connected the wild lands to its north with the rest of Siberia and the Soviet Union. Food, supplies, equipment, and workers all had to pass through Tiumen. And, just as the men from Siberia's eastern goldfields had poured into Irkutsk to spend the fruits of half a year's work in a fortnight's celebration in the days of the tsars, so workers from the Samotlor and Urengoi fields came to Tiumen to renew their contact with the world they had left behind.

Slightly farther north, Tobolsk, which stood very near the site of Ermak's victory over the armies of Kuchum Khan, enjoyed a similar revival. A trading center like Tiumen in the olden days, Tobolsk had also been a place of exile through which everyone sent to Siberia had been obliged to pass until the 1870s. The fallen Tsar Nicholas II, his wife, and his children had spent the winter of 1917–1918 in Tobolsk before being sent on to Ekaterinburg, but the city had never flourished in Soviet times. At the time of Khrushchev's fall, it had fewer than forty thousand inhabitants. Then, the population of Tobolsk more than doubled in two decades, largely because of a huge petrochemical complex built there in the 1970s to produce synthetic rubber products and plastic resins.[7]

Although Tobolsk and Tiumen both lay farther south, a cluster of boomtowns grew up within the Tiumen Region's oil and gas lands themselves. Set on the western and eastern edges of the Samotlor oil fields, Surgut and Nizhnevartovsk grew from tiny frontier settlements to cities of nearly a quarter of a million each between 1965 and 1985. Both became key links or the new rail and pipe lines the Russians built to supply the Samotlor and Urengoi fields, and both continue to exhibit reminders of the uncontrolled growth that Soviet bureaucratic planning claimed to be able to avoid. In keeping with Brezhnev's perennial insistence upon putting production ahead of public services, housing and shops came much later to Surgut and Nizhnevartovsk than workers did. As late as 1985, workers were still living in trailers and shacks without running water and electricity.

In Surgut and Nizhnevartovsk, rusting junk still mixes with the pre-fabricated cast concrete buildings that sprouted side by side with tattered shacks built of scrap lumber and packing crates. Roads still remain unpaved, and heat comes from primitive boilers that proudly pour pollution skyward as a sign of Soviet-style progress. In natural-gas boomtowns like Iamburg and Novyi Urengoi, the same clutter—and the same massive day-to-day misery amid vast sources of natural wealth—accompanied the Soviet efforts to reap the world's largest reserves of natural gas. As at other remote Siberian projects in the 1970s and 1980s, Soviet planners tried to lure workers into rough lands with promises of high pay, only to have the workers who took the bait refuse to stay on without life's basic amenities.[8]

If Siberia's workers suffered hardships at Urengoi and Samotlor, so did the Arctic environment. Because the Soviet Union did not produce off-road vehicles with wide soft tires that could cross the tundra without cutting it, the spring and summer landscape quickly became a sea of mud churned up by heavy equipment passing over a fragile tundra that takes hundreds of years to heal its wounds.[9] Now mixed with oil that has oozed from thousands of wells, puddles of tundra meltwater fill every tire track and depression with black, watery slime. Pollution does its work quickly here, not just on the tundra but in the rivers, which regenerate very slowly in the cold temperatures. With more than a hundred and fifty tons of sturgeon being taken by local fishermen every year, the lower reaches of the Ob River used to be one of the most fertile sturgeon fishing grounds in Siberia. Now spilled oil has poisoned the fish and reduced the catch to almost nothing.[10] In 1990, some Western sources estimated that oil spills caused by improperly laid pipelines, faulty equipment, leaking wells, and careless workers (who forgot to close valves and shut off faucets) amounted to some seven million barrels a year.[11]

Despite Soviet leaders' oft-repeated promises of progress and a higher quality of life, massive pollution may well stand as their major legacy. If so, the leakage from oil wells and pipelines make up only a small part of a disastrously large array of human and environmental crises. Pollution from plants built during the eras of Stalin, Khrushchev, and Brezhnev, floods of unprocessed human waste from new and poorly planned cities, immense quantities of chemicals leaching into rivers and streams from improperly applied fertilizers, and vast quantities of chemical and nuclear waste strewn in out-of-the-way places all threaten to produce the largest man-made disaster in human history. Once honored as symbols of Soviet industrial might, Magnitogorsk, Cheliabinsk, Novokuznetsk, Kemerovo, Norilsk, and a score of other cities that arose in the Siberian wilderness after the Bolshevik Revolution have now become centers of pollution so toxic that the population in them enjoys a life expectancy lower than the people of Paraguay and suffers an infant mortality rate that stands on a par with that of China and Sri Lanka.[12]

Living mainly to fulfill the quotas of today and believing for too long in their power to transform the reality of tomorrow by proclaiming it to be different from what it really was, Siberia's Soviet masters poisoned its water, air, and soil while proclaiming their respect for Nature. "When historians finally conduct an autopsy on Soviet Communism," two experts recently wrote as they surveyed the future through a glass that had turned almost too dark to see, "they may reach the verdict of death by ecocide."[13] Exploited for the benefit of others, drained of its wealth, and poisoned to a point beyond which complete recovery may no longer be possible, Siberia may bear the burden of that terrible verdict most heavily of all.

52

Siberia's Soviet Heritage

During the 1980s, the Siberian industrial centers, which had been the pride of Stalin, Khrushchev, and Brezhnev, came to be recognized as some of the most polluted places in the world. Thick clouds of sulfur dioxide and industrial dust hung perpetually over Kemerovo and Novokuznetsk, two of Stalin's proudest achievements in the Kuzbass, just as they did over the city of the Magnetic Mountain at Magnitogorsk. At Bratsk, the village-turned-industrial-giant, people choked on the fumes from the great aluminum smelter that Khrushchev's power station had brought into being. Norilsk, the great industrial complex built by NKVD slaves to mine the rich uranium, copper, nickel, and platinum deposits of the lands above the Arctic Circle, suffered the dirtiest air of any Siberian city. The quarter of a million people who lived there in the 1980s enjoyed the dubious honor of sharing among themselves more than two and a quarter million tons of industrial pollutants that its mills poured into the atmosphere every year.[1] "The sickest children in the country," the writer of an article in the Soviet magazine *Chemistry and Life* reported sadly, "live at Norilsk."[2]

Everywhere, Siberia's Soviet masters had transformed the fragile ecology of the tundra and taiga that for tens of thousands of years had boasted some of the planet's purest water, air, and soil into some of the most noxious surroundings on earth. By the late 1980s, it had become clear that some of the most vaunted Soviet achievements had in fact been the products of callous decisions by leaders anxious to barter their citizens' health and comfort in order to continue their self-proclaimed mission to surpass the West. Now painful reminders that the Bolshevik dream had failed, these had not been milestones on the road to building a society in which the well-being of citizens took precedence. Instead, they became a series of smeary blots on the first authoritative map of air pollution that the Soviet Academy of Sciences published in 1990.

After more than seven decades of promises of a better world to come, Siberia's Soviet heritage combined a Third World standard of living with a level of public health that was scarcely better than in the days of the tsars. Siberia's pollution stretched from the Urals to the Pacific, and from the Arctic Ocean to the mountains beyond Central Asia. Studies warned anyone who dared to read them that Siberia's great rivers—even the rushing Angara that poured in a torrent from the southern end of Lake Baikal—had become dangerously polluted. Now called "an aqueduct for poisons,"[3] the Angara carried 257,000 tons of chlorides, 140,000 tons of sulfates, 10,000 tons of nitrates, and 30,000 tons of organic wastes every year from factories built along its banks in the days of Khrushchev and Brezhnev.[4]

Not surprisingly, the center of Siberia's pollution and the center of the Bolshevik vision of a brave new world beyond the Urals coincided. Making a wide sweep from the Ural industrial centers at Cheliabinsk and Sverdlovsk (its tsarist name of Ekaterinburg was restored in 1990) through Magnitogorsk, Novokuznetsk, and Kemerovo, what has been described as "a vast toxic rust belt of mines and metallurgical combines"[5] stretched across the western third of Siberia from the northwest to the southeast. From not far beyond its eastern end, the ancient Andronovo people had ruled the Minusinsk and Altai lands in the long-ago days before the Huns had burst out of Mongolia.[6] No more than four hundred miles to the south and just beyond the southeastern limits of what continues to be the heart of the Siberian industrial fortress that Stalin had built to arm the Soviet Union, the remnants of the ancient Silk Road still formed an enduring monument to the vital lifeline that once connected China with the trading centers of ancient Persia and Rome. The romance of the Silk Road had survived for the better part of three millennia; that of Stalin's effort faded in less than a sixtieth of that time.

In the 1930s, the rise of Magnitogorsk, Novokuznetsk, Kemerovo, and Cheliabinsk had stirred the imaginations of thousands of men and women who, believing the poetic slogan "We were born to make a fairy tale a reality,"[7] had greeted the appearance of each gigantic factory city as new proof that a better future was on the way. At some point beyond the present, life would become easier, with the hardest work being done by machines, which would lift the burden of heavy labor from the shoulders of Soviet men and women forever. That vision had drawn Jack Scott to Magnitogorsk from Madison, Wisconsin, and it had become the shining point of light around which he and his Russian wife, Masha, had built their lives as Young Communists. In much the same way, America's "Big Bill" Haywood had devoted several years to recruiting workers from the United States for the Autonomous Industrial Colony of the Kuzbass, where, while struggling against the emptiness of the Siberian steppe, the dream of building a world in which working men and women would enjoy the full fruits of their labor stood forth as a beacon for all who dared to follow it.

As the huge blast furnaces and mills of Siberia's "rust belt" had taken shape, such men and women had cheered the great chimneys that poured smoke skyward as monuments to a brave new and better world. Open hearths became the soaring cathedrals of Siberia's modern age, and the smoking, humming industrial city became one of the most revered icons of socialist life. Soaring columns of airborne soot stood as symbols of hope. Gigantic furnaces, huge open-pit mines, and endless blocks of apartment buildings built of modern steel and concrete but without sewers became living proof that the Bolshevik vision was coming to life. Poets spoke not of Nature's beauty, but of smokestacks and steam turbines. Novelists wrote of hydroelectric dams and blast furnaces, and painters filled their canvases with factory chimneys belching the rich yellow-black smoke of progress. In winter, the smoke lay parallel to the earth, kept from rising high by the weight of Siberia's Arctic air. In summer it soared toward the heavens, spreading its clouds of poisons across tens of thousands of square miles of the Eurasian heartland to prove that the fetters of capitalism were being broken by toiling men and women who had vowed to build a better world. "The Magnitogorsk steel plant," one Soviet writer announced proudly in 1932, "is living proof of what Bolsheviks are able to achieve."[8]

During and after the Brezhnev era, the promise became as poisonous as the vision of progress had been alluring. In Novokuznetsk, clouds of dust perpetually clogged the lungs of the six hundred thousand humans who lived and worked within reach of the very mills that had been cheered as symbols of Soviet achievement half a century earlier. Now ranked as the fifth most polluted city in what was once the Soviet Union, Novokuznetsk boasts nearly six hundred times more benzopyrene in its air than the allowable maximum, and its people suffer lung cancer at rates that are a third higher than the norm for other Soviet industrial cities. As people began to ask if the proud mills that once armored half the tanks the Red Army sent into combat during World War II even need to run at all, their chimneys continued to spout almost nine hundred thousand tons of pollutants into the atmosphere. Did the Soviet Union need the steel that the filthy foundries and mills of Novokuznetsk produced? Probably not. It would be better, one of Gorbachev's advisers argued at one point, to make fewer (but better) tractors and combines and save the steel used to make so many poor ones.[9]

Not far from Novokuznetsk, planners of the Stalin era built almost two thirds of the factories of Kemerovo in residential neighborhoods, upon which they continue to pour a rich mixture of sulfur dioxide, hydrogen sulfide, solid phenols, sulfuric acid, and nitrous oxide at the rate of more than eight tons an hour. At modern-day Kemerovo, the air has become so foul that it would require a million additional cubic meters of fresh air every day just to get its nitrous oxide content down to a safe level. Once the route of trappers heading east and the artery that carried prison barges on the last leg of their journey from Tiumen to Tomsk, the Tom River has become a sewer into which Kemerovo's mills now pour forty-two times the allowable amount of oil products, thirty-four times the formaldehyde, forty times the arsenic, five times the nitrates, and more than twice the phenol. Soaring rates of chronic bronchitis, kidney disease, and endocrine system disorders are the daily lot of Kemerovo's half a million workers, whose children suffer extraordinarily high rates of retardation.[10] Most would rather live somewhere else; for every twenty people who arrive, nineteen others leave.[11]

In Nizhnii Tagil, the site of Nikita and Akinfii Demidov's early foundries, a ton and a half of industrial pollutants confronts each of the city's four hundred thousand people every year. Cement dust, so thick that residents can feel it between their teeth, and excessive quantities of nitrogen dioxide, ammonia, and formaldehyde continue to cause an epidemic of childhood diseases and birth defects. Still farther north in Norilsk, where once proud smokestacks pour 1.2 million tons of sulfur dioxide into the atmosphere, children suffer some of the highest rates of blood and kidney diseases anywhere in the former Soviet Union, while the city's men have the highest incidence of lung cancer in the world. Workers in the foundries of Norilsk wear gas masks from the time they start work until they finish, and all the berries and mushrooms within a twenty-mile radius of the city are toxic.[12] "The Soviet Union is an exceptional country," one of its economists remarked bitterly not long before it broke apart. "Exceptions were given to build a lot of polluting enterprises."[13] The poisons of Kemerovo, Novokuznetsk, Nizhnii Tagil, and Norilsk all demonstrate how unexceptional those exceptions have been.

If the dream that lured Siberia's builders of the 1930s and 1940s has soured in these cities, it has turned completely rotten in Magnitogorsk. Proclaimed by its founders to be a "garden city" in the making, Magnitogorsk now stands prominently among what some experts have called "the most poisoned and poisonous of Soviet industrial cities." Every year, its open-hearth furnaces belch forth ten tons of pollutants for every man, woman, and child living there. One fourth of the city's mothers deliver children with congenital birth defects, and only one infant in four is born completely healthy. Slightly more than half of the 438,000 residents of Magnitogorsk suffer from respiratory illnesses, including two thirds of its children, who visit special clinics every day to receive "oxygen cocktails" made of fruit juice, herbs, and sugar laced with pure oxygen. Yet, to care for these legions of sick, Magnitogorsk has only half of the physicians it is supposed to have. Doctors have been leaving, not only because of the city's unhealthful environment but because they can find no place there to live.[14] "We whipped it like a beaten horse," one fatalistic worker said of the great mill that Jack Scott and his comrades had raised from the empty steppe in the 1930s. "What we have now is what we have."[15]

Siberia's Soviet heritage comprises more than just the products of the gigantomania that ruled the years of Stalin and the time of Khrushchev. All across Siberia, smaller industries have also left their stain, each connected to the rest by a telltale trail of pollution. Every year, nine tons of pollution for each man, woman, and child pour from the smokestacks of Karabash, a town on Siberia's western edge, filling the lungs of its eighteen thousand copper-foundry workers with soot and rendering one out of every two of its young men unfit for military service. In 1987, the town's rate of first-time cancer diagnoses reached 3.3 per thousand, nearly twice the rate in the United States.[16] "Why don't you quit, get out of here?" one worker was asked. "Where to?" he replied. "It's the same everywhere."[17]

Yet some places are worse. Almost forty years ago a failed cooling mechanism at Kyshtym, a Siberian nuclear weapons site near Cheliabinsk, spewed between seventy and eighty tons of radioactive material over an area that, after being kept secret for thirty-two years, was introduced to the world in 1989 as the "East Ural Radioactive Trace." In 1958, a year after the Kyshtym accident, eleven thousand people had to be evacuated and farming banned. Now there are reports of high rates of leukemia and other forms of cancer among the survivors, even though Soviet officials insisted at the time that "[no] deviations in the incidence of diseases of the blood" had been detected.

Not far from Kyshtym, an even worse disaster occurred at Lake Karachai. Many years after the fact, it was discovered that officials at a top-secret weapons-making plant had pumped nuclear wastes containing "nearly twenty-four times the radioactive content of the debris released by the Chernobyl reactor failure" into the shallow lake's bottom. For years, the waste leached into the region's groundwater and poisoned anyone who ignored the warning signs that forbade swimming. Then, in the summer of 1967, a windy drought dried the lake and blew the radioactive dust onto the lands to its east. More than twenty years later, radiation levels in that part of Siberia still stand at 600 roentgens an hour, enough, one report stated, "to provide a lethal dose" in sixty minutes.[18]

Nuclear wastes buried under water (or simply poured into it) form another deadly part of Siberia's Soviet heritage. Although the disaster at Lake Karachai may have been one of a kind, the once pure waters of Siberia's Arctic and Pacific coasts are now also laced with radioactive pollutants dumped from Soviet nuclear submarines that continue to kill fish and other forms of wildlife in the millions.[19] For years, Soviet officials insisted that the mass kills reported periodically by foreign ships in these waters were natural incidents that gave no cause for concern. Now experts are telling a very different tale. "The USSR has 500 million cubic meters of radioactive open water," a high-level commission reported in 1990. This could, "in theory," its authors warned, "cause irreparable harm to 7.5 million people who live near the Iset, Irtysh, and Ob Rivers."[20]

The impact of Siberia's Soviet heritage does not stop with the people living in its industrial centers or along its polluted coasts and waterways for, as the authors of a brilliant recent study about Soviet environmental pollution remind their readers, "ecocide is not just an urban phenomenon."[21] When the near failure of Khrushchev's virgin lands project convinced the masters of Soviet agriculture to pour massive quantities of fertilizers, herbicides, and pesticides upon their tired fields, large sections of Siberia's southwest suffered ruinous amounts of chemical poisoning. In particular, DDT, which the Soviet Union banned in 1970 with considerable fanfare because the United States had not yet outlawed it (and did not until two years later), was widely used in secret for another twenty years. Until well into the 1980s, DDT was used around Kemerovo to kill forest ticks that carried encephalitis, with the result that the fish in the region's rivers now contain an average of nearly one percent DDT by weight. Around Sverdlovsk/Ekaterinburg to the north and west, the land has absorbed such huge quantities of highly toxic insecticides that numbers of workers have died while picking onions and weeding carrots and turnips.[22]

All across Siberia and the lands touching its southern edge, such poisoning of the land grew steadily worse throughout the 1970s and 1980s. Around the dying Aral Sea, once the center of the great Muslim cultures that the armies of Chingis Khan overwhelmed so long ago, chemicals poured on the cotton fields began to turn the land into desert. "There is no water for the people," one novelist wrote in 1983. "Where are we to find water for the trees?"[23] By the mid-1980s, food and water in that region had become so toxic that four out of every five pregnant women suffered from anemia and new mothers could not nurse their infants for fear of poisoning them. The land itself was drying up. By the late 1980s, the Aral Sea was shrinking so rapidly because of Soviet efforts to divert the waters that fed it that the fishing port of Muynak, to which over a hundred million pounds of fish were brought each year in the 1950s, stood more than forty miles inland.[24] It is an appalling inheritance, the irresponsible product of policies made by cynical men. The lands of Kazakhstan and Uzbekistan, one high official told an All-Union Party Conference in 1988, had begun "a triumphant march backward."[25]

At the center of the tragedy of Siberia's Soviet heritage stands Lake Baikal, the "pearl of Siberia," its "holy sea," and a symbol that every inheritance holds something of value. More than any other part of Siberia, Lake Baikal was spared the benefits and burdens of Soviet-style progress until the late 1950s. During the first forty years of Bolshevik power, the size of Irkutsk more than tripled, and during those days industries took hold along the banks of the city's Angara River. But since the Angara was Baikal's only exit, it kept the pollution from these new mills away from the lake until the late 1950s, when the men from Moscow decided to launch a great socialist leap forward that would bring industry to the shores of Lake Baikal itself. Although this was done over the objections of the entire Siberian Division of the Academy of Sciences, the Communist party proclaimed its effort to be a triumph in social engineering that would bring into the modern world the nomadic Buriat natives, who lived much as they had in the days of Chingis Khan.[26]

So-called strategic national interest, not concern for the Buriats' well-being, underlay this new wave of Soviet progress. Anxious to produce heavy-duty cellulose tire cord for air force fighters and bombers, Siberia's Kremlin masters had decided to build a huge processing plant at Baikalsk on the lake's southern tip to take advantage of its especially pure water. A few years later, a second plant rose at Selinginsk on the lake's southeastern shore to process the wood pulp needed at Baikalsk. Ironically, even before the plant at Baikalsk was finished, the Soviet Union had no need for its main product, for petroleum-based cord had replaced that made from cellulose as the standard for military planes and heavy trucks throughout the world. By the 1970s, the Baikalsk plant had shifted over to turning out civilian tires, ordinary twine, wrapping paper, and nutrient yeast, none of which had any strategic value and all of which could have been manufactured almost anywhere else in the Soviet Union.[27]

For Lake Baikal, the result of manufacturing large quantities of these ordinary products was to have tens of thousands of tons of untreated waste pumped into the waters at its southern end. In response to rising protests from concerned laymen and scientists (including a warning from the famous novelist Mikhail Sholokhov that "later generations will not forgive us if we do not conserve this glorious sea"),[28] the Soviet government in 1975 banned any discussion of ecological questions in the press and ignored its promises to process the wastes thoroughly before pumping them into the lake. In 1986, when the defenders of Lake Baikal took advantage of the first stirrings of *glasnost* to speak out against the cellulose works, the Baikalsk plant pumped almost sixty thousand tons of improperly treated waste into the lake. Two years later, it dumped nearly three times more. The same year, in combination with the plant at Selinginsk, Baikalsk also poured nearly a hundred thousand tons of pollutants into the atmosphere.[29]

In quantitative terms, such pollution seemed very minor compared with the destruction the Soviets had wrought upon Siberia's rivers, the tundras of the Tiumen Region, and the virgin lands to the south. All told, the pollutants pumped from Baikalsk during almost a quarter of a century touched fewer than eight square miles of the bottom of a lake whose surface area is more than fifteen hundred times that large. But, as a report from the Academy of Sciences officially warned, although "Baikal is not easy to pollute, it will be impossible to clean up."[30] Dependent upon hundreds of billions of tiny whiskered crustacean *epischura* to purify its waters by consuming algae and bacteria, Baikal seemed certain to turn foul if the wastes from the Baikalsk and Selinginsk mills interrupted the *epischura*'s fragile life cycle. Within the tiny eight-square-mile area touched by the by-products of cellulose-making, scientists found that the *epischura* was dying out and that worms and algae were taking its place.[31] "Nature is taking its revenge," one of Baikal's defenders wrote. "By destroying Baikal, we are destroying the basis of our own life. . . . Life," he concluded, "first appeared in water—pure water, not water that has first gone through a pulp plant."[32]

"We," in fact, meant the Russian-Soviet masters who had exploited Siberia for so long. The fight to save Lake Baikal rekindled a sense of division between east and west and helped give a common identity to the "Siberians" that was far broader than any known in earlier times. Who were the "Russians" and who were the "Siberians"? The answer had seemed obvious in the days of Chingis Khan, Ermak, and the great fur rush, but it was becoming less clear by the time of Shelikhov, Speranskii, and Kennan's journey. By the 1870s, "Siberians" could no longer be defined simply as Buriats, Iakuts, Chukchi, or members of a hundred other tribes whose ancestors had lived in the lands east of the Urals before the Russians came. "Siberians" now had to include onetime exiles, Russian settlers, and any others who thought of "Siberia" as a land separated from European Russia by history and destiny.

That had been the view of Nikolai Iadrintsev, the brilliant nineteenth-century ethnographer, historian, and journalist who had insisted that the "Siberian" was a "unique ethnic type." Even those who had been born west of the Urals but had come to Siberia to build new lives, Iadrintsev had insisted, thought of "Russians" as foreigners and defined themselves in terms of their new land. A type of rugged individualism not often seen in European Russia ruled their lives.[33] Men and women like Iadrintsev had believed that Siberians must inevitably go a different way from their Russian masters, a view that was shared by other prominent Russians who felt drawn to Siberia. "Just as America separated from its metropolis," the great short story writer and playwright Anton Chekhov once wrote to a friend, "I am convinced that Siberia will someday totally separate from Russia."[34]

The coming of the Trans-Siberian Railroad had tied Siberia and Russia closer together and postponed any debate about how and under what conditions Siberians and Russians might follow separate paths. A quarter century later, the Bolshevik Revolution had turned the relations between "Russia" and "Siberia" firmly back onto the course they had taken in earlier times, when the men in Moscow had worked to squeeze every advantage from Siberia that they possibly could. Siberia's minerals, its forests, the power of its rivers, and, as in the case of Lake Baikal, even the purity of its water, were to be used to the advantage of the Russians, just as its furs, iron, and gold had been used in tsarist times. For more than half a century, Moscow's new rulers had spoken and the

"Siberians" had obeyed. Regional party officials, commandants of forced-labor camps, directors of collective farms, and factory managers spoke with all the absolute authority of any military governor of tsarist times, but an undercurrent of thought similar to Iadrintsev's had survived nonetheless. With the coming of *glasnost* in the 1980s, this sense of regionalism had again come to the fore, and, as in earlier times, it called for restructuring Siberia's relationship to Russia, beginning by reconsidering the meaning of "Russian" and "Siberian."

This task was taken up by a group of Siberian village prose writers, the most prominent of whom is Valentin Rasputin, a passionate "Siberian" patriot who nonetheless sees Siberia's future as a part of Russia's. For Rasputin, patriotism does not mean separating Siberia from Russia, but "serving Russia by way of Siberia."[35] The relationship between the two, he argues, has to be different, based more upon trust, mutual benefit, and respect for that rare brand of individualism that seems so common among "Siberians" and so rare among "Russians." The time has passed when Siberia can be exploited by Russians, its wealth seized and carried away to be used west of the Urals. Now, he argues, Siberia and Russia must be equals, with an equal respect for each other's people, history, and environment. Siberia can no longer serve as Russia's "appendage or rental property," Rasputin insists. Siberia cannot continue to be the victim of a way of thinking that decrees that although the Russians "might use up, wear out, or squander [something] in their own economic sphere today, they would find something to replace it with tomorrow in Siberia."[36]

Rasputin's is not the only modern-day vision, nor is it necessarily the best, for the rules that have shaped Siberia's course since the days of Ermak may no longer apply in the uncertain world that has emerged after Gorbachev. Definitions of nationality, wealth, and Siberia's friends and enemies may be very different in the twenty-first century than they are now, and it is by no means certain what forces for change will guide those Siberians who look east rather than west. Vladivostok, after all, is nearer to San Francisco than to Moscow, and Beijing and Tokyo are much closer than that. In that context, the sort of independence from Russia that Chekhov and Iadrintsev once thought possible could still become Siberia's path in the turmoil that inevitably lies ahead in the lands that were once a part of the Soviet Union. It is important to remember that a Siberia entirely separate from Russia would be almost a third again as large as the United States, and it would be even richer in natural wealth.

With or without Russia, Siberia now has the potential to shape the course of world events in ways we cannot yet determine. Within the boundaries of this formidable continent, distance takes on different dimensions and so does time. These all foster unique visions of the past and present that people unaccustomed to Siberia's vastness find awkward to comprehend and even more difficult to act upon. Like Lake Baikal, which has survived longer than any other lake but remains the world's most unstable body of water because of its position in one of our planet's most complicated seismic fault zones, Siberia's future remains tangled in contradictions that are in part the product of the experiences of the men and women who have shaped her past and present. Were not people drawn to Siberia "to feel in themselves the boundary between the temporal and the eternal, the inconstant and the true, the ruined and the preserved?" Rasputin once asked. "We have only one Siberia," he concluded in 1984. "Here the human race is now being tested to see what it has become in the present and what can be expected of it in the future."[37]

Acknowledgments

Among the many libraries, archives, and institutions to which I am indebted for help over the past quarter century, the following come most readily to mind: The Academy of Sciences of the USSR, Leningrad (now St. Petersburg) Branch; Archives de la Guerre, Service Historique de l'Armée de la Terre, Château de Vincennes, Vincennes; The Bakhmetieff Archive of Russian and East European History and Culture, Columbia University, New York; The Central State Historical Archives, Leningrad/St. Petersburg; The Fulbright-Hays Faculty Research Abroad Program, U.S. Department of Education, Washington, D.C.; The Harriman Institute, Columbia University, New York; The Hoover Institution, Stanford, California; The Imperial War Museum, London; The International Research and Exchanges Board, Washington, D.C.; The Kennan Institution, Woodrow Wilson Center, The Smithsonian, Washington, D.C.; The Library of Congress, Washington, D.C.; The Lenin Library, Moscow; The National Endowment for the Humanities, Washington, D.C.; The Russian and East European Center, University of Illinois at Urbana-Champaign, Urbana; The Regenstein Library, The University of Chicago, Chicago; St. Antony's College, Oxford; The Saltykov-Shchedrin Public Library, Leningrad/St. Petersburg; and the Slavic Library, University of Helsinki, Helsinki.

Beyond the help of these many benefactors, I have incurred larger personal and intellectual debts that require further comment. It continues to be a great pleasure to acknowledge my intellectual debt to Marc Raeff, now Bakhmetieff Professor of Russian History Emeritus at Columbia University, whose pioneering work on Mikhail Speranskii first drew my attention to Siberia more than three decades ago and whose ideas about the history of the Russian Empire continue to influence my own.

Among all the other learned men and women with whom I have had the privilege of discussing the problems of Siberia's past and present in Moscow, St. Petersburg, Helsinki, Paris, Oxford, London, New York, Urbana, Stanford, and Washington, D.C., over the years, I am most grateful of all to Professor James Gibson of the Department of Geography at York University. A friend of nearly thirty years' standing who also is one of the world's leading experts on Siberian geography, Jim read through an earlier version of this book to point out ways in which it could be strengthened and made more precise. To say that I have benefited from his generosity is an understatement.

At the University of Illinois Library, the Slavic Reference Service's Helen Sullivan deserves a special note of thanks. Able to locate the "unfindable" and supply information almost at a moment's notice, Helen is truly a historian's librarian. Having her and her colleague Bob Burger just a phone call away has made writing this book a great deal easier and my progress on it considerably quicker.

Among the people at Northern Illinois University to whom I owe special thanks, Jerrold Zar, Dean of the Graduate School and Associate Provost for Research, came to my aid on several occasions. James Norris, Dean of the College of Liberal Arts and Sciences, offered well-timed logistical support, and his friendship has added much pleasure to the years during which this book has dominated my life. Over the dozen years we have known each other, Jim has probably long since ceased to count the times I have picked his brain about the history of mining, industry, and America's past in general.

Working with Robert Loomis, Vice President and Executive Editor at Random House, has been a delight, the likes of which too few authors have the opportunity to enjoy these days. Bob is a "book builder" in every sense of the word, and I am much indebted to him for the persistent questions and gentle prodding that led me to rethink much and clarify even more as my vision of this book began to come into focus. I also continue to be grateful to Robert Gottlieb, who has been a part of my work for almost fifteen years. As one of those rare literary agents who temper their demands for hard work with enthusiasm and reassurance, Robert has helped me to shape this book since its first brief incarnation in outline form.

As generous and helpful as all these people have been, my wife, Mary, towers above them all. As friend, consultant, and editor par excellence she has given more to me than she will ever know. Although I have not always been ready to accept her advice, I have usually lived to regret those times when I did not. This book has profited immensely from her careful, exacting criticism, which has obliged me to reshape chapters again and again. Dedicating the final product to her is but another small payment against a large (and growing) debt that is forever destined to remain unpaid.

W. Bruce Lincoln

DeKalb, Illinois
All Saints' Day, 1992

Key to Abbreviations

JHG	*Journal of Historical Geography.*
JNCBRAS	*Journal of the North China Branch of the Royal Asiatic Society.*
KA	*Krasnyi Arkhiv.*
KiS	*Katorga i Ssylka: Istoriko-revoliutsionnyi vestnik.*
MERSH	*The Modern Encyclopedia of Russian and Soviet History.*
NG	*The National Geographic Magazine.*
PHR	*Pacific Historical Review.*
PR	*Proletarskaia Revoliutsiia.*
RBS	*Russkii Biograficheskii Slovar'.*
RS	*Russkaia Starina.*
S	*Survey: A Journal of Soviet and East European Studies.*
SIE	*Sovetskaia Istoricheskaia Entsiklopediia.*
SR	*Slavic Review.*
SS	*Soviet Studies: A Quarterly Review of the Social and Economic Institutions of the USSR.*
SSE	*Sibirskaia Sovetskaia Entsiklopediia.*
TsGIAL	Tsentral'nyi Gosudarstvennyi Arkhiv v Leningrade.
VI	*Voprosy Istorii.*

Notes

Prologue

1. George Kennan, *Siberia and the Exile System* (New York, 1891), I, pp. 55–56.
2. Charles Wenyon, *Across Siberia on the Great Post-Road* (London, 1896), p. 26.
3. Quoted in Matthew of Paris, *English History from the Year 1235 to 1273,* translated from the Latin by the Reverend J. A. Giles (London, 1852), I, pp. 469, 471.

Chapter 1. The Fury of God

1. Matthew of Paris, *English History,* I, p. 469.
2. *Ibid.,* p. 131.
3. *Ibid.*
4. Quoted in *ibid.*
5. *Ibid.,* pp. 312–313.
6. Henry W. C. Davis, "Matthew of Paris," *EB* (New York, 1911), XVII, pp. 898.
7. Quoted in Matthew of Paris, *English History,* pp. 471, 469.
8. Edward Gibbon, *The History of the Decline and Fall of the Roman Empire* (London, 1887), VIII, p. 14.
9. Quoted in Matthew of Paris, *English History,* pp. 469–470.
10. Quoted in *ibid.,* pp. 341–347.
11. Quoted in Henry H. Howorth, *History of the Mongols from the 9th to the 19th Century* (London, 1876), I, p. 153.
12. Matthew of Paris, *English History,* II, p. 280; J. J. Saunders, *The History of the Mongol Conquests* (New York, 1971), p. 89.
13. Quoted in Matthew of Paris, *English History,* I, pp. 467, 473.
14. *Ibid.,* II, pp. 30, 131.
15. George Vernadsky, *The Mongols and Russia* (New Haven and London, 1953), p. 1.

Chapter 2. "Great Khan of All the People Living in Felt Tents"

1. Quoted in B. Ia. Vladimirtsev, *The Life of Chingis-Khan*, translated from the Russian by Prince D. S. Mirsky (London, 1930), p. 17. See also Francis Woodman Cleaves, *The Secret History of the Mongols for the First Time Done into English out of the Original Tongue and Provided with an Exegetical Commentary* (Cambridge, Mass., and London, 1982), pp. 18–22; Vernadsky, *The Mongols and Russia, passim.*

2. Cleaves, *Secret History of the Mongols*, p. 24.

3. *Ibid.*, pp. 1–18; J. J. Saunders, *History of the Mongol Conquests*, pp. 45–47.

4. René Grousset, *Empire of the Steppes: A History of Central Asia*, translated from the French by Naomi Walford (New Brunswick, 1970), p. 199.

5. Thomas T. Allsen, *Mongol Imperialism: The Policies of the Grand Qan Mongke in China, Russia, and the Islamic Lands, 1251–1259* (Berkeley, Los Angeles, and London, 1987), pp. 6–7; Vernadsky, *The Mongols and Russia*, pp. 20–28; Grousset, *Empire of the Steppes*, pp. 197–208.

6. Cleaves, *Secret History of the Mongols*, pp. 125–126.

7. Saunders, *History of the Mongol Conquests*, pp. 47–49; René Grousset, *Conqueror of the World*, translated from the French by Marian McKellar and Denis Sinor (New York, 1966), pp. 59–74.

8. Saunders, *History of the Mongol Conquests*, p. 53.

9. Cleaves, *Secret History of the Mongols*, p. 124.

10. Quoted in Henry H. Howorth, *History of the Mongols*, I, p. 110; On the devastation, see also Vernadsky, *The Mongols and Russia*, pp. 112–113; Grousset, *Empire of the Steppes*, pp. 197–208.

11. B. Vladimirtsev, *Le Régime social des Mongols: Le féodalism nomade*, translated by Michel Carsow (Paris, 1948), pp. 43–45, 56–99; H. D. Martin, *The Rise of Chingis Khan and His Conquest of North China* (Baltimore, 1950), pp. 17–33; John of Plano Carpini, "History of the Mongols," in Christopher Dawson, ed., *The Mongol Mission* (New York, 1955), pp. 33–37; Vernadsky, *The Mongols and Russia*, pp. 112–113; Grousset, *Empire of the Steppes*, pp. 216–226.

12. John of Plano Carpini, "History," pp. 33–37; Vernadsky, *The Mongols and Russia*, pp. 116–119; W. Barthold, *Turkestan down to the Mongol Invasion*, 3rd ed. (London, 1968), pp. 383–384.

13. René Grousset, *Conqueror of the World*, pp. 189–197; Martin, *Rise of Chingis Khan*, p. 168.

14. Quoted in Barthold, *Turkestan*, pp. 393–394.

15. *Ibid.*, pp. 399–403.

16. M. le Baron C. d'Ohsson, *Histoire des Mongols, depuis Tchinguiz-Khan jusqu'à Timour Bey or Tamerlan* (Amsterdam, 1852), I, pp. 289–290.

17. Ala-ad-Din Ata-Malik Juvaini, *The History of the World Conqueror*, translated from the text of Mirza Muhammad Qazvini by John Andrew Boyle (Cambridge, Mass., 1958), I, pp. 97–98.

18. *Ibid.*, p. 106.

19. Quoted in Grousset, *Conqueror of the World*, p. 223.

20. *Ibid.*, pp. 224–225.

21. Quoted in Juvaini, *History of the World Conqueror*, I, p. 116.

22. Grousset, *Conqueror of the World*, p. 226.

23. Juvaini, *History of the World Conqueror*, I, p. 178.

24. d'Ohsson, *Histoire des Mongols*, I, p. 291.

25. Juvaini, *History of the World Conqueror*, I, pp. 97–128, 150–178; Barthold, *Turkestan*, pp. 413–414, 436, 447.

26. Juvaini, *History of the World Conqueror*, I, p. 97.

27. Barthold, *Turkestan*, pp. 404–427; Grousset, *Empire of the Steppes*, pp. 236–247; Vernadsky, *The Mongols and Russia*, pp. 35–41; B. Grekov and A. Iakoubovski, *La Horde d'or et la Russie: La Domination Tatare aux XIIIe et XIVe siècles de la mer jaune à la mer noire,*

translated from the Russian by François Thuret (Paris, 1961), pp. 190–195; S. A. Zenkovskii, ed., *Medieval Russia's Epics, Chronicles, and Tales* (New York, 1954), p. 195.

28. Quoted in George Vernadsky, *Kievan Russia* (New Haven, 1948), p. 239.

29. Rashid al-Din, *The Successors of Genghis Khan*, translated from the Persian by John Andrew Boyle (New York, 1971), p. 17; Grousset, *Empire of the Steppes*, pp. 253–268; Vernadsky, *The Mongols and Russia*, pp. 45–58.

30. Grousset, *Empire of the Steppes*, p. 254.

Chapter 3. Batu's Winter War

1. N. M. Karamzin, *Istoriia Gosudarstva Rossiiskago*, 5th ed. (St. Petersburg, 1842), III, col. 166.

2. Serge A. Zenkovskii, ed. and trans., *Medieval Russia's Epics, Chronicles and Tales*, pp. 201–202.

3. Karamzin, *Istoriia*, III, col 169–171; S. M. Solov'ëv, *Istoriia Rossii s drevneishikh vremen* (Moscow, 1960), III, pp. 141–142.

4. Iu. A. Limonov, *Vladimiro-Suzdal'skaia Rus': Ocherki sotsial'no-politicheskoi istorii* (Leningrad, 1987), pp. 112–115; A. A. Kataev, "Tatary i poraboshchenie imi Rusi," in M. V. Dovnar-Zapol'skii, ed., *Russkaia istoriia v ocherkakh i stat'iakh* (Moscow, 1909), pp. 571–574; Karamzin, *Istoriia*, III, cols. 171–172; Solov'ëv, *Istoriia*, III, pp. 142–143.

5. Karamzin, *Istoriia*, III, cols. 172–174; IV, cols. 1–7; Solov'ëv, *Istoriia*, III, pp. 142–144.

6. Vernadsky, *The Mongols and Russia*, p. 52.

7. Karamzin, *Istoriia*, IV, col. 9.

8. Quoted in Gudzy, *History of Early Russian Literature*, translated by Susan Wilbur Jones (New York, 1949), p. 210.

9. B. D. Grekov and A. Iu. Iakubovskii, *Zolotaia orda i ee padenie* (Moscow and Leningrad, 1950), pp. 214–217; Karamzin, *Istoriia*, IV, cols. 9–12.

10. John of Plano Carpini, "History," pp. 29–30.

11. Thomas T. Allsen, "Mongol Census Taking in Rus', 1245–1275," *Harvard Ukrainian Studies*, V, No. 1 (March 1981), pp. 33–53, and especially pp. 47–52; A. N. Nasonov, *Mongoly i Rus' (Istoriia tatarskoi politiki na Rusi)* (Moscow and Leningrad, 1940), pp. 14–20, 50–68; V. V. Kargalov, "Sushchestvovali li na Rusi 'voenno-politicheskaia baskacheskaia organizatsiia' mongol'skikh feodalov?" *IstSSSR*, No. 1 (1962), pp. 161–165; V. V. Kargalov, "Baskaki," *VI*, No. 5 (1972), pp. 212–215; Vernadsky, *The Mongols and Russia*, p. 87.

12. Quoted in Nasonov, *Mongoly i Rus'*, p. 111.

13. L. V. Cherepnin, *Obrazovanie russkogo tsentralizovannogo gosudarstva V XIV–XV vekakh* (Moscow, 1960), pp. 497–519; M. K. Liubavskii, *Ocherk istorii litovsko-russkago gosudarstva* (Moscow, 1915), pp. 41–53; A. E. Presniakov, *Lektsii po russkoi istorii* (Moscow, 1938), II, pt. 1, pp. 44–65; B. N. Floria, "Litva i Rus' pered bitvoi na Kulikovskom pole," in L. G. Beskrovnyi, ed., *Kulikovskaia bitva: Sbornik statei* (Moscow, 1980), pp. 142–173; Vernadsky, *The Mongols and Russia*, pp. 233–240; E. Golubinskii, *Istoriia russkoi tserkvy* (Moscow, 1911), pp. 98–145.

14. Robert O. Crummey, *The Formation of Muscovy, 1304–1613* (London and New York, 1987), pp. 44–48.

15. V. L. Egorov, "Zolotaia orda pered kulikovskoi bitvoi," in Beskrovnyi, ed., *Kulikovskaia bitva*, pp. 174–213; G. A. Fedorov-Davydov, *Obshchestvennyi stroi Zolotoi Ordy* (Moscow, 1973), pp. 145–152; Grekov and Iakubovskii, *Zolotaia orda*, pp. 261–294; Cherepnin, *Obrazovanie*, pp. 530–556.

Chapter 4. On Kulikovo Field

1. Quoted in V. V. Kargalov, *Kulikovskaia bitva* (Moscow, 1980), p. 97.

2. George Vernadsky, Ralph T. Fisher, Jr., Alan D. Ferguson, Andrew Lossky, and

Sergei Pushkarev, eds., *A Source Book for Russian History from Early Times to 1917* (New Haven and London, 1972), I, p. 56.

3. L. G. Beskrovnyi, "Kulikovskaia bitva," in L. G. Beskrovnyi, ed., *Kulikovskaia bitva: Sbornik statei* (Moscow, 1980), pp. 222–245; Edward D. Sokol, "The Battle of Kulikovo," *MERSH*, XVIII, pp. 152–159; Kargalov, *Kulikovskaia bitva*, pp. 72–117; David M. Goldfrank, "Dmitrii Ivanovich Donskoi," *MERSH*, IX, pp. 170–177; and Jeremiah Curtin, *The Mongols in Russia* (Boston, 1908), pp. 368–391.

4. Vernadsky, *The Mongols and Russia*, pp. 245–248.

5. Quoted in Grousset, *Empire of the Steppes*, pp. 414–415; see also pp. 409–419.

6. *Ibid.*, pp. 406–408, 436–438; B. D. Grekov, L. V. Cherepnin, and V. T. Pashuto, eds., *Ocherki istorii SSSR: period feodalizma IX–XV vv.* (Moscow, 1953), II, pp. 228–230, 244–246, 654–660; Vernadsky, *The Mongols and Russia*, pp. 248–250.

7. Vernadsky, *The Mongols and Russia*, p. 266.

8. Cherepnin, *Obrazovanie*, p. 646; see also pp. 629–647.

9. *Ibid.*, 647–681.

10. Grekov, Cherepnin, and Pashuto, eds., *Ocherki istorii SSSR*, II, pp. 654–666; Grousset, *Empire of the Steppes*, pp. 435–456.

11. Cherepnin, *Obrazovanie*, pp. 743–771, 787–824; Crummey, *Formation of Muscovy, 1304–1613*, pp. 56–77; V. N. Bernadskii, *Novgorod i novgorodskaia zemlia v XV veke* (Moscow and Leningrad, 1961), pp. 252–263; Vernadsky, *The Mongols and Russia*, pp. 314–332.

12. Crummey, *Formation of Muscovy*, pp. 97–99.

13. Bernadskii, *Novgorod*, pp. 264–313; Cherepnin, *Obrazovanie*, pp. 862–896; George Vernadsky, *Russia at the Dawn of the Modern Age* (New Haven and London, 1959), pp. 42–62, 96–100; Crummey, *Formation of Muscovy*, pp. 84–93.

14. G. F. Miller, *Istoriia Sibiri* (Moscow and Leningrad, 1937), I, pp. 204–205; George V. Lantzeff and Richard A. Pierce, *Eastward to Empire: Exploration and Conquest on the Russian Open Frontier to 1750* (Montreal and London, 1973), pp. 48–49.

15. The view that Ivan became an invalid, incapacitated by a disease, alcohol, and drugs, and that he may not even have been literate has been set forth in a brilliant essay by Edward L. Keenan, *The Kurbskii-Groznyi Apocrypha* (Cambridge, Mass., 1971). Impressive critiques of Keenan's work have been written by the Soviet scholar R. G. Skrynnikov, *Perepiska Groznogo i Kurbskogo. Paradoksy Edvarda Kinana* (Leningrad, 1973), and, more recently, by Niels Rossing and Birgit Rønne, *Apocryphal—Not Apocryphal?* (Copenhagen, 1980).

16. See Vernadsky, *The Mongols and Russia*, p. 256, note 38, and George Vernadsky, *The Tsardom of Moscow, 1547–1682* (New Haven and London, 1969), Pt. 1, pp. 2–6.

17. Crummey, *Formation of Muscovy*, pp. 151–155; A. N. Nasonov, L. V. Cherepnin, and A. A. Zimin, eds., *Ocherki istorii SSSR: Period feodalizma. Konets XV v.–nachalo XVII v.* (Moscow, 1955), pp. 350–369.

Chapter 5. Anika and His Sons

1. "Stroganovy," *RBS*, vol. Sme–Suv, pp. 471–472.

2. " 'Kupchaia' na tret' varnitsy bez tsyrena i tret' varnichnogo mesta, kuplennykh Anikoi Fëdorovichem Stroganovym u Iakova Fëdorova syna Bizimova," 18 fevralia 1526g.; " 'Kupchaia' na varnitsu s tsyrenom i so vsem 'nariadom, chto v varnitse,' kuplennuiu Anikoi Fëdorovichem Stroganovym u Avdot'i Maksimovoi docheri u Stepanovskoi zheny Zuesa i ee vnuka Vasil'ia Ontomanova," 3 iiunia 1526g.; " 'Kupchaia' na varnitsu so vsem varnichnym inventarem i s varnichnym mestom, kuplennymi Anikoi Stroganovym u Vasil'ia i Dmitriia Varonitsynykh," 15 iiulia 1540g., all in A. A. Vvedenskii, ed., *Torgovyi dom XVI–XVII vekov* (Leningrad, 1924), pp. 86–88.

3. "Luka Koz'mich Stroganov," *RBS,* vol. Sme–Suv, p. 506.

4. Yuri Semënov, *Siberia: Its Conquest and Development,* translated from the German by J. R. Foster (Baltimore, 1963), pp. 26–27.

5. A. A. Vvedenskii, "Anika Stroganov v svoëm Sol'vychegodskom khoziaistve," in *Sbornik statei po russkoi istorii pòsviashchennykh S. F. Platonovu* (Petersburg, 1922), pp. 91–101; Vvedenskii, *Dom Stroganovykh v XVI–XVII vekakh* (Moscow, 1962), pp. 19–23; J. H. Shennan, "The Conquest of Siberia," *HT,* XIX, No. 2 (February 1969), pp. 102–103.

6. Miller, *Istoriia Sibiri,* I, p. 207.

7. Semënov, *Siberia: Its Conquest and Development,* p. 39.

8. Vvedenskii, "Anika Stroganov v svoëm Sol'vychegodskom khoziaistve," p. 107; Vvedenskii, *Dom Stroganovykh,* pp. 52–53.

9. N. V. Ustiugov, *Solevarennaia promyshlennost' Soli Kamskoi v XVII veke: K voprosu o genezise kapitalisticheskikh otnoshenii v russkoi promyshlennosti* (Moscow, 1957), pp. 123–132.

10. "Charter granted by Tsar Ivan Vasil'evich to Grigorii Stroganov on financial, juridical and trade privileges in the empty lands along the river Kama," April 4, 1558, in Terence Armstrong, ed., *Yermak's Campaign in Siberia: A Selection of Documents,* translated from the Russian by Tatiana Minorsky and David Wileman (London, 1975), pp. 281–282.

11. Quoted in Lantzeff and Pierce, *Eastward to Empire,* p. 85.

12. "Zhalovannaia gramota tsaria Ivana Vasil'evicha Grigoriiu Stroganovu o finansovykh, sudebnykh i torgovykh l'gotakh na pustye mesta po reke Kame," 4 aprelia 1558g., appendix 2 in Miller, *Istoriia Sibiri,* I, pp. 332–334.

13. "Charter granted by Tsar Ivan Vasil'evich to Iakov Stroganov on financial, juridical and trade privileges with regard to the salt-works on the river Chusovaia," March 25, 1568, in Armstrong, ed., *Yermak's Campaign,* pp. 284–287.

14. "Anika Fëdorovich Stroganov," *RBS,* vol. Sme–Suv, pp. 493–494; "Grigorii Anikievich Stroganov," *RBS,* vol. Sme–Suv, p. 495; Vvedenskii, *Dom Stroganovykh* (Moscow, 1962), pp. 25–26; "Zhalovannaia gramota tsaria Ivana Vasil'evicha Iakovu Stroganovu o finansovykh, sudebnykh i torgovych l'gotakh na solenoi promysel po reke Chusovoi," 25 marta 1568g., appendix 3 in Miller, *Istoriia Sibiri,* I, pp. 333–337; "Gramota tsaria Ivana Vasil'evicha v slobodku na Kame Iakovu i Grigoriiu Stroganovym o posylke ratnykh liudei dlia privedeniia i pokornosti cheremisov i drugikh narodov, proizvodivshikh grabezhi po reke Kame," appendix 4 in Miller, *Istoriia Sibiri,* I, pp. 338–339; "Iakov Anikievich Stroganov," *RBS,* vol. Sme–Suv, p. 531; Vernadsky, *The Tsardom of Moscow,* I, pt. 1, pp. 176–177.

15. "Zhalovannaia gramota tsaria Ivana Vasil'evicha Iakovu i Grigoriiu Stroganovym ob osvobozhdenii na 20 let ot raznykh podatei i povinnostei ikh zemel' i liudei na Takhcheiakh i na Tobole," appendix 5 in Miller, *Istoriia Sibiri,* I, pp. 339–341; see also pp. 206–207, note 3; V. I. Ogorodnikov, *Ocherk istorii Sibiri do nachala XIX stoletiia* (Vladivostok, 1924), II, pp. 21–22; Vvedenskii, *Dom Stroganovykh,* pp. 33–37.

16. R. G. Skrynnikov, *Sibirskaia ekspeditsiia Ermaka* (Novosibirsk, 1986), pp. 83–92.

17. Quoted in Lantzeff and Pierce, *Eastward to Empire,* p. 86.

18. Skrynnikov, *Sibirskaia ekspeditsiia Ermaka,* pp. 92–99; Ogorodnikov, *Ocherk istorii Sibiri,* II, pp. 18–20; Boris Nolde, *La Formation de l'Empire Russe: Etudes, Notes et Documents* (Paris, 1952), I, pp. 156–159; Vvedenskii, *Dom Stroganovykh,* pp. 76–79; Sergius Yakobson, "The Russian Conquest of Siberia," *HT,* XXII, No. 10 (October 1972), pp. 702–703; Shennan, "Conquest of Siberia," pp. 102–103.

19. "Ivan Vasil'evich's letter to the settlement on the Kama to Iakov and Grigorii Stroganov on the sending of fighting men for the subduing of the Cheremis and other peoples marauding on the river Kama," August 6, 1572, in Armstrong, ed., *Yermak's Campaign,* p. 288.

20. Skrynnikov, *Sibirskaia ekspeditsiia Ermaka*, pp. 100–103.

21. C. V. Bakhrushin, " 'Puti v Sibir' v XVI–XVIIvv.," in Bakhrushin, *Nauchnye trudy*, III, pt. I, pp. 96–97; "Gramota tsaria Ivana Vasil'evicha," pp. 338–339.

22. Vvedenskii, *Dom Stroganovykh*, pp. 102–103.

23. "Nikita Grigor'evich and Maksim Iakovlevich Stroganovy," *RBS*, vol. Sme–Suv, pp. 507–509.

Chapter 6. Ermak's "Conquest"

1. Quoted in Edward D. Sokol, "Ermak Timofeevich," *MERSH*, X, p. 226.

2. Skrynnikov, *Sibirskaia ekspeditsiia Ermaka*, pp. 177–178, 182–183; Crummey, *Formation of Muscovy*, p. 209.

3. Vvedenskii, *Dom Stroganovykh*, p. 98; "Francisco Pizarro," *EB*, XXI, pp. 690–691; "Hernando Cortés," *EB*, VII, pop. 205–207.

4. Skrynnikov, *Sibirskaia ekspeditsiia Ermaka*, pp. 168–169; S. V. Bakhrushin, "Puti v Sibir' v XVI–XVIIvv.," pp. 102–103; Miller, *Istoriia Sibiri*, I, pp. 215–217.

5. Skrynnikov, *Sibirskaia ekspeditsiia Ermaka*, pp. 169–170; Miller, *Istoriia Sibiri*, I, pp. 219–220.

6. Skrynnikov, *Sibirskaia ekspeditsiia Ermaka*, p. 218.

7. *Ibid.*, pp. 168–221; Miller, *Istoriia Sibiri*, I, pp. 229–231. For some examples of historians' disagreements about the chronology of Ermak's campaign, see the note by S. V. Bakhrushin (who also gets the date of the Tobolsk battle wrong) in Miller, *Istoriia Sibiri*, I, p. 492.

8. Skrynnikov, *Sibirskaia ekspeditsiia Ermaka*, p. 219.

9. Raymond Fisher, *The Russian Fur Trade, 1550–1700* (Berkeley, 1943), p. 119.

10. Miller, *Istoriia Sibiri*, I, pp. 251–253; John F. Baddeley, *Russia, Mongolia, and China, Being Some Record of the Relations Between Them from the Beginning of the XVIIth Century to the Death of the Tsar Alexei Mikhailovich* (London, 1919), II, p. 160.

11. Baddeley, *Russia, Mongolia, and China*, I, p. lxxiii; "Gramota tsaria Ivana Vasil'evicha Semenu, Maksimu, i Nikite Stroganovym o prigotovlenii k vesne 15 otrugov dlia liudei i zapasov, napravliaemykh v Sibir'," 7 ianvaria 1584g., appendix 4 in Miller, *Istoriia Sibiri*, I, pp. 343–344.

12. Quoted in Lantzeff and Pierce, *Eastward to Empire*, p. 105.

13. Skrynnikov, *Sibirskaia ekspeditsiia Ermaka*, pp. 234–235, 249–262; Fisher, *Russian Fur Trade*, pp. 26–27.

14. See, for example. V. F. Miller, *Istoricheskie pesni russkogo naroda XVI–XVII vekov* (Petrograd, 1915), pp. 475–540.

15. Baddeley, *Russia, Mongolia, and China*, I, p. lxxiii.

Chapter 7. The Siberians

1. Henry N. Michael, "Absolute Chronologies of Late Pleistocene and Early Holocene Cultures of Northeastern Asia," *AA*, XXI, No. 2 (1984), pp. 1–68; Iu. A. Mochanov, *Drevneishie etapy zaseleniia chelovekem Severo-Vostochnoi Azii* (Novosibirsk, 1977); A. P. Okladnikov et al., eds., *Istoriia Sibiri* (Leningrad, 1968), I, pp. 37–65; M. G. Levin and L. P. Potapov, eds., *Narody Sibiri* (Moscow and Leningrad, 1956), pp. 23–29. On the peoples of Siberia's Arctic frontier, see especially the excellent introduction of Yuri Slezkine's *Russia and the Peoples of Siberia's Arctic Frontier* to be published by Cornell University Press in 1994. See also James Forsyth, *A History of The Peoples of Siberia: Russia's North Asian Colony, 1581–1990* (Cambridge, 1992), which appeared only after the research for this book was completed.

2. Levin and Potapov, eds., *Narody Sibiri*, pp. 30–41; Okladnikov et al., eds., *Istoriia Sibiri*, I, pp. 76–79; N. N. Dikov, *Drevnie kul'tury Severo-Vostochnoi Azii: Aziia na styke s*

Amerikoi v drevnosti (Moscow, 1979), pp. 16–54, 134–141; V. V. Bobrov, "On the Problem of Inter-Ethnic Relations in South Siberia in the Third and Early Second Millennium B.C.E.," in D. B. Shimkin, ed., *Studies in North Asiatic Archaeology, Neolithic to Medieval by the Faculty of Archaeology, Kemerovo State University* (Urbana, 1988), pp. 62–65.

3. S. V. Kiselëv, *Drevniaia istoriia iuzhnoi Sibiri* (Moscow, 1951), pp. 23–66.

4. *Ibid.*, pp. 67–105, 172–180.

5. Levin and Potapov, eds., *Narody Sibiri*, p. 56.

6. Kiselëv, *Drevniaia istoriia iuzhnoi Sibiri*, pp. 334–361; A. P. Okladnikov et al., eds., *Istoriia Sibiri* (Leningrad, 1968), I, pp. 227–233; Owen Lattimore, "Caravan Routes of Inner Asia," *GJ*, LXXII, No. 6 (December 1928), pp. 497–528; F. S. Drake, "China's North-west Passage: A Chapter in Its Opening," *JNCBRAS*, LXVI (1935), pp. 40–49; Grousset, *Empire of the Steppes*, pp. xxii–xxiii, 39–42.

7. Levin and Potapov, eds., *Narody Sibiri*, p. 68.

8. *Ibid.*, pp. 65–80; Okladnikov et al., eds., *Istoriia Sibiri*, I, pp. 227–233; Kiselev, *Drevniaia istoriia iuzhnoi Sibiri*, pp. 334–392; I. A. Sher, "On the Sources of the Scythic Animal Style," in Shimkin, ed., *Studies in North Asiatic Archaeology*, pp. 142–173.

9. "Kirgizskaia Sovetskaia Sotsialisticheskaia Respublika," *SIE*, VII, col. 254–258; Levin and Potapov, eds., *Narody Sibiri*, pp. 378–380; Grousset, *Empire of the Steppes*, pp. 124–128, 216–217.

10. G. V. Glinka, ed., *Aziatskaia Rossiia* (St. Petersburg, 1914), I, pp. 153–163; Levin and Potapov, eds., *Narody Sibiri*, pp. 379–383.

11. Glinka, ed., *Aziatskaia Rossiia*, I, pp. 132–143; Levin and Potapov, eds., *Narody Sibiri*, pp. 217–266.

12. Quoted in *A Handbook of Siberia and Arctic Russia*, compiled by the Geographical Staff of the Naval Intelligence Division, Naval Staff, the Admiralty (London, 1920), p. 175.

13. *Ibid.*, pp. 172–177; Glinka, ed., *Aziatskaia Rossiia*, I, pp. 123–132; Levin and Potapov, eds., *Narody Sibiri*, pp. 701–729.

14. Glinka, ed., *Aziatskaia Rossiia*, I, pp. 145–150; Levin and Potapov, eds., *Narody Sibiri*, pp. 267–302.

15. Quoted in Kennan, *Siberia and the Exile System*, II, p. 22.

16. Glinka, ed., *Aziatskaia Rossiia*, I, pp. 106–115; Levin and Potapov, eds., *Narody Sibiri*, pp. 554–569; Miller, *Istoriia Sibiri*, I, p. 285.

17. Levin and Potapov, eds., *Narody Sibiri*, pp. 899–900; Ia. P. Al'kor and L. K. Drezen, eds., *Kolonial'naia politika tsarizma na Kamchatke i Chukhotke v XVIII veke. Sbornikh arkhivnykh materialov* (Leningrad, 1935), pp. 174–188.

18. Levin and Potapov, eds., *Narody Sibiri*, pp. 896–933, 950–977; Glinka, ed., *Aziatskaia Rossiia*, I, pp. 95–103; *A Handbook of Siberia and Arctic Russia*, pp. 96–113.

19. James R. Gibson, *Feeding the Russian Fur Trade: Provisionment of the Okhotsk Seaboard and the Kamchatka Peninsula 1639–1856* (Madison, Wis., 1969), pp. 25–26.

20. Quoted in Baddeley, *Russia, Mongolia, and China*, II, p. 271.

Chapter 8. To the Great Ocean

1. Valentin Rasputin, "Your Siberia and Mine," in Valentin Rasputin, *Siberia on Fire*, selected, translated, and with an introduction by Gerald Mikkelson and Margaret Winchell (DeKalb, Ill., 1989), p. 176.

2. Belov, *Arkticheskoe moreplavanie s drevneishikh vremen do serediny XIX veka* (Volume I of *Istoriia otkrytiia i osvoenniia Severnogo morskogo puti*) (Moscow, 1956), pp. 523–526; Bakhrushin, " 'Puti v Sibir' v XVI–XVIIvv.," pp. 72–136; A. V. Efimov, *Iz istorii velikikh russkikh geograficheskikh otkrytii v Severnom Ledovitom i Tikhom Okeanakh XVII—pervaia polovina XVIIIvv.* (Moscow, 1950), pp. 49–71.

3. S. V. Bakhrushin, *Ocherki po istorii kolonizatsii Sibiri v XVI i XVIIvv.* (Moscow, 1927), pp. 61–142; M. V. Belov, *Arkticheksoe moreplavanie, passim.*

4. Gibson, *Feeding the Russian Fur Trade*, pp. 61–62.

5. R. M. Kabo, *Goroda Zapadnoi Sibiri: Ocherki istoriko-ekonomicheskoi geografii XVII–pervaia polovina XIXvv.* (Moscow, 1949), pp. 84–85; P. N. Butsinskii, *Zaselenie Sibiri i byt pervykh ee nasel'nikov* (Kharkov, 1889), pp. 103–142; Okladnikov et al., eds., *Istoriia Sibiri*, II, pp. 271–272.

6. Okladnikov et al., eds., *Istoriia Sibiri*, II, p. 263.

7. Mark Bassin, "Expansion and Colonialism on the Eastern Frontier: Views of Siberia and the Far East in Pre-Petrine Russia," *JHG*, XIV, No. 1 (January 1988), pp. 7–8.

8. Belov, *Arkticheskoe moreplavanie*, pp. 112–120; Inna Lubimenko, "A Project for the Acquisition of Russia by James I," *EHR*, XXIV (1914), pp. 246–256.

9. See, for example, the hair-raising account of a journey from Tobolsk to Mangazeia in the 1640s in N. S. Orlova, ed., *Otkrytiia russkikh zemleprokhodtsev i poliarnykh morekhodov XVII veka na severo-vostoke Asii. Sbornik dokumentov* (Moscow, 1951), pp. 80–82.

10. Belov, *Arkticheskoe moreplavanie*, pp. 120–127; Terence Armstrong, *Russian Settlement in the North* (Cambridge, England, 1965), pp. 17–19.

11. Okladnikov et al., eds., *Istoriia Sibiri*, II, pp. 271–272.

12. V. I. Ogorodnikov, *Ocherk istorii Sibiri*, II, pt. 1, pp. 64–70; V. K. Andreevich, *Istoricheskii ocherk Sibiri* (St. Petersburg, 1889), I, pt. 1, pp. 72–81; S. B. Okun', "Materialy k istorii Buriatii v XVII v.," *KA*, LXXVI (1936), pp. 174–175; Lantzeff and Pierce, *Eastward to Empire*, pp. 146–152.

13. V. I. Ogorodnikov, *Ocherk istorii Sibiri*, II, pt. 1, 49.

14. Quoted in Armstrong, *Russian Settlement*, pp. 32–33.

15. Ogorodnikov, *Ocherk istorii Sibiri*, II, pt. 1, pp. 49–51; Okladnikov et al., eds., *Istoriia Sibiri*, II, pp. 46–50; Belov, *Arkticheskoe moreplavanie*, pp. 142–143; Fisher, *Russian Fur Trade*, p. 97.

16. Okladnikov et al., eds., *Istoriia Sibiri*, II, p. 49; Gibson, *Feeding the Russian Fur Trade*, p. 8.

17. S. A. Tokarev, Z. V. Gogolev, and I. S. Gurvich, eds., *Istoriia iakutskoi ASSR* (Moscow, 1957), II, pp. 32–38, 68–71.

Chapter 9. Searching for Grain

1. "Akty o plavanii pis'mennago golovy Vasil'ia Poiarkova iz Iakutska v Okhotskoie more," posle 12 iiunia 1646g., in *DAI*, III, document No. 12, pp. 50–52.

2. *Ibid.*, pp. 52–60.

3. See, for example, E. G. Ravenstein, *The Russians on the Amur: Its Discovery, Conquest, and Colonisation* (London, 1861), p. 19, note "c."

4. L. S. Berg, *Ocherki po istorii russkikh geograficheskikh otkrytii* (Moscow and Leningrad, 1949), pp. 145–148; Ogorodnikov, *Ocherk istorii Sibiri*, II, pt. 1, pp. 75–79; Lantzeff and Pierce, *Eastward to Empire*, pp. 155–158.

5. "Akty o plavanii pis'mennago golovy Vasil'ia Poiarkova iz Iakutska v Okhotskoie more," posle 12 iiunia 1646g., p. 59.

6. *Ibid.*, pp. 52–60. See also F. A. Golder, *Russian Expansion on the Pacific, 1641–1850* (Gloucester, Mass., 1960), pp. 35–37.

7. F. G. Safronov, *Erofei Khabarov* (Khabarovsk, 1983), pp. 9–46; "Erofei Pavlovich Khabarov-Sviatitskii," *SIE*, XV, col. 477; "Nakaz Iakutskago voevody Dimitriia Frantsbekova opytovshchiku Erofeiu Khabarovu, o pokhode v Daurskuiu zemliu," 6 marta 1649g., in *AI*, IV, document No. 31, pp. 67–72; Lantzeff and Pierce, *Eastward to Empire*, pp. 159–160.

8. Safronov, *Erofei Khabarov*, pp. 47–48; "Nakaz Iakutskago voevody Dimitriia Frantsbekova," 6 marta 1649g., *AI*, IV, document No. 31, pp. 67–70; Golder, *Russian Expansion on the Pacific*, pp. 38–43.

9. Rasputin, "Your Siberia and Mine," p. 176.

10. Quoted in Bassin, "Expansion and Colonialism," p. 13.

11. "Nakaz Iakutskago voevody Dimitriia Frantsbekova," 6 marta 1649g., *AI*, IV, document No. 31, pp. 67–70; "Voevodskaia otpiska Tsariu ob otpuske Khabarova v Dauriiu, o voennykh ego deistviiakh," in *AI*, IV, document No. 31, pp. 74–75; Safronov, *Erofei Khabarov*, pp. 49–51; Lantzeff and Pierce, *Eastward to Empire*, pp. 160–161.

12. Ogorodnikov, *Ocherk istorii Sibiri*, I, pt. 1, p. 86.

13. "Otpiska Iakutskomu voevode Dimitriiu Frantsbekovu sluzhivago cheloveka Erofeia Khabarova, o voennykh deistviiakh ego na reke Amure," Avgust 1652g., *DAI*, III, document No. 102, pp. 359–371; Safronov, *Erofei Khabarov*, pp. 52–55; Golder, *Russian Expansion on the Pacific*, pp. 45–47.

14. Bassin, "Expansion and Colonialism," p. 13.

15. "Otpiska sluzhivago cheloveka Terentiia Ermolina, ob ostavlenii im v Tungurskom zimov'e porokha i svintsa, poslannykh k prikaznomu cheloveku Erofeiu Khabarovu, i o plavanii po reke Amuru, avgusta 1652g., in *DAI*, III, document No. 101, pp. 356–359; Ravenstein, *Russians on the Amur*, pp. 19–21; Safronov, *Erofei Khabarov*, pp. 52–55; Golder, *Russian Expansion on the Pacific*, pp. 45–47.

16. Ogorodnikov, *Ocherk istorii Sibiri*, I, pt. 1, p. 88; Safronov, *Erofei Khabarov*, pp. 52–53.

17. Ogorodnikov, *Ocherk istorii Sibiri*, I, pt. 1, pp. 88–89.

18. Lantzeff and Pierce, *Eastward to Empire*, p. 246, note 14.

19. Ogorodnikov, *Ocherk istorii Sibiri*, I, pt. 1, pp. 90–91; Golder, *Russian Expansion on the Pacific*, pp. 49–50; Ravenstein, *Russians on the Amur*, pp. 21–28; Safronov, *Erofei Khabarov*, pp. 53–56; "Otpiska sluzhivago cheloveka Ivana Uvarova Iakutskomu voevode Dimitriiu Frantsbekovu, o plavanii ego dlia otyskaniia Erofeia Khabarova po reke Amuru i Vostochnomu Okeanu i o priobytii na reku Tugir'," 30 iiunia 1652, *DAI*, III, document No. 100, pp. 354–356; "Otpiska prikaznago cheloveka Onufriia Stepanova Iakutskomu voevode Mikhailu Lodyzhenskomu, o deistviiakh ego na reke Amure po ot"ezde Erofeia Khabarova v Moskvu," v nachale avgusta 1654g., *DAI*, III, document No. 122, pp. 523–528; Golder, *Russian Expansion on the Pacific*, pp. 49–50; Ravenstein, *Russians on the Amur*, pp. 21–28.

20. Safronov, *Erofei Khabarov*, pp. 57–58.

21. Quoted in *ibid.*, p. 65.

22. *Ibid.*, pp. 65–70; Ogorodnikov, *Ocherk istorii Sibiri*, I, pt. 1, pp. 95–97; Lantzeff and Pierce, *Eastward to Empire*, pp. 166–167.

23. Ogorodnikov, *Ocherk istorii Sibiri*, I, pt. 1, p. 94.

24. Lantzeff and Pierce, *Eastward to Empire*, p. 165.

25. S. V. Bakhrushin, *Ocherki po istorii*, p. 167.

26. *Ibid.*, pp. 167–168; Golder, *Russian Expansion on the Pacific*, pp. 62–65; V. K. Andreevich, *Istoriia Sibiri*, II, pp. 42–46.

27. Mark Mancall, *Russia and China: Their Diplomatic Relations to 1728* (n.p., 1971), pp. 127–162.

Chapter 10. Discovering a Passage Between Two Continents

1. F. A. Golder, *Russian Expansion on the Pacific*, p. 78.

2. Belov, *Arkticheskoe moreplavanie*, pp. 108–120.

3. A. P. Okladnikov, *Russkie poliarnye morekhody XVII veka u beregov Taimyra* (Moscow and Leningrad, 1948), pp. 93–95.

4. M. I. Belov, *Podvig Semëna Dezhnëva* (Moscow, 1973), pp. 20–54; V. A. Samoilov, *Semën Dezhnëv i ego vremia* (Moscow, 1945), pp. 43–44; M. I. Belov, ed., *Russkie morekhody v Ledovitom i Tikhom okeanakh: Sbornik dokumentov o velikikh russkikh geograficheskikh otkrytiiakh na severo-vostoke Azii v XVII veke* (Moscow and Leningrad, 1952), pp. 35–41.

5. "Nakaznaia pamiat' Iakutskago voevody Ivana Akinfova kazach'emu piatidesiatniku Ivanu Rebrovu, o priniatii v svoe vedenie Kovymskago ostroga i o sbore iasaka i

kosti ryb'iago zuba s Iukagirov i Chukchei," 30 iiunia 1652g., in *DAI*, III, document No. 98, pp. 350–352; Belov, *Podvig Semëna Dezhnëva*, pp. 61–68, 81–83; Golder, *Russian Expansion on the Pacific*, p. 72; D. M. Lebedev, *Geografiia v Rossii XVII veka: Ocherki po istorii geograficheskikh znanii* (Moscow and Leningrad, 1949), pp. 58–59; A. V. Efimov, *Iz istorii velikikh russkikh geograficheskikh otkrytii*, pp. 54–56.

6. Lantzeff and Pierce, *Eastward to Empire*, p. 187.

7. Belov, *Podvig Semëna Dezhnëva*, pp. 39–55, 60–61, 66–68, 73; Belov, ed., *Russkie more khody*, pp. 35–41.

8. Quoted in Belov, *Podvig Semëna Dezhnëva*, p. 76; Belov, *Arkticheskoe moreplavanie*, pp. 148–156.

9. Belov, *Podvig Semëna Dezhnëva*, pp. 88–110.

10. L. H. Neatby, *Discovery in Russian and Siberian Waters* (Athens, Ohio, 1973), pp. 40–49.

11. Belov, *Arkticheskoe moreplavanie*, pp. 164–165, 203–215; R. H. Fisher, "Semën Dezhnëv and Professor Golder," *PHR*, XXV (1956), pp. 281–292.

12. "Otpiski Iakutskomu voevode Ivanu Akinfovu sluzhivykh liudei Semëna Dezhnëva i Nikity Semënova, o pokhode ikh na reku Anadyr, o voennykh deistviiakh protiv inorodtsev i proch.," 4, i posle 15, aprelia 1655, in *DAI*, IV, document No. 7, pp. 25–26. There is a truncated translation of this report in Golder, *Russian Expansion on the Pacific*, pp. 282, 287.

13. *Ibid.*, p. 26.

14. Belov, *Podvig Semëna Dezhnëva*, pp. 88–126; I. P. Magidovich and V. I. Magidovich, *Ocherki po istorii geograficheskikh otkrytii* (Moscow, 1983), II, pp. 291–293.

15. Belov, *Arkticheskoe moreplavanie*, pp. 162–168; Belov, *Podvig Semëna Dezhnëva*, pp. 127–138, 67–75. *DAI*, IV, documents No. 4, 6, 8, 10, 19, and 20 are the most important for studying Dezhnëv's voyage, in addition to Dezhnëv's own report (document No. 7) and several others published by Nikolai Ogloblin in *Zhurnal Ministerstva Narodnago Prosveshcheniia*, No. 12 (1890), pp. 300–307. See also N. N. Ogloblin, *Semën Dezhnëv* (St. Petersburg, 1890). On the vast quantities of prehistoric ivory that would be unearthed in Siberia in the years to come, see E. W. Pfitzenmayer, *Les Mammouths de Sibirie: La découverte de cadavres de mammouths préhistoriques sur les bords de la Berezovka et de la Sanga-Iourakh* (Paris, 1939).

16. Lantzeff, *Siberia in the Seventeenth Century; A Study of the Colonial Administration* (Berkeley and Los Angeles, 1943), pp. 89–91.

17. Golder, *Russian Expansion on the Pacific*, pp. 97–99.

Chapter 11. Life on the Siberian Frontier

1. Even in the 1890s, it still *seemed* this way to the London physician Charles Wenyon, although Wenyon's feeling that "from one town to the next is sometimes as far as the whole length of England" was more the result of the journey's boredom than of measured distances. See Charles Wenyon, *Across Siberia on the Great Post-Road*, p. 26.

2. Fisher, *Russian Fur Trade*, pp. 108–122, 179–180, 184–185, 191–193; N. Rozhkov, *Sel'skoe khoziaistvo moskovskoi Rusi v XVI veke* (Moscow, 1899), pp. 259–265; Jerome Blum, *Lord and Peasant in Russia from the Ninth to the Nineteenth Century* (Princeton, 1961), pp. 235–239; Butsinskii, *Mangazeia i mangazeiskii uezd*, p. 1.

3. Fisher, *Russian Fur Trade*, pp. 175–178.

4. P. N. Butsinskii, *Zaselenie Sibiri*, pp. 139–140; F. A. Golder, *Russian Expansion on the Pacific*, p. 19, note 8.

5. George V. Lantzeff, *Siberia in the Seventeenth Century*, pp. 47–61.

6. Golder, *Russian Expansion on the Pacific*, pp. 22–23, especially notes 16 and 18.

7. *Ibid.*, p. 23; Yuri Semënov, *The Conquest of Siberia*, translated from the German by E. W. Dickes (London, 1944), p. 95.

8. Semënov, *Conquest of Siberia,* pp. 95–96.

9. "Mirskaia chelobitnaia tsariu Mikhailu Fedorovichu torgovykh i promyshlennykh liudei o nasiliiakh iakutskago voevody Petra Golovina," 1645g., ne ranee noiabria 21, in Ia. P. Al'kor and B. D. Grekov, *Kolonial'naia politika moskovskogo gosudarstva v Iakutii XVII v.* (Leningrad, 1936), p. 28. See also "Chelobytnaia Iakutskikh sluzhilykh liudei Vasil'ia Burga s tovarishchami, o pritesneniiakh ikh voevodoiu Vasil'em Pushkinym, ostavlenii imi Iakutska i stranstvovanii po rekam Iane, Indigirke, i Kovyme, dlia priiska novykh zemel' i iasachnago sbora s inorodtsev," 9 iiunia–1 sentiabria 11649g., in *DAI,* document No. 56, p. 211.

10. Golder, *Russian Expansion on the Pacific,* p. 19.

11. Russians at Tobolsk, for example, seized Kuchum Khan's successor at a ceremonial dinner and massacred his escort. Miller, *Istoriia Sibiri,* I, pp. 275–277. See also Butsinskii, *Zaselenie Sibiri,* p. 327; Butsinskii, *Mangazeia i mangazeiskii uezd,* p. 22; Lantzeff, *Siberia in the Seventeenth Century,* pp. 96–107; Ogorodnikov, *Ocherk istorii sibiri,* II, pp. 40–65; Fisher, *Russian Fur Trade,* pp. 33–45.

12. Fisher, *Russian Fur Trade,* pp. 49–50; S. V. Bakhrushin, "Iasak v Sibiri v XVIIv.," in Bakhrushin, *Nauchnye trudy,* III, pt. 2, pp. 49–57.

13. Bakhrushin, "Iasak v Sibiri v XVI v.," in Bakhrushin, *Nauchnye trudy,* III, pt. 2," pp. 58–60; Fisher, *Russian Fur Trade,* pp. 58–59, 68–69, 108–130, 140–142, 161–163, 179–180, 184–185, 191–193; A. A. Tirov, ed., *Sibir' v XVIIv. Sbornik starinnykh russkikh statei o Sibiri i prilezhashchikh k nei zemliakh* (Moscow, 1890), pp. 9–22; Butskinskii, *Mangazeia i mangazeiskii uezd,* pp. 26–27; Bakhrushin, "Puti v Sibir' v XVI–XVIIvv.," pp. 105–110.

14. Fisher, *Russian Fur Trade,* pp. 208–209; Mancall, *Russia and China,* pp. 11–13, 36–37.

15. Bassin, "Expansion and Colonialism," pp. 8–10, 14–15.

16. Kabo, *Goroda Zapadnoi Sibiri,* pp. 84–85; Butsinskii, *Zaselenie Sibiri* (Kharkov, 1889), pp. 103–142.

17. Okladnikov et al., eds., *Istoriia Sibiri,* II, p. 263.

18. *Ibid.,* pp. 271–272.

19. F. Kudriavtsev and G. Vendrikh, *Irkutsk: Ocherki po istorii goroda* (Irkutsk, 1971), pp. 13–19; V. P. Sukachev, *Irkutsk: Ego mesto i znachenie v istorii i kul'turnom razvitii Vostochnoi Sibiri* (Moscow, 1891), pp. 1–4.

20. Quoted in Bassin, "Expansion and Colonialism," p. 16.

21. V. I. Shunkov, *Ocherki po istorii kolonizatsii Sibiri v XVII–nachale XVIII vekov* (Moscow and Leningrad, 1946), pp. 137–173, 45–46; James R. Gibson, *Feeding the Russian Fur Trade,* p. 223; Lantzeff, *Siberia in the Seventeenth Century,* pp. 157–158, 167–169; P. A. Slovtsov, *Istoricheskoe obozrenie Sibiri* (St. Petersburg, 1886), I, p. 85; Vernadsky, *Tsardom of Moscow,* pt. 2, p. 673.

22. Quoted in F. Martens, *Sobranie traktatov i konventsii, zakliuchennykh Rossieiu s inostrannymi derzhavami* (St. Petersburg, 1892–1894), XIII, p. lxxiv.

23. Quoted in A. A. Brikhner, *Istoriia Petra Velikago* (St. Petersburg, 1882), IV, p. 461.

Chapter 12. The Demidovs, Frontier Iron, and Tsar Peter

1. Quoted in P. N. Miliukov, *Gosudarstvennoe khoziaistvo Rossii v pervoi chetverti XVIII stoletiia i reforma Petra Velikago* (St. Petersburg, 1892), p. 528.

2. Thomas Esper, "Military Self-Sufficiency and Weapons Technology in Muscovite Russia," *SR,* XXVIII (1969), pp. 187–197; S. G. Strumilin, *Istoriia chërnoi metallurgii v SSSR* (Moscow, 1954), I, pp. 16–32.

3. Quoted in P. G. Liubomirov, *Ocherki po istorii metallurgicheskoi i metaloobrabatyvaiushchei promyshlennosti v Rossii (XVII, XVIII i nachalo XIX vv.)* (Leningrad, 1937), pp. 65–66; Hugh D. Hudson, Jr., *The Rise of the Demidov Family and the Russian Iron industry in the Eighteenth Century* (Newtonville, Mass., 1986), p. 38.

4. Quoted in Hudson, *Rise of the Demidov Family,* p. 61.

5. *Ibid.*, pp. 37–38; Roger Portal, *L'Oural au XVIIIe siècle: Etude d'histoire économique et sociale* (Paris, 1950), pp. 54–55.

6. B. B. Kafengauz, *Istoriia khoziaistva Demidovykh v XVIII–XIX vv. Opyt issledovaniia po istorii ural'skoi metallurgii* (Moscow and Leningrad, 1949), pp. 82–89.

7. Quoted in Hudson, *Rise of the Demidov Family*, p. 38.

8. E. P. Karnovich, *Zamechatel'nye bogatstva chastnykh lits v Rossii: Ekonomichesko-istori-cheskoe izsledovanie* (St. Petersburg, 1874), pp. 194–195; I. Kh. Gamel, *Opisanie tul'skago oruzheinago zavoda v istoricheskom i tekhnicheskom otnoshenii* (Moscow, 1826), pp. 31–37.

9. Kafengauz, *Istoriia khoziaistva Demidovykh*, pp. 86–94.

10. Hudson, *Rise of the Demidov Family*, p. 39.

11. Kafengauz, *Istoriia khoziaistva Demidovykh*, pp. 160–163.

12. P. I. Liashchenko, *Istoriia narodnogo khoziaistva SSSR* (Moscow, 1956), I, p. 443; A. Cherkas, "Nikita Demidych Demidov," *RBS*, vol. Dab–Diad, pp. 217–219.

13. Portal, *L'Oural au XVIIIe siècle*, pp. 57–58.

14. Quoted in Hudson, *Rise of the Demidov Family*, p. 53.

15. S. G. Strumilin, *Chërnaia metallurgiia v Rossii i v SSSR: Tekhnicheskii progress za 300 let* (Moscow and Leningrad, 1935), pp. 155–166; Kafengauz, *Istoriia khoziaistva Demidovykh*, pp. 188–203; Hudson, *Rise of the Demidov Family*, pp. 49–50.

16. Kafengauz, *Istoriia khoziaistva Demidovykh*, pp. 400–401.

17. Joseph T. Fuhrmann, *The Origins of Capitalism in Russia: Industry and Progress in the Sixteenth and Seventeenth Centuries* (Chicago, 1972), pp. 48–49.

18. Quoted in Hudson, *Rise of the Demidov Family*, p. 51.

19. A. A. Kuzin, *Istoriia otkrytii rudnykh mestorozhdenii v Rossii do serediny XIX v.* (Moscow, 1961), pp. 52–70.

20. Z. G. Karpenko, *Gornaia i metallurgicheskaia promyshlennost' zapadnoi Sibiri v 1700–1860 godakh* (Novosibirsk, 1963), pp. 47–48, 57–58; Kuzin, *Istoriia otkrytii rudnykh mestorozhdenii*, pp. 193–194; Kafengauz, *Istoriia khoziaistva Demidovykh*, pp. 167–168.

21. Hudson, *Rise of the Demidov Family*, pp. 80–114.

Chapter 13. Bering's First Voyage

1. B. P. Polevoi, "Vodnyi put' iz Ledovitogo Okeana v Tikhii: Zabytii nakaz A. A. Viniusa 1697 goda," *Priroda*, No. 5 (1965), p. 94; A. V. Efimov, *Iz istorii russkikh geografiches-kikh otkrytii* (Moscow, 1949), pp. 104–105; A. I. Andreev, "Ekspeditsii V. Beringa," *Izvestiia Vsesoiuznogo Geograficheskogo Obshchestva*, 75, No. 2 (mart–aprel' 1943), pp. 4–5; L. S. Berg, *Otkrytie Kamchatki i ekspeditsiia Beringa, 1725–1742gg* (Moscow and Leningrad, 1946), pp. 9–10.

2. Quoted in B. P. Polevoi, "The Discovery of Russian America," in S. Frederick Starr, ed., *Russia's American Colony* (Durham, N.C., 1987), pp. 18–19.

3. Quoted in *ibid.*, pp. 17–18.

4. Raymond Fisher, *Bering's Voyages: Whither and Why?* (Seattle and Washington, 1977), *passim*, reevaluates much of the long-standing evidence and shows that although Peter the Great often spoke of finding a Northeast Passage and supported a number of efforts to do so, he had a very different purpose in mind; B. A. Polevoi, "Glavnaia zadacha pervoi kamchatskoi ekspeditsii po zamyslu Petra I," *Voprosy geografii Kamchatki*, No. 2 (1964), pp. 88–94.

5. Polevoi, "Discovery of Russian America," pp. 19–20.

6. Quoted in Golder, *Russian Expansion on the Pacific*, pp. 133–134, note 296.

7. Polevoi, "Discovery of Russian America," pp. 21–23.

8. M. I. Belov, *Arkticheskoe moreplavanie s drevneishikh vremën*, pp. 251–252.

9. V. A. Divin, *Velikii russkii moreplavatel' A. I. Chirikov* (Moscow, 1953), p. 43.

10. *Ibid.*, pp. 27–36; Leonhard Stejneger, *Georg Wilhelm Steller: The Pioneer of Alaskan Natural History* (Cambridge, 1936), pp. 96–97.

11. Quoted in Semënov, *Siberia: Its Conquest and Development,* p. 143.

12. Peter Lauridsen, *Vitus Bering: The Discoverer of Bering Strait,* translated from the Danish by Julius E. Olsen, with an introduction by Frederick Schwatka (Chicago, 1889), pp. 19–24.

13. L. S. Berg, *Otkrytie Kamchatki i ekspeditsii Beringa, 1727–1742* (Moscow and Leningrad, 1946), pp. 83–85; F. A. Golder, ed., *Bering's Voyages: An Account of the Efforts of the Russians to Determine the Relation of Asia to America* (New York, 1922), I, pp. 15–16; Divin, *Velikii russkii moreplavatel' A. I. Chirikov,* pp. 42–47; Golder, *Russian Expansion on the Pacific,* pp. 134–138.

14. Berg, *Otkrytie Kamchatki i ekspeditsii Beringa,* pp. 85–87; Divin, *Velikii russkii moreplavatel' A. I. Chirikov,* pp. 45–47; Golder, *Russian Expansion on the Pacific,* pp. 137–139; Lauridsen, *Vitus Bering,* pp. 24–27.

15. Peter Dobell, *Travels in Kamtchatka and Siberia; With a Narrative of a Residence in China* (London, 1830), I, pp. 100, 102.

16. "Bering's Report," in Golder, ed., *Bering's Voyages,* I, pp. 16–17; Divin, *Velikii russkii moreplavatel' A. I. Chirikov,* pp. 47–49; Golder, *Russian Expansion on the Pacific,* pp. 137–140.

17. "Bering's Report," p. 18.

18. *Ibid.*

19. *Ibid.,* p. 19; Berg, *Otkrytie Kamchatki i ekspeditsii Beringa,* p. 88.

20. "Bering's Report," p. 19.

21. Quoted in Golder, *Russian Expansion on the Pacific,* p. 148.

22. "Bering's Report," p. 25.

23. Golder, *Russian Expansion on the Pacific,* p. 165.

24. Quoted in Polevoi, "The Discovery of Russian America," p. 23.

25. Quoted in *ibid.,* p. 170.

Chapter 14. The Great Northern Expedition

1. Belov, *Arkticheskoe moreplavanie,* I, pp. 264–271; Lauridsen, *Vitus Bering,* pp. 65–74.

2. Stejneger, *Georg Wilhelm Steller,* pp. 92–95; Lauridsen, *Vitus Bering,* pp. 64–69.

3. Lauridsen, *Vitus Bering,* pp. 65–73.

4. Stejneger, *Georg Wilhelm Steller,* pp. 94–95.

5. Quoted in Golder, *Russian Expansion on the Pacific,* p. 250.

6. Golder, *Russian Expansion on the Pacific,* pp. 171–173; Berg, *Otkrytie Kamchatki i ekspeditsii Beringa,* pp. 130–132.

7. Quoted in Golder, ed., *Bering's Voyages,* I, p. 33.

8. The following discussion of the expeditions that explored the Arctic coast from Arkhangelsk to Berëzov is drawn mainly from the following: Belov, *Arkticheskoe moreplavanie,* I, pp. 272–289; Berg, *Otkrytie Kamchatki i ekspeditsiia Beringa,* pp. 312–315; Golder, *Russian Expansion on the Pacific,* pp. 232–234.

9. Quoted in Berg, *Otkrytie Kamchatki i ekspeditsiia Beringa,* p. 314.

10. The following materials on Ovtsyn's explorations from Tobolsk to Eniseisk are taken mainly from Belov, *Arkticheskoe moreplavanie,* I, pp. 289–296; Berg, *Otkrytie Kamchatki i ekspeditsiia Beringa,* pp. 315–317; Golder, *Russian Expansion on the Pacific,* pp. 234–236.

11. Golder, *Russian Expansion on the Pacific,* p. 236.

12. My account of Minin's effort to circumnavigate the Taimyr peninsula from the west and the efforts by the Pronchishchevs and Khariton Laptev to accomplish the same feat from the east is based mainly upon the following: Belov, *Arkticheskoe moreplavanie,* I, pp. 296–315; Berg, *Otkrytie Kamchatki i ekspeditsiia Beringa,* pp. 317–337; Golder, *Russian Expansion on the Pacific,* pp. 236–241.

13. Quoted in Belov, *Arkticheskoe moreplavanie,* I, p. 306.

14. Berg, *Otkrytie Kamchatki i ekspeditsiia Beringa,* p. 327.

15. My brief discussion of the explorations of Lasinius and his successor Dmitrii Laptev is much indebted to the materials found in Belov, *Arkticheskoe moreplavanie,* I, pp.

315–327; Berg, *Otkrytie Kamchatki i ekspeditsiia Beringa*, pp. 337–342; Golder, *Russian Expansion on the Pacific*, pp. 242–247; Stejneger, *Georg Wilhelm Steller*, pp. 187–192.

16. Lauridsen, *Vitus Bering*, pp. 65–73.

17. Stejneger, *Georg Wilhelm Steller*, pp. 100–106; S. M. Troitskii, "Gerard Fridrikh Miller," *SIE*, IX, col. 442; J. L. Black, "Gerhardt-Friedrich Müller," *MERSH*, XXIII, pp. 169–174; S. P. Krasheninnikov, *Opisanie zemli Kamchatki* (Moscow and Leningrad, 1949), pp. 22–25 (part of N. N. Stepanov's lengthy introductory essay, "Stepan Petrovich Krasheninnikov i ego trud *Opisanie zemli Kamchatki*").

18. Stejneger, *Georg Wilhelm Steller*, pp. 106–109; Krasheninnikov, *Opisanie zemli Kamchatki*, pp. 26–27.

19. Troitskii, "Gerard Fridrikh Miller," col. 442; Black, "Gerhardt-Friedrich Müller," pp. 169–174; Hans Rogger, *National Consciousness in Eighteenth-Century Russia* (Cambridge, Mass., 1960), pp. 202–213; Stejneger, *Georg Wilhelm Steller*, 107–115.

20. N. N. Stepanov, ed., *S. P. Krasheninnikov v Sibiri: Neopublikovannye materialy* (Moscow and Leningrad, 1966), 18–33; E. A. P. Crownhart-Vaughan, "Introduction," in S. P. Krasheninnikov, *Explorations of Kamchatka: A Report of a Journey Made to Explore Eastern Siberia in 1735–1741, by Order of the Russian Imperial Government*, translated with introduction and notes by E. A. P. Crownhart-Vaughan (Portland, 1972), pp. xxv–xxvii.

21. Krasheninnikov, *Opisanie zemli Kamchatki*, p. 529.

22. *Ibid.*, p. 530.

23. *Ibid.*, p. 193.

24. *Ibid.*, pp. 357, 366, 368, 393, 395, 368.

25. Quoted in Stejneger, *Georg Wilhelm Steller*, p. 199.

26. *Ibid.*, pp. 133–203.

27. *Ibid.*, pp. 232–234, 243–244.

28. *Ibid.*, pp. 232–243, 482–500; Krasheninnikov, *Opisanie zemli Kamchatki*, pp. 30–51.

Chapter 15. The Russians "Discover" America

1. This discussion of the background of the Gvozdev-Fedorov expedition, as well as the material on it in the chapters that follow, is drawn from the following: L. G. Kamanin, *Pervye issledovateli dal'nego vostoka* (Moscow, 1951), pp. 69–78; Berg, *Otkrytie Kamchatki i ekspeditsii Beringa*, pp. 96–103; Belov, *Arkticheskoe moreplavanie*, I, pp. 258–263; Golder, *Russian Expansion on the Pacific*, pp. 151–164.

2. Quoted in Golder, *Russian Expansion on the Pacific*, pp. 161–162.

3. Lauridsen, *Vitus Bering*, pp. 93–97.

4. *Ibid.*, 79–94.

5. Quoted in Stejneger, *Georg Wilhelm Steller*, pp. 99–100.

6. Lauridsen, *Vitus Bering*, pp. 83–94.

7. On Spanberg's voyages to the Kuriles and Japan, see Belov, *Arkticheskoe moreplavanie*, I, p. 327; Golder, *Russian Expansion on the Pacific*, pp. 220–231.

8. Quoted in Golder, *Russian Expansion on the Pacific*, p. 227, note 448.

9. *Ibid.*, p. 250, note 458.

10. Quoted in Divin, *Velikii russkii moreplavatel' A. I. Chirikov*, p. 105; see also pp. 94–105; Golder, *Russian Expansion on the Pacific*, pp. 169–177.

11. Berg, *Otkrytie Kamchatki i ekspeditsiia Beringa*, pp. 187–188; Golder, *Russian Expansion on the Pacific*, pp. 178–181.

12. On Steller's unpleasant relations with Bering and his crew, see especially G. W. Steller, "Journal of a Sea Voyage from the Harbor of Petropavlovsk in Kamchatka to the Western Coasts of America and the Happenings of the Return Voyage," published as pp. 9–241 of Golder, ed., *Bering's Voyages*, 2, pp. 27–32.

13. Berg, *Otkrytie Kamchatki i ekspeditsiia Beringa*, pp. 189–190; Belov, *Arkticheskoe moreplavanie*, I, pp. 330–331. On the courses sailed by the *St. Peter* and *St. Paul*, see "Chart of

the Voyage of Bering and Chirikov in the 'St. Peter' and 'St. Paul,'" in Golder, ed., *Bering's Voyages*, I, after p. 348.

14. Steller, "Journal," p. 40.

15. *Ibid.*, p. 37.

16. *Ibid.*, p. 34.

17. Quoted in Stejneger, *Georg Wilhelm Steller*, p. 270.

18. *Ibid.*, p. 46; See also pp. 35–37, 49–51.

19. *Ibid.*, pp. 53–54.

20. *Ibid.*, p. 34.

21. "Chart of the Voyage of Bering and Chirikov in the 'St. Peter' and 'St. Paul,'" in Golder, ed., *Bering's Voyages*, I, after p. 348.

22. Steller, "Journal," pp. 77–85; Stejneger, *Georg Wilhelm Steller*, pp. 292–293.

23. Sven Waxell, *The Russian Expedition to America*, with an introduction and notes by M. A. Michael (New York, 1962), pp. 99–100.

24. Sven Waxell, "Report on the Voyage of the *St. Peter*," in Golder, ed., *Bering's Voyages*, I, p. 276.

25. Steller, "Journal," p. 100.

26. *Ibid.*, p. 129.

27. Quoted in *ibid.*, p. 137.

28. Quoted in *ibid.*, p. 133.

29. *Ibid.*, p. 146.

30. Waxell, *Russian Expedition*, p. 110.

31. Steller, "Journal," pp. 157–158.

32. Stejneger, *Georg Wilhelm Steller*, pp. 292–293.

33. Waxell, *Russian Expedition*, pp. 114–115.

34. Steller, "Journal," pp. 211–212.

35. *Ibid.*, p. 212.

36. *Ibid.*, p. 181.

37. *Ibid.*

38. *Ibid.*, p. 241.

39. G. W. Steller, Letter to Professor Johann Gmelin, November 4, 1742, in Golder, ed., *Bering's Voyages*, II, p. 245.

40. Belov, *Arkticheskoe moreplavanie*, I, p. 331.

41. Golder, *Russian Expansion on the Pacific*, p. 187.

42. A. I. Chirikov, "Report on the Voyage of the 'St. Paul,'" in Golder, ed., *Bering's Voyages*, I, pp. 312–323.

43. *Ibid.*, pp. 319, 321, 322.

44. Golder, *Russian Expansion on the Pacific*, p. 189.

45. Gibson, *Feeding the Russian Fur Trade*, p. 28.

46. Steller, "Journal," p. 220.

47. James R. Gibson, "Russian Dependence upon the Natives of Alaska," in Starr, ed., *Russia's American Colony*, p. 78.

48. Gibson, *Feeding the Russian Fur Trade*, p. 28.

Chapter 16. The "Russian Columbus"

1. Gibson, *Feeding the Russian Fur Trade*, pp. 31–32.

2. Steller, "Journal," p. 221.

3. James R. Gibson, *Imperial Russia in Frontier America: The Changing Geography of Supply of Russian America, 1784–1867* (New York, 1976), pp. 35–37; Steller, "Journal," pp. 224–226.

4. Gibson, *Feeding the Russian Fur Trade*, p. 17.

5. S. B. Okun', *Rossiisko-Amerikanskaia Kompaniia* (Moscow and Leningrad, 1939), pp. 20–21.

6. *Ibid.*, p. 44.

7. P. N. Golovin, *The End of Russian America: Captain P. N. Golovin's Last Report, 1862,* translated with introduction and notes by Basil Dmytryshyn and E. A. P. Crownhart-Vaughan (Portland, 1979), p. 27.

8. Semënov, *Siberia: Its Conquest and Development,* p. 187.

9. James R. Gibson, *Imperial Russia in Frontier America,* p. 5n.

10. Quoted in P. A. Tikhmenev, *A History of the Russian-American Company,* translated and edited by Richard A. Pierce and Alton S. Donnelly (Seattle and London, 1978), p. 12.

11. *Ibid.*, pp. 13–14.

12. *Ibid.*, pp. 15–18.

13. Quoted in Marc Raeff, *Siberia and the Reforms of 1822* (Seattle, 1956), p. 7.

14. Okun', *Rossiisko-Amerikanskaia Kompaniia,* pp. 28–30.

15. Quoted in Tikhmenev, *History of the Russian-American Company,* pp. 23–24; see also Okun', *Rossiisko-Amerikanskaia Kompaniia,* pp. 28–30.

16. Quoted in Semenov, *Siberia: Its Conquest and Development,* p. 195.

17. Michel Poniatowski, *Histoire de la Russie d'Amérique et de l'Alaska* (Paris, 1978), pp. 78–84; Gibson, *Imperial Russia in Frontier America,* p. 8.

18. Okun', *Rossiisko-Amerikanskaia Kompaniia,* pp. 32–37.

19. Poniatowski, *Histoire de la Russie d'Amérique,* p. 164.

20. Okun', *Rossiisko-Amerikanskaia Kompaniia,* pp. 38–49.

21. K. T. Khlebnikov, *Baranov: Chief Manager of the Russian Colonies in America,* translated by Colin Bearne, edited by Richard A. Pierce (Kingston, Ontario, 1973), pp. 1–5.

22. Gibson, *Imperial Russia in Frontier America,* p. 10; K. T. Khlebnikov, *Zapiski o koloniiakh v Amerike,* edited by S. G. Fëdorova (Moscow, 1985), pp. 41–44.

23. Khlebnikov, *Zapiski,* pp. 70–71.

24. Quoted in Gibson, *Imperial Russia in Frontier America,* p. 15.

25. *Ibid.*, pp. 11–15; Okun', *Rossiisko-Amerikanskaia Kompaniia,* pp. 50–62.

26. Quoted in Richard A. Pierce, *Russia's Hawaiian Adventure, 1815–1817* (Berkeley, 1965), p. 197; see also *passim;* Gibson, *Imperial Russia in Frontier America,* pp. 141–149; Poniatowski, *Histoire de la Russie d'Amérique,* pp. 217–231.

27. Gibson, *Imperial Russia in Frontier America,* pp. 11, 160–163. See also Khlebnikov, *Baranov,* pp. 77–80; Poniatowski, *Histoire de la Russie d'Amérique,* pp. 249–259.

28. V. K. Andreevich, *Istoricheskii ocherk Sibiri,* V, pp. 159–160.

29. Captain John Dundas Cochrane, *Narrative of a Pedestrian Journey through Russia and Siberian Tartary, from the Frontiers of China to the Frozen Sea of Kamtchatka* (London, 1824), I, p. 399.

30. N. M. Iadrintsev, *Russkaia obshchina v tiurme i ssylke* (St. Petersburg, 1872), pp. 552–555; Marc Raeff, *Siberia and the Reforms of 1822,* pp. 18–19; François-Xavier Coquin, *La Sibérie: Peuplement et Immigration Paysanne au XIXe Siècle* (Paris, 1969), pp. 25–37, 45–59.

Chapter 17. At the Threshold of a New Era

1. Clifford M. Foust, *Muscovite and Mandarin: Russia's Trade with China and Its Setting, 1727–1805* (Chapel Hill, N.C., 1969), pp. 24–43.

2. *Ibid.*, p. 36.

3. Cochrane, *Narrative of a Pedestrian Journey,* II, pp. 167–168.

4. Kennan, *Siberia and the Exile System,* II, pp. 103–104.

5. Quoted in Foust, *Muscovite and Mandarin,* p. 80.

6. Lindon W. Bates, *The Russian Road to China* (Boston and New York, 1910), p. 176.

7. Cochrane, *Narrative of a Pedestrian Journey,* II, p. 170.

8. Foust, *Muscovite and Mandarin,* pp. 355–359.

9. *Ibid.*, pp. 358–359.

10. Quoted in *ibid.*, p. 164.

11. *Ibid.*, pp. 165–185.

12. *Ibid.*, pp. 346–351.

13. Kudriavtsev and Vendrikh, *Irkutsk*, pp. 35–73; Okladnikov et al., eds., *Istoriia Sibiri*, II, pp. 274–277.

14. N. M. Iadrintsev, *Sibir' kak koloniia* (St. Petersburg, 1882), p. 300; Okladnikov et al., eds., *Istoriia Sibiri*, II, pp. 336–337; William Tooke, *View of the Russian Empire During the Reign of Catharine the Second and to the Close of the Eighteenth Century*, 2nd ed. (London, 1800), I, pp. 591–594, and, most particularly, Slezkine's forthcoming *Russia and the Peoples of Siberia's Arctic Frontier*, Chapter 3.

15. Dobell, *Travels*, II, p. 87; Cochrane, *Narrative of a Pedestrian Journey*, I, pp. 210, 213; II, p. 125.

16. Okladnikov et al., eds., *Istoriia Sibiri*, II, pp. 271–272.

17. Kabo, *Goroda Zapadnoi Sibiri*, pp. 84–85; Butsinskii, *Zaselenie Sibiri*, pp. 103–142; Okladnikov et al., eds., *Istoriia Sibiri*, II, pp. 263–266.

18. Dobell, *Travels*, p. 113.

19. *Ibid.*, p. 115.

20. L. G. Beskrovnyi, ed., *Opisanie Tobol'skogo namestnichestva, sostavlennoe v 1789–1790gg.* (Novosibirsk, 1982), pp. 246–251.

21. Iadrintsev, *Russkaia obshchina*, p. 551.

22. Foust, *Muscovite and Mandarin*, p. 102.

23. Quoted in John Ledyard, *John Ledyard's Journey Through Russia and Siberia, 1787–1788*, edited with an introduction by Stephen D. Watrous (Madison, 1966), p. 72.

24. Quoted in *ibid.*

25. Dobell, *Travels*, p. 88.

26. Ledyard, *John Ledyard's Journey*, p. 70.

27. Donald W. Treadgold, *The Great Siberian Migration: Government and Peasant in Resettlement from Emancipation to the First World War* (Princeton, 1957), p. 32.

28. M. T. Florinsky, *Russia: A History and An Interpretation* (New York, 1968), I, p. 384.

29. Iadrintsev, *Sibir' kak koloniia*, pp. 300–305.

30. Raeff, *Siberia and the Reforms of 1822*, pp. 35–37.

31. A. P. Shchapov, "Sibirskoe obshchestvo do Speranskago," in A. P. Shchapov, *Sochineniia A. P. Shchapova* (St. Petersburg, 1908), III, p. 709.

Chapter 18. Governor-General Speranskii

1. Marc Raeff, *Michael Speransky: Statesman of Imperial Russia, 1772–1839* (The Hague, 1957), pp. 1–79, 170–202.

2. Raeff, *Siberia and the Reforms of 1822*, pp. 21–46.

3. *Ibid.*, pp. 25–27.

4. *Ibid.*, pp. 44–46.

5. Quoted in Raeff, *Michael Speransky*, p. 252.

6. Raeff, *Siberia and the Reforms of 1822*, p. 70.

7. Quoted in Baron M. A. Korf, *Zhizn' Grafa Speranskago* (St. Petersburg, 1861), II, p. 200.

8. Quoted in *ibid.*, pp. 201–202.

9. Raeff, *Michael Speransky*, pp. 257–259.

10. *Ibid.*, pp. 255–257; Raeff, *Siberia and the Reforms of 1822*, pp. 41–42.

11. Gibson, *Feeding the Russian Fur Trade*, pp. 222–223.

12. Raeff, *Michael Speransky*, pp. 257–258; Raeff, *Siberia and the Reforms of 1822*, pp. 42–43.

13. Raeff, *Siberia and the Reforms of 1822*, p. 111.

14. *Ibid.*, pp. 62–63, 112–124.

15. Quoted in *ibid.*, p. 69.

16. Quoted in Raeff, *Michael Speranskii*, p. 267.

17. *Ibid.*, p. 260.

18. The complete Statutes of 1822 on Siberia are published in *Polnoe sobranie zakonov rossiiskoi imperii s 1649g.* 2nd ed. (St. Petersburg, 1830), XXXVIII (1822–1823), Nos. 29124–29134, pp. 342–565. These are carefully discussed in Raeff, *Siberia and the Reforms of 1822*, pp. 53–128.

Chapter 19. *Katorga* and *Ssylka*

1. These quotes are from V. N. Dvorianov, *V Sibirskoi dal'nei storone: Ocherki istorii politicheskoi katorgi i ssylki 60-e gody XVIIIv.–1917g.*, 2nd ed. (Minsk, 1985), p. 24; N. M. Iadrintsev, *Russkaia obshchina*, p. 504.

2. S. V. Maksimov, *Sibir' i katorga* (St. Petersburg, 1891), III, pp. 281–288.

3. F. G. Safronov, "Ssylka v Vostochnuiu Sibir' v pervoi polovine XVIIIv.," in M. Goriushkin, ed., *Ssylka i katorga v Sibiri (XVIII–nachalo XXv.)* (Novosibirsk, 1975), pp. 15–16.

4. Iadrintsev, *Russkaia obshchina*, p. 546.

5. A. D. Kolesnikov, "Ssylka i zaselenie Sibiri," in Goriushkin, ed., *Ssylka i katorga v. Sibiri*, pp. 50–51.

6. F. A. Kudriavtsev, "Uchastniki narodnykh dvizhenii pervoi poloviny XIX veka na katorge," in *Ssyl'nye revoliutsionery v Sibiri (XIXv.–fevral' 1917g.)* (Irkutsk, 1974), II, pp. 4–7; Maksimov, *Sibir' i katorga*, II, p. 319; III, pp. 361–378.

7. Dvorianov, *V Sibirskoi dal'nei storone*, p. 54.

8. Quoted in Anatole G. Mazour, *Women in Exile: Wives of the Decembrists* (Tallahassee, 1975), p. v.

9. Quoted in *ibid.*, p. x.

Chapter 20. Two Princesses

1. The account of Ekaterina Laval's early life that follows is much indebted to I. N. Kologrivov, "Ekaterina Ivanovna Trubetskaia," *Sovremennye zapiski*, LX (1936), pp. 206–212; Mazour, *Women in Exile*, pp. 13–20.

2. Mazour, *Women in Exile*, p. 17.

3. The account of Mariia Volkonskaia's (née Raevskaia) early life that follows comes from M. N. Volkonskaia, *Zapiski* (St. Petersburg, 1916); Mazour, *Women in Exile*, pp. 57–64.

4. B. L. Mozdalevskii and A. A. Sivers, eds., *Vosstaniia dekabristov: Materialy* (Leningrad, 1925), VIII, pp. 57–58, 297–298.

5. Marc Raeff, *The Decembrist Movement* (Englewood Cliffs, N.J., 1966), pp. 1–29; V. I. Semevskii, *Politicheskie i obshchestvennye idei dekabristov* (St. Petersburg, 1909), pp. 286–377; M. V. Nechkina, *Dvizhenie Dekabristov* (Moscow, 1955), I, pp. 304–342.

6. Mozdalevskii and Sivers, eds., *Vosstaniia dekabristov*, VIII, pp. 57–58, 186–187, 297–298, 405–406.

7. For a brief discussion of the very murky events surrounding Alexander's death and Nicholas's accession, see W. Bruce Lincoln, *Nicholas I: Emperor and Autocrat of All the Russias* (London, 1978), pp. 18–38.

8. Quoted in Mozdalevskii and Sivers, eds., *Vosstaniia dekabristov*, I, p. 187.

9. Nicholas I, "Zapiska Nikolaia I o vstuplenii na prestol'," in B. E. Syroechkovskii, ed., *Mezhdutsarstvie 1825 goda i vosstanie dekabristov v perepiske i memuarakh chlenov tsarskoi sem'i* (Moscow and Leningrad, 1926), pp. 28–35; A. E. Presniakov, *14 dekabria 1825 goda* (Moscow and Leningrad, 1926), pp. 101–132; Lincoln, *Nicholas I*, pp. 39–47; Anatole G. Mazour, *The First Russian Revolution 1825: The Decembrist Movement: Its Origins, Development, and Significance* (Berkeley, 1937), pp. 169–180.

10. Nicholas I, "Zapiska Nikolaia I o vstuplenii na prestol'," pp. 29–30.

11. *Ibid.;* Grand Duke Mikhail Pavlovich, "Vospominaniia velikago kniazia Mikhaila Pavlovicha o sobytiiakh 14 dekabria 1825g.," in Syroechkovskii, ed., *Mezhdutsarstvie,* p. 62.

12. Quoted in Mazour, *Women in Exile,* p. 18.

13. Quoted in *ibid.,* p. 18.

14. *Ibid.,* p. 19.

15. Quoted in *ibid.,* p. 63.

16. Quoted in *ibid.,* p. 57.

17. Kennan, *Siberia and the Exile System,* II, p. 287; see also Semënov, *Geografichesko-statisticheskii slovar' rossiiskoi imperii* (St. Petersburg, 1865–1887), I, p. 30.

18. Quoted in S. B. Okun', *Dekabrist M. S. Lunin* (Leningrad, 1962), p. 256.

19. Quoted in Mazour, *First Russian Revolution,* p. 239.

20. M. K. Azadovskii and I. M. Trotskii, eds., *Vospominaniia Bestuzhevykh* (Moscow, 1931), p. 256.

21. Quoted in Glynn Barratt, *M. S. Lunin: Catholic Decembrist* (Mouton, 1976), p. 79.

22. Quoted in Dvorianov, *V Sibirskoi dal'nei storone,* p. 47.

23. Nechkina, *Dvizhenie Dekabristov,* II, p. 430.

24. Quoted in Azadovskii and Trotskii, eds., *Vospominaniia Bestuzhevykh,* p. 209.

25. Dvorianov, *V Sibirskoi dal'nei storone,* p. 47.

26. Mazour, *First Russian Revolution,* p. 248.

27. Quoted in Mazour, *Women in Exile,* p. 104.

28. *Ibid.,* pp. 99–105.

29. Quoted in *ibid.,* p. 99.

30. M. N. Gernet, *Istoriia tsarskoi tiurmy* (Moscow, 1961), II, p. 205.

31. Quoted in Dvorianov, *V Sibirskoi dal'nei storone,* p. 52.

32. Quoted in Mazour, *First Russian Revolution,* p. 233.

33. Quoted in Mazour, *Women in Exile,* p. 70.

34. Dvorianov, *V Sibirskoi dal'nei storone,* p. 53.

35. Quoted in Mazour, *Women in Exile,* p. 70.

36. Quoted in *ibid.*

37. Quoted in *ibid.,* p. 54.

38. Quoted in *ibid.,* p. 77.

39. Maksimov, *Sibir' i katorga,* II, pp. 320–332; Iadrintsev, *Russkaia obshchina,* pp. 563–568; Dvorianov, *V Sibirskoi dal'nei storone,* pp. 260–261.

40. F. M. Dostoevskii, *Zapiski iz mërtvogo doma,* in *Polnoe sobranie sochinenii v tridtsati tomakh* (Leningrad, 1972), IV, p. 20.

Chapter 21. Dostoevskii in the "House of the Dead"

1. "Vsepoddanneishaia dokladnaia zapiska grafa Uvarova [k Ego Imperatorskomu Velichestvu Nikolaiu Pavlovichu] 21 marta 1849g." (including Nicholas I's marginal comments) TsGIAL, fond 772, opis' 1, delo No. 2242/6–42; see also "Otnoshenie Deistvitel'nago Tainago Sovetnika Dmitriia Buturlina 17-go marta 1849g., k Ministru Nadvornago Prosveshcheniia Grafu S. S. Uvarovu" (konfidential'no), TsGIAL, fond 772, opis' 1, delo No. 2242/1–3; M. Lemke, *Ocherki po istorii russkoi tsenzury i zhurnalistiki stoletiia* (St. Petersburg, 1904), pp. 183–308; A. S. Nifontov, *Rossiia v 1848 godu* (Moscow, 1949), pp. 223–227; A. V. Golovnin, "Prodolzhenie zapisok A. V. Golovnina s dekabria 1870g. po fevral' 1871g.," TsGIAL, fond 851, opis' 1, delo No. 9/7–8; N. Rodzianko, "Nabliudeniia za dukhom i napravleniem zhurnala *Biblioteka dlia chteniia*" (mai 1850), TsGIAL, fond 772, opis' 1, delo No. 2423/16; M. M. Pogodin, *Istoriko-politicheskie pis'ma i Zapiski v prodolzhenii krymskoi voiny, 1853–1856gg.* (Moscow, 1874), p. 257; Lemke, *Ocherki po istorii russkoi tsenzury,*

pp. 239, 266–269; A. V. Nikitenko, *Dnevnik* (Moscow, 1955), I, pp. 312–313; "Konfidential'noe pis'mo Barona Korfa Ministru Vnutrennikh Del L.A. Perovskomu," 21 iiunia 1850g., TsGIAL, fond 1287, opis' 35, delo No. 97/1–2.

2. Lincoln, *Nicholas I*, pp. 303–310; J. H. Seddon, *The Petrashevtsy: A Study of the Russian Revolutionaries of 1848* (Manchester, 1985), pp. 24–31.

3. Seddon, *The Petrashevtsy*, p. 237.

4. *Ibid.*, pp. 14–15.

5. Quoted in Leonid Grossman, *Dostoevskii* (Moscow, 1965), p. 152.

6. F. M. Dostoevskii, *Pis'ma* (Moscow and Leningrad, 1928), I, p. 128.

7. Quoted in Grossman, *Dostoevskii*, p. 154.

8. S. V. Kodan, "Petrashevtsy na Nerchinskoi katorge," *Ssyl'nye revoliutsionery v Sibiri (XIXv.–fevral' 1917g.)* (Irkutsk, 1981), VI, pp. 8–9; Seddon, *The Petrashevtsy*, p. 237.

9. Quoted in Grossman, *Dostoevskii*, p. 157.

10. Quoted in *ibid.*, p. 161.

11. Kniaz E. E. Ukhtomskii, *Puteshestvie Gosudaria Imperatora Nikolaia II na Vostok (v 1890–1891)* (St. Petersburg, 1897), VI, pp. 130–131; Kennan, *Siberia and the Exile System*, II, pp. 421–422.

12. Quoted in Grossman, *Dostoevskii*, p. 164.

13. Dostoevskii, *Zapiski iz mërtvogo doma*, p. 55.

14. *Ibid.*, p. 10.

15. Gernet, *Istoriia tsarskoi tiurmy*, II, p. 515.

16. *Ibid.*, pp. 54–56.

17. Kennan, *Siberia and the Exile System*, II, p. 307.

18. Dostoevskii, *Zapiski iz mërtvogo doma*, p. 11.

19. *Ibid.*, pp. 62–63.

20. *Ibid.*, p. 20.

21. Gernet, *Istoriia tsarskoi tiurmy*, II, pp. 516–517.

22. Kennan, *Siberia and the Exile System*, I, pp. 142–143.

23. V. A. Tsie, "Zapiska o merakh, neobkhodimykh dlia sokrashcheniia perepiski i uproshcheniia deloproizvodstva v gosudarstvennykh uchrezhdeniiakh" (1856g.), GPB, fond 833, delo No. 292/1–4.

24. *Kolokol*, No. 13 (15 aprelia 1858g.), in *Kolokol: Gazeta A. I. Gertsena i N. P. Ogareva* (Moscow, 1961), I, p. 98.

Chapter 22. The Search for Gold

1. Herodotus is quoted in V. V. Danilevskii, *Russkoe zoloto: Istoriia otkrytiia i dobychi do serediny XIXv.* (Moscow, 1959); see also Okladnikov et al., eds., *Istoriia Sibiri*, II, pp. 397–398.

2. Okladnikov et al., eds., *Istoriia Sibiri*, pp. 393–394; Danilevskii, *Russkoe zoloto*, pp. 15–29.

3. Danilevskii, *Russkoe zoloto*, pp. 30–32.

4. *Ibid.*, pp. 79–86; Kennan, *Siberia and the Exile System*, II, p. 304.

5. Danilevskii, *Russkoe zoloto*, p. 315.

6. *Ibid.*, pp. 32, 34, 51, 257.

7. *Ibid.*, pp. 55–58; Kuzin, *Istoriia otkrytii*, pp. 277–279.

8. Danilevskii, *Russkoe zoloto*, pp. 114–127.

9. *Ibid.*, pp. 114–120; Thomas Witlam Atkinson, *Oriental and Western Siberia: A Narrative of Seven Years' Explorations and Adventures in Siberia, Mongolia, the Kirghis Steppes, Chinese Tartary, and Part of Central Asia* (Philadelphia, 1859), p. 103.

10. Danilevskii, *Russkoe zoloto*, pp. 114–127, 257.

11. *Ibid.*, pp. 249–250, 255; V. I. Semevskii, *Rabochie na Sibirskikh zolotykh promyslakh* (St. Petersburg, 1898), pp. 4–5; Kuzin, *Istoriia otkrytii*, pp. 288–290; Okladnikov et al., eds., *Istoriia Sibiri*, II, pp. 405–415; R. M. Kabo, *Goroda Zapadnoi Sibiri*, p. 156.

12. Okladnikov et al., eds., *Istoriia Sibiri,* II, p. 399; Danilevskii, *Russkoe zoloto,* pp. 253–255.

13. *Ibid.;* Perry McDonough Collins, *A Voyage down the Amoor: With a Land Journey Through Siberia, and Incidental Notices of Manchooria, Kamschatka, and Japan* (New York, 1860), pp. 125–126.

14. Dobell, *Travels,* I, p. 12.

15. Okladnikov et al., eds., *Istoriia Sibiri,* II, pp. 400–402.

16. *Ibid.,* p. 398; Semevskii, *Rabochie na sibirskikh zolotykh promyslakh,* pp. 7–8, 121–131; P. P. Semënov, ed., *Zhivopisnaia Rossiia. Otechestvo nashe v ego zemel'nom, istoricheskom, plemennom, ekonomicheskom i bytovom znachenii* (St. Petersburg and Moscow, 1895), XII, pt. 1, p. 91.

17. Semevskii, *Rabochie na sibirskikh zolotykh promyslakh,* pp. 117–120.

18. Okladnikov et al., eds., *Istoriia Sibiri,* II, pp. 400–402.

19. Atkinson, *Oriental and Western Siberia,* pp. 261–262; Okladnikov et al., eds., *Istoriia Sibiri,* II, pp. 401–402.

20. Okladnikov et al., eds., *Istoriia Sibiri,* II, p. 361; N. M. Iadrintsev, *Sibir' kak koloniia,* pp. 150–151.

Chapter 23. Muravëv Takes the Amur

1. M. I. Veniukov, "Graf Nikolai Nikolaevich Murav'ëv-Amurskii," *RS,* XXXII (1883), pp. 523–524; Ivan Barsukov, *Graf Nikolai Nikolaevich Murav'ëv-Amurskii po ego pis'mam, offitsial'nym dokumentam, rasskazam sovremennikov i pechatnym istochnikam (Materialy dlia biografii)* (Moscow, 1891), I, pp. 1–174.

2. Semënov (ed.), *Zhivopisnaia Rossiia,* XII, pt. 2, pp. 283–284.

3. Barsukov, *Graf Nikolai Nikolaevich Murav'ëv-Amurskii,* I, pp. 170–174; Ravenstein, *The Russians on the Amur,* pp. 203–212; Semënov, *Siberia: Its Conquest and Development,* pp. 247–248.

4. N. N. Murav'ëv, "Prichiny neobkhodimosti zaniatiia ust'ia r. Amura i toi chasti ostrova Sakhalina, kotoraia emu protivolezhit', a takzhe levago berega Amura" (1849–1850), in Barsukov, *Graf Nikolai Nikolaevich Murav'ëv-Amurskii,* II, p. 47.

5. *Ibid.,* p. 48.

6. N. N. Murav'ëv, "Nachal'niku Glavnago Morskago Shtaba Ego Imperatorskago Velichestva, gospodinu general-ad"iutantu Men'shikovu" 1 ianvaria 1850, in Barsukov, *Graf Nikolai Nikolaevich Murav'ëv-Amurskii,* II, p. 52.

7. Quoted in Karl Baedeker, *Russia 1914* (Leipzig, 1914), p. 539.

8. Barsukov, *Graf Nikolai Nikolaevich Murav'ëv-Amurskii,* I, pp. 177–178.

9. Quoted in *ibid.,* p. 179.

10. *Ibid.,* pp. 181–184.

11. *Ibid.,* 238–239.

12. Quoted in *ibid.,* p. 321.

13. Quoted in *ibid.,* p. 346.

14. Quoted in *ibid.,* p. 343.

15. *Ibid.,* pp. 362–370.

16. *Ibid.,* pp. 371–398, 405–421.

17. Harmon Tupper, *To the Great Ocean: Siberia and the Trans-Siberian Railway* (Boston, 1965), p. 43.

18. Major Perry M. Collins, *Overland Explorations in Siberia, Northern Asia, and the Great Amoor River Country; Incidental Notices of Manchooria, Mongolia, Kamschatka, and Japan, with Map and Plan of an Overland Telegraph Around the World, Via Behring's Strait and Asiatic Russia to Europe* (New York, 1864), pp. 1–2.

19. Letter to General Mikhail Korsakov, March 9, 1857, in *ibid.,* p. 384.

20. Collins to General Nikolai Muraviev-Amurskii, April 4, 1857, in *ibid.,* p. 390.

21. Quoted in Barsukov, *Graf Nikolai Nikolaevich Murav'ëv-Amurskii,* I, p. 514.

22. Quoted in Semënov, *Siberia: Its Conquest and Development,* p. 281.

23. Maksimov, *Sibir' i katorga*, II, pp. 320–332; Dvorianov, *V Sibirskoi dal'nei storone*, pp. 260–261; Iadrintsev, *Russkaia obshchina*, pp. 563–568; Kennan, *Siberia and the Exile System*, I, pp. 245–247.

24. Henry Lansdell, *Through Siberia*, 4th ed. (London, 1883), pp. 662–663.

Chapter 24. Kennan's Journey

1. Kennan, *Siberia and the Exile System*, I, pp. 27–30.

2. *Ibid.*, pp. vi–vii, iv.

3. A. I. Ivanchin-Pisarev, "Iz moikh vospominanii (Po doroge v Sibir', v Krasnoiarske i v Minusinske)," *KiS*, LVIII (1929), p. 304.

4. *Ibid.*, pp. 303–304; Vishnevetskii, "Eniseiskaia ssylka v 1878–1893 godakh," *KiS*, LXIX (1930), p. 157.

5. Kennan, *Siberia and the Exile System*, I, p. 84.

6. *Ibid.*, pp. 84–86.

7. Ekaterina Breshkovskaia, *The Little Grandmother of the Russian Revolution: Reminiscences and Letters of Catherine Breshkovsky*, edited by Alice Stone Blackwell (Boston, 1919), p. 95.

8. Kennan, *Siberia and the Exile System*, I, pp. 86–89.

9. *Ibid.*, pp. 94, 90–91.

10. *Ibid.*, pp. 99–101; Joseph Frank Payne, Arthur Shadwell, and Harriet L. Hennessy, "Plague," *EB*, XXI, pp. 694–695.

11. Kennan, *Siberia and the Exile System*, I, pp. 110–119.

12. *Ibid.*, pp. 296–301.

13. *Ibid.*, p. 297.

14. Ekaterina Breshkovskaia, *Hidden Springs of the Russian Revolution: Personal Memoirs of Katerina Breshkovskaia*, edited by Lincoln Hitchinson (Stanford, 1931), p. 183.

15. Leo Deutsch, *Sixteen Years in Siberia: Some Experiences of a Russian Revolutionist*, translated by Helen Chisholm (New York, 1904), pp. 152–153.

16. Kennan, *Siberia and the Exile System*, I, p. 314.

17. *Ibid.*, p. 315.

18. *Ibid.*, p. 309.

19. This paragraph and the ones that follow about convict convoys rely mainly upon the accounts of S. Maksimov (who based his report on conditions in the 1860s), George Kennan (who observed a number of convict convoys in 1885), Ekaterina Bresho-Breshkovskaia (a revolutionary populist noblewoman who was sent to Siberia in 1878), and Lev Deich (one of Russia's first Marxists, who crossed Siberia in a convict convoy in the same year as Kennan). See Maksimov, *Sibir' i katorga*, I, pp. 48–88; Kennan, *Siberia and the Exile System*, I, pp. 369–409; Deutsch, *Sixteen Years in Siberia, passim;* and Breshkovskaia, *Hidden Springs*, pp. 161–259.

20. Quoted in Maksimov, *Sibir' i katorga*, I, p. 81.

21. Deutsch, *Sixteen Years in Siberia*, p. 160.

22. Quoted in Maksimov, *Sibir' i katorga*, I, p. 73.

23. Kennan, *Siberia and the Exile System*, I, p. 391.

24. *Ibid.*, II, pp. 8–9.

25. *Ibid.*, pp. 145–146.

26. *Ibid.*, p. 146.

27. *Ibid.*, pp. 146–147.

28. *Ibid.*, pp. 159–160.

29. Lansdell, *Through Siberia*, II, pp. 76–77.

30. Kennan, *Siberia and the Exile System*, II, p. 289.

31. *Ibid.*, pp. 300, 317.

32. *Ibid.*, pp. 314–315.

33. *Ibid.*, p. 315.
34. *Ibid.*, p. 305.
35. Deutsch, *Sixteen Years in Siberia*, p. 204.
36. Kennan, *Siberia and the Exile System*, II, p. 455.
37. *Ibid.*, p. 456.

Chapter 25. The "Politicals"

1. Israel Getzler, *Martov: A Political Biography of a Russian Social Democrat* (Cambridge, 1967), p. 38.
2. Quoted in Adam Ulam, *Stalin: The Man and His Era* (New York, 1973), p. 123.
3. Quoted in Getzler, *Martov*, p. 39.
4. V. M. Andreev, "Chislennost' i sostav politicheskikh ssyl'nykh v vostochnoi Sibiri v 70–90kh godakh XIX veka," in *Ssyl'nye revoliutsionery v Sibiri* (Irkutsk), V, p. 69; A. D. Margolis, "O chislennosti i razmeshchenii ssyl'nykh v Sibiri v kontse XIXv.," in Goriushkin, ed., *Ssylka i katorga v Sibiri*, pp. 233–235; E. N. Koval'skaia, "Zhenskaia katorga: Iz vospominanii E. N. Koval'skoi," in *Kariiskaia tragediia (1889): Vospominaniia i materialy* (St. Petersburg, 1920), p. 12; Kennan, *Siberia and the Exile System*, II, p. 149.
5. Deutsch, *Sixteen Years in Siberia*, p. 188.
6. *Ibid.*
7. Anton Chekhov, *The Island: A Journey to Sakhalin*, translated by Luba and Michael Terpak (New York, 1967), pp. 331–332.
8. The material in the preceding paragraphs comes from the following: A. Fomin, "Kariiskaia tragediia 1889g. po dokumentam," in A. Dikovskaia-Iakimova and V. Pleskov, eds., *Kara i drugie tiurmy Nerchinskoi katorgi: Sbornik vospominanii, dokumentov, i materialov* (Moscow, 1927), pp. 120–137; Koval'skaia, "Zhenskaia katorga," pp. 5–29; G. F. Osmolovskii, "Kariiskaia tragediia," in *Kariiskaia tragediia*, pp. 30–55; V. Petrovskii, "Kariiskie sobytiia," in *Kariiskaia tragediia*, pp. 56–75; Deutsch, *Sixteen Years in Siberia*, pp. 266–290; Kennan, *Siberia and the Exile System*, II, pp. 212–216, 266–272.
9. Deutsch, *Sixteen Years in Siberia*, pp. 291, 153; N. M. Iadrintsev, *Sibir' kak koloniia*, p. 217.

Chapter 26. "By Administrative Process"

1. Kennan, *Siberia and the Exile System*, I, pp. 245–247.
2. *Ibid.*, pp. 80, 272.
3. *Ibid.*, pp. 263–264.
4. N. M. Iadrintsev, *Sibir' kak koloniia*, p. 217.
5. *Ibid.*, pp. 216–220.
6. *Ibid.*, p. 217.
7. Kennan, *Siberia and the Exile System*, II, pp. 38–39.
8. *Ibid.*, p. 41.
9. *Ibid.*, pp. 47–51.
10. *Ibid.*, pp. 55–56.
11. *Ibid.*, p. 52.
12. Quoted in *ibid.*, p. 22.
13. Quoted in *ibid.*
14. M. Poliakov, "Vospominaniia o Kolymskoi ssylke (1889–1896)," *KiS*, XLV, p. 158.
15. *Ibid.*, p. 162.
16. *Ibid.*, pp. 158, 160, 171, 169.
17. Quoted in Kennan, *Siberia and the Exile System*, II, p. 23.
18. Poliakov, "Vospominaniia o Kolymskoi ssylke," XLV, p. 171.

Chapter 27. Lenin in Exile

1. A. P. Meshcherskii, "Osobennosti, partiinyi sostav politicheskoi ssylki v Sibiri v kontse XIX–nachale XX veka," in *Ssyl'nye revoliutsionery v Sibiri*, I, p. 135.

2. Lenin to M. I. Ul'ianova, March 10, 1897, in A. G. Ivan'kov, *Lenin v sibirskoi ssylke, 1897–1900* (Moscow, 1962), p. 30.

3. Ivan'kov, *Lenin v sibirskoi ssylke*, p. 68.

4. Quoted in *ibid.*, p. 46; see also pp. 38–47.

5. Lenin to M. A. Ul'ianova and A. I. Ul'ianova-Elizarova, April 17, 1897, in Lenin, *Sochineniia*, 4th ed. (Moscow, 1957), XXXVII, p. 37.

6. Lenin to M. A. and M. I. Ul'ianova, May 18, 1897, in Lenin, *Sochineniia*, XXXVII, p. 42; Lenin to M. A. Ul'ianova, September 30, 1897, in *ibid.*, p. 62; Lenin to M. A. Ul'ianova, October 12, 1897, in *ibid.*, p. 63.

7. Lenin to M. A. and M. I. Ul'ianova, May 18, 1897, in Lenin, *Sochineniia*, XXXVII, pp. 43, 42; Lenin to M. A. Ul'ianova and A. I. Ul'ianova-Elizarova, in *ibid.*, p. 51; Lenin to M. A. Ul'ianova, August 17, 1897, in *ibid.*, p. 58; Lenin to M. A. Ul'ianova, February 7, 1898, in *ibid.*, p. 83.

8. Lenin to M. A. Ul'ianova, February 7, 1898, in Lenin, *Sochineniia*, XXXVII, p. 83.

9. Quoted in Louis Fischer, *The Life of Lenin* (New York, 1964), p. 32.

10. Lenin to M. A. and M. I. Ul'ianova, May 18, 1897, in Lenin, *Sochineniia*, XXXVII, p. 41. This description of Shushenskoe is taken from Lenin's letters to his mother, sisters, and brother-in-law, and from Bertram D. Wolfe, *Three Who Made a Revolution: A Biographical History* (New York, 1948), pp. 134–137; Fischer, *Life of Lenin*, pp. 31–33; Ivan'kov, *Lenin v sibirskoi ssylke*, pp. 111–126.

11. Lenin to M. A. Ul'ianova, May 7, 1897, in Lenin, *Sochineniia*, XXXVII, p. 40.

12. Lenin to M. A. Ul'ianova, February 7, 1898, in Lenin, *Sochineniia*, XXXVII, pp. 82–85; Lenin to M. A. Ul'ianova and M. I. Ul'ianova, February 28, 1898, in *ibid.*, pp. 91–93.

13. Lenin to M. A. Ul'ianova, May 10, 1898, in Lenin, *Sochineniia*, XXXVII, pp. 102–103.

14. Nadezhda K. Krupskaia, *Memories of Lenin*, translated by Eric Verney (New York, n.d.), pp. 31–32.

15. *Ibid.*, p. 32, 35.

16. Quoted in *ibid.*, p. 35.

17. *Ibid.*, p. 30.

18. Quoted in Isaac Deutscher, *The Prophet Armed: Trotskii, 1879–1921* (New York and London, 1963), p. 43.

19. Quoted in Wolfe, *Three Who Made a Revolution*, pp. 622–623.

Chapter 28. An Iron Road Across Asia

1. Quoted in Steven Marks, *Road to Power: The Trans-Siberian Railroad and the Colonization of Asian Russia, 1850–1917* (Ithaca, N.Y., 1991), p. 126.

2. *Ibid.*, pp. 133, 179–185; V. F. Borzunov, *Proletariat Sibiri i Dal'nego Vostoka nakanune pervoi russkoi revoliutsii (po materialam stroitel'stva transsibirskoi magistrali, 1891–1894gg.)* (Moscow, 1965), pp. 18, 26–42, 78–79; S. V. Sabler and I. V. Sosnovskii, *Sibirskaia zheleznaia doroga v eia proshlom i nastoiashchem. Istoricheskii ocherk*, edited by A. N. Kulomzin (St. Petersburg, 1903), p. 157; Tupper, *To the Great Ocean*, pp. 103–106.

3. Quoted in Marks, *Road to Power*, p. 130.

4. *Ibid.*, p. 105.

5. A. A. Polovtsov, *Dnevnik gosudarstvennogo sekretaria A. A. Polovtsova*, edited by P. A. Zaionchkovskii (Moscow, 1966), II, p. 343.

6. Quoted in Sabler and Sosnovskii, *Sibirskaia zheleznaia doroga*, p. 69.

7. Quoted in *ibid.*, p. 76.

8. Quoted in S. G. Svatikov, *Rossiia i Sibir' (k istorii sibirskogo oblastnichestva v XIXv.)* (Prague, 1930), p. 89.

9. Marks, *Road to Power*, pp. 49–50.

10. N. M. Iadrintsev, *Sibir' kak koloniia*, pp. 51, 59, 63; see also pp. 50–85.

11. Quoted in Marks, *Road to Power*, pp. 87–88.

12. Svatikov, *Rossiia i Sibir'*, p. 85.

13. Marks, *Road to Power*, p. 90.

14. *Ibid.*

15. Quoted in *ibid.*, p. 91.

16. Quoted in *ibid.*, p. 90.

17. Quoted in Theodore H. von Laue, *Sergei Witte and the Industrialization of Russia* (New York and London, 1963), p. 25.

18. Sabler and Sosnovskii, *Sibirskaia zheleznaia doroga*, p. 91.

19. Quoted in Marks, *Road to Power*, pp. 104–105.

20. Quoted in *ibid.*, p. 92.

21. Quoted in *ibid.*

22. A. I. Dmitriev-Mamonov and A. F. Zdziarskii, eds., *Guide to the Great Siberian Railway*, translated by L. Kukol-Yasnopolsky, revised by John Marshall (St. Petersburg, 1900), p. 76.

23. Quoted in Tupper, *To the Great Ocean*, p. 4.

24. Ukhtomskii, *Puteshestvie Gosudaria Imperatora Nikolaia II*, VI, *passim*.

25. K. P. Pobedonostsev, *Pis'ma Pobedonostseva k Aleksandru III* (Moscow, 1926), II, pp. 99–100.

26. Quoted in Harrison Salisbury, *Black Night, White Snow: Russia's Revolutions, 1905–1917* (New York, 1978), p. 176.

27. Sabler and Sosnovskii, *Sibirskaia zheleznaia doroga*, p. 129; S. I. Vitte, *Vospominaniia* (Moscow, 1960), I, pp. 433–435.

28. Marks, *Road to Power*, pp. 122–125.

29. Quoted in Princess Catherine Radziwill, *Memories of Forty Years* (London, 1914), p. 244.

30. Quoted in Marks, *Road to Power*, p. 130.

31. Quoted in *ibid.*

32. *Ibid.*, pp. 149–153; Liashchenko, *History of the National Economy of Russia, to the 1917 Revolution*, translated by L. M. Herman (New York, 1949), pp. 560–561; Peter Gatrell, *The Tsarist Economy, 1850–1917* (New York, 1986), pp. 153–155.

Chapter 29. Building the World's Longest Railroad

1. Sabler and Sosnovskii, *Sibirskaia zheleznaia doroga*, pp. 74–76.

2. Quoted in Lindon Bates, *The Russian Road to China*, pp. 54–55.

3. A. A. Polovtsov, *Dnevnik gosudarstvennogo sekretaria A. A. Polovtsova*, II, p. 453.

4. Marks, *Road to Power*, pp. 127–128.

5. Olga Crisp, *Studies in the Russian Economy Before 1914* (London, 1976), p. 27.

6. Quoted in Marks, *Road to Power*, p. 152.

7. *Ibid.*, pp. 149–153; Liashchenko, *History of the National Economy of Russia*, pp. 560–561; Gatrell, *The Tsarist Economy*, pp. 153–155.

8. Marks, *Road to Power*, p. 176.

9. Sabler and Sosnovskii, *Sibirskaia zheleznaia doroga*, 228–231, 240–247; Dmitriev-Mamonov and Zdziarskii, eds., *Guide to the Great Siberian Railway*, pp. 188, 371, 441–442; Tupper, *To the Great Ocean*, pp. 106, 175–179, 184–190; "Zapiski po sooruzheniiu mostov

cherez bol'shiia reki na Iuzhno- i Severno-Ussuriiskoi zheleznoi dorogakh," in Ministerstvo Putei Soobshcheniia, *Otchet po postroike Severno-Ussuriiskoi zheleznoi dorogi, 1894–1897* (St. Petersburg, 1900), pp. 271–300.

10. Sabler and Sosnovskii, *Sibirskaia zheleznaia doroga*, pp. 158, 199–203, 240–247; Dmitriev-Mamonov and Zdziarskii, eds., *Guide to the Great Siberian Railway*, pp. 168–170, 327–347; Tupper, *To the Great Ocean*, pp. 183–184, 175–179; Reverend Francis E. Clark, *A New Way Around an Old World* (New York and London, 1901), pp. 129–130.

11. V. F. Borzunov, *Proletariat Sibiri i Dal'nego Vostoka*, pp. 16–22; Donald W. Treadgold, *Great Siberian Migration*, p. 32.

12. Treadgold, *Great Siberian Migration*, pp. 26–42.

13. Sabler and Sosnovsksii, *Sibirskaia zheleznaia doroga*, pp. 152–156; Dmitriev-Mamonov and Zdziarskii, eds., *Guide to the Great Siberian Railway*, pp. 179–181, 191, 213.

14. Quoted in Tupper, *To the Great Ocean*, p. 115.

15. Quoted in Borzunov, *Proletariat Sibiri i Dal'nego Vostoka*, p. 92.

16. Marks, *Road to Power*, p. 181.

17. Borzunov, *Proletariat Sibiri i Dal'nego Vostoka*, p. 133.

18. *Ibid.*, pp. 132–138.

19. Quotes are from *ibid.*, pp. 124–126.

20. David McCullough, *The Path Between the Seas: The Creation of the Panama Canal, 1870–1914* (New York, 1977), pp. 173, 610.

21. Sabler and Sosnovskii, *Sibirskaia zheleznaia doroga* pp. 247–248; Tupper, *To the Great Ocean*, pp. 324–331.

22. Borzunov, *Proletariat Sibiri i Dal'nego Vostoka*, pp. 139–147.

23. Z. Vol'skii, *Vsia Sibir': Spravochnaia kniga po vsem otrasliam kul'turnoi i torgovo-promyshlennoi zhizni Sibiri* (St. Petersburg, 1908), pp. 250–252.

24. Sabler and Sosnovskii, *Sibirskaia zheleznaia doroga*, pp. 217–220; Tupper, *To the Great Ocean*, pp. 234, 338.

25. Fraser, *Real Siberia*, pp. 133–134.

26. Marks, *Road to Power*, p. 201.

27. Tupper, *To the Great Ocean*, pp. 117, 248.

28. Marks, *Road to Power*, p. 196.

29. Quoted in Tupper, *To the Great Ocean*, p. 251.

30. Marks, *Road to Power*, p. 206.

31. *Ibid.*, p. 217.

Chapter 30. Amur River Boats and Russia's Manchurian Connection

1. Quoted in Marks, *Road to Power*, p. 104; Sabler and Sosnovskii, *Sibirskaia zheleznaia doroga*, p. 91.

2. Tupper, *To the Great Ocean*, pp. 234–235.

3. Clark, *New Way Around an Old World*, p. 132.

4. Dmitriev-Mamonov and Zdziarskii, eds., *Guide to the Great Siberian Railway*, p. 376.

5. Fraser, *Real Siberia*, p. 151.

6. *Ibid.*, pp. 150–151; Clark, *New Way Around an Old World*, p. 130.

7. Dmitriev-Mamonov and Zdziarskii, eds., *Guide to the Great Siberian Railway*, p. 518.

8. Fraser, *Real Siberia*, pp. 159–160.

9. Clark, *New Way Around an Old World*, pp. 103, 100.

10. Fraser, *Real Siberia*, pp. 162–163.

11. Harry de Windt, *The New Siberia* (London, 1896), pp. 227–228.

12. Clark, *New Way Around an Old World*, pp. 71, 101.

13. Wirt Gerrare [William Oliver Greener], *Greater Russia: The Continental Empire of the Old World* (New York, 1903), p. 160.

14. Bates, *Russian Road to China*, pp. 121–122.

15. Lionel F. Gowing, *Five Thousand Miles in a Sledge: A Mid-Winter Journey Across Siberia* (London, 1889), pp. III, 137, 136, 149.

16. Clark, *New Way Around an Old World*, p. 87.

17. Fraser, *Real Siberia*, p. 179; see also pp. 167–180.

18. Gerrare, *Greater Russia*, p. 199.

19. Dmitriev-Mamonov and Zdziarskii, eds., *Guide to the Great Siberian Railway*, p. 444.

20. Clark, *New Way Around an Old World*, p. 198.

21. On the coronation of Nicholas and Aleksandra, see W. Bruce Lincoln, *The Romanovs: Autocrats of All the Russias* (New York, 1981), pp. 618–628; S. S. Ol'denburg, *Tsarstovanie Imperatora Nikolaia II* (Belgrade, 1939), I, pp. 59–61.

22. B. A. Romanov, *Russia in Manchuria (1892–1906)*, translated by Susan Wilbur Jones (Ann Arbor, 1952), pp. 81–93; Andrew Malozemoff, *Russian Far Eastern Policy, 1881–1904. With Special Emphasis on the Causes of the Russo-Japanese War* (Berkeley and Los Angeles, 1958), pp. 76–84; von Laue, *Sergei Witte and the Industrialization of Russia*, pp. 150–152.

23. The protocol for this bribe was written in Witte's hand and dated Moscow, May 23, 1896. See Romanov, *Russia in Manchuria*, pp. 402–403, note 74.

24. Sabler and Sosnovskii, *Sibirskaia zheleznaia doroga*, pp. 235–248; Tupper, *To the Great Ocean*, pp. 320–331.

25. Tupper, *To the Great Ocean*, pp. 331–335.

Chapter 31. Lake Baikal

1. Valentin Rasputin et al., *Baikal* (Moscow, 1985), unpaginated.

2. *Ibid.;* Tupper, *To the Great Ocean*, pp. 217–219, 224.

3. Okladnikov et al., eds., *Istoriia Sibiri*, II, p. 51.

4. Semënov, *Siberia: Its Conquest and Development*, 93.

5. Don Belt, "The World's Great Lake," *NG* (June 1992), p. 17.

6. *Ibid.*, p. 20; Rasputin et al., eds., *Baikal, passim;* Dmitriev-Mamonov and Zdziarskii, eds., *Guide to the Great Siberian Railway*, pp. 334–337.

7. Rasputin et al., *Baikal, passim*.

8. Fraser, *The Real Siberia*, pp. 132, 135.

9. Marks, *Road to Power*, p. 204.

10. Tupper, *To the Great Ocean*, p. 337.

11. Quoted in *ibid.*, pp. 337–338.

12. *Ibid.*, pp. 337–340; Sabler and Sosnovskii, *Sibirskaia zheleznaia doroga*, pp. 213–220.

13. Quoted in Sabler and Sosnovskii, *Sibirskaia zheleznaia doroga*, p. 443.

14. Quoted in S. G. Svatikov, *Rossiia i Sibir'*, pp. 52, 89.

15. Quoted in Marks, *Road to Power*, p. 80.

Chapter 32. "A Small Victorious War"

1. N. A. Voloshinov, "Sibirskaia zheleznaia doroga," *IzIRGO*, XXVII (1891), p. 14.

2. *Ibid.*, p. 15.

3. Konstantin Mochul'skii, *Vladimir Solov'ëv: Zhizn' i uchenie*, 2nd ed. (Paris, 1951), pp. 253–261; Samuel Cioran, *Vladimir Solov'ev and the Knighthood of the Divine Sophia* (Waterloo, Iowa, 1977), pp. 62–67.

4. Valerii Briusov, "Griadushchie gunny," in *Sobranie sochinenii v semi tomakh* (Moscow, 1973), I, p. 433.

5. Quoted in Laue, *Sergei Witte*, p. 189.

6. Quoted in John Albert White, *The Diplomacy of the Russo-Japanese War* (Princeton, 1964), p. 49.

7. I. I. Rostunov, "Proiskhozhdenie voiny," in I. I. Rostunov, ed., *Istoriia Russko-Iaponskoi voiny, 1904–1905gg.* (Moscow, 1977), pp. 48–54.

8. A. Svechin, *Russko-Iaponskaia voina, 1904–1905gg. po dokumental'nym dannym truda vo-enno-istoricheskoi komissii i drugim istochnikam* (Oranienbaum, 1910), pp. 2–4; Malozemoff, *Russian Far Eastern Policy*, pp. 52–58.

9. Malozemoff, *Russian Far Eastern Policy*, pp. 177–207; Romanov, *Russia in Manchuria*, pp. 248–308; Laue, *Sergei Witte*, pp. 243–248.

10. Quoted in Semënov, *Siberia: Its Conquest and Development*, p. 347.

11. McDonald, *United Government and Foreign Policy in Russia*, pp. 31–75.

12. Quoted in David Walder, *A Short Victorious War: The Russo-Japanese Conflict, 1904–1905* (London, 1973), p. 43.

13. Quoted in Semënov, *Siberia: Its Conquest and Development*, p. 350.

14. A. N. Kuropatkin, "Dnevnik A. N. Kuropatkina," *KA*, II (1922), p. 78.

15. Vitte, *Vospominaniia*, II, p. 292.

16. *Ibid.*

17. Quoted in *ibid.*, p. 291.

18. Kuropatkin, "Dnevnik," p. 106.

19. *Ibid.*, pp. 109–110.

20. V. A. Glukhov, "Oborona Port-Artura," in Rostunov, ed., *Istoriia Russko-Iaponsksoi voiny*, p. 248.

21. Voenno-istoricheskaia komissiia po opisaniiu Russko-Iaponskoi voiny, *Russko-Iaponskaia voina, 1904–1904: Oborona Kvantuna i Port-Artura* (St. Petersburg, 1910), VIII, pt. 2, appendix, pp. 181–186; *The Official History of the Russo-Japanese War* (London, 1909), III, pp. 139–140.

22. V. I. Vinogradov and Iu. F. Sokolov, "Operatsii v Man'chzhurii," in Rostunov, ed., *Istoriia Russko-Iaponskoi voiny*, pp. 270–294; V. Marushevskii and P. Orlov, *Boevaia rabota russkoi armii v voinu 1904–1905gg.* (St. Petersburg, 1910), II, pp. 1–103.

23. Quoted in Walder, *A Short Victorious War*, p. 268.

24. A. N. Kuropatkin, *Opisanie boevykh deistvii Man'chzhurskikh armii pod Mukdenom s 4-go fevralia po 4-e marta 1905 goda* (Moscow, 1907), I–III, *passim*; Vinogradov and Sokolov, "Operatsii v Man'chzhurii," pp. 295–306; Voenno-istoricheskaia komissiia, *Russko-Iaponskaia voina*, V, pt. 1, pp. 1–40; appendices Nos. 1 and 3, pp. 4–63, 78–90.

25. Quoted in Vitte, *Vospominaniia*, II, p. 384.

26. *Ibid.*

27. Voenno-istoricheskaia komissiia, *Russko-Iaponskaia voina*, VII, pp. 205–229; Iu. I. Chernov, "Tsusima," in Rostunov, ed., *Istoriia Russko-Iaponskoi voiny*, pp. 324–348.

28. Quoted in Shumpei Okamoto, *The Japanese Oligarchy and the Russo-Japanese War* (New York and London, 1970), p. 111.

29. Quoted in Eugene P. Trani, *The Treaty of Portsmouth: An Adventure in American Diplomacy* (Lexington, Ky., 1969), p. 53.

30. White, *Diplomacy of the Russo-Japanese War*, pp. 206–309; Okamoto, *Japanese Oligarchy*, pp. 150–163; Trani, *Treaty of Portsmouth*, pp. 118–155.

Chapter 33. The Immigrants

1. Treadgold, *The Great Siberian Migration*, p. 32.

2. Glinka, ed., *Aziatskaia Rossiia*, I, pp. 444–450.

3. Fraser, *Real Siberia*, p. 50.

4. *Ibid.*

5. Alexander Michie, *The Siberian Overland Route from Peking to Petersburg* (London, 1864), p. 320.

6. Glinka, ed., *Aziatskaia Rossiia*, I, pp. 187–188.

7. Treadgold, *Great Siberian Migration*, pp. 32–34, 95–96; P. I. Popov, "Pereselenie krest'ian i zemleustroistvo Sibiri," in A. K. Dzhivelegov et al., eds., *Velikaia reforma: Russkoe obshchestvo i krest'ianskii vopros v proshlom i nastoiashchem* (Moscow, 1911), VI, p. 253.

8. Fraser, *Real Siberia*, pp. 15–16, 70.
9. Quoted in Treadgold, *Great Siberian Migration*, p. 142.
10. Quoted in *ibid.*, p. 144.
11. Quoted in *ibid.*, p. 176.
12. *Ibid.*, p. 34.
13. Quoted in *ibid.*, p. 158.
14. Quoted in *ibid.*
15. P. P. Semënov [Tian-Shanskii], *Puteshestvie v Tian'-Shan'* (Moscow, 1958), pp. 46–47.
16. Quoted in Florinsky, *Russia*, II, p. 1223.
17. Semënov, *Siberia: Its Conquest and Development*, pp. 308–314.
18. Treadgold, *Great Siberian Migration*, pp. 176–179, 206.
19. Glinka, ed., *Aziatskaia Rossiia*, I, pp. 285–360; Dmitriev-Mamonov and Zdziarskii, eds., *Guide to the Great Siberian Railway, passim;* Baedeker, *Russia 1914, passim.*
20. Glinka, ed., *Aziatskaia Rossiia*, I, p. 190.
21. Bates, *Russian Road to China*, pp. 85, 84.
22. Fraser, *Real Siberia*, p. 83.

Chapter 34. Siberia's Wild East
1. Fraser, *Real Siberia*, pp. 88–89.
2. Glinka, ed., *Aziatskaia Rossiia*, I, pp. 348–349; Dmitriev-Mamonov and Zdziarskii, eds., *Guide to the Great Siberian Railway*, pp. 306–308.
3. Gowing, *Five Thousand Miles in a Sledge*, p. 207.
4. Lansdell, *Through Siberia*, I, p. 265.
5. Clark, *New Way Around an Old World*, p. 156.
6. Fraser, *Real Siberia*, p. 83.
7. Quoted in Tupper, *To the Great Ocean*, p. 203.
8. Bates, *Russian Road to China*, p. 110.
9. Quoted in Tupper, *To the Great Ocean*, pp. 209–210.
10. V. P. Sukachev, *Irkutsk*, pp. 108–110.
11. Lansdell, *Through Siberia*, pp. 258, 255, 267.
12. Fraser, *Real Siberia*, pp. 86–89.
13. de Windt, *New Siberia*, p. 138.
14. Clark, *New Way Around an Old World*, p. 20.
15. Fraser, *Real Siberia*, p. 207.
16. Kennan, *Siberia and the Exile System*, II, p. 128.
17. Glinka, ed., *Aziatskaia Rossiia*, I, p. 349.
18. Quoted in Tupper, *To the Great Ocean*, pp. 350, 349.
19. Fraser, *Real Siberia*, p. 211.
20. Kennan, *Siberia and the Exile System*, II, p. 323.
21. Tupper, *To the Great Ocean*, pp. 206–208.
22. Glinka, ed., *Aziatskaia Rossiia*, II, p. 426.
23. Okladnikov et al., eds., *Istoriia Sibiri*, III, pp. 212–221, 251–298.
24. Quoted in Gernet, *Istoriia tsarskoi tiurmy*, IV, pp. 21–23. The precise figure for 1912 is 1,859,314.
25. Quoted in *ibid.*, p. 23.
26. Okladnikov et al., eds., *Istoriia Sibiri*, III, pp. 355–356; "Lenskii rasstrel 1912," *SIE*, VIII, cols. 583–584.
27. Quoted in Tokarev et al., eds., *Istoriia Iakutskoi ASSR* II, p. 393.

Chapter 35. The Lena Goldfields Massacre

1. Okladnikov et al., eds., *Istoriia Sibiri*, III, p. 192.
2. *Ibid.*, p. 194.
3. *Ibid.*, pp. 188–189.
4. *Ibid.*, pp. 186, 195–196.
5. *Ibid.*, pp. 186–186.
6. *Ibid.*, pp. 341–348.
7. *Ibid.*, pp. 181–182.
8. P. Pospelov, ed., *Lenskie priiski: Sbornik dokumentov* (Moscow, 1937), pp. 11–12, 68–69; M. I. Lebedev, *Vospominaniia o Lenskikh sobytiiakh 1912 goda* (Moscow, 1962), pp. 17–18, 27–29.
9. Pospelov, ed., *Lenskie priiski*, p. 227; "Lensko-Vitimskii Zolotonosnyi Raion," *SSE*, III, cols. 77–83; "Lenskoe Zoloto-Promyshlennoe Tovarishchestvo," *SSE*, III, cols. 84–85; "Lenskii rasstrel 1912," *SIE*, cols. 583–584; Lebedev, *Vospominaniia*, pp. 30–33. These high profits were the result of having lowered the cost of extracting gold by a third. Although the introduction of steam-powered earthmoving equipment helped to accomplish that feat, it was mainly the result of company managers having raised fines and sold poorer quality food in minefield stores. Miners complained that the bread sold in company stores "often" had horse manure added to it, and one widely believed report claimed that store managers mixed chopped horse penises into the meat they sold (Pospelov, ed., *Lenskie priiski*, p. 263; Lebedev, *Vospominaniia*, p. 119).
10. Quoted in Lebedev, *Vospominaniia*, p. 57.
11. *Ibid.*, pp. 46–48, 55–57; Pospelov, ed., *Lenskie priiski*, p. 174.
12. Lebedev, *Vospominaniia*, pp. 58–63; Pospelov, ed., *Lenskie priiski*, pp. 257–258.
13. Tokarev et al., eds., *Istoriia Iakutskoi ASSR*, II, p. 393.
14. Lebedev, *Vospominaniia*, pp. 66–67; Pospelov, ed., *Lenskie priiski*, p. 260; see also pp. 255–261.
15. Lebedev, *Vospominaniia*, pp. 78–117.
16. Tokarev et al., eds., *Istoriia Iakutskoi ASSR*, II, p. 394.
17. Pospelov, ed., *Lenskie priiski*, pp. 280–281.
18. Quoted in Lebedev, *Vospominaniia*, p. 178.
19. Quoted in *ibid.*, p. 172.
20. Pospelev et al., eds., *Lenskie priiski*, pp. 286–287.
21. Quoted in Lebedev, *Vospominaniia*, pp. 177, 183.
22. *Ibid.*, pp. 178–182.
23. Quoted in *ibid.*, p. 233.
24. *Ibid.*, p. 235.
25. Quoted in *ibid.*, p. 235.
26. *Ibid.*, pp. 237–239.
27. *Ibid.*, pp. 240–242; "Lenskii rasstrel 1912," col. 584.
28. Pospelev, ed., *Lenskie priisksi*, p. 300.
29. Okladnikov et al., eds., *Istoriia Sibiri*, III, pp. 360–361; Tokarev et al., eds., *Istoriia Iakutskoi ASSR*, II, pp. 394–395; Lebedev, *Vospominaniia*, pp. 268–274; Florinsky, *Russia*, II, p. 1229.

Chapter 36. "I Hate the Autocracy So Much"

1. Dvorianov, *V Sibirskoi dal'nei storone*, pp. 183, 271; N. N. Shcherbakov, "Chislennost' i sostav politicheskikh ssyl'nykh Sibiri (1907–1917gg.)," in *Ssyl'nye revoliutsionery v Sibiri*, I, pp. 204–210; K. Nikitin, *Tsarskii flot pod krasnym flagom* (Moscow, 1931), pp. 194–196; Okladnikov et al., eds., *Istoriia Sibiri*, III, p. 299.
2. Florinsky, *Russia*, II, p. 1195.

3. R. H. Bruce Lockhart, *British Agent* (New York and London, 1933), p. 292.

4. Quoted in I. Steinberg, *Spiridonova: Revolutionary Terrorist*, translated by Gwenda David and Erich Mosbacher (London, 1935), p. 44.

5. Count Ottokar von Czernin, *In the World War* (New York and London, 1920), p. 245.

6. Quoted in Steinberg, *Spiridonova*, p. 33.

7. I. Kakhovskaia, "Iz vospominanii o zhenskoi katorge," *KiS*, XXIII (1926), p. 170.

8. *Ibid.*, pp. 171–174.

9. *Ibid.*, p. 176.

10. *Ibid.*, pp. 176–178.

11. *Ibid.*, pp. 172–173.

12. *Ibid.*, p. 180.

13. Quoted in Steinberg, *Spiridonova*, p. 144.

14. Quoted in *ibid.*, p. 145.

15. Quoted in *ibid.*, 145–146.

16. Dvorianov, *V Sibirskoi dal'nei storone*, pp. 203–205.

Chapter 37. Before the Storm

1. Liashchenko, *Istoriia*, II, pp. 522–525; Glinka, ed., *Aziatskaia Rossiia*, II, pp. 405–407.

2. Liashchenko, *Istoriia*, II, pp. 525–526; Glinka, ed., *Aziatskaia Rossiia*, II, pp. 258–259, 332–338; Levin and Potapov, eds., *Narody Sibiri*, p. 142.

3. Semenov, *Conquest of Siberia*, p. 103.

4. Liashchenko, *Istoriia*, II, pp. 526–527; Glinka, ed., *Aziatskaia Rossiia*, II, pp. 339–380.

5. Quoted in *Handbook of Siberia and Arctic Russia*, pp. 172, 175.

6. Glinka, ed., *Aziatskaia Rossiia*, I, p. 123.

7. *Ibid.*, pp. 123–130; Levin and Potapov, eds., *Narody Sibiri*, pp. 706–713; Okladnikov et al., eds., *Istoriia Sibiri*, III, p. 192.

8. Levin and Potapov, eds., *Narody Sibiri*, pp. 217–266; Okladnikov et al., eds., *Istoriia Sibiri*, III, pp. 87–89; Glinka, ed., *Aziatskaia Rossiia*, I, pp. 132–143.

9. Levin and Potapov, eds., *Narody Sibiri*, pp. 267–328; Tokarev et al., eds., *Istoriia Iakutskoi ASSR*, II, pp. 313–319; Okladnikov et al., eds., *Istoriia Sibiri*, III, pp. 90–95; Glinka, ed., *Aziatskaia Rossiia*, I, pp. 144–150.

10. Violet Conolly, *Beyond the Urals: Economic Developments in Soviet Asia* (London: 1967), pp. 41–43.

11. Glinka, ed., *Aziatskaia Rossiia*, II, p. 417.

12. Conolly, *Beyond the Urals*, pp. 16, 42.

13. Fraser, *Real Siberia*, p. 4.

14. *Ibid.*, pp. 44, 5, 48.

15. George Frederick Wright, *Asiatic Russia* (New York, 1902), II, p. 453.

16. Quoted in Conolly, *Beyond the Urals*, p. 19.

Chapter 38. War and Revolution

1. Quoted in Pierre Renouvin, *The Immediate Origins of the War (28th June–4th August 1914)*, translated by T. C. Hume (New York, 1969), p. 245.

2. Viscount Edward Grey, *Twenty-Five Years, 1892–1916* (London, 1925), II, p. 20.

3. Maurice Paleologue, *La Russie des Tsars pendant la Grande Guerre* (Paris, 1921), I, p. 44.

4. P. N. Miliukov, *Vospominaniia, 1859–1917* (New York, 1955), II, p. 183–184.

5. Viktor Chernov, *Rozhdenie revoliutsionnoi Rossii (fevral'skaia revoliutsiia)* (Paris, Prague, and New York, 1934), p. 75.

6. Quoted in Florinsky, *Russia,* II, p. 1378.

7. Iu. N. Danilov, *Rossiia v mirovoi voine, 1914–1915gg.* (Berlin, 1924), pp. 238–249; A. Kolenkovskii, *Manevrennyi period pervoi mirovoi imperialisticheskoi voiny 1914g.* (Moscow, 1940), pp. 297–303.

8. A. A. Manikovskii, *Boevoe snabzhenie russkoi armii v mirovuiu voinu,* 2nd ed. (Moscow and Leningrad, 1930), I, pp. 149–151, 154–164, 298, 364–365, 398. See also "Russian Munitions Tables," August 1916 and December 1917, AG, file 10N90; "Situation de l'armament de l'armée russe, février 1917, AG, file 10N73; and Major C. Dunlop, Reports to Major General C. E. Caldwell, AG, file 10N93.

9. See the reports of Major C. Dunlop to Major General C. E. Caldwell, AG, file 10N93.

10. *Ibid.;* Okladnikov et al., eds., *Istoriia Sibiri,* III, p. 438.

11. See and compare Collins, *Overland Explorations in Siberia, Northern Asia, and the Great Amoor River Country, passim;* H. H. Fisher, "The American Railway Mission to Russia," with marginal notes and comments by John F. Stevens, HIA John Frank Stevens Papers, File No. 1, pp. 1–6; John Frank Stevens, "Memorandum on Russia," Hoover Institution Archives, John Frank Stevens Papers, File 1, *passim;* "The American Commercial Invasion of Russia," *Harper's Weekly,* XLVI (March 22, 1902), pp. 361–363.

12. Okladnikov et al., eds., *Istoriia Sibiri,* III, pp. 437–439.

13. *Ibid.,* pp. 440–443. According to Okladnikov's calculations, Siberia's peasants were farming 16,585,098 acres in 1912. By 1917, that amount had risen to 24,154,954 acres. For discussions in high government circles about the importance of farm machinery for increasing harvests, see "O meropriiatiiakh Ministerstva Zemledeliia, vyzvannykh obstoiatel'stvami voennago vremeni i potrebnykh dlia osushchestvleniia etikh meropriiatii kreditakh," 10 oktiabria 1916g., TsGIAL, fond 1276, opis' 12, delo No. 1062, sheets 31–32; "Predstavlenie ministra zemledeliia A. A. Bobrinskago v Sovet Ministrov o vliianii voiny na sostoianie sel'skago khoziastva i neobkhodimykh meropriiatiiakh dlia ego pod"ema," 10 oktiabria 1916g., in A. N. Anfimov et al., eds., *Ekonomicheskoe polozhenie Rossii, nakanune velikoi oktiabr'skoi sotsialisticheskoi revoliutsii. Dokumenty i materialy* (Leningrad, 1967), III, p. 16.

14. Elsa Brändström, *Among Prisoners of War in Russia and Siberia,* translated from the German by C. Mabel Rickmers (London, 1930), pp. 102–104.

15. *Ibid.,* p. 109.

16. Quoted in *ibid.,* pp. 131–132.

17. A. Kh. Klevanskii, *Chekhoslovatskie internatsionalisty i prodannyi korpus: Chekhoslovatskie politicheskie organizatsii i voinskie formirovaniia v Rossii, 1914–1921gg.* (Moscow, 1965), pp. 32–35.

18. M. E. Solov'ëv, "Partiia Bol'shevikov—organizator pobedy fevral'skoi burzhuazno-demokraticheskoi revoliutsii v 1917g. v Rossii," in S. I. Murashov, ed., *Partiia bol'shevikov v gody pervoi mirovoi voiny. Sverzhenie monarkhii v Rossii* (Moscow, 1963), pp. 199–200; M. I. Akhun and V. A. Petrov, *1917 god v Petrograde: Khronika sobytii i bibliografiia* (Leningrad, 1933), pp. 2–3; E. N. Burdzhalov, *Vtoraia russkaia revoliutsiia* (Moscow, 1967), I, pp. 85–93; I. I. Mints, *Istoriia velikogo oktiabria* (Moscow, 1967), I, pp. 470–472; I. P. Leiberov, *Na shturm samoderzhaviia. Petrogradskii proletariat v gody pervoi mirovoi voiny i fevral'skaia revoliutsiia* (Moscow, 1979), pp. 113–115; F. A. Romanov, *Rabochee i professional'noe dvizhenie v gody pervoi mirovoi voiny i vtoroi russkoi revoliutsii (1914–fevral' 1917 goda). Istoricheskii ocherk* (Moscow, 1949), pp. 194–195.

19. "Doklad Petrogradskago okhrannago otdeleniia osobomu otdelu departamenta politsii, oktiabr' 1916g.," in M. N. Pokrovskii, ed., "Politicheskoe polozhenie Rossii nakanune fevral'skoi revoliutsii v zhandarmskom osveshchenii," *KA,* XXVI (1926), pp. 10–12; Tsuyoshi Hasegawa, *The February Revolution: Petrograd 1917* (Seattle and London, 1981), p. 200.

20. V. V. Shul'gin, *Dni* (Belgrade, 1925), p. 139.

21. Quoted in Raymond Pearson, *The Russian Moderates and the Crisis of Tsarism, 1914–1917* (London, 1977), pp. 132–133.

22. Quoted in Okladnikov et al., eds., *Istoriia Sibiri*, III, p. 447.

23. *Ibid.*, pp. 445–447.

24. *Ibid.*, pp. 447–474.

25. *Ibid.*, pp. 475–478, 485–487; IV, pp. 27–47.

Chapter 39. The Czech Legion

1. Klevanskii, *Chekhoslovatskie internatsionalisty*, pp. 9–112; Josef Kalvoda, "Czech and Slovak Prisoners of War in Russia During the War and Revolution," in Samuel R. Williamson, Jr., and Peter Pastor, eds., *Essays on World War I: Origins and Prisoners of War* (New York, 1983), pp. 215–226.

2. V. Vladimirova, *God sluzhby sotsialistov kapitalistam: Ocherki po istorii kontr-revoliutsii v 1918 godu* (Moscow and Leningrad, 1927), pp. 219–223; Klevanskii, *Chekhoslovatskie internatsionalisty*, pp. 128–147; Kalvoda, "Czech and Slovak Prisoners of War in Russia," pp. 227–230.

3. Trotskii's order is published in V. Maksakov and A. Turunov, *Khronika grazhdanskoi voiny v Sibiri, 1917–1918* (Moscow, 1926), p. 168.

4. Quoted in S. P. Mel'gunov, *Tragediia Admirala Kolchaka: Iz istorii grazhdanskoi voiny na Volge, Urale, i v Sibiri* (Belgrade, 1930), I, p. 73.

5. Česja družina. Hlavní štab, "The Operations of the Czechoslovak Army in Russia in the Years 1917–1920," HIA, Českoslovencky strelecky pulk, xx517–10.v., pp. 5–8; A. M. Nikolaev, "1918: Vtoroi god rossiiskoi grazhdanskoi voiny," A. M. Nikolaev Collection, Bakhmetieff Archive, Columbia University, New York, pp. 38–40, P. S. Parfenov, *Grazhdanskaia voina v Sibiri, 1981–1920* (Moscow, 1924), pp. 26–27; A. E. Antonov, *Boevoi vosemnadtsatyi god. Voennye deistviia Krasnoi armii v 1918–nachale 1919g.* (Moscow, 1961), pp. 62–66. For detailed maps of the Czech Legion's positions at a number of points in 1918–1919, see the file about its movements in Bakhmetieff Archive, Denikin Collection, Box 23.

6. Quoted in White, *Siberian Intervention*, pp. 239–240.

7. Quoted in Betty Miller Unterberger, *America's Siberian Expedition, 1918–1920* (Durham, N.C., 1956), p. 60.

8. Mel'gunov, *Tragediia Admirala Kolchaka*, I, p. 193; 9. W. Bruce Lincoln, *Red Victory*, p. 235; White, *Siberian Intervention*, p. 197.

10. John Ward, *With the "Die-Hards" in Siberia* (London, 1920), p. 268.

11. Baron P. N. Wrangel, *The Memoirs of General Wrangel: The Last Commander-in-Chief of the Russian National Army*, translated by Sophie Goulston (London, 1930), p. 6; S. N. Shishkin, *Grazhdanskaia voina na Dal'nem Vostoke* (Moscow, 1957), pp. 13–14, 22–26; L. H. Grondijs, *Le Cas-Koltchak: Contribution à l'histoire de la révolution russe* (Leiden, 1939), pp. 485–489; Kommissiia po istorii oktiabr'skoi revoliutsii i R. K. P. (bol'shevikov), *Revoliutsiia na Dal'nem Vostoke* (Moscow and Petrograd, 1923), I, p. 79; "Ataman Grigorii Mikhailovich Semënov," in Anatolii Markov, "Entsiklopediia belogo dvizheniia," HIA, Anatolii Markov Collection, file 1, pp. 614–614a.

12. Wrangel, *Memoirs of General Wrangel*, pp. 6–7.

13. N. M. Riabukhin, "The Story of Baron Ungern-Sternberg Told by His Staff Physician N. M. Riabukhin (Ribo)," HIA, N. M. Riabukhin Collection, file 1, p. 12; see also pp. 1–42; Boris Volkov, "Ob Ungerne," HIA, Boris Volkov Collection, file 2, pp. 1–53.

14. Wrangel, *Memoirs of General Wrangel*, pp. 6–7.

15. Lincoln, *Red Victory*, pp. 255–257; N. A. Andriushkevich, "Posledniaia Rossiia (vospominaniia o Dal'nem Vostoke)," *BD*, IV, pp. 120–137; White, *Siberian Intervention*, pp. 198–199, 266–267.

16. Baron Aleksei Budberg, *Dnevnik belogvardeitsa (kolchakovskaia epopeia)*, edited by

P. E. Shchegolov (Leningrad, 1929), p. 11; Baron Aleksei Budberg, "Dnevnik," *ARR*, XII, p. 290.

17. K. V. Gusev, *Partiia eserov: Ot melko-burzhuaznogo revoliutsionarizma k kontrrevoliutsii* (Moscow, 1975), pp. 230–233; G. K. Gins, *Sibir', soiuzniki, i Kolchak, 1918–1920* (Peking, 1921), I, 74–83, 86–131; Maksakov and Turunov, *Khronika grazhdanskoi voiny v Sibiri*, pp. 197–199, 208–209, 224–225.

18. V. V. Garmiza, "Iz istorii samarskoi uchredilki," *Istoricheskie zapiski*, VIII (1940), pp. 34–35; William Henry Chamberlin, *The Russian Revolution* (New York, 1965), II, pp. 15–18; K. V. Gusev and Kh. A. Eritsian, *Ot soglashatel'stva k kontrrevoliutsii: Ocherki istorii politicheskogo bankrotstva i gibeli partii sotsialistov-revoliutsionerov* (Moscow, 1968), pp. 323–352; Nikolaev, "1918," pp. 41–42.

19. George F. Kennan, *The Decision to Intervene* (Princeton, 1958), p. 105.

20. Quoted in *ibid.*, p. 101.

21. A. Zaitsov, *1918 god: Ocherki po istorii russkoi grazhdanskoi voiny* (Paris, 1934), p. 126; G. V. Kuz'min, *Razgrom interventov i belogvardeitsev v 1917–1922gg.* (Moscow, 1977), pp. 84–86.

22. Quoted in Kennan, *Decision to Intervene*, pp. 396–397.

23. "*Aide-Memoire* of the Secretary of State to the Allied Ambassadors," July 7, 1918, reprinted in Unterberger, *America's Siberian Expedition*, pp. 236–237.

Chapter 40. "Pitch-forked into the Melee"

1. Graves, *America's Siberian Adventure*, p. 3.

2. Quoted in *ibid.*, p. 4.

3. *Ibid.*, p. 55.

4. *Ibid.*, pp. 55–56.

5. *Ibid.*, p. 354.

6. White, *Siberian Intervention*, pp. 156–159, 239–240; "American Commercial Invasion of Russia," pp. 362–363.

7. Fisher, "American Railway Mission," pp. 1–6; John Frank Stevens, "Memorandum on Russia," HIA, John Frank Stevens Papers, file No. 1.

8. C. K. Cummings and Walter W. Petit, *American-Russian Relations, March 1917–March 1920: Documents and Papers* (New York, 1920), pp. 28–29.

9. Kennan, *Decision to Intervene*, p. 88.

10. V. G. Boldyrev, *Direktoriia. Kolchak. Interventy: Vospominaniia* (Novonikolaevsk, 1925), p. 75.

11. Gins, *Sibir', soiuzniki, i Kolchak*, p. 133; see also pp. 183–184; N. N. Golovin [Golovine], *Rossiiskaia kontrrevoliutsiia v 1917–1918gg.* (Paris, 1937), VIII, pp. 66–70.

12. Boldyrev, *Direktoriia*, p. 83.

13. *Ibid.*, p. 31; see also pp. 33–34.

14. Quoted in Mel'gunov, *Tragediia Admirala Kolchaka*, I, p. 194.

15. Boldyrev, *Direktoriia*, pp. 35–36; Golovin, *Rossiiskaia kontrrevoliutsiia*, VIII, pp. 77–78.

16. "Konstitutsiia ufimskoi direktorii: Akt ob obrazovanii vserossiiskoi verkhovnoi vlasti, 8–23 sentiabria 1918g.," *ARR*, XII, p. 189.

17. S. Piontkovskii, ed., *Grazhdanskaia voina v Rossii (1918–1921gg.): Khrestomatiia* (Moscow, 1925), p. 286.

18. Lincoln, *Red Victory*, pp. 236–238.

19. Quoted in Mel'gunov, *Tragediia Admirala Kolchaka*, I, p. 233.

20. Boldyrev, *Direktoriia*, p. 85.

21. Quoted in Chamberlin, *Russian Revolution*, II, p. 177.

22. Quoted in Boldyrev, *Direktoriia*, p. 91.

23. Graves, *America's Siberian Adventure*, p. 79.

24. *Ibid.*, pp. 91, 93.

25. *Ibid.*, p. 81.

Chapter 41. Siberia's Supreme Ruler

1. P. M. Bykov, "Poslednie dni poslednego tsaria," *ARR*, XVII (1926), p. 313.

2. J. C. Trewin, *Tutor to the Tsarevich* (London, 1975), pp. 111–112.

3. L. Trotskii, *Trotsky's Diary in Exile*, translated by Elena Zarudnaia (New York, 1963), p. 81.

4. This brief description of the Romanovs' last days and execution has been summarized from my longer account in *Red Victory*, pp. 148–155, which was based upon the following Russian sources: N. Sokolov, *Ubiistvo tsarskoi sem'i* (Berlin, 1925), pp. 142–148, 212–238; Bykov, "Poslednie dni," pp. 313–315; S. P. Mel'gunov, *Sud'ba imperatora Nikolaia II posle otrecheniia* (Paris, 1951), pp. 382–402; General M. K. Diterikhs, *Ubiistvo tsarskoi sem'i i chlenov doma Romanovykh na Urale* (Vladivostok, 1922), *passim*; E. E. Alfer'ev, ed., *Pis'ma tsarskoi sem'i iz zatocheniia* (Jordanville, N.Y., 1974), pp. 395–410. Most recently, Edvard Radzinsky's *The Last Tsar: The Life and Death of Nicholas II*, translated by Marian Schwartz (New York, 1992) has added additional details.

5. L. Trotskii, *Trotsky's Diary in Exile*, p. 81.

6. "Vyderzhki iz rechi lidera omskikh k.-d. Zhardetskogo na s"ezde torgovo-promyshlennikov v Omske v iiule 1918g.," No. 80 in Maksakov and Turunov, *Khronika grazhdanskoi voiny v Sibiri*, pp. 207–208.

7. Boldyrev, *Direktoriia*, p. 87.

8. Quoted in Richard Ullman, *Intervention and the War: Anglo-Soviet Relations, 1917–1920* (Princeton, 1961), p. 272.

9. Elena Varneck and H. H. Fisher, eds., *The Testimony of Admiral Kolchak and Other Siberian Materials*, translated by Elena Varneck (Stanford, 1935), p. 142.

10. Kolchak's press conference of November 28, 1918, quoted in Golovin, *Rossiiskaia kontrrevoliutsiia*, IX, pp. 83–87.

11. Lincoln, *Red Victory*, pp. 241–245.

12. Quoted in Richard Ullman, *Britain and the Russian Civil War, November 1918–February 1920* (Princeton, 1968), p. 34.

13. Quoted in A. G. Lipkina, *1919 god v Sibiri* (Moscow, 1962), p. 52.

14. N. V. Ustrialov, "Dnevnik," HIA, Ustrialov Collection, box 1, pp. 5–6; G. Z. Ioffe, *Kolchakovskaia avantiura i ee krakh* (Moscow, 1983), pp. 221–222; Gins, *Sibir'*, II, pp. 206, 220–221.

15. Richard Luckett, *The White Generals: An Account of the White Movement and the Russian Civil War* (New York, 1971), p. 263.

16. Quoted in Lipkina, *1919 god v Sibiri*, pp. 45–46.

17. Budberg, *Dnevnik belogvardeitsa* pp. 96–97.

18. Luckett, *White Generals*, p. 263.

19. N. Kakurin, *Kak srazhalas' revoliutsiia* (Moscow and Leningrad, 1925), II, pp. 123–126; J. V. Stalin, *Works* (Moscow, 1953), IV, pp. 202–204, 213–214, 229.

20. Quoted in White, *The Siberian Intervention* (Princeton, 1950), p. 119.

21. Quoted in Mel'gunov, *Tragediia Admirala Kolchaka*, III, p. 57.

22. Budberg, *Dnevnik*, pp. 218, 97.

23. Ustrialov, "Dnevnik," p. 1.

24. Lincoln, *Red Victory*, pp. 264–265.

25. Quoted in S. F. Naida et al., eds., *Istoriia grazhdanskoi voiny v SSSR* (Moscow, 1959), IV, p. 143; see also pp. 134–148; Ia. Zhigalin, "Partizanskoe dvizhenie v zapadnoi Sibiri," PR, 11, No. 10 (1930), pp. 98–114; John Erikson, *The Soviet High Command: A Military-Political History, 1918–1941* (London, 1962), pp. 64–65.

26. Quoted in A. S. Bubnov, S. S. Kamenev, R. P. Eideman, and M. N. Tukhachevskii, eds., *Grazhdanskaia voina, 1918–1921* (Moscow, 1928), III, pp. 328–329.

27. Gins, *Sibir'*, II, pp. 294–295.

28. Budberg, *Dnevnik*, p. 187.

29. Ustrialov, "Dnevnik," p. 16.

30. Budberg, *Dnevnik,* pp. 156, 291.

31. Vladimir Molotov, *Bolsheviki Sibiri v period grazhdanskoi voiny (1918–1919gg.)* (Omsk, 1949), p. 130.

32. General Zankevich, "Obstoiatel'stva, soprovozhdavshiia vydachu Admirala Kolchaka revoliutsionnomu pravitel'stvu v Irkutske," *BD,* II (1927), pp. 150–154.

33. Lincoln, *Red Victory,* p. 267.

34. B. M. Shereshevskii, *V bitvakh za dal'nii vostok (1920–1922gg.)* (Novosibirsk, 1974), pp. 157–181; B. M. Shereshevskii, *Razgrom Semënovshchiny (aprel'–noiabr' 1920g.)* (Novosibirsk, 1966), pp. 95–127, 203–235; Canfield F. Smith, *Vladivostok under Red and White Rule: Revolution and Counterrevolution in the Russian Far East, 1920–1922* (Seattle and Washington, 1975), pp. 72–274; John Channon, "Siberia in Revolution and Civil War, 1917–1921," in Alan Wood, ed., *The History of Siberia from Russian Conquest to Revolution* (London and New York, 1991), pp. 175–176.

Chapter 42. The Bolsheviks Take Siberia

1. E. Z. Volkov, *Dinamika narodonaseleniia SSSR za vosem'desiat let* (Moscow, 1930), pp. 185–191; Ian Mawdsley, *The Russian Civil War* (Boston, 1987), pp. 285–287; Frank Lorimer, *The Population of the Soviet Union: History and Prospects* (Geneva, 1946), pp. 40–41.

2. L. Kritsman, *Geroicheskii period velikoi russkoi revoliutsii* (Moscow, n.d. [1924]), p. 162; see also Silvana Malle, *The Economic Organization of War Communism, 1918–1921* (Cambridge, 1985), pp. 508–511; Mawdsley, *Russian Civil War,* pp. 187–288; Alex Nove, *An Economic History of the USSR* (London, 1969), pp. 86, 94.

3. R. S. Livshits, "Razmeshchenie promyshlennosti v dorevoliutsionnoi Rossii," *Izvestiia Akademiia Nauk SSSR* (1955), pp. 220–223; Glinka, ed., *Aziatskaia Rossiia,* II, pp. 413–446; Conolly, *Beyond the Urals,* pp. 33–41; Boris Baievsky, *Siberia: Its Resources and Possibilities,* U.S. Department of Commerce Trade Promotion Series No. 36 (Washington, D.C., 1926), pp. 25, 65.

4. Quoted in Conolly, *Beyond the Urals,* pp. 60–61.

5. Quoted in Stephen F. Cohen, *Bukharin and the Bolshevik Revolution: A Political Biography, 1888–1938* (Oxford, 1980), p. 133.

6. Lenin, *Collected Works,* XXXII, pp. 215–216.

7. Okladnikov et al., eds., *Istoriia Sibiri,* IV, pp. 177–189.

8. *Ibid.,* pp. 189–191.

9. *Ibid.,* pp. 196, 201.

10. Stalin, *Works,* XIII, pp. 40–41.

11. *Ibid.*

12. Okladnikov et al., eds., *Istoriia Sibiri,* IV, pp. 193–194; T. F. Gorbachev et al., *Kuznetskii ugol'nyi bassein* (Moscow, 1957), 74–82.

13. Okladnikov et al., eds., *Istoriia Sibiri,* IV, p. 195.

14. Tupper, *To the Great Ocean,* p. 414.

15. *"Kuzbas": An Opportunity for Engineers and Workers* (New York, 1922), p. 26.

16. *"Kuzbas,"* p. 1. On Haywood's involvement in recruiting volunteers for the Kuzbass colony, see Peter Carlson, *Roughneck: The Life and Times of Big Bill Haywood* (New York, 1983), pp. 318–320, a reference for which I am indebted to my colleague J. Carroll Moody.

Chapter 43. Jack Scott and Siberia's Magnetic Mountain

1. Quotes from John Scott, *Behind the Urals: An American Worker in Russia's City of Steel,* enlarged edition prepared by Stephen Kotkin (Bloomington, Ind., 1989), pp. xii–xiii. Scott's account is amazingly accurate and revealing. It can be supplemented by I. F. Galigusov and M. E. Churilin, *Flagman otechestvennoi industrii: Istoriia Magnitogorskogo*

metallurgicheskogo kombinata imeni V. I. Lenina (Moscow, 1978), pp. 21–64; Iu. Petrov, *Magnitka* (Moscow, 1971), pp. 4–89; M. E. Churilin, ed., *Magnitka* (Cheliabinsk, 1971), 31–91.

2. Quoted in Scott, *Behind the Urals*, pp. xi–xii.

3. *Ibid.*, p. 3.

4. *Ibid.*

5. *Ibid.*, pp. 57–58.

6. A. Malenky, *Magnitogorsk: The Magnitogorsk Metallurgical Combine of the Future* (Moscow, 1932), pp. 47–48.

7. *Ibid.*, p. 52.

8. *Ibid.*, pp. 33–34.

9. *Ibid.*, p. 47.

10. *Ibid.*, p. 50.

11. Quoted in *ibid.*, p. 56.

12. Stephen Kotkin, *Steeltown, USSR: Soviet Society in the Gorbachev Era* (Berkeley and Los Angeles, 1991), pp. 243–244.

13. Scott, *Behind the Urals*, p. 5.

14. *Ibid.*

15. *Ibid.*

16. *Ibid.*, p. xv.

17. *Ibid.*, pp. 5–6.

18. *Ibid.*, 142–143.

19. *Ibid.*, p. 5.

20. *Ibid.*, p. 92.

21. *Ibid.*, pp. 117–133.

22. Galigusov and Churilin, *Flagman otechestvennoi industrii*, p. 59; Scott, *Behind the Urals*, p. 231.

23. Kotkin, *Steeltown, USSR*, pp. xiv–xv.

Chapter 44. Edible Fossils

1. A. Solzhenitsyn, *Arkhipelag Gulag, 1918–1956: Opyt khudozhestvennogo issledovaniia* (Paris, 1973), I–II, p. 6.

2. David J. Dallin and Boris I. Nikolaevsky, *Forced Labor in Soviet Russia* (New Haven, 1947), p. 149.

3. Quoted in *ibid.*, p. 153.

4. *Ibid.*, pp. 153–154; E. G. Shirvindt, *Nashe ispravitel'no-trudovoe zakonodatel'stvo* (Moscow, 1925), *passim.* See also Shirvindt's small pamphlet in English, *Russian Prisons* (London, 1928).

5. Quoted in Dallin and Nikolaevsky, *Forced Labor in Soviet Russia*, p. 166.

6. *Ibid.*, p. 156.

7. Solzhenitsyn, *Arkhipelag Gulag*, I, p. 6.

8. Dallin and Nikolaevsky, *Forced Labor in Soviet Russia*, pp. 165–166.

9. *Ibid.*, p. 190. Less than half of one percent of the OGPU labor camp inmates at this time could be classified as common criminals.

10. Quoted in *ibid.*, p. 208.

11. *Ibid.*, p. 211.

12. Solzhenitsyn, *Arkhipelag Gulag*, II, p. 196.

13. *Ibid.*, pp. 206–207.

14. *Ibid.*, p. 206.

15. Elinor Lipper, *Eleven Years in Soviet Prison Camps* (Chicago, 1951), p. 79.

16. *Ibid.*, p. 80.

17. Quoted in Robert Conquest, *Kolyma: The Arctic Death Camps* (London, 1978), p. 30.

18. Quoted in *The Dark Side of the Moon,* with a preface by T. S. Eliot (New York, 1947), p. 197.

19. Michael Solomon, *Magadan* (Princeton, New York, Philadelphia, and London, 1971), p. 85.

20. Quoted in *ibid.,* p. 89.

21. Dallin and Nikolaevsky, *Forced Labor in Soviet Russia,* pp. 118–122.

22. Lipper, *Eleven Years in Soviet Prison Camps,* p. 101.

23. Dallin and Nikolaevsky, *Forced Labor in Soviet Russia,* pp. 129–131.

24. Solomon, *Magadan,* pp. 103–104.

25. Conquest, *Kolyma,* pp. 105–106.

26. Vladimir Petrov, *Soviet Gold: My Life As a Slave Laborer in the Siberian Mines,* translated from the Russian by Mirra Ginsburg (New York, 1949), pp. 285–286.

27. *Ibid.,* p. 284.

28. *Ibid.,* p. 305.

29. *Dark Side of the Moon,* p. 145.

30. Solzhenitsyn, *Arkhipelag Gulag,* II, p. 197.

31. Conquest, *Kolyma,* pp. 126–127.

32. Lipper, *Eleven Years in Soviet Prison Camps,* p. 204.

33. *Ibid.,* p. 203.

34. Petrov, *Soviet Gold,* p. 324.

35. Gustav Herling, *A World Apart,* translated from the Polish by Joseph Marek (London, 1951), p. 141.

36. Quoted in Conquest, *Kolyma,* p. 133.

37. Solzhenitsyn, *Arkhipelag Gulag,* II, p. 223.

38. Lipper, *Eleven Years in Soviet Prison Camps,* pp. 259–260.

39. *Ibid.,* p. 159.

40. Solomon, *Magadan,* p. 141.

41. Lipper, *Eleven Years in Soviet Prison Camps,* p. 157.

42. Solzhenitsyn, *Arkhipelag Gulag,* II, p. 228.

43. Solomon, *Magadan,* p. 100.

44. Solzhenitsyn, *Arkhipelag Gulag,* II, p. 231.

45. Lipper, *Eleven Years in Soviet Prison Camps,* p. 150.

46. *Ibid.,* p. 269–270; Conquest, *Kolyma,* pp. 67–68.

47. Lipper, *Eleven Years in Soviet Prison Camps,* p. 111; Conquest, *Kolyma,* pp. 68–69.

48. Quoted in Lipper, *Eleven Years in Soviet Prison Camps,* p. 112.

49. Soloman, *Magadan,* p. 79.

50. *Ibid.,* p. 80.

51. Conquest, *Kolyma,* p. 68.

52. Solomon, *Magadan,* pp. 184–186.

53. Conquest, *Kolyma,* pp. 216–217.

54. Quoted in *ibid.,* p. 217.

55. *Ibid.,* pp. 110–111.

56. *Ibid.,* p. 229; see also pp. 220–231.

57. *Ibid.,* p. 228.

58. Quoted in Dallin and Nikolaevsky, *Forced Labor in Soviet Russia,* p. 223.

59. Quoted in *ibid.;* see also pp. 217–224.

60. Vladimir V. Tchernavin, *I Speak for the Silent Prisoners of the Soviets,* translated from the Russian by Nicholas M. Oushakoff (Boston and New York, 1935), p. 252.

61. George Kitchin, *Prisoner of the OGPU* (London, 1935), p. 268.

62. Quoted in Conquest, *Kolyma,* p. 212; see also pp. 211–212.

63. Owen Lattimore, "New Road to Asia," *NG,* LXXXVI, No. 6 (December 1944), p. 657.

Chapter 45. Socialist Reconstruction

1. Tupper, *To the Great Ocean*, pp. 418–420.

2. Quoted in *ibid.*, pp. 407–408.

3. *Ibid.*, pp. 408–409.

4. Baievsky, *Siberia*, p. 9.

5. These comparative population figures are compiled from the raw material supplied in S. V. Utechin, *A Concise Encyclopedia of Russia* (New York, 1964), *passim.*

6. Okladnikov et al., eds., *Istoriia Sibiri*, IV, pp. 312–317.

7. *Ibid.*, pp. 324–329.

8. *Ibid.*, pp. 359–371.

9. M. Gor'kii et al., eds., *Belomorsko-Baltiiskii Kanal imeni Stalina: Istoriia stroitel'stva* (Moscow, 1934), *passim.*

10. Dallin and Nikolaevsky, *Forced Labor in Soviet Russia*, pp. 211–216; Conolly, *Beyond the Urals*, pp. 83–84; Tupper, *To the Great Ocean*, pp. 415–419.

11. S. Swianiewicz, *Forced Labor and Economic Development: An Enquiry into the Experience of Soviet Industrialization* (London, 1965), pp. 39, 290–302.

12. Quoted in Geoffrey Hosking, *The First Socialist Society: A History of the Soviet Union from Within* (Cambridge, Mass., 1990), p. 160.

13. *Ibid.*, p. 128; see also Teodor Shanin, *The Awkward Class: Political Sociology of a Peasantry in a Developing Society, Russia 1910–1925* (Oxford, 1972).

14. Quoted in Hosking, *First Socialist Society*, p. 163.

15. *Ibid.;* see also Moshe Lewin, *Russian Peasants and Soviet Power* (London, 1968).

16. Hosking, *First Socialist Society*, p. 166; Nicholas V. Riasanovsky, *A History of Russia* (New York, 1977), p. 551.

17. Okladnikov et al., eds., *Istoriia Sibiri*, IV, p. 330.

18. Quoted in *ibid.*, p. 336.

19. *Ibid.*, 331–338.

20. *Ibid.*, p. 346.

21. *Ibid.*, pp. 339–340.

22. John D. Littlepage and Demaree Bess, *In Search of Soviet Gold* (New York, 1938), pp. 184–185, 187.

23. Conolly, *Beyond the Urals*, pp. 89–91; Naum Jasny, *The Soviet Economy of the Plan Era* (Stanford, 1951), pp. 632–633.

Chapter 46. The Great Relocation

1. G. S. Kravchenko, *Voennaia ekonomika SSSR 1941–1945* (Moscow, 1963), p. 100.

2. Voznesenskii, *Voennaia ekonomika SSSR*, p. 41.

3. *Ibid.*, pp. 39–41.

4. Liashchenko, *Istoriia*, III, pp. 512–514; Okladnikov et al., eds., *Istoriia Sibiri*, V, pp. 83–85; Conolly, *Beyond the Urals*, pp. 99–101.

5. Conolly, *Beyond the Urals*, pp. 103–104; Liashchenko, *Istoriia*, III, p. 512.

6. Liashchenko, *Istoriia*, III, pp. 520–525.

7. Kravchenko, *Voennaia ekonomika*, p. 105.

8. Quoted in M. K. Kozybaev, "Iz Istorii deiatel'nosti 'Komissii AN SSSR po mobilizatsii resursov Urala, Zapadnoi Sibiri, i Kazakhstana na nuzhdy oborony," *Izvestiia Akademii Nauk Kazakhskoi SSSR. Seriia istorii, arkheologii i etnografii*, pt. 1, XVIII (1962), p. 62.

9. *Ibid.*, pp. 62–69.

10. Liashchenko, *Istoriia*, III, pp. 514–517.

11. Okladnikov et al., eds., *Istoriia Sibiri*, V, pp. 90–91.

12. Iu. A. Vasil'ev, *Sibirskii Arsenal: Deiatel'nost' partiinykh organizatsii Sibiri po razvitiiu promyshlennosti v period Velikoi Otechestvennoi voiny 1941–1945gg.* (Sverdlovsk, 1965), pp. 100–107.

13. V. T. Aniskov, *Kolhoznoe krest'ianstvo Sibiri i Dal'nego Vostoka—frontu 1941–1945gg.* (Barnaul, 1966), pp. 114–115, 136–137; Frank A. Durgin, Jr., "The Virgin Lands Programme, 1954–1960," *SS,* XIII (1962), p. 256.

14. Voznesenskii, *Voennaia ekonomika SSSR,* p. 42.

15. Okladnikov et al., eds., *Istoriia Sibiri,* V, pp. 130–131.

16. Quotes are from *ibid.,* p. 131.

17. Hosking, *First Socialist Society,* p. 262.

18. John Erikson, "Military and Strategic Factors," in Alan Wood, ed., *Siberia: Problems and Prospects for Regional Development* (London, 1987), p. 181.

19. *Ibid.,* pp. 132–141, 161–162.

20. Quoted in *ibid.,* p. 138.

21. Voznesenskii, *Voennaia ekonomika SSSR,* pp. 159–162.

Chapter 47. Stalin's Last Years

1. Okladnikov et al., eds., *Istoriia Sibiri,* V, p. 175.

2. *Ibid.,* pp. 177–178.

3. Quoted in Alan Wood, "From Conquest to Revolution: The Historical Dimension," in Wood, ed., *Siberia,* p. 55.

4. Voznesenskii, *Voennaia ekonomika SSSR,* pp. 49–51.

5. *Ibid.,* pp. 51–53.

6. *Ibid.,* p. 48.

7. Quoted in Conolly, *Beyond the Urals,* p. 244.

8. Hoskings, *First Socialist Society,* pp. 326–328.

9. Quoted in *ibid.,* p. 331; see also pp. 330–333.

10. Theodore Shabad, "Economic Resources," in Wood, ed., *Siberia,* pp. 62–63.

11. Conolly, *Beyond the Urals,* p. 244.

12. Okladnikov et al., eds., *Istoriia Sibiri,* V, pp. 214–215.

13. Conolly, *Beyond the Urals,* pp. 250–251.

Chapter 48. Virgin Lands

1. J. W. Cleary, "The Virgin Lands," *S,* No. 56 (July 1965), pp. 95–96.

2. Roy D. Laird, "Agriculture under Khrushchev," *S,* No. 56 (July 1965), p. 106.

3. Quoted in Conolly, *Beyond the Urals,* p. 223; see also pp. 222–224.

4. Quoted in S. A. Neishtadt, *Ekonomicheskoe razvitie Kazakhskoi SSR (period sotsializma i razvernutogo stroitel'stva kommunizma)* (Alma-Ata, 1960), p. 181.

5. Conolly, *Beyond the Urals,* p. 221.

6. *Ibid.,* p. 227; Durgin, "Virgin Lands Programme," pp. 255–258; Laird, "Agriculture under Khrushchev," p. 107.

7. Durgin, "Virgin Lands Programme," pp. 274–275.

8. *Ibid.,* pp. 271–272.

9. Quoted in *ibid.,* p. 271.

10. *Ibid.,* pp. 271–273.

11. *Ibid.,* p. 273.

12. Quoted in Cleary, "Virgin Lands," pp. 99–100.

13. Quoted in *ibid.,* p. 99.

14. Durgin, "Virgin Lands Programme," p. 274.

15. *Ibid.*, p. 259.

16. Quoted in Violet Conolly, *Siberia Today and Tomorrow: A Study of Economic Resources, Problems, and Achievements* (London and Glasgow, 1975), p. 134; see also Conolly, *Beyond the Urals*, p. 223.

17. Cleary, "Virgin Lands," p. 101.

18. Violet Conolly, "Siberia: Yesterday, Today, and Tomorrow," in Rodger Swearingen, ed., *Siberia and the Soviet Far East: Strategic Dimensions in Multinational Perspective* (Stanford, 1987), p. 17.

19. Quoted in Conolly, *Behind the Urals*, pp. 225–226.

20. Conolly, *Siberia Today and Tomorrow*, pp. 228–229.

21. *Ibid.*, p. 132; Okladnikov et al., eds., *Istoriia Sibiri*, V, p. 345.

22. Conolly, "Siberia" p. 22; Conolly, *Siberia Today and Tomorrow*, pp. 136–139.

23. Conolly, *Siberia Today and Tomorrow*, p. 134.

24. Quoted in Conolly, "Siberia" p. 9.

25. Quoted in John Sallnow, "Siberia's Demand for Labour: Incentive Policies and Migration, 1960–1985," in Alan Wood and R. A. French, eds., *The Development of Siberia: People and Resources* (New York, 1989), p. 202.

26. Conolly, *Siberia Today and Tomorrow*, p. 133.

27. Liashchenko, *Istoriia*, III, pp. 520–525.

Chapter 49. Bratsk Power Station

1. A. S. Bondarenko, *Energetiki Sibiri (1917–1977gg.)* (Novosibirsk, 1981), pp. 22–23.

2. Lincoln, *Red Victory*, p. 354; L. M. Maksakova, *Agitpoezd "Oktiabr'skaia Revoliutsiia," 1919–1920gg.* (Moscow, 1956), pp. 9–20.

3. M. Davydov and M. Tsunts, *Ot Volkhova do Amura* (Moscow, 1958), p. 159.

4. *Ibid.*, pp. 134–135.

5. Iu. V. Mochalova, ed., *Podvig na Enisee: Iz istorii stroitel'stva Krasnoiarskoi GES* (Moscow, 1972), p. 10.

6. Bondarenko, *Energetiki Sibiri*, pp. 22–33.

7. Quoted in Conolly, *Beyond the Urals*, p. 63.

8. Semënov, *Geografichesko-statisticheskii slovar' Rossiiskoi Imperii*, I, p. 313; Davydov and Tsunts, *Ot Volkhova do Amura*, p. 142.

9. S. V. Utechin, *Concise Encyclopedia of Russia*, p. 72.

10. Davydov and Tsunts, *Ot Volkhova do Amura*, pp. 143–146; Conolly, *Siberia: Today and Tomorrow*, p. 82.

11. Davydov and Tsunts, *Ot Volkhova do Amura*, pp. 150–151; C. E. Nemasov, "Pis'mo Geroia Sotsialistichesakogo Truda Nemasova C. E., o tom, kak on stal geroem," 24 dekabria 1961g., in V. F. Mal'tsev, ed., *Bratskaia GES: Sbornik dokumentov i materialov*, II, pp. 26–36.

12. "Pis'mo Geroia Sotsialisticheskogo Truda Nemasova," p. 26.

13. Davydov and Tsunts, *Ot Volkhova do Amura*, p. 146.

14. Evgenii Evtushenko, *Stikhi i poema: Bratskaia GES* (Moscow, 1967), p. 183.

15. Conolly, *Siberia: Today and Tomorrow*, pp. 82–83.

16. *Ibid.*, p. 83.

17. *Ibid.*, pp. 84–86.

18. Quoted in *ibid.*, p. 86.

19. *Ibid.*, p. 87.

20. *Ibid.*, pp. 88–89.

21. *Ibid.*, pp. 83–84; Bondarenko, *Energetiki Sibiri*, pp. 145–161.

22. Victor L. Mote, "The Baykal-Amur Mainline: Catalyst for the Development of

Pacific Siberia," in Theodore Shabad and Victor L. Mote, eds., *Gateway to Siberian Resources (the BAM)* (Washington, D.C., 1977), pp. 95–97.

23. *Ibid.*, p. 67; Victor L. Mote, "The Communications Infrastructure," in Swearingen, ed., *Siberia and the Soviet Far East,* pp. 49–52; Mike Edwards, "Siberia: In from the Cold," *NG* (March 1990), p. 30.

Chapter 50. The BAM

1. M. K. Baidman et al., eds., *Razvitie narodnogo khoziaistva Sibiri* (Novosibirsk, 1978), pp. 269–276; Mote, "Communications Infrastructure," pp. 41–43; Mote, "Baykal-Amur Mainline," pp. 63–65.

2. Mote, "Communications Infrastructure," pp. 43–45; Okladnikov et al., eds., *Istoriia Sibiri,* V, pp. 232–233; Tupper, *To the Great Ocean,* pp. 412–413.

3. Baidman et al., eds., *Razvitie narodnogo khoziaistva Sibiri,* pp. 276–278; Mote, "Baykal-Amur Mainline," pp. 38–39; Mote, "Communications Infrastructure," pp. 45–46.

4. Quoted in Violet Conolly, "The Baikal-Amur Railway (the BAM)," in Wood, ed., *Siberia,* p. 167.

5. *Ibid.*, pp. 166–167; Mote, "Baykal-Amur Mainline," pp. 80–84; Oleg A. Kibal'chich, "The BAM and Its Economic Geography," in Shabad and Mote, eds., *Gateway to Siberian Resources,* p. 148.

6. Mote, "Baykal-Amur Mainline," pp. 67–68.

7. *Ibid.*, pp. 79, 93–96; Kibal'chich, "BAM and Its Economic Geography," p. 148.

8. Mote, "Baykal-Amur Mainline," p. 80.

9. *Ibid.*, pp. 91–92; Conolly, "Baikal-Amur Railway," pp. 158–159.

10. Mote, "Baykal-Amur Mainline," pp. 91–92; Conolly, "Baikal-Amur Railway," pp. 162–166.

11. Mote, "Baykal-Amur Mainline," pp. 49–52.

12. Conolly, "Baikal-Amur Railway," p. 159.

13. *Ibid.*, p. 168.

14. Edwards, "Siberia," p. 31.

Chapter 51. The Riches of Samotlor and Urengoi

1. Quoted in Conolly, *Siberia Today and Tomorrow,* p. 64; see also pp. 64–65.

2. Theodore Shabad, "Siberian Resource Development in the Soviet Period," in Shabad and Mote, eds., *Gateway to Siberian Resources,* pp. 35–36; David Wilson, "The Siberian Oil and Gas Industry," in Wood, ed., *Siberia,* pp. 96–102.

3. Wilson, "The Siberian Oil and Gas Industry," pp. 98–101, 111–113.

4. *Ibid.*, pp. 123–124; Conolly, *Siberia Today and Tomorrow,* pp. 68–69; Shabad, "Siberian Resource Development," pp. 37–39.

5. Wilson, "Siberian Oil and Gas Industry," pp. 124, 98.

6. Edwards, "Siberia," p. 10.

7. Shabad, "Siberian Resource Development," p. 39.

8. Wilson, "Siberian Oil and Gas Industry," pp. 118–119; Edwards, "Siberia," pp. 35–36.

9. Edwards, "Siberia," pp. 35–36.

10. *Ibid.*, p. 35.

11. Peter Gumbel and James Tanner, "Tired Mammoth," *Wall Street Journal,* August 22, 1990, pp. A1–A4.

12. Murray Feshbach and Alfred Friendly, Jr., *Ecocide in the USSR: Health and Nature under Seige* (New York, 1992), p. 4.

13. *Ibid.*, p. 1.

Chapter 52. Siberia's Soviet Heritage

1. Feshbach and Friendly, *Ecocide*, p. 10.
2. Quoted in *ibid.*, p. 99.
3. *Ibid.*, p. 98.
4. *Ibid.*
5. *Ibid.*, p. 101.
6. Levin and Potapov, eds., *Narody Sibiri*, p. 56; S. V. Kiselev, *Drevniaia istoriia iuzhnoi Sibiri* (Moscow, 1951), pp. 23–66.
7. Quoted in Boris Komarov, *The Destruction of Nature in the Soviet Union*, translated by Michel Vale and Joe Hollander, with a foreword by Marshall I. Goldman (White Plains, N.Y., 1980), p. 27.
8. Quoted in Scott, *Behind the Urals*, p. xx.
9. Edwards, "Siberia," pp. 23–24, 28; Feshbach and Friendly, *Ecocide*, p. 10.
10. Feshbach and Friendly, *Ecocide*, p. 10.
11. Edwards, "Siberia," p. 31.
12. Feshbach and Friendly, *Ecocide*, pp. 100–103.
13. Quoted in Edwards, "Siberia," p. 27.
14. Kotkin, *Steeltown, USSR*, pp. xiii, 135; Feshbach and Friendly, *Ecocide*, pp. 92–93, 184, 214.
15. Quoted in Feshbach and Friendly, *Ecocide*, p. 105.
16. *Ibid.*, pp. 9, 105.
17. Quoted in *Ibid.*, p. 105.
18. *Ibid.*, pp. 174–175.
19. *Ibid.*, p. 174.
20. Quoted in *ibid.*, p. 176.
21. *Ibid.*, p. 49.
22. *Ibid.*, pp. 65–68.
23. Quoted in Rusi Nasar, "Fact in Fiction," *The Washington Post* (June 4, 1989), p. B3.
24. Feshbach and Friendly, *Ecocide*, pp. 73–74, 78–79.
25. Quoted in *ibid.*, p. 80.
26. *Ibid.*, p. 117.
27. *Ibid.*, pp. 118–119; Komarov, *Destruction of Nature*, pp. 5–11.
28. Quoted in Komarov, *Destruction of Nature*, p. 5.
29. Feshbach and Friendly, *Ecocide*, pp. 117–119.
30. Quoted in Komarov, *Destruction of Nature*, p. 16.
31. *Ibid.*, p. 10.
32. Quoted in Michael Dobbs, "Russians Fight to Save Lake Baikal," *The Washington Post* (October 11, 1990), p. A26.
33. Marks, *Road to Power*, pp. 50–52.
34. Quoted in *ibid.*, p. 51, note 14.
35. Valentin Rasputin, "Your Siberia and Mine," p. 172.
36. *Ibid.*, p. 176.
37. *Ibid.*, p. 179.

Works and Sources Cited

The following list of works and sources cited is provided for the reader's reference in identifying the abbreviated citations used in the end notes. It is not intended to be a bibliography, nor is it a compilation of the hundreds of additional volumes consulted (but not cited) in the research for this book.

"*Aide-Memoire* of the Secretary of State to the Allied Ambassadors," July 7, 1918. Reprinted in Unterberger, *America's Siberian Expedition*, pp. 236–238.

Akhun, M. I., and V. A. Petrov. *1917 god v Petrograde: Khronika sobytii i bibliografiia.* Leningrad, 1933.

Akty istoricheskie sobrannye i izdannye arkheograficheskoiu kommissieiu. 4 vols. St. Petersburg, 1842.

"Akty o plavanii pis'mennago golovy Vasil'ia Poiarkova iz Iakutska v Okhotskoie more," posle 12 iiunia 1646g., in *DAI*, III, document No. 12, pp. 50–52.

Alfer'ev, E. E., ed. *Pis'ma tsarskoi sem'i iz zatocheniia.* Jordanville, N.Y., 1974.

Al'kor, Ia. P., and L. K. Drezen, eds. *Kolonial'naia politika tsarizma na Kamchatke i Chukhotke v XVIII veke. Sbornik arkhivnykh materialov.* Leningrad, 1935.

Al'kor, Ia. P., and B. D. Grekov. *Kolonial'naia politika moskovskogo gosudarstva v Iakutii XVIIv.* Leningrad, 1936.

Allsen, Thomas T. "Mongol Census Taking in Rus', 1245–1275," *Harvard Ukrainian Studies*, V, No. 1 (March 1981), pp. 33–53.

————. *Mongol Imperialism: The Policies of the Grand Qan Mongke in China, Russia, and the Islamic Lands, 1251–1259.* Berkeley, Los Angeles, and London, 1987.

"The American Commercial Invasion of Russia," *Harper's Weekly*, XLVI (March 22, 1902), pp. 361–363.

Andreev, A. I. "Ekspeditsii V. Beringa," *Izvestiia Vsesoiuznogo Geograficheskogo Obshchestva*, Vol. 75, No. 2 (mart–aprel' 1943), pp. 3–44.

Andreev, V. M. "Chislennost' i sostav politicheskikh ssyl'nykh v vostochnoi Sibiri v 70–90kh godakh XIX veka," in *Ssyl'nye revoliutsionery v Sibiri*, V, pp. 52–71.

Andreevich, V. K. *Istoricheskii ocherk Sibiri.* 6 vols. St. Petersburg, 1889.

Andriushkevich, N. A. "Posledniaia Rossiia (vospominaniia o Dal'nem Vostoke)," *BD,* IV, pp. 120–137.

Anfimov, A. N., et al., eds. *Ekonomicheskoe polozhenie Rossii, nakanune velikoi oktiabr'skoi sotsialisticheskoi revoliutsii. Dokumenty i materialy.* Vol. 3. Leningrad, 1967.

Aniskov, V. T. *Kolkhoznoe krest'ianstvo Sibiri i Dal'nego Vostoka—frontu 1941–1945gg.* Barnaul, 1966.

Antonov, A. E. *Boevoi vosemnadtsatyi god. Voennye deistviia Krasnoi armii v 1918–nachale 1919g.* Moscow, 1961.

Armstrong, Terence. *Russian Settlement in the North.* Cambridge, England, 1965.

———, ed. *Yermak's Campaign in Siberia: A Selection of Documents.* Translated from the Russian by Tatiana Minorsky and David Wileman. London, 1975.

"Ataman Grigorii Mikhailovich Semënov," in Anatolii Markov, "Entsiklopediia belogo dvizheniia." HIA. Anatolii Markov Collection, file 1, pp. 614–614a.

Atkinson, Thomas Witlam. *Oriental and Western Siberia: A Narrative of Seven Years' Explorations and Adventures in Siberia, Mongolia, the Kirghis Steppes, Chinese Tartary, and Part of Central Asia.* Philadelphia, 1859.

Azadovskii, M. K., and I. M. Trotskii, eds. *Vospominaniia Bestuzhevykh.* Moscow, 1931.

Baddeley, John F. *Russia, Mongolia, and China, Being Some Record of the Relations Between Them from the Beginning of the XVIIth Century to the Death of the Tsar Alexei Mikhailovich.* 2 vols. Moscow, 1919.

Baedeker, Karl. *Russia 1914.* Leipzig, 1914.

Baidman, M. K., et al., eds. *Razvitie narodnogo khoziaistva Sibiri.* Novosibirsk, 1978.

Baievsky, Boris. *Siberia: Its Resources and Possibilities.* U.S. Department of Commerce Trade Promotion Series No. 36. Washington, D.C., 1926.

Bakhrushin, S. V. *Ocherki po istorii kolonizatsii Sibiri v XVI i XVIIvv.* Moscow, 1927.

———. "Iasak v Sibiri v XVI v.," in Bakhrushin, *Nauchnye trudy* (Moscow, 1954), III, pt. 2, pp. 49–85.

———. "Puti v Sibir' v XVI–XVIIvv.," in Bakhrushin, *Nauchnye trudy,* III, pt. 1, pp. 72–136.

Barratt, Glynn. *M. S. Lunin: Catholic Decembrist.* Mouton, 1976.

Barsukov, Ivan. *Graf Nikolai Nikolaevich Murav'ëv-Amurskii po ego pis'mam, offitsial'nym dokumentam, rasskazam sovremennikov i pechatnym istochnikam (Materialy dlia biografii).* 2 vols. Moscow, 1891.

Barthold, W. *Turkestan down to the Mongol Invasion.* 3rd ed. London, 1968.

Bassin, Mark. "Expansion and Colonialism on the Eastern Frontier: Views of Siberia and the Far East in Pre-Petrine Russia," *JHG,* XIV, No. 1 (January 1988), pp. 3–21.

Bates, Lindon. *The Russian Road to China.* Boston and New York, 1910.

Belov, M. I. *Arkticheskoe moreplavanie s drevneishikh vremën do serediny XIX veka* (Volume I of *Istoriia otkrytiia i osvoeniia Severnogo morskogo puti*). Moscow, 1956.

———. *Podvig Semëna Dezhnëva.* Moscow, 1973.

———, ed. *Russkie morekhody v Ledovitom i Tikhom okeanakh: Sbornik dokumentov o velikikh russkikh geograficheskikh otkrytiiakh na severo-vostoke Azii v XVII veke.* Moscow and Leningrad, 1952.

Belt, Don. "The World's Great Lake," *NG* (June 1992), pp. 2–39.

"Bering's Report," in Golder, ed., *Bering's Voyages,* I, pp. 8–20.

Berg, L. S. *Ocherki po istorii russkikh geograficheskikh otkrytii.* Moscow and Leningrad, 1949.

———. *Otkrytie Kamchatki i ekspeditsii Beringa, 1727–1742.* Moscow and Leningrad, 1946.

Bernadskii, V. N. *Novgorod i novgorodskaia Zemlia v XV veke.* Moscow and Leningrad, 1961.

Beskrovnyi, L. G. "Kulikovskaia bitva," in Beskrovnyi, ed., *Kulikovskaia bitva,* pp. 222–245.

———. *Kulikovskaia bitva: Sbornik statei.* Moscow, 1980.

———, ed. *Opisanie Tobol'skogo namestnichestva, sostavlennoe v 1789–1790gg.* Novosibirsk, 1982.

Black, J. L. "Gerhardt-Friedrich Müller," *MERSH,* XXIII, pp. 169–174.

Blum, Jerome. *Lord and Peasant in Russia from the Ninth to the Nineteenth Century.* Princeton, 1961.

Bobrov, V. V. "On the Problem of Inter-Ethnic Relations in South Siberia in the Third and Early Second Millennium B.C.E.," in Shimkin, ed., *Studies in North Asiatic Archaeology.*

Boldyrev, V. G. *Direktoriia. Kolchak. Interventy: Vospominaniia.* Novonikolaevsk, 1925.

Bondarenko, A. S. *Energetiki Sibiri (1917–1977gg.).* Novosibirsk, 1981.

Borzunov, V. F. *Proletariat Sibiri i Dal'nego Vostoka nakanune pervoi russkoi revoliutsii (po materialam stroitel'stva transsibirskoi magistrali, 1891–1894gg.).* Moscow, 1965.

Brändström, Else. *Among Prisoners of War in Russia and Siberia.* Translated from the German by C. Mabel Rickmers. London, 1930.

Breshkovskaia, Ekaterina. *Hidden Springs of the Russian Revolution: Personal Memoirs of Katerina Breshkovskaia.* Edited by Lincoln Hitchinson. Stanford, 1931.

———. *The Little Grandmother of the Russian Revolution: Reminiscences and Letters of Catherine Breshkovsky.* Edited by Alice Stone Blackwell. Boston, 1919.

Brikhner, A. A. *Istoriia Petra Velikago.* St. Petersburg, 1882.

Briusov, Valerii. "Griadushchie gunny," in *Sobranie sochinenii v semi tomakh* (Moscow, 1973), I, pp. 433–434.

Bubnov, A. S., S. S. Kamenev, R. P. Eideman, and M. N. Tukhachevskii, eds. *Grazhdanskaia voina, 1918–1921.* 3 vols. Moscow, 1928.

Budberg, Baron Aleksei. "Dnevnik," *ARR,* XII, pp. 197–290, XIII, pp. 197–312.

———. *Dnevnik belogvardeitsa (kolchakovskaia epopeia).* Edited by P. E. Shchegolov. Leningrad, 1929.

Burdzhalov, E. N. *Vtoraia russkaia revoliutsiia.* 2 vols. Moscow, 1967.

Butsinskii, P. N. *Zaselenie Sibiri i byt pervykh ee nasel'nikov.* Kharkov, 1889.

Bykov, P. M. "Poslednie dni poslednego tsaria," *ARR,* XVII (1926), pp. 305–316.

Carlson, Peter. *Roughneck: The Life and Times of Big Bill Haywood.* New York, 1983.

Česja družina. Hlavni štab, "The Operations of the Czechoslovak Army in Russia in the Years 1917–1920." HIA. Československencky strelecky pulk, xx517–10.v.

Chamberlin, William Henry. *The Russian Revolution.* 2 vols. New York, 1965.

Channon, John. "Siberia in Revolution and Civil War, 1917–1921," in Wood, ed., *History of Siberia,* pp. 158–180.

"Charter granted by Tsar Ivan Vasil'evich to Grigorii Stroganov on financial, juridical and trade privileges in the empty lands along the river Kama," April 4, 1558, in Armstrong, ed., *Yermak's Campaign,* pp. 281–284.

"Charter granted by Tsar Ivan Vasil'evich to Iakov Stroganov on financial, juridical and trade privileges with regard to the salt-works on the river Chusovaia," March 25, 1568, in Armstrong, ed., *Yermak's Campaign,* pp. 284–287.

Chekhov, Anton. *The Island: A Journey to Sakhalin.* Translated by Luba and Michael Terpak. New York, 1967.

Cherepnin, L. V. *Obrazovanie russkogo tsentralizovannogo gosudarstva v XIV–XV vekakh.* Moscow, 1960.

Cherkas, A. "Nikita Demidych Demidov," *RBS,* vol. Dab–Diad, pp. 217–219.

Chernov, Iu. I. "Tsusima," in Rostunov, ed., *Istoriia Russko-Iaponskoi voiny,* pp. 324–348.

Chernov, Viktor. *Rozhdenie revoliutsionnoi Rossii (fevral'skaia revoliutsiia).* Paris, Prague, New York, 1934.

Chirikov, A. I. "Report on the Voyage of the 'St. Paul,' " in Golder, ed., *Bering's Voyages,* I, pp. 312–323.

Churilin, M. E., ed. *Magnitka.* Cheliabinsk, 1971.

Cioran, Samuel. *Vladimir Solov'ev and the Knighthood of the Divine Sophia.* Waterloo, Ia., 1977.

Clark, Reverend Francis E. *A New Way Around an Old World.* New York and London, 1901.

Cleary, J. W. "The Virgin Lands," *S,* No. 56 (July 1965), pp. 95–105.

Cleaves, Francis Woodman. *The Secret History of the Mongols for the First Time Done into English out of the Original Tongue and Provided with an Exegetical Commentary.* Cambridge, Mass., and London, 1982.

Cochrane, Captain John Dundas. *Narrative of a Pedestrian Journey through Russia and Siberian Tartary, from the Frontiers of China to the Frozen Sea of Kamtchatka.* 2nd ed. 2 vols. London, 1824.

Cohen, Stephen F. *Bukharin and the Bolshevik Revolution: A Political Biography, 1888–1938.* Oxford, 1980.

Collins, Perry McDonough. *A Voyage down the Amoor: With a Land Journey Through Siberia, and Incidental Notices of Manchooria, Kamschatka, and Japan.* New York, 1860. 2nd ed. 1864.

———. *Overland Explorations in Siberia, Northern Asia, and the Great Amoor River Country.* New York, 1864.

Conolly, Violet. "The Baikal-Amur Railway (the BAM)," in Wood, ed., *Siberia*, pp. 158–170.

———. *Beyond the Urals: Economic Developments in Soviet Asia.* London, 1967.

———. *Siberia Today and Tomorrow: A Study of Economic Resources, Problems, and Achievements.* London and Glasgow, 1975.

———. "Siberia: Yesterday, Today, and Tomorrow," in Swearingen, ed., *Siberia and the Soviet Far East*, pp. 1–39.

Conquest, Robert. *Kolyma: The Arctic Death Camps.* London, 1978.

Coquin, François-Xavier. *La Sibérie: Peuplement et Immigration Paysanne au XIXe Siècle.* Paris, 1969.

"Cortés, Hernando," *EB*, VII, pp. 205–207.

Crisp, Olga. *Studies in the Russian Economy Before 1914.* London, 1976.

Crownhart-Vaughan, E. A. P. "Introduction," in S. P. Krasheninnikov, *Explorations of Kamchatka: A Report of a Journey Made to Explore Eastern Siberia in 1735–1741, by Order of the Russian Imperial Government.* Translated with introduction and notes by E. A. P. Crownhart-Vaughan. Portland, 1972.

Crummey, Robert O. *The Formation of Muscovy, 1304–1613.* London and New York, 1987.

Cummings, C. K., and Walter W. Petit. *American-Russian Relations, March 1917–March 1920: Documents and Papers.* New York, 1920.

Curtin, Jeremiah. *The Mongols in Russia.* Boston, 1908.

Czernin, Count Ottokar von. *In the World War.* New York and London, 1920.

Dallin, David J., and Boris I. Nikolaevsky. *Forced Labor in Soviet Russia.* New Haven, 1947.

Danilevskii, V. V. *Russkoe zoloto: Istoriia otkrytiia i dobychi do serediny XIXv.* Moscow, 1959.

Danilov, Iu. N. *Rossiia v mirovoi voine, 1914–1915gg.* Berlin, 1924.

The Dark Side of the Moon. With a preface by T. S. Eliot. New York, 1947.

Davis, Henry W. C. "Matthew of Paris," *EB*, XVII, pp. 898–899.

Davydov, M., and M. Tsunts. *Ot Volkhova do Amura.* Moscow, 1958.

Dawson, Christopher, ed. *The Mongol Mission.* New York, 1955.

Deutsch, Leo. *Sixteen Years in Siberia: Some Experiences of a Russian Revolutionist.* Translated by Helen Chisholm. New York, 1904.

Deutscher, Isaac. *The Prophet Armed: Trotskii, 1879–1921.* New York and London, 1963.

de Windt, Harry. *The New Siberia.* London, 1896.

Dikov, N. N. *Drevnie kul'tury Severo-Vostochnoi Azii: Aziia na styke s Amerikoi v drevnosti.* Moscow, 1979.

Dikovskaia-Iakimova, A., and V. Pleskov, eds. *Kara i drugie tiurmy Nerchinskoi katorgi: Sbornik vospominanii, dokumentov, i materialov.* Moscow, 1927.

Diterikhs, General M. K. *Ubiistvo tsarskoi sem'i i chlenov doma Romanovykh na Urale.* 2 vols. Vladivostok, 1922.

Divin, V. A. *Velikii russkii moreplavatel' A. I. Chirikov.* Moscow, 1953.

Dmitriev-Mamonov, A. I., and A. F. Zdziarskii, eds. *Guide to the Great Siberian Railway.* Translated by L. Kukol-Yasnopolsky, revised by John Marshall. St. Petersburg, 1900.

Dobbs, Michael. "Russians Fight To Save Lake Baikal," *The Washington Post* (October 11, 1990), pp. A25–26.

Dobell, Peter. *Travels in Kamtchatka and Siberia; With a Narrative of a Residence in China.* 2 vols. London, 1830.

"Doklad Petrogradskago okhrannago otdeleniia osobomu otdelu departamenta politsii, oktiabr' 1916g.," in Pokrovskii, ed., "Politicheskoe polozhenie Rossii," *KA,* XXVI (1926), pp. 1–35.

Dopolneniia k aktam istoricheskim, sobrannye i izdannye arkheograficheskoiu kommissieiu. Vols. 3 and 4. St. Petersburg, 1848.

Dostoevskii, F. M. *Pis'ma.* 3 vols. Moscow and Leningrad, 1928.

——. *Zapiski iz mërtvogo doma,* in *Polnoe sobranie sochinenii v tridtsati tomakh.* Vol. 4. Leningrad, 1972.

Drake, F. S. "China's North-west Passage: A Chapter in Its Opening," *JNCBRAS,* LXVI (1935), pp. 40–49.

Dunlop, Major C. Reports to Major General C. E. Caldwell. AG. File 10N93.

Durgin, Frank A. "The Virgin Lands Programme, 1954–1960," *SS,* XIII (1962), pp. 255–280.

Dvorianov, V. N. *V Sibirskoi dal'nei storone: Ocherki istorii politicheskoi katorgi i ssylki 60-e gody XVIIIv.–1917g.* 2nd ed. Minsk, 1985.

Dzhivelegov, A. K., et al., eds. *Velikaia reforma: Russkoe obshchestvo i krest'ianskii vopros v proshlom i nastoiashchem.* 6 vols. Moscow, 1911.

Edwards, Mike. "Siberia: In from the Cold," *NG* (March 1990), pp. 2–39.

Efimov, A. V. *Iz istorii velikikh russkikh geograficheskikh otkrytii v Severnom Ledovitom i Tikhom Okeanakh XVII—pervaia polovina XVIIIvv.* Moscow, 1950.

Egorov, V. L. "Zolotaia orda pered kulikovskoi bitvoi," in Beskrovnyi, ed., *Kulikovskaia bitva,* pp. 174–213.

Erikson, John. "Military and Strategic Factors," in Wood, ed., *Siberia: Problems and Prospects for Regional Development,* pp. 171–192.

——. *The Soviet High Command: A Military-Political History, 1918–1941.* London, 1962.

Esper, Thomas. "Military Self-Sufficiency and Weapons Technology in Muscovite Russia," *SR,* XXVIII (1969), pp. 187–197.

Evtushenko, Evgenii. *Stikhi i poema: Bratskaia GES.* Moscow, 1967.

Fedorov-Davydov, G. A. *Obshchestvennyi stroi Zolotoi Ordy.* Moscow, 1973.

Feshbach, Murray, and Alfred Friendly, Jr. *Ecocide in the USSR: Health and Nature under Seige.* New York, 1992.

Fischer, Louis. *The Life of Lenin.* New York, 1964.

Fisher, H. H. "The American Railway Mission to Russia." With marginal notes and comments by John F. Stevens. HIA. John Frank Stevens Papers, File No. 1, pp. 1–6.

Fisher, Raymond. *Bering's Voyages: Whither and Why?* Seattle and Washington, 1977.

——. *The Russian Fur Trade, 1550–1700.* Berkeley, 1943.

——. "Semën Dezhnëv and Professor Golder," *PHR,* XXV (1956), pp. 281–292.

Floria, B. N. "Litva i Rus' pered bitvoi na Kulikovskom pole," in Beskrovnyi, ed., *Kulikovskaia bitva,* pp. 142–173.

Florinsky, M. T. *Russia: A History and an Interpretation.* New York, 1968.

Fomin, A. "Kariiskaia tragediia 1889g. po dokumentam," in Dikovskaia-Iakimova and Pleskov, eds., *Kara i drugie tiurmy Nerchinskoi katorgi,* pp. 120–137.

Forsyth, James. *A History of the Peoples of Siberia: Russia's North Asian Colony, 1581–1990.* Cambridge, U.K., 1992.

Foust, Clifford M. *Muscovite and Mandarin: Russia's Trade with China and Its Setting, 1727–1805.* Chapel Hill, N.C., 1969.

Fraser, John Foster. *The Real Siberia, Together with an Account of a Dash Through Manchuria.* New York, 1904.

Fuhrmann, Joseph T. *The Origins of Capitalism in Russia: Industry and Progress in the Sixteenth and Seventeenth Centuries.* Chicago, 1972.

Galigusov, I. F., and M. E. Churilin. *Flagman otechestvennoi industrii: Istoriia Magnitogorskogo metallurgicheskogo kombinata imeni V. I. Lenina.* Moscow, 1978.

Gamel, I. Kh. *Opisanie tul'skago oruzheinago zavoda v istoricheskom i tekhnicheskom otnoshenii.* Moscow, 1826.

Garmiza, V. V. "Iz istorii samarskoi uchredilki," *IZ*, VIII (1940), pp. 33–43.

Gatrell, Peter. *The Tsarist Economy, 1850–1917.* New York, 1986.

Gernet, M. N. *Istoriia tsarskoi tiurmy.* 5 vols. Moscow, 1961.

Gerrare, Wirt [William Oliver Greener]. *Greater Russia: The Continental Empire of the Old World.* New York, 1903.

Gerson, Lennard D. *The Secret Police in Lenin's Russia.* Philadelphia, 1976.

Getzler, Israel. *Martov: A Political Biography of a Russian Social Democrat.* Cambridge, U.K., 1967.

Gibbon, Edward. *The History of the Decline and Fall of the Roman Empire.* London, 1887.

Gibson, James R. *Feeding the Russian Fur Trade: Provisionment of the Okhotsk Seaboard and the Kamchatka Peninsula 1639–1856.* Madison, Wis., 1969.

———. *Imperial Russia in Frontier America: The Changing Geography of Supply of Russian America, 1784–1867.* New York, 1976.

———. "Russian Dependence upon the Natives of Alaska," in Starr, ed., *Russia's American Colony,* pp. 77–104.

Gins, G. K. *Sibir', soiuzniki, i Kolchak, 1918–1920.* 2 vols. Peking, 1921.

Glinka, G. V., ed. *Aziatskaia Rossiia.* 2 vols. St. Petersburg, 1914.

Glukhov, V. A. "Oborona Port-Artura," in Rostunov, ed., *Istoriia Russko-Iaponsksoi voiny,* pp. 165–258.

Golder, F. A., ed. *Bering's Voyages: An Account of the Efforts of the Russians to Determine the Relation of Asia to America.* 2 vols. New York, 1922.

———. *Russian Expansion on the Pacific, 1641–1850.* Gloucester, Mass., 1960.

Goldfrank, David H. "Dmitrii Ivanovich Donskoi," *MERSH,* IX, pp. 170–177.

Golovin [Golovine], N. N. *Rossiiskaia kontrrevoliutsiia v 1917–1918gg.* 8 vols. Paris 1937.

Golovin, P. N. *The End of Russian America: Captain P. N. Golovin's Last Report, 1862.* Translated with introduction and notes by Basil Dmytryshyn and E. A. P. Crownhart-Vaughan. Portland, 1979.

Golovnin, A. V. "Prodolzhenie zapisok A. V. Golovnina s dekabria 1870g. po fevral' 1871g.," TsGIAL, fond 851, opis' 1, delo No. 9.

Golubinskii, E. *Istoriia russkoi tserkvy.* Moscow, 1911.

Gorbachev, T. F., et al. *Kuznetskii ugol'nyi bassein.* Moscow, 1957.

Goriushkin, M., ed. *Ssylka i katorga v Sibiri (XVIII–nachalo XXv.).* Novosibirsk, 1975.

Gor'kii, M., et al., eds. *Belomorsko-Baltiiskii Kanal imeni Stalina: Istoriia stroitel'stva.* Moscow, 1934.

Gowing, Lionel F. *Five Thousand Miles in a Sledge: A Mid-Winter Journey Across Siberia.* London, 1889.

"Gramota tsaria Ivana Vasil'evicha Semenu, Maksimu, i Nikite Stroganovym o prigotovlenii k vesne 15 otrugov dlia liudei i zapasov, napravliaemykh v Sibir'," 7 ianvaria 1584g., appendix 4 in Miller, *Istoriia Sibiri,* I, pp. 343–344.

"Gramota tsaria Ivana Vasil'evicha v slobodku na Kame Iakovu i Grigoriiu Stroganovym o posylke ratnykh liudei dlia privedeniia i pokornosti cheremisov i drugikh narodov, proizvodivshikh grabezhi po reke Kame," appendix 4 in Miller, *Istoriia Sibiri,* I, pp. 338–339.

Graves, William S. *America's Siberian Adventure, 1918–1920.* New York, 1941.

Grekov, B., and A. Iakoubovski. *La Horde d'or et la Russie: La Domination Tatare aux XIIIe et XIVe siècles de la mer jaune à la mer noire.* Translated from the Russian by François Thuret. Paris, 1961.

Grekov, B. D., L. V. Cherepnin, and V. T. Pashuto, eds. *Ocherki istorii SSSR: period feodalizma IX–XV vv.* Vol. 2. Moscow, 1953.

————, and A. Iu. Iakubovskii. *Zolotaia orda i eë padenie.* Moscow and Leningrad, 1950.

Grey, Viscount Edward. *Twenty-Five Years, 1892–1916.* 2 vols. London, 1925.

Grondijs, L. H. *Le Cas-Koltchak: Contribution à l'histoire de la révolution russe.* Leiden, 1939.

Grossman, Leonid. *Dostoevskii.* Moscow, 1965.

Grousset, René. *Conqueror of the World.* Translated from the French by Marian McKellar and Denis Sinor. New York, 1966.

————. *Empire of the Steppes: A History of Central Asia.* Translated from the French by Naomi Walford. New Brunswick, 1970.

Gudzy, N. K. *History of Early Russian Literature.* Translated by Susan Wilbur Jones. New York, 1949.

Gumbel, Peter, and James Tanner. "Tired Mammoth," *Wall Street Journal,* August 22, 1990, pp. A1–A4.

Gusev, K. V. *Partiia eserov: Ot melko-burzhuaznogo revoliutsionarizma k kontrrevoliutsii.* Moscow, 1975.

————, and Kh. A. Eritsian. *Ot soglashatel'stva k kontrrevoliutsii: Ocherki istorii politicheskogo bankrotstva i gibeli partii sotsialistov-revoliutsionerov.* Moscow, 1968.

A Handbook of Siberia and Arctic Russia. Compiled by the Geographical Staff of the Naval Intelligence Division, Naval Staff, the Admiralty. London, 1920.

Hasegawa, Tsuyoshi. *The February Revolution: Petrograd 1917.* Seattle and London, 1981.

Herling, Gustav. *A World Apart.* Translated from the Polish by Joseph Marek. London, 1951.

Hosking, Geoffrey. *The First Socialist Society: A History of the Soviet Union from Within.* Cambridge, Mass., 1990.

Howorth, Henry H. *History of the Mongols from the 9th to the 19th Century.* London, 1876. 3 vols in 4 parts.

Hudson, Hugh D., Jr. *The Rise of the Demidov Family and the Russian Iron Industry in the Eighteenth Century.* Newtonville, Mass., 1986.

Iadrintsev, N. M. *Russkaia obshchina v tiurme i ssylke.* St. Petersburg, 1872.

————. *Sibir' kak koloniia: K iubileiu trekhsotletiia.* St. Petersburg, 1882.

Ioffe, G. Z. *Kolchakovskaia avantiura i ee krakh.* Moscow, 1983.

"Ivan Vasil'evich's letter to the settlement on the Kama to Iakov and Grigorii Stroganov on the sending of fighting men for the subduing of the Cheremis and other peoples marauding on the river Kama," August 6, 1572, in Armstrong, ed., *Yermak's Campaign,* pp. 288–289.

Ivanchin-Pisarev, A. I. "Iz moikh vospominanii (po doroge v Sibir', v Krasnoiarske i v Minusinske)," *KiS,* LVIII (1929), pp. 303–312.

Ivan'kov, A. G. *Lenin v sibirskoi ssylke, 1897–1900.* Moscow, 1962.

Jasny, Naum. *The Soviet Economy of the Plan Era.* Stanford, 1951.

John of Plano Carpini, "History of the Mongols," in Christopher Dawson, ed., *The Mongol Mission.* New York, 1955.

Juvaini, Ala-ad-Din Ata-Malik. *The History of the World Conqueror.* Translated from the text of Mirza Muhammad Qazvini by John Andrew Boyle. 2 vols. Cambridge, Mass., 1958.

Kabo, R. M. *Goroda Zapadnoi Sibiri: Ocherki istoriko-ekonomicheskoi geografii XVII–pervaia polovina XIXvv.* Moscow, 1949.

Kafengauz, B. B. *Istoriia khoziaistva Demidovykh v XVIII–XIX vv. Opyt issledovaniia po istorii ural'skoi metallurgii.* Moscow and Leningrad, 1949.

Kakhovskaia, I. "Iz vospominanii o zhenskoi katorge," *KiS,* XXII (1926), pp. 145–162; XXIII (1926), pp. 170–185.

Kakurin, N. *Kak srazhalas' revoliutsiia.* 2 vols. Moscow and Leningrad, 1925.

Kalvoda, Josef. "Czech and Slovak Prisoners of War in Russia During the War and Revolution," in Williamson and Pastor, eds., *Essays on World War I,* pp. 215–226.

Kamanin, L. G. *Pervye issledovateli dal'nego vostoka.* Moscow, 1951.

Karamzin, N. M. *Istoriia Gosudarstva Rossiiskago.* 5th ed. 4. vols. St. Petersburg, 1842.

Kargalov, V. V. "Baskaki," *VI*, No. 5 (1972), pp. 212–215.

———. "Sushchestvovala li na Rusi 'voenno-politicheskaia baskacheskaia organizatsiia' mongol'skikh feodalov?" *IstSSSR*, No. 1 (1962), pp. 161–165.

———. *Kulikovskaia bitva.* Moscow, 1980.

Kariiskaia tragediia (1889): Vospominaniia i materialy. St. Peterburg, 1920.

Karnovich, E. P. *Zamechatel'nye bogatstva chastnykh lits v Rossii: Ekonomichesko-istoricheskoe izsledovanie.* St. Petersburg, 1874.

Karpenko, Z. G. *Gornaia i metallurgicheskaia promyshlennost' zapadnoi Sibiri v 1700–1860 godakh.* Novosibirsk, 1963.

Kataev, A. A. "Tatary i poraboshchenie imi Rusi," in Dovnar-Zapol'skii, ed., *Russkaia istoriia,* pp. 564–575.

Keenan, Edward L. *The Kurbskii-Groznyi Apocrypha.* Cambridge, Mass., 1971.

Kennan, George. *Siberia and the Exile System.* 2 vols. New York, 1891.

Kennan, George F. *The Decision to Intervene.* Princeton, 1958.

"Khabarov-Sviatitskii, Erofei Pavlovich," *SIE*, XV, col. 477.

Khlebnikov, K. T. *Baranov: Chief Manager of the Russian Colonies in America.* Translated by Colin Bearne, edited by Richard A. Pierce. Kingston, Ontario, 1973.

———. *Zapiski o koloniiakh v Amerike.* Edited by S. G. Fedorova. Moscow, 1985.

Kibal'chich, Oleg A. "The BAM and Its Economic Geography," in Shabad and Mote, *Gateway to Siberian Resources,* pp. 145–154.

"Kirgizskaia Sovetskaia Sotsialisticheskaia Respublika," *SIE*, VII, col. 254–258.

Kiselev, S. V. *Drevniaia istoriia iuzhnoi Sibiri.* Moscow, 1951.

Kitchin, George. *Prisoner of the OGPU.* London, 1935.

Klevanskii, A. Kh. *Chekhoslovatskie internatsionalisty i prodannyi korpus: Chekhoslovatskie politicheskie organizatsii i voinskie formirovaniia v Rossii, 1914–1921gg.* Moscow, 1965.

Kodan, S. V. "Petrashevtsy na Nerchinskoi katorge," in *Ssyl'nye revoliutsionery v Sibiri,* VI, pp. 7–21.

Kolenkovskii, A. *Manevrennyi period pervoi mirovoi imperialisticheskoi voiny 1914g.* Moscow, 1940.

Kolesnikov, A. D. "Ssylka i zaselenie Sibiri," in Goriushkin, ed., *Ssylka i katorga v Sibiri,* pp. 38–58.

Kologrivov, I. N. "Ekaterina Ivanovna Trubetskaia," *Sovremennye zapiski,* LX (1936), pp. 206–212.

Kolokol: Gazeta A. I. Gertsena i N. P. Ogareva. 11 vols. Moscow, 1961–1967.

Komarov, Boris. *The Destruction of Nature in the Soviet Union.* Translated by Michel Vale and Joe Hollander, with a forward by Marshall I. Goldman. White Plains, N.Y., 1980.

Kommissiia po istorii oktiabr'skoi revoliutsii i R. K. P. (bol'shevikov). *Revoliutsiia na Dal'nem Vostoke.* Vol. 1. Moscow and Petrograd, 1923.

"Konfidential'noe pis'mo Barona Korfa Ministru Vnutrennikh Del L. A. Perovskomu," 21 iiunia 1850g., TsGIAL, fond 1287, opis' 35, delo No. 97/1–2.

"Konstitutsiia ufimskoi direktorii: Akt ob obrazovanii vserossiiskoi verkhovnoi vlasti, 8–23 sentiabria 1918g.," *ARR*, XII, pp. 189–193.

Korf, Baron M. A. *Zhizn' Grafa Sperakskago.* St. Petersburg, 1861.

Kotkin, Stephen. *Steeltown, USSR: Soviet Society in the Gorbachev Era.* Berkeley and Los Angeles, 1991.

Koval'skaia, E. N. "Zhenskaia katorga: Iz vospominanii E. N. Koval'skoi," in *Kariiskaia tragediia,* pp. 5–29.

Kozybaev, M. K. "Iz istorii deiatel'nosti 'Komissii AN SSSR po mobilizatsii resursov Urala, Zapadnoi Sibiri, i Kazakhstana na nuzhdy oborony," *Izvestiia Akademii Nauk Kazakhstoi SSSR. Seriia istorii, arkheologii i etnografii,* pt. 1, XVIII (1962).

Krasheninnikov, S. P. *Opisanie zemli Kamchatki.* Moscow and Leningrad, 1949.

Kravchenko, G. S. *Voennaia ekonomika SSSR 1941–1945.* Moscow, 1963.

Kritsman, L. *Geroicheskii period velikoi russkoi revoliutsii.* Moscow, n.d. [1924].

Krupskaia, Nadezhda K. *Memories of Lenin.* Translated by Eric Verney. New York, n.d.

Kudriavtsev, F., and G. Vendrikh. *Irkutsk: Ocherki po istorii goroda.* Irkutsk, 1971.

Kudriavtsev, F. A. "Uchastniki narodnykh dvizhenii pervoi poloviny XIX veka na katorge," in *Ssyl'nye revoliutsionery v Sibiri,* II, pp. 3–10.

" 'Kupchaia' na tret' varnitsy bez tsyrena i tret' varnichnogo mesta, kuplennykh Anikoi Fëdorovichem Stroganovym u Iakova Fëdorova syna Bizimova," 18 fevralia 1526g., in Vvedenskii, ed., *Torgovyi dom,* p. 86.

" 'Kupchaia' na varnitsu s tsyrenom i so vsem 'nariadom, chto v varnitse,' kuplennuiu Anikoi Fëdorovichem Stroganovym u Avdot'i Maksimovoi docheri u Stepanovskoi zheny Zuesa i ee vnuka Vasil'ia Ontomanova,' 3 iiunia 1526g., in Vvedenskii, ed., *Torgovyi dom,* pp. 86–87.

" 'Kupchaia' na varnitsu so vsem varnichnym inventarem i s varnichnym mestom, kuplennymi Anikoi Stroganovym u Vasil'ia i Dmitriia Varonitsynykh," 15 iiulia 1540g., in Vvedenskii, ed., *Torgovyi dom,* pp. 87–88.

Kuropatkin, A. N. "Dnevnik A. N. Kuropatkina," *KA,* II (1922), pp. 5–112; V (1924), pp. 82–101; VII (1924), pp. 55–69; VIII (1925), pp. 70–100; LXVIII (1935), pp. 65–90; LXIX–LXX (1935), pp. 101–127.

————. *Opisanie boevykh deistvii Man'chzhurskikh armii pod Mukdenom s 4-go fevralia po 4-e marta 1905 goda.* 3 vols. Moscow, 1907.

"Kuzbas": An Opportunity for Engineers and Workers. New York, 1922.

Kuzin, A. A. *Istoriia otkrytii rudnykh mestorozhdenii v Rossii do serediny XIX v.* Moscow, 1961.

Kuz'min, G. V. *Razgrom interventov i belogvardeitsev v 1917–1922gg.* Moscow, 1977.

Laird, Roy D. "Agriculture under Khrushchev," *S,* No. 56 (July 1965), pp. 106–117.

Lansdell, Henry. *Through Siberia.* 4th ed. 2 vols. London, 1883.

Lantzeff, George V. *Siberia in the Seventeenth Century: A Study of the Colonial Administration.* Berkeley and Los Angeles, 1943.

————, and Richard A. Pierce. *Eastward to Empire: Exploration and Conquest on the Russian Open Frontier to 1750.* Montreal and London, 1973.

Lattimore, Owen. "Caravan Routes of Inner Asia," *GJ,* LXXII, No. 6 (December 1928), pp. 497–528.

————. "New Road to Asia," *NG,* LXXXVI, No. 6 (December 1944), pp. 641–676.

Laue, Theodore H. von. *Sergei Witte and the Industrialization of Russia.* New York and London, 1963.

Lauridsen, Peter. *Vitus Bering: The Discoverer of Bering Strait.* Translated from the Danish by Julius E. Olsen, with an introduction by Frederick Schwatka. Chicago, 1889.

Lebedev, D. M. *Geografiia v Rossii XVII veka: Ocherki po istorii geograficheskikh znanii.* Moscow and Leningrad, 1949.

Lebedev, M. I. *Vospominaniia o Lenskikh sobytiiakh 1912 goda.* Moscow, 1962.

Ledyard, John. *John Ledyard's Journey Through Russia and Siberia, 1787–1788.* Edited with an introduction by Stephen D. Watrous. Madison, 1966.

Leiberov, I. P. *Na shturm samoderzhaviia. Petrogradskii proletariat v gody pervoi mirovoi voiny i fevral'skaia revoliutsiia.* Moscow, 1979.

Lemke, M. K. *Ocherki po istorii russkoi tsenzury i zhurnalistiki stoletiia.* St. Petersburg, 1904.

Lenin, V. I. *Collected Works.* Vol. 32. Moscow, 1965.

————. *Sochineniia.* 4th ed. Vol. 37. Moscow, 1957.

"Lenskii rasstrel 1912," *SSE,* VIII, cols. 583–584.

"Lenskoe Zoloto-Promyshlennoe Tovarishchestvo," *SSE,* III, cols. 84–85.

"Lensko-Vitimskii Zolotonosnyi Raion," *SSE,* III, cols. 77–83.

Levin, M. G., and L. P. Potapov, eds. *Narody Sibiri.* Moscow and Leningrad, 1956.

Lewin, Moshe. *Russian Peasants and Soviet Power.* London, 1968.

Liashchenko, P. I. *History of the National Economy of Russia to the 1917 Revolution.* Translated by L. M. Herman. New York, 1949.

————. *Istoriia narodnogo khoziaistva SSSR.* 3 vols. Moscow, 1956.

Limonov, Iu. A. *Vladimiro-Suzdal'skaia Rus': Ocherki sotsial'no-politicheskoi istorii.* Leningrad, 1987.

Lincoln, W. Bruce. *Nicholas I: Emperor and Autocrat of All the Russias* London, 1978.

————. *Red Victory: A History of the Russian Civil War.* New York, 1989.

————. *The Romanovs: Autocrats of All the Russias.* New York, 1981.

Lipkina, A. G. *1919 god v Sibiri.* Moscow, 1962.

Lipper, Elinor. *Eleven Years in Soviet Prison Camps.* Chicago, 1951.

Littlepage, John D., and Demaree Bess. *In Search of Soviet Gold.* New York, 1938.

Liubavskii, M. K. *Ocherk istorii litovsko-russkago gosudarstva.* Moscow, 1915.

Liubomirov, P. G. *Ocherki po istorii metallurgicheskoi i metalloobrabatyvaiushchei promyshlennosti v Rossii (XVII, XVIII i nachalo XIX vv.).* Leningrad, 1937.

Livshits, R. S. "Razmeshchenie promyshlennosti v dorevoliutsionnoi Rossii," *Izvestiia Akademii Nauk SSSR* (1955), pp. 220–223.

Lockhart, R. H. Bruce. *British Agent.* New York and London, 1933.

Lorimer, Frank. *The Population of the Soviet Union: History and Prospects.* Geneva, 1946.

Lubimenko, Inna. "A Project for the Acquisition of Russia by James I," *EHR,* XXIV (1914), pp. 246–256.

Luckett, Richard. *The White Generals: An Account of the White Movement and the Russian Civil War.* New York, 1971.

Magidovich, I. P., and V. I. Magidovich. *Ocherki po istorii geograficheskikh otkrytii.* 2 vols. Moscow, 1983.

Maksakov, V., and A. Turunov. *Khronika grazhdanskoi voiny v Sibiri, 1917–1918.* Moscow, 1926.

Maksakova, L. M. *Agitpoezd "Oktiabr'skaia Revoliutsiia," 1919–1920gg.* Moscow, 1956.

Maksimov, S. V. *Sibir' i katorga.* 3 vols. St. Petersburg, 1891.

Malenky, A. *Magnitogorsk: The Magnitogorsk Metallurgical Combine of the Future.* Moscow, 1932.

Malle, Silvana. *The Economic Organization of War Communism, 1918–1921.* Cambridge, England, 1985.

Malozemoff, Andrew. *Russian Far Eastern Policy, 1881–1904. With Special Emphasis on the Causes of the Russo-Japanese War.* Berkeley and Los Angeles, 1958.

Mal'tsev, V. F. ed. *Bratskaia GES: Sbornik dokumentov i materialov.* Vol. 2. Irkutsk, 1965.

Mancall, Mark. *Russia and China: Their Diplomatic Relations to 1728.* N.p., 1971.

Manikovskii, A. A. *Boevoe snabzhenie russkoi armii v mirovuiu voinu.* Vol. 1. 2nd ed. Moscow-Leningrad, 1930.

Margolis, A. D. "O chislennosti i razmeshchenii ssyl'nykh v Sibiri v kontse XIXv.," in Goriushkin, ed., *Ssylka i katorga v Sibiri,* pp. 223–237.

Markov, Anatolii. "Entsiklopediia belogo dvizheniia." HIA. Anatolii Markov Collection, file 1.

Marks, Steven. *Road to Power: The Trans-Siberian Railroad and the Colonization of Asian Russia, 1850–1917.* Ithaca, 1991.

Martin, H. D. *The Rise of Chingis Khan and His Conquest of North China.* Baltimore, 1950.

Martens, F. *Sobranie traktatov i konventsii, zakliuchennykh Rossieiu s inostrannymi derzhavami.* 15 vols. St. Petersburg, 1892–1894.

Marushevskii, V., and P. Orlov. *Boevaia rabota russkoi armii v voinu 1904–1905gg.* 2 vols. St. Petersburg, 1910.

Matthew of Paris. *English History from the Year 1235 to 1273.* Translated from the Latin by the Reverend J. A. Giles. 3 vols. London, 1852.

Mawdsley, Ian. *The Russian Civil War.* Boston, 1987.

Mazour, Anatole G. *The First Russian Revolution 1825: The Decembrist Movement: Its Origins, Development, and Significance.* Berkeley, 1937.

————. *Women in Exile: Wives of the Decembrists.* Tallahassee, 1975.

McCullough, David. *The Path between the Seas: The Creation of the Panama Canal, 1870–1914.* New York, 1977.

Mel'gunov, S. P. *Sud'ba imperatora Nikolaia II posle otrecheniia.* Paris, 1951.

———. *Tragediia Admirala Kolchaka: Iz istorii grazhdanskoi voiny na Volge, Urale, i v Sibiri.* 2 vols. Belgrade, 1930.

Meshcherskii, A. P. "Osobennosti, partiinyi sostav politicheskoi ssylki v Sibiri v kontse XIX–nachale XX veka," *Ssyl'nye revoliutsionery v Sibiri* (Irkutsk, 1973), I, pp. 125–143.

Michael, Henry N. "Absolute Chronologies of Late Pleistocene and Early Holocene Cultures of Northeastern Asia," *AA,* XXI, No. 2 (1984), pp. 1–68.

Michie, Alexander. *The Siberian Overland Route from Peking to Petersburg.* London, 1864.

Mikhail Pavlovich, Grand Duke. "Vospominaniia velikago kniazia Mikhaila Pavlovicha o sobytiiakh 14 dekabria 1825g., in Syroechkovskii (ed.), *Mezhdutsarstvie,* pp. 49–63.

Miliukov, P. N. *Gosudarstvennoe khoziaistvo Rossii v pervoi chetverti XVIII stoletiia i reforma Petra Velikago.* St. Petersburg, 1892.

———. *Vospominaniia, 1859–1917.* 2 vols. New York, 1955.

Miller [Müller], G. F. *Istoriia Sibiri.* 2 vols. Moscow and Leningrad, 1937.

Miller, V. F. *Istoricheskie pesni russkogo naroda XVI–XVII vekov.* Petrograd, 1915.

Ministerstvo Putei Soobshcheniia. *Otchët po postroike Severno-Ussuriiskoi zheleznoi dorogi, 1894–1897.* St. Petersburg, 1900.

Mints, I. I. *Istoriia velikogo oktiabria.* 2 vols. Moscow, 1967.

Mochalova, Iu. V., ed. *Podvig na Enisee: Iz istorii stroitel'stva Krasnoiarskoi GES.* Moscow, 1972.

Mochanov, Iu. A. *Drevneishie etapy zaseleniia chelovekem Severo-Vostochnoi Azii.* Novosibirsk, 1977.

Mochul'skii, Konstantin. *Vladimir Solov'ëv: Zhizn' i uchenie.* 2nd ed. Paris, 1951.

Molotov, Vladimir. *Bol'sheviki Sibiri v period grazhdanskoi voiny (1918–1919gg.).* Omsk, 1949.

Mote, Victor L. "The Baykal-Amur Mainline: Catalyst for the Development of Pacific Siberia," in Shabad and Mote, eds., *Gateway to Siberian Resources (The BAM),* pp. 63–116.

———. "The Communications Infrastructure," in Swearingen, ed., *Siberia and the Soviet Far East,* pp. 40–73.

Mozdalevskii, B. L., and A. A. Sivers, eds. *Vosstaniia dekabristov: Materialy.* Vol. 8. Leningrad, 1925.

Murashov, S. I., ed. *Partiia bol'shevikov v gody pervoi mirovoi voiny. Sverzhenie monarkhii v Rossii.* Moscow, 1963.

Murav'ëv, N. N. "Nachal'niku Glavnago Morskago Shtaba Ego Imperatorskago Velichestva, gospodinu general-ad iutantu Men'shikovu" 1 ianvaria 1850, in Barsukov, *Graf Nikolai Nikolaevich Murav'ëv-Amurskii,* II, p. 52.

———. "Prichiny neobkhodimosti zaniatiia ust'ia r. Amura i toi chasti ostrova Sakhalina, kotoraia emu protivolezhit, a takzhe levago berega Amura" (1849–1850), in Barsukov, *Graf Nikolai Nikolaevich Murav'ëv-Amurskii,* II, pp. 47–56.

Naida, S. F., et al., eds. *Istoriia grazhdanskoi voiny v SSSR.* Vol. 4. Moscow, 1959.

"Nakaz Iakutskago voevody Dimitriia Frantsbekova opytovshchiku Erofeiu Khabarovu, o pokhode v Daurskiiu zemliu," 6 marta 1649g., in *AI,* IV, document No. 31, pp. 67–72.

"Nakaznaia pamiat' Iakutskago voevody Ivana Akinfova kazach'emu piatidesiatniku Ivanu Rebrovu, o priniatii v svoe vedenie Kovymskago ostroga i o sbore iasaka i kosti ryb'iago zuba s Iukagirov i Chukchei," 30 iiunia 1652g., in *DAI,* III, document No. 98, pp. 350–352.

Nasar, Rusi. "Fact in Fiction," *The Washington Post* (June 4, 1989), p. B3.

Nasonov, A. N. *Mongoly i Rus' (Istoriia tatarskoi politiki na Rusi).* Moscow and Leningrad, 1940.

———, L. V. Cherepnin, and A. A. Zimin, eds. *Ocherki istorii SSSR: Period feodalizma. Konets XV v.–nachalo XVII v.* Moscow, 1955.

Neatby, L. H. *Discovery in Russian and Siberian Waters.* Athens, Ohio, 1973.

Nechkina, M. V. *Dvizhenie Dekabristov*. 2 vols. Moscow, 1955.

Neishtadt, S. A. *Ekonomicheskoe razvitie Kazakhskoi SSR (period sotsializma i razvërnutogo stroitel'stva kommunizma)*. Alma-Ata, 1960.

Nemasov, C. E. "Pis'mo Geroia Sotsialisticheskogo Truda Nemasova C. E., o tom, kak on stal geroem," 24 dekabria 1961g., in Mal'tsev, ed., *Bratskaia GES*, II, pp. 26–36.

Nicholas I. "Zapiska Nikolaia I o vstuplenii na prestol," in Syroechkovskii, ed., *Mezhdutsarstvie*, pp. 9–35.

Nifontov, A. S. *Rossiia v 1848 godu*. Moscow, 1949.

Nikitenko, A. V. *Dnevnik*. 3 vols. Moscow, 1955.

Nikitin, K. *Tsarskii flot pod krasnym flagom*. Moscow, 1931.

Nikolaev, A. M. "1918: Vtoroi god rossiiskoi grazhdanskoi voiny," A. M. Nikolaev Collection, Bakhmetieff Archive, Columbia University, New York.

Nolde, Boris. *La Formation de l'Empire Russe: Etudes, Notes et Documents*. Paris, 1952.

Nove, Alex. *An Economic History of the USSR*. London, 1969.

"O meropriiatiiakh Ministerstva Zemledeliia, vyzvannykh obstoiatel'stvami voennago vremeni i potrebnikh dlia osushchestvleniia etikh meropriiatii kreditakh," 10 oktiabria 1916g., TsGIAL, fond 1276, opis' 12, delo No. 1062.

The Official History of the Russo-Japanese War. 3 vols. London, 1909.

Ogloblin, N. N. *Semën Dezhnëv*. St. Petersburg, 1890.

Ogorodnikov, V. I. *Ocherk istorii Sibiri' do nachala XIX stoletiia*. 2 vols. Irkutsk, 1920; Vladivostok, 1924.

d'Ohsson, M. le Baron C. *Histoire des Mongols, depuis Tchinguiz-Khan jusqu'à Timour Bey or Tamerlan*. 4 vols. Amsterdam, 1852.

Okamoto, Shumpei. *The Japanese Oligarchy and the Russo-Japanese War*. New York and London, 1970.

Okladnikov, A. P. *Russkie poliarnye morekhody XVII veka u beregov Taimyra*. Moscow and Leningrad, 1948.

———, et al., eds. *Istoriia Sibiri'*. 5 vols. Leningrad, 1968.

Okun', S. B. *Dekabrist M. S. Lunin*. Leningrad, 1962.

———. "Materialy k istorii Buriatii v XVII v.," *KA*, LXXVI (1936), pp. 156–191.

———. *Rossiisko-Amerikanskaia Kompaniia*. Moscow and Leningrad, 1939.

Ol'denburg, S. S. *Tsarstvovanie Imperatora Nikolaia II*. 2 vols. Belgrade, 1939.

Orlova, N. S., ed. *Otkrytiia russkikh zemleprokhodtsev i poliarnykh morekhodov XVII veka na severo-vostoke Asii. Sbornik dokumentov*. Moscow, 1951.

Osmolovskii, G. F. "Kariiskaia tragediia," in *Kariiskaia tragediia*, pp. 30–55.

"Otnoshenie Deistvitel'nago Tainago Sovetnika Dmitriia Buturlina 17–go marta 1849g., k Ministru Narodnago Prosveshcheniia Grafu S. S. Uvarovu" (konfidential'no), TsGIAL, fond 772, opis' 1, delo No. 2242/1–3.

"Otpiska Iakutskomu voevode Dimitriiu Frantsbekovu sluzhivago cheloveka Erofeia Khabarova, o voennykh deistviiakh ego na reke Amure," Avgusta 1652g., *DAI*, III, document No. 102, pp. 359–371.

"Otpiski Iakutskomu voevode Ivanu Akinfovu sluzhivykh liudei Semena Dezhneva i Nikity Semenova, o pokhode ikh na reku Anadyr, o voennykh deistviiakh protiv inorodtsev i proch.," 4, i posle 15, aprelia 1655, in *DAI*, IV, document No. 7, pp. 16–27.

"Otpiska prikaznago cheloveka Onufriia Stepanova Iakutskomu voevode Mikhailu Lodyzhenskomu, o deistviiakh ego na reke Amure po ot" ezde Erofeia Khabarova v Moskvu," v nachale avgusta 1654g., *DAI*, III, document No. 122, pp. 523–528.

"Otpiska sluzhivago cheloveka Ivana Uvarova Iakutskomu voevode Dimitriiu Frantsbekovu, a plavanii ego dlia otyskaniia Erofeia Khabarova po reke Amuru i Vostochnomu Okeanu i o pribytii na reku Tugir'," 30 iiunia 1652, *DAI*, III, document No. 100, pp. 354–356.

"Otpiska sluzhivago cheloveka Terentiia Ermolina, ob ostavlenii im v Tungurskom zimov'e porokha i svintsa, poslannykh k prikaznomu cheloveku Efofeiu Khabarovu, i o plavanii po reke Amuru, avgusta 1652g., in *DAI*, III, document No. 101, pp. 356–359.

Paleologue, Maurice. *La Russie des Tsars pendant la Grande Guerre.* 3 vols. Paris, 1921.

Parfenov, P. S. *Grazhdanskaia voina v Sibiri, 1918–1920.* Moscow, 1924.

Payne, Joseph Frank, Arthur Shadwell, and Harriet L. Hennessy. "Plague," *EB*, XXI, pp. 693–705.

Pearson, Raymond. *The Russian Moderates and the Crisis of Tsarism, 1914–1917.* London, 1977.

Petrov, Iu. *Magnitka.* Moscow, 1971.

Petrov, Vladimir. *Soviet Gold: My Life As a Slave Laborer in the Siberian Mines.* Translated from the Russian by Mirra Ginsburg. New York, 1949.

Petrovskii, V. "Kariiskie sobytiia," in *Kariiskaia tragediia,* pp. 56–75.

Pfitzenmayer, E. W. *Les Mammouths de Sibirie: La découverte de cadavres de mammouths préhistoriques sur les bords de la Berezovka et de la Sanga-Iourakh.* Paris, 1939.

Pierce, Richard A. *Russia's Hawaiian Adventure, 1815–1817.* Berkeley, 1965.

Piontkovskii, S., ed. *Grazhdanskaia voina v Rossii (1918–1921gg.): Khrestomatiia.* Moscow, 1925.

Pobedonostsev, K. P. *Pis'ma Pobedonostseva k Aleksandru III.* 2 vols. Moscow, 1926.

Pogodin, M. M. *Istoriko-politicheskie pis'ma i zapiski v prodolzhenii krymskoi voiny, 1853–1856gg.* Moscow, 1874.

Pokrovskii, M. N., ed. "Politicheskoe polozhenie Rossii nakanune fevral'skoi revoliutsii v zhandarmskom osveshchenii," *KA*, XXVI (1926), pp. 1–35.

Polevoi, B. P. "The Discovery of Russian America," in Starr, ed., *Russia's American Colony,* pp. 13–31.

———. "Glavnaia zadacha pervoi kamchatskoi ekspeditsii po zamyslu Petra I," *Voprosy geografii Kamchatki,* No. 2 (1964), pp. 88–94.

———. "Vodnyi put' iz Ledovitogo Okeana v Tikhii: Zabytii nakaz A. A. Viniusa 1697 goda," *Priroda,* No. 5 (1965), p. 94.

Poliakov, M. "Vospominaniia o Kolymskoi ssylke (1889–1896)," *KiS*, XLV (1928), pp. 158–172, XLVII (1928), pp. 113–122.

Polnoe sobranie zakonov rossiiskoi imperii s 1649g. 2nd. ed. St. Petersburg, 1830.

Polovtsov, A. A. *Dnevnik gosudarstvennogo sekretaria A. A. Polovtsova.* Edited by P. A. Zaionchkovskii. 2 vols. Moscow, 1966.

Poniatowski, Michel. *Histoire de la Russie d'Amérique et de l'Alaska.* Paris, 1978.

Popov, P. I. "Pereselenie krest'ian i zemleustroistvo Sibiri," in Dzhivelegov et al., eds., *Velikaia reforma,* VI, pp. 249–267.

Portal, Roger. *L'Oural au XVIIIe siècle: Etude d'histoire économique et sociale.* Paris, 1950.

Pospelov, P., ed. *Lenskie priiski: Sbornik dokumentov.* Moscow, 1937.

"Predstavlenie ministra zemledeliia A. A. Bobrinskago v Sovet Ministrov o vliianii voiny na sostoianie sel'skago khoziastva i neobkhodimykh meropriiatiiakh dlia ego pod"ema," 10 oktiabria 1916g., in Anfimov et al., eds., *Ekonomicheskoe polozhenie Rossii,* III, p. 16.

Presniakov, A. E. *14 dekabria 1825 goda.* Moscow and Leningrad, 1926.

———. *Lektsii po russkoi istorii.* 2 vols. Moscow, 1938.

Radziwill, Princess Catherine. *Memories of Forty Years.* London, 1914.

Radzinsky, Edvard. *The Last Tzar: The Life and Death of Nicholas II.* Translated by Marian Schwartz. New York, 1992.

Raeff, Marc. *The Decembrist Movement.* Englewood Cliffs, N.J., 1966.

———. *Michael Speransky: Statesman of Imperial Russia, 1772–1839.* The Hague, 1957.

———. *Siberia and the Reforms of 1822.* Seattle, 1956.

Rashid al-Din. *The Successors of Genghis Khan.* Translated from the Persian by John Andrew Boyle. New York, 1971.

Rasputin, Valentin, et al. *Baikal.* Moscow, 1985.

———. "Your Siberia and Mine," in Valentin Rasputin, *Siberia on Fire.* Selected, translated, and with an introduction by Gerald Mikkelson and Margaret Winchell. DeKalb, Ill., 1989.

Ravenstein, E. G. *The Russians on the Amur: Its Discovery, Conquest, and Colonisation, with a Description of the Country, Its Inhabitants, Productions, and Commercial Capabilities; and Personal Accounts of Russian Travellers.* London, 1861.

Renouvin, Pierre. *The Immediate Origins of the War (28th June–4th August 1914).* Translated by T. C. Hume. New York, 1969.

Riabukhin, N. M. "The Story of Baron Ungern-Sternberg Told by His Staff Physician N. M. Riabukhin (Ribo)." HIA. N. M. Riabukhin Collection, file 1.

Riasanovsky, Nicholas V. *A History of Russia.* New York, 1977.

Rodzianko, N. "Nabliudeniia za dukhom i napravleniem zhurnala *Biblioteka dlia chteniia* (mai 1850), TsGIAL, fond 772, opis' 1, delo No. 2423.

Rogger, Hans. *National Consciousness in Eighteenth-Century Russia.* Cambridge, Mass., 1960.

Romanov, B. A. *Russia in Manchuria (1892–1906).* Translated by Susan Wilbur Jones. Ann Arbor, 1952.

Romanov, F. A. *Rabochee i professional'noe dvizhenie v gody pervoi mirovoi voiny i vtoroi russkoi revoliutsii (1914–fevral' 1917 goda). Istoricheskii ocherk.* Moscow, 1949.

Rossing, Niels, and Birgit Rønne. *Apocryphal—Not Apocryphal?* Copenhagen, 1980.

Rostunov, I. I., ed. *Istoriia Russko-Iaponskoi voiny, 1904–1905gg.* Moscow, 1977.

———. "Proiskhozhdenie voiny," in Rostunov, ed., *Istoriia Russko-Iaponskoi voiny,* pp. 22–65.

Rozhkov, N. *Sel'skoe khoziaistvo moskovskoi Rusi v XVI veke.* Moscow, 1899.

"Russian Munitions Tables," August 1916 and December 1917. AG. File 10N90.

Sabler, S. V., and I. V. Sosnovskii. *Sibirskaia zheleznaia doroga v eia proshlom i nastoiashchem. Istoricheskii ocherk.* Edited by A. N. Kulomzin. St. Petersburg, 1903.

Safronov, F. G. *Erofei Khabarov.* Khabarovsk, 1983.

———. "Ssylka v Vostochnuiu Sibir' v pervoi polovine XVIIIv.," in Goriushkin, ed., *Ssylka i katorga v Sibiri,* pp. 15–37.

Salisbury, Harrison. *Black Night, White Snow: Russia's Revolutions, 1905–1917.* New York, 1978.

Sallnow, John. "Siberia's Demand for Labour: Incentive Policies and Migration, 1960–1985," in Wood and French, eds., *The Development of Siberia,* pp. 188–207.

Samoilov, V. A. *Semën Dezhnëv i ego vremia.* Moscow, 1945.

Saunders, J. J. *The History of the Mongol Conquests.* New York, 1971.

Sbornik statei po russkoi istorii posviashchennykh S. F. Platonovu. St. Petersburg, 1922.

Scott, John. *Behind the Urals: An American Worker in Russia's City of Steel.* Enlarged edition prepared by Stephen Kotkin. Bloomington, Ind., 1989.

Seddon, J. H. *The Petrashevtsy: A Study of the Russian Revolutionaries of 1848.* Manchester, 1985.

Semënov [Tian-Shanskii], P. P. *Geografichesko-statisticheskii slovar' rossiiskoi imperii.* 5 vols. St. Petersburg, 1865–1887.

———. *Puteshestvie v Tian'-Shan'.* Moscow, 1958.

———, ed. *Zhivopisnaia Rossiia. Otechestvo nashe v ego zemel'nom, istoricheskom, plemennom, ekonomicheskom i bytovom znachenii.* Vol. 12 (in 2 parts). St. Petersburg and Moscow, 1895.

Semënov, Yuri. *The Conquest of Siberia.* Translated from the German by E. W. Dickes. London, 1944.

———. *Siberia: Its Conquest and Development.* Translated from the German by J. R. Foster. Baltimore, 1963.

Semevskii, V. I. *Politicheskie i obshchestvennye idei dekabristov.* St. Petersburg, 1909.

———. *Rabochie na Sibirskikh zolotykh promyslakh.* St. Petersburg, 1898.

Shabad, Theodore. "Economic Resources," in Wood, ed., *Siberia: Problems and Prospects for Regional Development,* pp. 62–95.

——. "Siberian Resource Development in the Soviet Period," in Shabad and Mote, *Gateway to Siberian Resources,* pp. 1–62.

——, and Victor L. Mote, eds. *Gateway to Siberian Resources (the BAM).* Washington, D.C., 1977.

Shanin, Teodor. *The Awkward Class: Political Sociology of a Peasantry in a Developing Society, Russia 1910–1925.* Oxford, 1972.

Shchapov, A. P. "Sibirskoe obshchestvo do Speranskago," in Shchapov, *Sochineniia,* III, pp. 643–717.

——. *Sochineniia A. P. Shchapova.* Vol. 3. St. Petersburg, 1908.

Shcherbakov, N. N. "Chislennost' i sostav politicheskikh ssyl'nykh Sibiri (1907–1917gg.)," in *Ssyl'nye revoliutsionery v Sibiri,* I, pp. 199–242.

Shennan, J. H. "The Conquest of Siberia," *HT,* XIX, No. 2 (February 1969), pp. 101–107.

Sher, I. A. "On the Sources of the Scythic Animal Style," in Shimkin, ed., *Studies in North Asiatic Archaeology,* pp. 142–173.

Shereshevskii, B. M. *Razgrom Semënovshchiny (aprel'–noiabr' 1920g.).* Novosibirsk, 1966.

——. *V bitvakh za dal'nii vostok (1920–1922gg.).* Novosibirsk, 1974.

Shimkin, Dmitrii, ed. *Studies in North Asiatic Archaeology.* Urbana, Ill. 1988.

Shirvindt, E. G. *Nashe ispravitel'no-trudovoe zakonodatel'stvo.* Moscow, 1925.

——. *Russian Prisons.* London, 1928.

Shishkin, S. N. *Grazhdanskaia voina na Dal'nem Vostoke.* Moscow, 1957.

Shul'gin, V. V. *Dni.* Belgrade, 1925.

Shunkov, V. I. *Ocherki po istorii kolonizatsii Sibiri v XVII–nachale XVIII vekov.* Moscow and Leningrad, 1946.

"Situation de l'armament de l'armée russe, février 1917." AG. File 10N73.

Skrynnikov, R. G. *Perepiska Groznogo i Kurbskogo. Paradoksy Edvarda Kinana.* Leningrad, 1973.

——. *Sibirskaia ekspeditsiia Ermaka.* Novosibirsk, 1986.

Slezkine, Yuri. *Russia and the Peoples of Siberia's Arctic Frontier.* Forthcoming (1994), Cornell University Press.

Slovtsov, P. A. *Istoricheskoe obozrenie Sibiri.* St. Petersburg, 1886.

Smith, Canfield F. *Vladivostok under Red and White Rule: Revolution and Counterrevolution in the Russian Far East, 1920–1922.* Seattle and Washington, 1975.

Sokol, Edward D. "The Battle of Kulikovo," *MERSH,* XVIII, pp. 152–159.

——. "Ermak Timofeevich," *MERSH,* X, pp. 224–226.

Sokolov, N. *Ubiistvo tsarskoi sem'i.* Berlin, 1925.

Solomon, Michael. *Magadan.* Princeton, New York, Philadelphia, and London, 1971.

Solov'ëv, M. E. "Partiia Bol'shevikov—organizator pobedy fevral'skoi burzhuazno-demokraticheskoi revoliutsii v 1917g. v Rossii," in Murashov, ed., *Partiia bol'shevikov v gody pervoi mirovoi voiny,* pp. 186–255.

Solov'ëv, S. M. *Istoriia Rossii s drevneishikh vremen.* Vol. III. Moscow, 1960.

Solzhenitsyn, A. *Arkhipelag Gulag, 1918–1956: Opyt khudozhestvennogo issledovaniia.* 2 vols. Paris, 1973.

Ssyl'nye revoliutsionery v Sibiri (XIXv.–fevral' 1917g.). 8 vols. Irkutsk, 1973–1985.

Stalin, J. V. *Works.* 13 vols. Moscow, 1953–1955.

Starr, S. Frederick, ed. *Russia's American Colony.* Durham, N.C., 1987.

Steinberg, I. *Spiridonova: Revolutionary Terrorist.* Translated by Gwenda David and Erich Mosbacher. London, 1935.

Stejneger, Leonhard. *Georg Wilhelm Steller: The Pioneer of Alaskan Natural History.* Cambridge, Mass., 1936.

Steller, G. W. "Journal of a Sea Voyage from the Harbor of Petropavlovsk in Kamchatka to the Western Coasts of America and the Happenings of the Return Voyage," in Golder, ed., *Bering's Voyages,* II, pp. 9–241.

———. Letter to Professor Johann Gmelin, November 4, 1742, in Golder, ed., *Bering's Voyages,* II, p. 245.

Stepanov, N. N., ed. *S. P. Krasheninnikov v Sibiri: Neopublikovannye materialy.* Moscow and Leningrad, 1966.

Stevens, John Frank. "Memorandum on Russia." HIA. John Frank Stevens Papers. File No. 1.

"Stroganov, Anika Fedorovich," *RBS,* vol. Sme–Suv, pp. 491–495.

"Stroganov, Grigorii Anikievich," *RBS,* vol. Sme–Suv, pp. 495–498.

"Stroganov, Iakov Anikievich," *RBS,* vol. Sme–Suv, p. 531.

"Stroganov, Luka Koz'mich," *RBS,* vol. Sme–Suv, p. 506.

"Stroganovy," *RBS,* vol. Sme–Suv, pp. 471–476.

"Stroganovy, Nikita Grigor'evich i Maksim Iakovlevich," *RBS,* vol. Sme–Suv, pp. 507–513.

Strumilin, S. G. *Chërnaia metallurgiia v Rossii i v SSSR: Tekhnicheskii progress za 300 let.* Moscow and Leningrad, 1935.

———. *Istoriia chërnoi metallurgii v SSSR.* Vol I. Moscow, 1954.

Sukachev, V. P. *Irkutsk: Ego mesto i znachenie v istorii i kul'turnom razvitii Vostochnoi Sibiri.* Moscow, 1891.

Svatikov, S. G. *Rossiia i Sibir' (k istorii sibirskogo oblastnichestva v XIXv.).* Prague, 1930.

Svechin, A. *Russko-Iaponskaia voina, 1904–1905gg. po dokumental'nym dannym truda voenno-istoricheskoi komissii i drugim istochnikam.* Oranienbaum, 1910.

Swearingen, Roger, ed. *Siberia and the Soviet Far East: Strategic Dimensions in Multinational Perspective.* Stanford, 1987.

Swianiewicz, S. *Forced Labor and Economic Development: An Enquiry into the Experience of Soviet Industrialization.* London, 1965.

Syroechkovskii, B. E., ed. *Mezhdutsarstvie 1825 goda i vosstanie dekabristov v perepiske i memuarakh chlenov tsarskoi sem'i.* Moscow and Leningrad, 1926.

Tchernavin, Vladimir V. *I Speak for the Silent Prisoners of the Soviets.* Translated from the Russian by Nicholas M. Oushakoff. Boston and New York, 1935.

Tikhmenev, P. A. *A History of the Russian-American Company.* Translated and edited by Richard A. Pierce and Alton S. Donnelly. Seattle and London, 1978.

Tirov, A. A., ed. *Sibir' v XVIIv. Sbornik starinnykh russkikh statei o Sibiri i prilezhashchikh k nei zemliakh.* Moscow, 1890.

Tokarev, S. A., Z. V. Gogolev, and I. S. Gurvich, eds. *Istoriia Iakutskoi ASSR.* 3 vols. Moscow, 1957.

Tooke, William. *View of the Russian Empire During the Reign of Catharine the Second and to the Close of the Eighteenth Century.* 2nd ed. 3 vols. London, 1800.

Trani, Eugene P. *The Treaty of Portsmouth: An Adventure in American Diplomacy.* Lexington, Ky., 1969.

Treadgold, Donald W. *The Great Siberian Migration: Government and Peasant in Resettlement from Emancipation to the First World War.* Princeton, 1957.

Trewin, J. C. *Tutor to the Tsarevich.* London, 1975.

Troitskii, S. M. "Gerard Fridrikh Miller," *SIE,* IX, col. 442.

Trotskii, L. *Kak vooruzhalas' revoliutsiia (na voennoi rabote).* 3 vols. Moscow, 1923–1925.

———. *Trotsky's Diary in Exile.* Translated by Elena Zarudnaia. New York, 1963.

Tsie, V. A. "Zapiska o merakh, neobkhodimykh dlia sokrashcheniia perepiski i uproshcheniia deloproizvodstva v gosudarstvennykh uchrezhdeniiakh," (1856g.), GPB, fond 833, delo No. 292/1–4.

Tupper, Harmon. *To the Great Ocean: Siberia and the Trans-Siberian Railway*. Boston, 1965.

Ukhtomskii, Kniaz' E. E. *Puteshestvie Gosudaria Imperatora Nikolaia II na Vostok (v 1890–1891)*. 6 vols. St. Petersburg, 1897.

Ulam, Adam. *Stalin: The Man and His Era*. New York, 1973.

Ullman, Richard. *Britain and the Russian Civil War, November 1918–February 1920*. Princeton, 1968.

—————. *Intervention and the War: Anglo-Soviet Relations, 1917–1920*. Princeton, 1961.

Unterberger, Betty Miller. *America's Siberian Expedition, 1918–1920*. Durham, N.C., 1956.

Ustiugov, N. V. *Solevarennaia promyshlennost' Soli Kamskoi v XVII veke: K voprosu o genezise kapitalisticheskikh otnoshenii v russkoi promyshlennosti*. Moscow, 1957.

Ustrialov, N. V. "Dnevnik." HIA. Ustrialov Collection. Box 1.

Utechin, S. V. *A Concise Encyclopedia of Russia*. New York, 1964.

Varneck, Elena, and H. H. Fisher, eds. *The Testimony of Admiral Kolchak and Other Siberian Materials*. Stanford, 1935.

Vasil'ev, Iu. A. *Sibirskii Arsenal: Deiatel'nost' partiinykh organizatsii Sibiri po razvitiiu promyshlennosti v period Velikoi Otechestvennoi voiny 1941–1945gg*. Sverdlovsk, 1965.

Veniukov, M. I. "Graf Nikolai Nikolaevich Murav'ëv-Amurskii," *RS*, XXXII (1883), pp. 523–526.

Vernadsky, George. *Kievan Russia*. New Haven, 1948.

—————. *The Mongols and Russia*. New Haven and London, 1953.

—————. *Russia at the Dawn of the Modern Age*. New Haven and London, 1959.

—————. *The Tsardom of Moscow, 1547–1682*. 2 parts. New Haven and London, 1969.

—————, Ralph T. Fisher, Jr., Alan D. Ferguson, Andrew Lossky, and Sergei Pushkarev, eds. *A Source Book for Russian History from Early Times to 1917*. Vol. 1. New Haven and London, 1972.

Vinogradov, V. I., and Iu. F. Sokolov, "Operatsii v Man'chzhurii," in Rostunov, ed., *Istoriia Russko-Iaponskoi Voiny*, pp. 259–323.

Vishnevetskii. "Eniseiskaia ssylka v 1878–1893 godakh," *KiS*, LXIX (1930), pp. 157–175.

Vitte, S. Iu. *Vospominaniia*. 3 vols. Moscow, 1960.

Vladimirova, V. *God sluzhby sotsialistov kapitalistam: Ocherki po istorii kontr-revoliutsii v 1918 godu*. Moscow and Leningrad, 1927.

Vladimirtsev, B. Ia. *The Life of Chingis-Khan*. Translated from the Russian by Prince D. S. Mirsky. London, 1930.

—————. *Le Régime social des Mongols: Le féodalism nomade*. Translated by Michel Carsow. Paris, 1948.

Voenno-istoricheskaia komissiia po opisaniiu Russko-Iaponskoi voiny. *Russko-Iaponskaia voina, 1904–1904: Oborona Kvantuna i Port-Artura*. 8 vols. St. Petersburg, 1910.

"Voevodskaia otpiska Tsariu ob otpuske Khabarova v Dauriiu, o voennykh ego deistviiakh," in *AI*, IV, document No. 31, pp. 74–75.

Volkonskaia, M. N. *Zapiski*. St. Petersburg, 1916.

Volkov, Boris. "Ob Ungerne." HIA. Boris Volkov Collection. File 2.

Volkov, E. Z. *Dinamika narodonaseleniia SSSR za vosem'desiat let*. Moscow, 1930.

Voloshinov, N. A. "Sibirskaia zheleznaia doroga," *IzIRGO*, XXVII (1891), pp. 11–39.

Vol'skii, Z. *Vsia Sibir': Spravochnaia kniga po vsem otrasliam kul'turnoi i torgovo-promyshlennoi zhizni Sibiri*. St. Petersburg, 1908.

Voznesenskii, N. *Voennaia ekonomika SSSR v period otechestvennoi voiny*. Moscow, 1948.

"Vsepoddanneishaia dokladnaia zapiska grafa Uvarova [k Ego Imperatorskomu Velichestvu Nikolaiu Pavlovichu] 21 marta 1849g." (including Nicholas I's marginal comments) TsGIAL, fond 772, opis' 1, delo No. 2242/6–42.

Vvedenskii, A. A. *Dom Stroganovykh v XVI–XVII vekakh*. Moscow, 1962.

—————, ed. *Torgovyi dom XVI–XVII vekov*. Leningrad, 1924.

"Vyderzhki iz rechi lidera omskikh k.-d. Zhardetskogo na s"ezde torgovo-promyshlennikov v Omske v iiule 1918g.," No. 80 in Maksakov and Turunov, *Khronika grazhdanskoi voiny v Sibiri*, pp. 207–208.

Walder, David. *A Short Victorious War: The Russo-Japanese Conflict, 1904–1905*. London, 1973.

Ward, John. *With the "Die-Hards" in Siberia*. London, 1920.

Waxell, Sven. "Report on the Voyage of the *St. Peter*," in Golder, ed., *Bering's Voyages*, I, pp. 270–282.

———. *The Russian Expedition to America*, with an introduction and notes by M. A. Michael. New York, 1962.

Wenyon, Charles. *Across Siberia on the Great Post-Road*. London, 1896.

White, John Albert. *The Diplomacy of the Russo-Japanese War*. Princeton, 1964.

———. *The Siberian Intervention*. Princeton, 1950.

Williamson, Samuel R., Jr., and Peter Pastor, eds. *Essays on World War I: Origins and Prisoners of War*. New York, 1983.

Wilson, David. "The Siberian Oil and Gas Industry," in Wood, ed., *Siberia*, pp. 96–129.

Wolfe, Bertram D. *Three Who Made a Revolution: A Biographical History*. New York, 1948.

Wood, Alan. "From Conquest to Revolution: The Historical Dimension," in Wood, ed., *Siberia: Problems and Prospects for Regional Development*, pp. 35–55.

———. *Siberia: Problems and Prospects for Regional Development*. London, 1985.

———, ed. *The History of Siberia from Russian Conquest to Revolution*. London and New York, 1991.

———, and R. A. French, eds. *The Development of Siberia: People and Resources*. New York, 1989.

Wrangel, Baron P. *The Memoirs of General Wrangel: The Last Commander-in-Chief of the Russian National Army*. Translated by Sophie Goulston. London, 1930.

Wright, George Frederick. *Asiatic Russia*. New York, 1902.

Yakobson, Sergius. "The Russian Conquest of Siberia," *HT*, XXII, No. 10 (October 1972), pp. 700–705.

Zaitsov, A. *1918 god: Ocherki po istroii russkoi grazhdanskoi voiny*. Paris, 1934.

Zankevich, General. "Obstoiatel'stva, soprovozhdavshiia vydachu Admirala Kolchaka revoliutsionnomu pravitel'stvu v Irkutske," *BD*, II (1927), pp. 148–157.

"Zapiski po sooruzheniiu mostov cherez bol'shie reki na Iuzhno- i Severno-Ussuriiskoi zheleznoi dorogakh," in Ministerstvo Putei Soobshcheniia, *Otchët po postroike Severno-Ussuriiskoi zheleznoi dorogi*, pp. 271–300.

Zenkovskii, S. A. ed. *Medieval Russia's Epics, Chronicles, and Tales*. New York, 1954.

"Zhalovannaia gramota tsaria Ivana Vasil'evicha Grigoriiu Stroganovu o finansovykh, sudebnykh i torgovykh l'gotakh na pustye mesta po reke Kame," 4 aprelia 1558g., appendix 2 in Miller, *Istoriia Sibiri*, I, pp. 332–334.

"Zhalovannaia gramota tsaria Ivana Vasil'evicha Iakovu i Grigoriiu Stroganovym ob osvobozhdenii na 20 let ot raznykh podatei i povinnostei ikh zemel' i liudei na Takhcheiakh i na Tobole," appendix 5 in Miller, *Istoriia Sibiri*, I, pp. 339–341.

"Zhalovannaia gramota tsaria Ivana Vasil'evicha Iakovu Stroganovu o finansovykh, sudebnykh i torgovykh l'gotakh na solenoi promysel po reke Chusovoi," 25 marta 1568g., appendix 3 in Miller, *Istoriia Sibiri*, I, pp. 333–337.

Zhigalin, Ia. "Partizanskoe dvizhenie v zapadnoi Sibiri," *PR*, 11, No. 10 (1930), pp. 98–114.

Index

About the Author

A leading American authority on Russia and the former Soviet Union, W. BRUCE LINCOLN is the author of ten books, including the widely praised *The Romanovs: Autocrats of All the Russias, Nicholas I: Emperor and Autocrat of All the Russias, In War's Dark Shadow: Russians Before the Great War, Passage through Armageddon: The Russians in War and Revolution*, and *Red Victory: A History of the Russian Civil War*. During more than four years spent in Russia and Eastern Europe, he has been a Research Fellow at the Institutes of History at Moscow and Leningrad State universities, and, on three occasions, a Senior Research Fellow at the Institute of History of the Leningrad Branch of the Academy of Sciences of the U.S.S.R. He also has been a Senior Research Fellow at Columbia University's Harriman Institute, a Visiting Fellow at the Hoover Institution, a Fulbright-Hays Fellow, and a Guggenheim Fellow. A Distinguished Research Professor at Northern Illinois University, he lives with his wife, Mary, in DeKalb, Illinois.

About the Type

The text of this book was set in Janson, a misnamed typeface designed in about 1690 by Nicholas Kis, a Hungarian in Amsterdam. In 1919 the matrices became the property of the Stempel Foundry in Frankfurt. It is an old-style book face of excellent clarity and sharpness. Janson serifs are concave and splayed; the contrast between thick and thin strokes is marked.